INTERNAL MIGRATION

A Comparative Perspective

COMMITTEE ON COMPARATIVE URBAN ECONOMICS

ADVISORY BOARD

Abram Bergson	Harvard University
Kenneth E. Boulding	University of Colorado
Evsey D. Domar	Massachusetts Institute of Technology
John T. Dunlop	Harvard University
Wassily Leontief	New York University
Harvey S. Perloff	University of California at Los Angeles
Paul A. Samuelson	Massachusetts Institute of Technology
Jan Tinbergen	Erasmus University of Rotterdam

PLANNING COMMITTEE

Alan A. Brown	University of Windsor
Benjamin Chinitz	State University of New York at Binghamton
Ronald W. Crowley	Ministry of State, Urban Affairs, Canada
Zbigniew M. Fallenbuchl	University of Windsor
Janos Horvath	Butler University
Julius Margolis	University of Pennsylvania
Egon Neuberger	State University of New York at Stony Brook
Martin Pfaff	University of Augsburg
Jerome Rothenberg	Massachusetts Institute of Technology

INTERNAL MIGRATION
A Comparative Perspective

Edited by

Alan A. Brown
Department of Economics
University of Windsor
Windsor, Ontario
Canada

Egon Neuberger
Department of Economics
State University of New York
Stony Brook, New York

ACADEMIC PRESS   NEW YORK   SAN FRANCISCO   LONDON
A Subsidiary of Harcourt Brace Jovanovich, Publishers

ACADEMIC PRESS, INC.
111 Fifth Avenue, New York, New York 10003

United Kingdom Edition published by
ACADEMIC PRESS, INC. (LONDON) LTD.
24/28 Oval Road, London NW1

Library of Congress Cataloging in Publication Data

Main entry under title:

Internal migration.

Includes bibliographies.
1.   Migration, Internal—Addresses, essays,
lectures.   I.   Brown, Alan A.   II.   Neuberger, Egon.
HB1951.I54   301.32'6   76-51730
ISBN 0–12–137350–9

PRINTED IN THE UNITED STATES OF AMERICA

CONTENTS

List of Contributors   ix
Preface   xiii

1   Comparative Analysis of Internal Migration:
        An Overview   1
        Alan A. Brown and Egon Neuberger

PART I

Migration and Development: Interactions

2   Migration and Socioeconomic Development:
        Today and Yesterday   11
        Joseph J. Spengler and George C. Myers

3   Internal Migration and Economic Development:
        An Overview   37
        Robert E. B. Lucas

4   The Functions and Dynamics of the Migration Process   61
        Peter A. Morrison

PART II

Methodology: Models, Measurement
and Theoretical Reflections

5   Policy-Oriented Interregional Demographic Accounting
        and a Generalization of Population Flow Models   75
        William Alonso

6   Forecasting Migration in a Regional General Equilibrium
       Context   91
       Owen P. Hall, Jr. and Joseph A. Licari

7   Some Aspects of Measuring Internal Migration   103
       Eduardo E. Arriaga

8   Measurement of Internal Migration from Census Data   121
       K. C. Zachariah

9   Internal Migration:
       Measurement and Models   135
       Julius Margolis

PART III

The Effect of Migration
on Regions and Individuals

10   The Effect of Outmigration on Regions of Origin   147
       Kingsley Davis

11   A Migrant's-Eye View of the Costs and Benefits of
       Migration to a Metropolis   167
       Donald J. Bogue

12   On the Microeconomics of Internal Migration   183
       Jerome Rothenberg

PART IV

Selected Case Studies

Section A

Migration in the West

13   Internal Migration in the Mature American City   209
       James T. Little and Charles L. Leven

14   Urban Growth and Decline in the United States:
       A Study of Migration's Effects in Two Cities   235
       Peter A. Morrison

15   Population Distribution:
           Perspectives and Policies   255
           Ronald W. Crowley

Section B

Migration in Eastern Europe

16   Economizing on Urbanization in Socialist Countries:
           Historical Necessity or Socialist Strategy   277
           Gur Ofer

17   Internal Migration and Economic Development under
           Socialism: The Case of Poland   305
           Zbigniew M. Fallenbuchl

18   Yugoslav Development and Rural–Urban Migration:
           The Evidence of the 1961 Census   329
           Oli Hawrylyshyn

Section C

Special Constraints:
Causes and Consequences

19   The Demographic Effect of Migration on an Urban
           Population:
           Migration to and from West Berlin, 1952–1971   349
           Frederick W. Hollmann

20   Ethnicity as a Barrier to Migration in Yugoslavia:
           The Evidence from Interregional Flows and Inmigration
           to Belgrade   379
           Oli Hawrylyshyn

21   The Influence of Social and Geographical Mobility on the
           Stability of Kinship Systems:
           The Serbian Case   401
           E. A. Hammel

22   Residence and Work Place in Dynamic Tension:
         A Study in the Dual Labor Market of a South African
         Plant   417
            Arnt Spandau

                              PART V

                    **Migration: Disciplinary
                    and Systemic Comparisons**

23   Internal Migration:
         A Comparative Disciplinary View   443
            Joseph S. Berliner

24   Internal Migration:
         A Comparative Systemic View   463
            Egon Neuberger

Author Index   481
Subject Index   487

LIST OF CONTRIBUTORS

Numbers in parentheses indicate the pages on which the authors' contributions begin.

William Alonso (75), Center for Population Studies, Harvard University, Cambridge, Massachusetts

Eduardo E. Arriaga (103), International Statistical Programs Center, Bureau of the Census, Washington, D. C.

Joseph S. Berliner (443), Department of Economics, Brandeis University, Waltham, Massachusetts

Donald J. Bogue (167), Community and Family Study Center, The University of Chicago, Chicago, Illinois

Alan A. Brown (1), Department of Economics, University of Windsor, Windsor, Ontario, Canada

Ronald W. Crowley* (225), General Policy & Research Branch, Ministry of State for Urban Affairs, Ottawa, Ontario, Canada

Kingsley Davis (147), Department of Sociology and Population Research Laboratory, University of Southern California, Los Angeles, California.

Zbigniew M. Fallenbuchl (305), Department of Economics, University of Windsor, Windsor, Ontario, Canada

Owen P. Hall, Jr. (91), TRW Energy Systems Group, 1 Space Park, Redondo Beach, California

* Present address: Ministry of State for Urban Affairs, 373 Sussex Drive, Ottawa, Ontario, Canada.

E. A. Hammel (401), Department of Anthropology, University of California, Berkeley, California

Oli Hawrylyshyn (329, 379), Department of Economics, Queen's University, Kingston, Ontario, Canada

Frederick W. Hollmann† (349), Population Studies Center, Department of Sociology, University of Pennsylvania, Philadelphia, Pennsylvania

Charles L. Leven (209), Institute for Urban and Regional Studies, Washington University, St. Louis, Missouri

Joseph A. Licari (91), Brookings Fellow, Department of Commerce, Office of Policy Development, Washington, D. C.

James T. Little (209), Institute for Urban and Regional Studies, Washington University, St. Louis, Missouri

Robert E. B. Lucas (37), Economics Department, Boston University, Boston, Massachusetts

Peter A. Morrison (61, 235), The Rand Corporation, Santa Monica, California

George C. Myers (11), Department of Sociology and Center for Demographic Studies, Duke University, Durham, North Carolina

Julius Margolis (135), Department of Economics, University of Pennsylvania, Philadelphia, Pennsylvania

Egon Neuberger (1, 463), Department of Economics, State University of New York, Stony Brook, New York

Gur Ofer (277), Department of Economics (and Russian & Slavic Studies), The Hebrew University of Jerusalem, Jerusalem, Israel

Jerome Rothenberg (183), Department of Economics, Massachusetts Institute of Technology, Cambridge, Massachusetts

Arnt Spandau (417), Department of Business Economics, University of the Witwatersrand, Johannesburg, South Africa

† Present address: 4111 Boone Lane, Sacramento, California 95821.

Joseph J. Spengler (11), Department of Economics, Duke University, Durham, North Carolina

K. C. Zachariah (121), Population and Human Resources Division, International Bank for Reconstruction and Development, Washington, D. C.

PREFACE

This multidisciplinary comparative study of internal migration in several regions of the world is the culmination of several years' collaboration by leading anthropologists, demographers, economists, and sociologists. It fills a gap in the migration literature by providing the opportunity for scholars in these fields to ask new questions and give new answers to the key problems in the study of internal migration, in a comparative context, and to address the problems in regions of varying levels of economic development, and with different economic systems.

This book is the third in a series of publications sponsored by the Committee on Comparative Urban Economics (CCUE). The first publication was a two-volume set of proceedings from the Conference on Comparative Urban Economics and Development: Models, Issues, Policies, held at the University of Windsor in November 1972, in collaboration with the Association for the Study of the Grants Economy (ASGE).[1]

The second publication, also sponsored jointly by CCUE and ASGE, representing the proceedings of the Conference on Grants and Exchange in Urbanized Societies in August 1972 in Augsburg, F. R. of Germany, was published in 1976 by North Holland Publishing Company.[2] This book as well as the two-volume Windsor set, covered a very broad territory and served as introductions to more specialized volumes.

At the Windsor Conference, a planning group consisting of CCUE members and participants from various East European countries met to discuss research priorities and the means to implement them. Migration was selected as one of the important topics to be discussed, and subsequent to the meeting, representatives of the Polish Economic

[1] Alan A. Brown, Joseph A. Licari, and Egon Neuberger (Eds.) *Urban and Social Economics in Market and Planned Economies: Policy, Planning, and Development* (Vol. 1) and *Urban and Social Economics in Market and Planned Economies: Housing, Income, and Environment* (Vol. 2). New York: Praeger and Windsor, Ontario: University of Windsor Press, 1974.

[2] M. Pfaff (Ed.). *Grants and Exchange*. North Holland Publishing, 1976.

xiii

Society extended to CCUE an invitation to collaborate in organizing a conference on this topic to be held in Warsaw in the summer of 1974. The conference was supported by generous grants by the Ford Foundation and the International Research and Exchanges Board and representatives of these foundations (Allen Kassof, Ivo J. Lederer, William C. Pendleton, and Louis Winnick) provided invaluable advice to us at every stage of the conference planning and the preparation of this book.

We planned the Western participation in the Warsaw Conference, while professors Antoni Kuklinski and Aleksander Lukaszewicz, representing the Polish Economic Society and the Polish Academy of Sciences, planned the Eastern participation. Shortly before the conference was to meet it was found that virtually no Soviet and East European participants, other than Polish scholars, would have been able to participate. Therefore, the conference had to be cancelled.

Following a long period of negotiations regarding various possible forms of collaboration between CCUE and the Polish Economic Society, it was finally decided that the best way of utilizing the papers submitted by Western scholars was to publish this volume under CCUE auspices. We have been advised that the Polish Economic Society is publishing the Eastern papers in Poland.

The decision to publish the Western papers separately enabled us to invite a number of additional Western scholars to contribute to the volume. We believe that this has resulted in a better and more coherent volume and justifies the delay in the publication of the papers that were to have been presented at the conference. The book is no longer merely a set of conference presentations, but rather a multidisciplinary, comparative approach to the important problem of internal migration in countries with differing economic systems.

We owe a great debt to several scholars, especially Kingsley Davis, Eugene Hammel, Simon Kuznets, and George J. Stolnitz, without whose aid we could not have planned and executed this volume. In addition, the members of the CCUE Advisory Board and Planning Committee have provided us with important advice at crucial stages, particularly Abram Bergson, Benjamin Chinitz, Evsey Domar, Zbigniew Fallenbuchl, Julius Margolis, and Jerome Rothenberg.

CHAPTER 1

Comparative Analysis of Internal Migration: An Overview

Alan A. Brown
Egon Neuberger

This volume represents a multidisciplinary multiregional comparative approach to the study of internal migration. Although the literature on internal migration is certainly voluminous, there has been a conspicuous dearth of volumes treating the problem from different disciplinary approaches and concentrating on more than one region of the world. The purpose of this volume is to make a contribution toward filling this gap.

The problem of migration is a prime example of a subject that requires the skills and approaches of scholars from several disciplines; neither the questions that must be asked nor the methods of analysis required to answer them are within the province of any single discipline. It is for this reason that the contributors to this book include anthropologists, demographers, economists, and sociologists. It is clear that those belonging to other disciplines, such as history, law, political science, and psychology, have much to contribute, but the editors felt that the optimal degree of disciplinary diversification is not necessarily the maximal one. The disciplines represented in this book are sufficient to have resulted in the asking of many of the important questions and the exploration of many of the possible methodologies for dealing with them.

We believe that the publication of this volume will contribute to the field of internal migration in the following ways:

(1) It brings together for the first time a large number of leading scholars from several disciplines, both those who are well-known experts on migration and those who turn to this field for the first time; their respective contributions differ, of course, since the former can draw on their long study of this subject, while the latter bring to it the freshness of seasoned scholars who approach a new challenge.

(2) The book stresses both directly and indirectly the comparative aspect, in terms of discipline, economic system, and level of economic development.

(3) It provides a combination of analytical surveys of the existing literature, contributions to the tool chest of the student of migration, and examinations of some particularly interesting and significant case studies.

I. Migration and Development: Interactions

The first part of the book begins with a section that presents three analytical surveys of the literature on internal migration. These chapters cover the many-faceted interrelations between migration and socioeconomic development. They provide both a wide sweep of the historical record and an in-depth analysis of some of the economic models that have been developed to try to explain internal migration, and they provide an invaluable guide to any scholar interested in this important topic.

The paper by Spengler and Myers (Chapter 2) provides a panoramic and encyclopedic view of the literature on migration and provides an invaluable bibliography for the student of migration. It goes far back in history to deal with land-settling migrations, and then discusses the more recent literature on the macro- and micro-objectives of migration, the increasing freedom for the individual to move, the environmental, systemic, and technological changes that underlie the migration–development interactions (with the anticipated employment opportunities as the major force attracting migrants, and natural and cultural amenities forming a strong secondary motivation), and the problem of the optimum size of the city.

Lucas (Chapter 3) presents a thorough analytical survey of recent theoretical contributions to the comparative statics, and to a lesser extent, the dynamics, of the role of internal migration (primarily rural to urban migration) in promoting economic development through increased efficiency of resource allocation. Thus, his paper complements the paper by Spengler and Myers by treating the migration–development nexus from the point of view of comparing and analyzing formal economic models developed for studying the process in less developed countries.

Morrison (Chapter 4) provides a survey of the literature dealing with the determinants of migration, the "beaten path" syndrome, the effect of migration on the individual migrants, and the effect of migration on the areas of origin and destination. This survey serves as an excellent introduction to the third section of the book, where the problem of internal migration is viewed from the vantage point of the individual migrant and the region of origin.

II.   Methodology: Models, Measurement, and Theoretical Reflections

This section begins with two treatments of the problem of model building for the analysis of migration. The paper by Alonso (Chapter 5) presents a general model that includes the push, pull, and gravity models as special cases as well as a discussion of interregional demographic accounts for forecasting and policy evaluation. The paper by Hall and Licari (Chapter 6) pushes the model-building literature in another direction by providing a methodology for building a regional general equilibrium model that includes economic, demographic, and environmental interrelationships. The purpose of their model is to forecast regional immigration and a demonstration case is presented for the Los Angeles metropolitan area.

The next two papers in this section, by Arriaga (Chapter 7) and Zachariah (Chapter 8), deal with the problems of measurement of internal migration. They concentrate on the ways in which one can compensate for the inadequacies in the existing data bases.

The final paper in this section, by Margolis (Chapter 9), provides critical insights into the methodological problems connected with migration by a leading economist who has not specialized in the general topic of migration.

III.   The Effect of Migration on Regions and Individuals

This section consists of papers by Davis (Chapter 10), Bogue (Chapter 11), and Rothenberg (Chapter 12) dealing with the problem of internal migration as seen by the regions of origin and the individual migrants themselves. We had commissioned a leading economist to contribute a paper dealing with the problem of internal migration from the vantage point of the regions of destination, but he was unable to complete his assignment due to illness and pressure of other work.

Davis argues for using agricultural population or labor force, rather than rural population, for studies of the causation of rural–urban migration; for stressing the impacts of fertility as well as of migration in determining population in "sending" regions; and, most important, that rural outmigration often contributes to the development and well-being of sending regions, despite the usual assumption that rural "depopulation" is an unmitigated evil.

Bogue, although an eminent sociologist and demographer, argues for adapting the economists' cost–benefit approach to the study of individual migration decisions. His approach includes the pull and push factors as important partial components of costs or benefits. He presents a summary two-by-two matrix in which the potential costs of migrating include such cost factors as transportation, problems of finding employment and housing, need to adapt to new surroundings; and the costs of not migrating constitute such push factors as difficulties of finding a local job, unsatisfactory family or social relationships, and political conditions. The potential benefits of migrating include such pull factors as higher pay, better employment opportunities and social services, and a more interesting life, while the benefits of not migrating may include inexpensive housing, food, and recreation, daily contact with family and friends, and assured social status.

Rothenberg approaches the same problem as Bogue—the individual decision-maker's decision whether or not to migrate. His central thesis is that the migrant is not a random cross section of the population, but is rather a member of a self-selected subset of the population with special features that make him evaluate the costs or benefits of migrating or not migrating differently from the rest of the population. This approach permits an analysis of migratory moves that would otherwise seem paradoxical, for example, a move from an origin with opportunities on the average greater than those of the destination. Rothenberg's formulation leads him to investigate four basic elements of the decision to migrate or not migrate: the benefits of a move, the costs of a move, the extent of information about the benefits and costs, and the utility evaluation of each bundle of benefit and cost components by the particular agent making the decision.

The papers by Bogue and Rothenberg provide fascinating evidence that leading exponents of two disciplines can arrive at quite similar analytical approaches to the important question of analyzing the individual decision of whether or not to migrate.

IV.   Selected Case Studies

The second half of the book presents a series of case studies of migration in specific regions or in countries within a given region, with an emphasis on the United States and Eastern Europe.

A.   MIGRATION IN THE WEST

This section presents a paper by Little and Leven (Chapter 13) on internal migration in the mature American city, a paper by Morrison (Chapter 14) on urban growth and decline in the United States, and a paper by Crowley (Chapter 15) dealing with government policies for controlling migration in Western market economies.

Little and Leven provide an analytical treatment of the problems of migration within mature American metropolitan areas. They attempt to explain some of the causes of "urban decay," the deterioration of the position of the central city in terms of incomes, tax base, depopulation of neighborhoods, decline in city services, and decay, abandonment, and demolition of housing and commercial and public structures, both in general terms and in the specific case of St. Louis. They attempt to explain the fact that decay and abandonment occur in the United States but not in other countries. They show that changing incomes, falling internal transportation costs, and some degree of "snobbishness" provide some of the explanatory variables, but argue that these are hardly unique American characteristics. Thus, they tend to attribute the blame for decay and abandonment in the United States to fundamental differences between U.S. housing and urban development policies and those in other countries.

Morrison studies the two broad trends in twentieth-century urbanization in the United States—urban formation followed by metropolitan dispersal. He provides a case study of two extreme cases: San Jose, California, one of the fastest growing metropolitan centers, and St. Louis, Missouri, one of the most rapidly declining central cities. Some of the important conclusions of his study are the shift from rural–urban to urban–urban flows, the hypermobility of San Jose's population (a point bearing on Rothenberg's argument that migrants tend to be different from nonmigrants), the fact that for most practical purposes the "central city" is no longer the "real city," except in name, and the fact that a population decline tends to acquire its own dynamic.

Crowley explores the difficult problem of attempting to establish the optimum population size for a city. He then analyzes some of the causes for the divergence of actual from optimal distributions of population and the range of policies available to correct nonoptimal population distributions, either by direct countervaillants or by indirect influences over individual migration decisions.

B. MIGRATION IN EASTERN EUROPE

This section presents four papers on internal migration in East European countries. They stress the impact of a lower stage of economic development and the existence of a socialist planned system on the patterns of internal migration. The first chapter, by Ofer (Chapter 16), explores the interesting question of whether the lower level of urbanization relative to the degree of industrialization is a result of socialist development strategy or of historical legacies and concludes that both of them operated to bring about the same results. The second chapter, by Fallenbuchl (Chapter 17), analyzes the interrelationships between changing levels of economic development and socialist development strategies in Poland, as they affect the rate and pattern of internal migration. Fallenbuchl argues that under socialism one would expect a lower propensity to migrate due to the expected greater degrees of income equality, maintenance of full employment, and more uniform economic and social development of the regions. He shows that a country like Poland, which is in the process of building the socialist system according to the Soviet model and attempting to accelerate its economic development by stressing industrial rather than agricultural development, will have strong pull and push effects. Fallenbuchl presents an extremely useful analysis of the nature of Polish migrations and shows which of the theoretical expectations are met and which are not.

The chapter by Hawrylyshyn (Chapter 18) explores the relevance of Ravenstein's Laws of Migration as reflected in the relationship between level of development and rural–urban migration in Yugoslavia. Ravenstein's wave theory is represented only in a weak sense in Yugoslavia, since there was a lot of "leapfrogging" from villages directly to cities. For a country at Yugoslavia's level of economic development there has been considerable interurban migration, and industrialization is proceeding with several growth poles, instead of being concentrated in the largest city as is true in many less-developed countries.

C. SPECIAL CONSTRAINTS: CAUSES AND CONSEQUENCES

This section treats the causes and consequences of political, social, and racial constraints on internal migration. The section includes treatment by Hollman (Chapter 19) of the impact of political barriers (the

Berlin Wall) on the demographic composition of a city's population, the significance of ethnic affinities on the patterns of migration within Yugoslavia by Hawrylyshyn (Chapter 20), the impact of migration on kinship ties by migrants in Belgrade by Hammel (Chapter 21), and the formation of a dual labor market in a South African plant due to the existence of the apartheid policy by Spandau (Chapter 22).

These four papers provide important evidence of the impact of such barriers on migration and make it clear that political, social, and racial variables can have significant explanatory power in analyzing the causes and consequences of migration in certain cases.

V. Migration: Disciplinary and Systemic Comparisons

The concluding part of the book explores two important and relatively neglected aspects of the study of internal migration: first, a paper by Berliner (Chapter 23) on the manner in which different scholarly disciplines approach this topic and, second, a paper by Neuberger (Chapter 24) on the interrelations between different economic systems and the nature of internal migration.

Berliner makes the important point that most people who write about migration are not interested in migration at all, but only in its consequences. This is certainly true of economists, sociologists, anthropologists, and social psychologists, whose work constitutes a major part of the literature on migration. Only demographers, and to a lesser extent geographers and historians, care about migration per se. Thus, it comes as no surprise that most disciplines approach the question of the causes of migration in a very similar manner and then stress the question that really fascinates them—the consequences of migration—from the viewpoint of their disciplinary emphasis. Berliner evaluates the contributions by various disciplines within the context of their "bullishness" or "bearishness" on the issue of the ultimate consequences of migration for human welfare. While weighing the costs and benefits of migration to society in a most judicious manner, Berliner tends to stress the negative effects somewhat more than the positive ones. For economists, this is a useful corrective to the usual notion that migration is necessary for labor mobility and therefore clearly has positive results.

Neuberger treats the heretofore neglected topic of the interrelations between migration and various systemic variables. He utilizes the approach he developed for his book *Comparative Economic Systems: A Decision-Making Approach,* which concentrates attention on three systemic structures: the decision-making, information, and motivation structures. He argues that one reason why the systemic variables are usually ignored in studies of migration is because they generally tend to influence migration only indirectly and because slow, gradual, migratory moves do not tend to have a significant impact on the nature of the economic system in the area of origin or of destination. Neuberger compares the decision-making, information, and motivation variables in extreme pure models of planned and market systems, and in a mixed system—having a centralized information but decentralized decision-making structure. He also analyzes the welfare economic implications for migration of different economic systems, stressing the problems of interdependencies, externalities, and norms and the definition of optimal migration flows.

In fact, the Berliner and Neuberger papers tie together in a coherent manner the contributions made to the disciplinary and systemic analysis of migration in the various studies included in this volume. Thus, these papers serve the function of concluding the volume by synthesizing many of the important contributions by the other contributors.

PART I

Migration and Development: Interactions

CHAPTER 2

Migration and Socioeconomic Development: Today and Yesterday

Joseph J. Spengler
George C. Myers

I. Overview

Our purpose in this paper is to set migration within a context sufficiently broad so as to encompass both it and socioeconomic development, together with their interrelation over time.

Today, throughout the world, migration is contributing to economic and social development by enabling man to overcome "the tyranny of space," the primary policy objective of regional science.[1] Migration consists of a variety of movements that can be described in the aggregate as an evolutionary and development-fostering process operating in time and space to correct rural–urban, interurban, and interregional imbalances. It also may spread information, when migrants are more skilled than those living in the regions of destination, and it may break the cake of custom enveloping migrants and make the latter a dynamic force.[2] Migration also carries human capital to regions of destination (giving rise to migrant remittances), entails investment in the

---

[1] On this tyranny, see Warntz (1967), Isard and Reiner (1966), and Long (1971). For a general approach, see Hoover (1971), Richardson (1969), and Perlman et al. (1972). For an earlier analysis, see National Resources Planning Board (1943).

[2] See Marshall (1927), Clark (1951), and Plummer (1932). On the adverse effects of migration in the form of brain drain, see Ranis (1972), Adams (1968), and Bhagwati (1972).

employment of migrants, permits acquisition of new skills, and accentuates economic cycles (e.g., the 20-year cycle). (See Kuznets, 1961; Thomas, 1954; Abramovitz, 1968; and Spengler, 1958. Bhagwati, 1972, proposes that developed countries compensate underdeveloped ones for losses imposed on the latter by "brain drain.") The migratory process can be expected to slow down, at least in relative terms, as major imbalances diminish and the rate of population growth declines in sending areas. (For a full discussion of the changes in relative movement over time related to levels of urbanization and nonagricultural employment, see Parrish, 1973.) Moreover, the types and character of migration may be altered drastically in this process, especially with an increase in interurban migration and decline in rural to urban movement.

Because migration is a development-fostering process, its history runs back to ancient times, as does that of socioeconomic development. Migration can therefore be fruitfully examined in terms of its past as well as its current contribution. For the content of its contribution, together with its purpose, has reflected changes in man's socioeconomic and physical environment, along with changes in his technology. Moreover, migration has become more of a gross process over time, a process punctuated by cycles, longer-run trends, and reverse movements, which make less perceptible both its final net movements and effects and the actual role of the pecuniary and nonpecuniary stimuli motivating individuals to move.

An understanding of migratory processes, as well as attempts to regulate their rate and course, must take into account both their shorter-run and their longer-run advantages and costs, together with how they are perceived in the light of the available information.[3] Prospective environmental and sociostructural changes also may enter into expectations.

In the vast literature on migration, it is the moves themselves that have been stressed, at least until recently, together with the pecuniary and nonpecuniary motives that activate individuals. It is, however, the impact upon socioeconomic structure that needs to be stressed. This is particularly true with respect to the establishment and growth of cities, the major loci of employment opportunities and hence the demographic magnets to which potential migrants traditionally have been attracted. It is through changes in socioeconomic structure, as a function, in part, of

---

[3] On the subjective aspects of costs, advantages, and choice, see Shaw (1975), Fabricant (1970), Cebula and Vedder (1973), Nelson (1959), Sjaastad (1962), Trott (1972), Wolpert (1965), Ichimura (1966), Stouffer (1960), and Riew (1973). On interracial differences in expectations, see Pack (1973).

migration, that nations attempt to overcome "the tyranny of space."[4] A major component of this structure, given a sufficiency of transport, is the urban center, since most, though not all, expanding employment opportunities are situated in such centers.[5]

Today's man differs from yesterday's in that his propensity to move, temporarily or "for keeps," appears to be greater and obstacles in the way of his movement fewer. Hence, not only interurban but also rural–urban balance is more easily achieved than in Adam Smith's day. Then, so Smith tells us, despite the relative significance of small increments of income, rural man's propensity to move even a short distance was very low, often requiring a wage increase of one-fifth or more to be activated.[6] For this reason among others, so long as an increase in the labor force was the main source of increase of output, state policy usually was oriented to encouraging inmigration and discouraging outmigration.

A full understanding of the role played by migration in socioeconomic development requires one to view it historically, since its form and role have changed somewhat over time. Whether essentially unidirectional or partially reciprocal in flow, migration is an equilibrating process serving (a) to improve relations between man's numbers and his physical environment or (b) to reduce disparity between communities or regions in different stages of development or (c) to give rise to an increase in the overall productivity of the factoral equipment of a region or a country, an increase analogous to that in overall output resulting from an increase in trade between two regions differing substantially in factoral structure. Whereas equilibration of the (a) type was dominant before the late nineteenth century, equilibration of the last two types has predominated since.

Defined in most general terms, migration, as here employed, is voluntary movement through sociocultural space. The migration with which we are concerned refers to movement along a *geographical* vector and, as a rule, also includes movement along an *economic* vector, from

[4] Perhaps the most detailed and systematic study of a country's migratory history is Kuznets and Thomas (1964).

[5] See Ward (1963). On the migrant-attracting power of urban situations, see Somermeyer (1971) and Mathur (1970). On urban-oriented industries, especially in cities of 100,000 or more, and employment, see Czamanski (1964). Urban centers are of limited use, of course, to farmers supplying a world market (see Higgs, 1969). On nonurban employment, see Goodstein (1970).

[6] "It appears evidently from experience that a man is of all sorts of luggage the most difficult to be transported [Smith, 1937]." Also, see Marx. On migration-affecting conditions, see Deane (1965). On samples of past views of rural–urban relations, see Sorokin, Zimmerman, and Galpin (1930).

one set of employment opportunities to another. The other conditions that affect a decision to move may be viewed as elements generating a third, or *social*, vector. Impetus to movement originates either in the set of conditions actually incident upon a potential mover at a point of origin or in the set of conditions anticipated at the chosen point of destination or in a combination of these sets. The former are experienced, whereas the latter are perceived on the basis of information much more complete today than formerly.

While this description of the migratory process fits the movement of an individual or household, it can be made to fit a group, long the predominant type, since the members must form a consensus of sorts before undertaking to move as a group. Migration may, therefore, be individual, collective, or mixed in character. Migration on the part of an individual, or an individual and other members of a family, reflects an expectation that the individual will be better off at the point of destination than at the point of provenance. This expectation, in turn, reflects information (or misinformation) at the person's disposal, the mode of interpreting this information, and the estimate of the various costs of moving; together with a capacity to liquidate these costs and determine the prospective return over costs. Even then, the response to a given expectation of net advantage is conditioned by what may be called a propensity to move (or mobility threshold) that varies with individuals. When a number of individuals move together as a group, the migration may be described as collective, even though this migration is sponsored, with the sponsor bearing some of the costs of movement. For then each migrant (or household) will decide as an individual migrant, with the contribution of the sponsor entering into the calculations and the estimate of net return over costs. When migration from one point to another is both collective and individual, it may be called mixed, although individual movement usually comes in the wake of initial collective movements.

II. Migration in History

Throughout most of man's history, migration was of the (a) type—essentially unidirectional and contributive to the settlement of unexploited territory. Requisite for such settlement was an originating population with few opportunities that might be deemed attractive or even adequate. Illustrative of such land-settling migration—usually somehwat organized and hence collective–have been settlement in China and settlement carried out by the Greeks, by some of Rome's invaders, by the colonizers of medieval Europe, and by many who moved to the New World.[7] The impetus for this migration, while influenced by expected conditions at points of destination, usually originated predominantly in the pressure of numbers upon inelastic sources of livelihood in areas of origin (e.g., shortage of accessible land and other complements to labor). (See Thomas, 1954, pp. 94–96, on "the driving forces in the old world." Also, see Thomas, 1941; Songre, 1973; and Guade, 1972.) In spite of high levels of mortality and even periodic upsurges in mortality, spurts of population growth were possible[8] and could generate pressure, especially if agricultural and other conditions were static or were subject to fluctuation (see Wrigley, 1969, especially Chapter 3).

Migration of form (b) and form (c) could become important only after technological progress (especially industrialization) became significant. Typically, such development would proceed at different rates for countries or for subregions of a country. For only then could a potentially migratory category of population come into existence—either because a community's agriculture no longer required the whole of its current agricultural labor force or because communities, especially urban communities, came to differ from one another in terms of realizable average income or standard of living. Significant differences could not emerge, however, until technological progress became sufficiently pronounced; mere regional redistribution of political power and income could have but little continuing effect. The effects of progress were not conspicuous, however, especially in the first millenium of the Christian era. Nor, despite spurts of change, were they notable in the second millenium.

In Europe, over the whole period 1000–1850, per capita product grew by only about 0.16% per year and at an even lower rate up to the year 1700. (See Kuznets, 1971, p. 94n; also, Clark's (1957) comparison of ancient and nineteenth-century wages.) That output grew slowly is confirmed also by the fact that Europe's population grew by only about 1.6% per decade between 1000 and 1750 (see Kuznets, 1971, p. 25n). Even so, by the eighteenth century, the average standard of living of the English and the Dutch was appreciably better than that of the French, and nearly three times as high as that of India in the 1950s (see Deane,

---

[7] See Thucydides, Plato, Lot (1937, 1945). Clapham and Power (1941), Woytinsky and Woytinsky (1953), and Ho (1959). Today one finds examples of such movement in the USSR, Indonesia, and, to a somewhat lesser extent, in several Latin American countries.

[8] Even with a life expectancy of only 30 years at birth, a gross reproduction rate of about 2.5 (roughly equivalent to a birth rate of around 41) could give rise to a natural increase of around 7.5 per 1000 per year, enough to double a population in 93 years. So long as cities remained "consumers of men," however, rural areas had to supply the natural increase.

1965, pp. 6–7; also, Kuznets, 1965). After the late eighteenth century, average product in Western Europe began to pull farther away from that in Eastern and Southern Europe (see Kuznets, 1971, Chapter 1). As a result, migration was easily set in motion toward the relatively high income countries, provided that they did not erect barriers against inmigration.

Improvements in agriculture also could set migration in motion toward cities within countries experiencing such improvements and toward foreign countries. Let P' denote a country's rate of population growth, y' the rate of growth of average income, e the income elasticity of demand for agricultural products, a' the rate of growth of agricultural output per agriculturalist, and A' the rate of growth of the agricultural labor force. Then, in the absence of international trade, so long as (P' + ey') approximates (A' + a') > (P' + ey'), there will be pressure upon some of the agricultural population to emigrate; with $a' = (P' + ey')$, the equivalent of the natural increase of A (i.e., A') will tend to move; and with $a' > (P' + ey')$, the farm population and hence the rural population will tend to decline. (For a model, see Simon, 1957; and Berry and Soligo, 1968.) Should this country engage in trade, the growth of aggregate demand for domestic farm produce, here designated by (P' + ey'), will be reduced or increased accordingly as net imports or net exports grow and thus diminish or increase the annual amount of produce required of the domestic farm population. The tendency of a "surplus" rural population to migrate is conditioned, of course, by the state of urban employment opportunities as well.

Because output per agriculturalist a grew so slowly in the nineteenth and early twentieth centuries, migration out of rural areas did not begin to reduce the rural population in most countries until late in the nineteenth or early in the present century. (See Weber, 1899; and Haufe, 1936. On the causes and consequences of internal migration in Europe, see Parrish, 1973.) In relative terms, outmigration was small. For example, while 52 million people emigrated from Europe between 1846 and 1932, this amounted to something like 0.2% or less of the European population subject to emigration and corresponded to a rate of natural increase of around 1% per year over that period. Accordingly, in many countries, rural outmigration, even though augmented by emigration abroad, was insufficient to reduce rural population until industrialization and related agglomerative forces became powerful, mainly in the present century. Indeed, as late as 1920, about 54% of the population of Europe (exclusive of the Soviet Union) and 85% of the Soviet Union's remained rural. Nor was outmigration sufficient to decrease the *size* of Europe's rural population between 1920 and 1960, although it finally reduced slightly that of the developed world as a whole. At the same time, the rural population of the less-developed regions increased by about 50%, although the rural fraction declined from about 92% to about 80% (see United Nations, 1969, 1971).

Urbanward migration was held in check, at least until recently, not only by a shortage of city-developing physical and human capital but also by the slow rate of progress in agriculture, long a leading source of constraint upon economic development. The number of persons 100 agriculturalists could support in the early nineteenth century, say around 25 to 30, did not increase appreciably in spite of increases in output per agriculturalist and per acre. Accordingly, the whole of rural natural increase was not available for urbanward or transoceanic migration. The great increases in potential, especially in output per acre, itself a source of increase in output per agriculturalist, dates mainly from the 1930s, when indices of output in agriculture accelerated. This pointed to a future in which 100 agriculturalists might support 1000 or more nonagriculturalists and thus make possible a reduction in the rural fraction of a nation's population to one-fifth or less. The increase to date is due in part to a shifting of food-producing functions away from the farm. It should be added, of course, that removal of an emerging agricultural labor surplus calls for avoidance of depression, fairly full employment, and adequate investment in regions in which labor is plentiful.[9]

III. Objectives of Migration

The overall objective of migration, as treated in this paper, namely social and economic development, may be examined in both its *macro* and in its *micro* aspects.

A. MACRO ASPECTS

Of the forms that migration assumes, rural to urban movement has been quantitatively by far the most important. Rural–urban imbalance, which rests upon differences between the agricultural and the nonagricultural labor force, is the chief type of imbalance that migration can do most to correct. This imbalance may be described as a form of migratory lag, and its correction as the macro-objective of the migratory process.

[9] It is estimated that for every farm worker in the United States, there are about two farm-support workers situated off the farm (see Pimental *et al.* 1973). On migration in times of depression and prosperity, see Goodrich (1935), Bachmura (1939). On the changing state of agriculture, see Clark (1957), Brown (1965), and Woytinsky and Woytinsky (1953). On conditions in Europe, see Dewhurst (1961), Svennilson (1954), and Kuznets (1966).

As suggested previously, it is the result of a failure of the once overwhelmingly important component of the labor force (the agricultural) to decline in size as its potential capacity to supply produce continues to exceed, if not to outstrip, the capacity of the market to absorb this produce, subject as it was and often is to a declining income–elasticity of demand. Correction of this imbalance between the agricultural and the nonagricultural labor force will virtually correct rural–urban imbalance, even though a substantial proportion of the rural population normally is engaged in nonagricultural activities.[10] Correction of this imbalance also will greatly contribute to achievement of the micro-objectives of migration.

The extent of the migration needed to correct rural–urban imbalance by the year 2000 exceeds anticipations should the target rural fraction of the total population as of the year 2000 be set at, let us say, one-fourth. It is now expected that by 2000 world population will total 6.5 to 7.0 billion, of which only about 43% will be urban. (The estimates given are based upon United Nations, 1971, 1969. On limits to the augmentation of employment in rural areas, see Warriner, 1970.) In 1970, the world's urban population was approximately 1.35 billion, of whom only 635 million lived in less-developed regions. By the end of this century, it is estimated that four-fifths of the population of the developed world will be urban. Increasing the urban fraction to 75% in the world as a whole entails growth of the world's urban population by about 70%, or 4½% per year. This entails an increase of about 500% in the urban population of the less-developed world, or about 6% per year. Of this 6%, one-fifth or more would be contributed by natural increase and the balance by net inmigration.

Whether capital formation in rural and urban areas in the less-developed world will permit so high a rate of migration to urban centers is doubtful. Colin Clark has inferred that the nonagricultural labor force cannot economically be increased by more than 3% to 4% per year and that an agriculturally occupied population cannot be reduced by more than 1% per year.[11] While the latter constraint, which allows for only a

[10] For example, in the United States in 1970 about 27% of the population was rural, whereas only 4.9% fell in the farm population category, which constituted only about 18% of the rural population. The latter percentage, however, is much higher in most countries.

[11] See Clark (1942, 1967). Even in the rapidly growing Soviet Union in the period 1959–1970, the rural population decreased by only 3% and rural to urban inmigration accounted for only 45% of the 36% increase in population defined as "urban" (see Harris, 1971). In Japan, the population living in places of 10,000 population and over increased by only 258% or about 4¼% per year, between 1888 and 1918. Meanwhile, Japan's population increased by about 45%, and that in places under 10,000 by about 15%. The fraction of the population living in places 10,000 and over rose from about 13% in 1888 to about 32% in 1918 (see Taeuber, 1958).

25% reduction in the agricultural population by 2000, may be relaxed somewhat, it indicates that full achievement of the macro-objective is difficult unless past constraints can be relaxed.

By the close of this century, rural overpopulation will be pronounced only in the less-developed countries, given the high rates of natural increase in these countries and the dearth of physical and human capital essential for industrialization and efficient urbanization. Correction of the rural–urban imbalance in most less-developed countries is virtually contingent upon a marked reduction of fertility. If this can be achieved, then the aggregate amount of investment required to finance agricultural improvement, migration, and employment in cities for inmigrants from rural areas will be more manageable. Let us postulate a country whose population is growing by 2.5% per year while the urban population, initially 20% of the total, grows by 5% per year. In this situation, about 55 years must pass before the rural population is reduced to one-fourth of the total. A period of only about 36 years will suffice if the annual rate of natural increase approximates 1¼%.

A delay in reducing fertility in high-fertility countries will intensify perpetuation of a rural–urban imbalance. To illustrate, if a country is delayed for 10 years in reducing fertility to the replacement level, then the eventually attained stationary population will be about 20% to 25% larger than it would otherwise have been. There is some evidence for European countries that fertility reductions in rural areas may have been delayed by the wide availability of urbanward migration (see Friedlander, 1969). The growth of cities and their attractiveness for migrants may, in fact, serve to maintain high fertility among those remaining in rural areas, thus continuing the imbalance.

While the macro-objective of migration was formerly served by international as well as by rural–urban migration, this former source of relief is currently much less significant (see the many papers in Tapinos, 1974; also Myers, 1974). Indeed, the effects of emigration would seem to weaken countries when it drains away their superior manpower. Formerly, the job requirements for labor migrants were not technically very exacting, with the result that immigrants could find employment quite easily in receiving countries. This is no longer true today. (See Thomas, 1954, pp. 152ff., 163ff.; also Adams, 1968; and Böhning, 1975. On occupational maldistribution, see Clark, 1957, Chapter 10. Even in modern agriculture, the skill requirements have become so great that persons of limited skill are nearly as unemployable there as in urban settings. See Smith, 1970.) Emigrants from rural areas in underdeveloped countries are generally not equipped to meet most job requirements in advanced countries, with the result that the "new movement" tends to be selective of more skilled urban migrants. This is true also of migrants within advanced countries who originate in and move out of "cultural deprived" areas into more developed areas. In addition to general economic fluctuations (e.g., the recent oil crisis), problems associated with the admission of unskilled immigrants, together with the slowing down of natural population increase in immigrant-receiving countries and a consequent fear of qualitative dilution of their populations by inflows of less qualified immigrants, will increasingly make for the erection of barriers against immigrants from less-developed countries. The correction of rural–urban imbalance for these countries, no longer possible through external migration, will have to be sought by internal adjustments. Cultural, linguistic, skill, job, and (consequent) income differences slow down assimilation processes and thus impose on the receiving state a variety of costs which, were they incident upon responsible employers of immigrants, would diminish the desirability of seeking foreign workers. The solution of assimilation problems is more difficult today than in pre-1914 America or in the interwar period in Europe, where the gap between immigrant and native was narrower and more easily bridged. Today, a country's low-income wage earners are better able to resist politically the competition of immigrants, while the higher income groups, to whom immigrants are complements rather than competitors are less able to facilitate immigration.[12]

Intranational as well as international reduction of rural–urban imbalance was much easier to achieve in the late nineteenth and earlier twentieth centuries, when the creation of industrial and urban opportunities was less costly in terms of capital and less demanding in terms of job requirements. Sweden's experience affords a good example (see Thomas, 1941, Chapter 3). It remains possible, given judicious use of capital and sufficient access to foreign markets, for some of today's underdeveloped countries to develop the manufacture and export of labor-oriented goods and services and, thereby, establish domestic outlets for their excess agricultural populations (see Ohlin, 1933; also Marsden, 1970; Sternberg, 1971; and Baranson, 1971).

B. MICRO ASPECTS

The prime concern in this regard is improvement in the distribution of the urban population among regions and communities of diverse size. This entails enquiry both into the forces that govern urban population

---

[12] On Europe, see Nielsen (1972). A vast literature on immigrant assimilation appeared in the United States in the late nineteenth and early twentieth centuries. On migration and rural–urban imbalance in Europe in the first half of this century, see Svenillson (1954). On the impact of inmigration, see Reder (1963), Spengler (1958) and Thomas (1958).

distribution and into methods of control designed to internalize externalities, prevent distortion of time horizons, and check other forces making for maldistribution of the urban population.

Optimizing population distribution has been handicapped in the past by the heavy inflow of migrants of rural origin and, increasingly, by the fact that the distribution of natural increase in urban areas has corresponded closely to that of the distribution of the urban population itself. To the extent that the population was suboptimally distributed, this has tended to perpetuate suboptimal distribution. With the decline of the rate of population growth to around zero, however, and the stabilization of the age structure, rural–urban imbalance will eventually be eliminated and corrective influences, including public measures, will greatly reduce interurban and interregional imbalance. So long as an economy remains dynamic, however, even though a population be stationary, the interoccupational distribution of the labor force will remain subject to changes that may call for interurban and related changes as well. For, since progress in the production of goods and services tends to vary with category, as does the elasticity of demand for goods and services, interoccupational mobility results and sometimes gives rise to movement in geographical space.

IV. Freedom to Locate

Populations exercise much more freedom of choice today than in the past with respect to location in geographical space. Today, individual men and their impedimenta are more mobile than formerly. Moreover, today's migrants find that the potential situations from among which they may choose are made up in far greater measure than formerly of ubiquities, and they are hence less subject to the constraints imposed by nonubiquities. Furthermore, the flow of relevant information is far greater today, and hence man's capacity to anticipate and surmount the constraints imposed by nonubiquities is greater.

In Adam Smith's day, the costliness of land transport and the relative weightiness of subsistence and land-oriented raw materials greatly limited the locational options available to employment-providing entrepreneurs, tying them largely to fertile areas and places served by water transport (see Smith, 1937, pp. 18–19, 147–148, 206–207, 382–383; also Deane, 1965, Chapter 5, pp. 73–76, 83, 156–162; Dean, 1938, Chapter 3; Clark, 1957, pp. 405–420, and Clark and Haswell, 1964). Under these circumstances, cities seldom could attain significant size unless situated on suitable waterways and capable of commanding and drawing adequate subsistence, usually with the assistance of ecclesiastical and tax revenues.

These conditions have changed markedly over the past 175 years, initially with the improvement of means of water carriage and later with continuing improvement of the means of communication and transport, as steam and electric rail systems, and eventually motor carriers, came into use. Workers and hence population became increasingly "footloose," along with economic activities. For example, even as late as 1935, 28% of the American labor force was located in close proximity to resources. Allowing for the servicing of this population, about two-fifths of the country's poppulation was tied to nonubiquities. By 1970, this fraction had declined to something like one-tenth, in part because, as noted earlier, some functions formerly performed on the farm had been shifted to urban communities. (See Pimental, 1973. The 1935 estimate is based on National Resources Committee, 1939. On the role of resources, see Klaussen, 1973, and Chisholm, 1963.) According to Dziewonski (1970), however, the development of specialization of functions in Polish cities of intermediate size entailed a decline in ubiquitous functions, a reduction in the appropriateness of central place theory, and greater randomness of city location. Finally, it may be noted that the growth in the number of pensioned retired persons is increasing the pull of nonubiquities, in the form of natural amenities, given that other conditions are satisfactory.[13]

As conditions increasingly favored movement, the importance of migration as a population redistributing agent increased, more so in the United States than in a more densely populated country like Japan (see Suzuki, 1970). As Eldridge reports, migration has been "a far more potent factor in redistributing the population of the United States than has differential natural increase," at least for the period 1870–1950 (in Kuznets and Thomas (Eds.) 1964, Volume III, Chapter 2, especially p. 56). "Indices of dispersion, urbanization, and interstate displacement due to migration," Eldridge also reports, display similar and highly correlated patterns of change. "Both dispersion and urbanization have been essential to the development of a single integrated economic and social system occupying the available territory [Kuznets and Thomas, 1964, Volume 3, Chapter 7, p. 226]." (See Kuznets and Thomas, 1964, Volume 3, Chapter 7, p. 226; also Thomas's comments in *ibid.*, Volume 3, pp. 319ff., especially page 368. See Kuznets, A. R. Miller, And R. A.

---

[13] On the role of natural and cultural amenities, see Cebula and Vedder (1973) and Greenwood (1970). Also pertinent are Riew (1973), Yamada (1972), Fuchs (1962), and Ullman (1954).

Easterlin in Kuznets and Thomas, 1964, Volume 2, p. 78. See also Williamson, 1965.) These migratory trends apparently contributed to increasing similarity among states of the industrial distribution of the labor force, with the exception of agricultural and household service workers.

V. Population and Employment: Distribution in Space

The distribution of a country's population tends to correspond quite closely to the distribution of employment. Employment, in turn, tends to expand in areas where a great deal already exists, signifying the presence of both employment opportunity and diversified manpower, and in areas of potential opportunity, where "job makers" seek "job takers." Over the long range, therefore, given the incapacity of rural employment to keep pace with a growing rural population of working age, migrants will be drawn to existing towns and cities or areas in which new cities are coming into existence. (See Ward, 1963; Czamanski, 1964; and Blanco, 1963. Parasitic cities attract mainly consumer-oriented activities; see Hoselitz, 1955.) In view of what has been said, it is evident that inquiry into the forces underlying migration is subject to two conditions: (a) it should *not* be assumed that migration takes place within a fixed socioeconomic framework and eventuates in a necessarily stable interurban and/or rural–urban equilibrium; (b) underlying migratory movements play an important role in determining location of communities and economic activities, including technological changes that destabilize intra- and interurban equilibrium. Accordingly, migratory and developmental processes are interrelated and interact.

The distribution of towns and cities depends upon (a) historical factors, (b) physical or biospheric environmental conditions, (c) the determinants of industrial organization (e.g., economies of scale and agglomeration, means of transport and communication, stability of interurban networks), and (d) the changing state of technology that conditions both the economic availability and use of components of the environment and the functioning of elements in the system of industrial organization. While changes in the significance of these determinants may temporarily modify the importance of migration, its national importance tends to decline as a nation's rate of population growth approaches zero and the settlement process nears completion.

Outmigration may reduce but it cannot eliminate interurban and interregional differences. There is also a need, especially in less advantaged areas, for inflows of agents complementary to labor—capital, expertise and entrepreneurs (see Bachmura, 1939; and Sjaastad, 1960). As outmigration is generally selective with respect to age, skill, training, education, enterprise, and so on, and thus carries off human capital (even to the extent of depopulating small communities), it may be in order to utilize some of the resulting monetary returns to areas of destination for the benefit of areas of origin. Such transfers (in excess of ordinary immigrant remittances) may facilitate adjustment in areas undergoing depopulation and help to offset losses imposed on less developed countries by "brain drain."[14]

Two limitations upon population capacity levels have their basis in a country's physical environment—it circumscribes the areas within which particular activities can be carried on economically, and it sets upper limits to the rate at which activities based on environmental components (e.g., particular minerals) can be carried on. Nonubiquitous environmental components, such as arable land, water, minerals, and so on, limit locational options unless these components are sufficiently transportable to surmount their uneven distribution in space. This unevenness may be further accentuated through depletion of stocks of natural resource inputs. Transportation cannot, of course, surmount topographic or climatic limitations, or greatly ease regional inequality in the distribution of economically accessible water supplies.

Of the natural factors affecting locations selectively, the most important are energy and water, each of which is essential to the performance of many economic functions. Marked changes in the cost of energy inputs produce change, not only in the relative costs and prices of products of transport-sensitive industries (see Fahle and Hertzfeld, 1972, pp. 193–195; and Clark, 1967, Chapters 8–9) but in a variety of energy-sensitive prices, which can lead to greater emphasis on energy-conserving methods (see Lincoln, 1973). Rising energy costs also are likely to lead to changes in both the physical structure of urban areas and the modes of construction employed.[15]

Because energy costs are likely to increase substantially over time and because water supplies often are not augmentable in keeping with rapidly growing per capita water consumption (e.g., in the United States

[14] See, for example, Hoover (1971), Bowman and Myers (1967), Adams (1968), and Gupta (1973). On the localized impact of outmigration, see Beale (1964, 1969). See also Ranis (1972). The Japanese Ministry of Home Affairs has issued a White Paper on Depopulation as a result of a decline of 10% or more in the population of 1,047 cities, towns, and villages since 1960 (see Consulate General, 1974).
[15] See Lincoln (1973). On alternative urban patterns, see Dantzig (1974), Clawson (1973), Owen (1972), and Medvedkov (1970). See also Fals and Moses (1972), Pred (1966), Kulski (1967), Rasmussen (1966), Bourne (1971), and Lave (1970).

over the next 50 years, a number of regions are destined to become water-deficit areas; United States Water Resources Council, 1968, especially Part 6; and Ridker, 1972). Optimization of population distribution calls for feasible accommodation of the distribution of economic activities to the prospective availability of both water and energy of suitable form. Such action is indicated because neglect of prospective water and energy shortages would, in time, call for difficult and expensive adjustments. Somewhat comparable to the dangers inherent in neglect of prospective energy and water shortages are the dangers inherent in overloading ecosystems through excessive inmigration and settlement of regions with limited carrying capacity. Dangers of this sort are most likely to arise in tropical areas; a sequel to high rates of natural increase and consequent excessive movement of population into these areas (see Janzen, 1973; Gómez-Pompa, Vázquez, and Guevara, 1972; Meggers, 1973; Odum, 1969; and Nelson, 1973).

Two sets of issues are encountered in considering the location-determining influence of industrial organization: those associated with urban and metropolitan complexes and those associated with the development of such complexes in regions currently lacking them. Concentration of economic activities formerly had its origin in the ease of communication and transportation associated with propinquity, but this source has lost importance, given modern communication, computerization, transportation, and costs of congestion. (On proximity, see Fals and Moses, 1972, p. 82. On coping with costs of congestion, see Lave, 1970; and Make, 1970.) Concentration continues to have its origin in economies of scale in production or distribution (on scale economies, see Alonso, 1967; also von Böventer, 1963; Chenery and Taylor, 1968; and Chenery, 1971), in advantages of urban situation and economies of agglomeration (see Shefer, 1973; on labor costs, see von Böventer, 1963, pp. 186–187; Fuchs, 1962, pp. 108–119; and Mera, 1973), and in the complementarity of undertakings and interindustry linkages.[16]

Over time, centripetal forces have tended to outweight centrifugal forces in the determination of the location of economic activities and hence of the nonagricultural population. This predominance of centripetal forces could, however, diminish in the future. When there is a range of comparably efficient plant sizes, concern with congestion costs may favor the choice of smaller sizes. Furthermore, miniaturization of optimum plant size, perhaps a feasible objective of engineering technol-

---

[16] See Duncan et al. (1960), Streit (1970), Hodge and Wong (1972), Czamanski (1971), Lasuen (1969), and Thompson (1972). On coping with excessive suburbanization, see Bradford and Kelejian (1973).

ogy, could contribute to this result (witness the reduction in computer size, explosives, etc.). Increases in output per worker tend to reduce plant size in terms of workers. Increases in the relative importance of services reduces centripetal tendencies. Improvement in means of transportation and communication can have a similar effect. Insofar as competition is restrained and larger communities are allowed to exploit smaller communities, removal of constraints upon competition will favor the deconcentration of economic activities. In the United States, competitive and other forces have been powerful enough to reduce the concentration of the total *urban* population in places over 250,000. The population declines being experienced since 1970 both in the rings as well as in the central cores of the largest metropolitan areas in the United States, along with the apparent growth of nonmetropolitan areas, would signify important centrifugal forces operating of late (see Morrison, 1975; and Beale, 1975). Should the tendency for the relative cost of services to rise prove more powerful in larger than in smaller urban centers, decentralization would be favored (on the rising costs of services, see Baumol and Oates, 1972).

VI. Amenities

While anticipated employment opportunity—a type of opportunity migrants associate positively with the size and degree of urbanization of potential destinations—is a major force attracting migrants, the presence of natural (e.g., pleasant climate) or "cultural" amenities tends to reinforce other forces of attraction. Information in sufficient quantity is essential, of course, if potentially attractive forces are to be actualized. Having once been set in motion, the magnetic power of these forces may for a time become highly cumulative—as in California (see Greenwood, 1970; also Suzuki, 1970, pp. 335–352). With the reduction of the work day and the growth of discretionary time and income, the demand for amenities normally increases, and their availability becomes an important locational factor. Moreover, when other conditions are not too dissimilar, the availability of amenities may be the deciding locational factor for potential enterprisers.

Three issues, always of importance, emerge as corollaries to the increasing importance of amenities: (a) Are amenities positively correlated with urban size? (b) Can *new* urban centers be established in regions where natural amenities abound? (c) Do the tastes and desires of a city's residents have much influence upon its growth in size? The answer to (a) is not simple, as a "metropolitan" region may embrace a number of cities, and hence a large population, and yet not include a very large city. The answer to (b) is affirmative but subject to conditions to be noted. The answer to (c) is currently in the negative. For, although the overriding concern of most members of a city's labor force is employment, individuals are seldom presented with comparable employment options located in cities of different size. Of course, if desirable employment is not to be found in a city of desirable size, a person must trade-off between the type of employment and size of city. Given the possibility of stationary population and labor force, employers may well be under greater pressure to adjust his choice of city size to the tastes of the labor force in the future.

The growth of a city's population is less susceptible to the corrective forces of natural selection than is the growth of a firm or of a plant (see Stigler, 1968, Chapter 7). A firm or plant is subject to a single decision maker and hence is unlikely to be allowed to grow beyond a point where costs increase faster than returns. This point is not absolutely fixed, of course, but tends to move as conditions change, among them both the degree of competition to which a firm or plant is subject and the extent to which it can shift some costs to others. A city, by contrast, is *acephalous* and hence free of control by a single decision maker who could, in effect, internalize all costs and benefits of city growth and bring growth to a stop when, at the margin, costs have caught up with benefits. A city, moreover, is far less flexible, far less capable of speedily correcting mistakes, than is a firm or plant, most of whose components are shortlived or easily metamorphosable in keeping with changing needs. A city's growth pattern resembles that of a coral reef. Even though it is already too large, it will tend to expand so long as a firm entering it or its immediate environs is free to impose part of the costs of establishing itself on the city and profit therby, even though, were *all* of this firm's costs and benefits internalized, locating within the city in question would not be profitable. Moreover, unless amenities and disamenities are included with conventional benefits and costs, growth may continue even though it is not in keeping with the all-inclusive total and marginal cost–benefit ratios (see Ullman, 1962, pp. 7–27; also Barr and Leven, 1962).

That which constitutes satisfactory city size is elusive, for it varies with a city's structure, with the position of a city in a regional context, with the kinds of activities assembled within a city, and with the weights attached to various amenities and the stability of these weights. The information that is accumulated respecting amenities and disamenities is typically incomplete in that it is subjective. Moreover, the decision as to where to reside and work is dominated by the location of a jobholder's current job. For, as suggested earlier, a jobholder seldom has concrete alternatives that are richer in amenities than his current position. Thus, a person is not prone to move unless his source of employment shifts or a concrete preferable alternative is presented.

Until research into city size takes these conditions and potentials into full account, findings that report on correlations between overall per capita welfare and city size are incomplete and possibly misleading. To these shortcomings may also be added the failure to allow fully for the tendency of the cost of government, the inequity in the distribution of these costs, and perhaps the costs of other services as well to increase with city size. (On city size, see, for example, Hoover, 1971; Ullman, 1962; and Alonso, 1971, expecially his excellent bibliography, pp. 82–83. Many of the papers in Commission on Population and the American Future, 1973, deal with aspects of city size and location.) The conditions referred to in this and earlier paragraphs make it difficult to determine optimum city size under various conditions.[17] Even so, the concept is useful since it keeps in the forefront the need to check the growth in size of communities when it appears that further growth will not be advantageous on balance.

What it is that constitutes optimum city size may turn, in part, on a country's stage of development. There may exist, for instance, a choice between one or two cities with something like optimum size according to advanced-country criteria and five or six smaller cities. The latter option, though inferior to the former in the short run, may be preferable in the long run. For then, a large and hence more dispersed number of potential growth poles will be available to stimulate and give direction to urbanization and economic development. While the initial cost of the second option will be higher, its positive impact is likely to be greater in the long run and more conducive to economic development.

The creation of new cities is essential both to regional economic development and to control of city size, especially the maintenance of average city size. While it is possible for one large corporation to launch a new city, the cooperation of several major sources of employment may be essential. Establishment of an urban economic base is vital to the initiation of trade with other urban centers and source of supplies. Then the development of residentiary activities can get under way and stimulate the further growth both of these activities and of the urban base, as well as respond to increase in the latter. While there is

[17] On optimum city size, see *ibid.*, Whitman (1972), Harris (1972), and Evans (1972). Mera (1973) concludes that decentralization makes for less inequality but at the expense of efficiency.

considerable disagreement regarding the role of the urban economic base, this role is critical only in the initiatory stage, thereafter varying with the character and growth pattern of a city.[18]

VII. Conclusion

From our review of work on migration, we can conclude that its study needs to be systematized and subordinated both to inquiry into all relevant social and physical parameters and to inquiry into the optimization of the distribution of economic activities and population in space. This type of inquiry includes inter alia inquiry into the optimization of city sizes and city systems, the limitational impact of nonubiquitous natural or biospheric elements, the options respecting the ratio of amenities to disamenities, and the means suited to shunting to responsible parties all costs and all benefits flowing from their location-affecting actions. Such internalization calls for a long view, not only in the preparation of location-affecting plans but also in the costing and financing of undertakings over time. It is essential that replacement funds be accumulated at all levels as rapidly as depreciation and obsolescence consume property, be it residential, commercial, industrial, public, or eleemosynary in form, for then the financial means to countervail urban and other forms of blight will always be at hand and users of all forms of property will become obligated to pay the full cost of its use. Out of inquiries along the lines just suggested should flow an awareness of the degree to which countries can be divided into relatively self-sufficient and politically autonomous regions and thereby reduce a nation's transportation and congestion costs as well as the oppressive, inefficient, and wasteful concentration of political and economic power to which countries over the world are increasingly becoming subject. Regional solutions also might be found for the financing of cultural amenities (e.g., theatre, orchestra) that require, for their support, sufficiently large and continuous audiences. The search for regional solutions will be accentuated if the relative costs of energy and transportation rise, thus increasing the cost of population scatter that stems from the present practice of many urban workers living in rural nonfarm areas.

It is desirable that countries and regions that are victimized by the "skill drain" be compensated for this loss by the countries and regions

---

[18] On the role of the urban base, see Dziewonski (1967), Fahle and Hertzfeld (1972), Ullman and Dacy (1960), Ullman (1962), Anderson (1970), Thompson (1965), Perloff and Wingo (1968), Rodwin (1970), Richardson (1969), and Hoover (1971).

benefiting from the inmigration of superior human capital. Otherwise, international and interregional income disparity is accentuated and the capacity of economically depressed areas to progress is reduced. While freedom to migrate is an essential "right," the advantage conferred on the immigrant-receiving country needs to be paid for, much as the influx of physical capital must be paid for (see Bhagwati, 1972).

References

Abramovitz, M. The passing of the Kuznets cycle. *Econimica*, 1968, *35*, 349–367.

Adams, W. (Ed.). *The brain drain*. New York. Macmillan, 1968.

Alonso, W. A reformulation of classical location theory and its relation to rent theory. *Papers of the Regional Science Association*, 1967, *19*, 23–44.

Alonso, W. The economics of urban size. *Papers of the Regional Science Association*, 1971, *26*, 67–82; 82–83 (Bibliography)

Anderson, R. J., A note on economic base studies and regional econometric forecasting models. *Journal of Regional Science*, 1970, *10*, 325–334.

Bachmura, F. T. Man–Land equalization through migration. *American Economic Review*, 1939, *49*, 1004–1017.

Baranson, J. Automated manufacturing techniques in developing economies. *Finance and Development*, December 1971, *8*, 10–17.

Barr, J. L., and C. L. Leven. The spatial dimension of the economy as a social outcome. In M. Perlman, D. J. Leven, and B. Chinitz (Eds.), *Spatial, regional, and population economics*. New York: Gordon and Breach, 1972.

Baumol, W. J., and W. E. Oates. The cost disease of the personal services and the quality of life. *Skandinaviska Enskilda Banken Quarterly Review*, 1972, *2*, 44–54.

Beale, Cl L. Rural depopulation in the Unites states. *Demography*, 1964, *1*, 264–272.

Beale, C. L. Natural decrease of population: The current and prospective status of an emergent American phenomenon. *Demography*, 1969, *6*, 91–100.

Beale, C. L. *The revival of population growth in nonmetropolitan America*. Washington, D.C.: U.S. Department of Agriculture, 1975.

Berry, R. A., and R. Soligo. Rural–urban migration, agricultural output, and the supply price of labour in a labour-surplus economy. *Oxford Economic Papers*, 1968, *20*, 220–249.

Bhagwati, J. N. *Economics and world order*. London; Macmillan, 1972.

Blanco, C. The determinants of interstate population movements. *Journal of Regional Science*, 1963, *5*, 77–84.

Böhning, W. R. Mediterranean workers in Western Europe: Effects on home countries of employment. Geneva: International Labour Office, 1975.

Bourne, L. S. (Ed.). *Internal structure of the city*. New York: Oxford University Press, 1971.

Bowman, M. J., and R. G. Myers. Schooling, experience, gains and losses in human capital through migration. *Journal of the American Statistical Association*, 1967, *62*, 875–898.

Bradford, D. F., and H. J. Kelejian. An econometric model of the flight to the suburbs. *Journal of Political Economy*, 1973, *81*, 566–589.

Brown, L. *Increasing world food output*. Washington, D.C.: U.S.D.A., 1965.

Buchanan, J. M. *Cost and choice*. Chicago: Markham, 1969.

Cebula, R. J., and R. K. Vedder. A note on migration, economic opportunity, and the quality of life. *Journal of Regional Science*, 1973, *13*, 205–211.

Chenery, H. B. Growth and structural change. *Finance and Development*, September 1971, *8*, 16–29.

Chenery, H. B., and L. Taylor. Development patterns: Among countries and over time. *Review of Economics and Statistics*, 1968, *50*, 391–416.

Chisholm, M. Tendencies in agricultural specialization and regional concentration in industry. *Papers of the Regional Science Association*, 1963, *10*, 157–162.

Clapham, J. H., and E. Power (Eds.). *The Cambridge economic history of Europe*, (Vol. 1). Cambridge: Cambridge University Press, 1941.

Clark, C. *The economics of 1960*. London: Macmillan, 1942.

Clark, C. *The conditions of economic progress* (2nd ed.). London: Macmillan, 1951.

Clark, C. *The conditions of economic progress* (3rd ed.). London: Macmillan, 1957.

Clark, C. *Population growth and land use*. London: Macmillan, 1967.

Clark, C. and M. R. Haswell. *The economics of subsistence agriculture*. New York: St. Martin's, 1964.

Clawson, M. *Modernizing urban land policy*. Baltimore: 1973.

Commission on Population and the American Future. *Research reports* (Vols. 3 and 5). Washington, D.C., 1973.

Consulate General of Japan, New York. *Japan report*. January 1, 1974.

Czamanski, S. A model of urban growth. *Papers of the Regional Science Association*, 1964, *13*, 177–200.

Czamanski, S. Some empirical evidence of the strengths of linkages between groups of related industries in urban regional complexes. *Papers of the Regional Science Association*, 1971, *27*, 137–150.

Dantzig, G. B. *Compact city*. San Francisco: W. H. Freeman, 1974.

Dean, W. H., *The theory of the location of economic activities*, Ann Arbor: University of Michigan Press, 1938.

Deane, P. *The first industrial revolution* Cambridge: Cambridge University Press, 1965.

deJong, G. F., and W. L. Donnelly. Public welfare and migration. *Social Science Quarterly*, 1973, *54*, 529–544.

Dewhurst, J. F., et al. *Europe's needs and resources*. New York: Twentieth Century Fund, 1961.

Duncan, O. D., et al., *Metropolis and region*. Baltimore: Johns Hopkins, 1960.

Dziewonski, K. Overlooked aspects of the concept of the urban economic base. *Papers of the Regional Science Association*, 1967, *18*, 139–146.

Dziewonski, K. Specialization and urban systems. *Papers of the Regional Science Association*, 1970, *24*, 39–45.

Evans, A. W. The pure theory of city size in an industrial economy. *Urban Studies*, 1972, *9*, 49–77.

Fabricant, R. A. An expectational model of migration. *Journal of Regional Science*, 1970, *10*, 13–24.

Fahle, V. L., and H. R. Hertzfeld. The role of transport costs and market size in threshold models of industrial location. *Papers of the Regional Science Association*, 1972, *28*, 189–202.

Fals, R. L., and L. N. Moses. Land-use theory and the spatial structure of the nineteenth-century city. *Papers of the Regional Science Association*, 1972, *28*, 219–280.

Friedlander, D. Demographic responses and population change. *Demography*, 1969, *6*, 359–381.

Fuchs, V. Statistical explanations of the relative shift of manufacturing among regions of the United States. *Papers of the Regional Science Association,* 1962, *8,* 105–126.

Gaude, J. Agricultural employment and rural migration in a dual economy. *International Labour Review,* 1972, *106,* 475–490.

Gómez-Pompa, A., C. Vázquez, and S. Guevara. The tropical rain forest: A nonrenewable resource. *Science,* 1972, *177,* 762–765.

Goodrich, C. *Migration and economic opportunity.* Philadelphia: University of Pennsylvania Press, 1935.

Goodstein, M. E. A note on urban and nonurban employment growth in the South, 1940–1960. *Journal of Regional Science,* 1970, *10,* 397–402.

Greenwood, M. J. Lagged response in the decision to migrate. *Journal of Regional Science,* 1970, *10,* 375–384.

Gupta, M. L. Outflow of high-level manpower from the Philippines. *International Labor Review,* 1973, *107,* 167–191.

Harris, B. Externalities and urban decision-making. In M. Perlman, C. J. Leven, and B. Chinitz (Eds.), *Spatial, regional, and population economics.* New York: Gordon and Breach, 1972.

Harris, C. D. Urbanization and population growth in the Soviet Union, 1959–1970. *Geographical Review,* 1971, *61,* 102–124.

Haufe, H. *Die Bevölkerung Europas.* Berlin: Junker und Dünnhaupt, 1936.

Higgs, Robert. The growth of cities in a midwestern region, 1870–1900. *Journal of Regional Science,* 1969, *9,* 369–76.

Ho, Ping-ti. *Studies in the population of China, 1368–1953.* Cambridge, Massachusetts: Harvard University Press, 1959.

Hodge, G., and C. K. Wong. Adapting industrial complex analysis to the realities of regional data. *Papers of the Regional Science Association,* 1972, *28,* 145–166.

Hoover, E. M. *An introduction to regional economics.* New York: Alfred A. Knopf, 1971.

Hoselitz, B. Generative and parasitic cities. *Economic Development and Cultural Change,* 1955, *3,* 278–294.

Ichimura, S. An econometric analysis of domestic migration and regional economy. *Papers of the Regional Science Association,* 1966, *16,* 67–79.

Isard, W., and T. A. Reiner. Regional science: Retrospect and prospect. *Papers of the Regional Science Association,* 1966, *16,* 1–16.

Janzen, D. H. Tropical agraecosystems. *Science,* 1973, *182,* 1212–1219.

Klaussen, T. A. Regional comparative advantage in the United States. *Journal of Regional Science,* 1973, *13,* 97–106.

Kulski, J. E. *Land of urban promise.* Notre Dame, Indiana: Notre Dame University Press, 1967.

Kuznets, S. *Capital in the American economy.* Princeton, N. J.; Princeton University Press, 1961.

Kuznets, S. *Economic growth and structure.* New York: 1965.

Kuznets, S. *Modern economic growth: Rate, structure, and spread.* New Haven, Conn.: 1966.

Kuznets, S. *Growth of nations,* Cambridge, 1971.

Kuznets, S., and D. S. Thomas (Eds.). *Population redistribution and economic growth: United States, 1870–1950* (3 vols.). Philadelphia: Population Studies Center, University of Pennsylvania, 1964.

Lasuen, J. On growth poles. *Urban Studies,* 1969, *6,* 137–161.

Lave, L. B. Congestion and urban location. *Papers of the Regional Science Association,* 1970, *25,* 133–150.

Lincoln, G. A. Energy conservation. *Science,* 1973, *153,* 155–162.

Long, W. H. Demand in space: Some neglected aspects. *Papers of the Regional Science Association,* 1971, *27,* 45–60.

Lot, F. *Les invasions barbares et le peuplement de L'Europe* (2 vols.). Paris: Payot, 1937.

Lot, F. *Les invasions germaniques.* Paris: Payot, 1945.

Make, W. R. Spatial-economic decentralization and mergers in a metropolitan region. *Papers of the Regional Science Association,* 1970, *25,* 119–132.

Marsden, K. Progressive technologies for developing countries. *International Labour Review,* 1970, *101,* 475–502.

Marshall, A. *Industry and trade.* London: 1927.

Marx, K. *Capital* (trans. Samuel Moore and Edward Aveling). Chicago: Charles H. Kerr, 1906.

Mathur, V. K. Occupational composition and its determinants: An intercity size class analysis. *Journal of Regional Science,* 1970, *10,* 81–92.

Medvedkov, Y. Internal structure of a city: An ecological assessment. *Papers of the Regional Science Association,* 1970, *27,* 95–118.

Meggers, B. J., E. S. Ayensu, and W. D. Duckworth (Eds.). *Tropical forest ecosystems in Africa and South America.* New York: Smithsonian Institution Press, 1973.

Mera, K. On the urban agglomeration and economic efficiency. *Economic Development and Cultural Change,* 1973, *21,* 309–324.

Morrison, P. A. The current demographic context of national growth and development. Santa Monica, Calif.: Rand, 1975.

Myers, G. C. Migration and the labor force. *Monthly Labor Review,* 1974, *97,* 12–16.

National Resources Committee. *The structure of the American economy.* Washington, D. C., 1939.

National Resources Planning Board. *Industrial location and national resources.* Washington, D. C., 1943.

Nelson, P. Migration, real income and information. *Journal of Regional Science,* 1959, *1,* 43–74.

Nelson, M. *The development of tropical lands.* Baltimore: Johns Hopkins University Press, 1973.

Nielsen, J. A dilemma: Migrant workers flood Europe. *European Community,* November 1972, pp. 7–12.

Odum, E. P. The strategy of ecosystem development. *Science,* 1969, *164,* 262–270.

Ohlin, B. *Interregional and international trade.* Cambridge: Harvard University Press, 1933.

Owen, W. *The accessible city.* Washington, D. C.: 1972.

Pack, J. R. Determinants of migration to central cities. *Journal of Regional Science,* 1973, *13,* 249–260.

Parrish, W. L., Internal migration and modernization: The European case. *Economic Development and Cultural Change,* 1973, *21,* 591–609.

Perlman, M., C. J. Leven, and B. Chinitz (Eds.). *Spatial, regional, and population economics.* New York: Gordon and Breach, 1972.

Perloff, H., and L. Wingo (Eds.). *Issues in urban economics.* Baltimore, Johns Hopkins University Press, 1968.

Pimental, D., L. E. Hurd, O. C. Bellottis, M. J. Forster, I. N. Oka, O. D. Sholes, and R. J. Whitman, Food production and the energy crisis. *Science,* 1973, *182,* 444.

Plato, *Laws* (B. Jowett, trans.). New York: Random House, 1937, 707–709.

Plummer, A. The theory of population: Some questions of quantity and quality. *Journal of Political Economy*, 1932, *40*, 617–637.

Pred, A. R. *The spatial dynamics of U.S. urban-industrial growth, 1800–1914.* Cambridge, Massachusetts: MIT Press, 1966.

Ranis, G. (Ed.). *The gap between rich and poor nations.* London: Macmillan, 1972.

Rasmussen, T. E. The development of a planned plurinuclear city region: Greater Oslo. *Papers of the Regional Science Association*, 1966, *16*, 105–116.

Reder, M. W. The economic consequences of increased immigration. *Review of Economics and Statistics*, 45, 1963, 221–230.

Richardson, H. W. (Ed.). *Regional economics.* New York: St. Martin's Press, 1971.

Ridker, R. G. Future water needs and supplies. In *Papers of Commission on Population Growth and the American Future* (Vol. 3). Washington, D. C.: U.S. Government Printing Office, 1972.

Riew, J. Migration and public policy. *Journal of Regional Science*, 1973, *13*, 65–76.

Rodwin, L. *Nations and cities.* Boston: Houghton-Mifflin, 1970.

Shaw, R. P. *Migration theory and fact.* Philadelphia: 1975.

Shefer, D. Localization economics in SMSAs: A production function analysis. *Journal of Regional Science*, 1973, *13*, 55–64.

Simon, H. A. Productivity and the urban-rural balance. In H. A. Simon (Ed.), *Models of man.* New York: Wiley, 1957.

Sjaastad, L. A. The relationship between migration and income in the United States. *Papers of the Regional Science Association*, 1960, *6*, 47; 52–54.

Sjaastad, L. A. Costs and returns of human migration. *Journal of Political Economy*, 1962, *70*, Part 2, 80–93.

Smith, A. *An inquiry into the nature and causes of the wealth of nations.* New York: 1937. (Originally published 1776.)

Smith, T. L. Farm labor trends in the United States. *International Labour Review*, 1970, *102*, 149–169.

Somermeyer, W. H. Multi-polar flow models. *Papers of the Regional Science Association*, 1971, *26*, 131–44.

Songre, A. Mass emigration from Upper Volta: The facts and implications. *International Labour Review*, 1973, *108*, 209–225.

Sorokin, P. A., C. C. Zimmerman, and C. J. Galpin (Eds.). *A systematic source book in rural sociology* (2 vols.). Minneapolis: University of Minnesota Press, 1930.

Spengler, J. J. The economic effects of migration. In *Selected studies of migration since World War II.* New York: Milbank Memorial Fund, 1958, pp. 172–192.

Spengler, J. J. Effects produced in receiving countries by pre-1939 immigration. In B. Thomas (Ed.)., *The economics of international immigration* (2nd ed.). London: 1973. (Originally published 1958).

Sternberg, M. J. Agrarian reform and employment: Potential and problems. *International Labour Review*, 1971, *103*, 453–476.

Stigler, G. *The organization of industry.* Homewood, Illinois, Irwin, 1968.

Stouffer, S. A. Intervening opportunities and competing migrants. *Journal of Regional Science*, 1960, *2*, 1–26.

Streit, M. P. Spatial associations and economic linkages between industries. *Journal of Regional Science*, 1970, *9*, 177–188.

Suzuki, K. The variation of regional population in Japan. *Journal of Regional Science*, 1970, *10*, 325–334.

Svennilson, I. *Growth and stagnation in the European economy.* Geneva: 1954.

Taeuber, I. B. *The population of Japan.* Princeton, N. J.: Princeton University Press, 1958.

Tapinos, G. (Ed.). *International migration.* Paris: CICRED, 1974.

Thomas, B. (Ed.). *The economics of international immigration.* (2nd ed.). London: Macmillan, 1954, 1973.

Thomas, D. S. *Social and economic aspects of Swedish population movements, 1750–1933.* New York: Macmillan, 1941.

Thomas, B. *Migration and economic growth.* Cambridge: Cambridge University Press, 1954.

Thompson, W. R. *A preface to urban economics.* Baltimore: Johns Hopkins University Press, 1965.

Thompson, W. R. The national system of cities as an object of public policy. *Urban Studies,* 1972, *9,* 99–116.

Thucydides. *The complete writings* (R. Crowley, trans.). New York: Random House, 1934.

Trott, C. E. Differential responses in the decision to migrate. *Papers of the Regional Science Association,* 1972, *28,* 203–219.

Ullman, E. L. Amenities as a factor in regional growth. *The Geographical Review,* 1954, *44,* 119–132.

Ullman, E. L. The nature of cities reconsidered. *Papers of the Regional Science Association,* 1962, *9,* 7–27.

Ullman, E. L., and M. E. Dacy. The minimum requirements approach to the urban economic base. *Papers of the Regional Science Association,* 1960, *6,* 175–194.

United Nations. *Growth of the world's urban and rural population, 1920–2000.* New York, 1969.

United Nations. *The world population situation in 1970.* New York, 1971.

United States Water Resources Council. *The nation's water resources.* Washington, D.C., 1968.

von Böventer, E. Towards a united theory of spatial economic structure. *Papers of the Regional Science Association,* 1963, *10,* 163–187.

Ward, B. City structure and interdependence. *Papers of the Regional Science Association,* 1963, *10,* 207–221.

Warntz, W. Global science and the tyranny of space. *Papers of the Regional Science Association,* 1967, *19,* 7–19.

Warriner, D. Some problems of rural–urban migration. *International Labour Review,* 1970, *101,* 441–451.

Weber, A. F. *The growth of cities.* New York: Columbia University Press, 1899.

Whitman, M. V. N. Place prosperity and people prosperity: The delineation of optimum policy Areas. In M. Perlman, C. J. Leven, and B. Chinitz (Eds.), *Spatial, regional, and population economics.* New York: Gordon and Breach, 1972.

Williamson, J. G. Regional inequality and the process of national development: A description of the patterns. *Economic Development and Cultural Change,* 1965, *13*(4), Part 2.

Wolpert, J. Behavioral aspects of the decision to migrate. *Papers of the Regional Science Association,* 1965, *15,* 159–169.

Woytinsky, W. S., and E. S. Woytinsky. *World population and production.* New York: Twentieth Century Fund, 1953.

Wrigley, E. A. *Population and history.* New York: McGraw-Hill, 1969.

Yamada, H. On the theory of residential location: Accessibility, space, leisure, and environmental quality. *Journal of Regional Science,* 1972, *29,* 125–135.

CHAPTER 3

Internal Migration and Economic Development: An Overview

Robert E. B. Lucas

The subject matter of this overview is the role of population migration in promoting economic development through increased efficiency of resource allocation, with marginal comments on at least some aspects of distributional implications. The study is limited to observations on internal, rather than international, migration and focuses primarily upon economies in which factors of production are predominantly owned by the private sector.

The existing literature on this topic is quite enormous, and I shall therefore outline only some of the more important issues and contributions. In particular, the focal theme is the idea, prevalent in both analyses and policy positions, that there exists a migration "problem" in developing countries, calling for some form of corrective policy intervention.

Most of the discussion at hand can be adequately illustrated within a two-sector general equilibrium framework. The two sectors—labeled agriculture and manufacturing—are assumed to be located in rural and urban locations, respectively, so that reallocation of laborers between sectors requires migration, though some reservations about these labeling conventions must be expressed at appropriate points.

The paper is divided into two major parts—the first dealing with comparative static analysis, the second very briefly introducing certain aspects of time into the problem—followed by a few concluding remarks.

I. Comparative Static Analysis

This section deals with that branch of the migration literature which examines the properties of an equilibrium of the two-sector economy when endowments of population and other resources are given. Essentially, the objective of most contributions drawn upon here is to discern whether there exists some form of policy intervention that will "improve" upon the equilibrium described, and the optimal form of that intervention.

The section is organized into four subsections: The first establishes, as a reference point, a very simple model in which migration leads the economy to technical efficiency; the second considers various market pathologies in the rural sector which have been suggested as reasons for a breakdown in efficiency; urban pathologies are confined to the third section; and the fourth mentions some limitations of the existing models.

1. FACTOR PRICE EQUALIZATION

In the field of interregional trade, the factor price equalization theorem states that free movements of produced commodities alone is sufficient to generate equality of absolute real factor prices in both regions under certain assumptions (see Samuelson, 1949). However, probably the most useful aspect of this theorem is the fact that the conditions necessary for this result are very restrictive. For example, incomplete specialization of production is generally necessary for full factor price equality, so that trade in agricultural and manufactured goods alone, between rural and urban sectors, will not serve to establish equal real wages for labor in both regions.

Yet such factor price equality may be necessary for technical efficiency. Suppose that output for the two sectors is given by the production functions:

$$Q_i = Q^i(K_i, N_i) \qquad i = r, u. \tag{1}$$

where K_i is the amount of capital employed in sector i, N_i is the number of workers employed in sector i, and subscripts r and u stand for rural and urban, respectively. A necessary condition for the maximization of the value of output $[P \cdot Q_r + Q_u$, where P is the commodity terms of trade], subject to full employment of both factors, and a given P is:[1]

$$P \cdot (\partial Q_r / \partial N_r) = (\partial Q_u / \partial N_u). \tag{2}$$

---

[1] We shall suppose throughout that this is a small open economy, so that P is given exogenously.

If, in addition, labor is hired in both sectors up to the point at which workers receive a wage (w_i; $i = r, u$) equal to the value of marginal product, then (2) is satisfied when:

$$P \cdot (\partial Q_r / \partial N_r) = w_r = w_u = (\partial Q_u / \partial N_u). \tag{3}$$

Given that commodity trade alone does not complete the central equality in (3), the issue is whether migration will do so.[2] Suppose, then, that workers shift their employment from low-wage to high-wage areas and continue to shift until no wage-differential remains (this simple model is already implicit in the writings of Adam Smith, 1812, pp. 218–219), that is,

$$\dot{N}_u \gtreqless 0 \quad \text{as} \quad w_u \gtreqless w_r. \tag{4}$$

It then follows, from an assumption of diminishing marginal productivity of labor, that migration leads to an equilibrium in which labor is used efficiently and serves to promote an equal distribution of wages between urban and rural locations. This situation is depicted in Figure 3.1, with a stable equilibrium division of labor at point a.[3]

Wherein then lies the migration problem?

2. RURAL SECTOR PATHOLOGIES

One of the fundamental assumptions of the foregoing is that rural workers are paid the value of their marginal product. In recent decades, the validity of this condition has been questioned in the context of LDCs, many economists arguing that two widespread phenomena in rural, peasant economies serve to disturb this equality—the phenomena of disguised unemployment and sharecropping.

A. Disguised Unemployment

i. THE EARLY VIEW. Lewis (1954) maintains that in some countries, so many workers are crowded onto so little land that workers may be withdrawn from agriculture without reducing production. In other words, the economy is operating, supposedly in equilibrium, somewhere to the right of b in Figure 3.1, in the range where $\partial Q_r / \partial N_r = 0$. Migration is prevented from moving the system toward point a, despite the migration rule (4), because according to Lewis $w_u = w_r$ at some

---

[2] Notice that movement of capital until $P \cdot \partial Q_r / \partial K_r = \partial Q_u / \partial K_u$ is not typically sufficient to give (2).

[3] The stability conditions are clearly more complex if changing demand patterns initiated by migration affect P, for then the value of marginal product curves themselves shift as laborers move.

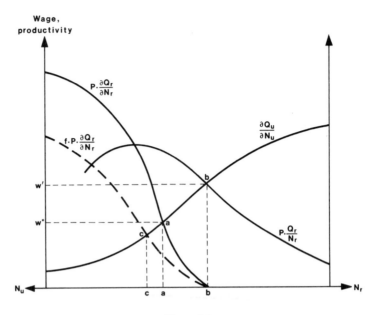

Figure 3.1

level, w', above w^*. The difficult part of the story is explaining why rural firms should continue to hire labor when $w_r > P \cdot \partial Q_r / \partial N_r$.

A popular response to this problem is to point to the profusion of family farms and suggest that the output of such farms is simply divided amongst the family members. In this fashion, the typical person receives a reward equal to the value of his average product on the farm (see Ranis and Fei, 1961). In other words, $w' = P \cdot Q_r / N_r$, as shown in Figure 3.1, and:

$$P \cdot (\partial Q_r / \partial N_r) < P \cdot (Q_r / N_r) = w_r = w_u = (\partial Q_u / \partial N_u). \qquad (5)$$

Clearly, the laissez-faire solution here allocates too much labor to the rural sector compared to the output-maximizing solution—or in other words, there is too little rural-to-urban migration if one starts with an entirely rural population. Notice that it is superfluous to this argument that $\partial Q_r / \partial N_r = 0$. As long as $P \cdot \partial Q_r / \partial N_r < \partial Q_u / \partial N_u$, the same conclusion follows (see Bhagwati and Chakravarty, 1969, who express skepticism concerning many of the attempted tests of this point).

This purported maladjustment of the market system has received widespread acceptance at the policy level, leading to various programs to extract the "surplus" laborers from agriculture and apply them to industry. In doing this, Lewis (1954) suggests that labor can be withdrawn from the rural sector without raising real wages beyond w'; however, a glance at Figure 3.1 shows that if $P \cdot Q_r / N_r$ is the supply curve of labor to the urban sector, this cannot be.[4]

The chief inadequacy of these early models is a failure to consider the behavior of individuals or families that might lead to the inefficient allocations described—an omission perhaps attributable to a lack of belief in any utilitarian sense of rationality amongst peasants. It is to this weakness that the recent literature, and I, now turn.

ii. INCOME MAXIMIZATION. Take first the case in which the sole private objective is one of maximizing income. Within this case, three separate institutional arrangements between the individual and his community (family) must be distinguished (much of this section and the next one, (iii), draw upon an excellent 1969 article by Stiglitz).

a. The Individualistic Economy. If any property is individually owned and each person seeks only to maximize his own earnings, it is clear that laborers will be applied to agriculture up to the point at which $w_u = P \cdot \partial Q_r / \partial N_r$, in the usual competitive fashion and not as in (5).

b. The Communal Economy. Suppose next that communal income is shared equally and that migrants away from the community retain membership. That such ties are maintained is evidenced by the flow of remittances between migrants and their home communities (see Johnson and Whitelaw, 1972). If the communal objective is income maximization, it again pays for members to work outside so long as external wages exceed the value of their marginal contribution to farm output, and the solution is the same as for the individualistic economy. This ought not to be surprising, for this may be viewed as an individualistic society in which persons choose to spend their maximal incomes on gifts to others—either through altruism or by perceiving such gifts as informal insurance or loan payments. Alternatively, however, one can imagine a benevolently despotic family head acting to maximize the communal income then sharing it.

c. The Mixed Economy. An interesting exception arises when the land (or K_r) is communally owned and its total produce shared amongst members, but outmigrants cease to be treated as community members and receive no rent from the land. In this event, the income-maximizing

---

[4] The last observation assumes a nonconstant average product of labor. However, as Stiglitz (1969) argues, if the factors other than laborers are in surplus then output is proportional to the number of laborers. Thus, the infinitely elastic supply case would correspond to a capital–land surplus economy and not to a labor surplus.

individual compares the value of his average product on the commune with his outside wage, and migration proceeds until (5) is satisfied. Notice that the source of the market "distortion" is plainly the lack of individual property rights over the land, for if the migrant could rent out his equal fraction of land after departing, migration would proceed until:

$$(K_r/N_r)\cdot\rho + w_u = w_r = P\cdot(Q_r/N_r) \tag{6}$$

where ρ is the rental price for K_r. If $\rho = P\cdot\partial Q_r/\partial K_r$, then, given constant returns to scale in the production of Q_r, it follows from Euler's theorem that $w_u = P\cdot\partial Q_r/\partial N_r$—the efficiency condition.

Having identified the primary source of the difficulty here as lack of individual property rights, it seems most likely (from the well-known trade theory dictum) that the first-best policy is to establish such rights, rather than tamper with wage subsidies or commodity terms of trade (see Bhagwati, 1971). However, before concluding that even this first-best policy is desirable, it should be noted that there exists a gap in the analysis. In particular, the above theory takes the property rights system as a datum, whereas the tendency today is to treat such rights as endogenous. Unfortunately, though, the theory of any efficiency considerations leading to the widespread establishment of communal property rights to land is not yet well developed (see however Demsetz, 1967; McCloskey, 1972; and Weitzman, 1974).

iii. ELASTICALLY SUPPLIED LABOR. The objective of income maximization, assumed in the previous subsection, implies that each person applies every available moment to earning activities, which is surely indefensible even in low-income societies. Some recent contributions to the behavioral theory of peasant economies therefore adopt a utility function, assumed common to each individual, in which utility depends both upon the individual's income and upon the hours worked—$U(Y, l)$ (see Sen, 1966; Berry and Soligo, 1968; and Stiglitz, 1969).

By embracing leisure as an objective, hours of work are rendered elastically supplied by a given work force, so the production functions (1) must generally be modified to:

$$Q_i = Q^i(K_i, N_i, l_i) \tag{7}$$

where l_i are the hours worked per worker in sector i. As far as total product maximization is concerned, it remains necessary for migration to proceed until the marginal contribution of an extra worker is equal in each sector. However, it is now vital that this marginal contribution be denoted *mutatis mutandis* and, in particular, after any adjustment in l_i.

Thus, the necessary condition on laborer allocation becomes:

$$\frac{dQ_u}{dN_u} = P \cdot \frac{dQ_r}{dN_r} \tag{8}$$

where, in general:

$$\frac{dQ_i}{dN_i} = \frac{\partial Q_i}{\partial N_i} + \frac{\partial Q_i}{\partial l_i} \cdot \frac{\partial l_i}{\partial N_i} . \tag{9}$$

We may continue to suppose for now that $w_u \cdot l_u = dQ_u/dN_u$, so that the condition (8) may be stated as:

$$w_u l_u = P \cdot \left[\frac{\partial Q_r}{\partial N_r} + \frac{\partial Q_r}{\partial l_r} \cdot \frac{\partial l_r}{\partial N_r} \right] . \tag{10}$$

The question now arises as to whether or not migration proceeds to establish (10), and this depends both upon the communal arrangements and upon the form of the production functions (7).

a. Homogeneous Man-hours: The Communal Economy. Sen (1966) and Berry and Soligo (1968) adopt a fairly traditional specification of (7):

$$Q_r = Q^r(K_r, L_r) \tag{11}$$

where $L_r = l_r \cdot N_r$. It follows that (9) is:

$$\frac{dQ_r}{dN_r} = \frac{\partial Q_r}{\partial L_r} \left[l_r + N_r \cdot \frac{\partial l_r}{\partial N_r} \right] . \tag{12}$$

Following Sen (1966), suppose that each community shares its income equally, and acts to maximize a Benthamite welfare function additive in utilities of both migrants and nonmigrants (this problem is not, however, explicitly considered by Sen, 1966). That is,

$$\max_{N_r, l_r, l_u} N_r \cdot U(Y, l_r) + (\bar{N}_r - N_r) \cdot U(Y, l_u) \tag{13}$$

subject to

$$\bar{N}_r \cdot Y = (\bar{N}_r - N_r) w_u \cdot l_u + P \cdot Q^r(K_r, N_r \cdot l_r)$$

where $\bar{N}_r$ is the community membership. Solving for the first-order conditions, gives $l_u = l_r$ and:

$$P \cdot (\partial Q_r/\partial L_r) = w_u = -\frac{\partial U/\partial l}{\partial U/\partial Y} . \tag{14}$$

Thus, although free migration equates the distribution of income and utility in this context, it serves to satisfy (10) and hence maximize output only if $\partial l_r / \partial N_r = 0$. The latter is highly unlikely, for, although there is no change in labor "earnings" from a marginal shift in laborers to manufacturing, holding l_r constant, the family does lose income through a fall in "rents" to their land. Thus $\partial U/\partial Y$ rises, given l_r, and l_r therefore begins to rise to reestablish the last equality in (14). In rising, l_r contributes to Y through (11), so the equilibrium adjustment depends on the forms of both (11) and the utility function.

In fact, Sen (1966) focuses on those properties required to make (12) zero, but any negative value of $\partial l_r / \partial N_r$ is sufficient for free rural to urban migration to be too little to generate maximal product: It is not necessary to be to the right of b in Figure 3.1, only to the right of a.

These issues have stimulated much interest, both theoretically and empirically, in the distinction between the marginal product of labor $(\partial Q/\partial L)$ and the *mutatis mutandis* marginal product of laborers (dQ/dN), apparently in the belief that this represents a market "failure." This belief, however, is only necessarily founded if one takes a narrow view of economic development—namely that of maximizing output. In a society adhering to consumer sovereignty, one must surely balance extra output against forgone leisure in considering the promotion of further migration, and it follows immediately from the communal welfare maximization assumed above that overall welfare cannot be improved.[5]

b. Seasonal Labor: The Individualistic Economy. So far, there is nothing to distinguish the "rural" sector as being agricultural. Indeed, since family enterprises are not uncommon in the traditional urban sectors and since plantations are frequently intermingled with peasant farms, the foregoing use of the terms *rural* and *urban* must be read with care. But Stiglitz (1969) introduces an element distinctly associated with arable farming—the seasonality of labor.

In this instance, labor productivity depends not only on the total number of man-hours but on their distribution over the seasons. Sen's production function does not capture this, for every man-hour is a perfect substitute for all others in (11). If output depends upon the season to which a man applies his hours and if there exists a natural upper limit on the hours per person that may be applied to any one

[5] This strong result depends upon the ability of the community to choose all relevant variables in (13). This follows the sense of Sen (1966); but contrast Stiglitz (1969), who assumes each individual to decide his own hours of work and hence (p. 24) reaches a weaker result on social welfare in the communal economy. In either case, zero marginal productivity of laborers does not imply zero social welfare cost for withdrawn laborers.

season, then a marginal hour worked by a given work force may contribute to the off-season, whereas an extra man can contribute also to the high-productivity season. In other words, the appropriate production function is typically (7). It may then be shown that even the simplest case—the individualistic economy of landless peasants—does not typically cause migration to maximize output.

The difficulty here really arises from the migration decision rule, which may be written:

$$\dot{N}_u \gtreqless 0 \qquad \text{as} \qquad U(Y_u, l_u) \gtreqless U(Y_r, l_r). \tag{15}$$

If $Y_i \equiv w_i \cdot l_i$, this reduces to (4); but, with seasonal labor, Y_i is not so defined. Rather, the income–leisure constraint is generally kinked for the individual, as shown by rr in Figure 3.2 for two seasons, owing to the seasonal marginal productivity differences. When migration ceases, the urban wage line (uu) must be tangential to the same indifference curve as rr. Consequently, free migration now results in equality of utility distribution, with rural workers earning less whilst enjoying greater leisure than their urban counterparts, or $w_u l_u > Y_r$. If the competitive agricultural sector pays a worker the value of his marginal product over

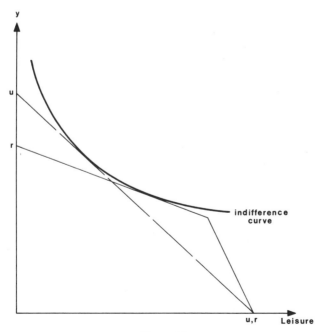

Figure 3.2

the year, ceteris paribus, then:

$$w_u l_u > Y_r = P \cdot \partial Q_r / \partial N_r \qquad (16)$$

and there is no reason to suppose in general that (10) is satisfied. Free, nonseasonal migration will not serve to maximize output, though again it may be shown that even if $dQ_r/dN_r = 0$, withdrawal of workers from agriculture into manufacturing adds nothing to social welfare at the margin, owing to leisure losses in the rural sector (for proof, see Stiglitz, 1969, pp. 23–24).

iv. DISGUISED UNEMPLOYMENT: A SUMMING UP. Whether there exists disguised unemployment in the rural sector such that free rural-to-urban migration is too little for the social good remains unresolved, though the theory has proceeded far from the original work by Lewis. The existence of communal land, to which one forfeits rights upon outmigration, does promote an inefficient allocation of inelastically supplied labor, ceteris paribus, though a broader view of efficiency must await inquiry into the reasons for establishing communal land. Similarly, the migrant-embracing communal economy and even the individualistic economy may fail to promote maximal output under free migration, once leisure enters the scenario. Yet, whether or not this failure ought to be deemed a market failure, really pivots on the evaluation of forgone leisure vis-à-vis gained output, and certainly some (though not all) institutional arrangements cannot be improved upon in this sense, despite sectoral inequality of marginal productivity of a given endowment of laborers.

B. Sharecropping

The practice of sharecropping—dividing output between landlord and tenant—is both old and widespread. The traditional view of this practice is essentially that of an excise tax, being most conveniently illustrated by returning to the production functions (1). If a farm tenant must pay some fraction, $(1 - f)$, of the value of his output to the landlord, then the tenant's profits are given by:

$$\pi = f \cdot P \cdot Q_r - w_r \cdot N_r. \qquad (17)$$

Hiring laborers (or retaining family members) so as to maximize profits, and assuming the migration rule (4), equilibrium is reached when:

$$w_u = w_r = f \cdot P \cdot \partial Q_r / \partial N_r. \qquad (18)$$

This is illustrated by point c in Figure 3.1, which, being to the left of a, is a position of excessive rural-to-urban migration, as compared to the output maximum.

This outlook remained the conventional wisdom until the appearance of Cheung's (1968) paper, which considers the problem of rental maximization for the landlord. This, Cheung writes as:

$$\max_{m,f,N_r} m \cdot (1 - f) \cdot P \cdot Q_r \qquad (19)$$

subject to

$$w_r \cdot N_r = f \cdot P \cdot Q_r$$

where m is the number of parcels into which the landlord's total holding is equally divided. The constraint on this problem is the competitive condition of zero normal profits in (17). It follows immediately from the necessary first-order conditions with respect to f and N_r that $w_r = P \cdot \partial Q_r / \partial N_r$, rather than (18), and there is no migration problem on this count.

Bardhan and Srinivasan (1971) subsequently question the validity of Cheung's novel position, chiefly on the grounds of the ability of atomistic landlords to decide individually upon f and to dictate N_r. Instead, Bardhan and Srinivasan allow the tenant to select the amount of labor to be applied to the rented land, and—assuming that the landlord will choose to work some of his own land with hired and own labor—they derive the demand and supply for sharecropped land as a function of f. The share, f, in their model is then determined by the market as if it were a price. Naturally, in this model, since tenants choose N_r, one again returns to the condition (18).

Which of these views is correct? To answer this, consider the following problem: How can a sharecropping tenant pay labor according to (18) and yet compete with labor-hiring landlords, who presumably hire until the value of the marginal product of laborers equals w_r? The answer offered by Bardhan and Srinivasan (1971) is that:

$$f \cdot P \cdot Q_{r1} = w_r = P \cdot Q_{r2} \qquad (20)$$

where Q_{r1} and Q_{r2} are the marginal products of laborers on the tenants' and landlords' farms, respectively. This of course implies that $Q_{r1} > Q_{r2}$, which is possible in competitive equilibrium only under two circumstances: that of diminishing returns to scale, and when landlords possess different production functions from tenants.[6] The most plausible

---

[6] In responding to Newberry (1974), Bardhan and Srinivasan (1974) stress the former circumstance, though I shall pursue the latter, in keeping with the rest of this paper.

reason for the latter arises from a discrepancy in effort or quality of work supplied when working for fixed wages as opposed to a share in output, an element omitted from the specification of (1).[7] For simplicity, let us insert this element by supposing it possible to raise the marginal productivity of the landlord's workers to Q_{r1} by incurring supervisory costs equal to γ at the margin. Hence, landlords will hire laborers up to Q_{r1} if:

$$w_r = P \cdot Q_{r1} - \gamma. \tag{21}$$

The apparent discrepancy between Cheung (1968) and Bardhan–Srinivasan (1971) is then resolved if Cheung's condition is seen as referring to marginal product in the sense of net contribution $P \cdot Q_{r1} - \gamma$, and if competition in the market sets:

$$f = 1 - \gamma / P \cdot Q_{r1} \tag{22}$$

as it must for wage labor and sharecropping to coexist under these conditions.[8] Sharecropping does not, then, act to lower the effective marginal product curve as shown in Figure 3.1, but rather, this curve remains intransigent under the offsetting effects of increased incentive versus lowered fraction of marginal product received. In other words, sharecropping does not induce any migration differing from the wage-labor economy and both are productively efficient (γ being a real cost), given the above assumptions.

Nevertheless, the above scenario is somewhat ambivalent, leaving landlords neutral between sharecropping and wage-labor uses of their lands. This ambivalence may generally be removed by the admission of riskiness in production, viewing sharecropping as a contractual mechanism for spreading these risks as well as providing work-effort incentives. Little is changed if both tenants and landlords are risk neutral, acting solely on the value of expected marginal products. More generally, interpersonal differences in attitudes toward risk and effort incentives yield inequalities in output per acre across farms and hence render agriculture "productively" inefficient, though again to conclude that welfare can necessarily be improved would be to override those taste factors leading to this dispersion (see particularly Stiglitz, 1974).

---

[7] Notice the comparison with piece-rate labor. I am very grateful to J. Hirshleifer and J. G. Riley for discussion of this topic. See also Stiglitz (1974) on elasticity of effort supply.

[8] Cheung (1968) and Newberry (1974) apparently are considering the case where supervisory costs may be incurred either under the wage or under the sharecropping system. Under the former these costs are prohibitive, but under sharecropping the landlord can select effort level at some cost, and output is net of these costs in (19). Indeed, these authors suggest that this sharecropping supervisory cost comprises only the cost of enforcing an explicit contract.

3. URBAN PATHOLOGIES

Thus far, it is assumed that the wage paid to an urban migrant is equal to the value of his marginal contribution to output in the manufacturing or modern sector. Yet a prevalent feature of urban centers in capitalist LDCs is a high rate of unemployment, in the sense that a substantial fraction of the available urban work force is not employed in modern manufacturing.

Todaro (1969) therefore inquires into the causes of persistent rural-to-urban migration when there already exist many unemployed in the towns. Essentially, Todaro adopts a stochastic formulation of the urban wage, modifying (4) (or (15)) accordingly to:

$$\dot{N}_u \gtreqless 0 \quad \text{as} \quad w_u^e \gtreqless w_r \tag{23}$$

where w_u^e is the expected value of the stochastic w_u. Notice that, by relying upon the mean alone, Todaro is assuming risk neutrality on behalf of the individualistic migrants. Moreover, Todaro presumes that the expected urban wage is dependent upon the going manufacturing wage, w_u, and the employment rate $(N_u/N_u^*$, where N_u^* is the urban work force), which governs the probability of receiving w_u. Hence:[9]

$$w_u^e = E(w_u, N_u/N_u^*) \quad \text{with} \quad E_1 > 0 \quad \text{and} \quad E_2 > 0. \tag{24}$$

Consideration of the efficiency implications of a comparative static model embodying (23) and (24) commonly parallels the previous section in assuming productive efficiency within the other (now rural) sector, so that $w_r = P \cdot \partial Q_r/\partial N_r$.[10] Thus, migration ceases when:

$$P \cdot \frac{\partial Q_r}{\partial N_r} = E\left(w_u, \frac{N_u}{N_u^*}\right). \tag{25}$$

Analysis of the relationship of (25) to an efficient solution, together with the packaging of policy prescriptions to improve efficiency, cannot proceed independently of the source of unemployment in our comparative static framework, and two broad cases are distinguished below.

i. AN INSTITUTIONAL URBAN WAGE. The path-breaking model of Harris and Todaro (1970) is depicted in Figure 3.3. The ultimate cause

---

[9] In fact, Todaro (1969) employs $w_u^e = w_u \cdot N_u/N_u^*$. Stiglitz (1974) shows that this particular specification can stem from a number of alternative hiring models. However, each of these (and (24)) assumes a zero wage during unemployment. In practice, this is frequently unrealistic in LDCs—"unemployment" often corresponding to low-wage occupation in the urban traditional sector (see Herrick, 1974).

[10] Or $w_r \cdot l_r = P \cdot dQ_r/dN_r$ if labor is elastically supplied.

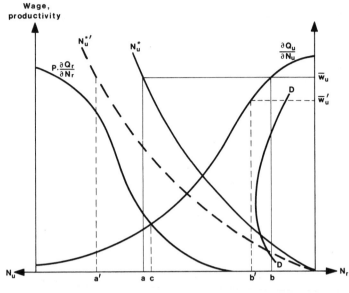

Figure 3.3

of urban unemployment in this framework is a "politically" determined urban minimum real wage, $\bar{w}_u$—perhaps maintained by minimum wage legislation. The competitive industrial sector hires labor up to point b, where $\bar{w}_u = \partial Q_u / \partial N_u$. The curve N_u^* may be read as a supply schedule of laborers to the urban sector—incorporating the discouraged migrant effect from unemployment—being the locus of solutions to (25). Notice that w_r is not held constant along N_u^*. N_r is total endowment of labor minus N_u^*, so (25) is an equation in w_u and N_u^* alone.[11] Given $\bar{w}_u$, one may then read employment in the urban sector at b, urban unemployment as ab, and residual employment in agriculture at a.

This system is of course inefficient. Laborers are unemployed and $P \cdot \partial Q_r / \partial N_r < \partial Q_u / \partial N_u$. It ought to be emphasized that the sole source of this inefficiency is the minimum wage, and the first-best policy is clearly removal of this rigidity, but such action may not be politically feasible.

A very standard second-best policy suggestion is a wage subsidy to urban employers, effectively lowering their observed wage from $\bar{w}_u$ to $\bar{w}_u'$, raising urban employment from b to b' in Figure 3.3. If the N_u^*

---

[11] N_u is, of course, a function of w_u alone, through $\partial Q_u / \partial N_u$, assuming K_u constant. The above also assumes P constant as before, a restriction not imposed by Harris and Todaro (1970).

curve were to remain fixed, unemployment would fall to ab'. But $\bar{w}_u$ observed by workers is unaltered, so by the conditions on (24), $w_u{}^e$ increases for any given w_u and $N_u{}^*$ must shift left as shown by $N_u^{*\prime}$. In fact it is possible that $a'b' > ab$, with unemployment magnified (indeed Harris and Todaro, 1970, Appendix II, indicate that for many African countries this is indeed likely). If the latter is true, then output may also fall, despite subtraction of workers from low marginal productivity agriculture and addition of them to higher marginal productivity industry, for the number of workers involved in the former (aa') then exceeds the latter (bb').

In essence, since there are two "problems" here— urban unemployment and induced migration—one might suppose that two instruments are generally required. Harris and Todaro advocate a policy package of urban wage subsidies and quantitative migration controls. By use of the latter, it is in principle possible to hold rural-to-urban migration constrained at point c in Figure 3.3 and simultaneously deploy wage subsidies to slide $\bar{w}_u{}'$ down $\partial Q_u/\partial N_u$ to c—the output-maximizing position that would be achieved in the absence of the sticky urban wage.

Harris and Todaro rightly express reservations about the ethical propriety of imposing physical restrictions upon internal migration. This aspect is taken up by Bhagwati and Srinivasan (1974), who show that such a policy instrument is not essential to achieving point c. Obviously, no free migration will occur under rule (23) if $w_r = \bar{w}_u$ and no unemployment is incurred. The latter condition is satisfied at point c when:

$$w_r - s_r = P \cdot (\partial Q_r/\partial N_r) = (\partial Q_u/\partial N_u) = \bar{w}_u - s_u \qquad (26)$$

where s_i is a wage subsidy to employers in sector i. It follows immediately (using $w_r = \bar{w}_u$) that $s_u = s_r$. In other words, an equal wage subsidy to both sectors achieves point c without resorting to direct migration controls—one policy solves both problems. One unfortunate feature of this solution is that of being a universal subsidy—rather than a tax-cum-subsidy—which raises the problem of financing without producing contervailing distortions (see Stiglitz, 1974).

ii. A LABOR-TURNOVER MODEL. Stiglitz (1974b) offers an alternative view of the fundamental source of urban unemployment. This model retains the essential rural and migration features of the Harris–Todaro model, so that (25) continues to hold, but a new element is inserted into urban employment. In particular, some cost, τ, is incurred in hiring new laborers, and employees possess a propensity to quit their firm governed by:

$$q = q \left(\frac{w_u}{E(w_u)}, \frac{w_u}{w_r}, \frac{N_u^* - N_u}{N_u^*} \right) \quad , q_i < 0, \quad i = 1, 2, 3 \quad (27)$$

where w_u is this firm's wage rate, $E(w_u)$ is the expected value of other urban wages. The cost of employing a laborer is then given by:

$$\tilde{w}_u = w_u + \tau \cdot q. \quad (28)$$

Stiglitz assumes that each firm acts as a monopolistic competitor, taking other urban wage offers, rural wages, and the unemployment rate as given, but varying own wage to minimize labor costs per worker. That is, the firm sets w_u at the minimum point of the U-shaped $\tilde{w}$ cost curve in Figure 3.4, at the point where extra wage costs would be just offset by decreasing turnover costs.

The profit-maximizing firm selects its labor force size such that $\tilde{w}_u$ equals the value of labor's marginal product, generating a downward-sloping demand for labor schedule with respect to $\tilde{w}_u$ as usual. This property also holds true for the urban market demand curve for labor, assuming with Stiglitz that all urban firms are identical, so $w_u = E(w_u)$. However, the market demand curve for urban labor is now backward-

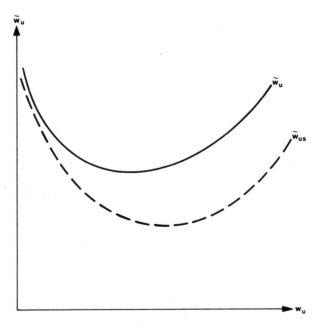

Figure 3.4

bending with respect to w_u in some part of its range, owing to the U-shaped relationship between $\tilde{w}_u$ and w_u. Such a backward-bending demand curve is shown by DD in Figure 3.3. w_u is set by firms at the point where DD becomes vertical, this being the minimum for $\tilde{w}_u$. N_u is then determined by DD, and N_u^* may be read from a curve equivalent to that marked in Figure 3.3, which leaves N_r as a residual. Thus, monopolistic competition in Stiglitz's model generates unemployment in equilibrium.

Stiglitz maintains that the output-maximizing solution must also embody unemployment, noting that the value of total output is now given by:

$$P \cdot Q_r + Q_u - \tau \cdot q \cdot N_u. \tag{29}$$

If the quit rate becomes very high as full employment is approached, then clearly turnover costs dominate and output is maximized short of zero unemployment. However, the competitive system described by Stiglitz will not generate the "optimal" amount of unemployment, owing ultimately to monopolistic competition in the model: Though each firm assumes w_r and $(N_r^* - N_r)/N_r^*$ given, changes in w_u by every identical firm will in fact change these values. In other words, whereas the firms in aggregate act as if DD were the locus of profit-maximizing solutions under alternative w_u, this is not in fact the case. Further, Stiglitz demonstrates, as in the Harris–Todaro case, that an urban wage subsidy alone will not guide the economy to the output-maximizing solution. It is clear that subtracting a subsidy from $\tilde{w}_u$ in (28) will increase urban demand for labor, but migration now serves to withdraw labor from the rural sector on two counts: first because of the initial drop in unemployment as in Harris–Todaro; but also because w_u rises. The latter may be seen in Figure 3.4, where the wage subsidy acts to lower $\tilde{w}_u$ but shifts its minimum w_u point to the right, as shown by $\tilde{w}_{us}$. (For proof that this is a shift to the right, see Stiglitz, 1974b, pp. 215–216.) In other words, as DD in Figure 3.3 shifts left, its turning point w_u rises and N_u^* shifts left on two counts.

However, Stiglitz does not really consider the Bhagwati–Srinivasan case of both rural and urban wage subsidies. In general, with these two instruments it is possible to manipulate both migration and urban unemployment—but to where should they be guided? Consider again the quit rate function (27). The recent literature on job search suggests that it may be quite rational for an individual to quit his job and invest in job search, providing there exists some dispersion of alternative wages (see Stiglitz, 1974, p. 198). Conversely, there remains no incentive to quit ($q = 0$) if $w_u = E(w_u) = w_r$. The former equality is assumed by Stiglitz, the latter is the condition of no migration with zero unemployment. In other words, Stiglitz's system is in a no-subsidy equilibrium at:

$$(\partial Q_u / \partial N_u) = \bar{w}_u = w_u = w_r = (\partial Q_r / \partial N_r) \cdot P. \tag{30}$$

Further, with $q = 0$ and full employment, (30) is obviously consistent with maximizing (29).

The conventional optimal solution is then an equilibrium in Stiglitz's system, sustainable under laissez-faire, provided that quit and search ceases when no spread in wages exists. The complication which this model does add is that monopolistic competitors preempt the Walrasian auctioneer in flexing wages toward the optimum: If this part of the story is true, then temporary wage subsidies may be necessary to nudge the economy toward output maximization, only to be disbanded upon arrival.

4. CONCLUDING REMARKS ON COMPARATIVE STATICS

Is there a migration problem in LDCs? The answer to this question is sought above by viewing the rural and urban sectors in turn, while presuming the other sector to be internally allocating laborers efficiently. For the most part, this latter presumption proves internally consistent within the partial approach, migration leading to an "efficient" allocation of laborers between sectors in a laissez-faire equilibrium. Here it must be emphasized that efficiency is defined in terms of individual preferences and may not be consistent with productive efficiency— particularly in the cases of elastically supplied hours of work and uncertainty in production under sharecropping. This generalization is not without exception—the case of a mixed economy, a communal economy where the individual chooses his hours of work selfishly, or Stiglitz's view of urban monopolistic competition may each generate equilibria inconsistent with maximal welfare under laissez-faire. The incidence of such cases, and the probability of government selecting an instrument set at a level so as actually to improve upon laissez-faire, are clearly empirical questions of some considerable import.

The foregoing analytical framework is, however, rather limited. For example, it is presumed throughout that labor is homogeneous. As long as markets are clearing in the usual competitive fashion, this restriction is not of great interest for efficiency. But study of a three-factor economy with unskilled labor capable of transformation into skilled at some cost—probably partially subsidized—might prove rewarding under some of the institutional frameworks discussed here.[12]

The comparative static models are further limited, by definition, to a timeless world. Thus, there is no migration in these models—always the question concerns equilibrium properties when migration ceases. Also, these are truly studies of migration effects in developing countries, rather than migration for development in the sense of factor accumulation. The next section therefore turns very briefly to certain elements of time relating migration to development.

II. Elements of Time

Three elements of time in relation to migration are distinguished for brief discussion here: migration as dynamic adjustment between comparative static solutions, migration as investment, and the role of migration in factor accumulation.

1. ONGOING MIGRATION: THE MIGRATION FUNCTION

The basic methodology of comparative statics is generally sound even though the economy is not in equilibrium, provided dynamic adjustment is toward such a solution. It is worth noting that the only constraints placed on the dynamics of migration in considering "stability" in the previous section are certain properties (such as (4), (5) and (23)) of the rate of migration function. No particular specification of such a function is required, and there is consequently no claim to a lack of influence from variables exogenous to the system. Indeed, it is not even required that, say, wage differentials (in (4)) should explain a large fraction of the rate of population flow.

A number of empirical studies confirm the qualitative nature of the inequality constraints in (4), though less attention is typically paid to the desired zero-migration property. (For a recent survey, see Krugman and Bhagwati, 1975.)

These qualitative results typically hold for both gross and net migration flow equations, the latter clearly being the relevant consideration in the above comparative static models. The existence of concurrent reverse migration is not an explicit part of the models in Section I, but the standard explanation postulates a heterogeneous labor force, with

---

[12] Bhagwati and Hamada (1974) undertake a Harris–Todaro type analysis with skilled and unskilled labor and an international brain drain. See also Todaro (1971).

each group behaving according to the decision rules of Section I—a hypothesis not yet subjected to much systematic testing.[13]

Unfortunately, most econometric studies of migration equations are open to substantial criticism at least on the grounds of both simultaneous equation and specification bias.[14] It seems unlikely that the qualitative nature of the results is reversed by these biases, but certainly the magnitude of the estimated coefficients is more dubious, the latter being essential to evaluation of the general repercussions of almost any policy intervention (or removal).

2. INVESTMENT IN MIGRATION: A HUMAN CAPITAL APPROACH

The human capital approach to migration, as developed by Sjaastad (1962), introduces an element of time into the migration decision criterion. Letting θ represent the costs initially incurred in migrating, the individualistic criterion (15) might be modified to:[15]

$$\dot{N}_u \gtreqless 0 \quad \text{as} \quad \int_t [U(Y_{ut}, l_{ut}) - U(Y_{rt}, l_{rt})]e^{-\phi t} - \theta \gtreqless 0 \quad (31)$$

where subscript t denotes value at time t, ϕ is a discount rate. This present value criterion, in other words, states that the individual views θ as an investment in access to an alternative location's utility stream.

Sjaastad's proposal is to employ this framework to evaluate whether too little or too much migration is undertaken. In particular, Sjaastad

---

[13] Stiglitz (1969) develops an interesting variant of the welfare-maximizing rural community, where members choose their own work hours under seasonal labor. Presumably $w_u >$ w_r at the margin of hours for a worker (cf. Figure 3.2), urban workers work longer and $U(Y, l_u) < U(Y, l_r)$. Thus, migrants must be coerced into migrating—perhaps at the promise of later return to the higher rural utility. In essence, this is a form of the target savings idea.

In the communal case where the commune selects l_u and l_r, it can be shown that $U(Y, l_u) = U(Y, l_r)$ only if

$$(\partial Q_r/\partial N_r) \cdot (\partial l_r/\partial Q_r) \cdot (N_r/l_r) = 1.$$

[14] Having treated these and other estimation issues elsewhere (Lucas, 1975), I shall not repeat the arguments here. In that paper, I also mention the difficulty of explaining why adjustment to any wage differential by a given population should be extended through time, unless one incorporates a learning-through-time feature.

A few studies using U.S. data have estimated migration functions in a simultaneous model, allowing both the flow of migrants to depend upon wage differentials and vice versa. See, for example, Muth (1971).

[15] The costs involved include transportation, foregone earnings, psychic costs of separation, and costs of information acquisition. Distance is commonly taken to be a proxy for these total costs in regression analysis, though Schwartz (1973) presents evidence favoring information costs as the predominant component.

considers computing the present value of earning differentials between locations and comparing these with estimated values of θ. This method is, however, subject to a number of unfortunate difficulties.

First, in view of (31) it is apparent that use of Y alone in computing present values is inadequate—the omission of leisure value being an error common to much of the human capital literature. Second, in general, Y in (31) includes the monetary equivalent of psychic earnings associated with alternative milieux. Sjaastad explicitly advocates omission of psychic earnings in computing present values, which is tantamount to denying some aspects of consumer preferences in defining optimal development. Third, there is an implicit assumption of equilibrium inherent in Sjaastad's view. Thus, if one finds the integral in (31) to be greater than θ, it is not clear in what sense this is inefficient as long as $\dot{N}_u > 0$. Finally, Sjaastad rightly emphasizes the possibility of a gap between the social and private evaluation of migration. Indeed, that is precisely what most of Section I is about, and one cannot test for the lack of such a discrepancy by assuming it away.

Nevertheless, the human capital framework has its useful points. By emphasizing the time investment nexus inherent in individuals' decisions, (31) indicates the importance of capital markets in determining migration responses through ϕ. If capital markets are "imperfect," one should then expect migration to be at an inefficient level, though it is well known that "imperfect" capital markets are frequently misdefined. Further, (31) reduces to (15) or (23) only if wages and expected wages respectively remain constant through time (ignoring compounded values of θ and changes in levels of unearned income). On the other hand, if there is a queue for employment, or random selection from the unemployment pool without replacement, then $w_u{}^e$ does vary through time (see Stiglitz, 1974, Appendix). Also, there is ample evidence that nominal wages grow with age.[16] Appropriate modifications of the comparative static conclusions are fairly trivial, but certainly testing causes of migration hypotheses in terms of current differentials alone may be misleading.

3. MIGRATION AND FACTOR ACCUMULATION

All of the preceding is essentially concerned with the role of migration in moving a developing economy onto an appropriately defined produc-

---

[16] The investment approach generates a widely confirmed hypothesis that the young have a greater propensity to migrate, ceteris paribus, owing to their longer recoupment period.

tion possibility frontier, constrained by a given capital stock and population. The extent to which these latter endowments are endogenous to a model of migration renders our analysis incomplete, for migration then influences the expansionary speed of the production frontier. This topic rightly deserves a separate overview, and only a few features are mentioned here.

The economic theory of fertility suggests that the demand for children depends—among other things—on income, cost of child-rearing, and tastes. Rural-to-urban migration generally influences each of these. In Section I, it was noted that the individualistic economy with seasonal rural labor generates lower income and greater leisure in rural, as compared to urban, locations. If, then, children are superior goods in terms of money income, continued migration should tend to enhance population growth, ceteris paribus. Counterbalancing this is the fact that child-rearing is likely to be much less costly in rural locations, where the relative price of foods is typically lower and children enter the work force at a younger age. Also operating in the latter direction is the taste factor from migration creating a sex imbalance in the two sectors. Notice, however, that one cannot conclude that migration does or does not promote fertility by simply comparing birthrates amongst migrants and rural dwellers; since migration is known to be selective with regard to age and education, at least these factors must be held constant in comparing.

The role of migration in growth through capital deepening is the subject of much attention in development literature, appearing in early Soviet discussion as the famous Proebrazhensky dilemma. (For an excellent formalization of Proebrazhensky's dynamic programming problem, see Bardhan, 1970, Chapter 9.) If manufacturing and agriculture are heroically viewed primarily as capital and consumer goods industries respectively, then the supply of extra capital depends upon migration in allocating laborers between sectors and hence industries. Imposing an optimization rule on the time path of consumer goods, then implies an optimal time path of labor allocation and hence migration.

These observations on the incompleteness of our outline of comparative statics does not imply irrelevance. Far from it. The issue of whether migration acts to place society at a position on the production possibility frontier at a point of tangency with the terms of trade, P, may be the *only* relevant question on the efficiency of migration for economic development as defined by consumer preferences. If there are no externalities involved in child rearing, and if P adequately reflects society's marginal rate of intertemporal substitution between present and future consumption, this is indeed probably true. An additional wrinkle appears in the analysis of a closed economy if—as is sometimes suggested—the distributional effects of migration influence the propensity to save; for then migration affects the demand for capital and consumer goods, and hence P. For the small open economy examined above, no extension is required, however, for any such demand shifts merely affect the volume of international trade in the two classes of goods.

III. Closing Remarks

In lieu of a conclusion, an economist's overview in an interdisciplinary volume of this nature should probably close with a bow to the limitations of existing economic methodology. In particular, the analysis throughout this paper tacitly presumes tastes of individuals, and the institutional extensions of those tastes in the form of communal arrangements, as data—or at least as exogenous to the migration process. This omission is not a consequence of complete unawareness of the likelihood that urbanization changes both tastes and institutions[17] but, rather, results from the great difficulties of evaluating these induced phenomena in any meaningful fashion.

References

Bardhan, P. K. *Economic growth, development and foreign trade.* New York: Wiley-Interscience, 1970.

Bardhan, P. K., and T. N. Srinivasan. Cropsharing tenancy in agriculture: A theoretical and empirical analysis. *American Economic Review,* vol. 61, 1971, *61,* 48–64.

Bardhan, P. K., and T. N. Srinivasan, "Cropsharing in Agriculture: Rejoinder," *American Economic Review,* vol. 64, December 1974, pp. 1067–69.

Berry, R. A., and R. Soligo. Rural–urban migration, agricultural output, and the supply price of labour in a labour-surplus economy. *Oxford Economic Papers,* 1968, *20,* 230–249.

Bhagwati, J. N. The generalized theory of distortions and welfare. In J. N. Bhagwati et al. (Eds.), *Trade, balance of payments and growth.* Amsterdam: North-Holland, 1971.

Bhagwati, J. N., and S. Chakravarty. Contributions to Indian economic analysis: A survey. *American Economic Review,* 1969, *59* supplement, 1–73.

Bhagwati, J. N., and K. Hamada. The brain drain, international integration of markets for professionals and unemployment. *Journal of Development Economics,* 1974, *1,* 19–42.

---

[17] See, for example, an interesting passage by Adam Smith on the effects of urbanization upon another institution—that of feudal war-lords: "Commerce and manufactures gradually introduced order and good government, and with them, the liberty and security of individuals, among the inhabitants of the country, who had before lived almost in a continual state of war with their neighbours, and of servile dependency upon their superiors. This, though it has been the least observed, is by far the most important of all their effects [Smith, 1812, Volume 3, p. 119]."

Bhagwati, J. N., and T. N. Srinivasan. On reanalyzing the Harris–Todaro model. *American Economic Review*, 1974, *64*, 502–508.

Cheung, S. N. S. Private property rights and sharecropping. *Journal of Political Economy*, 1968, *76*, 1107–1122.

Demsetz, H. Towards a theory of property rights, *American Economic Review*, 1967, *57*, 347–359.

Harris, J. R., and M. P. Todaro. Migration, unemployment and development: A two-section analysis. *American Economic Review*, 1970, *60*, 126–142.

Herrick, B. Urban self employment and changing expectations as influences on urban migration. Unpublished Discussion Paper No. 46, University of California, Los Angeles, February 1974.

Johnson, G., and W. E. Whitelaw. Urban–rural income transfers in Kenya: An estimated remittance function. Unpublished paper, Institute of Development Studies, University of Nairobi, 1972.

Krugman, P., and J. N. Bhagwati. The decision to migrate: A survey. *Journal of Development Economics*, 1975, 2.

Lewis, W. A. Economic development with unlimited supplies of labour. *The Manchester School*, 1954, *22*, 139–192.

Lucas, R. E. B. The supply-of-immigrants function and taxation of immigrants' incomes: An econometric analysis. *Journal of Development Economics*, 1975, *2*, 289–308.

McCloskey, D. N. The enclosure of open fields: Preface to a study of its impact on the efficiency of english agriculture in the eighteenth century, *Journal of Economic History*, 1972, *32*, 15–35.

Muth, R. F. Migration: Chicken or egg? *Southern Economic Journal*, 1971, *37*, 295–306.

Newberry, D. M. G. Cropsharing tenancy in agriculture: Comment. *American Economic Review*, 1974, *64*, 1060–1066.

Ranis, G., and J. C. H. Fei. A theory of economic development. *American Economic Review*, 1961, *51*, 533–565.

Samuelson, P. A. International factor–price equalization once again. *The Economic Journal*, 1949, *59*, 181–197.

Schwartz, A. Interpreting the effects of distance on migration. *Journal of Political Economy*, 1973, *81*, 1153–1169.

Sen, A. K. Peasants and dualism with or without surplus labor. *Journal of Political Economy*, 1966, *74*, 425–450.

Sjaastad, L. A. The costs and returns of human migration. *Journal of Political Economy*, 1962, *70*, 80–93.

Smith, A. *The Wealth of Nations*. Edinburgh: Cadell and Davies, 1812.

Stiglitz, J. E. Rural–urban migration, surplus labour, and the relationship between urban and rural wages. *Eastern Africa Economic Review*, 1969, *1*, 1–28.

Stiglitz, J. E. Incentives and risk sharing in sharecropping. *Review of Economic Studies*, 1974, *41*, 219–256. (a)

Stiglitz, J. E. Wage determination and unemployment in LDCs. *Quarterly Journal of Economics*, 1974, *88*, 194–227. (b)

Todaro, M. P. A model of labor migration and urban unemployment in less developed countries. *American Economic Review*, 1969, *59*, 138–148.

Todaro, M. P. Education and rural–urban migration: theoretical constructs and empirical evidence from Kenya. Paper presented at a Conference on Urban Unemployment in Africa, Institute of Development Studies, University of Sussex, September 1971.

Weitzman, M. L. Free access vs. private ownership as alternative systems for managing common property. *Journal of Economic Theory*, 1974, *8*, 225–234.

CHAPTER 4

The Functions and Dynamics of the Migration Process

Peter A. Morrison

I. Introduction

Urban populations form and redistribute themselves primarily through migration, but, until relatively recently, little was known in detail about why migration itself occurs. Prior to about 1960, studies of migration did little more than describe net migration patterns. While net figures offered some indication of a community's or a region's comparative "attractiveness," they were, for analytical purposes, statistical fictions. There are no "net migrants"; there are, rather, people who are arriving at places or leaving them. Why they are doing so is central to understanding the dynamics of urban growth and decline.

Since 1960, the scope and analytical precision of United States migration research have increased immensely. Information developed in surveys and residence histories has given us insight into the social and economic determinants of the *intent* to move and enabled us to identify factors that prompt or impede a subsequent *decision* to move. Residence histories have also illuminated the *sequences* of moves more directly than before, so that we can examine single moves within the context of a series of related acts. New sources of historical data, as well, have supplied important insights into the remarkable fluidity of nineteenth century urban populations (see Thernstrom, 1973; Chudacoff, 1972; Pierson, 1973; and Gitelman, 1974).

61

The studies based on these superior data sources have enlarged understanding of what causes migration to occur, what its effects are on migrants, and how it affects the places they leave and the places to which they go: Now, as in the past, the primary motives for, and the effects of, migration are connected with the workings of the national economy and social system. One characteristic of modern economies is the quick exploitation of newly developed resources or knowledge, a process that requires the abandonment of old enterprises along with the development of the new (see Lee, 1971, p. 20). Such economies depend on migration continuously to adjust the labor supply, away from dwindling opportunities toward multiplying ones—ostensibly to the benefit of both migrant and employer. Thus, the way population arranges and rearranges itself in space answers the changing economic needs both of individuals and of the nation.

Migration has also served, and appears to continue to serve, as an important vehicle of social mobility in a society that is stratified predominantly along lines of achievement rather than of ascription. Immigrants and, more recently, migrants from rural areas have congregated in cities, where access to the training needed for high-wage jobs in commerce and industry afforded them opportunities to improve their material well-being. In this way, social status came to rest more on personal achievement and less on a legacy of disadvantage imposed by racial or cultural prejudice. Today's intermetropolitan migrants also appear to benefit from the option to migrate, whether by increasing their income or by gaining access to avenues of opportunity not available in their former location.

But, while migration clearly provides a means of correcting economic imbalance and social disadvantage, it also is the source of selective and uneven urban growth.

II. Determinants of Migration

The dominant migratory pattern of the past—away from rural areas to urban centers—occurred for many reasons, which, taken together, reflect long-run demographic and economic adjustments. On the demographic side, rural population always grew more rapidly than urban population and still does.[1] While urban families produced slightly more offspring than were needed for generational replacement, rural families

---

[1] In 1972, for example, the cumulative fertility of women 35–44 years old who had ever married was 7% higher for nonmetropolitan women (and 21% higher for farm women) than for metropolitan women (U.S. Bureau of the Census, 1973).

produced substantially more. On the economic side, the mechanization of agriculture reduced absolutely the demand for labor in rural areas, especially in those farm occupations that were likely to be filled by blacks.

The combination of high fertility and shrinking labor demand in rural areas produced increasing unemployment and underemployment. Faced with this prospect, many people were drawn to urban centers, attracted by both jobs and the amenities of urban life heard about through relatives, friends, and, increasingly, the mass media.

By 1970, however, rural-to-urban movement was largely over. Now, the newcomers to a metropolitan area are likely to have moved there from other metropolitan areas, often over long distances. Viewed in the aggregate, their moves amount to a system for exchanging manpower among different metropolitan labor markets. How this system functions has been elaborated through a number of recent studies.

A. ECONOMIC PULL WITHOUT PUSH

The economic wisdom of migrants seems to be one-sided. Research findings on intermetropolitan migration, although not fully in agreement, indicate that migrants find their way to areas where labor is in demand, but they may not always leave places where labor is in oversupply.

Economic pull is clearly evident in migration studies. The demand for labor, gauged by relative wage rates and the availability of jobs, attracts inmigrants from economically healthy localities as well as from ailing labor market areas. Outmigration from a metropolitan area, however, appears to be spontaneous and, over the long term, insensitive to local labor market conditions.

The first indication of outmigration's economic insensitivity was given in Lowry's often-cited study of intermetropolitan migration (Lowry, 1966), which was later supported by numerous other studies (e.g., Alonso, 1971). Further support at the micro level came in a unique survey, which illuminated behavioral aspects of this push–pull asymmetry for actual and would-be migrants (see Lansing and Mueller, 1967). The investigators probed individuals' perceptions of local economic conditions and their motives for staying or leaving. The data obtained indicated that there was no obvious push for outmigration among residents of depressed areas, compared with residents of economically healthy areas.

Other investigators, however, report finding a relationship between outmigration and economic conditions at origin. According to Miller's research, the expected correlation between outmigration rates and income levels appears when state of birth is controlled (see Miller, 1973). Others assert that origin push surely is operative, but that it is masked by improper specification of the unemployment variable: Average or end-period unemployment rates have already been modified by the most recent corrective effects of outmigration. To avoid this problem, they developed such synthetic measures as "prospective" or "potential" unemployment, which were intended to indicate the actual economic pressure for outflow and its effect on outmigration (see Blanco, 1964, pp. 221–222; Mazek, 1966; and Olvey, 1970).

Ironically, the evidence on both sides rests partially or wholly on 5-year migration data from the 1960 Census, which show that outmigration rates, viewed in cross section, are at least as high in prosperous metropolitan areas as in depressed ones. The trouble is that in these data, long-term structural changes are amalgamated with short-term adaptive changes. It may be that the high outflows from fast-growing urban centers, like San Jose, California, reflect a hypermobile population base built up by wave after wave of inmigrants (see Morrison, 1971). And, conversely, low outflow rates from ailing urban centers like St. Louis, Missouri, may reflect the fact that such areas have already lost many of their mobile residents.

If push does operate in the short term, then, any trace of its effect may be obscured by the opposing structural effect of hypermobility. A recent study that examined this hypothesis using annual migration-flow data supports this interpretation. It concluded that metropolitan outmigration does respond to short-run changes in local employment growth but that, over the long term, it is economically insensitive (cf. Lowry, 1966; see Renshaw, 1970, 1974).

B. BEATEN PATHS

People move, or fail to move, for multiple and complex reasons. A national survey of migrants (see Lansing and Mueller, 1967) disclosed that:

- Two-thirds of all migrants consider no other destination than the place to which they actually move.
- Six out of ten migrants rely on only one source of information to explore job opportunities in a new place.
- Information about jobs is obtained most frequently from friends and relatives (49%) or through special trips to look the situation over (33%).

Because they rely so heavily on family and friends in deciding where to go, migrants often limit their destination choices to places where friends and relatives have already settled. This "beaten path" effect gives rise to a second important feature of metropolitan migration: A steady flow of migrants into a locality becomes, to a degree, self-perpetuating. Like a siphon, it draws ever more migrants to the same locale through ties with people left behind.

Economic pull without long-term push, reinforced by this beaten path effect, is a powerful force for selective and uneven urban growth. First, the metropolitan center that can remain an economically "live" magnet draws on a virtually unlimited supply of "urbanization on the move"— the pool of migrants from both prosperous and depressed areas. Second, its access to this pool broadens as early-arriving migrants broadcast information to other would-be migrants.

III. Individual Outcomes of Migration

How migration affects people's material wellbeing and personal satisfaction is somewhat ambiguous (see Duncan *et al.*, 1972, pp. 224–225). For one thing, migration is not equally advantageous for all types of people. The skilled or educated worker is better equipped to compete in new labor markets, and he stands to gain more from moving than do his less skilled or educated counterparts.

Moreover, whether the migration experience is "favorable" or not may depend on the norm of comparison selected. One possibility is to compare migrants and nonmigrants from the same place of origin. If the migrants are more successful, we may infer that their migration experience has been favorable. Recent studies, for example, report that rural–urban migrants enjoy greater economic success relative to their counterparts who stay behind (see Koshel, 1972; Price, 1971; Bowles, 1970; Collignon, 1973; and Morrison, 1972). In making this comparison, however, we cannot rule out the possibility that the migrant's advantage arises primarily from his access to a broader set of opportunities. One way of separating these interpretations is to compare migrants with nonmigrants in the communities of destination, where opportunities are presumably the same for inmigrants and natives alike.

Whichever comparison is made, a central ambiguity remains: whether the act of migration, by freeing an individual's energies, leads to subsequent observed improvements in his life; or whether, as a prism separates light, the act is merely selective of certain persons who would have improved their status irrespective of the decision to migrate. The personal initiative that predisposes a decision to migrate tends to be more characteristic of people who have had superior advantages in

TABLE 4.1

REPORTED EARNINGS AFTER MIGRATION FOR HEADS OF
FAMILIES IN THE LABOR FORCE[a]

	Percentage of moves in last 5 years	
	All moves	Moves to get a better job
Head's earnings after move		
Higher	65	73
Same	11	10
Lower	24	17
Total	100	100
Number of moves	401	139

[a] Migration is defined here as moving across the boundaries of labor market areas.

SOURCE: John B. Lansing and Eva Mueller, *The Geographic Mobility of Labor,* Survey Research Center, Institute for Social Research, Ann Arbor, Michigan, 1967, p. 247.

education and work experience—factors that make for improved outcomes. So, to an unknown extent, migration may simply move people likely to succeed anywhere to places where the opportunities for success are more readily available for everyone (see Blau and Duncan, 1967, p. 273).

In the studies reviewed here, the effects of migration have been gauged in three different ways: (1) by asking migrants for their own evaluation, (2) by comparing migrants with their counterparts who have not migrated, and (3) by estimating migration's "dividends" as an investment in human capital.

Regarding the first approach, it can be tricky to assess outcomes on the basis of how the individual migrant *perceives* the consequences of his action. Actual monetary improvements are meaningful only if they are perceived as gains; on the other hand, the individual's judgment may overstate his true gain if he fails to account for loss of purchasing power.

Migration's perceived effect on earnings is shown in Table 4.1. These data refer to heads of families in the labor force who, after migrating, were asked about their prior and subsequent earnings. Referring to their last move, 65% reported higher earnings after moving; 24% said they earned less. Of the 11% earning the same, some probably had made defensive moves to avoid circumstances in which earnings would otherwise have declined. The right-hand column shows that for persons

4 FUNCTIONS AND DYNAMICS OF THE MIGRATION

who moved with the intention of obtaining a better job, earnings were even more likely to have increased. According to people's own reports, then, migration tends to be accompanied by higher earnings, although it must be noted that many moves are made by young adults, who typically enjoy a rising income anyway.

People's overall evaluations, all things considered, are shown in Table 4.2. They, too, are highly favorable, although possibly influenced by ex post facto rationalization. The vast majority of moves (89%) are judged as a "good idea" or a "very good idea," without qualification by people's own criteria.

Comparing migrants with nonmigrants affords a second perspective on individual outcomes. Specifically, we can ask whether people who have moved enjoy higher incomes than those who have not moved, other things being equal. Lansing and Mueller's survey does not show migration to have any consistently favorable effect on subsequent income. To be sure, mean income for migrants is substantially higher than for nonmigrants, but the differential is attributable to occupational, educational, and racial differences between the two groups (see Lansing and Mueller, 1967, p. 83).

These cross-sectional data, however, afford only crude comparisons and have intrinsic limitations. For example, they do not compare the rural–urban migrant's earnings with those of his counterpart who remained behind, or with earnings of urban nonmovers at the destination. The evidence shows that, on the following points, migrants from rural to

TABLE 4.2

OVERALL EVALUATION OF MOVES

	Percentage of moves in last 5 years
Evaluation of the move	
Very good idea	14
Good idea	75
Good in some ways, not others	5
Poor idea	4
Very poor idea	2
Total	*100*
Number of moves	690

SOURCE: John B. Lansing and Eva Mueller, *The Geographic Mobility of Labor,* Survey Research Center, Institute for Social Research, Ann Arbor, Michigan, 1967, p. 250.

urban areas subsequently better their economic positions and attain parity with the urbanites they join:

- Relative to earnings at origin: "People who have left rural areas for urban areas now earn more on the average than those who remained in rural areas, and people who have left the Deep South now earn more on the average than those who remained there [Lansing and Morgan, 1967, p. 460]."
- Relative to earnings at destination: "Five years after moving, the migrants have earnings equal to those of . . . urban nonmovers of the same education, age, race, and sex [Wertheimer, 1970, p. 58]."

Thus, people do not consistently better their earnings when they migrate, given their initial personal attributes. However, our distinguishing among functionally different types of migration forces us to qualify. Certain kinds of migration are associated—and strongly so—with improved incomes and better employment prospects. Migrants from rural to urban areas and migration by disadvantaged blacks are the clearest cases in point (see Morrison, 1972).

Finally, migration can be viewed as an investment in human capital that incurs costs and yields returns. It is an investment with direct costs, opportunity costs, information costs, and psychological costs, and also with losses in the value of capital that is costly to transfer to a new location. Among the returns are changes in earnings and nonpecuniary benefits over subsequent years (e.g., the individual's full lifetime or his remaining years in the labor force). Since it is embodied in the individual himself, migration is an investment in *human* capital.

Migration may change the value of a person's existing stock of human capital by affording him the opportunity to work in another labor market where his stock of human capital is more highly valued. Migration also may enable him to add to his human capital stock—by obtaining on-the-job training at the destination, for example.[2]

The human capital approach is represented in a study of migration out of the South, which reports that "the present value of the expected income gains from moving out of the South is positively related to the probability of moving" [Bowles, 1969, pp. 1–2]. That is, the people who stand to gain most from moving are the ones most apt to do so. It also notes that the effect of income gain on the probability of moving appears

---

[2] This description of the human capital approach is drawn from, and developed more fully in, J. DaVanzo (1972).

to be increased by the level of schooling but reduced by the individual's age.[3]

IV. Effects of Migration on Places

In facilitating national economic growth and personal wellbeing, migration also affects the basic anatomy of local growth and decline. Additions of population through migration may stimulate further growth; subtractions may attenuate it.

Two explanations of how inmigration and employment growth reinforce one another have been offered. One is that employment growth acts as a magnet to attract available migrants (jobs draw migrants). Alternatively, differential employment growth itself may result from differential inmigration and its invigoration of local demand for goods and services (additions of migrants stimulate new jobs) (see Muth, 1971).

However useful this distinction may be in theory, it is difficult to make empirically. The weight of evidence points to the interpretation that migration and employment growth perpetuate each other (see Muth, 1971; Olvey, 1970; and Greenwood, 1973). That is, an influx of migrants tends to stimulate employment growth by increasing the demand for local goods and services, thereby drawing more migrants to fill new jobs. Three possible effects can be distinguished here: (1) the tendency for service jobs to increase in response to the demands of a population growing larger and more diverse; (2) the pull exerted by growing economies, which begin to evidence agglomeration opportunities; and (3) the tendency for migration to add more ambitious and enterprising workers, whose qualifications attract additional entrepreneurs. Because of their interaction, exogenous increases in either migration or employment lead to multiple increases in both (see Muth, 1971).

The self-perpetuating characteristic in a growing locality has its counterpart in a declining area. Part of the reason why outmigration and economic stagnation reinforce each other is that migration is adversely selective. Outmigration acts as an economic adjustment mechanism by

---

[3] See Apgar (1970). Although theoretically sound, this analysis suffers from several empirical faults. One is its focus on net, rather than gross, migration flows, which complicates interpretations of actual behavior. More important, though, the data supporting the analysis are contaminated by the influence of military-related migration, which accounts for a substantial share of long-distance moves by men. Other kinds of migration (e.g., return migration) that are responsive to different factors also are lumped together in the study.

reducing local labor surpluses and lessening competition for scarce employment. But what begins as an equilibrating force may lead to disequilibrium, as rich areas become richer and poor areas become poorer. At some point, outmigration accelerates local economic distress by reducing the productivity of the area's labor force and, hence, its attractiveness to new industry.

Since outmigration usually draws away the more highly qualified members of the labor force—the young, the educated, and the skilled— the labor force left behind tends to be overaged, undereducated, and underskilled. This effect often is further accentuated by inmigration of persons similar to those who have remained behind (see Lansing and Mueller, 1967, pp. 318–319). As a labor force declines in quality, distressed areas become less attractive to new industries that require a supply of skilled workers. Only marginal firms paying low wages want an undereducated, underskilled, and overaged labor force. Where down-side rigidity has kept wages high relative to productivity, an area fails to attract new employers and hence continues to lose labor, though perhaps too slowly (see Olvey, 1970, pp. 127–129).

Furthermore, since the people who stay are generally the less migra-tion prone, the remaining population shows a gradually reduced poten-tial for mobility. This means that stronger and stronger economic incentives would be necessary to induce additional people to move away in order to maintain any balance between population size and shrinking employment opportunities.

Prolonged and heavy outmigration, then, leaves behind those persons who are least able to cope with the unfavorable conditions that led others to depart in the first place. The remaining residents tend to lack the attributes and skills that would attract new employers who could offer them jobs or that would predispose them to move away as others before them did.

V. Summary

Migration promotes economic efficiency by rearranging workers so as to increase national output. In economically expanding localities, migra-tion responds vigorously to the demand for labor and has a multiplica-tive effect on this growth. In declining localities, it reduces imbalance between labor supply and demand in the near term, although its effectiveness diminishes with prolonged heavy outflow.

On the individual level, migration tends to be both economically rewarding and personally satisfying. Judged by objective measures, migrants often improve their earnings and occupational status, particularly where the move is rural-to-urban. And their own self-evaluations of moving suggest that migrants believe they are better off for having moved. Disadvantaged persons—blacks especially—benefit remarkably when they migrate, inviting the conclusion that moving offers people a major escape route from disadvantaged circumstances.

There is, however, in the combination of economic push without pull, which is reinforced by the beaten path effect, a powerful force for selective urban growth. Together, these factors have strengthened the reciprocal relationship between employment growth and migration.

References

Alonso, W. The system of intermetropolitan population flows. Working Paper No. 155, Center for Planning and Development Research, University of California, Berkeley, 1971.

Apgar, W. C. Migration as investment: Some further considerations. Discussion Paper No. 64, Program on Regional and Urban Economics, Harvard University, May 1970.

Blanco, C. Prospective unemployment and interstate population movements. *Review of Economics and Statistics*, 1964, *46*, 221–222.

Blau, P. M., and O. D. Duncan. *The American occupational structure*. New York: Wiley, 1967.

Bowles, G. K. A profile of the incidence of poverty among rural–urban migrants and comparative populations. Paper presented at the Annual Meeting of the Rural Sociological Society, Washington, D.C., 1970.

Bowles, S. Migration as investment: Empirical tests of the human investment approach to geographical mobility. Discussion Paper No. 51, Program on Regional and Urban Economics, Harvard University, July 1969.

Chudacoff, H. P. *Mobile Americans: Residential and social mobility in Omaha, 1880–1920*. New York: Oxford University Press, 1972.

Collignon, F. C. *The causes of rural-to-urban migration among the poor*. Institute of Urban and Regional Development, University of California, Berkeley, 1973.

DaVanzo, J. *An analytical framework for studying the potential effects of an income maintenance program on U.S. interregional migration*, The Rand Corporation, R-1081-EDA, December 1972.

Duncan, O. D., D. L. Featherman, and B. Duncan, *Socioeconomic background and achievement*. New York: Seminar Press, 1972.

Gitelman, H. M. *Workingmen of Waltham: Mobility in American urban industrial development, 1850–1890*. Baltimore: Johns Hopkins University Press, 1974.

Greenwood, M. J. A simultaneous equations model of urban growth and migration. n.d. (Mimeograph).

Greenwood, M. J. Urban economic growth and migration: Their interaction. *Environment and Planning*, 1973, *5*(1) 91–112.

Koshel, P. *Migration and the poor*. Working Paper No. 7, Office of Planning, Research, and Evaluation, U.S. Office of Economic Opportunity, Washington, D. C., July 1972.

Lansing, J. B., and J. N. Morgan. The effect of geographical mobility on income. *Journal of Human Resources*, 1967, *2*, 449–460.

Lansing, J. B., and E. Mueller. *The geographic mobility of labor*. Survey Researc Center, Institute for Social Research, Ann Arbor, Michigan, 1967.

Lee, E. S. Psychological and social effects of population growth. In International Union c Biological Sciences, *Proceedings of the Scientific Program, 17th General Assembl) National Academy of Sciences*, Washington, D. C., 1971.

Lowry, I. S. *Migration and metropolitan growth: Two analytical models*. San Francisc(Chandler, 1966.

Mazek, W. F. The efficacy of labor migration with special emphasis on depressed area: 1966. (Mimeograph).

Miller, E. Is out-migration affected by economic conditions? *Southern Economic Journa* 1973, *39*(3), 396–405.

Morrison, P. A. Chronic movers and the future redistribution of population. *Demograph) 1971, 8*, 171–184.

Morrison, P. A. *The impact and significance of rural–urban migration in the Unite States*. The Rand Corporation, P-4752, March 1972.

Muth, R. F. Migration: Chicken or egg? *Southern Economic Journal, 1971, 37*, 295–306.

Olvey, L. D. Regional growth and interregional migration—Their pattern of interactio1 Ph. D. dissertation, Department of Economics, Harvard University, 1970.

Pierson, G. W. *The moving American*. New York: Knopf, 1973.

Price, D. O. *Rural–urban migration and poverty: A synthesis of research findings with look at the literature*. U.S. Office of Economic Opportunity, Washington, D.C., Jul 1971.

Renshaw, V. The role of migration in labor market adjustment. Ph. D. dissertatio: Massachusetts Institute of Technology, 1970.

Renshaw, V. Using gross migration data compiled from the Social Security Sample Fil *Demography, 1974, 11*(1), 143–148.

Thernstrom, S. *The other Bostonians: Poverty and progress in the American metropoli 1880–1970*. Cambridge, Mass.: Harvard University Press, 1973.

U.S. Bureau of the Census, *Current population reports*, Series P-20, No. 248, April 1973

Wertheimer, R. F. *The monetary rewards of migration within the U.S.* The Urb; Institute, Washington, D.C., 1970.

PART II

Methodology: Models, Measurement and Theoretical Reflections

Policy-Oriented Interregional Demographic Accounting and a Generalization of Population Flow Models

William Alonso

In recent years, interest has been growing in demographic accounts analogous to such economic accounts as input–output. Stolnitz suggested in 1964 an expansion of the labor inputs in interregional input–output accounts, which would specify labor inputs by their characteristics and region of residence. Coefficients would be calculated in the usual manner based on current ratios, so that, for instance, expansion of an industry in one region would draw (import) female workers from another region. Rogers (1968) investigated a related approach. More recently, Stone (1966, 1970) has explored the design and use of demographic accounts for forecasting and for various areas of policy planning, but without interregional detail. Rees and Wilson (1973) have been publishing a series of papers on interregional demographic accounts, which carefully lay out the full framework of transformations among categories over a segment of time. Indeed, the interest is such that, in its Volume 5, Number 1 (1973) issue, the journal *Environment and Planning* devoted practically the entire issue to demographic accounts.

This paper has two purposes. The first is to discuss generally some of the uses of interregional demographic accounts for forecasting and policy evaluation. The second, more formal and technical, is to show that such accounts, by placing the phenomenon of migration in the context of a system, lead to some necessary but generally neglected

considerations of considerable importance both for theory and for
practical applications.

I. An Overview of One Model of Interregional Demographic Accounts and Its Uses

The discussion will be aided by a brief, impressionistic overview of such
a model, which I have developed (Alonso, 1973). It is, in many ways,
similar to the Wilson–Rees model, but stripped down from the full
complement of transitional categories to make it operational. A prototype of this model has been built for the United States, for 243 regions,
and it has been run by 5-year increments to the year 2000 for a variety of
forecasting and policy analysis projections.

The nation is divided into some set of regions, and data are gathered
on the population of the region, its birth and death rates, a square matrix
of gross migratory flows among regions,[1] and such other information as
may be needed for behavioral analysis. This information may include
such variables as local climates, geographic coordinates, local incomes
and levels of education, and so on. Needless to say, the practical
difficulties are great in gathering, cleaning up, and making consistent this
body of data; but that is not the topic of this paper.

The population of each region is advanced from period to period by
adding births, subtracting deaths, adding inmigrants and subtracting
outmigrants. For projection, it is necessary to have some functions or
constant relations to generate these components of change. By analogy,
these constant relations are, in an input–output system, the technical
coefficients, which state that the proportion of each input per unit of
output for each industry is constant. In the case of demographic
accounts there are several such relations, and they are considerably
more complicated.

In our model we collapsed birth and death rates into a local rate of
natural increase, for simplicity. This rate varies widely among regions,
from zero to rates typical of developing countries. Local rates of natural
increase were projected into later periods proportionately to alternative
projections of national natural increase, adjusted for the net migration
history of the region. This adjustment, which I call a "demographic
multiplier," is based on the fact that the overwhelming majority of
migrants are young and fertile, so that migratory gains or losses strongly

---

[1] In the United States, this matrix was produced by the Census by asking a 25% sample
of respondents where they lived 5 years previously.

affect the age composition of regions and consequently their rate of natural increase. This relation, as were all others, was calibrated by multiple regression to past experience.

Migration received the most attention in the model, on two grounds. First, migration is the form of demographic interaction among regions in the national system, and is thus the primary reason for thinking in a systems framework. Second, the United States has experienced a sharp decline in birth rates, so that interregional migration assumes the greatest potential for variations in local growth or decline.

Gross (that is to say, directional) migrations from each region to every other were projected for each period by an elaborate form of the gravity model (discussed in the second part of this paper) that considered incomes, population sizes, local climate, and lagged natural increase and net migration. These lagged variables are of great importance. Natural increase lagged by some 20 years serves to indicate the proportion of the population that is at an age with a high propensity to migrate, while similarly lagged (by about 5 years) past net migration indicates the proportion of the population who have been migrants in the past and who therefore have a high propensity to move. I believe it is such lagged variables, representing the effect of past history on present behavior, that account for much of the hysteresis or continuing momentum in population phenomena. But I shall refrain from a full presentation and interpretation of the variables used in my model because my purpose in this paper is to raise issues about the general logic of such models, rather than the particulars of one of them.

If such a model is to be used for projection or for policy, all of the variables for each locality must somehow be produced for each period, either endogenously (as in the moving forward of population stocks by adding and subtracting flows) or exogenously. Exogenously generated variables might be state variables, such as national crude birthrate projections, or policy variables, such as variations in local income through taxes or subsidies, policy-set limits to local populations, or any other, according to the ingenuity of the designer. In our model, various demographic variables were endogenously generated after setting the initial conditions, local climate was exogenous (assumed constant), and income was generated endogenously through an equation that was highly significant statistically but admittedly had a large error term. Income at each locality for each period was needed both for projection and because modifications on local income through taxes and subsidies were our principal policy or control variables.

With this model we explored for the national system of regions (in our case, the 200-odd metropolitan areas and the nonmetropolitan residue) the consequences of alternative national projections of birth rates, and of a dozen alternative policies, such as the favoring of small cities, alternative national growth centers policies, the favoring of certain regions, the favoring of the poorest regions, the interregional equalization of incomes, the maximization of total income. We also considered, but did not carry out, analysis of the optimal pattern of subsidies to growth centers to self-sustaining growth, the effects of growth centers upon the surrounding regions, and the effects of direct controls upon population movements or growth or decline of particular regions.

Quite obviously, such a model may be quite inaccurate, but still it may be better than any other way of exploring the future. Overall, my sense is that for a large demographic system, such as the United States or the European Common Market, in which substantial population movements are present or possible, this type of analysis is useful for what may be called normal effects. This means that for broad classes of regions or cities, the conclusions of this type of model will be better than other projective methods. But that for unusual circumstances (such as the Irish potato famine, massive depressions, radical sectoral shifts in the economy, cultural or religious paroxysms, and the like), the model is very limited, especially for particular localities. This, in other terms, is a reflection of the tendency of statistically formulated simulation or policy models to contain less variance within their range than is the case in reality. Most generally, it is an aspect of statistically calibrated models to concentrate on central, rather than extreme, values. Which is to say, in the end, that such models are evolutionary, rather than revolutionary. But this is a general characteristic, with its accompanying failings, rather than a particular failing of such models.

A final comment is needed in this general overview. This is that any such model will produce thousands or tens of thousands of numbers. They amount, in their output, to future censuses of the endogenously produced variables. And anyone who has tried to summarize past experience from the censuses will understand that the richness of the data and the permutations of combinations of those data can result in utter confusion in the interpretation of the output of any such model. From this it is obvious that it is necessary to reduce the output of such models to intelligible proportions, if they are to be of any use.

This takes two forms, for practical purposes. First, the initial disaggregation into regions will need to be recombined into categories (rich–big, Southern–small, and so forth) that are relevant for political or other purposes. Second, the model can only produce information in terms of variables that are endogenously produced. If the model does not produce, for instance, information about suicide rates or alienation, it is useless to ask it about them. On the other hand, combinations of variables and categories within the model can produce a great deal of information, such as national indices of population concentration or interregional income distribution (including the direct effect of such distributions and their secondary effects). A broad range of social indicators (to use that much abused term) can be generated from intelligently chosen permutations of the endogenous variables. In very simple terms, for classes of regions, such a model can produce data that are organizable to give insight on a number of matters. Such insight is based on information endogenously generated by the model (with the assumption of endogenous outputs) and consists in the intelligent reduction of thousands of numbers to a manageable few. The congruence of the dimensionality of the behavioral model to the dimensionality of the social purpose (or social indicators) is the key here. If the congruence is high, the model will be very useful within its reliability; if the congruence is low, whatever the statistical reliability of the model, it will be of little use.

II. Opportunity and Competition in a Migratory System[2]

Demographic accounting, by viewing population as a system of stocks and flows, permits a generalization of migratory relations that is of considerable theoretical interest, as well as being important for policy. I will show that, unless the interdependence of the system is explicitly considered, important variables will be omitted or assumptions will be made implicitly that would not be readily granted if made explicit. In other words, viewing migrations as a system does make a difference, and various approaches in the literature can be shown to be extreme special cases of a generalized formulation. For instance, I will show that those who study the relation of outmigration to local characteristics unknowingly assume a unit elasticity in the supply of jobs at the destination with respect to prospective migrants, while those who study inmigration as a function of local characteristics assume that outmigration in the rest of the system is unit elastic to the opportunities provided.[3]

---

[2] Since writing the following section, I believe I have improved the interpretation and derivation of the model, and I hope to present these advances in later papers.

[3] My discussion is limited here to gross migration. Net migration, which is the difference of gross outmigration from gross inmigration, has been much studied; but net migration is a statistical abstraction not a form of human behavior: People either come or go.

Let us start with the *push model*, which is currently the most active form of migration research in the United States. This model seeks to relate gross outmigration to a function v_i of local characteristics. This function may include the size and demographic characteristics of the population at i, local climate, and variables dealing with economics, with education, with culture, with past migration, and with any other of a vast number of considerations. Quite properly, the literature has concerned itself with the variables and form of the function v_i, but for our argument what goes into v_i is not important.

Consider, now, that every migrant leaving i must arrive at some destination. Call w_j the attractiveness or pulling power of a destination j. Again, a substantial literature addresses itself to the variables and functional form of w_j, but for our argument the specification does not matter. However w_j is constructed, the outmigrants from i will distribute themselves among their possible destinations in proportion to their respective pulling powers. That is to say, the migration from i to j will be

$$M_{ij} = v_i(w_j / \sum_k w_k), \tag{1}$$

where M_{ij} is the number of migrants from i to j, w_j is the pulling power of j, and v_i is the total number of gross outmigrants from i. However, the reader should keep in mind that, as we generalize the model, we shall refine the definition of these variables.

It may be that a relational term or function, t_{ij}, is relevant to link the attractive characteristics at j to the characteristics at i. This would refine Eq. (1) into

$$M_{ij} = v_i(w_j t_{ij} / \sum_k w_k t_{ik}). \tag{2}$$

In the literature, the most common form of this relational function is some negative power of distance between i and j, in which case we have a conventional gravity model, with a Huff (1961) normalization adjustment. But, of course, this relational function may take into account many other relations between origin and destination, such as functional distance, number of ex-residents of i now living at j, differences or commonalities in language, religion, ethnicity, or industrial composition, and so forth. Again, we are not concerned here with the insides of the relational function, since our argument is general. Indeed, if we chose to ignore it, we would only implicitly set $t_{ij} = 1$ in all cases. But it is worth noting that, whereas v_i consists of variables measured in i, and w_j of variables measured in j, t_{ij} must be constructed of variables measured in both i and j.

Continuing our exploration of the push model, by summing equations such as (2) for migrants from all origins into j, we obtain the gross inmigration into j:

$$\sum_i M_{ij} = \sum_i v_i(w_j t_{ij} / \sum_k w_k t_{ik}) = w_j \sum_i (v_i t_{ij} / \sum_k w_k t_{ik}).$$
(3)

This is the inmigration relation implied by push models. We will save its detailed examination until we have converted it to the general notation, but suffice it to say here that it states that gross inmigration will be proportional to the attraction of j and to the pool of migrants, after taking account of their alternative opportunities. In other words, that j will receive migrants in simple proportion to their availability, or that the absorptive capacity of j is unit elastic to the supply of migrants.

Consider now the implications of the *gravity model* approach. This begins not with the total departures from one place or the total arrivals at another but with the number of migrants between them, so that its basic relation is

$$M_{ij} = v_i w_j t_{ij}.$$
(4)

If we ask what the total arrivals at a destination j will be, we find

$$\sum_i M_{ij} = w_j \sum_i v_i t_{ij},$$
(5)

which is visibly different from what is implied by the push model as shown in Eq. (3).

Equally, if we ask what the gravity model assumes gross outmigration from i to be, we find

$$\sum_j M_{ij} = v_i \sum_j w_j t_{ij},$$
(6)

which contrasts with the push model's $\sum_j M_{ij} = v_i$. That is to say, the push model holds that outmigration is totally determined by local conditions at the origin, while the gravity model says that, given local conditions v_i, total departures will be unit elastic to the attraction of outside opportunities. This will be seen more clearly in the generalized notation, but it is of particular policy interest because of the lively debate between Lowry (1966) and a multitude of critics. I will not enter into the specifics of this argument, which has centered on the variables and structure of the push function, v_i. But it is worth noting that two different models are involved. Lowry's gravity model assumes full elasticity for push, while his critics use push models that assume zero elasticity.

A third common migration model, which may be called the *pull model*, focuses on the arrival of migrants at j and attributes it solely to characteristics at j; that is, its point of departure is $\Sigma_i M_{ij} = w_j$. From this it follows that total departures from i will be $\Sigma_j M_{ij} = v_i \Sigma_j (w_j t_{ij} / \Sigma_k v_k t_{kj})$, which obviously differs from what is assumed in the push model (that $\Sigma_j M_{ij} = v_i$) or in the gravity model as shown in Eq. (6). Similarly, the implicit form of the flows, $M_{ij} = v_i w_j t_{ij} / \Sigma_k v_k t_{kj}$, is obviously different from the other flow formulations.

A comparison with a fourth model, devised by Wilson (1970) in reference to traffic and frequently called the entropy model, will be postponed, because of its complexity, until we have presented the general model.

These different models, then, imply very different things, as can be seen once the system consequences of their various points of departure are spelled out. But they can be put in a common framework that shows them to be special cases of a general model. Their differences then reduce to whether they assume values of 0 or -1 for two key parameters that stand for elasticities, while in reality the values of these parameters are most probably intermediate between 0 and -1. The various models in the common notation are shown in Table 5.1.

Two variables must be defined, which I shall call competition, C, and opportunity, O. These variables, it must be stressed, bring in no new measurements but are merely combinations of the vs, ws, and ts. Two new parameters, α and β, are now raised as matters for empirical estimation, whereas their value has been assumed in existing models. The definition of these variables is made difficult because they are functions of each other and their definition and explication will have to be simultaneous.

Let us refine the definition of v_i to be the internally determined outmigration from i, or its internal propensity to produce migrants. Without yet defining opportunity O_i operationally, let us call α the elasticity of outmigration to opportunities. Thus, the total number of outmigrants from i will be $v_i O_i^\alpha$. The share of prospective migrants from i to j will depend on the attractive pull of j on i, $w_j t_{ij}$, and on the alternative opportunities available to migrants from i, resulting in $w_j t_{ij} / O_i$. Applying this share to the total migrants from i to all places, and summing over i, we obtain

$$\sum_i (v_i O_i^\alpha)(w_j t_{ij} / O_i) = w_j \sum_i v_i t_{ij} O_i^{\alpha-1}.$$

Dividing through by w_j to convert to prospective arrivals per unit of

TABLE 5.1

GENERAL MODEL OF INTERREGIONAL GROSS MIGRATION AND SPECIAL CASES[a]

	Flow from i to j M_{ij}	Departures $\sum_j M_{ij}$	Arrivals $\sum_i M_{ij}$	Opportunity O_i	Competition C_j	Elasticities	
						α	β
General model	$v_i w_j t_{ij} O_i^{\alpha-1} C_j^{\beta-1}$	$v_i O_i^{\alpha}$	$w_j C_j^{\beta}$	$\sum_j w_j t_{ij} C_j^{\beta-1}$	$\sum_i v_i t_{ij} O_i^{\alpha-1}$	$0 \le \alpha \le 1$	$0 \le \beta \le 1$
Push model	$v_i w_j t_{ij} O_i^{-1} C_j^{0}$	$v_i O_i^{0}$	$w_j C_j^{1}$	$\sum_j w_j t_{ij} C_j^{0}$	$\sum_i v_i t_{ij} O_i^{-1}$	0	1
Pull model	$v_i w_j t_{ij} O_i^{0} C_j^{-1}$	$v_i O_i^{1}$	$w_j C_j^{0}$	$\sum_j w_j t_{ij} C_j^{-1}$	$\sum_i v_i t_{ij} O_i^{0}$	1	0
Elastic gravity model (Lowry)	$v_i w_j t_{ij} O_i^{0} C_j^{0}$	$v_i O_i^{1}$	$w_j C_j^{1}$	$\sum_j w_j t_{ij} C_j^{0}$	$\sum_i v_i t_{ij} O_i^{0}$	1	1
Inelastic gravity model (Wilson)	$v_i w_j t_{ij} O_i^{-1} C_j^{-1}$	$v_i O_i^{0}$	$w_j C_j^{0}$	$\sum_j w_j t_{ij} C_j^{-1}$	$\sum_j v_i t_{ij} O_i^{-1}$	0	0

[a] The point of departure of the various special case models is indicated by a frame around the expression.

attraction at j, we arrive at our definition of competition

$$C_j = \sum_i v_i t_{ij} O_i^{\alpha-1}. \tag{8}$$

The interpretation of C_j, then, is that it is the potential number of migrants that might arrive at j per unit of its attractiveness, w_j, having taken account of the special relation of j with migrants from every source and their alternative opportunities. Most simply, it is the ex ante number of migrants per unit of pull at j; which is to say, the number that would arrive if competition did not matter. Competition may also be interpreted as the pool of migrants per opportunity at j.

The definition of opportunity, O_i, is similarly arrived at. We refine the definition of w_j to be the internally determined attractions or opportunities available to migrants at j. This basic attraction is modified by the propensity of opportunities at j to expand in response to additional supplies of (or demands by) prospective migrants, which is to say competition raised to an exponent (elasticity) β: C_j^β. Thus, the actual number of migrants who will arrive at j will be $w_j C_j^\beta$. From the point of view of a resident at i, these opportunities at j must be weighted by the relational function t_{ij} that may obtain between i and j and be discounted by the total number of migrants competing per unit of opportunity at j, which is to say, C_j. In brief, from the point of view of a resident at i, the opportunities at j are $w_j C_j^\beta t_{ij} / C_j = w_j t_{ij} C_j^{\beta-1}$. Summing over all the possible destinations, we obtain the total outside opportunities available to a resident of i:

$$O_i = \sum_j w_j t_{ij} C_j^{\beta-1}. \tag{9}$$

In our construction of O_i and C_j, we stated in passing that total departures from i will be $v_i O_i^\alpha$, and that total arrivals at j will be $w_j C_j^\beta$. Without deriving it, I will merely state here that the flow equation for migrants between i and j will be

$$M_{ij} = v_i w_j t_{ij} O_i^{\alpha-1} C_j^{\beta-1}. \tag{10}$$

In an appendix at the conclusion of this paper, I present in greater detail the structure of Eq. (10), but here I merely want to show its consistency with the total arrivals and departures. For departures, we merely sum over all possible destinations j:

$$\sum_j M_{ij} = \sum_j v_i w_j t_{ij} O_i^{\alpha-1} C_j^{\beta-1} = v_i O_i^{\alpha-1} (\sum_j w_j t_{ij} C_j^{\beta-1}).$$

But from Eq. (9) we see that the expression in the parentheses is precisely the definition of O_i, so that we have

$$\sum_j M_{ij} = v_i O_i^{\alpha-1} O_i = v_i O_i^{\alpha}.$$

In a parallel fashion, summing over the origins to obtain total arrivals at j, we have:

$$\sum_i M_{ij} = \sum_i v_i w_j t_{ij} O_i^{\alpha-1} C_j^{\beta-1} = w_j C_j^{\beta-1} \left(\sum_i v_i t_{ij} O_i^{\alpha-1} \right).$$

From Eq. (8) we see that the expression in the parentheses is the definition of C_j, so that we have

$$\sum_i M_{ij} = w_j C_j^{\beta-1} C_j = w_j C_j^{\beta}.$$

I fear that the reader will by now be confused to some degree and somewhat uncertain as to what he has been made to swallow. What I have presented is a highly circular or consistent set of very general relations, and it is possible to enter it from many points, to derive things otherwise, and indeed to explicate them quite differently. My greatest difficulty in writing this has been to choose the mode of presentation, where to break into the circle. Now it may be best to move on to the examination of the various models in the literature to see how they appear in this general framework. Table 5.1 is a summary of the discussion that follows, and the last column shows that the standard models differ from one another by assuming all the permutations of values of 0 or 1 for α or β; I shall argue and cite some evidence that the values are likely to be intermediate.

The *push model* assumes that outmigration is totally determined by local conditions at i and unaffected by opportunities, so that it assumes that $\alpha = 0$. Of necessity, this implies that in the flow equation O_i will have an exponent of $(\alpha - 1) = -1$; and, by following the algebra, that $\beta = 1$, which is to say that jobs at destinations expand as necessary to absorb migrants. In effect this assumes that jobs follow people. On the other hand, the *pull model* assumes precisely the opposite: that opportunities or jobs at destination are determined exclusively by local characteristics and are totally inelastic with respect to the flow of inmigrants. That is to say, that opportunities are inelastic to the pool of migrants, or $\beta = 0$. This is typical of economic base (and, more generally, of economic) approaches, which assume that people follow jobs, typically projecting $w_j(C_j^0)$ through some sectoral estimates in the growth of employment, and assuming that the flows of people will adjust exactly to these changes in employment through migration. Implicitly, such approaches assume that outmigration is exactly proportional, or unit elastic, at the origin to the demand for migrants at destination; which is to say, they assume that $\alpha = 1$. In reality, jobs chase people and people chase jobs.

The *gravity model* assumes both that outmigration is unit elastic to outside opportunities and that jobs at destination are unit elastic to prospective migrants; which is to say, it assumes $\alpha = \beta = 1$. By contrast, Wilson's entropy model, which was designed initially for modeling of intraurban traffic, assumes that both the rates of departure and the rates of arrival are fixed, or that they are both totally inelastic ($\alpha = \beta = 0$). This model is also, ultimately, a gravity model, but with very strong double proportionality controls. Hence, in Table 5.1 we have called it *inelastic gravity model*, whereas the Lowry type of model is called *elastic gravity model*. The push and the pull models might be called one-sided elastic gravity models.

Having now reduced these various models to a common framework, we see that they vary only in making diverse a priori assumptions about the elasticities α and β. Yet the values of their elasticities are, ultimately, an empirical matter and may even be expected to vary from time to time and place to place. Thus, in periods of general labor surplus, one may expect that people will tend to chase jobs more than the reverse; that is to say, that α will be relatively larger and β relatively smaller than in periods of full employment, when jobs will chase after workers. But in general, I would find it surprising if either were unit or zero elastic. Rather, it is as if these four existing approaches delimited the square with vertices at (0, 0), (0, 1), (1, 1), and (1, 0) in a space of coordinates α and β. In reality, under most circumstances, we would expect α and β to be a point inside this square. We would expect outmigration to respond somewhat to outside opportunities ($\alpha > 0$) but probably less than with full proportionality ($\alpha < 1$). It is possible that there may even be cases, such as gold rushes or other instances of exaggerated expectations, where α might be greater than 1. Similarly, we would expect the rate of arrivals to vary somewhat with the available pool of migrants ($\beta > 0$) but for competition among them to result in less than full proportionality ($\beta < 1$).

Indeed, in my empirical work (Alonso, 1973), I estimate $\alpha = .3$ and $\beta = .1$ for the United States in the period 1955–1960. It should be noted that this was a period of relative economic stagnation. The only other comparable figures of which I am aware are those of Muth (1971), who found a substantial elasticity of job formation to net migration, and Greenwood (1973), who found a similar elasticity for gross inmigration. Their figures cannot be directly compared, however, because they deal with actual, rather than potential, migration, as in C_j. I am not aware of any literature on estimates that would relate to the elasticity of outmigration.

If the case I have developed for including consideration of opportunity and competition is accepted, some practical considerations come to the fore, principally because it is laborious, expensive, and technically difficult to estimate them. From the perspective of scientific research, the question is whether omission of these variables is very damaging to traditional approaches. My judgment is that it is reasonably so. In the first place, competition and opportunity have substantial correlation with some of the variables, such as income, normally included in the specification of the functions v and w. Hence, there will be bias, as some of their effect will be attributed to such correlated variables as may be included, or, in the case of negatively correlated variables, be missed. Secondly, because variables with such elasticities will have important second-order effects, given the range of values of C and O, there will be substantial loss of accuracy for projection.

For policy, these considerations are amplified by others. The inclusion of these systemic variables and estimation of their parameters will clearly be relevant to such matters as the determination of the number and location of growth centers undertaken at one time, to the choice among policies of regional development versus policies of aid to migration, to an estimation of the effects of a growth center upon its surrounding region, and so forth. Government intervention may take the form of affecting variables within the functions v and w, such as the number of jobs, local incomes, tax rates, levels of education, provision of housing, or any others. This may also take the form of action upon the relational function t_{ij}, by improving transportation or lowering its cost, by programs of resettlement grants and helping to find jobs, by travel and residence permits, and so forth. Whatever the policy variables acted upon, they will be aspects of the functions of local characteristics, v and w, or aspects of the relational functions, t_{ij}. These, in turn, will change the values of the systemic functions of opportunity and competition at all other locations to a lesser or greater extent. Thus, as systemic characteristics have local consequences, local actions in turn change the web of systemic relations.

III.   Appendix: A Parsing of the General Flow Relation

In the general formulation, the equation for the flow of migrants from i to j is

$$M_{ij} = v_i w_j t_{ij} O_i^{\alpha-1} C_j^{\beta-1}. \tag{10}$$

The structure of this relation is more intelligible if we rewrite it as follows:

$$M_{ij} = (v_i O_i^{\alpha})[w_j(w_j C_j^{\beta}/w_j C_j)t_{ij}O_i^{-1}],$$

where the expression within the first parenthesis is the total number of migrants to leave i, and the expression within the bracket is the share who will arrive at j. Within the bracket:

w_j	basic attraction of j;
$w_j C_j^{\beta}$	total number of migrants who will arrive at j from all origins;
$w_j C_j$	ex ante number of migrants who would arrive at j from all origins, i.e., the number who would arrive if they could all be accommodated;
$w_j C_j^{\beta}/w_j C_j$	the number of actual places at j per seeker; this, of course, reduces to $C_j^{\beta-1}$; thus the initial attraction w_j is weighted by the ratio of places to seekers;
t_{ij}	a further weighting taking account of any special relations from i to j.

Thus far, the expression within the bracket reduces to $w_j C_j^{\beta-1}t_{ij}$, which is the opportunities at j from the point of view of a migrant from i. Thus, we divide this by O_i, the opportunities at all other places in the system, similarly defined from the point of view of i, to obtain the proportion of migrants from i who will go to j.

Similarly, the terms of the flow equations can be regrouped so as to be interpreted as the total arrivals at j times the share of these arrivals coming from i.

Acknowledgment

This work was supported by a grant from the National Science Foundation.

References

Alonso, W. *National interregional demographic accounts: A prototype*. Monograph No. 17, Institute of Urban and Regional Development, University of California, Berkeley, 1973.

Greenwood, M. J. Urban economic growth and migration: Their interaction. *Environment and Planning*, 1973, 5(1).

Huff, D. Ecological characteristics of consumer behavior. *Papers of the Regional Science Association*, 1961.

Lowry, I. *Migration and metropolitan growth: Two analytical models*. San Francisco: Chandler, 1966.

Muth, R. Migration: Chicken or egg? *Southern Economic Journal*, January 1971.
Rees, P. H., and A. G. Wilson. Accounts and models for special demographic analysis I: Aggregate population. *Environment and Planning*, 1973, 5(1).
Rogers, A. *Matrix analysis of interregional population growth and distribution.* Los Angeles: University of California Press, 1968.
Stolnitz, G. Manpower movements: A proposed approach to measurement. In Werner Hirsch (Ed.), *Elements of regional accounts,* Baltimore: Johns Hopkins Press, 1964.
Stone, R. Input–output and demographic accounting: A tool for educational planning. *Minerva*, 1966.
Stone, R. An integrated system of demographic, manpower, and social statistics and its links with the system of national economic accounts. United Nations, Economic and Social Council, E/CN.3/394, 1970.
Wilson, A. *Entropy in urban and regional modelling.* London: Pion, 1970.

CHAPTER 6

Forecasting Migration in a Regional General Equilibrium Context

Owen P. Hall, Jr.
Joseph A. Licari

Migration flows are determined by a complex interaction of economic, environmental, and demographic factors. However, models for forecasting regional migration are conventionally based upon partial equilibrium assumptions. The economic, environmental, and nonmigration demographic factors are forecasted exogenously without explicit concern for the influence of migration. Migration is then forecast as a function of these exogenous forces.

The purpose of this paper is to present a methodology for forecasting regional inmigration flows as part of a full regional general equilibrium system of economic, demographic and environmental interrelationships. A demonstration case is given for the Los Angeles metropolitan area and it is shown that the general equilibrium forecasts can differ greatly from those derived from various partial equilibrium processes.

In the section to follow, we summarize alternative models of migration and describe the general characteristics of our empirical general equilibrium approach. Results are then presented for the experimental application of the interactive model to the Los Angeles region. We conclude with a brief general assessment of the implications of the model and empirical results for regional migration forecasting.

I. Models of Regional Migration Flows

Neoclassical models of interregional migration rely on economic factors related to regional differences in labor market conditions to

TABLE 6.1

BASIC LINKAGES IN THE GENERAL EQUILIBRIUM MODEL

Linkage	Relationship
Economic → Demographic	Birth rate = f (personal income, employment)
	Migration = f (employment)
Demographic → Economic	Labor force = f (population)
Economic → Environmental	Stationary sources = f (output)
	Mobile sources = f (personal income)
Environmental → Economic	Consumption = f (mobile control costs)
	Investment = f (stationary control costs)
Demographic → Environmental	Mobile sources = f (population)
	Stationary sources = f (population)
Environmental → Demographic	Migration = f (air quality)

explain observed flow patterns. Key explanatory variables here include levels or growth rates of gross regional product, personal income, unemployment, and employment. These in turn are defined either with respect to the particular region in question, or in relative terms to capture somewhat more explicitly the "push–pull" phenomena involved.[1] Under certain conditions, the feedback from migration to the labor market itself is crucial, and this requires a simultaneous equation approach.[2]

Recent studies have tended to broaden the explanatory factors considered to include both demographic and quality-of-life indicators, as well as the traditional labor market factors. Among the demographic variables investigated have been accumulated past migration (Greenwood, 1970, 1971; and Levy and Wadycki, 1973) and percentage of nonwhite population (Cebula and Vedder, 1973; and Pack, 1973). Quality-of-life indicators have included local temperature variations (Cebula and Vedder, 1973; and Greenwood, 1970), housing stock and quality (Pack, 1973), frequency of crimes or political violence (Cebula and Vedder, 1973; and Schultz, 1971), and air pollution (Cebula and Vedder, 1973). The introduction of both demographic and quality-of-life factors is a recognition that the decision to migrate involves cost–benefit calculations not fully represented by labor market data and that the implied

[1] Fabricant (1970) has developed a related model that introduces certain expectational considerations as well.

[2] This situation is particularly important in LDGs, where outmigration from rural areas is not only a function of urban labor market conditions but a strong determinant of those conditions. See Annable (1972) for an application of this approach.

weighting and discounting processes vary among different types of individuals.

It is our purpose here neither to add to these lists of empirical factors influencing migration patterns nor to investigate in detail the applicability of any proposed set of factors to any particular region. We intend, rather to use a small subset of these factors as the basis for a simple migration model embedded within the full set of general equilibrium relationships defining a region, and to demonstrate empirically that such a coupled model is feasible and likely to provide migration forecasts differing from those derived from uncoupled models.

A. THE GENERAL INTERACTIVE MODEL

The interactive nature of migration described in the model is illustrated schematically in Figure 6.1. For simplicity, air pollution is used as a proxy for the quality of life of the region.[3] The figure describes the general nature of interaction between environmental, demographic, and economic factors within the region. The important linkages are further summarized in Table 6.1. In this interpretation, migration is simply one

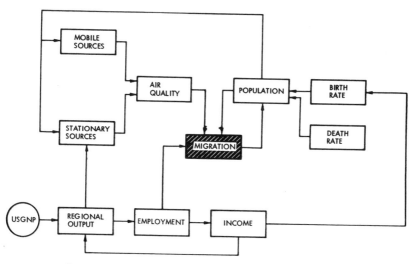

Figure 6.1 Schematic of regional general equilibrium model.

[3] This is more a reflection of the increased perception of environmental quality issues in most metropolitan areas than an assumption that other quality indexes are not important. It is not unreasonable to assume that air quality considerations, especially since the mid-1960s, have begun to influence decisions to locate, either for residence or for business. In addition, air quality indexes in many metropolitan areas in the United States have tended to move with certain other quality indicators, especially crime rates, since about 1960.

of the phenomena serving to couple the multidimensional system into an internally consistent whole. Net inmigration is directly influenced by local labor market conditions (employment), demographic factors (population),[4] and local air quality. Net inmigration in turn is one of the determinants of population change, which indirectly influences both air quality and regional output. A demographic model utilizes these migration estimates to predict population by sex and age cohorts.

II. A Demonstration for the Los Angeles Metropolitan Area

Let us now describe an experimental application of the ideas presented in Section I to the Los Angeles metropolitan area, using 1960–1970 data. In an earlier study, we estimated a small econometric model for the Los Angeles SMSA (Hall and Licari, 1974). The specific set of employment, income, and production relationships serve to define the economic components of our general interactive model.

Concern for air quality in the region is among the more critical parameters for major metropolitan areas due to a combination of meteorological peculiarities and extreme reliance on private automobiles for transportation. In Los Angeles, the major air pollutant is photochemical smog. Therefore, photochemical oxidant concentrations were selected as the measure of air quality, with the specific air quality index being the number of days during the year for which pollutant concentrations exceeded governmentally established health standards.[5] The air quality model consists of relations describing the pollutant generation from both mobile and stationary sources and the conversion of these rates into estimated average days exceeding standards.[6]

A. MODEL LINKAGES

The key linkage relations for the model appear in Table 6.2. These equations were estimated using Los Angeles regional data from 1960–1970. The structural linkages evolve from the general equilibrium model

---

[4] Population can be viewed here as a proxy for population density or as a proxy for past migration along the lines employed by Greenwood and others (see Greenwood, 1970; and Levy and Wadycki, 1973).

[5] Cebula and Vedder (1973), in their study of migration, employed the average absolute concentration of particulates as an air quality indicator. This however fails to reflect accurately the nature of episodes that so often characterize air quality problems. Our index handles this situation much more explicitly.

[6] Much of the air quality model involved use of nonstatistical engineering relations, rather than statistically estimated functions (for details, see Hall, 1974).

TABLE 6.2

Statistically Estimated Linkage Equations for the Los Angeles Region[a]

Dependent variable	Equation estimate	$\bar{R}^2$	DW
Migration	$\text{MIG} = 820.6 - 0.489\,\text{SMOG}_{-1} - 0.120\,\text{POP}_{-1}$ $\qquad\qquad\quad (1.60) \qquad\qquad (5.55)^b$ $+ 0.021\,\text{TEMP}_{-1}$ (0.966)	0.850	1.12
Labor force	$\text{LF} = 178.8 + 0.867\;\text{TEMP} + 0.107\,\text{POP}$ $\qquad\qquad (10.11)^b \qquad\quad (1.71)$	0.994	1.25
Birth rate	$\ln\text{BR} = 7.551 + 1.11\,\ln\text{TEMP}_{-1}$ $\qquad\qquad\qquad (1.08)$ $- 1.54\,\ln\text{PY}_{-1}$ $\quad (2.38)^c$	0.919	0.72
Automobile population	$\text{CARS} = -1113.4 + 0.0548\,\text{PY}_{-1}$ $\qquad\qquad\qquad\qquad (1.99)^d$ $+ 0.527\,\text{POP}$ (1.55)	0.955	2.68
Truck population	$\text{TRUK} = -3.790 + 0.0019\,\text{GRP}$ $\qquad\qquad\qquad (21.53)^b$	0.977	2.41

[a] This table contains only those linkage equations that were statistically estimated. Other linkage equations following from Table 6.1 were described by linear functions with simple point estimates of coefficients due to limited data.
[b] Significant at the 0.01 level.
[c] Significant at the 0.05 level.
[d] Significant at the 0.10 level.
Definitions of variables in Table 6.2:

BR	= Birth rate, births/mother
CARS	= Automobile population, thousands
GRP	= Gross regional product, millions of dollars/year
LF	= Regional labor force, thousands
MIG	= Net inmigration, persons/year
POP	= Regional population, thousands
PY	= Regional personal income, millions of dollars/year
SMOG	= Days per year exceeding state pollution standard
TEMP	= Total regional employment, thousands
TRUK	= Truck population, thousands

perspective in Table 6.1. While a number of alternative simple specifications of the migration equation were estimated—nonlinear and linear with various explanatory variables lagged and unlagged—the linear form given in Table 6.2 performed as well as or better than all others. Two observations regarding this migration equation are worth noting. First, $\bar{R}^2$ was maximized, with all explanatory variables lagged one period. This is certainly consistent with popular views of a lagged response of migration to changes in economic, demographic, and environmental factors (see, for example, Lianos, 1972). Second, all signs of the estimated structural coefficients are consistent with theoretical expectations. The attraction of the region should vary directly with the environmental quality or inversely with the number of days exceeding standards (SMOG). One would also expect net inmigration to vary directly with labor market conditions (TEMP) and inversely with population density, crowding, and congestion (POP).[7] This simple model explains 85% of variations in net inmigration for Los Angeles during the decade of the 1960s. The structural coefficients for the other linkage equations estimated statistically for this illustration were either of the correct sign or, when not, were statistically insignificant.

B. SIMULATION RESULTS

One attractive characteristic of the Los Angeles region for purposes of this demonstration is the major dynamic interaction of economic, demographic, and environmental phenomena occurring during the 1960s and projected for the 1970s due to complex changes in population growth, economic structure, and air quality. These factors are reflected in our empirical results. Let us first turn to performance of the full model over the sample period. These results appear in Figure 6.2. The model follows actual population changes very closely (the mean absolute percentage of error was 0.6). It also replicates historical migration data well, generally reflecting not only the reversal from net inmigration to net outmigration over the decade but also the second-order accelerations and decelerations within the same period.[8]

The results of forecasts for the period 1971–1980 with the general equilibrium model are given in Figures 6.3, 6.4, and 6.5. Because considerable variation is possible in regional air quality, depending upon legislated standards, forecasts were made for two possible environmental conditions. The first, a baseline case, assumes that the federal emission control standards for post-1974 motor vehicles and the interim standards for the few preceding years are met by all new vehicles in the region. The second, an active control scenario, assumes that additional stationary and mobile source restrictions will be implemented, since the baseline case fails to meet federally established air quality standards by 1980.

---

[7] As Laber (1972) has argued, a negative sign for this coefficient is consistent with a partial adjustment migration model.

[8] Since regional net inmigration experienced such a dramatic reversal, the mean absolute percentage of error for our predicted figures, 32%, is not a meaningful statistic.

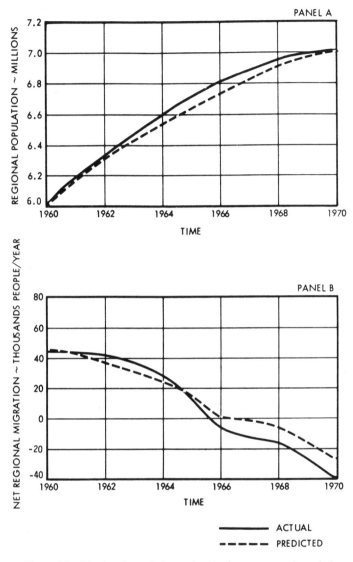

Figure 6.2 Simulated population and migration over sample period.

.Figure 6.3 demonstrates that major improvements in air quality are projected during the 1970s, with most gains coming after 1974, upon the introduction of less polluting motor vehicles, and, in the scenario case, of additional control measures. The impact on migration and population growth of these environmental changes coupled with simultaneously

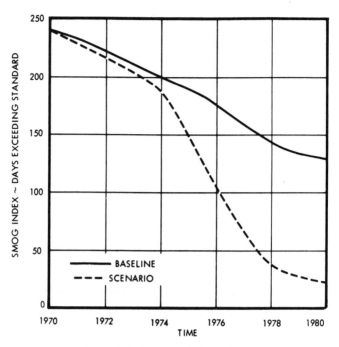

Figure 6.3 Forecasted air quality.

projected changes in economic conditions appears in Figure 6.4. Panel A indicates that the effects on birth rates of slow growth in employment and personal income, combined with low migration rates, lead to fairly stable population projections. At the same time, in both cases, the model projects a "reversal of the reversal" in net inmigration. Due to improved environmental conditions, a stabilizing regional population, and a slowly rising regional employment, the net outmigration observed during the late 1960s and projected for the early 1970s is reversed at mid-decade and a return to a positive net inmigration is forecasted by the end of the decade. The higher end-of-decade net inmigration projected under the control scenario is a direct reflection of the impact of environmental factors on migration.

C. COMPARATIVE FORECASTS FOR THE PERIOD 1971–1980

To highlight the differences between the general equilibrium and other forecasts of migration for the 1970s, we have summarized these forecasts in Figure 6.5. The "naive" forecast is simply a direct linear extrapolation of the pattern of the late 1960s. The simple equation forecast employs the migration function given in Table 6.2 with simple linear extrapolations of air quality, total employment, and population for the 1970s. Comparison with the interactive model forecast clearly shows how decoupled forecasting procedures will fail to pick up turning points such as the trend reversal in migration predicted for mid-decade. The official state forecast does follow the general trend of the interactive forecast but fails to indicate turning points and appears generally biased

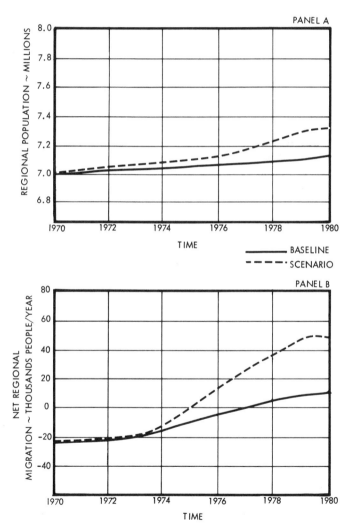

Figure 6.4 Forecasted population and migration.

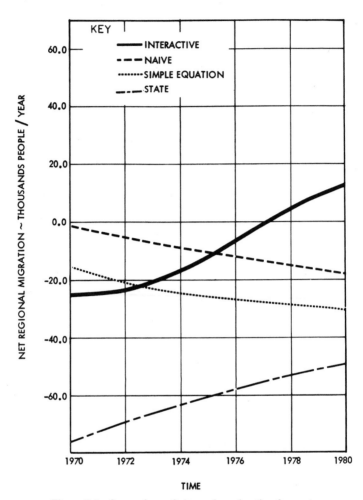

Figure 6.5 Comparison of alternative migration forecasts.

downward. It fails entirely to project a return to positive net inmigration by 1980.[9]

III. Concluding Remarks

In this paper we make a simple point: Migration flows emerge from a full set of interactive relationships for any region. One needs to consider

[9] The wide variations in all four estimates also suggest the difficulty of projecting regional migration flows with an accuracy typical of other kinds of forecasts.

the general equilibrium nature of the region in forecasting future migration patterns. Given the availability of regional data, it is possible to link economic, environmental, and demographic models into a simultaneous system of statistical and nonstatistical relations, of which one linkage is the migration equation itself. Our demonstration for the Los Angeles region shows a considerable variation between interactive model forecasts and those from decoupled procedures, although the historical data necessary to confirm relative projection accuracies are not yet available. Nonetheless, for regions undergoing major changes in the economic, demographic, or environmental areas, or where migration is the primary source of regional population growth, forecasts ignoring feedbacks accounted for in a general equilibrium model are likely to be in considerable error.

References

Annable, J. E. Internal migration and urban unemployment in low-income countries: A problem in simultaneous equations. *Oxford Economic Papers*, 1972, *24*, 399–412.

Cebula, R. J., and R. K. Vedder. A note on migration, economic opportunity, and the quality of life. *Journal of Regional Science*, 1973, *13*, 205–211.

Fabricant, R. A. An expectational model of migration. *Journal of Regional Science*, 1970, *10*, 13–24.

Greenwood, M. J. Lagged response in the decision to migrate. *Journal of Regional Science*, 1970, *10*, 375–384.

Greenwood, M. J. A regression analysis of migration to urban areas of a less-developed country: The case of India. *Journal of Regional Science*, 1971, *11*, 253–262.

Hall, O. P. Regional policy analysis by computer simulation. Unpublished Ph.D. disseration, University of Southern California, 1974.

Hall, O. P., and J. A. Licari. Building small region econometric models: Extension of Glickman's structure to Los Angeles. *Journal of Regional Science*, 1974, *14*(3), 337–353.

Laber, G. Lagged response in the decision to migrate: A comment. *Journal of Regional Science*, 1972, *12*, 307–310.

Levy, M. B., and W. J. Wadycki. The influence of family and friends on geographic labor mobility: An international comparison. *Review of Economics and Statistics*, 1973, *55*, 198–203.

Lianos, T. P. The migration process and time lags. *Journal of Regional Science*, 1972, *12*, 425–433.

Pack, J. R. Determinants of migration to central cities. *Journal of Regional Science*, 1973, *13*, 249–260.

Schultz, T. P. Rural–urban migration in Colombia. *Review of Economics and Statistics*, 1971, *53*, 157–163.

CHAPTER 7

Some Aspects of
Measuring Internal Migration

Eduardo E. Arriaga

I. Introduction

The concept of migration is easily understood in general terms, but it presents certain problems of definition. Since migration depends on several aspects and characteristics of a population, such as region of residence, distance separating inhabited places, time of settlement, individual motivations, purposes of the move, and other economic and social characteristics, it is impossible to have an accurate and all-encompassing definition of what constitutes an internal migrant. Hence, one of the difficulties involved in measuring migration is the lack of a perfect delineation of what internal migration is.

Another problem in measuring migration is the one related to the difficulties in collecting information on the subject. In most cases, the migration is measured by using indirect information, which does not yield the best estimates of the total number of migrants during a particular period of time.

Finally, in analyzing migration, special attention has to be given to how the estimates arrived at should be interpreted, bearing in mind the types and sources of information used and the procedures selected for use in the particular study or analysis.

Since it is impossible here to cover all possibilities, this paper is limited to a discussion of some of the procedures for measuring migration in relation to the information available. After a brief analysis of the sources of migration information, some procedures for estimating numbers of migrants and some of the possible ways of calculating migration rates are presented.

II. Information on Migration

There are three principal sources of information from which migration can be estimated: a) population registers, b) surveys, and c) population censuses (see United Nations, 1970).

A. Population Registers

Population registers keep a record of all population movements. Therefore, in theory, they constitute the best source of information about migrants. However, in practice, not all moves or changes are reported or registered. Hence, such registers do not necessarily present the best population information about migration. Nevertheless, it has to be said that when population registers are properly kept they permit one to identify migrants and to obtain information about their place of birth, previous residence, and many other demographic, social, cultural, and economic characteristics. Under a system of population registers, the problem would not lie in the process of estimating the number of migrants but, rather, in the process of registering all people who move—those moving into and out of any place.

B. Surveys

Surveys can be a good procedure for estimating migrants to particular areas and, principally, for obtaining the characteristics and motivations of migrants and the purposes of the move. If they are truly representative of the population under study, surveys are probably the best source for studying migration. They can be highly accurate in detecting the number of migrants and can also be conducted for the specific purpose of determining the characteristics desired for a particular investigation—which is an advantage over the other sources. The problem with surveys is not in obtaining information about migrants but, rather, in designing the survey. One difficulty is that, if not undertaken on a national scale, surveys do not give a comprehensive and accurate measure of internal migration. A local survey permits establishing only inmigration into a particular place, not necessarily outmigration from such a place. Neither do surveys detect those persons who move into a place but move out again before the date of the survey.

C. Censuses

Censuses can be useful in estimating migration if they incorporate certain tabulations. Unlike migration surveys, censuses are supposed to include all persons in an area; thus their problem is not one of representativeness but of including the appropriate information. If adequate information on migrants is tabulated, censuses can be an excellent source for estimating migration. The problem, however, is one of reliability. For instance, censuses may have different degrees of enumeration completness in different areas, and they may contain errors or biases either because the interviewee does not respond properly or because the interviewer does not have proper training or for both of these reasons. Nevertheless, in most cases, migration is measured by using census information, since it is usually the only source of data available.

III. Census Information for Measuring Migration

Two kinds of information for estimating migration can be found in censuses: 1) General information, collected for whatever purpose, that will permit making an estimate of migrants and 2) information that was specifically collected for the purpose of estimating migration. In both cases, only net migration over a particular period of time will be detected and the results will differ according to the information collected and the calculation procedures used.

A. General Information That May be Used for Measuring Migration

Among the different kinds of information collected in a census, population of particular places or areas—where possible by age and sex—is the most commonly used for estimating migration. If such information is available at two different dates (t and $t + m$), net migrants surviving at time $t + m$ can be estimated by the following equation

$$SM^{t+m} = P_i^{t+m} - P_i^t - NG_i^{t,t+m} \qquad (1)$$

where SM^{t+m} is the migrants surviving to year $t + m$, P_i^t and P_i^{t+m} are the populations of place i at time t and $t + m$, respectively, and $NG_i^{t,t+m}$ is the natural growth of place i during the interval $t, t + m$.

Unfortunately, in most cases, information about the natural increase for particular places—births and deaths—is not available, and an estimate of natural increase is required. These estimates can introduce some biases or errors. For instance, if an estimate of the rate of natural increase is available, migrants can be calculated by comparing the actual population at time $t + m$ with an expected population, assuming that no migration since year t would have occurred. This expected population is frequently estimated as

$$EP_i^{t+m} = P_i^t e^{mr} \tag{2}$$

where r is an estimate of the rate of annual natural increase of place i. Thus, the difference between the actual population in place i and the estimated population gives the number of migrants, together with births and deaths of migrants, during the m-year period

$$MG_i^{t,t+m} = P_i^{t+m} - EP_i^{t+m} . \tag{3}$$

The births and deaths of migrants occurring in the inmigration place constitute the natural effect of migration. This natural effect has to be separated from the total number of migrants since such effect is not part of total migration. For this purpose, some assumptions must be made about the number of migrant births and deaths, or directly about the natural increase of migrants. A factor has already been developed for separating migrants from their natural effect (see Arriaga, 1968). This factor is computed as

$$MF = \frac{P^{t+m} - P^t}{m(e^r - 1)P^{t+m}} \tag{4}$$

where P^{t+m} and P^t are the total population of the country at time $t + m$ and t, respectively, and r is the natural growth rate of the country's population. Multiplying this factor by the number of migrants and their natural effect, an estimate of the surviving migrants in place i at year $t + m$ is obtained:

$$SM_i^{t+m} = MF \cdot MG_i^{t,t+m} . \tag{5}$$

When the age structure of the population of a place is available, and in addition mortality is known, a net cohort of surviving migrants at time $t + m$ can be estimated by comparing the population in a particular age group at time $t + m$ with the expected population at the same age and year. For instance, the number of net surviving migrants in place i at time $t + m$ during the m-year period pertaining to the cohort whose age was x, $x + n$ in year t would be

$$_iSM_{x+m,x+m+n}^{t+m} = {_iP_{x+m,x+m+n}^{t+m}} - {_iS_{x,x+n}^{t,t+m}} \cdot {_iP_{x,x+n}^t} \tag{6}$$

where $_iP_{x,x+n}^t$ and $_iP_{x+m,x+m+n}^{t+m}$ are the population of place i of x, $x + n$ and $x + m$, $x + m + n$ years old at year t and $t + m$, respectively, and $_iS_{x,x+n}^{t,t+m}$ is the survival ratio for the cohort c, $c + n$ years old at year t living in place i during the next m years. Two problems usually have to be faced: a) availability of the $_iS_{x,x+n}^{t,t+m}$ values and b) migration in the interim since birth of the group aged 0 to m at time $t + m$.

For the first case, the survival ratio for the whole country can be used to estimate the survival ratio for place i. That is:

$$_iS_{x,x+n}^{t,t+m} \doteq \frac{P_{x+m,x+m+n}^{t+m}}{P_{x,x+n}^t} . \tag{7}$$

Another possibility is to use life tables for estimating the survival ratio for place i:

$$_iS_{x,x+n}^{t,t+m} \doteq \frac{L_{x+m,x+m+n}}{L_{x,x+n}}. \tag{8}$$

Usually the first procedure is preferable to the second. The life table procedure implies a perfect enumeration of censuses at the beginning and end of the migration period in relation to completeness and age misreporting, which would never happen in actuality. Hence, the number of migrants estimated by using life table survival ratios reflects census errors rather than migration. On the other hand, the first procedure implies only that errors in each census are approximately the same in all places as well as that mortality is the same in all areas. Although neither assumption represents actuality, the first is more acceptable. If mortality differentials by places or areas are known, the census survival ratios can be modified accordingly.

To assume that mortality is almost the same in all areas will not produce significant bias in industrialized countries because actual mortality differentials are relatively small. Thus, the assumption will not greatly affect the estimation of migrants during intercensal periods—usually 10 years. Most of the migrants are between ages 15 and 45, an age span in which mortality is low in any area of an industrialized country. However, in less developed countries, mortality differentials could be significant even in ages of low mortality. Hence some assumptions will have to be made. A possibility is to adjust the census survival ratios according to the relative difference between two survival ratios for the same age and period from two different life tables—those pertaining to the estimated levels of mortality for the whole country and those pertaining to the particular place i.

To sum up, the estimation of migrants by indirect information would give an estimate of the net migration of a particular place. But this procedure would not reveal the previous place(s) of residence of the inmigrants nor the destinations of the outmigrants.

B. Information Directly Related to Migrants

Four types of data have usually been tabulated concerning migrants: a) place of enumeration by place of birth, b) place of enumeration by duration of residence, c) place of enumeration by place of last residence, and d) place of enumeration by place of residence at a particular date. Each one of these characteristics might also be cross-tabulated by other characteristics, such as age, sex, labor force, education, family composition, civil status, and so on, for the purpose of relating migration to some demographic, social, or economic aspects of the population.

First, each of the possible tabulations will be discussed briefly, then, two detailed examples of the use of such tabulations will be presented.

(a) Information about population enumerated in a particular place j at time t born in place i, $BP_{j,i}^t$ gives the number of lifetime migrants born in place i living at place j in year t. Unfortunately this tells us nothing about when they came to place j. However, if there are two censuses, at times t and $t + m$, the difference, $BM_{j,i}^{t,t+m} = BP_{j,i}^{t+m} - BP_{j,i}^t$, gives the net number of surviving migrants born in place i who came to (or left) place j during the intercensal period of m years.

This tabulation identifies where migrants were born but not where they migrated from.

(b) Information about duration of residence in the place of enumeration, if it is tabulated by intervals of several years, permits estimating not only the number of inmigrants to a particular place but also the intensity of such migration during the time. However, it does not give any information about where migrants came from nor about any outmigration that might have taken place.

(c) Enumeration by place of last residence has a certain similarity to enumeration by place of birth, although the migration period would be equal to or shorter than when place of birth is used. If there is more than one census available with this information, migration for the intercensal period can be estimated by similar procedures to those outlined in (a).

(d) Enumeration by place of residence at particular dates permits estimating for particular periods of time the net surviving migrants at the census date without the need for more than one census. In addition, if the tabulation is presented for several dates, some trends of migration can also be calculated. Particular attention should be given to the population born during the interim since the last period of reference. For instance, if the last period of reference is 5 years—that is, place of residence 5 years prior to the census date—particular consideration should be given to children under 5 years of age.

Since the estimation of migrants is frequently based on place of enumeration by place of birth or on place of enumeration by residence w years prior to the census, what follows is a method for estimating migrants and migration rates from these two different kinds of information.

IV. Migration Estimates Based on Information on Place of Enumeration by Place of Birth

Where there is only one census with information on place of residence by place of birth, only lifetime migration can be estimated. In such a case, migration rates cannot be calculated, only ratios or percentages. For instance, the following matrix can be made for the census year t.

Place of Birth

$$
\begin{array}{c}
\text{Place of} \\
\text{Enumeration}
\end{array}
\begin{array}{l}
BP^t_{1,1} BP^t_{1,2} \cdots BP^t_{1,i} \cdots BP^t_{1,s} \\
BP^t_{2,1} BP^t_{2,2} \cdots BP^t_{2,i} \cdots BP^t_{2,s} \\
\vdots \quad \vdots \quad \vdots \quad \vdots \\
BP^t_{j,1} BP^t_{j,2} \cdots BP^t_{j,i} \cdots BP^t_{j,s} \\
\vdots \quad \vdots \quad \vdots \quad \vdots \\
BP^t_{s,1} BP^t_{s,2} \cdots BP^t_{s,i} \cdots BP^t_{s,s}
\end{array} = A^t \tag{9}
$$

in which $BP^t_{j,i}$ means the population born in place i enumerated in place j; such population can be considered as the net lifetime migration of those born in place i and migrating to place j. Foreigners born in different countries can be grouped in additional column $P^t_{s,s+1}$ if they are included in the analysis. The population enumerated in place j would be

$$
BCP_j{}^t = \sum_{i=1}^{s} BP^t_{j,i} \tag{10}
$$

and the population born in place i

$$
BBP_i{}^t = \sum_{j=1}^{s} BP^t_{j,i} . \tag{11}
$$

Therefore, the total net lifetime migration into place j surviving at year t, would be

$$
BI_j{}^t = BCP_j{}^t - BP^t_{j,j} . \tag{12}
$$

Similarly, the net lifetime outmigration of those born in place i from place of birth to any other place and surviving at year t would be

$$
BE_i{}^t = BBP_i{}^t - BP^t_{i,i} . \tag{13}
$$

With the previous estimation of migrants, several ratios or percentages can be computed to analyze the internal migration movement—always keeping in mind that the data refer to lifetime migration. This fact will reduce considerably the possibilities for analysis.

The situation will be much better if information on place of enumeration by place of birth is available for more than one census. Then, migration can be estimated for an intercensal period—usually 10 years. For instance, the information of each census can be tabulated as in matrix A^t for the years t and $t + m$. The difference between the two matrices will give the changes of the population born in particular place i and enumerated in place j. These differences can be considered as intercensal migration.

$$BM^m = A^{t+m} - A^t \qquad (14)$$

for each individual element of the matrix

$$BM_{j,i}^m = BP_{j,i}^{t+m} - BP_{j,i}^t ; \qquad j \neq i \qquad (15)$$

where $BM_{j,i}^t$ is the net migration to place j of those persons born in place i during the m-year period who survive up to year $t + m$. The exception will be for $BM_{j,j}^t$, which would represent not migration but the change in the number of those born and residing in the same place during the m period.

The $BM_{j,i}^m$ can be positive, negative, or zero. Zero will be considered as no surviving migrants from i to j; positive, as inmigration to place j by those born in i—but not necessarily coming from k; and negative, as outmigration from place j of those born in place i. (Deaths would be considered as outmigration.)

The total net migration to place j of those born outside of place j during the m-year period would be

$$BI_j{}^m = \sum_{i=1}^{s} BM_{j,i}^m - BM_{j,j}^m . \qquad (16)$$

Similarly the total net surviving outmigrants born in place i, from place i to any other place would be

$$BE_i{}^m = \sum_{j=1}^{s} BM_{j,i}^m - BM_{i,i}^m . \qquad (17)$$

It should be borne in mind that place of birth is not necessarily the same as place of previous residence (i.e., place of origin). Those born in a particular place who have migrated into the area of enumeration might have come from any area of the country. Taking this fact into account, the following annual average rates can be computed.

The annual average migration rate to place j of those born outside j during the m-year period will be

$$BIR_j^m = z \frac{BI_j^m}{BCP_j^{t+m} + BCP_j^t} \tag{18}$$

where BCP_j^t and BCP_j^{t+m} are the enumerated census population in place j at years t and $t + m$, respectively, and z is a constant for obtaining the annual rate. This is calculated as:

$$z = \frac{2 \times 1000}{m} \tag{19}$$

where m is the number of years of the intercensal period, 2 stands for the average population at the middle of the period, and 1000 is a constant used to express the rate per thousand of population.

This rate is the net surviving number of migrants born outside of place j who have left (or come to) place j during the m-year period, per thousand persons living in place j.

The annual average migration rate—in most cases the rate of outmigration—of those born in place i in relation to those living in i is

$$BER_i^m = z \frac{BE_i^m}{BCP_i^{t+m} + BCP_i^t} \tag{20}$$

which gives us the annual average number of net migrants born in place i who have left (or come to) place i during the m-year period, per thousand persons living in place i.

A rate similar to BER_j^m can be calculated, but instead of referring to each thousand of population residing in i, it can be calculated per thousand of population born and residing in j.

$$EBR_j^m = z \frac{BE_j^m}{BP_{j,j}^{t+m} + BP_{j,j}^t} . \tag{21}$$

This rate gives the annual net average number of migrants born in j who have left (or come to) place j during the m-year period, per thousand of population born and living in place j.

The addition of the previous two rates (Eqs. (18) and (20)) for a particular place j gives the net annual migration rate for place j—for those born in j as well as for those born outside of j

$$MR_j^m = BIR_j^m - BER_j^m . \tag{22}$$

Migration rates for migrants born in any place can be calculated in relation to any other place. That is, the rate BIR_j^m can be decomposed into rates indicating where migrants were born. Each of these components rates are

$$SIR_{j,i}^m = z \frac{BM_{j,i}^m}{BCP_j^{t+m} + BCP_j^t}. \tag{23}$$

This rate indicates the annual average number of net migrants born in place i coming to (or leaving) place j during the m-year interval, per thousand of population residing in place j.

A similar rate can be calculated in relation to the number of migrants born in a particular area i who are contributing to the population change of place j in relation to those residing in place i

$$SER_{j,i}^m = z \frac{BM_{j,i}^m}{BCP_i^{t+m} + BCP_i^t}. \tag{24}$$

This rate refers to the annual average number of net migrants born in place i who have arrived at (or left) place j, per thousand of population residing in i.

Finally, an additional computation can be made from the census information on place of birth, namely, the attraction that a particular area j exerts on the population born in area i and living outside of the area j. This attraction rate is

$$BAR_{j,i}^m = z \frac{BM_{j,i}^m}{(BBP_i^{t+m} - BP_{j,i}^{t+m}) + (BBP_i^t - BP_{j,i}^t)} \tag{25}$$

where BBP_i^t and BBP_i^{t+m} are the total population born in place i and enumerated in any other place (Eq. (11)). This rate is the annual average number of net migrants born in place i who have come to (or left) place j during the m-year period, per thousand of population born in i and living outside of j.

V. Migration Estimates Based on Information on Place of Enumeration by Place of Residence m Years prior to the Census Date

This information has two advantages over place-of-birth data. It gives direct information about places of residence of migrants to a particular place during the last n years, and it requires only *one* census to obtain annual rates. However, special attention should be given to those children born between the date of reference for establishing the previous residence and the census date. These children under age n—assuming that the question in the census was, "Where did you live n years ago?''—were not alive n years ago and therefore did not have a place of residence. If they are included as having resided in the present place of residence, those who have migrated will not be detected. A possible solution is to have two separate tables—one showing the population n years of age or over by place of residence n years ago, the other the population under n years of age by place of birth. Since the period of reference is usually 5 years, the tabulation of those under age 5 by place of birth would give a good estimate of their migration movement. Assuming that there is information for both tabulations, the census information can be used for constructing two matrices, which would be similar to the one made previously for the information on place of birth. For the population under age n the matrix will be exactly the same as before (Eq. (9)). However, each element will be symbolized as $CH_{j,i}^t$, indicating the children under age n born in place i and enumerated at place j in the year t. The other matrix would be for the population n years old and over. Each element of this would be $RP_{j,i}^t$, representing the population residing in place i n years ago, but living in place j at the census date t. Each column of the matrix will indicate the place of previous residence (or place of birth for children under age n), and each line the place of residence at the census date. Those in the diagonal would be considered to be those who did not migrate during the n years—although this procedure would include people who were living in place i n years ago, went to another place, and then returned to place i before the census was taken. In this respect, the migration estimated by using this information is net migration.

The number of net migrants to place j during the last n years prior to the census would be

$$RP_j^n = \sum_{i=1}^{s} RP_{j,i}^t - RP_{j,j}^t + \sum_{i-1}^{s} CH_{j,i}^t - CH_{j,j}^t . \qquad (26)$$

Similarly, the number of net outmigrants from place i would be

$$RE_i^n = \sum_{j=1}^{s} RP_{j,i}^t - RP_{i,i}^t + \sum_{j=1}^{s} CH_{j,i}^t - CH_{i,i}^t . \qquad (27)$$

As in the previous case, several rates can be estimated. The main difference in calculating the rates would be to estimate the population at the middle of the n-year period of reference—at year $t - \dfrac{n}{2}$. For simplification, the mean year of the n-year period is represented by $w = t - \dfrac{n}{2}$.

Therefore, the population resident in place j at year w is

$$RP_j^w = \frac{1}{2} \left(\sum_{i=1}^{s} RP_{j,i}^t + \sum_{j=1}^{s} RP_{j,i}^t + \sum_{i=1}^{s} CH_{j,i}^t + \sum_{j=1}^{s} CH_{j,i}^t \right). \qquad (28)$$

This population is used as a base for calculating the following annual rates, in which k is the constant for expressing the rates per thousand of population per year.

$$k = 1000/n. \qquad (29)$$

The annual average net inmigration rate to place j during the n-year period, per thousand of population residing in place j, is

$$RIR_j^n = k(RI_j^n/RP_j^w). \qquad (30)$$

The annual average net outmigration rate from place i during the n-year period, per thousand of population residing in place i, is

$$RER_i^n = k(RE_i^n/RP_i^w). \qquad (31)$$

The annual average net inmigration rate from place i to place j during the n-year period, per thousand of population residing in place j, is

$$RIR_{j,i}^n = k(RP_{j,i}^t + CH_{j,i}^t)/(RP_j^w). \qquad (32)$$

The annual average net outmigration rate from place i to place j during the n-year period, per thousand of population residing in place i, is

$$RER_{j,i}^n = k(RP_{j,i}^t + CH_{j,i}^t)/(RP_i^w). \qquad (33)$$

This last rate can also be considered as the attraction rate that place j exerted on those residing in place i.

All the rates dealt with so far were based on census information pertaining to *surviving* migrants, and they would be useful for estimating net surviving migrants during particular periods. To obtain the net number of migrants arriving in a particular place—although some of them will die later—the previous rates can be adjusted to take into account those who have died, as long as information about the rate of migrant mortality is available. If survival ratios are available for the period for which rates were calculated $(SR^{t-n,t})$, then each rate should be divided by one-half $(1 + SR^{t-n,t})$, since migrants would have been exposed to the mortality of the migration place for only one-half of the period, on the average.

VI. Comparison of Different Procedures

Faced with several possibilities for analyzing migration, the question is which procedure the researcher should use. There is no single answer to this question; it would depend not only on the information available but also on the information sought. For instance, if age and sex of migrants is sought and no direct information on these characteristics is available, then the method of cohort survivors should be applied. However, such procedures will not yield any information about numbers of inmigrants and outmigrants nor about the places of origin of migrants.

If information about the areal origin of migrants is sought, then, data on place of birth or residence n years before the census date will be useful. If both are available, an analysis of both should be made. In general, the place of residence n years ago would be more efficient in identifying not only migrants, but also their places of origin. Information by place of birth will permit analysis of the movement of persons with certain origin, particularly if the country's population has marked regional characteristics.

Migration rates vary as a consequence not only of the procedure used but also of the detail of the information used. For instance, when using the cohort survival procedure, if 10-year age groups instead of 5-year age groups are used, the migration estimates will differ. Similarly, the smaller the geographic unit considered for measuring migration, the better the estimate of migrants, when the variable used is place of birth or residence n-years before.

As an illustration, several rates were calculated. For instance, by using the cohort survival procedure for native population of the states of California and Florida in the United States, the net annual migration rates (inmigration) during the period 1960–1970 were 8.1 and 16.2, respectively. That is, an annual average of 8.1 native persons of the United States per thousand native residents of California who were alive in 1970 moved to California during the period 1960–1970. The same would hold for the state of Florida, where the net annual average of migrants was 16.2 per thousand.

If migration is estimated by using information on place of enumeration by place of birth in 1960 and 1970, the following rates can be estimated. As in the previous case, only native population is considered. In this case, the rates can be separated for those born outside of each state and those born in each state. These were:

	California	Florida
Annual average net inmigration rate for those born outside of each state (per thousand)	8.9	18.7
Annual average net outmigration rate for those born in each state (per thousand)	3.9	4.4
Annual average net migration rate (per thousand)	5.0	14.3

The rates shown in the last line mean exactly the same as the rates given earlier based on the cohort survival procedure—for California, a net annual total of 5.0 U.S. native migrants per thousand native residents of the state arrived in California during the intercensal period 1960–1970. For both states, the rates based on place of birth are lower than those based on cohort survival: 8.1 versus 5.0 for California, and 16.2 versus 14.3 for Florida. The differences may be due to misreporting of characteristics in the census, or to underenumeration in each state in relation to the whole country or to both of these. Another possibility is that, since both states have experienced a large foreign-born immigration during the decade, some foreigners might have been reported as native and as being born in the state of enumeration in the 1970 census.

Another comparison of procedures can be done, comparing data on place of enumeration by place of birth and data on place of enumeration by previous residence n years ago. In a specific case, the 1960 and 1970 information by place of birth and by place of residence 5 years prior to the 1970 United States census was used (see Tables 7.1 and 7.2). The calculations were made for each of the nine continental subdivisions of the country—each subdivision having several states. The equations used were numbers (18), (20), (30), and (31). The comparison is not perfect,

TABLE 7.1

INTERNAL MIGRATION AMONG GEOGRAPHICAL DIVISIONS IN THE UNITED STATES CALCULATED BY USING INFORMATION ON NATIVE POPULATION BY PLACE OF ENUMERATION AND PLACE OF BIRTH IN THE 1960 AND 1970 POPULATION CENSUSES (RATES PER THOUSAND)[a]

| | Annual net migration rates for the population born | | |
Geographical division	Outside the division (1)	Inside the division (2)	Total (1) + (2)
New England	4.11	−3.64	.53
Middle Atlantic	.96	−4.26	−3.30
East North Central	1.70	−3.08	−1.38
West North Central	1.50	−1.67	− .17
South Atlantic	6.44	−2.36	4.08
East South Central	2.60	−2.65	− .05
West South Central	2.66	−2.56	.10
Mountain	6.99	−6.50	.49
Pacific	5.00	−3.31	1.69

[a] Positive and negative rates mean inmigration and outmigration, respectively.

TABLE 7.2

INTERNAL MIGRATION AMONG GEOGRAPHICAL DIVISIONS IN THE UNITED
STATES CALCULATED BY USING INFORMATION ON POPULATION ENUMERATED
BY RESIDENCE 5 YEARS PRIOR TO THE 1970 POPULATION CENSUS (RATES PER
THOUSAND)

Geographical division	Annual net migration rates		
	Inmigration (1)	Outmigration (2)	Total (1) − (2)
New England	18.61	14.69	3.92
Middle Atlantic	12.08	12.41	−.33
East North Central	13.51	13.28	.23
West North Central	16.61	19.52	−2.91
South Atlantic	24.86	15.31	9.55
East South Central	18.24	20.56	−2.32
West South Central	19.52	15.63	3.89
Mountain	40.14	33.74	6.40
Pacific	26.73	15.40	11.33

since place of birth pertains only to native population, while the estimate of migrants by place of residence 5 years earlier includes *all* population *living* in the continental United States in 1970. However, the rates are presented because they show a great variation, more than would be expected from the inclusion or exclusion of the foreign born or because the annual rates are for periods of different length. That is, part of the variation is due to the procedure used. The higher rates obtained by using place of residence 5 years earlier would indicate that more migrants are identified by this procedure than when data are by place of birth.

Detecting migration from census information depends mainly on the information that has been tabulated. If more than one procedure is possible, then more than one attempt should be made to identify migrants and calculate rates of migration. After comparing results and keeping in mind the purposes of the analysis, the relative value of each procedure—based on the results yielded by it—can be judged.

VII. Conclusions

This paper has considered only a few of all the possible ways of estimating migration, not only because of the limitations of space but also because such possibilities depend on the information available and the specific purposes of each study. *The main problem in estimating migration is not a methodological one but, rather, a problem of data.*

Migration methodology is a somewhat simple analysis of the available information for estimating the number of migrants during a period and for establishing exactly what the migration information means. Rates are usually calculated by computing ratios that represent an average annual number of migrants in relation to a specific population—usually estimated at the middle of the migration period.

The problem lies in collecting the information and in producing the data tabulations. The information about migrants may be subject to errors of reporting because of misinterpretation of place of residence, place of birth, or period of reference, because of lack of money or knowledge; or even because of deliberate misreporting. In addition, there are errors that originate with interviewers or with the registration system as well as coding errors when tabulations are being prepared.

Finally, the available tabulations of migration information do not always permit one to make good estimates of migratory movement, particularly in relation to places of origin and in relation to the sex and age characteristics of migrants. Countries can improve tabulations concerning migrants, particularly in relation to publishing information already collected such as on the demographic, cultural, or economic characteristics of migrants.

References

Arriaga, E. E. Components of city population growth in selected Latin American countries. *Milbank Memorial Fund Quarterly, 46*(2), Part 1, April 1968, pp. 237–252.

Bogue, D. J., *Methods of studying internal migration.* Technical paper prepared for Regional Seminar on Population in Central and South America, Rio de Janeiro, Brazil, December 1955.

Das Gupta, A. Types and measures of internal migration. In International Union for the Scientific Study of Population, *International Population Conference,* Vienna, 1959, pp. 619–624.

Eldridge, H. T. A cohort approach to the analysis of migration differentials. *Demography,* 1964, *1*(1), 212–219.

Elizaga, J. C. A study of migration to Greater Santiago (Chile). *Demography,* 1966, *3*(2), 352–377.

Hamilton, C. H. Practical and mathematical considerations in the formulation and selection of migration rates. *Demography,* 1965, *2*, 429–443.

Hamilton, C. H. Effect of census errors on the measurement of net migration. *Demography,* 1966, *2*(2), 393–415.

Siegel, J. S., and C. H. Hamilton. Some considerations in the use of the residual method of estimating net migration. *Journal of the American Statistical Association,* 1952, *47*, 475–500.

Stone, L. O. Evaluating the relative accuracy and significance of net migration estimates. *Demography,* 1967, *4*(1), 310–330.

United Nations. *Methods of measuring internal migration.* Manual 6, ST/SOA/Series A/ 47, New York, 1970.

Wunsch, G. Le calcul des soldes migratoires par la méthode de la "population atten- due"—caractéristiques et évaluation des biais. *Population et famille* (Brussels), 1969, *18*, 49–62.

Zitter, M., and E. S. Nagy. Use of Social Security's Continuous Work History Sample for measurement of net migration by geographic area. *Proceedings of the American Statistical Association,* Social Statistics Section, Washington, D.C., 1969, pp. 235–260.

CHAPTER 8

Measurement of Internal Migration from Census Data

K. C. Zachariah[1]

I. Introduction

Population census has been and still is the principal source of data for measuring internal migration in most countries of the world, including such countries as Japan, the Netherlands, and Sweden, which have a system of continuous registration of their population. Censuses are taken only periodically, usually once in 10 or 5 years, and questions directly related to migration are few, usually one but sometimes two or three. These limitations of census as a source of migration data are more than compensated for by the enormous potential for preparing detailed cross-classification of migration data with other demographic and socio-economic characteristics normally obtained in censuses. This aspect of census data is particularly important because, aside from measurement of the volume of migration, most other migration analysis would require a considerable degree of cross-classification of migrants by demographic and socioeconomic characteristics. Even in the comparison of migration rates of different socioeconomic groups, control for age–sex differences is essential. The prime position of census as a source of migration data is

[1] The author is a staff member of the International Bank for Reconstruction and Development. However, this paper is not an official Bank document and the views expressed here are not necessarily those of the Bank. It was prepared for presentation at the Warsaw Conference on Migration.

thus as much due to the near universality of the system of census taking as it is due to the enormous scope for basic cross-classification of these data with other characteristics.

The system of population registration is potentially the most valuable source of migration data. But, as presently organized—with the system existing in a fairly satisfactory manner in only a few countries, tabulation and publication of migration data delayed considerably or not carried out at all, and cross-classification of migrants with socioeconomic characteristics rarely undertaken—it remains still, at least from the international point of view, a potential source, rather than an actual one. In a United Nations survey conducted in 1962, it was found that, of the 57 countries presumed to have some "system" of population registration, only 9 reported that they provided statistical data on internal migration (United Nations, 1970, p. 50).

Census data refer to *migrants* and nonmigrants, while population registers are concerned with the event of *migration*. As a result, there are systematic differences between data derived from censuses and from population registers. Census data have other limitations and differences when being compared with those from other sources. It is rarely that information on repeated movements, and accompanying changes in occupation and other socioeconomic characteristics, are obtained in population censuses. Similarly, reasons for migration are rarely inquired into; nor do censuses usually provide supplementary information that would make it possible to classify migrants into meaningful types. Lack of such supplementary information can sometimes adversely affect the usefulness of the data.[2] These problems are easily handled in sample surveys, which allow the exploration of the migration process in greater depth by means of a larger set of questions. Thus, although census data are adequate for a variety of migration studies, they need to be supplemented with data from carefully conducted sample surveys when in-depth analysis of the migration process is envisaged.

The present paper is confined to census data alone. It deals with the measurement of internal migration and provides some illustrations of the use of such measures for analytical purposes. As the topic is fairly well covered in some of the recent literature (Everett, 1957; Eldridge and Thomas, 1964; United Nations, 1970), no attempt has been made here to go into technical details.

---

[2] For example, in India it is customary for a woman to return to her father's household to bear the first child and sometimes the second and subsequent children. This practice gives rise to some spurious migration as measured from birthplace statistics. There is no way to separate such marriage ancillary migration from other types of migration.

II. Measurement of Migration

Some measures of migration, such as net intercensal migration, can be estimated from census data even without any direct question on migration, but other measures, such as gross migration flows, can be obtained only with a direct question on migration in the census. We shall first discuss measures that do not require a direct question, the so-called indirect measures.

A. INDIRECT MEASURES OF MIGRATION:

Estimates of net migration for regions, administrative areas, urban areas, and so forth can be made with as little census data as the total count (with or without an age–sex breakdown) at two or more censuses. The quality of the estimates will, of course, depend on the quality of the census enumeration and the use of supplementary information. The method consists in estimating the expected intercensal population growth in the absence of migration and comparing it with the actual growth. The difference is taken as the net effect of intercensal migration. There are two main approaches for estimating the expected growth in the absence of migration: (i) through vital statistics and (ii) through estimates of the probability of survival.

Where reliable vital statistics are available, net migration may be obtained as a balance between total growth and natural increase. Thus,

$$\text{Net } M = (P_{t+n} - P_t) - (B - D),$$

where P_t and P_{t+n} are total population at two successive censuses, and B and D are the total births and deaths during the interval. In cases where statistics on births and deaths are not available, the second factor, $(B - D)$, may be substituted with:

$$\frac{P_{t+n} + P_t}{2} \cdot n \cdot r$$

where r is an estimate of the annual rate of natural increase, which, in some cases, may be taken as equal to the national growth rate.

The vital statistics method of estimating net migration is particularly useful for estimating net migration totals for towns and cities for which migration (direct method) data are not separately tabulated. Even in countries where the vital statistics are generally poor, very often those of cities are reliable enough for their use in estimating net migration. The method has a built-in capacity to take care of some degree of underregistration of vital events.

The second approach, using survival probability, may be expressed symbolically as:

$$\text{Net } M(x) = P_{x+n,t+n} - SP_{x,t}$$

where $M(x)$ is net migration among survivors of persons aged x at the first census in a given area, $P_{x,t}$ is the population aged x years in that area at the first census, $P_{x+n,t+n}$ is the population aged $x+n$ years in the same area at the second census taken n years later, and S is the survival ratio, which may be estimated either from the censuses or from life tables, according to the availability of the relevant data. In the census survival ratio method, S is estimated by the ratio

$$\bar{P}_{x+n,t+n} \div \bar{P}_{x,t}$$

where the $\bar{P}$'s refer to the national totals. Alternately, S may be estimated from the life table function

$$L_{x+n} \div L_x$$

of the area for the intercensal period.

The data requirement is minimal for the census survival ratio method; all that is needed is the number of persons classified by age and sex enumerated at two successive censuses for the area for which the migration estimate is required and for the country as a whole. However, the application of the method to a particular situation requires the fulfilment of a number of conditions. These are not always realized, especially in countries where regional variations in mortality levels are great. In such situations, use of the life table survival ratios could result in more accurate estimates of net migration. It is not intended to give in this paper a detailed discussion of all the conditions underlying the use of survival probability method and their effects on migration estimates; these are available in several places in the literature (Lee, 1957; United Nations, 1970). What is attempted here is merely to show that estimates of net migration useful for the analysis of population growth and other analytical studies can be obtained with some of the most readily available census data even without any outside data or a separate census question on migration. Of course, the scope of measurement and the analysis can be greatly improved with data from one or more questions directly related to migration.

B. MIGRATION ESTIMATES BASED ON DIRECT QUESTIONS

Census data on migration flows and characteristics of migrants can only be produced by asking a direct question on one or another aspect of the migration status of the enumerated population. The questions usually asked for this purpose are:

(i)   Place of birth
(ii) Duration of residence
(iii) Place of last residence
(iv) Place of residence at a fixed prior date.

The question on birthplace is the one most commonly used and the one given first priority in the United Nations recommendations for the 1960 and 1970 rounds of censuses. The other questions are relatively new, but they are finding increasing acceptance in recent censuses, not in place of the question on birthplace but in addition to it. Thus in the 1971 census of India, all the above questions except (iv) were asked.

These questions serve the main purpose of classifying the enumerated population into two groups: migrants and nonmigrants. As should be expected, the basis for the classification is not the same for the different questions (see Table 8.1), and, consequently, measures of migration derived from these various questions are different quantitatively and even conceptually. Thus, migration estimates obtained from a question on duration of residence must be greater than the estimates produced by the question on place of birth, as the former counts persons who return to their birthplace as migrants, while the latter classifies them as

TABLE 8.1

CRITERIA FOR CLASSIFYING MIGRANTS AND NONMIGRANTS BY CENSUS
QUESTIONS ON MIGRATION

Questions	Migrant	Nonmigrant
1. Place of birth	Person who is enumerated in a place different from the place where he was born	Person who is enumerated in the place where he was born
2. Duration of residence	Person who has lived in the place of enumeration for a period less than his age	Person who has lived in the place of enumeration all his life
3. Place of last residence	Person whose place of last residence is different from the place of enumeration	Person who has lived in the place of enumeration all his life
4. Place of residence at a fixed prior date.	Person whose place of residence at the census date differs from his place of residence at the specified prior date.	Person whose residence at the census date is the same as that at the specified prior date

TABLE 8.2

TYPES OF MIGRATION MEASURES THAT CAN BE DERIVED FROM DATA BASED ON
USUAL QUESTIONS RELATED TO MIGRATION

Questions	Type of migration measures	Main advantages and disadvantages
1. Place of birth	Lifetime inmigration by place of origin; lifetime outmigration by place of destination; net balance of lifetime migration between any two places Data from more than one census can be used to estimate intercensal net migration among persons born within, and among those born outside	*Advantages:* The question is easily understood; provides the geographical configuration of migration *Disadvantages:* Timing of migration unknown (recent migration flows may be very much different from lifetime migration flows); assumes a single movement directly from area of birth to area of enumeration; exclusion of return migrants
2. Duration of residence	Inmigration by duration of residence in the place of enumeration Data from more than one census can be used to derive estimates of remigration by year of arrival for intercensal periods	*Advantages:* Takes care of return migration; provides the timing of the last move *Disadvantages:* Migration cohorts may be decimated by remigration and deaths, both factors influenced by duration of residence; place of origin not given, consequently no data on outmigration; no distinction between immigrants and inmigrants
3. Place of last residence	Inmigrants by place of last residence; outmigrants by place of present residence; net balance of migration between any two places	*Advantages:* Provides information on direct moves; otherwise, similar to Question 1 *Disadvantages:* Lack of time reference
4. Place of residence at a fixed prior date	Inmigrants by place of residence x years ago; outmigrants by place of present residence; net migration between places	*Advantages:* Migration time span is clear-cut *Disadvantages:* Persons born during the interval not included; difficult to estimate intercensal migration

nonmigrants. Conceptually, questions (i) and (iii) lack the essential time element involved in migration measures. With data from these questions it is impossible to say how many persons migrated during a given period of time. On the other hand, question (ii) provides the time element but is silent on the spatial aspect; that is, it is impossible to distribute the inmigrants by their area of origin or to measure outmigration, either collectively or by area of destination. Question (iv) is the only one that provides information on the temporal as well as spatial aspects. With this question it is possible to give the number of persons who moved in (or out) during a known fixed period and how many of them came from each of the origins (or went to each of the destinations). Apparently, this is the most satisfactory single question on migration in population census. Yet, as noted above, this is the only one not included in the recent Indian census. It is feared that people will have difficulty in recalling where they were living at some arbitrary date in the past and that it will be easier for them to recall place of last residence or duration of present residence.

Table 8.2 gives a brief summary of the type of migration estimates that can be made from these census questions and some of their advantages and disadvantages. Details of the method of estimation and the relative accuracy of the census data and of the migration estimates are discussed elsewhere (United Nations, 1970). The main conclusion of this discussion is that, if only one question is asked, the best seems to be one on place of residence at a fixed prior date. But migration estimates from this question have several drawbacks, and the desire to confine the inquiry on migration status to a single question should not be allowed to outweigh considerations of the quality and usefulness of the results. With regard to these latter considerations, two questions, one on duration of residence and the other on place of birth or place of last residence, are of particular value.

III. Characteristics of Migrants:

Migration is a highly selective process. Migrants' characteristics usually differ from those of nonmigrants, not only at the place of origin but also at the place of destination. Among migrants themselves, there are large differences between old-timers and new arrivals. Information on the nature and degree of such selectivity and differentials is one of the principal bases for the analysis of the determinants and consequences of internal migration. It has also an important bearing on methods of migration analysis. Inasmuch as migrants and nonmigrants differ considerably with respect to age–sex distribution, comparison of migration rates would require corrections or adjustments for these demographic structural differences. Similarly, classification of migrants by their duration of residence and elimination of the effect of the distribution of migrants by length of residence are essential in analytical studies, especially in cases where the migrants include persons with varying lengths of residence in the place of enumeration. This is usually the case with birthplace data or with data based on place of last residence. Control for differences in age, sex, and, in some cases, duration of residence is essential when overall migration rates are compared.

As noted above, study of the characteristics of migrants involves their comparison with those of nonmigrants. In migration studies it is as important to know in what ways and by how much the migrants differ from the nonmigrants as it is to know how many or what proportion of the migrants are clerks or craftsmen, how many are illiterate, and so on. For such comparisons, all the census tabulations produced for the migrants should also be available for the nonmigrants (or the total population). Otherwise, the scope of analysis will have to be compromised very much and limited to descriptive aspects.

As mentioned earlier, the greatest strength of the census as a source of migration data is its ability to provide data on a range of characteristics of the migrants and of the nonmigrants. In principle, it should be possible to classify the migrants (and the nonmigrants at destination) by all the characteristics obtained in censuses—age, sex, educational attainment, marital status, occupation, industry—and to cross-classify them by two or more of them. In practice, cross-tabulation of migrants by their demographic and socioeconomic characteristics has not been widely undertaken. There is, however, a welcome change in recent census tabulations, especially those done with the help of high-speed electronic computers, which make the preparation of cross-tabulations of the characteristics of the migrants fairly easy. Even with hand tabulation, it should be possible to derive the basic cross-tabulations for the more critical sections of the population of a country.[3] With proper cross-classifications, census data are ideally suitable for analyzing migration differentials, as they provide characteristics of the migrants and nonmigrants at destination. A major drawback of these data is that they are inadequate for studying migration selectivity, especially for

[3] A good example is the tabulation of migration data for "million cities" in the 1961 census of India.

those characteristics that undergo change with migration (occupation, industry, income, educational attainment, etc.). It is rarely that censuses attempt to trace a migrant's characteristics before migration; that is, at the place of origin. Therefore, except for such characteristics as sex, which does not change, or age, which can be estimated if duration of residence and present age are available,[4] it is impossible to work out the migrants' characteristics before migration and compare them with those of the nonmigrant population at the place of origin. This deficiency of the census data is particularly serious because differentials at destination may be quite different from differentials at origin and the latter are more basic to an understanding of the determinants of migration, especially the "push" factors that make the migrants leave their native place.

Migration differentials (at origin or at destination) may be measured in terms of (i) differential proportion or (ii) differential ratios (or rates). Thus if $M_1, M_2, \ldots M_n$ represent the distribution of migrants at the place of destination with respect to some characteristic (e.g., occupation) and $N_1, N_2, \ldots N_n$ represent the distribution of nonmigrants with respect to the same characteristic, a measure of migration differential by the differential proportion method is given by:

$$\frac{M_i}{M} - \frac{N_i}{N}$$

where $M = M_1 + M_2 + \ldots M_n$ and $N = N_1 + N_2 + \ldots N_n$, and by the differential ratio method is given by:

$$\frac{M_i}{N_i} - \frac{M}{N}.$$

These two measures are not the same, but indices of migration differential could be the same if the proper denominator is used to calculate them. Thus, if N_i/N is used in the first case and M/N in the second, the two indices will be the same.

In using indices of migration differentials for identifying factors associated with migration, it is important to bear in mind that *crude* index of migration differentials (an index based on classification by a single characteristic), as in the case of zero-order correlation coefficients, can sometimes be misleading. Inferences based on *specific* index of migration differentials (an index based on multiple classification) can be quite different from those based on a crude index.

---

[4] Even in these cases, selective attrition of migration cohorts through deaths and remigration could make the estimation difficult.

IV. Analytical Studies on the Determinants and Consequences
of Internal Migration

Factors associated with internal migration may be analyzed on the basis of (i) questions on reasons for migration, (ii) correlates of temporal fluctuations of migration time series, (iii) comparative analysis of the characteristics of the areas of origin and of destination, and (iv) comparative analysis of the characteristics of migrants and nonmigrants at origin and at destination. As mentioned earlier, reasons for migration are generally not asked in national censuses; census-based analysis of the determinants of migration has to follow one or the other of the other three approaches. A few examples of these three ways of using census data for such analysis are given below.

An outstanding example of the use of census data for the analysis of factors associated with migration with the help of temporal correlations is the University of Pennsylvania multivolume study (Eldridge and Thomas, 1964). In this study, estimates of migration were obtained from census age data as well as from birthplace data for intercensal periods during the period 1870–1950. These estimates, together with their age–sex characteristics, were used in the analysis of the interrelationship between migration and economic changes. A general hypothesis underlying the study was that migration responds positively to variations in economic activity and that variations in economic activity are identifiable with variations in economic opportunities. The analysis presents convincing evidence of high positive association between decadal swings in migration and in economic activity.

> The differential timing of economic opportunities, as indicated by decadal swings upward and downward, has been perfect in conformity with, and probably accounts for, the relative amplitudes of rises and falls . . . in the interstate redistribution of total and urban population and of the nonagricultural labor force; in comprehensive measures of interstate migration of the total population and especially when each of the two main component color-nativity groups are isolated [Eldridge and Thomas, 1964, p. 333].

Supporting evidence of the close interrelationship between migration and economic changes was given on the basis of age–sex differentials in rates of displacement due to migration in prosperous and depressed decades and by cohort analysis. For every subgroup for which data could be assembled, it was found that age-specific displacement rates in prosperous decades exceeded those in depressed decades by wide margins. Similarly, as cohorts of migrants passed from one decade to another, migration rates were found to be consistently higher in prosperous decades than in depression periods.

An alternative approach in the use of census data for analyzing the factors associated with migration is given in a set of three closely related studies—on the United States, Brazil, and Ghana (Beals, 1967; Sahota, 1968; and Sjaastad, 1961). The distinguishing feature of these studies lies not only in their method of analysis (econometric method) and their major conclusions (see next paragraph) but also in the nature of the migration data used by them (lifetime migration estimates for major geographic subdivisions, derived from census question on birthplace). Unlike the Pennsylvania study, which uses data from a series of nine censuses and applies elaborate demographic techniques to derive migration estimates, these three studies use raw migration data from a single census on the basis of the most widely used question.

The models used in these studies are formulated in the framework of the economic costs and returns from migration. The explanatory variables include education, urbanization, density, distance, wages, income, and so on. The studies found that distance is a strong deterrent to migration, and they hypothesized that distance proxies to a significant extent for the costs of migration. Migration is found to be highly responsive to earning or income differentials between the sending and receiving areas. Education is found to be an important factor promoting migration, not only directly but also indirectly, by influencing other variables conducive to migration. However, in the Ghana study, a negative correlation between migration and education was obtained; there was no evidence that education caused migration except insofar as it increased income potential and reduced a person's abhorrence of cultural and social adjustment. This is an interesting finding, and it would be of considerable interest to see how far other developing countries show similar results. Also, from the methodological point of view, it would be instructive to check whether or not the conclusion would be affected if an alternate approach of measuring educational selectivity after controlling for *income*, age, and sex was followed.

An example of the use of extensive cross-tabulation of migrants by socioeconomic characteristics, and analysis of the factors associated with migration by the method of migration differentials, is the study of migration in Greater Bombay (Zachariah, 1968). The distinguishing feature of this study is the detailed tabulation of migrants by educational attainment, industry, occupation, employment status, work status, religion, and marital status—each of which is further cross-classified by age, sex, duration of residence, and state of birth (identifying rural and

urban areas separately). The study was undertaken to develop methodological procedures that would lend themselves to repetition in other
cities in India, and beyond India in other developing countries, where
similar census questions on migration could be formulated and tabulations carried out within the limitations imposed by a high degree of
illiteracy of the population being enumerated and a low degree of
professionalization of the enumerators and tabulators.

The basic strengths and weaknesses of census data are reflected in
this study. For example, the analysis could throw considerable light on
the consequences of migration—its effect on the supply of labor and of
skills in the city, on the industrial and occupational composition of the
labor force, and on the demographic factors of the city population.
Similarly, the analysis could provide some insight into the migrant's
assimilation process, according to the length of time a migrant has been
in the city, the effect on his earning capacity, educational attainment,
type of job and so on. On the other hand, all that the study could show
with respect to selectivity was that the migrants were better educated
and had a higher proportion of males in the young adult age groups than
did the nonmigrants in the states of origin. These are important
conclusions, but they are insufficient for understanding the process of
outmigration from the villages to Bombay city.

V. Conclusions

Methods of measuring internal migration from census data have
advanced a great deal in recent years. Some of them, like the census
survival ratio method and the place of birth method (without the age
breakdown), have been tested in a variety of data situations and their
strengths and weaknesses have been pointed out. These tests have
indicated that, although these methods have a built-in capacity to absorb
some of the errors of the basic data, uncritical applications of them,
without taking into consideration the nature and extent of errors in the
basic data and without checking whether the assumptions involved in
the method are fulfilled or not, can lead to erroneous conclusions about
the pattern of migration in a country. It is therefore necessary to check,
wherever possible, measures of migration derived from one type of
census data against those derived from other types, and with estimates
from sources other than census. Such consistency checks are particularly necessary in countries where the census data are subject to errors
of underenumeration, misreporting, digit preference, and so on, and
where regional differences in mortality levels are great.

A recent development, which is likely to have considerable impact on methods of measuring migration from census data, is the production in an increasing number of censuses of cross-tabulations of one type of migration data (e.g., birthplace data) with other types (e.g., duration of residence data) and for the same type by age, duration of residence, place of origin, and so on. It is too early to envisage the full impact of these developments, but considerable refinement in the existing method- ology and new applications of census data for migration analysis can be expected. A recent development in the use of the census survival ratio method is a good indication. One of the limiting assumptions of this method is that the survival ratios are assumed to be the same in all geographic parts of the country. This assumption does not hold in many countries, especially in large ones with high mortality rates. With the availability of birthplace data by age and sex in two or more censuses, it is no longer necessary to make this assumption; estimates of age-specific survival ratios can be derived by regions of birth, and more accurate estimates of intercensal net migration can be obtained (for an illustrative example, see United Nations, 1970, p. 9).

Analysis of the extent of, and factors associated with, remigration and return migration is important in understanding the process of migration in a country. Census data are considered to be inadaquate for this purpose. Here again, recent developments indicate a variety of new possibilities. Cross-classification of birthplace data by place of residence x years before the census provides measures of return migration (those who were living outside the place of birth x years ago and had returned to it at the time of the census) and remigration (i.e., including those who were living outside the place of birth but were enumerated in a third place). Similarly, cross-tabulation of birthplace by duration of residence makes it possible to estimate intercensal remigration separately among persons born in an area and among earlier inmigrants to that area. With proper manipulation of the data, it is also possible to estimate remigra- tion during shorter periods of time (Zachariah, 1967). Where duration of residence data are available by age and sex at more than one census, much more refined estimates of remigration can be worked out (see United Nations, 1970, p. 16).

These are a few illustrations of some of the emerging applications of census data for migration analysis. These and the ones discussed earlier clearly indicate that the greatest asset of census data is their ability to provide cross-tabulations, not only of migrants by their demographic and socioeconomic characteristics, but also of migrants as defined by different questions. The full potential of this latter feature of census data will only be realized as more censuses produce such cross-tabulations and use them for migration analysis.

References

Beals, R. E., M. B. Levy, and L. N. Moses. Rationality and migration in Ghana. *Review of Economics and Statistics,* 1964, *49*(4), 480–86.

Eldridge, H. T., and D. S. Thomas. *Population redistribution and economic growth, United States, 1870–1950.* Vol. 3: *Demographic analyses and interrelations.* American Philosophical Society, Philadelphia, 1964.

Kuznets, S., A. R. Miller, and R. A. Easterlin. *Population redistribution and economic growth, United States, 1870–1950.* Vol. 2: *Analysis of economic changes,* American Philosophical Society, Philadelphia, 1960.

Lee, E. S., A. R. Miller, C. P. Brainerd, and R. A. Easterlin. *Population redistribution and economic growth, United States, 1870–1950.* Vol. 1: *Methodological considerations and reference tables,* American Philosophical Society, Philadelphia, 1957.

Sahota, G. S. An economic analysis of internal migration in Brazil, *Journal of Political Economy,* 1968, *76*(2), 218–244.

Sjaastad, L. A. Income and migration in the United States. Unpublished Ph.D. dissertation, University of Chicago, 1961.

United Nations. *Methods of measuring internal migration.* Manual 6, ST/SOA/Series A/ 47, New York, 1970.

Zachariah, K. C. Estimation of return migration from place-of-birth and duration-of-residence data. *Contributed Papers,* International Union for the Scientific Study of Population, Sydney, 1967, pp. 615–622.

Zachariah, K. C. *Migrants in Greater Bombay.* Bombay: Asia Publishing House, 1968.

CHAPTER 9

Internal Migration:
Measurement and Models

Julius Margolis

The understanding of migration, despite a huge literature and the relative ease of counting population, has been handicapped by a lack of clarity in what is to be measured and why. In very broad terms, the analyst wants to measure the permanent, spatial movements of population in relation to the growth and decline of different regions—usually defined in terms of economic activity. However, if the analyst seeks more specificity so that he can predict the populations that will move or the problems that will develop in the receiving or sending areas, he soon finds that his data are deficient and his theory too crude.

There is little doubt that net migration into an area is positively related to the demand for labor. The expansion of jobs is a magnet that pulls population. Though this is an important finding, it tells us far too little for purposes of areal planning or the design of national policies involving the flow of population. What are the remaining questions relevant to understanding and policy and not yet adequately resolved?

Do the migrants stay, return, or move on to still more attractive sites? Whence do they come? Do they leave areas of relative labor surplus or do they come from areas that are also growing? Is the movement of population consistent—over long periods of time, over changes in the business cycle, among different cultures—so that "laws" have generality?

Who are the migrants? Are they the uncommitted young? Are they the educated with more information available to them? And does

education imply a greater range of opportunities or a degree of specialization that restricts the range of opportunities? Are they being
"pushed" from their current locations or "pulled" to the new ones. Are
they permanent relocatees or persons "on the move"? Can they be
differentiated by psychological or sociological categories and, if so, is
this classification of interest for policy formulation?

Why have they moved? Is it for higher wages? A higher probability of
a job? A new occupation? Better long-run prospects? Are the advantages of the new site the dominating influence or do the disappointments
of the forsaken site dominate their decisions? Are differences in amenities, climate, style of life important? Do migrants have a propensity to
migrate? Or do they move with a specific job or other objective in mind?

Who benefits and who loses by migration? A more mobile population
would seem to lead to obvious efficiency gains for the nation. But does
large gross migration relative to net migration mean a great deal of
wasteful reshuffling of population or a socially desirable matching among
preferences, capabilities, and opportunities? Are there external economies associated with agglomeration and diseconomies associated with
increased congestion as well as with declines in population? Even
without externalities, gains and losses are not equally distributed and
their incidence is of concern to policy makers. Equally important, such
gains and losses give rise to political activities that seriously affect
policy choices.

There is no consensus about the answers to many of the above
questions. But is it even important to find answers to all of them?
Clearly, scientific curiosity is sufficient to justify research on these and
many other questions about migration. However, research talents are
scarce and policy relevance should influence the choice of questions.

My familiarity with migration had been restricted to intrametropolitan
movements. International and intranational migration studies seemed
mature and authoritative, when viewed from the confusions of intrametropolitan studies. Though sampling of the migration literature has
confirmed my view that migration over longer distances is better
understood, I have been impressed that great improvements in measurement and methodology are necessary before many useful hypotheses can
be accepted with confidence.

I. Data on Measures of Migration

The contemporary population is highly mobile. The revolutions in
transportation and communication technology have made it increasingly

cheap for humans to move long distances, and their movement has become more likely as they have found it easier to get information about alternative locations. However, movement is for many purposes, and increasing mobility means that the simple aggregates are a composite figure representing a great variety of behaviors. People jet to distant cities for luncheon meetings, they live in motels for short training courses, they have mobile homes following construction work, they advance up the corporate ladder but often with changes in branch location, they move with the expectation of moving on, and so on. The language of these illustrations is suggestive of the advanced industrial economy of the United States, but movements involving less than lifetime commitments are typical of underdeveloped areas as well.

Rather than the binary classification of migrant and nonmigrant presented in the census documents, it seems more realistic to think of a population of individuals who over their lifetime will be repeatedly confronted by the decision of whether or not to move a significant distance. Most of them for most of their years will rarely consider their options. Some restless ones will move repeatedly; some will never make a conscious decision either to stay put or to try their luck elsewhere. In any case, many will make moves of short as well as long duration (see Peterson, 1968, pp. 286–287).

The term *migration* conveys the sense of a permanent move, but the term *migrant* invokes the image of a person who is relatively footloose. In fact, a very large percentage of the immigration to an area consists of those who will leave subsequently. Even during the height of the mass immigration into the United States (1890–1910), with movement very costly, about 40% of the foreign migrants returned (see Kuznets and Rubin, 1954, Table 7).

Today, within the United States, for every permanent migrant to a region there are a large number who move on to other cities and regions, searching for greater advantages. Areas grow and others decline as a consequence of these flows. However, the net contribution of migration to population change is small relative to the impact of the gross flows, which do seriously affect the composition of population and pose severe problems to the areas. Areas of expanding economic growth attract net migrants, but they also have the larger flows of outmigration (see Morrison and Relles, 1975).

The migrant who moves for a fixed term or who moves with the intention of permanence but then returns or moves on to another area is missed in some census counts, while in others he is included but not distinguished from those who have made a permanent move. And, among the permanent movers, there will be the very large percentage who moved because their jobs were transferred or who, at least, had specific jobs promised them before they moved. The job transferees are a very different population from the unskilled unemployed, though the moves of both may be permanent. These different groups respond to different sets of influences that attract them to or repel them from specific sites. The groups cannot be disaggregated from census data, and, since the determinants of their behavior are not likely to be stable over time or over areas, the aggregate is a questionable variable, requiring explanation. Zachariah demonstrates that several census questions are necessary to establish the fact of migration and its minimum characteristics (see Zachariah, this volume, Chapter 8). Since censuses, even when they probe for migration, do not all use the same questions or the same subsets of questions, cross-national comparability is impaired and very few of them enable one to estimate directly the desired magnitude. For the analyst who restricts his study to net migration, Arriaga shows the versatility of demographic tests in estimating net flows; but the limitations of the basic data for causal analysis persist (see Arriaga, this volume, Chapter 7).

The limitations of census data at place of settlement are small relative to their limitations in regard to place of origin. To design policy or to understand behavior it is important to understand the push factors as well as the pull factors. Even if we had reliable data about the migrant's place of origin (was it a temporary or permanent residence?) we have hardly any information about his activities at the origin. Attributing mean characteristics to the migrant is very hazardous. After all the mean person did not migrate. Did the migrant have poorer opportunities than the stationary person? Did he have better opportunities elsewhere? Or did his perceptions of the relative gains and costs of migration differ from those of the nonmigrant?

The alternative to the occasional census is the sampling of special data, such as population registers, social security data, or special surveys. U.S. Social Security data deal with employed migrants and are therefore based on a biased sample. Population registers, while more inclusive, are rare, costly to maintain, limited in information, and not readily available for analysis. These bodies of data, despite their limitations are likely to be more useful than censuses for analytic purposes (see Morrison and Relles, 1975). There is no lack of migration data, but, like most other data, they are gathered for administrative objectives and there is reluctance to make significant changes or extensions to serve researchers or analysts, especially if the latter are in another agency or outside the government.

II. Models

Studies in the area of migration have had a very strong empirical bent. The conceptual and practical problems of data have preoccupied scholars, while a variety of ad hoc models of the process have been a substitute for theory. Models have ranged from simple gravity models, which proved to be very unsatisfactory, to complex and cumbersome systems of equations with excessive demands on data and computation.

The initial models were highly macroanalytical; they focused on the comparative attraction powers of places of origin and destination. It was not surprising that they were judged to be inadequate to explain the movements of a very mixed population. Subsequent models were more microanalytical and focused on the behavior of the migrants. The combination of the two holds the greatest promise, though clearly it will be difficult to achieve a successful grand model (see Morrison, 1973).

The simplest and earliest of the migration models, the gravity models, have been soundly criticized, but their basic ideas have persisted and have motivated many later and far more sophisticated models. The essential element of a gravity model is that migration between any two points is positively related to the size of the two places and inversely related to the distance between them. The motivation for the form is intuitively clear. The larger the cities or regions, the more likely that there will be interchanges of many sorts, which will encourage movement; the greater the distance between them, the less likely that there will be movement, since the costs will be greater. The simple gravity model fails to answer the dozens of questions that arise in studying migration. However, the variables can be and have been adjusted to take into account many factors, so that special populations or problems could be addressed (see Olsson, 1965).

The sophisticated gravity model uses several variables to capture the relative drawing power of areas, and the distance variable can be adjusted to account for different theories of the costs of movement. Instead of total population as a measure of size, subsets of the population more relevant to the problem can be used. If common sense or theory indicates that other variables are relevant—such as housing or housing vacancies, labor force, wage rates, unemployment rates, lot sizes, occupational composition, and so on—then these can be substituted. The variables can be assigned weights to better approximate behavioral assumptions; or a very different single aggregate, such as income, can be used, which better reflects relative opportunities in the two places.

The distance variable has proven to be the most perplexing. Statistical studies have demonstrated that its significance is highly volatile over time and space. This is not unreasonable, since the costs of transportation are small relative to the other costs involved in a move. Clearly, straight-line distance is much less important than economic or social distance. Recent studies have stressed the important roles of information, which decreases with distance, and the psychic costs of separation from friends and relatives, which increase with distance; both of these will vary with educational level, age, and cultural integration. In practice, the analyst can adjust for these factors through a modification of the distance variable or by a more elaborate specification of the variables that are assumed to attract. However, a proper treatment of economic and social distance requires a level of understanding about behavior that is not easily attainable.

The interaction of many variables in explaining movement has made it difficult to sort out the causative factors. Consider age. Clearly, young adults constitute the most mobile group, and they move the longest distances. However, among the young, it is the well-educated and trained that are the mobile group, not the unskilled. It is assumed that the educated have more information about opportunities and that distance is therefore less of an economic cost. Alternatively, it could be argued that the "trained" have a reduced set of alternative jobs in mind and have to travel longer distances to match skill with job. The budding professor is only an extreme case of the person who faces only a few openings per metropolitan area. In fact, we find that the percentage of professional and technical persons who move with a specific job in hand is twice the percentage of all other migrants in this category. Education increases information, and it brings the group into a market that is nationally organized. But, there is no analysis to separate out the hypotheses that the national market exists because the paucity of openings per site makes a national search necessary or that it exists because education makes it easier for the person to acquire information (see Greenwood, 1975, pp. 406–407). Whatever the causal factors in this case, the growing number of empirical studies and the expanding body of information about migration make it clear that more subtle behavioral theory is needed and that more disaggregated and complex models are required. Alonso's model illustrates this development (see Alonso, this volume Chapter 5).

Over time, the simple physical analogies have become dominated by the elaboration of explanatory variables, and at the same time alternative models based upon more simple theories from social science theory have been suggested and tested. The simplest derives from economics:

The individual is assumed to calculate a cost–benefit balance between alternative locations. He is assumed to compare the cost of movement with the present value of the difference in net advantages presented by the two sites over his expected life. Since it is extremely difficult to identify and measure all of the relevant factors, the model is rarely tested; however, the formulation is useful to the degree that it is suggestive for aggregative regression models (see Sjaastad, 1962).

Cost–benefit analyses of individual behavior raise the question as to whether we should pay most attention to the analyst's evaluation of the costs and benefits or the potential migrant's perception. Since it is the migrant's perception that controls movement, if the difference between the subjective and objective evaluation of the factors is great, the analyst will be driven to gather data that focus on the characteristics of the movers. For instance, it is observed that the volume of outmigration from an area is highly sensitive to the volume of immigration to that area. A large part of this relationship is due to the existence of a hypermobile population—a group that will make a sequence of moves. Are they hypermobile because they are less averse to risk, have higher aspiration levels, or are more willing to incur movement costs to get information about alternatives (see Lee, 1966)? Of course, if the answers to these questions add little insight into the causes or effects of migration, then the disaggregation is unnecessary. Current research indicates that disaggregation would be of value, not only to improve on predictive models but to design better policy instruments.

The proliferation of aggregative multiple regression analyses, suggested by economic wisdom, has had more the character of intelligent treatment of data than the testing of theoretically derived hypotheses. However, the recent growth of simultaneous equation models suggests a better balance between theory and empiricism, since the more rigid requirements regarding specification of the variables for more complex models has stressed theory in place of ad hocism. Single equation estimation has sometimes produced strange results for the influence of such variables as income growth, income levels, and unemployment rates. Clearly these variables influence migration, but at the same time their magnitudes are affected by migration (see Muth, 1971). For example, within a city, housing improvements in a ghetto area sometimes lead to reduced income in the area. This unanticipated consequence arises because the inflow of low-income persons is encouraged by subsidized housing and the outflow of higher-income persons is accelerated by the increase in low-income density.) The interaction effect between migration and its explanatory variables is complicated by the selection of the appropriate time interval. Migration is a flow responding to variables operating in an earlier time period and resulting in changes in those variables in a subsequent time period. Single equation, multiple regression studies, by ignoring interaction effects and relying on data dependent upon the vagaries of census reporting, have confused efforts at causal analysis. Because dating is critical for the causal specification of a simultaneous equation model, greater care about the appropriateness of data is required, and there are likely to be significant improvements in both data and models with the increasing use of simultaneous equation systems (see Greenwood, 1975, pp. 412, 418–421).

The most complex and sophisticated of the models derive from the sociological, rather than the economic, tradition. Though economic factors play a major role, models focusing on these factors simply do not tell us enough about the migration characteristics required by policymakers. Who moves may be as important for policymakers as the aggregate flows; and, of course, this applies equally to the characteristics of the nonmovers. The composition of the migratory flows, and of the populations that remain stationary, is important to an understanding of economic growth as well as for the formulation of housing, educational, tax, and other policies. Modelers have been driven to focus on diverse groups because of the inadequacy of the macromodels, but in fact disaggregation is needed both to understand the policy implications of migration and to evaluate the tools to influence migration.

The most straightforward mechanical approach is to characterize the flow of migrants as the result of the working out of a transition matrix of probabilities of movements among places. The model can be made specific to the age composition of the populations as well as to other factors, such as duration of residence, life cycle, home ownership, occupation, and so on. Again, we face the problem of increasing complexity, as additional numbers of interesting variables are introduced to account for differences in the population (see Ginsberg, 1973).

The most extreme form of this concern with the characteristics of movers has been the extension of models to search processes, that is, to the decision to move. Such models take explicit account of how individuals evaluate alternatives and then choose. Most persons are immobile, in that the push factors in their current location do not reach the threshold level that would prompt them to consider alternatives. For the potential movers who cross that threshold, there is a process of information gathering and evaluation which is necessary to choose a site or possibly to motivate them to stay put. These models of decision processes try to explain the behavior of individuals at different stages of the life cycle and of households that differ in their housing, occupational, educational, socialization, and other characteristics (see Wolpert, 1965).

This last group of models contrasts greatly with the initial set. Modeling initially focused on the characteristics of places. Models were enriched to explain the different pull and push factors of the set of areas under analysis. These macroanalytical models failed to account for many interesting phenomena, especially the differences among population groups, and this led to a shift of focus to the migrants or to those who remain stationary. Micromodeling is more appropriate for these purposes. The result has been a rich mixture of models and empirical findings, some confusion about the current state of reliable hypotheses, and a lack of integration between macro and micro models and between those dealing with movers and those dealing with places. (For a concise summary of the models, see Speare, Goldstein, and Frey, 1974, Chapter 7).

The thrust of research on migration has been on the determinants of the flows, not the consequences for the receiving or sending communities, and therefore it has not been as useful as possible for policy formulation. Population movements were seen as equilibrating factors, rather than as exogenous to the economy or, more realistically, as contributing significantly to regional growth and decline. Simple multiplier models are helpful to explain the amplification effects of changes in economic opportunities, but more is called for in understanding the process and in deciding what policies should be adopted. External economies of growth or diseconomies of decline are one set of phenomena that should be included in models if they are to be policy relevant; another set would be the changes in public facilities associated with populations of different compositions. Since modeling has not been concerned with policy, little can be said except that this is regrettable (see Greenwood, 1975, pp. 421–422).

References

Alonso, W. Policy-oriented interregional demographic accounting and a generalization of population flow models. This volume, Chapter 5.

Arriaga, E. E. Some aspects of measuring internal migration. This volume, Chapter 7.

Ginsberg, R. Stochastic models of residential and geographic mobility for heterogeneous populations. In E. Moore (Ed.), *Models of residential location and relocation in the city.* Northwestern University, Geography Department, 1973.

Greenwood, M. J. Research on internal migration in the United States: A survey. *Journal of Economic Literature,* 1975, *13*(2).

Kuznets, S., and E. Rubin. *Immigration and the foreign born.* Occasional Paper No. 46, National Bureau of Economic Research, New York, 1954.

Lee, E. A theory of migration *Demography*, 1966, *3*(1).

Morrison, P. A. Theoretical issues in the design of population mobility models. *Environment and Planning*, 1973, *5*(1).

Morrison, P. A., and D. Relles. *Recent research insights into local migration flows*. Paper P-5379, Rand Corporation, Santa Monica, 1975.

Muth, R. F., Migration: Chicken or egg? *Southern Economic Journal*, 1971, *37*(3).

Olsson, G. *Distance and human interaction*. Regional Science Research Institute, Philadelphia, 1965.

Peterson, W. Migration: Social aspects. In *International Encyclopedia of Social Sciences* (Vol. 10). New York: Crowell, 1968.

Sjaastad, L. A. The costs and returns of human migration. *Journal of Political Economy*, Supplement 1962, *70*(5).

Speare, A., S. Goldstein, and W. H. Frey. *Residential mobility, migration, and metropolitan change*. Cambridge, Mass. Ballinger, 1974.

Wolpert, J. Behavioral aspects of the decision to migrate. *Papers of the Regional Science Association*, 1965, *15*.

Zachariah, K. C. Internal migration: measurement and models. This volume, Chapter 8.

PART III

The Effect of Migration
on Regions and Individuals

The Effect of Outmigration
on Regions of Origin

Kingsley Davis

The momentous transition from an agrarian–handicraft to an urban–industrial technology, a transition now approximately at its midpoint for the world as a whole, entails migratory movements of unprecedented size. It has this effect for two reasons: First, the rise of urban–industrialism temporarily creates the widest disparity ever known between regions—that is, between regions that have made the transition and those that have not, or between those that are at different stages of the transition (see Davis, 1974, pp. 182–207). Second, the transition greatly enhances regional specialization, with the result that different regions within the same economy, presumably all participating in the same "stage" of development, have widely diverging manpower demands.

Regardless of the basis of the migration, I am confining my attention in the present paper to "sending" areas (those that have a net outmigration), and, among these, to only one great class—the agricultural regions. In the process of development during the last three centuries, it is the agricultural regions that have experienced the highest rates of outmigration and which therfore afford the best opportunity to explore its effects. In dealing with these areas, I shall examine first the magnitude and pattern of their outmigration, next the demographic causes and consequences, and finally the social and economic effects.

I. The Size and Pattern of Rural Outmigration

In all nations as they modernize, the volume of outmigration from rural areas is impressive. In absolute terms, it tends to be greatest when the nation is around the halfway point in the process of urbanization—that is, when it is 45% to 60% urban. Relative to the total population in the rural areas, however, the outmigration is greatest in the late stages of urbanization.

The precision with which this general pattern can be described depends on the type of agricultural area or population under discussion. If large politically defined areas, such as the states of the United States or the provinces of Canada, are taken as the units of analysis, then inevitably the urbanization of these units makes them increasingly unrepresentative of the "rural population" or "rural areas." If the rural population itself is taken, the precision is greater, but "rural" is mainly a geographical category that does not permit inferences to be automatically drawn concerning the industrial structure or other characteristics of the labor force. In the last analysis, as we shall see, the proper statistical approach to rural outmigration depends on the analytical question being posed. If the question is why certain large political regions send out more migrants than they receive and what the consequences are, one has to look at all the major demographic and industrial features of these regions, but if the question is why rural areas strictly defined or the farm population itself loses by migration, one can concentrate on a more limited range of causes and consequences.

By way of documenting the general pattern and showing how its precise measurement depends on the analytical question in view, let us take different populations as our units of analysis, beginning with large politically defined regions.

A. Large Politically Defined Areas

In the United States between 1920 and 1970, there were eight agrarian states that had not only about the lowest rates of population growth but also a net outmigration in every decade.[1] The average net outmigration

[1] The eight were Arkansas, Kansas, Mississippi, Montana, Nebraska, North Dakota, South Dakota, and West Virgina.

per decade in these states was as follows:

	Net outmigrants per 1000 middecade population
1920–1930	76.8
1930–1940	86.4
1940–1950	116.4
1950–1960	119.7
1960–1970	97.0

The rate kept rising until, late in the period, it was damped by the fact that urbanization within these states absorbed an increasing proportion of the exodus from rural areas. The eight states were, on average, only 23.1% urban in 1920 but 51.5% urban in 1970.

Similarly, in Canada, there were two agrarian provinces (Manitoba and Saskatchewan) that had a net outmigration in three successive decades between 1931 and 1961. The rates per decade for these two provinces combined were as follows:

	Net outmigrants per 1000 middecade population
1931–1941	109.8
1941–1951	122.2
1951–1961	42.0
1961–1971	99.7

In the third decade shown, the rate fell not only because the two provinces had become more urbanized (37.4% urban in 1931, 58.1% urban in 1961) but also because Canada had experienced a higher rate of international migration (see George, 1970, pp. 58–59, 67).

Finally, in Venezuela, eight provinces containing 43% of the country's total population in 1936 had, by a minimum estimate, net outmigration rates as follows (see Chen, 1968, pp. 32, 43, 53):

	Net outmigrants per 1000 population per decade
1936–1941	95.0
1941–1950	98.8
1950–1961	69.8

In all three cases, the net outmigration rate accelerated and then diminished. At first glance, this might leave the impression that the exodus from rural areas was slackening, but such a conclusion would be misleading; rather, the areas in question, the largest political units into which each nation is divided, did not remain as rural as they had been at the beginning. The proportion of the population defined as "rural" changed in each case as follows:

	Percentage of population rural
The eight agrarian states of the United States:	
1920	76.9
1970	48.5
The two agrarian provinces of Canada:	
1931	62.6
1961	41.9
The eight agrarian estados *of Venezuela:*	
1936	68.2
1961	57.2

Obviously, if the question concerns strictly rural migration, units must be found that represent more strictly the rural population. One way to do this is to deal with politically defined areas that are small.

B. SMALL POLITICAL UNITS

The smaller the area, the easier it is to find units that are and remain highly agricultural and have high rates of outmigration. Thus, in the United States between 1960 and 1970, among the total of counties in the entire nation, there were 2065, or 66.4% of all counties, that had decennial net outmigration. In 1183 of these, 38.1% of all counties, the net outmigration during the decade was 100 or more per 1000 population at the beginning of the decade, and in 429 counties the rate was 200 or more per 1000 (compiled from *County & City Data Book 1972,* 1973, Table 2). In Venezuela between 1950 and 1961, there were six districts (the next subdivision smaller than a state) in which the net outmigration averaged 451 per 1000 population per decade (see Chen, 1968, p. 67). Instead of diminishing recently, as it did in the *estados,* the outmigration rate in these districts increased.

II. The Cause of Outmigration from Rural Areas

The reason for being concerned about the units of analysis is that one does not have in mind simply a description of migratory currents but, rather, a theory of why they occur. By taking politically defined units that are primarily rural, one achieves an approximation—but only a rough one, because the units do not remain equally rural through time.

Alternatively, one can deal with the rural population as such, independently of politically bounded units. But whether or not this is a good procedure depends on the theory of what it is about rurality that is conducive to outmigration.

My interpretation is that rural outmigration is a geographical manifestation of an occupational exodus. In areas defined as rural, the chief industry is agriculture because agriculture has to be spread out over the land, whereas most other industries can be concentrated because they use land only as a site and not as an instrument of production. Other industries can thus crowd together in order to overcome the friction of space in the interchange of goods. Since many of them are new, created by technological innovation, they expand rapidly, whereas an old industry like agriculture, with inelastic demand, must reduce its labor force drastically as it substitutes machinery and fossil energy for human labor. As agriculture modernizes, the displacement of labor impels small or undercapitalized entrepreneurs to sell out and causes farm laborers to become unemployed. The newer industries, located together in urban areas, are, in many cases, because they are new, satisfying demands that never existed previously; hence they can offer jobs to erstwhile agriculturalists and their offspring. The result is a mass exodus from agriculture and hence from regions where agriculture is the predominant industry. The volume of outmigration is much the same, whether agriculture is managed by private entrepreneurs or by governmental agents.

If it is the exodus out of agriculture that chiefly explains rural outmigration, the rural population itself is not the most precise category in terms of which to measure the causation. A more crucial category is either the agricultural population or the agricultural labor force. This is particularly true when an attempt is being made to explain rates of change in outmigration. The reason for the imprecision of the rural concept is this: As modernization occurs, an increasing portion of the "rural" population is composed of nonagriculturalists. What happens is that the fringe around metropolitan areas expands because of the settlement of people with urban occupations, and yet much of it remains sufficiently sparse to continue to be characterized as rural. For this reason, in the later stages of development, the rural population is a heterogeneous category from the standpoint of occupation and income. In the United States, the nonfarm element in the "rural" population increased steadily. In 1880 it was 39%; by 1970 it was 82%. Similarly, in Sweden, the proportion of the "rural" population represented by the population dependent on agriculture was 87.6% in 1800 but only 38.9% in 1960. Increasingly, then, the term "rural" fails to describe the agricultural population.

TABLE 10.1

Decline in the Agricultural Labor Force in Sweden, the United States, and Poland

	Sweden		United States		Poland	
	Number[a] (in thousands)	Change per decade (in percentages)	Number[d] (in thousands)	Change per decade (in percentages)	Number (in thousands)	Change per decade (in percentages)
1880	902.2					
1900	832.4	− 3.9				
1920	724.7	− 6.7	11,449		10,244	
1930	707.6	− 2.4	10,472	− 8.5	9,577	−6.5
1940	687.7[b]	− 1.9	9,140	−12.7		
1950	578.7	−29.2	7,160	−21.7	7,016	—[e]
1960	408.1	−29.5	5,458	−23.8	6,546	−6.7
1970	315.0[c]	−40.4	3,462	−36.6	5,955	−8.4

[a] Males only.
[b] Relates to 1935, rather than to 1940. Rate calculated on decadal basis.
[c] Relates to 1965, rather than to 1970. Rate calculated on decadal basis.
[d] Includes only those employed in agriculture, not those unemployed but seeking work in that sector.
[e] Since Poland's boundaries were changed in connection with World War II, the rate of change from 1930 to 1950 cannot be determined on the basis of national figures.

Sources: For Sweden: Dorothy Thomas, *Social and Economic Aspects of Swedish Population Movements* (New York: Macmillan, 1941), pp. 94–96; United Nations, *Demographic Yearbook, 1956, 1964, 1972.* For the United States: *Historical Statistics of the United States to 1957; Statistical Abstract of the United States, 1971,* p. 210. For Poland: *Concise Statistical Yearbook of Poland, 1971.*

In the United States the farm population reached its maximum about 1916 or 1917, at which time its size was approximately 32.5 million. After that it declined relentlessly until in 1971 it was down to 9.4 million. In 25 advanced countries, Kumar found, between 1950 and 1960, an average reduction of 23.7% in the *agricultural labor force*, and in 21 countries he found an average reduction of 18.4% in the *agricultural population* (see Kumar, 1973, p. 93).

Once the agricultural contingent starts declining, it tends to drop very rapidly. In both the United States and Sweden the workers gainfully occupied in farming fell with increasing speed, as shown in Table 10.1.

III. The Effect of Outmigration on Population Growth

Granted that outmigration from rural regions is primarily a function of the exodus from agriculture, how does it affect population growth? In answering this question, one encounters difficulties. The actual population trend is not determined by migration alone but also by births and deaths; hence the same rate of outmigration will in one case (when natural increase is low) be associated with population decline and in another case (when natural increase is high) be associated with population increase. Worse yet, the three components of population change are mutually dependent. The impact of outmigration is not due solely to the migrants who leave but also encompasses the births and deaths they would have had if they had stayed. Of course, analyzing the demographic behavior of migrants (or of stay-at-homes, had the migrants stayed) is hazardous, because one cannot know for sure how the absence of outmigration would have affected their fertility and mortality. Simple as it may seem, therefore, the influence of outmigration on population change can be assessed only on the basis of assumptions— some of which are bound to be dubious.

With these difficulties in mind, we can examine some concrete cases, beginning with the history of advanced countries.

A. Depopulation of Rural Areas in Advanced Countries

Despite difficulties in assigning exact causation, we know that staggering reductions of the agricultural labor force have been associated with impressive losses of population in the agrarian regions of many industrial countries. For example, during the 30 years from 1871 to 1901, Ireland (which was a part of the United Kingdom until 1926) had an excess of births over deaths amounting to 6.3 per 1000 population per year, but net emigration was at more than twice this rate—14.2 per

1000—with the consequence that Ireland's population fell from 4,053,000 to 3,222,000 (computed from Kennedy, 1973, p. 212). In the United States, where we have already shown a high proportion of counties experiencing net outmigration, a high proportion also lost population. Between 1950 and 1960, when the total population grew by 18.5%, there were 782 counties (one-fourth of all the counties in the nation) where the population diminished by one-tenth or more (see Beale, 1964). Between 1960 and 1970, when the total population grew by 13.3%, the proportion of U.S. counties losing population was even greater: 1183 counties, 38.1% of all counties, lost one-tenth or more of their population (see *City and County Data Book 1972*, 1973). In Sweden, rural districts reached their maximum population in 1925; by 1965 their population was 13.4% smaller. By a stricter definition of "rural" (dispersed areas), the loss in Swedish rural regions was 17.7% in the 15 years from 1930 to 1945. In Australia between 1966 and 1971, the state of Victoria gained 275,944 inhabitants, 26.5% of this number directly by net inmigration, but 5 of the state's 10 subdivisions lost population (see Rowland, 1972, p. 124).

In interpreting these population declines, we must remember that the cause is not simply outmigration. High rates of outmigration have been found in rural regions where the population was growing rapidly. Thus Robert Gardner, in an unpublished paper prepared at the University of California, estimates the rural outmigration in European Russia between 1867 and 1896 as 4,637,200, yielding an exodus of 24 per 1000 population per decade; yet the rural population increased by 134 per 1000 per decade. Similarly, in Sweden between 1851 and 1910, the rural outmigration was 74 per 1000; nevertheless, the rural population grew by 48 per 1000 per decade (computed from *Historisk Statistik för Sverige*, 1969, p. 100). In order to cause a decline in population, rural outmigration must more than cancel out the rural natural increase. How much migration is required to do this depends on how high the natural increase is, which in turn depends on whatever factors govern rural fertility and mortality.

When rural depopulation eventually occurred in the industrial nations, it was caused by reduced fertility as well as by outmigration. For instance, when the United States agricultural labor force started to fall around 1917, the estimated fertility of the white population was already less than one-half of what it had been a century earlier. Although this reduction in fertility characterized the cities more than the countryside, it affected the countryside as well; and sometime around the 1920s the fertility reduction in rural areas began to exceed that in urban areas. The exact pattern in the United States is difficult to trace because nonregistration and underregistration of births was associated with rurality; but after 1930, when the registration area was virtually complete, the role of reduced fertility in the slow or negative population growth of rural areas can be shown by taking either the states that had the least population growth or the states that were most rural in 1930 and comparing their fertility with that of other states. As summarized in Table 10.2, the 10 most rural states in 1930, which were on average 76.9% rural at that date, had a more rapid decline in fertility than did the nation as a whole. In 1930 their fertility ratio was 31% higher than that of the nation, but by 1960 it was only 5% higher. Had their fertility remained at its 1920–1929 level (according to estimates corrected for underregistration), with mortality falling as it did and with the same rates of migration, their population would have increased during the period 1930–1970 slightly faster than that of the nation, instead of less than one-half as fast. The decline of population growth in these states was 66.8% due to net outmigration rates and 33.2% due to declining fertility.

Much the same finding emerges from a study of Sweden. There, in 1850, the fertility of rural districts was much higher than that of towns, but subsequently the rural rate dropped faster and by 1965 was lower

TABLE 10.2

FERTILITY DECLINE AND POPULATION CHANGE IN AGRICULTURAL AND SLOW-GROWTH STATES OF THE UNITED STATES, 1930–1970. BIRTHS PER 1000 WHITE WOMEN AGED 10–54[a]

	Registered		Adjusted for underregistration			
	1930	1940	1940	1950	1960	1970
10 states with least population growth[b]	63.2	56.5	61.5	78.5	76.2	58.7
10 most agricultural states in 1930[c]	73.2	64.4	72.5	84.0	78.1	59.1
United States as a whole	55.9	52.0	54.3	72.3	74.4	55.0
Percentage greater than United States as a whole:						
Low-Growth states	13.1	8.7	13.3	8.6	2.4	6.7
Most-agricultural states	30.9	23.8	33.5	16.2	5.0	7.5

[a] Unweighted averages.

[b] Arkansas, Iowa, Kansas, Mississippi, Nebraska, North Dakota, Oklahoma, South Carolina, South Dakota, West Virginia.

[c] Alabama, Arkansas, Idaho, Mississippi, New Mexico, North Carolina, North Dakota, South Carolina, South Dakota, West Virginia.

Sources: 1930–1940: *Vital Statistics Rates in the U.S., 1900–1940,* Table 47. 1940–1960: *Vital Statistics Rates in the U.S., 1940–1960,* Table 22. 1970: *Monthly Vital Statistics Report,* Vol. 22, No. 12, Supp., p. 9.

than urban fertility (see *Historisk statistik för Sverige,* 1969, p. 78).[2] If this drop had not occurred, the rural areas (which actually dropped in population by 19.5% between 1920 and 1945 and by 29.3% between 1950 and 1965) (see *Historisk statistik för Sverige,* 1969, p. 66) would have had no reduction in population.[3] Instead, with the same migration rates as those that actually prevailed, their population would have been 6.9% greater in 1960 than in 1920. If we take the difference between the rural population as it actually was in 1960 and as projected with the 1911–1920 vital rates and no migration, we find that the actual rates of outmigration explain 69% of the difference and declining fertility 31%. Thus, declining fertility must account for nearly one-third of the drop in Sweden's rural population between 1920 and 1960. This finding is remarkably similar to that for the 10 most rural states of the United States.

B. DELAYED RURAL DEPOPULATION IN UNDERDEVELOPED COUNTRIES

An absolute drop in the agricultural labor force, and hence in the population of agricultural regions, can be expected in all countries as they become developed. However, in present-day underdeveloped countries the depopulation of rural areas seems often to be delayed—that is, it appears to come at a later stage of development than it did in the history of the industrialized nations, and possibly at a slower rate after it starts. If so, the reason is not lack of rural outmigration, for that is occurring on a grand scale, but rather a higher rate of natural increase than the industrial nations ever exhibited. In general, due to much lower mortality and somewhat higher fertility, the natural increase of rural regions in present-day backward countries appears to be two to three times that found in industrial nations when they were at roughly the same stage of development. Accordingly, the same rate of outmigration that the advanced nations had will not now produce, in developing countries, an actual population decline in agricultural regions.

Evidence that the decline in agricultural population is now setting in at a later stage than it did historically in advanced countries is found by taking urbanization as an index of development. Among 14 countries for which data are available, those in which the downturn began before 1900 were 33.6% urban at the time, whereas those in which the switch came

[2] The ratio of children under age 15 to persons aged 15–64 was 50% higher in rural districts in 1850, but by 1965 it was 2.3% lower.

[3] An increase in fertility per woman would have been required to maintain the crude birth rate because of the changing age structure of the rural population, but the increase would have had to be only slight.

after 1900 were, on average, 41.8% urban. In 3 countries in which the decline started in the 1950s or 1960s—Chile, Mexico, and Portugal—the average proportion urban at the time was 48.9%.

Once the decline starts, however, its rate seems to be at least as fast. In four Latin American countries where the agricultural labor force declined between 1960 and 1970, the average drop was 10.9%. This exceeds the drop of 10.6% per decade in the United States and 5.3% in Sweden during the first 20 years after the downturn started. A rapid decline in the agricultural labor force, once it begins, is what one would expect from the lateness of the downturn. I have argued elsewhere that it is the size of the city population relative to the rural that determines the rate of exodus from the rural population (see Davis, 1972, pp. 317–319). If this is so, then the later in the process of development the agricultural decline starts, the faster it should be, because the relative size of the city population is greater.

If the absolute decline in the agricultural population now begins at a later stage, the question is, why? The answer, I believe, is the much higher rate of population growth in today's underdeveloped countries, which causes the agricultural population to expand despite a high rate of outmigration. The only exceptions are those less-developed countries that have reduced their fertility.

This view is confirmed by classifying underdeveloped countries according to their rate of population growth. Below are the rates for 13 nations grouped in this way.

	Average percentage population growth,[4] 1950–1970	Average percentage change in agricultural labor force[4]	
		1950–1960	1960–1970
Class I	0–35	−9.9	−28.4
Class II	36–70	15.2	7.6
Class III	71+	28.0	7.7

In this tabulation, all four of the nations with slow population growth are East European Communist states. It might be thought that the penchant of Communist regimes for the collectivization of agriculture is the reason for their declining agricultural labor force. However, it is just as plausible to attribute their decline to relatively slow population growth.

To make a more comprehensive test of the influence of overall population growth, one needs to hold constant the stage of development, and this requires more cases, or countries. To get more cases, we can

[4] The averages are unweighted. The countries in the first class are Hungary, Poland, Yugoslavia, Rumania; those in the second are Egypt, India, Chile; those in the third are Brazil, Mexico, Nicaragua, Philippines, Thailand, and Venezuela.

TABLE 10.3

RATES OF POPULATION GROWTH IN REGIONS AT A ROUGHLY SIMILAR
STAGE OF DEVELOPMENT

	Percentage urban in 1950	Percentage change per decade, 1950–1970	
		In total population	In rural population
Eastern Europe	42.4	8.2	−3.9
Southern Europe	40.4	8.7	−1.1
USSR	42.5	16.4	−5.7
South Africa	39.1	26.8	14.6
Caribbean	35.2	25.8	18.6
Tropical South America	35.8	33.9	14.5
Middle America	39.2	39.4	22.6

Source: K. Davis, *World Urbanization, 1950–1970,* Vol. 2 (Berkeley, Calif.:
Institute of International Studies, University of California, 1972), pp. 182–207.

switch from the agricultural labor force to the rural population. In Table
10.3 are shown seven regions which in 1950 were at a roughly similar
stage of development, as measured by the percentage of population that
was urban. Among these regions, the ones with the fastest overall
population growth had the speediest rate of increase in their rural
population. When a nation has a very high rate of natural increase, its
agricultural population does not decline until urbanization is so advanced that a modest rate of *migration into cities* will mean a large rate
of *outmigration from rural areas.* The size of the migration stream is
divided by a large base (the city population) to obtain the city rate and a
small base (the rural population) when urbanization is far advanced.

IV. Rural Depopulation and the Age Structure

That a disproportionate share of those who leave agricultural areas are
young adults is well known. In the United States in 1970, for example,
only 39.7% of males employed in agriculture, forestry, and fishing were
aged 20–44, whereas 54.2% of the total labor force were in these ages.
As a consequence, the median age of males employed in agriculture
was 46.1 years, whereas for males employed in all industries it was
40.2 years. The effect of outmigration on the age structure, however, is
modified and sometimes counterbalanced by the influence of natural

increase; and the influence of migration itself is partly indirect, coming through its effect on births. By selecting out young adults, outmigration lowers the rural crude birth rate, which then results in fewer children and hence an older population. On the other hand, a high rate of natural increase creates a young population with a high proportion of potential migrants.

To determine precisely the influence of outmigration on the rural age structure, one must follow the same procedure used in the case of the total population—that is, one must decompose the gross change into that due directly and indirectly to migration and that due directly and indirectly to natural increase. The result will depend on the stage of development. If the stage is early, rural fertility will tend to be high and outmigration relative to the existing rural population will be small; in that case the rural population will be young. In the late stages of development, when the agricultural population is near decline or has already started to fall, the rural birth rate will have been much reduced and the outmigration will have become stronger relative to the rural population. In that case, both outmigration and declining rural fertility give the rural areas an aged population.

Just how distorted the age structure can become is shown by the following data:

	Ratio of persons aged 15–39	
	To those aged 40+	To those aged 65+
Swedish rural districts		
1850	1.54	8.2
1970	0.75	2.5
U.S. rural–farm population		
1920	1.53	7.5
1970	0.67	2.5

Except in rate, the similarity of the two countries is amazing. In the case of Sweden, I have estimated that approximately 80% of this change in the age structure was due to outmigration, the rest to natural increase.[5]

V.   Outmigration and Sex Composition

In the Western world, migration out of rural areas characteristically involves more females than males, leaving a masculine sex ratio in the

---

[5] The estimate is made by assuming that without internal migration the age structure in the rural districts would have changed as it did in Sweden as a whole. The difference between the all-Swedish and the rural age structure is then attributed to internal migration.

working ages. By comparing the rural ratio at each age with that of the urban population, one can see the distortion produced by migration. Table 10.4 gives the data for Sweden. The excess of males in rural districts turns out to be even greater in the elderly ages than in the young working ages. The reason for this may be that elderly women, mostly widows, are in better economic circumstances than elderly men and can thus more often afford to remain in urban places. Elderly men, on the other hand, are more dependent on their own labor; in the countryside they not only can escape urban costs but can pick up some kinds of employment as well.

In Asian and African countries, on the other hand, outmigration from rural areas tends to be more masculine than feminine. The reasons for this are complex and differ somewhat from one region to another. In Asia and North Africa, the customary seclusion of women involves prejudice against their migrating to the city on an individual basis, but in Africa and Asia in general, and in Central Africa in particular, there is, or has been, great reliance on hoe and hand agriculture, both of which tend to be performed by women. Also, high agricultural density in these continents gives rise to surplus labor in off-seasons, thus facilitating migration to cities on a seasonal basis, the men being by tradition more mobile. Finally, the extremely high fertility and early marriage prevailing in Asia and Africa burden young women with children to a greater extent than was ever true in the West.

With modernization, the sex composition of rural populations in Asia and Africa is apparently beginning to be more masculine. Nevertheless, in Japan the rural population is still predominantly female in every age

TABLE 10.4

Sex Ratios in the Urban and Rural Population,
Sweden, 1970

| Age | Males per 100 females | | Rural as a percentate of all-Sweden |
	All-Sweden	Rural districts	
Under 15	105.7	107.1	1.3
15–29	105.4	133.6	26.7
30–39	102.2	110.4	8.1
40–64	99.3	113.1	14.0
65+	82.3	106.3	29.1

Source: United Nations, *Demographic Yearbook 1972*, pp. 198–99.

above 15, the urban population predominantly male in every age up to 45. Only at advanced ages—age 65 and over—is the sex ratio in Japanese cities more feminine than in the countryside. In its sex distribution, then, Japan differs from all Western industrial nations.

VI.   The Economic and Social Consequences of Outmigration

By now it should be clear that, strictly speaking, there are no concrete phenomena arising exclusively from outmigration. There are some in which outmigration figures prominently—such as the damping or elimination of rural population growth, the aging of the rural population, and sex distortion; but in all of these, other factors also play a role. The more economic or social the phenomenon in question, the less can it be attributed solely to migration, because the more numerous are the additional variables involved.

Official anxiety about the socioeconomic effects of rural outmigration usually displaces attention from the outmigration itself to the demographic changes it presumably engenders. Such concern unhesitatingly attributes the decline, aging, and sex distortion of the rural population to outmigration, and then focuses on the consequences of these intermediary factors. Unfortunately, the conclusions reached seem to be based more on preconceived notions than on empirical evidence.

A.   The Prejudice against Population Stability or Decline

Since, on the average, prosperous nations are more sparsely settled and have less population growth than poor nations, there is no a priori reason to believe that population growth promotes prosperity or its opposite promotes poverty. Why, then, is the fear of depopulation so deeply ingrained? The reasons appear to be as follows:

1. Throughout nearly all of human history, populations grew in good times and declined in bad times. Normally, when there was no flood, fire, famine, epidemic, or war, the birth rate exceeded the death rate. Occasionally, however, one or more disasters would arise to cause the death rate to shoot up and wipe out the accumulated population increase. Naturally, people came to equate population growth with normality, population decline with catastrophe.

2. In modern times, however, the salient demographic condition has been an almost universal and continuous excess of births over deaths. Therefore, in the cases in which population stability or decline has occurred, it has usually been caused mainly by outmigration. The assumption has arisen that, if conditions are good, people will not leave.

3. Population growth contributes to overall economic expansion—for example, a rise in national product. Such expansion is commonly confused with economic improvement.

4. The concept "economies of scale" is vaguely believed to have something to do with population size. Normally, the concept implies that if a firm's size increases, its cost per unit of product, other things equal, diminishes. But a firm's size does not depend on a country's population, and the costs to a firm do not equal the costs to a society. A system of reasoning applicable to business firms is not applicable to societies.

5. In economics there is a tendency to equate the wages paid to labor with the contribution of labor to the product. This leads to the belief that an increased labor force (population) will bring a commensurate increase in production. Naturally, since workers are human beings, wages remain a large proportion of the price of the product even when virtually all of the energy used is inanimate. This proportion of the price, however, does not represent the contribution of labor to the product but rather the role of labor in distribution. On the productive side, the smaller the number of workers in relation to product, the higher is the productivity, by definition. Maximizing workers in relation to resources therefore has a negative, rather than a positive, effect on development.

6. The idea that the political strength of a group is proportional to its numerical size leads to the feeling that lack of population growth is a danger to the collectivity. This idea is prevalent in France (see Sauvy, 1969, especially pp. 51–59, 283–319, 382–407). However, consensus, organization, and technology appear to be overriding factors in a group's political influence, and it is doubtful that these are positively associated with the group's numerical size.

B. A Case of Mistaken Identity

Even this brief list demonstrates the tendency to attribute to population change per se the effects of whatever it was that initially brought the population change. If a famine causes a negative natural increase, or unemployment a net exodus, these conditions, insofar as they persist, are necessarily regarded as unfavorable; but the population decline or stability itself is not at fault. In some cases, in fact, it is an amelioration or correction of the initial condition. Since the conditions giving rise to it are diverse, population stability is not, universally, even associated with economic disadvantage, much less does it give rise to it.

An obvious way to gauge the effect of outmigration is to ask what would have happened if the migration had not occurred. For example, if a region that actually experienced large outmigration had not experienced it, would its population have grown correspondingly, and if so, what would have been the economic result? Let us take West Virginia, a coal mining state, as an example. In 1970 it had 13% fewer people than it had in 1950, because its outmigrants more than canceled its excess of births over deaths. Had the migrants not left, what would have happened? Nobody knows, because there are several alternatives. If the migrants had not left, the West Virginians might have reduced their birth rate or suffered a rise in mortality or both; or they might have had the population growth that their actual natural increase (plus that of the migrants) would have given them. In the latter case, the state's population in 1970 would have been 27% greater, rather than 13% less, than it was in 1950. The population density in 1970 would have been 40% greater than it actually was. Suppose this prodigious population increase had taken place, with all other conditions in the United States remaining the same, what would have been the state's condition? The extra people would have had to make a living somehow in agriculture and mining (both depressed in the state) or in industries that would take advantage of low-cost labor. The per capita income would have deteriorated in comparison to that of people in the rest of the country. West Virginia would have been declared a disaster area eligible for federal relief.

What actually did happen to West Virginia? Its per capita income went up 13.5% faster than it did in the United States as a whole. Its school enrollment for youths aged 16–17 rose 53% faster than it did in the nation. The precentage of employed persons engaged in agriculture, forestry, and fishing dropped by 78.6%—9.1% faster than in the entire nation. By virtually any standard one cares to apply, West Virginia did well during its two decades of population decline.

Perhaps much the same result would have been obtained if, instead of sending out migrants, West Virginians had simply reduced their birth rate to the point where the state's population would have dropped 13% in two decades. This would have required the birth rate to be far below the death rate. In fact, the birth rate would have had to be reduced 86%! Instead of reproducing at a rate that would give her slightly over three children in her lifetime, each woman would have had to reproduce at a rate that would give her only 0.4 of a child. No wonder the state's people preferred outmigration.

West Virginia is not an isolated case. To get a wider sample and a longer period, I have taken the 10 states that showed the least population increase between 1920 and 1970 and have compared them with the 10 states that showed the most increase. The results, exhibited in Table

TABLE 10.5

PROGRESS IN STATES WITH THE SLOWEST AND FASTEST POPULATION GROWTH, UNITED STATES 1920–1970

| | Percentage increase per decade | | | | Education Index[b] |
	In total population	In percentage urban	In percentage in agriculture	In per capita personal income[a]	
10 population-loss states[c]	3.2	17.1	−30.6	61.6	11.3
10 population-gain states[d]	30.0	13.1	−27.1	55.4	3.7
United States as a whole	13.9	7.5	−33.2	52.1	4.1

[a] The period is 1929 to 1970, rather than 1920 to 1970.
[b] The index is composed by taking the years of schooling completed for persons aged 25–29 and for those aged 25+ and finding the ratio of the first to the second.
[c] Arkansas, Kansas, Mississippi, Montana, Nebraska, North Dakota, Oklahoma, South Dakota, Vermont, West Virginia.
[d] Arizona, California, Delaware, Florida, Maryland, Michigan, Nevada, New Mexico, Oregon, Washington.

Sources: Population: *Statistical Abstract of the United States, 1972*, p. 12; Urban: *U.S. Census 1970*, PC(1)-A1, Table 18. Agriculture: *U.S. Census, 1920*, Vol. 4, p. 50; and *1970 General Social and Economic Characteristics, U.S. Summary*, Table 170. Income: Statistical Abstract of the United States 1962, p. 319; and *1972*, p. 319. Education: *U.S. Census 1970*, PC(1)-D1, pp. 327–329.

10.5, indicate that the states in the second group were not buying prosperity with their rapid population growth but its opposite. They increased their population nearly 10 times as fast as the slow-growth states but improved their economic and social situation at a considerably less rapid rate.

Evidently, the outmigration states developed faster not only because their lesser population growth improved their ratio of resources to population but also because the outmigration was accompanied by development. If the exodus had been caused by a natural calamity—say, prolonged drought, soil erosion, or disease—the outmigration states would doubtless have been better off than they would have been without the exodus, but they would probably have lost ground in relation to other states.

Additional effects of outmigration derive from its economic and social selectivity. We have mentioned age and sex selection but not selection for other traits. Insofar as rural areas retain men more than women, they increase their average productivity per person; but insofar as they retain more children and aged persons, they decrease it. However, from a societal point of view, the countryside is a better place for aged persons to be. Their skills are more useful in a rural area, less expensive care is needed, and the milieu is freer from some of the diseases of old age, such as emphysema. Obtaining part-time and casual jobs in agricultural regions is less impeded by union and government rules. Since the aged must live somewhere, the countryside offers advantages.

As for other traits, space does not permit analysis here. However, there are two indicators that can be quickly mentioned. In the United States, the population-loss states sent out more farmers and more blacks than they sent people in general. Since neither class was high in the economic scale, this fact suggests that it is people of lesser material circumstance who leave in greater abundance. If so, the labor force tends to be upgraded by outmigration.

VII. Conclusion: The Misplaced Fear of Rural Depopulation

In sum, rural outmigration appears to contribute to the development and well-being of sending regions. If so, it is worth asking why the opposite is often assumed and why policy is sometimes aimed at slowing down the rural exodus.

The answer, I believe, is twofold. First, many governments are less concerned with rural areas than with the politically more potent cities. The influx into cities disturbs them because it seems to create urban unemployment and to lower the level of living in the cities. Second, insofar as officials worry about the countryside, they tend to revert to the old habit of associating population decline with catastrophe. They see empty farm houses, empty stores, schools, and churches in rural villages, and this seems to them to indicate economic decline. My suggestion is that the empty buildings be torn down, the areas they occupied plowed over. Visitors from government headquarters in the city will then see only green fields. They will then say how beautiful and productive the countryside is and will return to their offices without being reminded that the population in rural areas is declining.

References

Beale, C. L. Rural depopulation in the United States: Some demographic consequences of agricultural adjustments. *Demography* 1964, *1*, 264–272.

Chen, C.-Y. Movimientos migratorios en Venezuela. Caracas: Instituto de Investigaciones Economicas, Universidad Catolica Andres Bello, 1968.

County and city data book, 1972. Washington, D.C., United States Department of Commerce, 1973.

Davis, K. *World urbanization, 1950–1970* (Vol. 2). Berkeley: Institute of International Studies, 1972.

Davis, K. Human migration. *Scientific American,* 1974, *230*.

George, M. V. *Internal migration in Canada: Demographic analysis.* Ottowa: Dominion Bureau of Statistics, 1970.

Historisk statistik för Sverige. Vol. 1. *Befolkning 1720–1967* (2nd ed.). Stockholm: Statistiska Centralbyran, 1969.

Kennedy, R. E. *The Irish: Emigration, marriage, and fertility.* Berkeley: University of California Press, 1973.

Kumar, J. *Population and land in world agriculture.* Berkeley: Interntional Population and Urban research, Institute of International Studies, 1973.

Rowland, D. T. Aspects of rural depopulation in Victoria. *Proceedings,* 7th Geography Conference, New Zealand Geographical Society, Hamilton, 1972.

Sauvy, A. *General theory of population.* New York: Basic Books, 1969.

CHAPTER 11

A Migrant's-Eye View of the Costs and Benefits of Migration to a Metropolis[1]

Donald J. Bogue

I. A Rational-Behavioral Approach to Migration Study

Discussions of the forces that stimulate or retard migration have often been dichotomized into "push" and "pull" factors. It has been hypothesized that some migrants are primarily "pushed" out of a place of residence by a combination of unfavorable forces which made continued residence there undesirable, while others are induced to leave ("pulled" out) by attractive situations in other locations. From there, discussion has been extended to the comparative strengths of "push" and "pull" factors.

The purpose of this paper is to urge that this traditional dichotomy be abandoned in favor of a "cost–benefit" approach from the point of view of the individual migrant. Using this approach, the decision to migrate (or not to migrate) would be viewed as the outcome of a balancing of the benefits of migration against the costs of migration. By estimating the benefits and comparing them with the calculated costs, the potential migrant hypothetically arrives at an estimate of the net gain or loss that might come from migration. A similar calculation with respect to costs

[1] The study on which this article is based was financed by a grant from the Ford Foundation for research on "Problems of Living in the Metropolis."

(opportunity costs) and the benefits that might result from remaining in the place of residence would be anticipated. The potential migrant would then be expected to compare the net profit or loss from migrating with the net profit or loss that might result from staying at the place of residence. The decision to migrate or to remain would be based on an estimation of which course of action would yield the largest net gain or the smallest net loss.

It is useful to regard migration as a rationally planned action which is the result of a conscious decision, taken after a consideration or calculation of the advantages and disadvantages of moving and of staying. Whereas the push–pull theory tends to regard the migrant as the equivalent of a billiard ball which is set in motion by external forces, the cost–benefit approach sees the migrant as *putting himself in motion* (or remaining immobile) after taking stock of the external forces and interpreting their implications for his wellbeing. The push–pull approach would undertake to explain migration by correlating the volume and direction of migration flows with "objective" indices of external conditions. In contrast, *the cost–benefit approach would undertake to explain migration by collecting information about the particular combination of forces the individual migrant perceives and the interpretation he places upon them.* Such an explanation is "subjective," in that the raw data are the reports that individual people give of their perceptions of the positive or negative aspects of their present residence and of some other potential residence. But subjectivity need not imply irrationality; the opposite is intended here. There are undoubtedly many behaviors of individuals which cannot be adequately researched on the presumption that they are the result of careful and rational calculation of alternatives, based upon the actor's perception of his total situation; but it is believed that migration is one behavior which may be dealt with very adequately on such a premise.

It is believed that the rational decision making, or cost–benefit calculation, approach to migration is not only viable but is destined to replace the traditional push–pull point of view. There are at least two reasons for making this assertion: (a) In industrially developed nations the flow of mobility continues undiminished, but, increasingly, it is becoming simply a movement between similar environments (movement from one city to another, from one suburb to another, or from one rural residence to another), rather that a movement between highly dissimilar environments (such as movement from farm to city). Under such circumstances, correlations between the volume and composition of the major migration flows and the objective characteristics of the environment at origin or destination tend to be low. (b) It is possible to develop a cost–benefit hypothesis that will subsume the traditional push–pull situation as a special case, thereby reconciling the new with the old.

The present paper is a tentative step in this direction. Table 11.1 is an outline of the decision-making or cost–benefit matrix which, it is believed, realistically reflects the sets of calculations that a potential

TABLE 11.1

LISTING OF PROTOTYPICAL FACTORS THAT COMPRISE THE FOURFOLD
COST–BENEFIT MOBILITY MATRIX

Decision	Potential costs	Potential benefits
MIGRATE	(A)	(B)
	Transportation to new residence	Higher rate of pay
	Uncertainty of finding employment	Employment of choice or preference
	Housing while seeking employment	Improved housing
	Food while seeking employment	Better educational opportunities for children, self
	Clothing appropriate for employment	Better community service institutions
	Mistreatment by strangers	More interesting, exciting social life
	Lack of social status	
	Living in strange surroundings	Better race, ethnic, social conditions
	Need to use another language, improve speech	
	Need to change customary dress, behavior, daily habits	
	(Migration cost factors)	*(Migration pull factors)*
NOT MIGRATE	(C)	(D)
	Difficulties of finding local employment	Inexpensive housing, already available
	Lack of appropriate local employment	Inexpensive food, recreation, living
	Excessive domination by family	Daily contact with family
	Unsatisfactory local social relations	Daily contact with old friends, peers
	Unsatisfactory local institutions	Living in familiar surroundings
	Unsatisfactory race, ethnic, political conditions	Social status assured
		Convenience of continued use of traditional speech, dress, customs
		Assured employment (for some)
	(Migration push factors)	*(Migration counterinfluences)*

migrant makes in arriving at a decision to migrate or to stay in his present residence.

Table 11.1 is a 2 × 2 matrix in which there are two sets of costs and two sets of benefits: One set of costs and benefits is associated with mobility, the other with nonmobility. Cell (A) is a listing of the actual or potential costs of migration; often these are ignored in studies of migration. Cell (B) is seen to be a listing of the pull factors that are commonly hypothesized as stimulating migration. Cell (C) is a listing of the push factors that are commonly hypothesized as stimulating migration. Cell (D) is a listing of the potential benefits of not migrating; these also are often ignored in studies of migration.

It is the hypothesis of this article that if the perceived influence of cells (B) and (C) is greater than that of cells (A) and (D), there will be migration. When the perceived importance of cells (A) and (D) exceeds that of cells (B) and (C), there will be no migration. This model may be used to describe or explain the behavior either of individuals or of groups. Moreover, the indicators used to insert data into the cells of the matrix may be objective indices derived from census or community-based survey data or they may be subjective recordings of the impressions experienced by potential or actual migrants. In this article, we are interested in emphasizing the validity of research using the subjective-but-presumed-rational perceptions of individual persons.

II.   A Rough Quantification of the Model

The model proposed above has not yet been fully operationalized and tested with empirical data. However, data from a survey, "Problems of Living in the Metropolis," taken in Chicago in 1958–1959, permit insights into the problem. In this survey, samples of migrants were probed in depth concerning the reasons they would report for leaving their previous place of residence. These data provide subjective material concerning cells (B) and (C) in Table 11.1. Another set of questions was asked concerning how the migrants handled the costs of migration—itemized in cell (A).

Finally, some indirect data on the perceived benefits of not migrating—cell (D)—were obtained. Although the model proposed above was developed long after the data were collected, the data from this survey permit at least a rough illustration that the model has potential utility in future migration and mobility research.

The data that will be placed in each cell are discussed separately. The process is discussed not only in terms of migrants as a class, but also for four separate groups of migrants: white males, white females, nonwhite males, and nonwhite females.

A.   PUSH FACTORS IN MIGRATION

A battery of questions was asked of migrants concerning the factors that caused them to be discontented or maladjusted in their previous place of residence. The responses obtained were classified into six broad categories, reported in Table 11.2. (As will be shown later, only a minority of migrants mentioned any push factor at all.) Of those migrants who reported some expulsive reasons for leaving their former residence, the overwhelming majority of reasons given pertained to employment. Roughly 30% of the expulsive forces consisted of loss of employment—primarily of layoff. An additional 30% to 35% consisted of dissatisfaction with employment—because of the nature of the work, rate of pay, or conditions of work.

Dissatisfaction with life in the local community ranked third in importance. This category covered a very broad range of complaints, from dislike for the community itself to actively hostile relations with particular persons living there, which made it an undesirable place to stay.

Unsatisfactory social relations with family and relatives was mentioned by a small minority as a reason for leaving. Among the black population (most of whom had migrated from the South), race hostility or discrimination was mentioned by about 10% as a push factor. It does not seem to have been a major expulsive force.

TABLE 11.2

PUSH FACTORS IN MIGRATION TO CHICAGO, BY SEX AND RACE, 1958–1959

	Male		Female	
Push factors	White	Black	White	Black
Total	100.0	100.0	100.0	100.0
Different employment	43.2	31.1	29.6	21.2
Discharged or laid-off	30.2	34.7	22.4	36.0
Family	5.6	7.8	16.8	18.4
Social	16.0	14.0	26.4	16.2
Race	2.5	10.4	1.6	5.0
Health	2.5	2.1	3.2	1.1
Other	—	—	—	—
Number of respondents	162	193	125	179

Social (as contrasted with economic) factors looked somewhat more important as a push factor among females than among males. After allowance for the moderate response on race, the pattern of expulsive forces for blacks seem to have been nearly the same as for whites.

It had been hypothesized that one reason for blacks to migrate to Chicago is for persons with serious or chronic ailments to obtain adequate health care, which is said to be less accessible to them in the South. It was found that only a tiny proportion of all migrants (about 2% to 3%) gave this as a reason for moving, and that it was reported as frequently by white migrants as by black.

Table 11.2 makes it clear that the primary expulsive forces are linked to employment, but that there were substantial undercurrents of dissatisfaction with the local social environment and of family discord.

In constructing Table 11.2, only one push factor (the one that appeared to be strongest for the individual migrant) was tabulated. Undoubtedly push factors can operate in combination. Thus a combination of unsatisfactory employment and discontent with the local community could function to stimulate outmigration.

B. Pull Factors in Migration

The pull factors which caused migrants to choose Chicago as their point of destination were inventoried by a second battery of questions. The responses were classified into the broad categories shown in Table 11.3. In each case, the leading or most important factor mentioned by a migrant was tabulated.

For males, the overwhelming (60% or more of all responses) pull factor pertained to employment, which was also a highly important pull factor for females. Almost 20% of the white male migrants and almost 10% of the black male migrants already had employment arranged before leaving their former residence. Even where a definite job offer had not been arranged, a substantial proportion of the migrants of both sexes and races reported that they were attracted to Chicago because they perceived it to be a more favorable place to find satisfactory employment than alternative places they might have considered.

For females, the presence of family contacts (relatives already living in Chicago) was the prime pull factor that guided them there. For females, more than half of the responses pertaining to pull cited this as the major element in the decision. Apparently there is a feeling that the female migrant must be protected or sheltered—that she is less able to fend for herself alone in a strange city than her brother. Hence, she tends to choose a destination where there are relatives to receive and

TABLE 11.3

PULL FACTORS IN MIGRATION TO CHICAGO, BY SEX AND RACE, 1958–1959

	Male		Female	
Pull factors	White	Black	White	Black
Total	100.0	100.0	100.0	100.0
Employment arranged	19.4	9.3	6.1	4.1
Favorable employment situation	46.3	55.7	28.7	33.3
Family contacts	18.8	19.7	58.8	52.4
Other social contacts	1.9	0.3	0.7	1.4
Educational benefits	6.5	2.6	3.2	1.2
Institutional benefits	0.3	0.9	0.7	0.2
Familiarity with the city	3.2	4.6	0.7	3.6
Other factors	3.5	7.0	1.1	3.6
Number of cases	309	345	279	414

sponsor her. Family contacts were a prime reason for about one-fifth of the male migrants also.

The other categories of pull factors that had been hypothesized received very few responses. Educational benefits (for self or children) were mentioned by only a small minority. It had been hypothesized that some persons might move to Chicago because of the "institutional benefits" available—higher welfare payments, freedom to vote, greater range of and access to community services. But less than 1% of migrants mentioned these. The last two categories of Table 11.3 were constructed to code the vague and general responses given by the migrants.

Table 11.3 makes it clear that employment and family contacts almost exhaust the pull factors. Only a tiny fraction of the respondents reported being attracted to Chicago by factors other than these two. The oft-stated claim that people are attracted to big cities by the "bright lights" is not supported by these data. However, as was noted for the push factors, perhaps social, educational, and institutional factors (including "bright lights") were supplementary attractions, even though they were less strong than employment and family contacts.

C. THE COSTS OF MIGRATION

In order to change his residence, a typical migrant incurs a substantial financial cost. Not only must he transport himself, but he must have savings or other resources for lodging, meals, and other expenses while he searches for employment. If he lacks savings, he may compensate for

TABLE 11.4

How Migrants Met the Costs of Migration to Chicago

	Male		Female	
Type of help	White	Black	White	Black
Percentage having $100 or more on arrival	58.7	52.7	68.4	46.5
Percentage receiving help with lodging	58.2	63.7	68.1	67.1
Percentage receiving help with meals	12.3	21.0	13.5	13.0
Percentage receiving help in finding work	44.2	55.6	33.7	45.0
Percentage receiving help with a loan	24.6	24.8	17.4	30.4
Percentage receiving help with clothing	10.7	10.0	12.9	13.2
Percentage receiving advice and information	29.5	39.6	29.1	32.3
Percentage receiving help in some form	93.6	91.7	—	—
Percentage receiving moderate to lavish help (two or more kinds)	63.6	65.8	—	—

this by getting help from relatives, other persons, or institutions. Table 11.4 attempts to assemble some facts about how migrants met the costs of their migration.

Nearly one-half of the migrants claimed to have arrived in Chicago with less than $100 in cash to support themselves. They compensated for this by accepting various kinds of help:

60% received help with lodging
50% received help in finding work
20% received help in the form of a cash loan
20% received help with meals
15% received help with clothing

Each migrant could receive some, all, or none of these various kinds of help. The second-last line of Table 11.4 reports the proportion of male migrants who received one or more of these forms of help, while the last line reports the percentage of male migrants who received moderate-to-lavish help (two or more kinds). Almost all migrants received some help, and about two-thirds received help of more than one kind. The great preponderance of the help cited above was provided by family or other relatives (see next section).

From the data of Table 11.4, it is evident that, while a substantial share of migrants to Chicago had very limited resources with which to pay the costs, a majority compensated for this by getting help—primarily from relatives.

D. THE PAYOFF OF MIGRATION

In considering the costs of migration, it is useful to know how long it took the migrants to find jobs, the quality of the employment obtained, and the salaries earned. These items of information were obtained from the migrants; Table 11.5 summarizes the responses.

Migration paid off quickly and well for a majority of migrants:

50% found employment within 1 week of arriving in Chicago
70% were employed within 4 weeks
70% of first jobs were permanent jobs
85% of first jobs paid $100 per week or more

The typical "migration story" was to arrive in Chicago with $100 or slightly more in one's pocket and within 1 week to be employed at a permanent job paying $100 per week or more. (This is the retrospective story as told in 1958–1959, it refers to an era spanning the days of World War II and the first decade following. It probably is very different from what exists in the economically depressed 1970s.) The brief period of hiatus was supported or sponsored in a majority of cases by relatives or friends who gave one or more forms of assistance.

However, even though 50% or more of all migrants fell into the comfortable stereotype just described, it must not be overlooked that a small group of migrants did not have employment even after one month, that the first employment received by some was temporary, and that the wages received on the first job were low in a substantial minority of cases. Moreover, the persons who were interviewed for this study were, of course, the "survivors" of a larger group of arrivals. In a retrospective study such as the one that provided the data for this paper, the respondents defined as "migrants" were those who came to the city and

TABLE 11.5

FINANCIAL PAYOFF OF MIGRATION TO CHICAGO

Financial payoff	Male		Female	
	White	Black	White	Black
Percentage finding employment within one week	60.0	48.7	55.1	39.4
Percentage finding employment within four weeks	78.6	64.5	64.3	62.9
Percentage finding permanent work in first job	67.6	73.9	62.2	68.2
Percentage receiving $100 per week in first job	82.3	82.4	79.6	76.5

TABLE 11.6

MISGIVINGS ABOUT MIGRATION TO CHICAGO

	Male		Female	
Negative factors	White	Black	White	Black
Percentage feeling homesick	31.7	16.5	42.2	31.6
Percentage unhappy or having mixed feelings about migration	28.4	27.5	33.7	30.0

stayed. (The majority had resided in the city for 10 years or more at the time of the survey). It is unknown how many arrived in the city and then returned—because the costs were greater than their resources, because help could not be obtained, or because the advantages of the home community were found to outweigh those of Chicago after an on-the-spot comparison had been made. Thus, the migrants who failed to get an adequate payoff were missed by the study, making the picture rosier than it really is for the average migrant.

E. COUNTERINFLUENCES TO MIGRATION

When he leaves a community, a migrant often gives up a very substantial number of benefits. Panel D of Table 11.1 lists some of these. For the migration to be a "profitable" one, the rewards at the destination must exceed not only the costs of migration but also repay the migrant for the benefits he has renounced. The Chicago interviews contained very little and only indirect information concerning the advantages of staying in the former residence. Respondents were asked how they felt shortly after making the move to the city—how homesick they were and whether they were pleased or sorry they had moved. Table 11.6 presents tabulations of these responses. Nearly one-half of females, but only about one-fifth of males, reported being homesick. About 30% of the respondents either were unhappy or had mixed feelings about having moved. Thus, there is indirect evidence that a substantial minority of migrants experience counterinfluences to migration—even after having moved. It is not difficult to presume that it is these counterinfluences which cause many people who consider migration to abandon it because they perceive the benefits they enjoy at the current residence to be greater than the net benefits of migration—the costs of migration weighed against the benefits they would enjoy at the new site.

For a substantial proportion of the migrants (30% to 50%), it appears that the move to Chicago was not one of complete joy and satisfaction. Instead, there was a feeling of ambivalence and indecision, as homesickness for the former environment and disappointment with the new (in comparison with the old) caused some feelings of regret. Our interviews were all held with migrants who had remained in Chicago, so, obviously, these counterinfluences had not been sufficiently powerful to induce return migration. But, as noted earlier, there are an unknown number of migrants who came to Chicago and then moved again—because these counterinfluences were powerful enough in their individual cases.

III.   Some Detailed Relationships

In addition to these general findings, the interrelationships of the variables introduced in the analysis were explored. Space does not permit a reporting of the large number of statistical tables upon which the following findings are based.

A.   PUSH VERSUS PULL FACTORS AND THEIR CORRELATES

Tables 11.2 and 11.3, dealing with push and pull factors, respectively, coded only one push and one pull factor per respondent. However, a much more refined coding of the open-ended questions concerning the reasons for moving was performed. In this refined coding, *all* reasons for moving given by the respondents were classified. Then each respondent was classified into one of three categories:

a. Movement exclusively or primarily stimulated by push factors
b. Movement exclusively or primarily stimulated by pull factors
c. Movement stimulated by a combination of push and full factors

Table 11.7 shows that about two-thirds of all migrants were stimulated

TABLE 11.7

FACTORS THAT MOTIVATED MIGRATION TO CHICAGO

Incentive to move	Sex		Race	
	Male	Female	White	Black
Total	100.0	100.0	100.0	100.0
Primarily push factors	9.0	15.7	18.8	18.3
Primarily pull factors	64.4	67.5	65.9	64.4
Both	15.2	15.3	13.7	16.8
Unable to determine	1.4	1.5	1.7	1.3

predominantly by pull factors and only about 15% to 20% predominantly by push factors; about 15% migrated because of a combination of both push and pull factors. The proportions are amazingly similar for male and female and for black and white migrants. From this we must conclude that, from the point of view of the migrant, the decision to migrate appears to be based upon the opportunity for self-improvement or upward mobility much more than upon desperation or dire necessity. Since almost two-thirds of all migrants reported no push factors at all in their decision to migrate, we must presume that their decision to move was a choice between the better of two acceptable situations.

An effort was made to learn what aspects of migration appear to be correlated with particular mixtures of push and pull factors. The following conclusions were reached:

a. The amount of money resources the migrant possessed upon arrival was significantly associated with the mixture of push and pull factors. Migrants who left primarily because of push factors had significantly less money than migrants who came primarily because of pull factors. This was true for males and females, blacks and whites.

b. The amount of help given migrants was related to the mixture of push and pull factors. Migrants who were pushed out of their former residence tended to receive more help than migrants who were attracted to Chicago by pull factors. This was especially true for females and blacks.

c. Feelings of loneliness and homesickness were felt by a higher proportion of persons who were impelled to migrate primarily by pull factors and least by persons impelled primarily by push factors.

d. The average length of time required to find a job was essentially the same for those who came primarily because of push factors and those primarily influenced by pull factors. Moreover, the proportion whose first job was a permanent job was the same for both groups.

e. Migrants (who had moved more than once) who had left their previous residence primarily because of push factors also tended to leave their second residence primarily because of push factors.

B. AMOUNT OF HELP RECEIVED BY MIGRANTS (MALES ONLY)

As has been noted, some migrants reveived no help or very little help, while others received very generous help. An effort was made to find the correlates of this variation.

a. Migrants who arrived with less than $100 tended to receive much more generous help than migrants who arrived with greater financial resources. This was true for both black and white migrants. This is evidence that migrants who lack adequate financial resources for migration choose a destination where family or other resources will be available to help pay the costs.

b. Migrants who received the most help tended also to be the most lonesome and homesick for the previous residence. This suggests that migrants who have family resources in a metropolis may be more prone to migrate while still in an ambivalent state, whereas migrants who must be completely self-sufficient tend not to migrate until they have made a firm and stable decision.

c. Those who received the most generous help were migrants who had a close relative expecting them. Those who received least help had no one expecting them. This documents that most help is provided by families.

d. There was no relationship between the amount of help received and the time required to find employment.

e. As noted earlier, migrants who migrated primarily because of push factors received more help than did migrants who responded primarily to pull factors.

C. SATISFACTION AT HAVING MIGRATED

Feelings of unhappiness at having migrated to Chicago (appreciation of the advantages of the former residence) were found to have the following relationships with other variables of the study:

a. Feelings of happiness or unhappiness were not correlated with the mixture of push and pull factors that motivated migration.

b. Feelings of happiness or unhappiness were not correlated with the amount of money resources the migrant possessed at the time of arrival in Chicago.

c. Feelings of happiness or unhappiness were not correlated with the amount of help the migrant received.

d. Feelings of happiness or unhappiness were very highly correlated with feelings of homesickness or lonesomeness for the previous place of residence.

With the costs of migration having been met through personal or family resources and with financial payoff having been received rather promptly, the primary variable determining satisfaction or dissatisfaction with the move was a perception of the benefits and pleasures that had been renounced by leaving the former residence.

TABLE 11.8

Sources of Various Types of Help Given to Male Migrants to Chicago

Source of help	Housing	Loan of money	Clothing	Meals	Job help	Information
Total	100.0	100.0	100.0	100.0	100.0	100.0
No help	38.4	74.7	89.5	81.9	48.2	64.6
Family	25.7	10.8	5.4	6.8	18.4	11.3
Other relatives	20.3	8.4	3.0	6.2	16.0	11.2
Friends	10.9	3.5	0.8	3.0	12.3	9.5
Institutions	4.6	2.5	1.3	2.1	5.0	3.4

D.   HELP RECEIVED

In an effort to learn which groups of migrants received the most and the least help, relationships with other variables of the study were explored:

a. Migrants who had no one waiting for them upon their arrival in Chicago tended to receive no help or very little help. Those who had someone waiting for or expecting them tended to receive generous or even lavish help. The amount of help received was about the same if the person expecting the migrant was a nonrelative, a distant relative, or a primary relative.

b. Migrants who received no help required a longer time to find employment than those who received help. However, those who received lavish amounts of help also found employment only after an above average period of time.

c. The major proportion of all help given to migrants was provided by relatives; friends contributed a modest amount, but the contribution of institutions was negligible in comparison with the total volume of help given. Table 11.8 reports the sources of various kinds of help given to male migrants.

IV.   Implications

There has been a tendency in demography to deny the importance of social psychological variables (the perceptions, feelings, and beliefs of individuals). The "real" or "true" forces, it has been asserted, are objective and societal. Examples are interarea differentials in income, in unemployment rates, in environmental amenities, and so on. The choices, feelings, and perceptions of individuals, it is held, are epiphenomena which people may experience as these external forces exert their pressure.

This view, which has progressively been challenged in other areas, is seriously challenged by the model and the data presented here. Instead, it may be more fruitful to view the decision to migrate (or not to migrate) as a rational process, one involving the factors that each individual perceives and the action he takes on the basis of his calculations of the potential gains and costs of moving.

The day may soon arrive in many developed countries such as the United States where human migration will appear, from the aggregate point of view, as being purely circulatory—producing very little structural change either in the community of origin or in the community of destination. From the aggregate point of view this may appear to be a process of social waste—communities simply trading individuals with near-identical characteristics. Yet from the individual point of view, such movement may be highly functional and profitable. Individuals with highly specific skills will continue to seek those specific sites that can use their talents. In a democracy, as older workers retire from the labor force and make way for new generations of workers, residents of other regions can and should be able to compete with local residents to replace them. People living in different communities will fall in love and marry; one member of the couple must then migrate in order to form a family. Not all employers and employees are compatible, and labor mobility for individual workers will entail some geographic mobility. Retirement may cause individuals to want a complete change in their place of residence—for reasons of climate, to be near family or friends, or for other reasons. Under these circumstances, the subjective person-linked data of the type presented here may explain a far higher percentage of migration behaviors than do environmental and structural variables.

In making individual calculations of the costs and benefits of migration, it appears that economic and employment considerations weigh very heavily. The primary strategy for reducing costs seems to be to accept temporary assistance from a relative or friend already established in the place chosen as a destination. Once the decision to migrate is made and the move accomplished, a majority of migrants appear to settle in quickly, to be happy that they have moved, and to believe that they have enjoyed a net gain as a result. However, a substantial minority have mixed feelings at first, as they make comparisons between what they acquired and what they renounced by deciding to migrate.

CHAPTER 12

On the Microeconomics
of Internal Migration

Jerome Rothenberg

I. Introduction

This chapter is a discussion of the determinants of internal migration by individual decision makers. It comes on the heels of a substantial number of theoretical and econometric treatments over the last 10 or so years, dealing with developed economies like the United States as well as with less developed economies throughout the world.[1] Its justification, given this spate of research, is that it emphasizes an extreme disaggregated microlevel. Most treatments have dealt with migration flows on a much more aggregative level. They have been forced by the requirements of aggregation to use explanatory specifications that blur some important issues in the understanding of migration. The present focus on the individual potential migrant decision maker is designed to permit a judgment on the extent to which attention to aggregation problems may have led to misleading formulations, and to provide a renewed source of suggestions for strengthening empirical work in the field.

The paper does not pretend to provide strikingly original insights; nor to be adding a new model to the many already extant. It is attempting, rather, to draw together and examine critically, in a coherent manner and within an integrated decision framework, many of the variables,

---

[1] For example, see the 251-item bibliography relating primarily to U.S. internal migration in Greenwood (1975) and the 89-item bibliography referring primarily to less developed countries in Yap (1975).

factors, forces, and influences bearing on internal migration decisions. It is hoped that this comprehensive—but not exhaustive—critical compendium will offer a useful perspective and suggestion fund for more specialized theoretical and empirical work. No model can feasibly incorporate all or even most of the types of influence to be discussed here. But the paper will have served its purpose if it can help to clarify some discriminations, help to indicate why some analytic linkages should be abandoned and others forged in this complex, provocative field.

As noted, internal migration has been studied both in developed and in less developed systems. The explanatory structure has been quite similar for both, and the empirical findings do not strikingly differ for the two. Clearly, there are some institutional differences—barriers, opportunities, social forms—that would be expected to have some impact on the character of the migration process; but these have not led to significant differences in the kinds of theories being tested, or the outcomes of these tests. Something like a unitary basic approach has seemed warranted, with international differences calling for changes in detail but not in overall form. It is in this spirit that we shall propose a fundamental format for studying internal migration phenomena.

II. The Migrant and the Non-Migrant

A central thesis of the present paper is that the migrant is not a random cross-section of the population. He (she) is not the average person in some origin group, responding in an average way to a set of differential advantages connected with moving. In that kind of formulation, each average individual has a finite probability of becoming a migrant under each set of alternative opportunities, and a stochastic process determines which individuals actually migrate under each such set. In an aggregative treatment, especially where individual and group differences cannot be abstracted and documented, such a characterization may be as much as can be expected. But it may be seriously misleading. The migrant is in fact self-selected. Under any set of opportunities, it is no accident which individuals will choose to migrate and which to stay. The migrant has special features that make him evaluate the grounds for going or staying differently than those who stay.

What this means is that a given set of opportunities will induce a different amount of migration in populations of different composition.

This can be rationalized either by specifying a general set of inducements and constraints, with different evaluational parameter values for different parts of the population, or by specifying different sets of inducements and constraints specific to the different individuals and groups in the population. Both of these approaches will be used in this paper, when they seem appropriate.

Three types of migration movement have to be explained. First is the move that can be characterized in aggregative average terms as from an origin of inferior opportunities to a destination of superior opportunities. This is the form of migration most congenial to the conventional aggregate economic rationality model. Second is the move from an origin with opportunities on the average greater than those of the destination. Third is the staged migration where, for reasons of expense or staged information gathering, a move is made from origin i to some destination j which is envisaged as only a temporary resting place, rather than the true or final destination. Thus an observed move from i to j will not generally be explainable as the most advantageous available (utility maximizing). The second and third types will usually be difficult or impossible to explain in aggregate models dealing with average individuals. They require the agent-specific opportunities and constraints describable in disaggregated models. In such a context, the return home of disappointed earlier migrants, or the special opportunities open to a favored few in otherwise impoverished areas, can be easily understood and modeled. And the temporary expedient of partial moves, either half-heartedly sampled, or avowedly used as staging areas on the way to more seriously anticipated destinations, can be rationalized in strategic terms in such microapproaches. Our treatment of individual migration decisions will attempt to provide a single analytic framework that integrates all three types of move.

III.   A Calculus of Rational Migration Choice

The basic approach to individual migration decisions is to assume that each member of the population performs the following calculation: At each point of time he (she) perceives that a choice has to be made between remaining a resident of his (her) current region and moving to another region. Each region, including the current place of residence, is perceived as possessing a set of opportunities and constraints relevant to the calculation; in addition, if he (she) were to move, a set of costs would be incurred. By evaluating each of the regions as an alternative prospect in utility terms and subtracting the cost of moving to it in utility terms, the subject forms a utility level for each hypothetical course of action. If a move to any new region yields an expected utility level greater than that associated with remaining in the current region, the subject will become a migrant. He (she) will migrate to that region that promises the highest expected utility level.

This formulation, certainly a conventional one, requires four basic elements: the benefits characterization of a move to any new region, the costs involved in each such move, the character and extent of the information about these benefits and costs, and the utility significance of each component of benefits and costs—or, more appropriately, the utility evaluation by the particular agent making the decision of each bundle of benefit and cost components. In the paper to follow, we shall consider each of these elements in turn. Now, we shall simply list some of the items to be considered.

On the benefits side, we shall treat improvement in job prospects, in style of life, in the variety of private and public commodities available for consumption, in the quality of public services attainable, and in housing standards achieved, as well as the adventure of initiating a risky quantum change in the overall life situation.

On the cost of migration side, we shall treat moving costs, transition costs, loss of friends and relatives, change in style of life, and concern over a risky quantum change in the overall life situation.

Two items are treated both as benefit and as cost dimensions. This is to emphasize that each can be one or the other for different individuals. Neither is invariably a benefit or a cost for all individuals. Having both a cost and benefit dimension for the two better fits our emphasis on individual differences.

The calculation of benefits and costs for each hypothetical move depends on the relevant information available to the individual. Information is never perfect, and its adequacy differs for different potential moves. The sources and adequacy of information about different moves and how the information is integrated into the evaluation process are examined.

Finally, the individuality of the utility evaluation is treated. The concept of migrants as a self-selected group is stressed by considering individual and group differences in (1) commodity tastes, (2) present career situation, (3) attitudes toward risk, (4) situational mobility (family constraints, transportable property), and (5) significance of differences in prospects (due to age, sex, education, etc.).

IV.   Benefits from Migration: New versus Old Job Prospects: Risk, Search, and Job Markets

In all economic treatments of migration, improved income opportunities are accorded the premier influence. This is concurred in here. But the meaning and measurement of such improvement is by no means as simple as the treatment in some aggregative econometric models. A number of important and difficult issues have to be resolved in formulating this benefit dimension properly.

To begin, "the income" to be associated with a given region is generated through employment, but a given region does not represent either one particular job or one particular income. Two issues are involved here: (1) In any period, the particular employment situation enjoyed (or suffered) by an individual is not the only one possible to him—he may seek a different job of the same or other types in the same region or if currently unemployed, seek some job more intensely. (2) The income relevant to migration decisions is lifetime income, which results from a sequence of employment experiences—a career profile— and each region offers a variety of "career trees," in which each segment leads temporally to a different set of irreversible further opportunities. The individual's present job does not guarantee a single unique temporal path with a determinate income flow. Rather, it suggests only a given career tree—a distribution of possible sequential branches for which probabilities may be more or less solidly assigned.

Both of these considerations suggest that the decision to migrate should be integrated with labor market theory. Job search, job turnover, promotions, changes in occupation, voluntary unemployment are not independent of decisions to migrate. They are all simultaneous elements in the job change experience: Migration may sometimes accompany, sometimes give way to, combinations of these other elements. This section will concentrate primarily on job search considerations, the next section on lifetime income considerations.

A.   "Risk" and Active Choice

If the "income opportunity" associated with a region is a product of a career profile and this in turn is a stochastic variable, then the "income opportunity" is a risk prospect. Unlike some risk prospect choice situations, where the agent simply selects among risk prospects and then is passive while an intrinsically exogenous chance process determines the outcome, the job market choice situation is one in which the individual chooses among families of risk prospects (career trees) and then actively and progressively narrows down choice within each family. Within each region, a presently employed worker can at any time choose to look for the same kind of job in other firms of the same industry or in firms of a different industry, or he (she) can look for a different kind of job (either with or without additional training) in either the same or other industries. This voluntary search behavior is a variable involving amount and kind, where job content, training, firm, industry are dimensions defining the latter. Individuals with the same general skills may, in any observed period, experience quite different job–income outcomes, depending both on their past voluntary strategies with regard to search and on chance factors affecting success in search and performance.

The possibility of migrating to another region is the existence of a set of such alternative families of risk prospects (career trees). The decision to migrate to a particular destination is the selection of a different family of risk prospects about which the same kinds of decision concerning amount and kind of search will have to be made after—or in preparation for—migration.

B. SEARCH AND EXPERIENCE

These considerations are relevant to the comparison between income prospects in the present location versus those in alternative locations. If the individual has resided at his present location for any length of time, he has presumably already narrowed down the family of prospects characteristic of this location. Thus, he is not likely to have a present situation whose prospect he evaluates at the mean value for the entire original family of prospects relevant to a newcomer. Moreover, since the possibility of further search is not exhausted, even the present career tree, let alone the present income earned or the present wage rate, does not necessarily constitute an adequate representation of the income opportunity involved in remaining in the present region.

Newcomers to the region will tend to view its "opportunity" as a mean value and a completely unsampled set of possibilities—that is, a total population variance. Older residents will view it as a value adjusted for their actual achieved income level (relative to the mean) and a variance of possibilities smaller than the total by an adjustment that takes into account the degree to which they have already narrowed down the original set of prospects.

So a given set of individuals, alike in skills, tasks, and so on but differing in length of occupancy and in stochastic fortunes, may well differ in their evaluation of the income prospects for a given region. In predicting how many of the set will migrate elsewhere, it is therefore important to know something about these specific characteristics of the group: One should want to know where, within the forest of risk, each member of the group currently stands.

C. THE INDIVIDUALIZATION OF INCOME PROSPECTS

The foregoing suggests a general principle in the characterization of income prospects. It should be, to whatever extent possible, reflective of the situation of the particular individual or group being observed, rather than be the average of some larger group of which these are members. This is especially important if the individuals who turn out to be actual migrants are unrepresentative of the larger group; but this is exactly what is likely to be true if special characteristics affect the evaluation of the opportunities and costs reflected by different locational alternatives.

D. JOB SAMPLING AND VARIANCE

In contrasting the income significance of a region to residents of different durations, we described prospects in terms of a mean level and a variance. In portfolio theory, variance has been accorded an explanatory role as an adjunct to mean value. When extending the calculation of income prospects to potential residence locations, there is even more reason to include variance, as well as even higher moments, of the probability distribution of income prospects. Unlike the passive holding of a risky prospect, where an exogenous chance process selects outcomes, voluntary variable search affects the expected maximum value function. Search should be prolonged so long as the expected marginal increase in maximum value among the items sampled exceeds the marginal cost of additional sampling, and it should stop only when the two are equal. Finite sampling gives an expected value higher than the overall mean value of the unsampled distribution, while at the same time decreasing the remaining variance. Moreover, the expected payoffs to sampling are a positive function of the size of the original variance. The greater the variance, the greater the ability to use sampling of jobs to achieve an earnings sequence that exceeds the mean unsampled ("one shot") experience. Other characteristics of the original probability distribution also influence the payoff to sampling.[2]

[2] This whole section has benefited heavily from David (1974) and Renshaw (1970). The second source developed a framework that integrated migration with other forms of labor market adjustment. The first stressed the two-stage decision package including migration and variable job search and also developed the dependence of the gains from search on the variance of the original probability distribution of income prospects.

The money gains to sampling are independent of an individual's attitude toward risk. But of course the utility significance of such gains is dependent on such attitudes. The fact that the set of alternative migration destinations will generally contain a variety of mean–variance tradeoffs means that attitudes toward risk may be an important ground on the basis of which otherwise similar individuals (e.g., similar in skills, length of residence) will evaluate income prospects from the same set of prospects quite differently. These differences in evaluation refer both to the decision to migrate at all and to the relative attractiveness of different possible destinations.

E. Variance and Destination Size

The importance of variance as a migration incentive serves not only to self-select certain types of people as migrants but also to select certain regions as especially popular destinations for migrants, from whatever origins. If high variance is attractive, then it is the very large urban areas that are likely to provide it, because they have both the scale and the variety of jobs to make very different career patterns possible. Even largeness of market alone serves this, because natural job turnover then offers many attractive, if low probability, opportunities. Since large size is also generally associated with large variety, the variance of outcomes is even more pronounced in large metropolitan areas. These, then, come to exercise a migratory pull out of proportion to any advantage they may show in the mean level of their returns. Even mean income lower than that in some smaller destinations will be offset for many migrants by the more adventurous risks of "the big town."

F. Investment in Human Capital

Another personal characteristic enters to influence the evaluation of a given set of alternative income prospects. This is the investment in human capital. If an individual has just completed significant investment in human capital—say, by a quantum increase in education—then that part of the probability distribution of jobs previously most relevant to him is no longer so relevant. A new, higher skilled subset is now more appropriate. But this subset has not been sampled, and much or most of the individual's previous job experience is now irrelevant. Thus, he perceives his resident region's income opportunities almost like a newcomer, with little of the accumulated fruits of sequential sampling and career ladder climbing. As a result, his new situation in his resident region lacks the advantage of the higher-than-average perspective due to longer duration in comparison with a newcomer's average perspective of gains from the comparable job subset in other regions. A normal status quo advantage for his resident region is thus missing, and so he is more likely to migrate—despite the absence of any change in the objective opportunities available in different locations. In sum, significant new investment in human capital increases the probability of migration, a migration associated with a change in occupation.

V.   Benefits from Migration: New versus Old Job Prospects: Lifetime Earnings, Wage Rates, and Unemployment

A.   LIFETIME EARNINGS

The benefit calculation for income should refer to the present value of lifetime income differences between each potential migration destination and the present residence location, not just to the current period's differentials in such earnings. There are two important advantages of the lifetime formulation. First, it discriminates between decision makers of different remaining lifetimes in the labor force. Assume that the positive first-year earnings differential between some destination and the present location would remain unchanged over the remaining productive lifetime of two different individuals, but that individual A had 10 more years to work and individual B 30 more years. If only first-year differences were regarded, the migration incentive of the two individuals would be registered as equal. However, it is clear that individual B could count on a larger total lifetime gain from the migration than could individual A, and, with any significant but equal cost of migrating for the two, the overall gain for A might fall short of its cost while exceeding that same cost for B. So the probability of migration would differ under the lifetime earnings formulation, as it should.

Here is another example where the kind of advantage which migration brings favors certain kinds of individuals over others. Just as individuals with poorer than average chance earning outcomes and those with risk preference, with lesser job sampling experience in their current residences, and with new educations have somewhat higher probabilities of migrating for any given objective differences in job opportunities, so too, younger individuals are likely to be self-selected for migration because their migration investments have a longer payout period, and thus higher rates of return, than do those with fewer remaining work years.

The second advantage of the lifetime earnings formulation is that it discriminates different career profiles over time. Different occupations carry different patterns of skill and promotion ladders over time. Even the same occupation in two different places may bear different time profiles of advancement because of the different industries embedding them or different patterns of labor competition or firm vicissitudes in the two places. Moreover, a career profile that includes sequential changes in occupation as opportunities permit may certainly differ in two places if the scale, variety or health of job opportunities differ markedly in the two places.

Thus, the real nature of income opportunity in two different places depends on the expected time shape of earnings in both. The same first-year prospects may be consistent with very different subsequent prospects. Rational migration calculation should certainly take these different time shapes into account.

The self-selection engendered by this consideration is more complex. It depends on the matching of particular kinds of people with particular kinds of job market patterns. Different types of labor skill are likely to have different "natural" time profiles of earnings capacity. Different regions are also likely to differ in the skill mix of their distribution of jobs (because of different industry distributions, for example). Thus, certain skill types are likely to fare better over time in some regions than in others. A kind of comparative advantage may come to operate, such that skill type A would do better over time in region α than in region β, while skill type B would do better over time in β than in α. Individuals with skill A residing in region β would have a higher probability of migrating than would region β residents with skill B; and α residents with skill A would have a lower probability of migrating than those with skill B.

One further variable is introduced into the calculation of potential migration benefits that discriminates both among potential migrants and among potential destinations. That is the internal discount rate selected by each individual to convert expected income streams into a present value. The choice of any rate tends to discriminate among destinations insofar as they offer different typical earnings profiles over time. Insofar as different individuals express different time preference in their discounting, these same destination-specific variations in time profiles will tend to favor one set of destinations for one group of migrants, another set for a different group—including the decision whether or not to migrate at all.

B. WAGE RATES VERSUS EARNINGS

So far we have spoken of the job incentives for migration as "earnings differentials." There is an ambiguity in this. Earnings is the product of a wage rate and the number of labor units worked. But the latter is to some extent a voluntary response to the former. Insofar as units (hours) worked changes in the course of migration, the amount of leisure changes as well. To register gains in terms of earnings puts zero value on leisure (see Lucas, 1975a, p. 2, Footnote 2). The true utility value is a function of the price of leisure—namely, the wage rate—along with money income and the price of other commodities. It is appropriate to calculate prospective gains in terms of these arguments of the indirect utility function, rather than in terms of earnings. But this puts a heavy burden on specifying the appropriate utility function for theoretical analysis, although for econometric study the wage rate can simply be plugged in as the appropriate income prospect variable.

Despite the formal appropriateness of this modification, its practical significance may be much less. It is the endogeneity of the hours decision that is crucial here. Insofar as hours are conventional or employer-prescribed, the modification is unnecessary and possibly incorrect. But, in a large proportion of jobs, exogenous determination of hours worked is the prevailing pattern. So earnings may well be the better variable after all, despite its neglect of the value of leisure.

C. UNEMPLOYMENT

We have not raised the issue of unemployment. In speaking about voluntary job search we have implicitly introduced some voluntary unemployment. Indeed, choice of higher variance job distributions through migration is often associated with a voluntarily larger sampling of the new distribution—and thus longer voluntary unemployment after migration. But involuntary unemployment is different. Labor markets are certainly subject to cyclical periods of involuntary unemployment. But these are relatively short-term affairs. Some labor markets, however, experience persistent involuntary unemployment. A major contribution of the Harris–Todaro (1970) model is to stress the practical importance of such market situations and how it modifies migration incentives. Especially in less developed countries, (LDCs), urban areas may be characterized by dual markets, where the more desirable, regular jobs (in the so-called formal sector) carry significantly higher wave rates than jobs in the casual, informal sector. Yet labor competition between the two is not permitted to break down the sizable two-wage differential, and, instead, a relatively permanent queuing process occurs for the artificially limited jobs in the desirable sector. The queuing represents involuntary unemployment.

Dependably expected involuntary unemployment reduces the attractiveness of a given set of employment opportunities. Harris and Todaro suggest treating this in terms of *expected* earnings, where each prospective employment experience is multiplied by its probability of occurrence—an adjustment of our previous probability concept by introducing the unemployment rate, for example, valuation summarizing the overall risk prospect of a region multiplied by (1 − unemployment rate).

An adjustment of this sort may be appropriate for *beginning* earnings, but at least in the institutional queuing model it is inappropriate for *later* period earnings. Use of lifetime earnings markedly reduces the significance of such an adjustment to expected values. Indeed, it raises the question whether unemployment should not be treated differently.

If the expected period of unemployment generally comes just after migration, then it strikes at a time when the migrant is economically especially vulnerable—since his resources and productivity are likely to be lower than subsequently, and the social contacts that might help to support him over the postmigration transition period are few or nonexistent. Expected unemployment at that time strikes at his ability to become viable at the new destination—thus strikes at the practicability of migrating to that destination at all. Unemployment should thus be treated as a cost of migration rather than as an adjustment to expected gross lifetime advantages of the migration.

VI.   Benefits from Migration: Nonjob Benefits

A.   REAL INCOME DIFFERENTIALS

In the last section we spoke of earnings differentials as a chief incentive for migration. The differentials were expressed in nominal money terms. Clearly, the differentials that matter are "real-income" differentials. This calls for deflating the nominal amounts by the cost of living. This is easier said than done, however, in the present case. Since different regions are involved, we are speaking about using cost of living indices that compare living costs in different regions. Comparability is always a question for this kind of problem, but even more so here where the regions may differ markedly in character. Since so much migration is from backward rural areas to the largest, most developed urban areas in the nation, the market basket characteristics of origins and destinations will differ in extreme ways. The variety of goods available will be especially divergent, but the relative importance of different items will also show these differences. Under these circumstances the use of cost of living (consumer price) indices is highly suspect. Nonetheless, some procedure is needed to increase the comparability of the buying power of earnings in different locations.

A mechanical adjustment via cost of living indices will not achieve the purpose. Rather, these large differences in style and pattern of consumption should be introduced as explicit variables. They are part of the differential in opportunities that migration offers, just as are job differentials. Thus, we shall discuss them explicitly as separate components of the destination—specific bundles of attributes being evaluated by potential migrants. The overall treatment of nonjob benefits, therefore, is to make a cost of living adjustment for elements in the consumption bundle that are roughly comparable across locations and to supplement this by a separate listing of grossly noncomparable consumption aspects.

B. Utility Significance

The variety of private and public goods will vary appreciably from location to location, and especially between simple rural areas and large, sophisticated urban areas. The variety increases notably with size. This is a result of urban scale economies.

Increasing variety in itself should bear an unambiguously positive impact on an individual's welfare, since he can buy (use) everything that was available in a smaller variety situation, as well as various additional combinations. For the prospective migrant there is an element of self-selection in that the *utility significance* of the wider selection of commodities depends on the individual's tastes: Those who appreciate complex, sophisticated consumption will benefit more from such a widening of choice than those with simple tastes. This interpersonal discrimination is especially important in the migrations from simplest origins to most sophisticated destinations.

C. Style of Life

The availability of commodities is a perfectly objective attribute of a situation. Somewhat more elusive is the notion of what people do with this availability, their style of life. Yet the concept of a style of life is widely used and, while not capable of being brandished with unanimous agreement, does appear to be employed with a real convergence of understanding and does refer to something that is more than simply an assortment of goods.

The style of life in large, sophisticated urban areas differs appreciably from that in rural areas or small towns. The pattern of consumption is different; the tempo of living is different. The high degree of competitiveness and impersonality, the interest in change and newness for their own sake, the desire for elaboration of simple things into complex, the habituation and delight in meeting frequent challenges and risking much to accept them, the willingness to live surrounded by tension and danger—these and other elements characterize big city living; they represent quantum leaps from comparable elements in rural and small town living. For any one person, they are a function not only of what commodities are available but of the pattern of behavior of other people—a significant set of externalities.

The degree of differences in style of life depends on the nation being considered and the variety of destinations involved. The utility impact of such differences is potentially greater even than the migration differences in earnings, because these can constitute virtually different ways of life and involve the most basic values and attitudes of the individual. But this impact is subject to the widest differences among individuals. Individual "tastes" will determine whether the change of style from rural to big city life is a matter of gaining adventure and excitement, even liberation and rebirth, or subjecting oneself to insecurity, anxiety, and corruption, degrading and dehumanizing one's life.

So, style of life will strongly differentiate people. A given set of origin–destination differences will attract some in widely varying degrees, repel others in just as widely varying degrees. Among the individual differences that underlie these differences in utility impact are probably age, sex, degree of education, and attitudes toward risk and personal mobility (in terms of the intensity and complexity of familial relationships). The list is strikingly similar to that which underlies individual differences in the utility tradeoffs between men and variance in income prospects. It is not accidental. From an observational point of view it may be very difficult to disentangle income variance from style of life as a migration determinant: Areas offering high variance are also likely to offer "big city, sophisticated life styles." But there is probably a deeper psychological link as well. The behavioral and interpersonal ingredients making for one are also likely to make for the other. Working and consuming are never as psychologically distinct as their treatment in conventional economic analysis asserts.

D. QUALITY OF HOUSING

Differences in the quality of housing are often listed as a determinant of migration. This may be misleading. Insofar as housing is a private good and offered without subsidy in the private market or needing to be produced by the migrants themselves, differences in quality and price of housing among migration locations are already represented in the cost of living adjustment noted earlier and do not warrant separate treatment.

Indeed, in some nations, especially among the less developed countries, housing conditions in popular urban migration destinations are often worse than in the rural origins. Most of the poor migrants are crowded into shantytowns on the edges of the urban area, with poor, temporary shelter and no public services like water, sewage, electricity, and streets. This represents a negative differential consequence of migration. It should be registered by a cost of living adjustment which distinguishes the real cost of different qualities of private commodities like housing.

In some nations, urban housing is provided which is at least partly public in character—public housing, or publicly subsidized housing. In these cases, the cost of living adjustment would probably miss what are in effect public service benefits. These should be separately listed. Their utility impact on migrants—and thus on the migration decision—depends on the nature of the public service provision: size, character, and distribution. Here too, we should not expect the influence to be distributionally neutral but to promise differential advantages to different types of migrants.

E. GENERAL PUBLIC GOODS

The generalization of the public component of housing that warranted separate treatment is local public goods generally. While effective tax rates may be included in cost of living indices, the variety and quality of public services are rarely so. Welfare services, health care, education, and job training may be notably different in different regions. These surely can qualify as benefit dimensions of the migration decision alternatives. Even the negative "public goods" of quality of air and water and degree of congestion—so-called environmental quality— should be included in this context.

Indeed, some of the positive public services qualify for a second role as well. In discussing unemployment, we noted the especially vulnerable transition period of the migrant as embodying a migration cost which is a potentially important deterrent to migration. Just as expected unemployment rates might be treated as an element of those transition costs, so the availability of public services that provide a potential cushion against transition difficulties can be considered a diminution of expected transition costs. Different types of public services will of course differ in their playing of these twin roles. Moreover, the two roles will generally have different utility impact for potential migrants in different circumstances—since transition difficulties will loom larger for some than for others. Thus, for reasons over and above normal differences in tastes for collections of public services, a given complement of local public services may be evaluated differently by individuals in different circumstances; and different collections of public services will evoke different relative evaluations from different aggregations of individuals.

To summarize this section, regions will differ in providing the commodities and living patterns that are ingredients of the quality of life. They are as location-specific as are job opportunities, and they qualify as genuine dimensions of the location bundles evaluated by potential migrants. Like job opportunities, they are not neutral among individuals deciding whether and where to migrate. They exercise incentives that encourage a self-selection of the migrant from the nonmigrant and a specialized pairing of migrant with destination. As with employment opportunities, too, this self-selection requires that some of the benefits be disaggregated to show their differential incidence on different types of migrants. A larger part of these benefits, however, in comparison with job opportunities, can probably be expressed as general, or average, opportunities, potentially open to all migrants but differently evaluated by different individuals on the basis of their circumstances or tastes.

VII. Migration Costs

We shall mention five kinds of costs, but two of them have essentially already been listed as forms of nonjob benefits. Their dual inclusion will be explained later. The five are (1) moving costs, (2) transition costs, (3) loss of friends and relatives, (4) change in lifestyle, and (5) concern over uncertain prospects.

A. MOVING COSTS

Moving costs include personal transportation and the removal of personal property to the migration destination. The size of these costs is clearly a positive function of the amount of property possessed, the size of the family proposing to migrate, and the distance to be traveled. For a given set of potential benefits from migration, the existence of moving costs clearly has an unequal deterring impact on migration. Other things equal, it favors for migration (1) younger people, with weak familial obligations and a small amount of accumulated property, (2) individuals institutionally or culturally more mobile—in many societies, predominantly males, (3) small families or single persons, and (4) close destinations.

Especially where single young persons are involved, moving costs are one-time expenditures that are small relative to expected lifetime earnings differentials. On this score, they may not be expected to have a strong negative influence on migration. But they may represent large absolute amounts at one time. They may well be larger than the accumulated savings of just that group that is otherwise least deterred. In contexts where capital markets are notably imperfect, especially with regard to human capital (migration being a form of locational investment in human capital), this can stifle migration that would otherwise have been economically rational.

This factor is, of course, especially important for international migration, where significantly large minimum distances are involved. It is less so for internal migration, where distances can be graduated more continuously. One adjustment in internal migration is the strategy of staged migration, where a desired long distance move is broken into shorter-distance stages, the migrant stopping at each stage primarily to accumulate more capital in order to finance further stages—although unexpected good fortune in job search and experience at any stage can serve to short-circuit original migration plans.

Another impact of the minimum capital requirement to finance migration is that individuals (families) with adequate accumulated capital will be less deterred from migration *relative to* the favored categories listed above than sheer relative size of moving costs would suggest. The capital as well as the net returns flow dimensions of moving costs must be considered in order to compare the relative influence on different potential migrants. So, somewhat older, more successful, larger families may comprise a nontrivial share of actual migrants on this score.

B. Transition Costs

A second set of costs are transition costs. These are the costs of settling in to a new, unfamiliar milieu, where housing, shopping, and other contacts require gradual, possibly painful orientation periods. This set of costs often includes an indefinite period of unemployment, as the process of job search in a new location has to begin at the very beginning. These are in effect one-time setup costs—a necessary investment in "locational social capital." In international migration and even in some forms of internal migration, the learning of a new language is required.

While the same repertoire of information is required of everyone, individuals differ in how much they already know, in how difficult attainment of the rest is, and in how important this set of efforts is. The utility significance of the possibility of an initial period of unemployment is especially likely to differ among individuals. Since it occurs before the migrant has an opportunity to take advantage of the anticipated increment of earnings over his recent origin, his asset position is likely to be unusually weak. His vulnerability to a period of unemployment at that time may be very great. At one extreme, some migrants move with a job already arranged for, or have the kind of skills that practically guarantee a short initial unemployment period, or they come with adequate assets; at the other extreme, some have no specific job prospects, have skills not easy to fit quickly into the job market, and have nearly zero accumulated assets; and other migrants fit somewhere between these extremes. So the utility impact can range from trivial to very considerable among potential migrants.

As noted earlier, availability of certain local public services at the migration destination decreases the expected intensity of these costs. Thus, we can expect a double form of self-selection: by individuals and for destinations. If no destination has cost-moderating public services, the possible severity of settling-in costs may absolutely discourage any migration by those who would be especially hard hit. To the extent that such services are available, this group of individuals will be less deterred from migrating at all and will tend to select destinations possessing the highest levels of such services, all other things equal. Since prospective transition costs may, if unalleviated, exert an absolute veto on migration, this basis for selecting a migration destination may be extremely compelling.

C. Loss of Friends and Relatives

A third form of cost is the "loss" of friends and relatives. Since satisfactory close social relationships may be *the* dominant determinant of an individual's full welfare in the range of circumstances where basic biological needs are met at least at minimal levels, this "loss" may have large impact effects. On the other hand, new substitute social relations can often be created after a time in a new surrounding, so the utility loss is generally only temporary, and, with this in prospect, temporary deprivation probably does not have the absolute veto status that unattainability of travel costs, or even more, prospectively severe transition costs, may have.

Once again, this factor will vary considerably among individuals and destinations. The range and importance of close social contacts at the origin differ widely among individuals, as does perceived ability to create substitute relationships in new surroundings. While both have important idiosyncratic components, the latter consideration probably is closely related to age as well. Older people may have more deeply formed associations in their current location (a lifetime accumulation of this form of "social capital"); even more decisively, they probably feel less ability to re-create such relationships in a new location than do young people.

A discrimination by destination is important too. The "loss" of friends and relatives is not absolute simply because of moving away from them. Continued contacts with them are possible—although less frequent or protracted than previously. The expected degree of continued contact is probably strongly inversely related to distance in a nonlinear relationship: Degree falls away rapidly at first with distance, but progressively more slowly, until a nearly zero marginal impact of distance on degree is reached.

D. CHANGE IN LIFE STYLE

Change in style of life is listed here as a kind of cost. The same variable was earlier included as a form of benefit. The reason for duplicating it here is to separate the instances where it represents a positive incentive toward migration (benefit) from those where it is looked on with aversion. For a given set of life patterns in different locations the difference between these two attitudes seems entirely idiosyncratic: It depends on personality. This is an extreme aspect of the self-selection I have been emphasizing: where the very same prospects can be regarded as a gain by some, as a loss by others.

While the source of individual differences is personal, it has an external dimension as well. Different destinations will offer different styles of life, varying in degree of negative difference from the current style of life of individuals for whom this is a problem. The availability of graduated alternatives on this dimension will, as with other cost dimensions, decrease its net deterrent effect against all migration and convert its influence more toward that of informing a choice among potential destinations.

E. UNCERTAIN PROSPECTS

A final category of costs is the concern over what may be considered a quantum increase in the uncertainty of one's life, a dramatic loss of security. This is the mirror image of the perceived benefit from the adventure of significant change. Here, too, it is being included as a cost, to distinguish between situations in which significant change itself is prized or found repellent. It differs from the previous style of life category in that it is not so much the specific aesthetic–moral characteristics of the prospective new way of life but simply the *extent* of the change from the present that is decried.

Individual differences are very important here. Strong risk averters will be especially deterred. Another personal characteristic may be involved too. Up to now we have treated the strength of incentives to migrate as functions simply of the size of *differentials* between present and prospective locations, without having to ask as well about the *absolute* level of wellbeing achieved by a potential migrant in his present situation. This procedure is dictated by our conventional notion of rational choice. But an individual's attitude toward the newness of overall prospects—of substantial change in itself—may depend partly on whether he feels satisfied or unsatisfied in his present situation in an absolute sense, and in what degree. An individual feeling miserably unhappy in his present circumstances—not with respect to concrete alternatives but with his own sense of self, his hopes (or fantasies)—may be desperate enough to overcome whatever fears he may otherwise have about radical change in his life. An individual very happy currently in an absolute sense may satisfice—i.e., give vent to whatever risk conservatism he may have about his overall life prospects. In other words, he may leave well enough alone.

VI. Migration Choice: Information

Up to now we have spoken of the positive and negative influences bearing on the individual migration decision. Every one of them involves a factual content which has so far simply been assumed to be known with certainty. This assumption must now be called into question.

There is a critical asymmetry in the degree of certainty with which the different facts are known: The individual's actual present circumstances are presumably known with more certainty—less uncertainty—than any hypothetical or prospective circumstances. Moreover, there are likely to be important differences within the latter category. Alternative opportunities within the same location—obtainable by search behavior—are likely to be known better than opportunities at other locations.

The key variable underlying these degrees of uncertainty is information. Information is imperfect with respect to the several alternatives of choice. Information about the present location is imperfect in terms of future consequences resulting from a sheer continuance of present commitments, since these have stochastic elements that are intrinsically unknowable. This is of course shared for all alternative destinations as well. Moreover, opportunities inherent in the present location extend to situations that have not yet been sampled by additional search. The probabilities associated with these are not known with certainty either.

For alternative locations, information is likely to be even less satisfactory about (1) the mean and other moments of the distribution of outcome characteristics and (2) how well to trust the information that is available (i.e., the variance of the estimates in (1)).

The familiar self-selection of migrants applies here too: Individuals will differ with respect to the amounts of information they have about different destinations and with respect to their preference tradeoffs among prospects with different degrees of uncertainty.

Relevant information is available from general information media—TV, newspapers, books, magazines,—and from more personal sources, such as friends, relatives, and neighbors who have migrated and then either returned or remained in some form of direct or indirect correspondence. Empirical studies have established that the second channel is a very important one in influencing migration decisions. The amount and quality of information available from this source is probably a negative function of the distance between origin and each destination, and a positive function of the number of friends, relatives, and others from the same area who migrated to the destination earlier, and the number and recency of returnees.[3]

Information from general media is roughly equally available to all but is in fact used very differently by different individuals. The amount of voluntary exposure to this source, and the degree of efficiency in processing the information contained therein, are probably strongly positively associated with education level. As with the personal information channel, amount, and possibly also accuracy, of information about destination j in origin i are likely to be negatively related to distance between i and j. Here too, then, both individual and destination differences will interact to form double discriminations in the evaluational components that determine migration decisions.

Discrimination patterns concerning adequacy of information do not have quite the same significance in influencing migration as do discrimination patterns with respect to benefit and cost dimensions, however. In the latter they are unambiguous in direction of thrust. Here they are mediated by another idiosyncratic characteristic of the decision makers. Just because information at i is better (more trustworthy) concerning destination j than concerning destination k does not mean that j will exert greater attraction. Information about k may be less accurate—but

---

[3] As a determinant of migration from i to j, this stock of previous migrants from i to j proxies an additional consideration. It reflects the strength of previous incentives to migrate from i to j. Insofar as conditions have changed little, it therefore duplicates *all* of the aforementioned specific determinants. In empirical studies it must therefore be used with care.

more optimistic. If correctly compared with regard to trustworthiness by
an individual in i, it will have an effect similar to that of increasing the
variance of expected outcomes in k relative to j. But as noted earlier,
this higher variance may be an *attractive* characteristic for many people,
instead of a repellent one.

Most theoretical and empirical treatments of information have assumed that amount of information is unambiguously a positive attraction. To be consistent with the plunging propensities of some risk takers
(and the foregoing analysis suggests that the group of actual migrants
may well be less adversely affected by the prospect of risk than the
population as a whole), this can be interpreted as defining amount of
information as number of specific positive opportunities noted. But this
is surely a very special meaning of the term. Since part of the transmittal
of person-to-person information must consist of general descriptions and
promises as well as of specific instances, these general propositions may
be based on inadequate information at the destination sources. Amount
of information flow would help to correct (decrease the variance of)
these general assertions by increasing the size of the sample of such
assertions. But this does not prevent a very small sample of very
optimistic prognostications about a certain destination from becoming
more attractive to certain potential migrants than the more restrained,
better sampled claims about a different destination.

Thus it is not obvious that amount of information can be treated
unambiguously as a kind of benefit dimension. Its role in migration is
more complicated.

VII.   Migration Choice: Choice among Alternatives

From any origin, a given individual will choose, among all potential
destinations (including the status quo), that one promising the greatest
expected utility increase: a combination of the net effects of the various
benefit and cost dimensions discussed and the qualifications imposed by
relative degrees of information. This means that for this individual the
probabilities of a move by him from i to each of the alternative
destinations are all interdependent, since all alternatives are simultaneously competing against one another in the choice. This interdependence
has significance for the econometric procedures that can be used to
study migration choice empirically.[4]

For a given individual, the probability of moving from a given origin

---

[4] It has been suggested that this makes modeling the determinants of migration from
alternative origins to a single destination preferable to modeling the determinants of
migration from a single origin to alternative destinations. See, for example, Lucas (1975a).

to a particular destination depends on the net attractiveness of that particular move relative to that of all other possible moves (or remaining at the origin). If benefits from alternative moves are not positively associated with distance from origin to destination, then, since total costs *are* probably a monotonically increasing function of distance, the probability of a move from i to some j is partly a measure of the size of the set of intervening net opportunities—i.e., the attractiveness of all destinations closer than j.

With this role played by distance, the distance variable can now be seen as a composite of at least four distinct, but probably mutually consistent, roles in influencing migration:

a. It has a positive impact on moving costs

b. It has a positive impact on the utility significance of the "loss" of friends and relatives

c. It is inversely related to the adequacy of information about the destination

d. It is positively related to the maximum size of the net attractiveness of intervening destinations between i and j.

Thus, the overall negative impact carried by distance on the probability of choosing a particular destination is probably far in excess of the importance of sheer moving costs over that distance.

References

David, P. A. Fortune, risk, and the microeconomics of migration. In *Nations and Households in Economic Growth: Essays in Honor of Moses Abramovitz*. New York: Academic Press, 1974.

Greenwood, M. J., and L. E. Preston. Research on internal migration in the U.S.: A survey, *Journal of Economic Literature*, 1975, *13*(2).

Harris, J., and M. Todaro. Migration, unemployment and development: A two-sector analysis. *American Economic Review*, 1970, *60*(1).

Krugman, P., and J. Bhagwati. The decision to migrate: A survey. Massachusetts Institute of Technology, June 1975.

Lucas, R. E. B. The supply-of-immigrants function and taxation of immigrants' incomes: An econometric analysis. University of California, Los Angeles, April 1975. (a)

Lucas, R. E. B. Internal migration and economic development: An overview. University of California, Los Angeles, July 1975. (b)

Magoulas, G., K. Peschel, and M. Wadehn. Determinants of commuting and migration. Discussion Papers of the Institute of Regional Research at the University of Kiel, 1975.

Renaud, B. The specification and estimation of economic models of internal migration. International Bank for Reconstruction and Development, 1975.

Renshaw, V. The role of migration in labor market adjustment. Unpublished Ph. D. Dissertation, Massachusetts Institute of Technology, 1970.

Yap, L. Y. L. Internal migration in less developed countries: A survey of the literature. International Bank for Reconstruction and Development, Assignment #19, April 1975.

Selected Case Studies

SECTION A

Migration in the West

Internal Migration in
the Mature American City

James T. Little
Charles L. Leven

In the first half of this century, the United States became a nation of urbanites. This was reflected in rates of population growth for large urban areas well above that of the country as a whole. In the last two decades, however, there has been a reversal of this trend. More than half of the metropolitan areas with populations of more than one million are growing at rates less than the national rate of population growth. [By urban areas and metropolitan areas, we refer to Standard Metropolitan Statistical Areas (SMSAs), not simply central cities.] As shown in Table 13.1, these cities—predominantly located in the northeastern quarter of the country—had growth rates ranging from 14.8% for Baltimore and Kansas City to a negative .2% for the Pittsburgh metropolitan area. Intercensus estimates since 1970 indicate that several other of these metropolitan areas are now showing declining populations.

These SMSAs can properly be called mature urban areas. Their share of total population is constant or declining. Few of them are centers of rapidly growing industries, and thus their economic bases tend to be relatively fixed in composition and scale of employment. At the same time, these areas are not static. They have experienced internal shifts in population and employment location that have consequences as dramatic as those of rapid growth. In almost all the mature SMSAs, the population of the central city has declined. At the same time, suburban areas in these cities have shown rapid increases in population in many

TABLE 13.1

POPULATION GROWTH IN METROPOLITAN AREAS OF ONE MILLION POPULATION
OR MORE, 1960–1970

Metropolitan Area	Percentage change in population	Percentage change in central city population
Above the national average:		
Anaheim, California	101.8	0
San Bernardino, California	41.2	38.6
Houston, Texas	40.0	31.2
Dallas, Texas	39.0	24.2
Washington, D.C.	37.8	−1.0
Atlanta, Georgia	36.7	2.0
Miami, Florida	35.6	14.8
Denver, Colorado	32.1	4.2
San Diego, California	31.4	21.1
Seattle, Washington	28.4	−4.7
Minneapolis, Minnesota	22.4	−6.5
San Francisco, California	17.4	3.3
Los Angeles, California	16.4	23.3
Below the national average:		
Baltimore, Maryland	14.8	−3.6
Kansas City, Missouri	14.8	5.5
Paterson, New Jersey	14.5	0.8
St. Louis, Missouri	12.3	−17.0
Chicago, Illinois	12.2	−5.2
Detroit, Michigan	11.6	−9.5
Philadelphia, Pennsylvania	10.9	−2.7
Newark, New Jersey	9.9	−5.6
Milwaukee, Wisconsin	9.8	−3.3
Cincinnati, Ohio	9.2	−10.0
Cleveland, Ohio	8.1	−14.3
New York, New York	7.8	−5.6
Boston, Massachusetts	6.1	−8.1
Buffalo, New York	3.2	−13.1
Pittsburgh, Pennsylvania	−0.2	−13.9

Source: Census of Population, 1970

cases, to the point where the suburbs have a majority of the metropolitan population. The experience of the St. Louis SMSA typifies these trends: Between 1960 and 1970, the population of the city of St. Louis declined 17% while suburban St. Louis County grew by 35% and St. Charles County by 80%. Recent estimates show the population of the entire SMSA to be declining, but at the same time St. Charles County to be the fourth fastest growing county in the entire nation.

One manifestation of this trend is a phenomenon that has come to be known as "urban decay." (For a detailed description see Institute for Urban & Regional Studies, 1972). Together with declining central city population, the most overt symptoms of this process are depopulation of entire neighborhoods and the physical decay of dwelling units, leading ultimately to abandonment and demolition of structures and often accompanied by the abandonment and demolition of commercial structures and such public facilities as schools and fire and police stations. An important aspect of the urban decay process is the fall in the ratio of central city median family income to the SMSA median. This reflects the fact that the households that have left the central city were primarily those with higher incomes. Since, in the American system, many of the services to those with lower incomes are provided by local government, central city governments face a fiscal dilemma in that their tax base, taxable capacity, and tax collections have fallen faster than service demands. This fiscal dilemma has been offset in part by the expansion of state and federal grant-in-aid programs and the federal revenue-sharing plan, but many of the central city governments in the mature SMSAs remain in dire financial straits.

Our main concern here is to attempt to explain the internal population shifts that have produced the phenomenon of urban decay—in particular the spatial dynamics of the housing market and the implications of this dynamic for internal migration in such areas. In the mature SMSA, three factors have an important effect on the demand for housing and its spatial pattern. The first of these is change in the level of income. A change in the level of a family's income will in general change that household's most preferred housing; a generalized increase in income will produce a change in the most preferred housing bundle for a large segment of the population. Another aspect of this change stems from "life cycle effects." As a family moves through the life cycle, there is a change both in income and in family composition which changes its housing demand and thereby induces migration. If there are changes in the overall age distribution of the population, there will be a change in total demand and in the spatial pattern of population distribution.

The second factor in the spatial dynamic is the nature of the housing itself as a commodity. Conceptually, housing is a multidimensional commodity. With the purchase of a unit, a household acquires a particular structure, a location relative to employment and commercial centers, a physical and socioeconomic neighborhood, and the right to consume the goods and services provided by the relevant local government as well as the responsibility to pay a share of the costs of producing these goods and services. The latter three of these dimensions are spatial in nature and are essentially beyond the control of the individual household. Thus, in choosing housing, households face constraints on the spatial distribution of alternatives. As a result, changes in the spatial distribution of these dimensions change the spatial pattern of demand for housing and produce internal migration.

An important consequence of the multidimensionality of housing is its effect on dynamics at the neighborhood level. Actual or expected changes in the demographic or public sector dimensions of a neighborhood will produce changes in demand for housing in that neighborhood, with the result that actual changes are intensified and expectations frequently are self-fulfilling. This phenomenon manifests itself in high rates of outward migration, sharp changes in the value of housing units, and destabilization of expectations. Given the substitutability of housing across neighborhoods, this dynamic forms the basis of the larger dynamic which ultimately ends in abandonment, demolition, and neighborhood depopulation.

The third factor is the conditions for the supply of new housing and new space. New urban space is created through improvement in the transport system. Not only does an improved transport system reduce the access cost of existing urban locations, but also it results in absorption of rural land into the urban area. A second aspect of supply conditions is the existence of a well-developed, government-subsidized capital market for the construction of new housing. The net effect of the supply situation is that it allows households to "create" housing bundles which are preferable to those available, at a price that makes these new units economically viable.

In the following section, we consider these factors in somewhat more detail. We then proceed to show the effect of changes in income levels and transport costs on·the spatial distribution of population and income through the comparative statics of the Alonso–Muth–Beckmann type of residential location model. In the section following, we consider the neighborhood dynamic in more detail, developing the concept formally and drawing on some empirical data from the St. Louis metropolitan area. Finally, we return to the urban decay process and discuss the economic efficiency of the process and its effect on individual welfare.

I. Some Economic Aspects of Internal Migration

Perhaps the most elementary reason for interneighborhood migration would be a change in preferences for particular kinds of housing units by different kinds of families. It has often been argued, for example, that suburbanization is a result of a change in the modal preference among city dwellers from high access housing to lower density housing. One implication of this argument is that suburbs are a relatively recent phenomenon, as are trends toward lower central city densities. Historically, however, such is not the case. Low-density suburbs first appeared in the early nineteenth century, and the period 1870 to 1910 (predating the automobile) saw a period of suburbanization paralleled only by the post–World War II period (for a discussion of early suburbanization see Warner, 1963, and Holt, forthcoming, Chapters 3 & 4). Furthermore, average population densities of urban areas and central city densities have both been falling since the late nineteenth century (see Taeuber, 1973). Thus, it appears that no dramatic shift in preferences has occurred, even taking an 80-year period that includes the spread of automobile ownership.

Comparison of the suburbanization of the late nineteenth century and postwar suburbanization yields some insight into common forces producing both streams of internal migration. In both periods, transport systems experienced fundamental changes: In the earlier period, railways and electric trams became important modes, while in the latter period freeway technology was implemented. Furthermore, in both periods there was rapidly increasing family income. Thus, there is strong evidence to suggest that income level and transport costs have both been fundamental in determining urban form, along with kinds of housing and prevailing local government institutions.

Another dynamic of internal migration is changes in family composition. As household heads progress, from unmarried adults to young marrieds with small children to older couples whose children are grown to widowers and widows, their housing needs change drastically. Assuming a housing stock of unchanging physical characteristics, these changes in demand manifest themselves as orderly movements between neighborhoods, with unchanging family composition in a given neighborhood. However, as the data on neighborhood family and age composition for the St. Louis area shown in Table 13.2 indicate, significant changes within individual neighborhoods have occurred in a relatively short time span.

The central explanatory variable in most models of housing investment is the age of the housing stock. The roots of this theory are largely empirical. Homer Hoyt, for example, observed that as cities grow and age there is a tendency for higher income households to vacate existing dwelling units in favor of new housing. In turn, these households are replaced by households of somewhat lower income. The housing va-

TABLE 13.2

CHANGES IN POPULATION AND FAMILY COMPOSITION, ST. LOUIS, SELECTED NEIGHBORHOODS, 1960–1970

Area	Population 1970	Percentage population change 1960–1970	Percentage of population aged 65+		Percentage of population nonwhite		Percentage of families with female head		Percentage of families with children under 18	
			1960	1970	1960	1970	1960[a]	1970	1960	1970
Inner city:										
Census tract 1203	7,509	− 32.4	8.6	8.2	9.7	67.2	21.6	32.2	60.9	62.9
Census tract 1224	7,403	− 41.3	9.0	9.4	10.9	70.9	34.7	44.0	65.2	70.5
Census tract 1241	7,528	− 17.2	14.3	16.4	0.0	0.0	17.1	15.7	49.1	43.0
Outlying central city:										
Census tract 1022	8,274	− 24.4	16.5	23.8	0.0	0.0	12.8	11.5	34.4	33.1
Census tract 1065	7,337	− 10.1	7.3	8.7	79.8	96.0	24.9	24.4	51.6	52.1
Census tract 1076	4,168	+137.2	14.8	8.2	6.4	79.4	22.0	17.3	42.8	56.5
Inner suburbs:										
Wellston	7,050	− 11.6	10.7	8.1	8.7	69.0	16.3	26.9	53.9	61.5
University City	46,309	− 9.6	12.1	16.9	0.4	21.2	13.6	12.4	52.3	43.7
Webster Groves	27,455	− 6.9	10.5	11.9	3.8	5.1	9.8	8.7	57.4	52.6
Outer suburbs:										
Florissant	65,908	+ 72.7	2.3	3.1	0.1	0.3	2.9	4.7	80.0	73.3
Frontenac–Des Peres	7,001	+ 49.6	4.3	6.1	0.4	0.1	3.0	4.0	67.5	60.8
Kirkwood	31,769	+ 8.4	7.5	10.3	3.2	6.6	8.4	8.3	63.7	54.9
Exurbia:										
St. Charles	31,384	—[b]	7.1	7.8	1.2	1.6	8.7	7.7	67.2	61.7
St. Louis SMSA	2,363,017	+ 14.7	9.3	9.8	14.3	16.0	14.4	11.5	57.0	55.5

[a] Includes a small number of male household heads who are widowers.
[b] Not available due to census definition changes.
Source: U.S. Census.

214

cated by this second group of households is then reoccupied by households of still lower income. Thus, there is a general movement of households to newer housing, with the oldest units either abandoned or occupied by low income inmigrants, traditionally from smaller SMSAs or rural areas (see Hoyt, 1939, and, for an earlier example, see Park, Burgess, and McKenzie, 1925).

Two forces are seen as underlying this empirical tendency. The first is a preference on the part of higher income households for new housing. The second—and the more important—is the correlation between age and quality of housing. In other words, it is assumed that housing depreciates through normal use and therefore that the flow of services from a new house is ceteris paribus greater than that from an already standing unit. It is not clear, however, that quality per se is related to age. As Lowry points out, the physical quality of a unit depends on the maintenance pattern, and therefore a well-maintained older house can be of higher physical quality than a poorly maintained, recently constructed unit (see Lowry, 1960). A more fundamental way in which age is related to housing services is through the technology employed in the unit.

Clearly, the newer the house, the more modern are such features as the heating and cooling plant, the electric wiring, and the plumbing system. Thus, the observed premium for newer housing may be in part a premium paid for higher quality durables. However, older houses can be converted to newer technologies, even though it may be more expensive to convert an older house than a newer one. This would imply that two units with equivalent space and structural quality, but of different age, still might not sell for the same price, given the additional cost of converting the older house to the new technology. However, this is a price effect and not a preference effect, and changes in the conversion cost for the older house could reduce the apparent premium on "newness." It could even be argued that this price effect occurs because of market imperfections, in that loans for rehabilitation and upgrading are of shorter term and at higher interest rates than loans for new construction.

Empirically speaking, it is difficult to factor out the effect of age on housing values. As Hoyt observed and as Table 13.3 indicates, the age of a unit tends to be highly correlated with the socioeconomic characteristics of the neighborhood in which it is located. Using factor analysis to create composite measures of these interrelated variables and regressing the factors on housing values, we have shown that in St. Louis housing values are significantly related to these characteristics. As seen in Table 13.4, the independent contribution of age alone is fairly small, while median income in the neighborhood has a much greater influence on

TABLE 13.3

CORRELATION COEFFICIENTS: STRUCTURAL CHARACTERISTICS, AGE, AND NEIGHBORHOOD CHARACTERISTICS, ST. LOUIS, 1970

	Living area	Rooms	Baths	Years old	Percentage of renter occupants	Percentage of female-headed households	Percentage nonwhite	Percentage with nonwhite adjoining neighborhood	Median income
Living area	1.00								
Rooms	.81	1.00							
Baths	.53	.54	1.00						
Years old (age)	.23	.03	-.15	1.00					
Percentage of renter occupants	.32	.14	0	.58	1.00				
Percentage of female-headed households	.23	.05	-.13	.72	.72	1.00			
Percentage nonwhite	.10	.08	-.13	.52	.42	.77	1.00		
Percentage with nonwhite adjoining neighborhood	.08	-.03	-.17	.53	.38	.66	.72	1.00	
Median income	-.02	-.05	.27	-.65	-.65	-.53	-.56	-.60	1.00

TABLE 13.4

REGRESSION COEFFICIENTS OF STRUCTURAL, AGE AND NEIGHBORHOOD
VARIABLES ON SELLING PRICE OF OWNER-OCCUPIED HOUSING, ST. LOUIS, 1970

Characteristic	Coefficient
Living area (sq ft)	6.9
Rooms	3684.9
Bedrooms	3944.7
Baths	9242.4
Years old	−252.3
% Renter	−237.0
% Female heads	−794.3
% Nonwhite	−164.4
% NW-adj. tract	−137.8
Median income ($100)	250.0

property values. However, this by itself does not deny the role of age as
an explanatory factor. (For a complete description of these results, see
Little, 1976.)

Another way in which the effect of age on values can be determined is
through tracking of property values as aging and socioeconomic change
occurs. Recent experience in University City, an inner suburb of the St.
Louis metropolitan area (1970 population about 47,000), provides an
excellent example. During the latter part of the 1960s, the northern half
of University City experienced substantial racial change accompanied
by a fall in income rank. This change was accompanied by falling
housing prices (in real terms) and declining prices—standardized for
physical differences in the units—relative to neighborhoods with predominantly older housing. For example, one of these northern University City neighborhoods fell six ranks in terms of standardized price in a
sample of 30 neighborhoods over this period (see Little, 1976; and Little,
1973).

An examination of the effect of changes in racial composition,
changes in income, and the age of housing in neighborhoods on the
change in the price differentials is even more revealing. While older
neighborhoods did decline in value relative to newer neighborhoods, age
explained less than 1% of the variation in differentials. The most
powerful explanatory value was racial composition. That race should
explain more than income is somewhat surprising, given that the cross-
section analysis indicates that income differences in neighborhoods are
more important than race in explaining price differentials. It would

appear that the correlation between changes in neighborhood income and racial changes lies behind this apparent contradiction. Of neighborhoods included in the time series analysis, only neighborhoods experiencing racial change experienced income change. Thus, racial change also causes income change, and consequently the effect of changing racial composition on changes in interneighborhood price differentials reflects the income change as well. This could be interpreted as indicating that market participants consider racial change a signal of actual or impending income change, even without their having aversion to nonwhites, though such aversion could still be operating as an additional (though probably weaker) factor in its own right.

Given the importance of socioeconomic characteristics in explaining neighborhood price differentials, it follows from a revealed preference argument that such characteristics are an important element in households' preferences and, consequently, in the neighborhood pattern of demand for housing. Thus, changes in the characteristics of neighborhoods, or impending changes, are an important motivating force in internal migration patterns. It also follows that the larger the number of relatively low-income households in the urban area and the larger the number of nonwhites—especially if they have low incomes—the more probable are high rates of internal migration. This is borne out by the experience in the mature SMSAs. Almost all of these areas have a disproportionate number of families below the poverty line and relatively large nonwhite populations. At the same time, they have experienced and are experiencing sharp changes in the spatial pattern of housing demand and population distribution.

A further factor in the spatial pattern of housing demand is differences in public services. In the American political system, local decisions as to the public production of goods and services and the financing of this production represent a larger share of the total public sector than in most other Western nations. Furthermore, the typical SMSA has multiple municipalities offering differentiated services. St. Louis County, for example, has 97 different municipalities; Los Angeles County has 233 local governmental units, of which 76 are municipalities (the others are special districts). Thus, households, in choosing housing, in part choose the local public goods and services that best suit their preferences.

In a world of static local public sectors, that is fixed local budgets, these differences should produce no intraurban moves other than those stemming from life-cycle motivations. However, with changes in income and income distribution, static local budgets will lead to additional moves. As a household's income rises, its demand for public goods changes and it may find that the community in which it resides does not provide the bundle of public goods closest to its most preferred bundle. Thus, if housing that is equivalent in all other dimensions is available in another community, a move will result. If income change is at all general, there will be a tendency for house prices in the preferred community to be bid up as the housing demand shifts toward it. At the same time, falling prices in the former community might result in the inmovement of households who prefer the bundle of public goods available there to those available in their original community. Thus, a chain of moves can result.

Another important aspect of the local public sector is the overall progressivity of the local budget. While the major source of local funds—the property tax—is regressive, the benefits of local expenditures more than offset this effect, since they go more than proportionately to low-income households. Thus, high-income households usually pay a larger share of taxes than their share of benefits (see Netzer, 1966). This produces an incentive for higher-income households to break away from any political unit and form separate communities of their own. The further the income of a household from that of the modal voter, the stronger is this motivation. Thus, the desire on the part of higher-income households to escape the progressivity of the local public sector becomes an important factor in their outmigration from the central cities of mature urban areas. This also explains in part the declining ratio of central city median income to the median for the SMSA as a whole.

II. The Income–Transport Cost Dynamic

Here, we consider the effects of changing income and changing transport costs in a city where all households have the same preferences regarding housing, leisure, and all other goods, although differing in their incomes. All trips are to the central business district (CBD) and transport costs increase monotonically with distance from the center. Housing is produced with land and capital in varying proportions. Several well-developed models exist which analyze the equilibrium properties of such systems—for example those of Alonso (1970), Muth (1969), and Beckmann (1974). We consider the effect of changes in the level of aggregate income on the spatial income distribution and population distribution, through an analysis of the comparative statics of the Beckmann model.

All households are assumed to have a utility function of the form:

$$U = a_0 \log c + a_1 \log s + a_2 \log t \tag{1}$$

where s is the consumption of housing, t is the leisure time, and c is the consumption of other goods and services. Since preferences are homothetic—implying that income elasticities of demand for all commodities are unitary—demand behavior for all households can be generated from the behavior of a representative household with income y. This household maximizes its utility as constrained by its income and its total time endowment. The number of trips to the CBD is fixed, and travel time from any distance r from the city center increases monotonically with distance. It follows that the equilibrium pattern of housing prices must be:

$$p(r) = p_0(T - kr)^{a_2/a_1} \tag{2}$$

where $p(r)$ is the price of housing (per square foot) at distance r, p_0 is the price of housing at the boundary of the CBD, T is the total time endowment, and kr is the time consumed in CBD trips from distance r.

Equation (2) represents the spatial demand for housing in the sense that it represents the only spatial pattern of housing prices that is consistent with maximizing behavior. It should be noted that this demand is independent of the income of the representative household. Hence, an increase in the income of all households affects the equilibrium only in so far as it alters the price of housing at the boundary of the CBD.

The supply of housing is given by:

$$h = bx^\beta \tag{3}$$

where h is the amount of housing per unit of land, x is the amount of capital per unit of land, and $b > 0$, $0 < \beta < 1$. From (3) we obtain the housing supply function:

$$h(r) = b^{(1/c-\beta)}[\beta p(r)]^{\beta/1-\beta}/c \tag{4}$$

where c is the annual cost of capital.

The role of the market-clearing condition is to determine the price of housing at the boundary of the CBD. This is given by:

$$P_0 = [\bar{Y}/\gamma(r_0, r_1)]^{1-\beta} \tag{5}$$

where

$$\gamma(r_0, r_1) = \frac{r_0(T - kr_0)^{1+m}}{k(1 + m)} + \frac{(T - kr_0)^{2+m}}{k^2(1 + m)(2 + m)}$$

and

$$m = (a_2/a_1) \cdot (1/1 - \beta)$$

and r_0 is the inner radius of the residential zone (equal to radius of CBD) and r_1 is the outer limit of the zone which is equal to the maximum feasible distance, $r_{max} = T/k$. Thus, the boundary price depends on aggregate city income, the travel time from the inner radius of the CBD to the center of the CBD, and the parameters of the utility function and housing production function.

In the derivation of this CBD boundary price, we obtain a relationship between aggregate income and distance:

$$Y(r) = (a_0 + a_1/a_1)2\pi b^{1/(1-\beta)}(\beta/c)^{\beta/(1-\beta)}p(r)^{1/(1-\beta)}r \tag{6}$$

The sign of $dY(r)/dr$ is indeterminate, and thus the model makes no prediction as to the shape of the income gradient: It may be positively or negatively sloped depending on the values of the parameters of the system.

For our analysis, we are concerned principally with the effect of changes in aggregate city income and in travel costs on the spatial patterns of demand for housing, supply of housing, and income. First, we consider the effect of an increase in city income. Since travel costs do not change, the geographic extent of the residential zone remains constant. Furthermore, given the homotheticity of the utility functions, there are proportional increases in the demand for housing, access, and all other goods. Taking both the simple and the logarithmic derivatives of $p(r)$, $h(r)$, and $Y(r)$ with respect to $\bar{Y}$, we obtain:

$$\frac{dp(r)}{d\bar{Y}} = [(1 - \beta)/\bar{Y}]p(r) > 0; \qquad \frac{d^2 \log p(r)}{d\bar{Y}\,dr} = 0 \tag{7}$$

$$\frac{dh(r)}{d\bar{Y}} = (\beta/\bar{Y})h(r) > 0; \qquad \frac{d^2 \log h(r)}{d\bar{Y}\,dr} = 0 \tag{8}$$

$$\frac{dY(r)}{d\bar{Y}} = (1/\bar{Y})Y(r) > 0; \qquad \frac{d^2 \log Y(r)}{d\bar{Y}\,dr} = 0 \tag{9}$$

Thus, in the new equilibrium, house prices, supply of housing, and aggregate income are higher at all distances from the CBD. Also, the increase in these values is proportionate to the values in the old equilibrium. The increase in income therefore produces spatially proportionate growth. This implies that a growth in income should not produce migration, since the market responds by proportionately increasing the supply of housing at all distances. If we assume that the total number of households has remained fixed and that the income of each household has risen proportionately, each household is able to obtain exactly that amount of housing it wishes as its location in the initial equilibrium.

Let us now assume that the increase in income was not distributed over households in proportion to their initial income. Further, let us assume that the households which experience this more than proportionate increase in income live in the ring from r_0 to $\bar{r}$. The supply of housing in the new equilibrium increases in proportion to the increase in aggregate income at all distances. However, households living in the ring r_0 to $\bar{r}$ will increase their housing consumption more than proportionately, while those in the ring from $\bar{r}$ to r_{max} will increase their demand less than proportionately in the new equilibrium. This implies that as the housing market converges to the new equilibrium, some households will migrate from the inner ring to the outer ring. Under these assumptions, the number of households migrating between rings will depend on the differential rate of growth of incomes of the two groups: the larger the differential, the larger the flow of migrating households.

While this analysis probably does not explain the outflow of households from the central cities of mature SMSAs in the second half of the 1960s, it is consistent with the outward migration of lower-echelon white-collar and blue-collar workers during the 1950s. During that period, incomes of all occupational categories were rising, with these particular groups experiencing more rapid increases than the average. Since these households were predominantly located in the central cities as of 1950, this differential rate of income growth would produce outflows of these groups after that time.

It should be noted that, within this model, population increases are coincident with income increases. That is, an increasing population does produce an increase in aggregate SMSA income, and the effects of this change on the spatial pattern of housing demand and income distribution can be analyzed in terms of that income increase.

While income affects the spatial distribution of housing prices, land use, and income only through differential rates of income growth, changes in the transport system have a direct effect. In the model, these changes are reflected in changes in k: as improvements in the transport system reduce the time required for travel to the CBD, k falls. Similarly, as commercial establishments decentralize, the number of CBD trips is reduced. On the other hand, as population and congestion increase, k will rise.

The immediate effect of such changes in the transport system is a change in the effective size of the urban area. As k falls, r_{max} increases as the maximum feasible trip to the CBD increases. Similarly, an increase in k will produce a reduction in size. Intuitively then, without a change in aggregate city income, the total number of housing units in the developed area and its income should fall. This in fact is the case, but, unlike the case with income, these changes are not spatially symmetric.

For all three spatial distributions—$p(r)$, $h(r)$ and $Y(r)$—the derivatives with respect to k are positive if and only if:

$$P_0 \frac{a_1}{a_2} \frac{dp_0}{dk} \geq \frac{r}{T - kr} \tag{10}$$

The left side of this equality is independent of r, as it depends only on the change in the price of housing at the boundary of the CBD. As might be expected, this derivative is positive, which implies that increases in k lead to increases in the CBD boundary price and reductions in k lead to reductions in the CBD boundary price. The magnitude of the derivative depends on aggregate income, the total time endowment, and the parameters of the utility and housing supply functions. It should be noted that the greater the magnitude of $\bar{Y}$, the greater will be the magnitude of dp_0/dk.

The right-hand side of (10) is zero at the CBD and approaches infinity as r approaches r_{max}. This implies that there exists a distance, $\bar{r}$, such that for all distances greater than $\bar{r}$ the inequality (10) holds, with $\bar{r}$ strictly less than r_{max}. This implies that growth occurs in one portion and declines in another. For all distances less than $\bar{r}$, $dp(r)/dk$, $dh(r)/dk$, and $dY(r)/dk$ are negative and for all distances greater than $\bar{r}$, $dp(r)/dk$, $dh(r)/dk$, and $dY(r)/dk$ are positive. This implies that the amount of housing, the price of housing, and the income at any distance less than $\bar{r}$ fall as k falls and rise in the area in which r is greater than $\bar{r}$ (see Figure 13.1). Since we have assumed that the number of households and aggregate city income have not changed, this implies that the number of households residing in the inner ring must fall while rising in the outer ring or that households in the outer ring are replaced by higher income households from the inner ring. Thus, two possible migration patterns are possible: a net outmigration from the inner ring or a balancing flow in terms of number but accompanied by an increase in total income and housing consumption of households in the outer ring.

Clearly, this prediction bears up well under empirical verification. The migration patterns described have been manifest in all the mature SMSAs during or shortly following their adoption of expressway technology. Indeed, the declining density gradients of this century in American cities—as the automobile technology was adopted—would follow from the diminished transport times. (For an analysis of changes

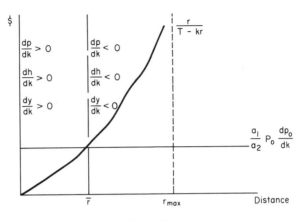

Figure 13.1

in density gradients over time, see Mills, 1972, Chapter 3; and Harrison and Kain, 1974.)

In the St. Louis metropolitan area, the first major expressways were completed in the late 1950s, with an extensive system in place by 1970. This development was accompanied by a fall in population of the inner ring in the periods 1950–1960 and 1960–1970. The inner ring of suburbs grew slightly during the first period but declined in population during the second. At the same time, outer ring suburbs were experiencing rates of population growth as high as 1000%.

While the Beckmann model does not directly yield predictions as to the length of the internal moves, it does suggest that longer moves will occur more frequently than shorter moves. Neighborhoods in the vicinity of $\bar{r}$ will be relatively stable, in that the demand for housing in these areas is not significantly altered relative to the initial equilibrium. The areas with the largest changes in income and supply of housing are those areas in the vicinity of the inner boundary of the outer limit of the city. Thus, the general pattern of migration could be expected to be of the "leapfrogging" type, in which migrating households move several neighborhoods farther away from the center, rather than to adjacent neighborhoods. Empirical evidence on migration patterns during the period 1967–1971 for one of the inner ring suburbs of St. Louis bears out this expectation. Nearly 60% of the outmigrant households moved more than 5 miles farther from the city center. Less than 10% of the outmigrants moved closer to the city center, and a significant number of this latter group were elderly people moving to public housing (for details, see Little, 1973).

However, other evidence gathered in this community suggests that the income–transport dynamic does not provide a complete explanation of mobility in the mature city. Since the community was located in the inner ring of suburbs, in the vicinity of the distance from the center at which no population changes occurred, it could be expected that housing prices would be relatively stable. Such was not the case: Prices of housing fell substantially in real terms during the period. There was no significant downgrading of the housing stock or removal of units during the period. On the other hand, substantial racial change did occur early in the period, with falls in real median income in the latter portion of the period. This suggests that housing demand as it manifests itself in bid prices depends not only on locational factors but also on the demographic composition of neighborhoods. In the next section, we show how households' preferences for the socioeconomic character of a neighborhood might affect equilibrium locations of households and prices.

III. The Neighborhood Preference Dynamic

As discussed in the previous section, part of the differentials in housing prices (standardized for structural differences) can be explained by differences in the socioeconomic characteristics of neighborhoods. This implies that an important element in the decisions of individual households is the "neighborhood" in which alternative units are located. More generally, it implies that locational decisions of households are interdependent; that is, the decisions of a household can affect the welfare of another household directly, rather than just through the effect of its decisions on aggregate demand for housing and on housing prices. In this section, we consider a rather simple example of the market allocation process which takes these interdependencies into account and illustrates how they lead to *continued* high rates of migration even in a situation where the number of units, the number of households, and the incomes of these households is fixed.

We assume three households (or equivalently three groups of identical households) and three identical housing units. Households incomes are the following:

Household 1:   income $840
Household 2:   income $1680
Household 3:   income $2520

It is also assumed that households have utility functions that are separable in housing, other commodities, and neighborhood. In particular, these utility functions generate bid functions for housing that depend on the particular assignment of households to locations, where the assignment is represented by a 3 × 3 permutation matrix P. The bid functions of the three households are given by:

$$b_{i1} = Y_1/100$$

$$b_{i2} = Y_2/100 - 50P_{i-1,1} - 50P_{i+1,1}$$

$$b_{i3} = Y_3/100 - 70P_{i-1,1} - 70P_{i+1,1}$$

where b_i is the bid price for the ith neighborhood by the jth household, y_j the income of the jth household and P_{i1} the element of the assignment matrix for individual 1. The bid functions represent the maximum amounts the households are willing to pay to live at each location. In this particular set of bid functions, household 1 is indifferent as to the identity of his neighbors (he would pay the same in any neighborhood), while households 2 and 3 prefer not to live next to household 1 and therefore are willing to pay a premium for any location that is not adjacent to 1's location. Given any initial assignment, the real estate market is assumed to operate so as to maximize the sum of bids; that is, to maximize $\Sigma_i \Sigma_j P_{ij}b_{ij}(P)$, subject to the constraint that the new assignment P be a permutation matrix. Thus, this is a linear assignment problem of the Koopmans–Beckmann type (see Koopmans and Beckmann, 1957).

Assume the households are initially assigned by:

$$P_i = \begin{pmatrix} 1 & 0 & 0 \\ 0 & 1 & 0 \\ 0 & 0 & 1 \end{pmatrix}$$

Given this assignment, the bid matrix is:

$$B(P_1) = \begin{pmatrix} 84 & 84 & 84 \\ 168 & 118 & 168 \\ 252 & 177 & 252 \end{pmatrix}$$

and the new assignment which results

$$P_2 = \begin{pmatrix} 0 & 1 & 0 \\ 1 & 0 & 0 \\ 0 & 0 & 1 \end{pmatrix}.$$

Thus, the new assignment results from an exchange between the low- and middle-income households. However, this new assignment generates the bid matrix:

$$B(P_2) = \begin{pmatrix} 84 & 84 & 84 \\ 118 & 168 & 118 \\ 177 & 252 & 177 \end{pmatrix},$$

and, with efficient operation of the real estate market, the new assignment would be:

$$P_3 = \begin{pmatrix} 0 & 0 & 1 \\ 1 & 0 & 0 \\ 0 & 1 & 0 \end{pmatrix},$$

which represents an exchange of locations between the low-income and the high-income households. This assignment produces the new bid matrix:

$$B(P_3) = \begin{pmatrix} 84 & 84 & 84 \\ 168 & 118 & 168 \\ 252 & 177 & 252 \end{pmatrix}$$

together with a new assignment:

$$P_4 = \begin{pmatrix} 0 & 1 & 0 \\ 1 & 0 & 0 \\ 0 & 0 & 1 \end{pmatrix}.$$

However, the assignment P_4 is identical with P_2 and thus, from this point on, the assignment will cycle between P_2 and P_3. The implication of this cycling is that the system never achieves an equilbrium assignment. This can be contrasted with the case in which the bid functions do not depend on the assignment; for example:

$$B_{i1} = Y_1/100$$

$$b_{i2} = Y_2/100$$

$$b_{i3} = Y_3/100$$

In this case, any assignment is stable.

Thus, with the introduction of these locational interdependencies, the possibility arises that the housing market is in perpetual disequilibrium, in the sense that there is always an exchange that will make the trading partners better off. However, as a consequence of this trade, a third party may experience changes in utility that are sufficient to induce him to engage in a trade to offset these utility changes. In the more general case, allowing for differences in structural and locational characteristics, the system may move to equilibrium. This system, however, is extremely sensitive to income changes, and it is possible that change in the income of the low-income household will set the system cycling.

It should be noted that, while the path would differ, the same general properties would hold if households 1 and 3 preferred not to live adjacent to the middle-income household. Thus, we are not asserting that income per se contributes to the instability but rather that some households care about the identity of their neighbors. In the current example, the preference for not living near the first household might result from the fact that he makes a practice of burning tires in his backyard or that he is of a different religion, race, or ethnic group. The essential point is that any positive or negative externality that is associated with particular individuals will contribute to the instability of the system and lead to high rates of internal migration.

It should also be noted that the example could be carried out in terms of prices. The assignment problem has associated with it a linear programming problem; the solutions to the dual of this linear program define prices which would support this equilibrium under normal utility-maximizing behavior. For example, the move from P_1 to P_2 involves a fall in price for both the first and the third locations. It is this effect that provides the theoretical rationale for the development of the interneighborhood price differentials described earlier. (For a complete discussion of this approach, see Little, 1974.)

The interpretation of this analysis is that an important motivation for internal moves is a decline in the welfare of a given household resulting from the moves of other households. These changes could be thought of as "passive filtering" (where a household stays in the same place but finds its neighborhood has "filtered," having the same effect as if the household had moved to a different neighborhood). It is based on the notion that changes in a neighborhood represent changes in the bundle of characteristics associated with units in it, in the same way that quality declines in structure are changes in the housing bundle. It can also be argued that, given the possibility of moving to new housing—that is, given that potential excess supplies of housing exist—entire neighborhoods could filter downward so far that no households would choose to occupy them. Thus, the process of neighborhood abandonment follows from the possibility and importance of downward filtering. Also, where transport and housing policies make new settlement zones continuously available at the margin, the cycle could spread out indefinitely. Here, too, it should be noted that, as a practical matter, "spread" will eventually be halted by rising opportunity costs; but, depending on transport costs and housing price differentials, considerable spread could occur, leaving abandoned property at the center to be recycled *eventually* by reoccupancy for new use.

It is also important to consider downward filtering in a dynamic context. As downward filtering occurs, the market value of units will fall. For owner occupants, this means a decline in the value of their most important asset. At the same time, they experience a decline in their utility, and they consider relocation. However, the cost of relocation has risen, since the value of their housing has fallen. Thus, as households perceive the probability of downward filtering increasing, a natural response is to move before the downward filtering and decline in values occur. Even if the downward filtering is not inevitable, the risk of occurrence may make such behavior rational. However, while such behavior may be rational, it cannot be argued that it is necessarily efficient. As Arrow has demonstrated, a requirement for market efficiency in the face of uncertainty is perfect insurance markets (see Arrow, 1964–1965). In the case of the housing market, no market for insuring against downward filtering exists. Thus, the only way in which households can insure against these risks is through relocation. However, the effect of covering risk in this way might be to bring about the very changes' that were expected. That is, as households leave a neighborhood in response to an increase in perceived risk, prices will fall and, as a consequence, lower income households will move in. If, in fact, neighborhood income is an element in households' preferences, then downward filtering will occur.

Together with the immobility of capital, the risk of declines in market value explains the phenomenon of abandonment of entire residential neighborhoods without subsequent reuse. (Over a very long time period, of course, reuse of some kind probably would take place, so long as the central business district itself had not migrated. See Alonso, 1964.) Since such neighborhoods are, for the most part, located adjacent to the lowest-income neighborhoods of the city, the risk of downward filtering for all but lowest-income housing is higher than it is for suburban neighborhoods. While the land in the abandoned neighborhood sells at a low price—in some cases, at a virtually zero price—reuse of the area requires that new capital be placed on the land. While loss on land would be negligible, since it is already at near zero value, losses on new physical capital might be substantial, since it could not be moved to a site where its value in use would be higher.

Another consequence of the risk of capital losses stemming from the downward filtering of neighborhoods is the unwillingness of financial institutions to lend in areas subject to this risk. For the financial institution, the risk–return combination associated with any mortgage depends on the mortgage interest rate, the risk of default associated with the borrower, and the expected value of the unit that serves as collateral. For neighborhoods in which the risk of downward filtering is high, both the expected value of the unit and the variance on the distribution (the measure of risk) increases. Thus, the financial institution will in general require a higher mortgage interest rate or will reduce risk through requiring a larger downpayment or a shorter term of the mortgage. Furthermore, if financial institutions select only portfolios which are risk–return efficient, it is possible that mortgages for housing in such neighborhoods will not be included in efficient portfolios.[1] The effect of the nonavailability of mortgage funds, or the availability of these funds only under much more stringent terms than those imposed for housing in low-risk neighborhoods, in turn intensifies the downward filtering and the consequent price declines.

Thus, the effect of an increase in the probability of downward filtering is that downward filtering in fact occurs. More succinctly, expectations are self-realizing. The end result may be a system of dynamically unstable expectations, which produces cycles of the kind considered above. This suggests that the observed high rates of change (and interneighborhood migration) are the result of expectations that "feed on themselves." The analysis also suggests that much of this process does not represent an improvement in welfare in contrast to migration motivated by changes in transport cost and income. Rather, mobility results from households attempting to insure themselves against declines in welfare. At the same time, the costs of the process are high: Capital is abandoned, not because it is obsolete in the production of housing services but, rather, because the risk of capital losses in the asset value of housing is high. In light of these costs, a strong case can be made for social actions that slow or halt this cycle.

IV. Conclusions

In the foregoing sections, we have tried to describe the pattern that internal migration within an SMSA might be expected to assume and the

---

[1] That financial institutions do "red line"—designate entire neighborhoods as unsuitable for mortgage lending, irrespective of the credit worthiness of the borrower—is well documented. For example, see Institute for Urban and Regional Studies (1972, p. 58), for a description of the way in which this practice is reinforced by the regulatory agencies. Our argument here is that such practices might be a rational response of financial institutions which balance their desire for higher profits against their aversion to higher risk. For a good summary of the capital asset pricing model on which this argument is based, see Jensen (1972).

nature of the new equilibrium internal population distribution, if any, to which it would lead, and we have attempted to illustrate this process using some selected data, mainly for the St. Louis area. To us, it would seem that the most salient aspect of the whole internal migration process within metropolitan areas is the very strong predilection of populations within such areas to move their places of residence. Stated differently, only very weak assumptions are needed to explain movement.

Specifically, changing distribution of family income *or* a reduction in unit intrametropolitan transport costs *or* a shift in the distribution of who is willing to live next to whom is sufficient to generate not only a few relocations but a whole chain of movement. Moreover, if the rise in income or fall in transport costs is continuous, or if the aversion of some groups to living near others is strong enough even initially, a continuous stream of internal migration may result. Perhaps this movement will recycle on to zones near the center with continuous recycling out and then back to the core. Perhaps the movement, at least in part, will involve spread of the area outward. In any event, continuous relocation of families is not an unlikely result. Whatever the case, as it occurs in mature American SMSAs, the process leaves behind it a path of decay and abandonment, which, while not permanent, shows prospects for reuse only after very long gestation periods or with massive public subsidy.

But the really interesting question is why decay and abandonment are peculiar to the American scene, since the individual behavior they assume would seem fairly typical, at least in most Western societies, even socialist ones. To reiterate, such a pattern depends on changing incomes, falling internal transport costs, and some degree of "snobbishness" which is class definable. These are hardly uniquely American characteristics. A priori one could expect the phenomenon to be somewhat more evident in American cities simply because, until recently, average family incomes were notably higher and effective transport costs may have been falling more rapidly due to the spread of automobile ownership, the low price of gas, and the very large investments in expressway construction. But this should produce a difference in degree rather than in kind. It is difficult to believe that externalities stemming from the effects of neighbors' characteristics on utility would be so much greater among Americans as to explain the difference; but we cannot, of course, disprove such a contention, and attempts to develop reasonable proxy measures for it would be a very worthwhile future research endeavor.

Any attempt to speculate about relative "snobbishness" aside, we can formulate more defensible and more important explanations for the observed differences in outcomes. These explanations lie in rather fundamental differences in housing and urban development policy, in respect to which American experience does appear to be highly distinctive and unfortunately, even if well meaning, often foolish.

The first policy has to do with the relative cost of new construction versus repair and modernization. In part since the 1930s, but definitely since the Housing Act of 1949, lower downpayments, longer terms, and, frequently, lower interest rates have been available for new housing than for the reconstruction of existing housing. And more favorable terms generally have been available for the financing of new as opposed to used housing. (An unfortunate exception to the latter is the sudden availability—and almost as sudden disappearance, once transition is completed—of FHA-insured mortgage finance in changing areas at the critical point in their transition where original inhabitants could otherwise only "escape" their old neighborhood at considerable capital loss.) Also, the favorable relative price structure for new housing is reinforced by construction trade union policies and local building codes which add a good deal of cost to rehabilitation through arbitrary rules and standards; essentially, the rules and standards are written so as to accommodate new housing construction most easily.

The second aspect of American policy that is crucial has to do with urban transportation. Only in part is this a matter of the switch from public to private auto-transportation. True, the switch to automobiles has freed urban development from dependence on densely settled transport corridors, and indeed, for those willing to purchase a new house, lower density living was made available at a rather low transport opportunity cost. But perhaps even more important than the automobile itself is the tendency of American cities to spend their transport investment dollars extensively rather than intensively. Specifically, urban transport investments have tended to increase the length of the longest trips (one can now go much further in an hour) than to shorten the time of nearer-distance trips. (The mode available and time required for a short-distance trip to the center or a short inner-city cross-town trip are about the same now as 40 years ago.) This too has sharply lowered the opportunity costs of spread.

Finally, a third distinctive aspect of American urban development policy has to do with zoning and land use control. In most American urban areas, almost any capital improvements and land use are permitted except in those areas where they are specifically prohibited. And even where zoning ordinances exist, they generally are written so as only to exclude lower but permit higher uses. For example, only single-family housing can be built in areas so zoned, but any kind of housing can be built in multiple-family zones; housing can be built in commercial zones, but industry cannot; anything can be built in heavy industry zones. One consequence of this legal stance is that zoning ordinances have little influence over the actual land use pattern; Houston, which has *no* zoning ordinance, is little different from other cities of its size and age (see Mandelker, 1970, pp. 21–56). The other consequence is that no effective barrier to incremental growth at the margin exists, again lowering the opportunity cost of spread. And if we add the possibility of spreading to a separate municipal jurisdiction, migrational tendencies are still further enforced by the possibility of escaping unfavorable property tax jurisdictions.

These conclusions seem to point out two important lessons, one for Americans and one for other Western, or maybe even developing, countries. For Americans, the lesson actually is a somewhat hopeful one. It says that the personal behavioral forces that produce destructive internal migration may not be much different than those at work in other cultures, at least developed ones, and that reversals of present trends may be possible by reformulation of existing public policies. The political resistance to such reformulation should not be underestimated, but it does not appear that we must reconstruct our Constitution or rework our psyches.

For non-Americans, the moral is simply the need for skepticism before adopting American policy solutions. Perhaps the rest of the world has already learned that lesson out of the experiences of the past few decades, but it seems worth reiterating once again. And even in developing countries, as incomes grow and transport technology improves, it does seem important to note that policies could be adopted that could reproduce much of the American experience, even though the cultural orientation and apparent life style demands of their peoples on the surface seem much different than those of Americans.

Acknowledgments

The authors wish to thank the U. S. Department of Housing and Urban Development and the National Science Foundation for support of work that was drawn on in this paper, and the research assistance of Jonathan Mark and Keith Ihlanfeldt.

References

Alonso, W. The historic and the structural theories of urban form: Their implications for urban renewal. *Land Economics,* May 1964, pp. 227–231.

Alonso, W. *Location and land use.* Cambridge, Mass.: Harvard University Press, 1970.

Arrow, K. J. The role of securities in the optimal allocation of risk bearing. *Review of Economic Studies*, 1964–1965.

Beckmann, M. J. Spatial equilibrium in the housing market. *Journal of Urban Economics*, 1974, *1*(1).

Harrison, D., and J. F. Kain. Cumulative urban growth and urban density functions, *Journal of Urban Economics*, 1974, *1*(1).

Holt, G. E. *The shaping of St. Louis*. Forthcoming.

Hoyt, H. *The structure and growth of residential neighborhoods in American cities*. Washington, D.C.: U.S. Government Printing Office, 1939.

Institute for Urban and Regional Studies. *Urban decay in St. Louis*. Springfield, Va., National Technical Information Service, No. PB-209-947, March 1972.

Jensen, M. C. The foundations and current state of capital market theory. In M. C. Jensen (Ed.), *Studies in the theory of capital markets*. New York: Praeger, 1972.

Koopmans, T. C., and M. Beckmann. Assignment problems and the location of economic activities. *Econometrica*, 1957, *25*(1), pp. 53–76.

Little, J. T. Housing market behavior and household mobility patterns in a transition neighborhood. Working Paper HMS 1, Institute for Urban and Regional Studies, Washington University, October 1973.

Little, J. T. Household preferences, relocation and welfare: An evaluation of the filtering concept. Working Paper HMS 2, Institute for Urban and Regional Studies, Washington University, March 1974.

Little, J. T. Residential preferences, neighborhood filtering and neighborhood change. *Journal of Urban Economics*, 1976, *3*.

Lowry, I. S. Filtering and housing standards: A conceptual analysis. *Land Economics*, 1960, *36*.

Mandelker, D. R. *The zoning dilemma*. Indianapolis: Bobbs-Merrill, 1970.

Mills, E. S. *Studies in the structure of the urban economy*. Baltimore: Johns Hopkins Press, 1972.

Muth, R. F. *Cities and housing*. Chicago: University of Chicago Press, 1969.

Netzer, D. *Economics of the property tax*. Washington, D.C.: The Brookings Institution, 1966.

Park, R. E., E. W. Burgess, and R. D. McKenzie (Eds.). *The city* Chicago: University of Chicago Press, 1925.

Taeuber, C. M. Measuring patterns of urban growth. Oak Ridge, Tenn.: ORNL UR-104, April 1973.

Warner, S. B. *Street car suburbs*. Cambridge, Mass.: Harvard University Press, 1963.

CHAPTER 14

Urban Growth and Decline in the United States: A Study of Migration's Effects in Two Cities

Peter A. Morrison

I. Introduction

The United States is a highly urbanized nation with space in abundance, yet large portions of its national territory are emptying out. In two out of every three counties during the 1960s, more persons moved out than in; and in one out of two, an absolute decline in residents was recorded. Increasingly, the population has concentrated in metropolitan centers or within commuting distance of them. In 1974, 73% of the population was classified as metropolitan (the figure had already reached 67% in 1960); over 95% of the population resided within the daily commuting field of a city.

Most Americans now live in metropolitan areas but shun their central cities. During the 1960s, the central cities' share of the metropolitan population fell from 50% to 46%. Rising incomes and extensive highway building within and to metropolitan areas have permitted more and more people to move out to the suburbs and indulge their taste for detached, single-family homes with yards; the exodus of whites has been hastened in certain instances by the rising percentage of nonwhites in central cities.

Changing technology and transportation costs have fostered industrial decentralization as well. The trends set in motion by these market forces have been inadvertently accelerated by federal policies. Both national mortgage insurance programs and tax laws encouraged homeownership following World War II, and highway construction programs increased homeowners' access to the suburbs.

As a result, an unprecedented number of the nation's central cities not only ceased to grow but lost population during the 1960s. Of the 292 municipalities designated as central cities of Standard Metropolitan Statistical Areas (SMSAs), 130 contained fewer inhabitants in 1970 than in 1960. The losers include 15 of the 21 central cities whose 1960 populations exceeded 500,000: Chicago, Philadelphia, Detroit, Baltimore, Cleveland, Washington, D.C., St. Louis, Milwaukee, San Francisco, Boston, New Orleans, Pittsburgh, Seattle, Buffalo, and Cincinnati. Of these, St. Louis suffered the sharpest drop. More recently, an increasing number of entire SMSAs have registered absolute population decline, suggesting an outward extension of processes previously observed only in the metropolitan core.

The counterpart of pervasive population decline is a highly selective pattern of growth, conferred by a national system of migration flows that has increasingly favored a certain few metropolitan areas. Between 1960 and 1970, 23 metropolitan areas grew by 20 percent or more because of net inmigration. As of 1965, these areas held only one-tenth of the entire metropolitan population, yet they drew seven-tenths of the cumulative net migration that fed metropolitan growth during the decade.

For any country, a study of urbanization might be organized around a variety of perspectives; whichever one is chosen, it imposes a selective focus. The duality of growth and decline, and its dependence on an intricate system of migration flows, are central features of the U.S. experience, and they provide the perspective adopted in this study. Migration is taken as a key observable phenomenon, expressing the urbanization process and hence promising insight into its workings. This chapter therefore examines U.S. migration, first from a broad analytical viewpoint and then through the experience of two specific cities.

Because national urbanization trends are more immediately palpable at the local than at the national scale, it is useful to examine them in concrete settings. Accordingly, Sections II and III present two specific metropolitan area case studies within which general urbanization phenomena are examined. San Jose, California, was chosen as a case study of rapid population growth in the low-density mode typical of the 1950s and 1960s. The city of St. Louis exemplifies central-city population decline within the core jurisdiction of a metropolitan area. Clearly, no single pair of urban centers can represent the diversity of experience and the variation of common themes that are represented in the several hundred centers, each with its own engaging history, of which the national urban fabric is composed. But despite the historically unique processes that have shaped each city, San Jose and St. Louis can be viewed as opposite extremes of a growth-decline continuum, thereby illuminating the common demographic processes at work in two highly contrasting settings and strengthening generalizations about these processes in other urban settings.

II. Growth in San Jose

Early in this century, population in urban centers grew mainly through rural-to-urban and international migration. These large migrations from outside the metropolitan system, along with the substantial cushion of natural increase, afforded all urban centers some measure of growth. In recent years, however, the intensification or reversal of some long-standing trends has altered the patterns of growth and distribution of the U.S. population.

For one thing, net growth from international migration has diminished both absolutely and as a percentage of the U.S. population. During the era of major immigration—1908 to 1915—the population increased 0.6% annually through net international migration; more recently, this increase has been only about 0.2%.

Second, the rate of rural–urban migration has also diminished, and, since 1970, actually reversed. The rural population's decline over recent decades has left a limited reservoir of potential migrants in the countryside. Equally significant is the fact that rural areas now retain a much higher proportion of their population growth than formerly.

Finally, the total fertility rate has declined to its lowest point in U.S. history. As of 1960, the hypothetical "average woman" implied by this rate would eventually bear 3.7 children over a lifetime; by 1974, this index had declined to 1.9.

As these traditional growth forces weakened, migration flows *among* metropolitan areas emerged as the principal determinants of urban growth. But intermetropolitan migration has favored a certain few metropolitan centers, which have experienced the bulk of available migratory growth (see Alonso and Medrich, 1972, pp. 229–265).

No metropolis demonstrates this effect more clearly than San Jose, whose rapidly expanding aerospace and service industries have attracted an extraordinary influx of new residents over the last two decades.

During the 1960s, metropolitan San Jose's population increased 66%, a rate surpassed by only four other SMSAs in the United States. One-third of this growth was due to natural increase, two-thirds to net inmigration. In 1965, fewer than 7 of every 1000 metropolitan Americans were residents of San Jose, but San Jose received 55 of every 1000 net migrants into metropolitan areas between 1960 and 1970.

Having more than tripled in population between 1950 and 1970, San Jose today bears the cumulative hallmarks of selective inmigration: Its population is young and highly migratory, and its age distribution— through the intensive addition of young adults of childbearing age—gives rise to many more births than deaths.

But this remarkable growth cannot be comprehended strictly in local terms. San Jose's experience is part of the expansion of California's entire metropolitan structure through migration to and within it (see Foley, et al., 1965).

A. Migration Flows Affecting San Jose

California draws migrants from great distances. The vast majority of them enter the state through Los Angeles, San Francisco, or San Diego. Table 14.1 shows that these centers act as national magnets, drawing migrants mostly from out of state. (Los Angeles and San Francisco also draw significant numbers of foreign immigrants.) Other than these metropolitan areas, the 10 other California metropolises in Table 14.1 draw migrants primarily from within the state. (All 16 of California's standard metropolitan statistical areas are shown in Figure 14.1.)

But large numbers of people use these cities only as gateways. Consider the flows in and out of San Francisco. Between 1965 and 1970, San Francisco received 269,000 out-of-state migrants and sent only 204,000 migrants to other states—a net population gain of 65,000 for San Francisco (and California). But San Francisco kept little of this gain: 249,000 of its residents moved to other places in California, but only 191,000 Californians moved to San Francisco; so the city lost 58,000 migrants to the rest of the state, of whom 23,000 ended up in San Jose. In fact, San Jose lures nearly as many migrants away from San Francisco and Los Angeles combined as it does from the remainder of the entire nation (Table 14.2). This abundant supply of new growth funneled into California through San Francisco and Los Angeles has undoubtedly been an important factor in San Jose's 44% population increase through migration during the 1960s.

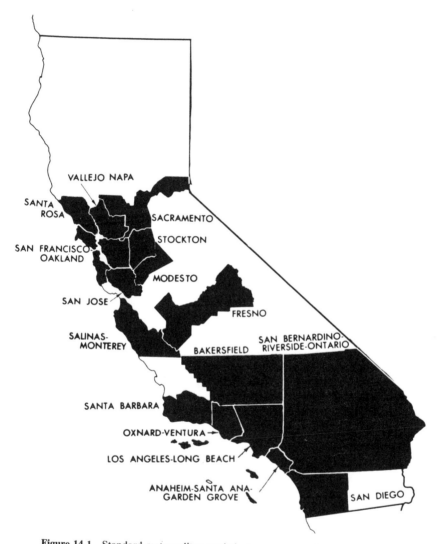

Figure 14.1 Standard metropolitan statistical areas, state of California, 1971.

B. REPERCUSSIONS OF RAPID MIGRATORY GROWTH

Rapid growth causes a number of repercussions, one of which is the youth-weighted age distribution that heavy inmigration typically confers. (Nationally, nearly one-third of all migrants are in their twenties—the peak childbearing age—and 16% are children 1 through 6 years old.) We

TABLE 14.1

DOMESTIC MIGRATION STREAMS INTO AND OUT OF CALIFORNIA'S METROPOLITAN AREAS, 1965–1970[a]

Metropolitan area[b]	Migrants to metropolitan area from		Migrants from metropolitan area to		Net migration to metropolitan area	
	California	Out of state	California	Out of state	California	Out of state
San Francisco	190,931	268,824	249,495	204,149	−58,564	+64,675
Los Angeles	265,500	649,166	414,096	516,019	−148,596	+133,147
San Diego	124,578	223,001	88,544	139,130	+36,034	+83,871
San Jose	132,223	102,416	92,875	67,043	+39,348	+35,373
Sacramento	67,055	52,245	77,359	50,631	−10,304	+1,614
Stockton	29,601	13,808	29,658	11,609	−57	+2,199
Fresno	39,296	15,731	47,972	18,704	−8,676	−2,973
San Bernardino–Riverside	150,470	112,553	107,600	91,728	+42,870	+20,825
Bakersfield	35,097	23,451	42,314	24,328	−7,217	−877
Santa Barbara	41,296	31,879	32,576	29,529	+8,720	+2,350
Santa Rosa	51,516	15,201	29,834	14,178	+21,682	+1,023
Modesto	35,493	21,793	31,797	20,801	+3,696	+992
Oxnard–Ventura	68,157	37,366	39,973	29,183	+28,184	+8,183

Source: U.S. Bureau of the Census, *Census of Population, 1970: Subject Reports*, Final Report PC(2)-2E, *Migration between State Economic Areas*, Government Printing Office, Washington, D.C., 1972.

[a] Excludes foreign migration. The Salinas–Monterey and Vallejo–Napa SMSAs are not shown, since they cannot be approximated with the State Economic Area data used here.

[b] These are Standard Metropolitan Statistical Areas, with the following exceptions: San Francisco here includes Solano County; Los Angeles combines the Los Angeles SMSA and the Anaheim–Santa Ana–Garden Grove SMSA; Sacramento excludes Placer and Yolo Counties; Santa Rosa includes Napa County; and Modesto includes Merced County.

TABLE 14.2

DOMESTIC MIGRATION STREAMS INTO AND OUT OF THE SAN JOSE SMSA, 1965–1970[a]

Metropolitan area[b]	Migrants from metropolitan area to San Jose	Migrants to metropolitan area from San Jose	Net migration to San Jose
San Francisco	55,674	32,241	+23,433
Los Angeles	23,741	15,363	+8,378
San Diego	5,553	4,008	+1,545
Sacramento	6,646	2,443	+4,203
Stockton	2,160	1,616	+544
Fresno	3,954	1,897	+2,057
San Bernardino–Riverside	3,219	2,504	+715
Bakersfield	1,970	968	+1,002
Santa Barbara	2,881	2,169	+712
Santa Rosa	2,340	2,875	−535
Modesto	2,788	2,428	+360
Oxnard–Ventura	1,265	1,452	−187
Rest of Calif.	20,032	22,911	−2,879
Rest of U.S.	102,416	67,043	+35,373

Source: U.S. Bureau of the Census. (See Table 14.1.)
[a] See footnote (a), Table 14.1.
[b] See footnote (b), Table 14.1.

can see the difference between a place that grows through migration and one that declines by comparing the San Jose SMSA with the city of St. Louis. While San Jose's population more than tripled between 1950 and 1970, mostly because of migration, St. Louis's declined 27%, as heavy outmigration more than canceled out its natural increase. Thus, compared with that of St. Louis, San Jose's age distribution shows a comparative surplus in the under-44 age brackets and a comparative deficit in the over-45 range (Figure 14.2). With relatively more potential parents, San Jose's population grew faster than St. Louis's. San Jose's 1960–1970 rate of natural increase was 21.6 per 100 residents in 1960; St. Louis's was only 7.3.

San Jose's rapid migratory growth also makes its population hypermobile. Since people who migrate tend to do so repeatedly, a population built up by waves of past inmigration is heavily weighted with chronically mobile people and therefore is subject to high rates of subsequent outmigration (see Morrison, this volume, Chapter 4). Consequently,

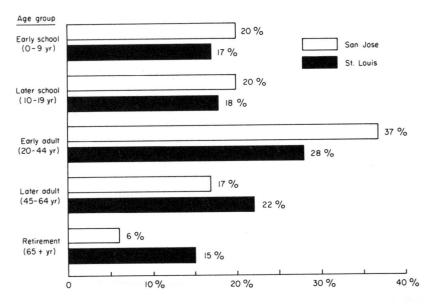

Figure 14.2 Contrasting age distributions: San Jose SMSA and the city of St. Louis, 1970.

there is a continual flow of migrants *through* San Jose. Annual net migration into metropolitan San Jose averaged nearly 4% during the 1960s. This net flow was composed of about 21 arrivals and 17 departures each year per 100 residents (or nearly 10 actual moves for each "net migrant" added).[1] About 7 of these 17 outmigrants, though, had moved into San Jose only the year before. Indeed, fully one-third of the migrants attracted to San Jose had moved away a year later.

Thus, San Jose's rapid population growth rests on a rather precarious arithmetic balance between inmigration and outmigration. Although many of its inmigrants soon depart, San Jose manages to grow by attracting more than enough new arrivals each year to offset this considerable loss. Any moderate decline in the rate of gross inmigration

---

[1] Based on data from the Social Security Continuous Work History Sample, which covers approximately 9 out of 10 wage and salary workers nationally. These data are not directly comparable to the census figures analyzed above. The social security data shown here refer only to employed civilians in social security–covered jobs—a subset of the entire population 5 years and older to which the census data refer. Thus, the Continuous Work History Sample excludes completely self-employed and unemployed workers, persons not in the labor force, and certain classes of workers (principally federal civilian employees, some state and local government employees, and railroad workers). We have also excluded migrants entering or leaving military service.

could easily bring net migration down to a small fraction of its present level (unless of course, outmigration declined as well). For example, if San Jose attracted only 16 (instead of 21) inmigrants per 100 residents, its net migratory gain would stand at less than 1% (instead of 4%) annually.[2]

On the other hand, because it is highly mobile, San Jose's population can probably accommodate change quite quickly. Adjustment to changes in the overall demand for labor, or to shifts in the mix of required skills, can occur promptly because of the brisk inflow and outflow of workers. For this reason, San Jose's labor market is likely to show an uncommon resilience to change.

III. Decline in the City of St. Louis

The St. Louis SMSA, shown in Figure 14.3, encompasses the city of St. Louis and six counties lying on either side of the Mississippi River: St. Louis, St. Charles, Franklin, and Jefferson Counties in Missouri; and St. Clair and Madison Counties in Illinois. The city of St. Louis is entirely separate in area and jurisdiction from the County of St. Louis. (Hereafter "St. Louis" will refer to the city, while St. Louis County will be so designated.) The closest metropolitan area of comparable size is the Kansas City SMSA, about 275 miles to the west.

In 1970, the population of metropolitan St. Louis was about 2.4 million. It had increased by 12 percent since 1960, a rate lower than the average national metropolitan increase of 17 percent. After 1970, population in metropolitan St. Louis, like that in 21 other formerly growing SMSAs, began to decline.

A. COMPARATIVE TRENDS IN ST. LOUIS AND ITS METROPOLITAN RING

St. Louis attained a peak population of 880,000 in the early 1950s. But by 1973, it had dwindled to a city of less than 570,000. During the 1960s, St. Louis's population declined 17% while its metropolitan ring population increased 29%. The central city decline was acute, compared with that of most cities. Examination of the demographic change components reveals why (see Table 14.3).

---

[2] This estimate is a rough approximation only. It assumes that the lower rate of inmigration would, by reducing the stock of chronic movers, lower the rate of subsequent outmigration from 17 to 15 per 100. All estimates here refer to the period to which these Continuous Work History Sample data apply (1957 through 1966) and to San Jose residents working in social security–covered jobs.

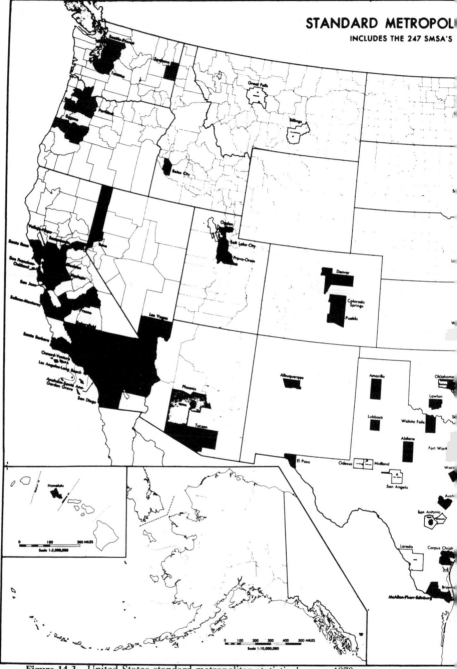

Figure 14.3 United States standard metropolitan statistical areas, 1970.

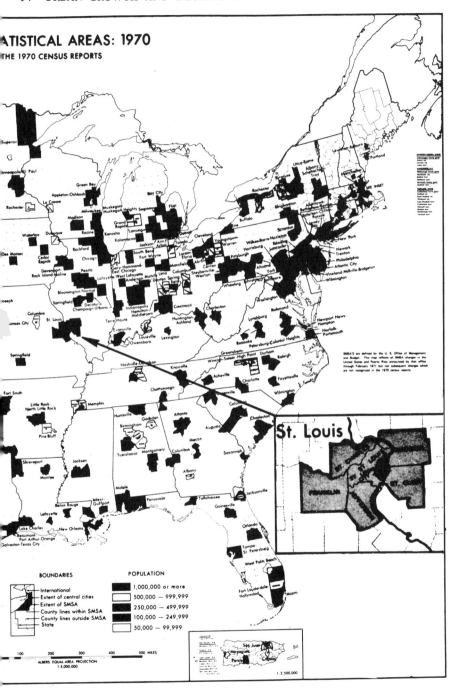

STATISTICAL AREAS: 1970
THE 1970 CENSUS REPORTS

St. Louis

SMSA'S are defined by the U. S. Office of Management and Budget. This map reflects all SMSA changes in the United States and Puerto Rico announced by that office through February 1971 but not subsequent changes which are not recognized in the 1970 census reports.

BOUNDARIES
- International
- Extent of central cities
- Extent of SMSA
- County lines within SMSA
- County lines outside SMSA
- State

POPULATION
- 1,000,000 or more
- 500,000 — 999,999
- 250,000 — 499,999
- 100,000 — 249,999
- 50,000 — 99,999

100   200   300   400   500 MILES
ALBERS EQUAL AREA PROJECTION
1:5,000,000

1:2,500,000

TABLE 14.3

COMPONENTS OF POPULATION CHANGE IN ST. LOUIS, 1960–1970[a]

Area	Total change	Natural increase[b]	Net migration
Both races			
St. Louis SMSA	12.3	11.5	0.8
St. Louis City	−17.0	7.3	−24.4
Remainder of SMSA			
(metropolitan ring)	28.5	13.8	14.7
Whites			
St. Louis SMSA	9.4	10.1	−0.7
St. Louis City	−31.6	2.4	−34.0
Remainder of SMSA			
(metropolitan ring)	26.6	13.3	13.3
Nonwhites[c]			
St. Louis SMSA	28.2	20.2	9.7
St. Louis City	18.6	19.5	−0.4
Remainder of SMSA			
(metropolitan ring)	53.8	22.0	37.2

Source: U.S. Bureau of the Census, *Census of Population and Housing: 1970; General Demographic Trends for Metropolitan Areas, 1960 to 1970,* Final Report PHC(2)-1, Tables 10–12; PHC(2)-27, Table 3; PHC(2)-15, Table 3.

[a] The rates given are per 100 1960 residents.

[b] Rate of increase attributed to excess of births over deaths.

[c] In this section, "Total change" applies only to the black population. "Natural increase" and "Net migration" apply to the nonwhite population as a whole, but virtually all nonwhites in the St. Louis SMSA are blacks.

The white population declined mostly because of massive outward migration, chiefly to the suburbs. Between 1960 and 1970, a net 34% of the white city dwellers moved away. But whites also declined because their death rate steadily approached their birth rate, and since 1965 has exceeded it. Those who remained in the city added only 2% to their numbers (nationally, the decade increase in the white metropolitan population was 11%).

The picture for blacks was very different. There was no gain or loss through net migration during the 1960s, but St. Louis's black population rose 19.5% through natural increase, very close to its national rate of 21.6%. Annual population estimates, however, show St. Louis's non-white population to have peaked in 1968 at around 269,000.[3] By 1973, it

---

[3] In St. Louis, blacks make up 99% of the nonwhite population. Hence the terms "nonwhite" and "black" are used synonymously in the following discussion.

is estimated to have dropped below 247,000. In view of the black population's positive natural increase, the only explanation is that blacks have been migrating out of the city since at least 1968 (and almost certainly before).

The number and composition of households in the city also changed during the decade. The number of households declined somewhat more slowly than the population (13% versus 17%), and the average size of a household went down slightly. Households of only one person increased from 21% in 1960 to 28% in 1970, a reflection primarily of the growing frequency of widowed elderly persons.

Demographic trends were somewhat more uniform outside the city (Table 14.3). Natural increase and net migration contributed equally to the white population's 26.6% increase during the 1960s. The black population's 53.8% suburban growth was attributable more to net migration than to natural increase.[4] St. Louis's suburbs attracted migrants largely from the city but also from outside the metropolitan area. Increasingly, migrants of both races entering the St. Louis SMSA bypassed the city and settled in the suburbs (mainly in St. Louis County). It can be seen in Figure 14.4 that the total stream of new

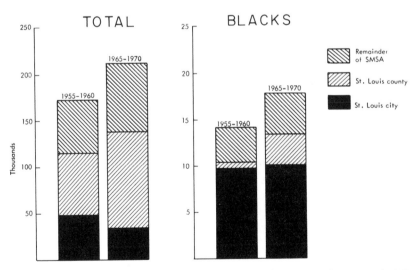

Figure 14.4 Destinations of migrants entering the St. Louis SMSA, 1955–1960 and 1965–1970 (persons 5 years old and over, residing outside SMSA or abroad 5 years perviously). Data shown for 1955–1960 for graph on the right refer to nonwhites.

[4] Suburban blacks registered a high overall rate of growth between 1960 and 1970 because their 1960 base was minuscule.

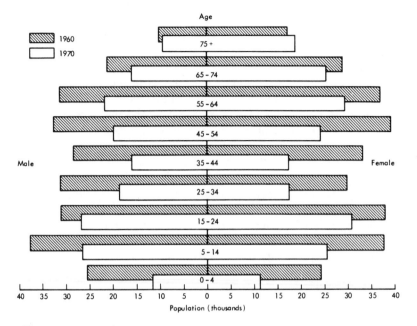

Figure 14.5   Age distribution of white population, St. Louis city, 1960 and 1970.

arrivals to St. Louis city between 1965 and 1970 was smaller (both absolutely and relatively) than it had been a decade earlier. For blacks, the inbound stream was numerically about the same; but in relative terms, newly arriving blacks increasingly favored the suburbs.

B. CONSEQUENCES OF DEMOGRAPHIC CHANGE

Persistent and severe migration away from St. Louis has altered the structure of its population. These changes bear heavily on the city's capacity to meet the needs of the increasingly disadvantaged population that remains and on this population's capacity to regenerate itself.

1. Diminished Replacement Capacity

The white population's capacity to replace itself diminished during the 1960s. Heavy and prolonged outmigration among whites drew away potential parents and left behind an elderly population that no longer replaces itself.

We can gauge the severity of the outmigration of young white adults by following individual age cohorts from 1960 to 1970 (Figure 14.5). For example, in the absence of migratory change, people 5 to 14 years old in 1960 would reappear as the same number of people 15 to 24 years old in 1970, less a small allowance for mortality. Since this allowance is negligible below age 45 (at most 5%), any sizable discrepancy between 1960 and 1970 indicates the extent of migration that has taken place in that cohort. Figure 14.5 provides stark evidence of extensive outmigration from St. Louis in the early adult years. For example, in 1960 there were 37,900 white females 15 to 24, but by 1970 only 17,900 aged 25 to 34 remained—a 53% reduction. There were 31,100 white males 25 to 34 in 1960, but only 15,900 aged 35 to 44 in 1970—a 49% reduction. Overall, 46% of whites 15 to 34 in 1960 were gone by 1970, leaving St. Louis with a sharply diminished pool of prospective parents.

The resultant modifications in replacement capacity are illustrated more directly in Table 14.4, from which we can see that:

- The proportion of women in the middle and later childbearing years declined. In 1960, white women aged 25 to 44 made up 22.1% of all white women in the city; by 1970 the figure had dropped to 17.6%. (Part of this drop stemmed from the changing national age distribution; for white women nationally, this age group declined from 26.4% to 23.5% of the total population between 1960 and 1970.)

TABLE 14.4

INDEXES OF CHANGE IN REPLACEMENT CAPACITY FOR ST. LOUIS'S BLACK AND WHITE POPULATION, 1960–1972[a]

Indicator	1960	1970	1972
Percentage of women in later childbearing years (age 25–44)			
White	22.1%	17.6%	N.A.
Black	27.1%	22.7%	N.A.
Percentage of population age 65+			
White	14.5%	19.2%	N.A.
Black	6.8%	8.3%	N.A.
Crude birth rate per thousand			
White	22.1	14.5	12.0
Black	34.4	25.1	24.9
Crude death rate per thousand			
White	14.8	17.7	18.0
Black	11.4	11.3	11.2

[a] N.A. = not available.

- The proportion of elderly whites rose. Whites 65 and over made up 14.5% of the population in 1960, but 19.2% in 1970. (The corresponding figure nationally was 10% in both years.)
- Partially as a result of these changes in age structure, the crude birth rate per 1000 whites declined from 22.1 in 1960 to 12.0 in 1972; and the crude death rate per 1000 whites rose from 14.8 to 18.0. (Part of this decline was, of course, a consequence of the national trend in the birth rate, which dropped nearly 25% during the 1960s.)

Since 1965, the white population has ceased to replace itself, its death rate having exceeded its birth rate. By 1973, the services of the undertaker exceeded those of the obstetrician by a margin of 5 to 3. Since it is now undergoing natural decrease, St. Louis's white population will continue to shrink whether or not net outmigration continues. Only a dramatic rise in fertility or a massive influx of childbearing families can alter this situation.[5]

The city's black population has not undergone severe migratory change and retains its strong replacement capacity: In 1972 its crude birth rate was 24.9 per 1000, and its crude death rate only 11.2. In 1969, however, the black population began to decline, indicating a net migratory loss severe enough to offset its natural increase. This recent shift could signify an increase in departing migrants, a reduction in entering migrants, or a combination of both. Indications favor the first of these explanations.[6]

2. Accumulation of Disadvantaged Citizens

As migration has changed the metropolitan-wide distribution of population, St. Louis has come to be composed disproportionately of those citizens who are disadvantaged or have special needs, as the following comparisons show:

- Between 1960 and 1970, the black percentage of the city's population rose from 29 to 41; it increased only from 6 to 7 in the rest of the metropolitan area.

---

[5] Because changes in fertility are difficult to forecast, a dramatic rise cannot be entirely ruled out, although it seems highly unlikely at this time. Foreseeable changes in mortality can have no appreciable bearing on the population's replacement capacity.

[6] Data in Figure 14.4 indicate that the gross number of black migrants entering St. Louis between 1965 and 1970 was about the same as between 1955 and 1960—around 10,000. Thus only an increase in gross outmigration could account for the change in net migration.

- The percentage of residents aged 65 years and older increased from 12 to 15 in the city; it stayed at 8 in the rest of the metropolitan area.
- For families and unrelated individuals, median income in the city was 79% of that for the St. Louis SMSA as a whole in 1959; by 1969 city income was only 68% of SMSA income.
- The proportion of relatively high-income families declined sharply. In 1959, 11% of families in the city had incomes at least double the city's median family income; 10 years later, only 4% had incomes double the 1969 median.
- The proportion of relatively low-income families rose slightly. In 1959, 16% of families in the city had incomes less than half the city's median family income; 10 years later, 21% had incomes less than half the 1969 median.

Through selective outmigration, then, problems of dependency and poverty—not exclusively problems *of* St. Louis—have come increasingly to be located *in* St. Louis.

C. THE POLICY DILEMMA: COPING WITH DECLINE

The degree of population decline in St. Louis may be exceptional, but St. Louis is no exception to the rule. The phenomenon of local population decline is widespread now—a characteristic of entire metropolitan areas, not just their central cities. The policy dilemma in coping with decline and its local consequences is likely to intensify during the 1970s.

The dilemma is this. The local official responsible for what happens in a place like St. Louis is understandably alarmed by severe population loss and the bleak future in store for the city if it continues. The city's boundaries, which have not changed since 1876, separate the problems within St. Louis from resources in its suburbs. But from the standpoint of individual welfare, it can be argued that the people who have left St. Louis now enjoy living conditions they prefer, and those who have remained benefit from a thinning out of people from formerly over-crowded areas.[7] Even the widespread abandoned housing in St. Louis can be viewed as a positive sign that many people have upgraded their living conditions, leaving behind a residue of housing no longer competi-

---

[7] Taking persons per room as the conventional index of overcrowding, census data show that only 12.7% of all occupied housing units in St. Louis contained more than one person per room in 1970, compared with 16.4% in 1960.

tive within the market. Both views have validity, the choice depending on whether one's perspective is that of a local policymaker or of a freely mobile citizen.

But the argument may amount to no more than a confusing piece of sophistry for the policymaker, or even for the objective student of urban affairs, who looks at careful statistics from respectable sources telling him unequivocally that St. Louis is much worse off than it used to be. Part of the confusion is due to the paradox that statistics can be deceptive even when they are accurate. They can mislead us here, for example, if they beguile us into confining our attention to the plight of *places*, whereas our central concern is with the wellbeing of *people*. It is hard to escape that situation, however. A major difficulty in our way is that standard social and economic statistics are compiled and organized mostly by areas, rather than by groups of people. Consequently, we can observe the experience of places but not of people. These experiences can differ sharply. For instance, black inmigrants from impoverished rural areas of states like Mississippi may be less affluent or employable, on the average, than the mostly white population they join in St. Louis. If this is true in St. Louis as it is in other cities,[8] then group indicators (e.g., of unemployment or poverty *among the migrants* now, compared with before they came to St. Louis) may show marked improvement. In short, the place we call St. Louis may be worse off because of inmigration while the inmigrant people are better off than they were.

IV. Summary and Conclusions

The population changes in San Jose and St. Louis between 1960 and 1970 exemplify the two broad trends—urban formation followed by metropolitan dispersal—that have shaped twentieth-century urbanization in the United States. The fact that these developmental trends were expressed through demographic processes found to be common to both cities, despite their contrasting recent experiences, suggests that generalizations can be made about the complex forces underlying urbanization in the United States.

The formation of metropolitan San Jose's population parallels the traditional process, whereby a region's growth comes to be focused, through migration, on a few urban centers. The modern variant is not characterized by a rural-to-urban shift, however, but by migration flows among urban areas, and particularly to a few most-favored areas, such as San Jose.

---

[8] Evidence on this point is reviewed in Chapter 4, Section III of this volume.

Migratory growth has left a powerful demographic legacy in San Jose. This legacy is also instructive for studying the migratory formation of any new city's population. Its demographic character determines its demographic destiny, whose likely variations we can now perceive with some clarity. San Jose's population is both youthful and chronically migratory. The presence of many prospective parents and relatively few elderly persons lays a broad foundation for the population's continued growth through natural increase, despite the national downturn in fertility.[9] Even without further net inmigration, the population of new cities like San Jose would continue to grow at a rate above average.

The hypermobility of San Jose's population (i.e., its propensity for further migration) also has an important bearing on the future. With about 21 migrants entering and 17 departing each year per 100 residents, San Jose's rapid migratory growth rests (as it would in other new cities) on a precarious arithmetic balance. A significant dip in local employment growth could easily reduce net migration to a small fraction of its present high level. Even a slight decline would result in the inflow no longer exceeding the high volume of outflow. Demographic analysis alone cannot foresee such an employment downturn, but if it happened, the migratory downturn probably would be swift. Hypermobility also works the other way; and, given San Jose's focal position in California's expanding metropolitan structure (with its virtually endless supply of migratory growth), net migration could resume with equal swiftness.

The outward dispersal of population from central cities that has occurred in St. Louis has been accelerating in other cities as well and will remain a prominent feature of U.S. urban growth. It may seem paradoxical that in a period noted for something called "urban growth" there are so many declining central cities, but that is merely one indication that the "central city" no longer is the *real* city, except in name. Real city or not, the central city can expect to come into political conflict with other jurisdictions created in the process of dispersion. In cities like St. Louis, where population is dispersing but old political boundaries are fixed, the problems of the central city are separated from the resources in the suburbs. Transitional problems associated with persistent and severe outmigration also arise: accumulation of disadvantaged citizens, declining demand for city housing, and a diminished replacement capacity in the population.

Carried far enough, the last of these results in natural decrease; and thereafter the population's decline acquires its own dynamic. As noted

[9] The exact rate of San Jose's natural increase, although dependent on the future course of U.S. fertility, will remain above the national metropolitan average.

earlier, the white population in St. Louis has reached this point: The number of persons dying now exceeds the number being born. For two reasons, this natural decrease can do little other than intensify. First, a substantial proportion of whites are either entering or already within the high-mortality age brackets. The white population's crude death rate therefore will continue to rise. Second, prospective parents are becoming scarce among St. Louis's whites, and the national evidence that parents in general will choose to have smaller families continues to mount. The white population's crude birth rate is therefore likely to fall, barring a dramatic increase in fertility or a strong and sustained inflow of child-bearing families. Nor is St. Louis's black population likely to grow substantially. It is expanding steadily through natural increase, but black migration out of the city is more than enough to cancel that increase.

Acknowledgments

Presented at the Conference on Contemporary Migration, Urbanization, and Socio-Economic Development, cosponsored by the Committee on Comparative Urban Economics and the Polish Economic Association, June 27–July 3, 1974, in Warsaw, Poland.

This chapter is drawn from two Rand Reports written by the author: *San Jose and St. Louis in the 1960s: A Case Study of Changing Urban Populations,* R-1313-NSF, 1973, prepared under Rand's Urban Policy Analysis Program with support from the National Science Foundation; and *Migration from Distressed Areas: Its Meaning for Regional Policy,* R-1103-EDA/FF/NIH, 1973, supported by the Economic Development Administration, The Ford Foundation and the National Institutes of Health. I thank Professor William Alonso of the University of California, Berkeley, and Professor Sidney Goldstein, Director of the Population Studies and Training Center, Brown University, for their helpful critiques of earlier drafts on which this chapter is based.

References

Alonso, W., and Medrich, E. Spontaneous growth centers in twentieth-century American urbanization. In Niles Hansen (Ed.), *Growth centers in regional economic development.* New York: Free Press, 1972.

Foley, D. L., R. L. Drake, D. W. Lyon, and B. A. Ynzenga. *Characteristics of metropolitan growth in California,* Vol. 1. Report, Center for Planning and Development Research, Institute for Urban and Regional Development, Berkeley, California, 1965.

Morrison, P. A. The functions and dynamics of the migration process. This volume, Chapter 4.

CHAPTER 15

Population Distribution:
Perspectives and Policies

Ronald W. Crowley

I. Introduction

For two generations now, governments have become increasingly concerned with questions related to the regulation of population growth and distribution. And it is not surprising, for the resolution of the most pressing societal problems may rest to a large extent with the ability to affect population growth in a manner consistent with other national goals.

This paper addresses some questions related to regulation of population. In particular, it is concerned with the instruments that are available for affecting and controlling population distribution. The concept of a population optimum is first analyzed. This is followed by a brief description of some population trends, the components of demographic change, and the factors influencing change. The nature of available policy instruments is then surveyed, and Canadian, U.S. and West European experiences with various policies are discussed. An assessment of the potential for nations to exert significant influence on their population distribution concludes the paper.

II. Optimum Population: Regulation and Incentives[1]

For any phenomenon, whether or not an optimum exists is an article of faith, even though the concept is well embedded in the theory and

[1] This section is based on Spengler (1973).

255

practice of the social sciences (Sauvy, 1969; Tisdell, 1975). All socioeconomic organizations appear to function differently at different sizes. But in the case of cities, for example, there are likely to be a number of possible optima. Extant research does not suggest that product per capita has declined as cities have grown; in fact, larger cities tend to have higher incomes than smaller ones. Even if certain costs are associated with size, there is a legitimate question whether a very large city may not serve an important role in the overall structure or hierarchy. Changing substitutability between telecommunications and transport as well as agglomeration economies may dramatically affect the optimum population size. Moreover, these factors may change the optimum faster, and by magnitudes greater, than any policy can change actual population size. Hence, it is probably more appropriate to think of a range of population sizes within which a city can function optimally, with the range defined by environmental circumstances, available technology, and institutional arrangements. In this context, the prime value of the concept of optimality is that it provides a guide to asking certain questions which can in turn lead to solutions.

At any rate, regulations and incentives are based on the notion that there exists something (i.e., a wellbeing function) which can be minimized or maximized, that it is advantageous to do so, and that a minimum or maximum position will not be reached automatically. Even setting aside the considerable difficulty of constructing a satisfactory index of wellbeing, it may be extremely difficult to correlate the index with variations in city size and type. Moreover, even if that were possible, it is not certain that the "peak" in question is the highest one or that a distribution problem does not remain. The value for a wellbeing function is likely to vary not only with city size but also with a city's internal structure and with its position in an urban network or hierarchy. Internal structure in turn is a reflection of the particular composition of activities within a city, as well as of their distribution in urban space (Crowley, 1973a).

Limits to increased efficiency occur because of constraints arising internally or externally. A city is a product of socioeconomic as well as physical factors. Some of these change more rapidly than others, with the result that they differentially impose limits. A city might be regarded as one large input–output system, with "conduits" along which flow the inputs and outputs of human activities. Being limited in size, these conduits are subject to increasing congestion and rising costs. As well, there may be increasing costs of coordination. Similarly, the physical, external environment of a city will set a limit to growth since, after a point, there are no substitutes for physical environment.

A tendency for a city to grow beyond some optimum size (or sizes) could reflect either a lack of homeostatic response or the generation of substantial externalities falling primarily on the residential sector but generated by the commercial–industrial sector. For cities, homeostatic mechanisms that compensate for maladjustments are generally weak, and they moderate only slightly the forces working toward concentration. In the past it was often assumed that self-correcting mechanisms were sufficient to minimize maladjustments in the system. Even if true, this argument neglected distributional considerations, institutional and historical constraints, and the effects of dynamic change. The high costs of information and the diverse impact of technological change affecting both actual and optimum populations were also ignored.

Socioeconomic organizations are generally of one of two types: (a) those subject to regulation through more or less centralized decision-making processes and sets of procedures and (b) those given a degree of direction by noncentralized "cues" and dispersed sets of decisions in the laissez-faire tradition. A city is essentially an organization of the latter sort. Unlike, say, a business firm, the index for maximization in a city is nebulous, badly defined, and difficult to achieve. The methods that have been generally applied to "determine" optimal size (for example, "survivorship" and models of revealed preference) are clearly less effective as measures of size for cities than for firms.

First, there are longer lags in the response to excess size by occupants of a city, and the information processes at work are less efficient in throwing up the anomalies likely to lead to a response. But also, the decision to move may not be as clearly associated with size or the index of wellbeing as one might expect. In fact, it is not size per se that stimulates outmigration but rather correlates of size, such as anomie and alienation, the absence of competitively priced inputs, and noxious environmental forces stemming from negative externalities (e.g., congestion, noise, blight, pollution, lawlessness, and lack of open space) (Wolpert, 1966). At least, these reasons appear to have been more dominant in the substantial exodus that took place from U.S. central cities during the 1960s.

With a variety of assumptions, it is not difficult to imagine a homeostatic system sensitive to increasing divergences from optimality. Such a system would require the internalization of externalities, functioning competition, and a price system that permitted shifting of costs among producers and consumers. This system might please economists, but the *economic* equilibrium implied may still not be at the level considered optimal, since the economic indicator might not be highly enough correlated with the index of wellbeing.

It is useful to distinguish between direct and indirect "causes" for the divergence of actual from optimal distributions of population. Indirect causes are primarily associated with public policies: national transport policies, distribution of regulatory power, the establishment of regional jurisdictions, and generally explicit or implicit policies concerning the size and distribution of a nation's population. Direct causes have seven principal sources:

a. *High sensitivity thresholds* may exist so that marginal changes are not consistently acted upon.

b. *Public policy decisions may be irreversible* or reversible only with long time lags [i.e., an inefficient indicator of divergences from optimality may be employed].

c. A city may *lack regulatory power* or the will to exercise it.

d. Opportunity for generating and capturing *urban rents* may stimulate speculators, due particularly to superior information.

e. *Externalities* may exacerbate growth trends because decision makers do not bear all costs of their decisions.

f. There may be a *lack of information on alternatives* or alternatives may be incorrectly evaluated or both of these may occur.

g. *Technological change* may affect either actual or optimum size.

Of these seven sources, urban rents, externalities, and lack of information are the most important because they probably result in an increasing divergence of actual and optimal population. High sensitivity thresholds and irreversible policy decisions work to reduce the degree of homeostatic response. Regulatory power and technological change are presumably institutionally determined and hence subject to discrete changes over the longer term.

III. The Problem: The Concentration of Population through Urbanization

A. GENERAL PATTERNS OF DEMOGRAPHIC CHANGE

The demographic history of most countries in this century suggests a strong tendency for population to cluster. This has been especially true in the period since the advent of industrialization and the decline of the agricultural sector. Table 15.1 provides illustration of the rapid movement toward urbanization in most highly industrialized countries. Generally, not only have urban populations grown substantially more rapidly than populations as a whole, but the most rapid urban growth has been in the largest cities. For example, in the period 1959 to 1969, the average annual growth rate of Canada's total population was 1.85%, but for

TABLE 15.1

PERCENTAGE OF ANNUAL POPULATION GROWTH IN SELECTED COUNTRIES[a]

	Total population growth 1959–1969	Urban population growth 1960–1970	Growth of population in cities over 100,000 1960–1970
United Kingdom	0.65	0.7	0.5
Austria	0.50	0.8	0.2
Belgium	0.60	1.1	1.4
Ireland	0.25	1.4	1.5
Luxembourg	0.80	1.4	—
Italy	0.85	1.5	2.8
Denmark	0.75	1.6	1.9
Greece	0.70	1.6	2.8
Sweden	0.70	1.6	3.5
Germany	1.05	1.7	1.6
Portugal	0.90	1.7	1.2
Spain	0.95	1.7	2.7
Netherlands	1.25	2.0	3.1
Norway	0.80	2.0	3.1
United States	1.35	2.1	2.8
France	1.05	2.2	3.5
Switzerland	1.70	2.5	2.9
Finland	0.70	2.7	2.6
Iceland	1.65	2.7	—
Australia	—	2.7	2.9
CANADA	1.85	2.8	3.3
Japan	1.05	3.7	4.0
Turkey	2.55	4.2	6.8
Yugoslavia	—	4.8	5.6
Average growth rate	1.03	2.27	2.88

[a] Countries are ordered by average annual growth rate in urban population, 1960–1970.
Source: Organization for Economic Cooperation and Development, Sector Group on the Urban Environment, *Urban Growth in OECD Countries,* U/ENV/71.6 (Paris, August 1971) Tables 1 and 4; and United Nations, *Demographic Yearbook 1970* (New York, 1971), Tables 5 and 9.

urbanized areas it was 2.8% and for cities over 100,000 it was 3.3%. For all OECD (Organization for Economic Cooperation and Development) countries together, these percentages were 1.03%, 2.27%, and 2.88%. The resulting concentration of population in only a few metropolitan areas is depicted in Table 15.2.

TABLE 15.2
POPULATION CONCENTRATION IN METROPOLITAN AREAS, OECD COUNTRIES, 1970

Country	Total population (millions)	Largest city		Two largest cities		Percentage of total population	
		Population	City	Population	Cities	Largest city	Two largest cities
Australia	12404	2720	Sydney	4920	Sydney Melbourne	21.9	39.7
Denmark	4963	1480	Copenhagen	1670	Copenhagen Arhus	29.8	33.6
Greece	8876	2425	Athens	2895	Athens Thessalonika	27.3	32.6
Ireland	2936	775	Dublin	905	Dublin Cork	25.4	30.8
Austria	7449	1890	Vienna	2145	Vienna Linz	25.4	28.8
United Kingdom	56065	11544	London	14525	London Manchester	20.6	25.9
Sweden	8083	1350	Stockholm	2000	Stockholm Goteberg	16.7	24.7
Portugal	9723	1500	Lisbon	2350	Lisbon Porto	15.4	24.2
CANADA	21673	2511	Montreal	4948	Montreal Toronto	11.6	22.8
Finland	4768	757	Helsinki	955	Helsinki Turku	15.9	20.0
France	51402	8714	Paris	9940	Paris Lyon	16.9	19.3

Norway	3876	Oslo	590	742	Oslo / Bergen	15.2	19.1
Belgium	9801	Brussels	1104	1778	Brussels / Antwerp	11.3	18.1
Netherlands	13110	Rotterdam	1222	2361	Rotterdam / Amsterdam	9.3	18.0
Switzerland	6270	Zurich	667	1037	Zurich / Basel	10.6	16.5
Spain	32958	Madrid	2990	5323	Madrid / Barcelona	9.0	16.2
Japan	102795	Tokyo	12199	15506	Tokyo / Osaka	11.9	15.1
Fed. Rep. Germany	61795	Essen	6789	9196	Essen–Dertmund–Duisberg / Hamburg	10.9	15.1
United States	206985	New York	16077	25550	New York / Los Angeles	7.8	12.3
Yugoslavia	20649	Zagreb	1165	2343	Zagreb / Belgrade	5.6	11.3
Turkey	35225	Istanbul	2600	3850	Istanbul / Ankara	7.4	10.9
Italy	53648	Rome	2920	4570	Rome / Milan	5.4	8.7

Source: See Table 15.1.

The increasing tendency toward clustering has imposed considerable pressures both on rapidly growing urban areas and on less rapidly growing rural areas. Some of these pressures have been: (1) the conversion of land from agricultural production to urban purposes, (2) the competition for and resulting price escalation of scarce urban land, (3) low-density suburbanization and the associated traffic congestion thereby generated, (4) lack of attention to the natural environment, (5) rapid increases in expenditures for public services, and (6) the spatial concentration of low-income families, with attendant effects. Finally, the process has tended to exacerbate regional disparities in income and opportunity.

B. FERTILITY AND MORTALITY

Population change obviously occurs through the three basic phenomena of birth, death, and migration (internal and external). The ability to differentially affect the death rate through social policy is limited. Similarly, birth rates, though more amenable to influence than death rates, are manipulatable only by affecting overall levels, rather than different levels among different regions of a country. Changing social attitudes toward family size have caused a substantial decline in the birth rate of many Western countries during the past two decades. Yet, in Canada as elsewhere, the highest rates of birth are often recorded in lagging peripheral regions where the capacity to absorb additions to the labor force is limited (Kalbach and McVey, 1971).

Will the current downward trends in fertility become a permanent feature of Western society? Demographers are cautious by experience in predicting future trends. Whatever the case, a critical element in population growth stabilization has been the dissemination of birth control information, and birth rates are probably more amenable to willful influence now than in the past. A review of the American experience in the late 1960s, revealed that 4 births in 11 were unplanned and 15% to 20% of children born were unwanted at time of conception (Spengler, 1973, p. 1). If such births did not take place, a stable population, where deaths approximately offset births, would be achieved in about six decades.

As a long-run policy, stabilizing overall population growth rates is an important aspect of regulating population distribution. However, a potentially superior lever rests in influencing migration decisions (Morrison, 1974). Whereas death rates are determined primarily by medical–health conditions and birth rates more by social and health factors, migration is the result of a decision based primarily on economic motives. One can attempt to work either through those forces that determine the demand for labor in any specific area or through those that cause people to want to move (supply). Obviously, the two sets of factors are closely related, and it is to them that we turn in Section IV.

C. MIGRATION: THE CANADIAN CASE

The role of migration in intensifying the concentration of people in urban areas is readily apparent in the Canadian situation. Only the three most economically advanced and urbanized provinces (Ontario, Alberta, and British Columbia) have consistently gained population through inmigration. Though this pattern holds for both internal and external migration flows, it is most clear for the latter. Montreal, Toronto, and Vancouver have collectively accounted for almost 70% of all foreign inmigrants to the 21 largest Canadian cities. About one-third of *all* immigrants to Canada chose Toronto during the 1966–1971 period. Indeed, Toronto's robust growth has not been due to internal migration but to immigration from abroad (see Table 15.3).

The detailed pattern of internal migration for Canada's metropolitan areas is less easily described than is immigration. In recent years, migration among urban areas has accounted for about 80% of the gain accruing to metropolitan areas through internal migration. This reverses the earlier situation whereby migration from farm to city was chiefly responsible for fueling urban growth.

The volume of internal migration has been high. For 1966–1971, almost one Canadian in five arrived in or departed from one of Canada's largest centers. Rates of internal migration, however, have varied considerably from one city to another and from one year to the next. If internal migration were the only source of population change, some of the largest cities in eastern and central Canada (e.g., Montreal, Hamilton, Winnipeg) would have lost population between 1966 and 1971 at the same time as other, far western centers (e.g., Calgary, Edmonton, Vancouver) were registering healthy gains. This may be misleading, since most outmigrants from an urban area have remained in what might be termed the "urban field" (cf. Hansen, 1974, for an examination of the U.S. situation). Hence, internal movements appear to be more responsible for the distribution of population among metropolitan areas than for the collective growth of the largest Canadian cities. In some specific cases, however, they can be important for the latter as well.

Migration, even when not contributing significantly to growth, has potential for imposing considerable changes on the demographic structure of an urban area. If flows of arriving and departing migrants differ

TABLE 15.3

SOME PARAMETERS OF CANADIAN URBAN MIGRATION, 21 METROPOLITAN AREAS, 1966–1971

Metropolitan areas[a]	Population 1971	Total net migration	Immigrants from elsewhere in Canada	Percentage of total Inmigrants to 21 cities	Immigrants from outside Canada	Percentage of total Inmigrants to 21 cities
Vancouver	1,082,352	+132,900	267,200	12.4%	84,100	10.7%
Edmonton	495,702	+38,900	152,500	7.1	25,600	3.2
Calgary	403,319	+51,200	148,900	6.9	27,700	3.5
Saskatoon	126,449	−1,100	68,300	3.2	4,700	.6
Regina	140,734	−6,700	55,200	2.6	3,900	.5
Winnipeg	540,262	+9,600	109,600	5.1	30,200	3.8
Thunder Bay	112,093	−3,000	27,900	1.3	4,100	2.0
Windsor	258,643	+9,600	33,800	1.6	15,900	2.0
London	286,011	+23,200	77,000	3.6	20,000	2.5
Sudbury	155,424	+13,800	56,200	2.6	5,200	.7
Kitchener	226,846	+23,400	60,200	2.8	18,300	2.3
Hamilton	498,523	+7,900	81,100	3.8	31,600	4.0
Toronto	2,628,043	+205,600	346,900	16.1	324,600	41.1
St. Catherine's	303,429	+9,300	55,600	2.6	12,600	1.6
Ottawa–Hull	602,510	+44,200	124,500	5.8	30,300	3.8
Montreal	2,743,208	+57,800	277,300	12.9	127,000	16.1
Quebec	480,502	+22,900	83,900	3.9	6,200	.8
Chicoutimi	133,703	−6,400	24,100	1.1	800	.1
Saint John	106,744	−2,900	18,400	.9	1,700	.2
Halifax	222,637	+3,000	52,900	2.5	6,700	.8
St. John's	131,185	−1,200	27,600	1.3	2,600	.3
21-city Total	11,678,319	—	2,149,100	100.0	783,800	100.0

[a] Aggregations of counties and census divisions correspond as closely as possible to census metropolitan areas; data were unavailable for Victoria.

Source: Special tabulation by Statistics Canada, based on Department of National Revenue information.

systematically from each other in sex, age, ethnicity, or occupational status, substantial alterations in the demographic structure of a region can occur without a noticeable change in its population size (Stone, 1969, p.7; Kalbach and McVey, 1971, p. 32).

D. Who Migrates and Why

An understanding of who and why is important if appropriate policies for influencing population distribution are to be formulated. Migration is selective of certain elements of the population according to sex, age, education, income, and employment status. Migrants tend to be younger than the population as a whole; males tend to predominate slightly among long distance (interprovincial) movers; females tend to predominate for short distance moves, especially to urban centers. Those who migrate, particularly those moving long distances, tend to have higher educational levels than those who stay. Substantial mobility is also experienced, however, at the opposite end of the economic spectrum. Income-specific migration rates in Canada (1966–1971) are best described by a U-shaped curve, peaking for the lowest and highest income earners (Courchene, 1974).

To explain why peoply migrate is enormously difficult. The literature on migration is extensive but relatively inconclusive. Researchers have been reluctant to generalize their findings and to set forth theoretical propositions (Lee, 1966, p. 51). One eminent demographer observed a number of years ago (and the situation is not much changed) that migration studies teach us only that migration is a nonrandom phenomenon (Bogue, 1959, p. 505).

The one conclusion of most migration studies is that the "economic" motive explains a substantial proportion of migration. Hence, policies that operate through labor markets and the other parameters of economic decision making are likely to prove at least partially effective. However, it is not clear that government action is necessarily beneficial, even when it does operate in this way. One recent study suggests that migration has tended to correct regional disparities, while government interventions have maintained them (Courchene, 1970). Several critical questions have yet to receive a satisfactory answer in the literature: Do people move to jobs, or do jobs move to people? and, How heavily do nonpecuniary factors—the bright lights, the wide selection of goods and services, cultural amenities and social opportunities—weigh in the decision of prospective migrants to larger centers?

IV. Approaches to Control: An Enumeration and Evaluation of the Available Policy Instruments

The above analysis suggests certain *direct* causes for the maladjustment of actual and optimal populations (Section II), as well as *indirect* causes for such maladjustment, manifest principally in the factors that motivate migration (Section III). If the analysis is valid, then two general policy approaches are indicated:

1. The establishment of *direct* countervaillants to particular sources of population maldistribution;
2. the formation of policies with respect to transportation, regional growth, industrial incentives, and the like, so as to de-fuse the forces leading to concentration *indirectly* through influencing the decision to migrate.

A. DIRECT COUNTERVAILLANTS

Of the problems outlined in Section II, *high sensitivity thresholds* and *irreversible policy decisions* may be treated jointly. It may be possible to utilize a number of distinct indicators differentially sensitive to different phenomena associated with variations in city size. In this way, policies can be linked to indicators that measure subthreshhold responses. Given the large number of possible indicators, those with which we are most concerned are those sensitive to changes and to the degree of intervention indicated. Indeed, my view is that the promise of the considerable study of indicators now under way lies not so much in establishing new general indicators as it does in establishing the utility of indicators regarding subcomponents of social and urban systems.

In the case of *insufficient regulatory power* at the city level, the appropriate solution is a redistribution of jurisdictional powers, possibly including the restructuring of local government. Forms of betterment taxation, though imperfect—as the British experience demonstrates—could contribute toward a solution through taxation of excessive *urban land rents*. Likewise, financial "carrots" or "sticks" can be used to ameliorate *externalities* once they have been identified and quantified. Public ownership of land around a city's boundaries, an option that has recently received attention, would permit more comprehensive planning of urban land use and a direct accountability for the size of urban agglomerations. The problems related to a *lack of knowledge of alternatives* will not be easily overcome, though presumably there is some scope through education and the institutionalized exchange of information. Uncertainty among those who attempt to formulate policies is further exacerbated by the need to anticipate *technological change,* a similarly difficult problem.

Notwithstanding the immense difficulties, many national governments have attempted to implement some variant of direct controls with respect either to employment or to land use and building development (e.g., OECD, 1973b). It is the latter that have been employed most frequently, though studies in the context of population distribution concentrate almost exclusively on the former. (It should be noted that these policies are not the same as the countervaillants discussed above, since they focus on symptoms rather than causes of maladjustment.)

Controls over the location of employment have taken the form of licensing industrial and office buildings in the United Kingdom, construction and occupancy permits in France, special construction–investment taxes in the Netherlands and Finland, and compulsory "consultations" in Sweden (OECD, 1974a, p. 7). The rationale for such policies is reduction of employment demand; but the difficulty is that governments are seldom willing to compromise possible damage to economic growth or to the "status" of their largest cities. Generally, controls have been applied only as a reluctant last resort after incentives have proved inadequate, and they are inevitably the least popular of program measures, always resisted and attacked (Sundquist, 1975, p. 270). As a result, the criteria for implementing such policies are "too easy" (OECD, 1974a, p. 7), and hence the controls are often not effective.

The number of possible controls on land use and building development is extremely wide, ranging from classic zoning through specific tax and grant inducements, to sophisticated systems for transferral of development rights (TDRs) (cf. OECD, 1973c). Although in operation throughout most Western countries, there is little favorable and some contrary evidence to suggest that such controls have a beneficial long-run effect on shaping or restraining urban growth (Crowley, 1973b, and Yeates, 1965). Many deleterious ramifications may also arise from the ad hoc and uneven application of rigid planning controls. Crude physical planning instruments intended to limit urban growth, such as the "freeze" on buildings above a designated height in Toronto, are largely an inappropriate means of achieving what is, to a great extent, a social goal. The establishment of such limits has, for example, been assailed by one Toronto researcher for generally resulting in the redistribution of wealth and social opportunities, largely in socially regressive directions against those who can least afford it (Bourne, 1975, p. 28).

A number of problems are posed by the direct implementation of controls on buildings, land, and employment. First, regulations are sometimes exercised within geographical boundaries inappropriate to the task. Since we are usually talking about an urbanized region, the appropriate focus for regulating urban growth is at the metropolitan and not at the central city level. A plan limited to a city is likely to be inadequate. Second, actions must be tempered by the consideration that control also provides greater scope for political chicanery. Third, and most important, controls are often imposed on strong market forces and, when in conflict, are subverted by such forces. Nevertheless, they probably do have potential where developed and used in concert with a battery of policies that indirectly influence population distribution, and it is to that option that we now turn.

B.   An Indirect Approach: Influencing the Migration Process

Though counter to fundamental values in Western society, always lurking in the background is the draconian possibility of a nation placing direct restraint on the mobility of its citizens. Whether such a drastic policy would prove successful if tried is a moot point. Where restrictions on migration have been imposed, mainly in East European countries, their effectiveness has been questionable. Available evidence suggests that East European urban centers have grown substantially, possibly as rapidly as they would have without the control measures. However, the reasons for these failures are far from clear, since there have been no comprehensive evaluations.

Given the tendency of foreign immigrants to cluster in the largest urban areas, Canadian policymakers have flirted with the idea of imposing restrictions as to where newcomers may settle (Department of Manpower and Immigration, 1975). According to the Parliamentary Committee on Immigration Policy, future immigrants could be required to sign contracts specifying where they would live and work for a few years. If the contract were violated, the persons could be expelled or denied social services.

A more acceptable, and generally more viable alternative for decentralizing urban growth is through a package of regional development policies (Morrison, 1973a,b). The issue of regional development is multifaceted and requires a full range of policy initiatives, some of which are listed in Table 15.4. To influence the distribution of the population, policies that affect the demand for labor (such as industrial incentive programs or foreign investment policies) or the supply of skills (such as manpower development–training programs) almost certainly have to be developed in concert. Programs to dissmeinate information on alternative employment opportunities, as well as programs to provide infrastructure—housing, transportation, utilities, and so on—either within

TABLE 15.4

REGIONAL DEVELOPMENT–POPULATION DISPERSAL POLICIES

I. *Policies to Affect the Demand for Labor through the Location of Industry*
   (a) Capital, labor and land subsidies to private sector locations (e.g., industrial incentives)
   (b) Provision of physical infrastructures to improve market operation (e.g., transportation, housing, utilities)
   (c) Government procurement policies
   (d) Decentralization of government offices and installations that directly provide as well as induce employment (e.g., defense cases, agricultural research installations, airports, hospitals, and universities)
   (e) Foreign investment policies.

II. *Policies to Affect the Labor Supply*
   (a) Mobility and retraining grants
   (b) Information on alternative employment opportunities
   (c) Contracts to settle in designated locations for landed immigrants.

III. *Comprehensive Packages*
   (a) Assistance to identified growth centers
   (b) New community development.

---

cities or between cities are also necessary. If regional development efforts are to result in the growth of alternative centers, governments cannot hedge on the provision of social infrastructure.

C. POPULATION DISTRIBUTION THROUGH REGIONAL DEVELOPMENT POLICY: A SURVEY OF EXPERIENCES

The countries of Western Europe—Britain, France, Italy, the Netherlands, and Sweden—have all attempted some form of comprehensive program for population dispersal and regional development (OECD, 1974b). In each country, the original stimulus for the growth policy was alleviation of the plight of economically depressed areas. But as the ill effects of overcongestion in the metropolitan centers became increasingly apparent, these countries adopted the broader goals of restraining growth in expanding areas, reducing interregional population flows, and even, in some cases, specifying in detail the geographical distribution of jobs and population. Simultaneously, program measures to achieve these ends broadened considerably. After their first halting steps to improve physical infrastructure, provide industrial parks, and offer limited aid for new enterprises through loans and tax concessions, the West European countries have erected complexes of mutually reinforcing policies. To stem the flow of migrants to the major urban centers, these nations have adopted, with varying degrees of emphasis, four approaches: (a) infrastructure improvement to prepare areas of economic decline and outmigration for industrial growth; (b) industrial incentives, including cash grants, to encourage investors to locate in "development areas"; (c) disincentives and moral suasion to discourage investment in the major metropolitan areas; and (d) decentralization of government agencies, universities, and state-controlled industries (Sundquist, 1975). The coordination of such programs is generally ensured through comprehensive regional development planning, which comprises a growth center strategy in all five nations and a new towns policy in Britain, Sweden, and France.

Though moving toward the same goals and gradually progressing in the same policy direction, regional development programs in the United States and Canada have not evolved to the same extent as they have in Europe. As in Europe, Canadian development efforts began with improvements to the physical infrastructure, largely in rural areas (Prairie Farm Rehabilitation Act, 1935; Maritime Marshlands Rehabilitation Act, 1948; Argriculture Rural Development Act, 1961) and then proceeded to the development of industrial parks and the provision of loans to prospective investors (Area Development Act, 1963). Priorities for the first initiatives were set according to the "worst first" rule, and programs focused on small, chronically depressed, peripheral areas (Brewis, 1969). Hence welfare, rather than development, principles were stressed; and equity considerations were accorded greater importance than efficiency. With the establishment of the Department of Regional Economic Expansion (DREE) in 1969, comprehensive regional development as a long-term federal government priority came into its own. A multidimensional approach to the pursuit of developmental opportunities by means of the coordinated application of public policies and programs at both the federal and provincial level has been urged by the Department. In effect, a two-pronged effort has been mounted by DREE, including incentive grants (Regional Development Incentives Act) designed to stimulate private capital investment in manufacturing and processing facilities, and the provision of physical as well as social infrastructure via its Special Areas Program. Though essentially uncoordinated, governmental activity has also involved mobility and retraining grants for labor and, more recently, a policy of decentralizing federal government offices and adapting procurement policies to regional development goals.

Yet, the full complement of programs and legislation necessary to support a national policy of population redistribution has never been enacted in Canada. Although the strategy has been favored in some circles, growth center policy has never become a major plank in the nation's regional development program. Unlike the European case, the application of the "new communities" policy in Canada has been limited to northern, single resource towns; it has been unrelated to the populous south and to providing suburbia with structure. That is, it has not been employed specifically as a technique for decentralizing growth.

With a substantial proportion of the manufacturing sector owned by foreign interests, and a heavy concentration of that industry in southwestern Ontario, foreign investment policy is probably critical for deflecting growth from the dense Windsor–Toronto corridor (Ray, 1969). Regional development objectives are, however, conspicuously absent from the foreign investment monitoring process. Perhaps this apparent shortcoming is understandable. Although programs for bolstering the economy of depressed areas have been in place for two decades, it is only recently that there has been any clear recognition of the need to restrain metropolitan growth and redistribute population.

In the United States, measures for population dispersal are still in the early stages of formulation. Indeed, among Western developed nations, the United States is most extreme in considering the geographic distribution of economic activity and population as a matter for market forces, rather than for national planning (Sundquist, 1975, p. 241). So far, only two kinds of program measures have been attempted—improvement of public services and infrastructure in depressed areas and loans or tax credits to influence the locational decisions of new enterprises. This state of affairs may be attributed principally to two factors; the reluctance of the U.S. government to intervene in the private market; and strong, regionally based interests, both metropolitan and rural, which have been unable to reach a consensus (Sundquist, 1975).

D. POPULATION DISTRIBUTION THROUGH REGIONAL DEVELOPMENT
    POLICY: THE LESSONS TO BE LEARNED FROM EXPERIENCE

A wide range of policies have been employed to effect population redistribution; while it is not possible to review them in detail, some of the more prominent are here briefly assessed.

a. *Infrastructure improvement* is a necessary though insufficient condition for regional expansion. The experience of European countries suggests that a minimum level of infrastructure is necessary for industrial development, but above that minimum, differences are of only minor importance.

b. *Financial incentives:* Loans and loan guarantees, though a popular measure in the United States and Canada, exert little influence on the locational decisions of strong, expanding companies with ample credit, although they may affect marginal enterprises. Tax concessions were once offered by most European countries, but direct subsidies in the form of cash grants are now preferred. To minimize subsidy budgets, most European countries, notably excepting Britain, have tried to employ rigorous eligibility tests. Generally, financial incentives are thought to be effective in transferring new industry to designated areas (Sundquist, 1975, pp. 228–229; and OECD, 1975). However, incentive grants have been, at best, marginal in affecting the location of tertiary activity (e.g., head offices). If the French experience is a reliable indicator, convincing the service sector to disperse is a very difficult matter (Sundquist, 1975, pp. 143–144).

c. *Government office dispersal* is probably overrated since it will usually have an appreciable impact only upon the capital area of a country. However, at the local level, the siting of large installations such as defense bases undoubtedly has a salutary economic influence.

d. *Government procurement preferences* have been given by European governments to suppliers located in development areas, but it is not clear how well they have worked. Judging from the brief U.S. experience, procurement preferences are an unsatisfactory way of stimulating regional development. Their principal effect has been to promote inefficiency and graft in administrative agencies.

e. *Growth center strategies and new town development:* Recognizing that lagging areas will rebound faster if investment is focused on a relatively few sites that exhibit potential for growth, many European countries have adopted growth center strategies. Given the limited knowledge at hand and the political pressures involved, the selection of growth centers has, in practice, been somewhat arbitrary. As a comprehensive development package aimed at decentralizing growth, the British new towns policy has met with a measure of success, particularly as it affects London (Rodwin, 1970; OECD, 1973a; OECD, 1974d). However, the lesson of the British new town experience is that the success of a population dispersal policy depends on the coordinated implementation of a *battery* of policies over a reasonably *long-term* planning span.

V. Conclusions

Ascertaining the goals of a country's policies is far easier than finding out what those policies have actually achieved. Nevertheless, it is possible to conclude that the achievement of objectives concerning population distribution depends on the formulation of a coherent, multifaceted policy package and its subsequent implementation over a lengthy period of time. For example, the dual approach of subsidizing migration, to help workers go where jobs are, and regional development, to create jobs where idle workers live, is likely to meet with greater success than either approach by itself. Second, though a federal form of government complicates the achievement of consensus on a national population policy, it may prove beneficial for the administration of regional development programs. Western European countries, particularly Italy, have found it necessary to establish and strengthen regional organizations for development planning purposes.

If a government has the political will to disperse population from the largest centers, there is a wide array of policies available for effecting such a goal. The burden lies in drawing upon extant experience to select the mix best suited to a particular country.

Acknowledgments

Director General, Research and Program Development, Department of Labour, Government of Canada. The views expressed in this chapter are those of the author and not necessarily those of the Government nor of the Department. Bob Kerton provided a helpfully harsh review of an earlier draft and Wayne Bond was of substantial assistance in a major overhaul of an earlier draft.

References

Bogue, D. J. Internal Migration. In P. M. Hauser and O. D. Duncan (Eds.), *The study of population*. Chicago: The University of Chicago Press, 1959.

Bourne, L. S. *Limits to urban growth: Who benefits, planning climate in Toronto*. Research Paper No. 68, Centre for Urban and Community Studies, University of Toronto, 1975.

Brewis, T. N. *Regional economic policies in Canada*. Toronto: Macmillan, 1969.

Courchene, T. J. Interprovincial migration and economic adjustment. *Canadian Journal of Economics*, 1970, *3*, 550–576.

Courchene, T. J. *Migration, employment and income*. C. D. Howe Research Institute, Montreal, 1974.

Crowley, R. W. Reflections and further evidence on population size and industrial diversification. *Urban Studies* 1973, *10*, 91–94.

Crowley, R. W. A case study of the effects of an airport on land values. *Journal of Transport Economics and Policy* 1973, *7*, 144–152. (b)

Hansen, N. The challenge of urban growth. Center for Economic Development, University of Texas, Austin, 1974.

Kalbach, W., and W. McVey. *The demographic bases of Canadian society*. Toronto: McGraw-Hill, 1971.

Lee, E. S. A theory of migration. *Demography*, 1966, *3*, 47–57.

Department of Manpower and Immigration. *Internal migration and immigrant settlement.* Ottawa, 1975.

Morrison, P. A. *How population movements shape national growth.* Santa Monica: Rand Corporation, 1973. (a)

Morrison, P. A. *Migration from distressed areas: Its meaning for regional policy.* Santa Monica: Rand Corporation, 1973. (b)

Morrison, P. A. Guiding urban growth: Policy issues and demographic constraints. Santa Monica: Rand Corporation, 1974.

OECD, Environment Directorate. Constraining the growth in employment of London, Paris and Randstad: A study of methods. By Gordon C. Cameron. U/CHG/73.472, Paris, 1973. (a)

OECD, Environment Directorate. National urban growth policies and strategies: An evaluation of experience in the OECD countries. By Philip H. Friedly. U/CHG/73.473, Paris, 1973. (b)

OECD, Environment Directorate. Policy instruments in the urban land market: Analyses and conclusions. By G. M. Neutze. U/CHG/73.474, Paris, 1973. (c)

OECD, Environment Directorate. The effectiveness of policy instruments to encourage the growth of small and medium-sized cities. By Harry W. Richardson. U/CHG/73.471, Paris, 1973. (d)

OECD, Environment Directorate. Policy instruments for influencing the form and structure of urban development and the distribution of urban growth: Review of case study papers. U/ENV/74.3, Paris, 1974. (a)

OECD, Industrial Committee. Re-appraisal of regional policies in OECD countries. IND/WP6 (74)4, Paris, 1974. (b)

OECD, Industrial Committee. Measuring the results of regional policies: Review studies made in the United Kingdom. IND/WP6 (75)27, Paris, 1975.

Ray, D. M. *Dimensions of Canadian regionalism.* Ottawa: Department of Energy, Mines, and Resources, Policy Research and Coordination Branch, Geographical Paper No. 49, 1969.

Rodwin, L. *Nations and cities.* Boston: Nations and cities: A comparison of strategies for urban gorwth, 1970.

Sauvy, A. *General Theory of Population.*, New York: Basic Books, 1969.

Spengler, J. J. On Regulating the size of cities. Discussion paper B.73.29 (rev), Ministry of State for Urban Affairs, Ottawa, 1973.

Stone, L. O. *Urban development in Canada.* Ottawa: Queen's Printer, 1967.

Stone, L. O. *Migration in Canada: Regional aspects.* Ottawa: Queen's Printer, 1969.

Sundquist, J. L. *Dispersing population: What America can learn from Europe.* Washington: Brookings Institution, 1975.

Tisdell, C. A. The theory of optimal city-sizes: Elementary speculations about analysis and policy. *Urban Studies,* 1975, *12,* 61–70.

Wolpert, J. Migration as an adjustment to environmental stress. *Journal of Social Issues,* 1966, *22*(4), 92–102.

Yeates, M. The effects of zoning on land values in American cities: A case study. In J. P. Whitton and P. D. Woods (Eds.) *Essays in geography for Austin Miller.* Reading: Reading University, 1965.

PART IV
Selected Case Studies

SECTION B
Migration in Eastern Europe

Economizing on Urbanization in Socialist Countries: Historical Necessity or Socialist Strategy

Gur Ofer

I. Introduction

The student of the demographic and industrial structures of the socialist countries of Eastern Europe is faced with a number of phenomena that are different from those usually observed in market economies and that create at least an impression of internal inconsistency. The socialist strategy of rapid industrialization, which has now been pursued for at least a generation, has succeeded in increasing the proportion of GNP from manufacturing and related industries to levels that are above the "normal" for market economies at similar stages of development. However, this high level of activity in manufacturing is not fully revealed by the demographic characteristics and by the distribution of the labor force by sector of origin of these East European countries during the 1960s. First, the proportion of the labor force employed in agriculture in these countries is much higher and, in some socialist countries, the proportion of labor employed in manufacturing and related industries lower than in the comparable market economies. Second, the share of the population that resides in urban locations, where normally most industrial activity takes place, is also much lower than in the corresponding market economies. This asymmetry between growth strategy and product structure on the one side, and labor

277

structure and demographic characteristics on the other, is one apparent inconsistency. A second is that the observed concentration of the population in rural areas and in agricultural pursuits still exists despite a dynamic growth of the urban sector in these countries over the last generation, accompanied by a no less impressive decline in the share of the labor force engaged in agriculture. Both processes were manifested in a massive rural-to-urban migration movement.

In an earlier paper (Ofer, 1974a) it was claimed that the apparent contradiction between intensive industrialization and the prevailing demographic and labor force structures can be explained by a strategy of economizing on urbanization which has been implemented by the socialist governments of the Soviet Union and the East European countries. That paper first made a theoretical case to justify such a policy on a priori grounds—given the growth and industrialization goals under socialism and the means available for their implementation. It then proceeded to demonstrate that such a policy has indeed been carried out, by comparing the industrial structure of input and output for socialist and nonsocialist countries around 1960 and by relating some of the structural deviations of the former to the pursuit of such a policy.

The main task of this paper is to extend that analysis historically to cover the period preceding the socialist takeover in those countries and to bring the findings up to date. Since urbanization is a dynamic–historical process, the economizing on urbanization hypothesis should be tested directly within the historical context of growth and structural changes. Such a test is essential in order to find out whether the deviant structures found in the socialist countries were actually created during the socialist period, and can thus be explained by the socialist growth strategy, or whether the deviant structures were inherited from the preceding regimes—and must then be explained by completely different factors.

A historical investigation is also required to explain the second apparent inconsistency mentioned above: that of dynamic rural-to-urban migration accompanied by persisting rural concentration. By investigating the initial economic and demographic situation in these countries more closely and by examining in detail the migration movement, different conclusions may be reached as to the true magnitude of this inconsistency. The bare essentials of the previous inquiry are presented here as a basic background.

Socialist growth strategy is defined as one aiming at the highest possible rates of growth of GNP. This aim is achieved by pushing the rate of investment to its maximum feasible level, concentrating at a very early stage on a self-industralization drive, that is, with minimum reliance on external trade for this purpose.[1] Being centrally planned, the socialist system can thus better perceive and take into account the social costs involved in urbanization than can the various private forces and government agencies operating in market economies. In addition, socialist planners regard the direct increase in consumption levels associated with urbanization as cost—an outlay that reduces the amount of investments that can be made. Finally, the planners are aware that migrants to urban areas create further pressures for a rise in living standards. Nevertheless, according to the socialist planners, industrial development must take place in urban concentrations in order to reap the desired economies of scale and the other external advantages provided by such concentrations. Since the bulk of the costs of urbanization—initial infrastructure investment as well as the continuous supply of services—are connected with the settlement of people rather than with the investment of capital in the cities, a policy planned to economize on urbanization, *given the high industrial production targets,* should include among its goals the limitation of rural-to-urban migration. Possessing almost absolute powers for planning and allocating inputs (including labor) and outputs, a socialist system can also be more efficient than a market economy in pursuing such a policy.

Different means are used. First, the levels of urban infrastructure and services per migrant are forced down. Second, policies are aimed at keeping the ratio of dependents and service workers to those "productively" employed in the manufacturing sector at the lowest possible level. Third, the number of migrants is reduced by improving the total productivity of inputs in the urban industries, by using higher capital–labor ratios—as compared with market economies—in those industries and lower capital–labor ratios in agriculture. While my earlier paper demonstrated the apparent use of most or all of the above policies, the application of an input substitution policy was especially emphasized.

In Section II of this paper, the presocialist structure of the East European countries is compared with the normal pattern in market economies. Because the structural deviations found are very similar to those of the socialist period, an attempt must be made to find out whether these similar deviation patterns result from the same or from different causes. The analysis of the differences in the economic and

---

[1] In the Soviet Union, industrialization was achieved with minimum reliance on foreign trade. As for the socialist countries of Eastern Europe, while not aiming at autarky, they have been following a trade policy strongly oriented toward import substitution of industrial goods. Thus, at a very early stage of development, their trade structure is biased against exporting primary goods and importing industrial goods. See discussions by Brown and Marer (Brown, 1968, oo. 57–63; and Brown and Marer, 1973, pp. 153–155).

historical conditions in the two periods seems to support the conclusion that the initial conditions—high concentrations of population and labor in the rural and agricultural sectors and a low level of development of the urban infrastructure—were highly conducive to the development and implementation of a policy of economizing on urbanization, a policy which is also a logical result of the socialist system and growth strategy.

This conclusion is further strengthened in Section III, where the urbanization process from 1950 to 1967, its size and structure, is described and the economic and demographic consequences of a more accelerated rural-to-urban migration—necessary if the gaps are to be narrowed—are analyzed.

II. A Comparison of the Presocialist and Socialist Structure of the East European Economies with Those of the Market Economies

To make this comparison, "normal" levels of various structural elements, such as the proportion of population residing in urban areas (UR) or the share of the labor force engaged in the main branches of the economy, are estimated for the market economies by correlating these levels with a corresponding rate of GNP per capita in the countries concerned. The general equation takes the form:

$$X = a + b \log Y \tag{1}$$

Where X is the structural variable and Y is GNP per capita.

As numerous studies have shown, GNP per capita, or a similar index approximating the level of economic development, is highly correlated with the structure of the economy. The deviations for the East European economies are then estimated by comparing the economic structure of each of these countries with the normal levels. Alternatively, all countries are included in the estimation process but a dummy variable of "being an East European country" (EE) for the presocialist period or "being a socialist country" (SC) is added to the above equation. In this fashion a "collective" deviation is estimated for all the East European countries.

The market economy group consists of 23 countries (a few less for 1940) with GNP per capita ranking with and above that of the 8 East European countries included.

The dates chosen to represent the presocialist period—the late 1930s (put as 1940 in the tables for convenience) and 1950—are far from ideal. The upheavals and disruptions of World War II make the late 1930s at best only the least disruptive, fairly recent, presocialist period. By 1950 all the East European countries under investigation had already been under socialist rule for several years. It is assumed, however, that many of their structural characteristics at that time were influenced more by their previous history than by the new economic system. The sources of the data, the information itself, and some references to its deficiencies, are presented in the Appendix Table 1. Additional problems with the data, which may affect the findings, are mentioned in the body of the text.

In Tables 16.1 and 16.2, the levels of urbanization and the labor force structures of the East European countries are compared with the normal levels for the prewar period and for 1950, and during the socialist

TABLE 16.1

URBANIZATION LEVELS, SOCIALIST AND NONSOCIALIST COUNTRIES, 1940–1967[a]

	1940		1950		1960		1967	
	Act.	Res.	Act.	Res.	Act.	Res.	Act.	Res.
Czechoslovakia	48	− 2	51	− 3	57	− 5	61	− 3
East Germany	67	15	69	19	72	11	73	9
Soviet Union	33	−10	39	− 9	48	− 9	55	− 7
Hungary	36	−11	35	−13	40	−15	44	−18
Poland	29	−13	36	−12	47	− 6	50	−11
Bulgaria	24	−16	29	−13	38	−12	48	−12
Rumania	24	−18	23	−20	35	−15	39	−21
Yugoslavia	15	−24	19	−22	28	−21	34	−24
Selected Coefficients of Equations:[b]								
SS_1 *(EE)*	−8.2		−8.2		−9.7		−9.4	
	(−1.3)		(−1.5)		(−1.7)		(−1.5)	
SC_2	−16.0		−15.7		−13.8		−16.8	
	(—)		(−2.6)		(−2.0)		(−2.5)	
SEE	14.4		12.0		14.3		13.4	
Log *y*	12.3		12.2		13.9		6.7	
	(2.1)		(3.4)		(2.9)		(1.2)	
Constant	−29.0		−27.0		−35.6		16.0	
	(−0.8)		(−1.1)		(−1.1)		(0.4)	

[a] Both actual and residual figures are rounded to the nearest percentage point.

[b] *SE* (or *EE* for 1940 and 1950) is the coefficient of "being a socialist country" (or an East European country in 1940) estimated from equations that include both socialist and nonsocialist countries; SC_1 is based on all socialist countries; SC_2 on all socialist countries except Czechoslovakia, East Germany, and the Soviet Union. SEE—the standard error of estimate, log *y*—the coefficient of GNP per capita, and constant are coefficients of the normal equations based on observations for non-socialist countries only. Figures in parenthesis are the corresponding t values of the coefficients.

Sources and other notes on the basic data: See Appendix Table 1.

TABLE 16.2

LABOR FORCE STRUCTURE OF SOCIALIST COUNTRIES FROM ESTIMATED LEVELS, 1940–1967[a]

	1940			1950			1960			1967		
	A	M	S	A	M	S	A	M	S	A	M	S
Czechoslovakia	3.8	5.1	-9.0	9.4	0.9	-9.9	6.0	7.4	-7.5	1.9	8.7	-8.7
East Germany	-13.5	16.9	-3.6	-13.6	17.4	-3.6	-3.6	11.1	-6.6	-3.5	11.0	-7.4
Soviet Union	8.7	-2.9	-5.9	11.2	-1.8	-9.0	11.3	-0.5	-10.7	8.0	-0.2	-7.9
Hungary	10.2	-7.5	-2.7	10.3	-5.3	-4.5	7.6	2.7	-10.3	4.1	4.3	-8.6
Poland	18.2	-11.2	-6.9	16.0	-3.2	-12.3	12.0	1.1	-13.1	11.4	1.3	-12.9
Bulgaria	27.2	-16.2	-11.0	28.4	-14.2	-13.9	19.9	-5.7	-14.2	11.8	0.5	-11.3
Rumania	27.8	-16.0	-11.8	29.3	-14.1	-14.9	29.7	-13.5	-16.2	26.5	-11.2	-14.8
Yugoslavia	25.2	-12.8	-12.4	22.8	-7.5	-15.0	20.1	-5.7	-14.4	21.8	-9.0	-13.2
Selected Coefficients of Equations[b]												
SC_1 (EE)	10.7	-3.6	-7.1	13.5	-3.5	-9.7	12.8	-0.5	-12.6	9.0	1.7	-10.9
	(5.7)	(-1.5)	(-2.3)	(3.1)	(-1.0)	(-4.2)	(3.7)	(-0.2)	(-6.6)	(2.5)	(0.6)	(-5.4)
SC_2	21.7	-12.7	-9.0	20.9	-8.8	-11.9	17.5	-4.0	-13.9	14.3	-2.2	-12.4
	(—)	(—)	(—)	(4.5)	(-2.4)	(-4.2)	(4.0)	(-1.2)	(-5.7)	(3.4)	(-0.7)	(-4.7)
SEE	11.8	9.0	5.4	8.7	7.1	5.5	8.2	6.5	5.1	6.4	5.2	4.7
Log y	-19.9	11.7	8.2	-17.7	11.2	6.4	-20.2	10.7	9.4	-15.9	4.7	10.8
	(-4.5)	(3.5)	(4.0)	(-6.7)	(5.2)	(3.8)	(-7.2)	(4.9)	(5.4)	(-5.2)	(1.9)	(4.7)
Constant	162.9	-38.5	-24.9	146.7	-33.6	-12.7	161.8	-31.0	-30.5	132.1	10.9	-40.3
	(5.8)	(-1.8)	(-1.9)	(8.5)	(-2.4)	(-1.2)	(8.4)	(-2.1)	(-2.6)	(5.9)	(0.6)	(-2.4)

[a] The sectors are: A = agriculture; M = manufacturing and mining, construction, transportation, and communications; S = services.

[b] See note [b] to Table 1.

Sources and other notes on the basic data: See Appendix Table 1.

period for 1960 and 1967. The results shown in the tables, together with the underlying data, demonstrate that the structural changes normally associated with a rise in GNP per capita are indeed taking place in the socialist countries. Together with a rise in Y, there are also increases in the levels of UR and in the M and S shares of the labor force, and a decline in the A labor share.[2] The differences investigated here, between socialist countries and market economies, thus fit into the framework of the same general theory.

By far the most striking result is that most of the structural anomalies observed in the socialist period, which hitherto have been explained by reference to the socialist system and growth strategy, show up extremely clearly in the presocialist period as well.

Thus, with respect to the level of urbanization (Table 16.1), we find in all of the East European countries—with the exception of Czechoslovakia and East Germany—for all of the years studied very large deficiencies as compared with normal levels. In most cases the deficiencies range between 10 and 20 percentage points, and in some cases they constitute more than 50 percentage points, of the normal level. The deficiencies in UR for the EE group (including Czechoslovakia and East Germany) do amount to between 8 and 10 points, but they are not highly significant.

Since here, and also in whàt follows, it is found that Czechoslovakia and East Germany behave differently from the other, less-developed East European countries[3] and since the Soviet Union in 1940 was already socialist and well into the 5-year plan era, we have also calculated SC_2, the collective deviation from the normal pattern for only five East European countries: Hungary, Poland, Rumania, Bulgaria, and Yugoslavia. When only these countries are included, the collected UR deviations are larger—about 16 points in the presocialist period, 14 in 1960, and almost 17 in 1967—all of which are statistically significant. In all cases, the deficiencies found in the level of urbanization are common to both the presocialist and the socialist period; even in 1967 the EE group was significantly underurbanized.

There is always the possibility that such findings result from inconsistencies between Eastern Europe and the market economies as to what constitutes an urban location or that the levels of GNP per capita assigned to the EE group are too high (thus overestimating their

---

[2] A = agriculture; M = mining, manufacturing, construction, transportation, and communications; S = public and private services.

[3] We refer below, p. 285, to the abnormal behavior pattern of Czechoslovakia and East Germany. The pattern of deviations for the Soviet Union is similar to that for other East European countries.

expected level of urbanization). As shown in the notes to Appendix Table 1, the definitions used for "urban" are those used by the individual countries and thus in principle they might not be fully consistent with one another. The view taken here, however, is that the different definitions are designed to account for special conditions in each country, that what is generally understood as "urban" will be so classified, and that the end result will be very similar in the different countries. In addition, after examining the individual definitions, we did not find any reason to believe that *as a group* the East European countries used a narrower definition of *UR* than do the market economy countries.[4] With respect to GNP per capita, we used the series that assigns the lowest values for the *EE* group, as compared to the market economies, and thus attempted to reduce the possible bias mentioned earlier.[5]

The urbanization gap of the *EE* group is also reflected in the labor force structure, as shown in Table 16.2. Here, the proportion of the labor force employed in the *A, M,* and *S* sectors of the East European economies are compared with those for the market economies. Just as there were large concentrations of the population in rural areas, so are there large surpluses in the *A* sector of all East European countries, with the exception of East Germany. (Even Czechoslovakia had a positive *A* gap until the late 1960s). The gaps exist not only in the 1960s but also in 1950 and 1940. They range between 10 and 20 points but in some cases reach 50% or more above the expected, or normal, levels. Taken as a group, the East European countries all show surpluses that are statistically significant: 10.7 points in 1940; 13.5 in 1950; 12.8 in 1960, and 9.0 in 1967. Here too, Czechoslovakia, and East Germany—especially the latter—behave quite differently, and the collective deviations based only on the five less-developed East European countries (SC_2) are very much larger: more than 20 points in the presocialist period, 17.5 points in 1960, and more than 14 points in 1967.

The observed deficiency in urban residence (Table 16.1) is found here to be unequally shared between the *S* and *M* sectors and to differ as between the presocialist and socialist periods. A larger share of the deficiency is borne by the *S* sector, which is smaller than normal by 5 to 12 points in the earlier period (group deviations of 7 to 12 points). These gaps tended to *increase* during the socialist period. Typical individual

---

[4] See Myers (1970, pp. 101–102) for a discussion on different *UR* definitions. See also note [d] in Table 16.3. See Konrad and Szelenzyi (1974) for a very forceful claim that the East European countries are severely underurbanized.

[5] For more on this point, including a sensitivity analysis of errors in GNP per capita, see Ofer (1974a, pp. 31–32).

gaps of 10 to 15 points and group gaps of 12 to 14 points are observed in 1960 (the gaps are only somewhat smaller in 1967). This slight difference in the S gap pattern between the two periods is much more pronounced in the pattern of the labor share of the M sector. Whereas for 1960 and 1967 one can no longer speak of a general pattern of M share deficiencies in the EE group—there are only small deficiencies in two or three countries—there were negative M gaps in 1940 and 1950 in all of these countries with the exception of East Germany, gaps that are not smaller than the corresponding ones in the S sector. The gap in the M sector thus constitutes the only observation that deviates from the paradoxical picture of similar demographic and structural deviations in the East European countries during the two periods. It may also provide the first clue to the resolution of this paradox.

With relatively minor exceptions, none of the typical "socialist" deviations found in the other six countries are observed for Czechoslovakia or East Germany. East Germany in fact, has shifted to the other side. The urbanization level and labor force structure in Czechoslovakia for 1940 are relatively close to the norm, and there are no important changes after the socialist takeover. Only in the S sector is there a consistently negative deviation of statistical significance. Because of a relatively inclusive definition of urbanization, the comparable gap in UR may be larger by a number of percentage points. This last comment also applies to East Germany, which uses an even more inclusive definition of UR; as a result, the large positive gap shown may be mostly artificial.[6] East Germany, part of a larger Germany before the war, started from a structure diametrically opposite to that of the other East European countries—a negative gap in A and a large positive gap in M (in 1940 and 1950) and developed toward a much more normal structure in UR, A, and M, associated, however, with some increase in the negative deviation of S, which is certainly characteristic of socialist economies. The different structural behavior of Czechoslovakia and East Germany may be a consequence of both countries having been already fairly well developed and industrialized before the socialist takeover and thus having had to adapt to the structural implications of the socialist growth strategy in a different way. In what follows, therefore, we concentrate on the behavior of the less-developed socialist countries, including the Soviet Union 20 years earlier, and return to Czechoslovakia and East Germany to test our conclusions.

[6] In East Germany every location with 2000 inhabitants or more is considered urban. Since 1970(?) Czechoslovakia, which used this definition in the past, uses a somewhat less inclusive definition (see Myers 1970, p. 102; and United Nations, *Demographic Yearbook,* 1970, p. 163).

There could be two opposing explanations for the similarity in the urbanization and labor gap patterns of the *EE* group over time; that is, provided that we rule out a third explanation—that the pattern of gaps is a result of consistent errors in the data. The first and more logical explanation is that it is not the socialist system as such but a number of geopolitical factors and historical developments common to most of these countries that can explain the structural differences—factors that prevailed even after the establishment of socialist regimes, which may even have prevailed over any socialist countertendencies. At the other extreme, there is the possibility that the same pattern of labor deviations in the two periods is explained by two entirely different sets of factors: that during the presocialist period there existed a number of common geopolitical and economic conditions which created structural deviations similar to those created by the completely different set of factors that emerged from the newly established socialist system and growth strategy.

Between the two extremes there exists a continuum of mixed possibilities, of some mutual relationships and effects of one set of factors on the other. We believe that the truth lies somewhere in this range. The proposition that is offered here is that two completely different sets of conditions and factors caused similar structural anomalies during the two periods, but that the initial structure at the time of the socialist takeover is a very important supporting condition for the kind of socialist growth strategy, and the socialist economic system, that has since been developed. Moreover, some important elements of what is known as the socialist strategy, which had developed earlier in the Soviet Union and were there influenced by conditions very similar to those in the other East European countries, were taken into consideration in formulating and carrying out the strategy in Eastern Europe.

That the pattern of the deviations in the output, labor, and demographic structures of these countries should have been completely different in the presocialist as compared with the socialist period should be obvious from what is widely known about the nature of these economies during the two periods. For a long time the economies of the less-developed countries of Eastern Europe were relatively stagnant and undeveloped, situated on the fringes of a developing and industrializing continent. Because of their proximity to the developed part of Europe, these areas experienced—in addition to the usual difficulties of any preindustrial economy—high rates of population growth (imported from the West in the form of means to lower the death rate). They also directed their trade, and thus their structures of production, to providing agricultural produce for the developed West, while at the same time

importing manufactured goods. Finally, they benefited to various degrees from the educational and cultural advances that took place in the
rest of Europe. As a result, these economies were able to grow slowly
along a path heavily dominated by primary production; they developed
with very little industrialization and thus not much urbanization. Before
World War II the East European economies were, with few exceptions,
agrarian societies dominated by small-scale, family-based, farming units.
This characteristic was further accentuated by a wave of land reforms—
which in most of these countries took place during the interwar period—
that supplied land to landless peasants, mainly at the expense of large
estates. The marked overconcentration of population in rural areas and
of the labor force in agriculture thus reflected the combined result of a
production structure biased toward higher A and lower M and S shares
(in real terms) and a phenomenon of disguised unemployment which had
developed over long periods of economic stagnation and abortive
attempts at industrialization.

The backwardness of these economies during the interwar period is
well documented. Moore's (1945) comprehensive comparative study
may provide the most suitable background for our analysis, since it
exhaustively discusses the main development problems of the area at
that time.[7] Of all the countries considered, Hungary was by far the most
industrialized; but its industrialization process had been very slow until
the last few years before the war, when it picked up momentum through
its trade with Nazi Germany (Eckstein, 1956, pp. 23–30). Even so, the
share of labor in the A sector declined only from about 60% to 50% from
1900 to 1949—a very slow structural change. That part of Poland which
had belonged to the Russian Empire before World War I had been an
important industrial center; but, after the separation, manufacturing
generally declined in Poland and did not start to improve until the late
1930s. As for Rumania, Bulgaria, and Yugoslavia, their level of industrialization—measured by the per capita production of manufacturers—
was at or below that of such countries as India, Syria, Brazil, or Turkey
in the 1960s (Montias, 1967, p. 45; and Moore, 1945, pp. 122–127).

The drastic changes that took place in the trade structure of the East
European countries between the two wars are duly recorded in one of
Hungary's statistical yearbooks.

---

[7] See especially Chapter 2 on surplus agricultural labor; Chapter 3 and Appendix 3,
which discuss in great detail the agrarian institutional setup and the effect of the land
reforms; and Chapter 4, pp. 122–128, in which the level of industralization in these
countries is described. Other sources on the period are Eckstein (1956), Gerschenkron
(1962), Montias (1967), and Rosenstein-Rodan (1958).

Before World War II, in compliance with the agrarian character of Hungary's economy, agricultural products and products of the food processing industry prevailed in the exports of the country. Historical causes also contributed to this development of our foreign trade pattern. In the Austro-Hungarian monarchy, Hungary played the role of the granary. Even after the dissolution of the monarchy, Hungary remained one of the important agricultural deliverers of Austria and Czechoslovakia, then in the 1930s, of Germany and Italy. This one-sideness of our exports made its detrimental effect felt in the second half of the 1930s, too, when the development of exports was slackened by the dragging agricultural crises accompanying the economic crises [Hungary, Central Statistical Office, 1970, p. 199].

All the causes of this situation disappeared almost immediately after the socialist takeover. The socialist policy of rapid growth (accompanied by a decline in the rate of population increase) could be expected to eliminate any unemployment, disguised or not, and the socialist strategy of early industrialization combined with an autarkic trade policy could be expected to shift the production structure away from the A sector toward the M sector. Further, such a redirection of the production structure could be anticipated from the high rate of investment and the low share of private consumption that form the basis of the rapid-growth policy. Thus, had the socialist growth strategy consisted *only* of the elements of rapid growth, heavy investment, industrialization, and autarky, the production, demography, and labor structure of the presocialist period should have veered rapidly toward the normal pattern or even led to gaps in the opposite direction. The positive labor output gaps in A should at least have been closed and the negative gaps in M been turned into positive ones. Since this is what happened to the real-product shares and gaps but not to the population and labor-gaps—that is, the latter have stayed more or less at the presocialist level—some other elements of the socialist system and growth strategy appear to be the cause. It is our argument that these other elements are—or are associated with—policies designed to economize on urbanization.

An earlier paper (Ofer, 1974b) presented a much more precise and detailed quantitative dynamic analysis to substantiate most of what is claimed here on the basis of impressionistic evidence. That paper showed that there were very marked changes—*as compared to normal patterns of changes*—in the trade and output structure of the East European economies away from agriculture and toward the M (but not the S) sector, but that these changes were not accompanied, as might have been expected, by equally intensive changes in the structure of the labor force.

In addition to the positivistic evidence for the presence of a policy of economizing on urbanization in the socialist countries, the foregoing analysis also offers insights into the motivations of these countries in following such a policy. First, the initial conditions of overconcentration of the population in rural areas were conducive to a policy of input substitution. It was only necessary to use the surplus labor as much as possible in agriculture and to develop the M sector in the cities with high capital–labor input ratios. Such a policy would have made less sense had there been an initially high concentration of population in urban centers. Secondly, the initially low level of urban infrastructure (not to speak of war damage) confronted the socialist countries with the difficulty of deciding how to utilize their then meager investment funds. Should, or could, they spend huge amounts of scarce investment funds to make up for the missing infrastructure? Or should they pursue instead policies that economized on urbanization costs and saved the investment funds for direct industrialization?

In light of such a hypothesis, the deviant behavior of East Germany and Czechoslovakia becomes clearer. With a relatively large urban infrastructure at the outset and with a large proportion of the population already having moved into urban locations from rural areas, there was both less to gain from a policy of economizing on urbanization and fewer limitations on urban growth. As a result we find only a limited and selective use of this policy in those countries (Ofer, 1974b, pp. 41–43).

This hypothesis–conclusion on the interaction between historical conditions and a new economic system is directly examined in the next section, in relation to evidence on the dynamics of the rural-to-urban migration movement and the demographic and investment aspects of the urbanization process in the less-developed socialist countries.

III. Urbanization and Rural-to-Urban Migration

Table 16.3 presents more detailed information on the urbanization process in the less-developed East European countries since 1950. Notwithstanding what was said in the previous section, the data in the table give the impression of a rather dynamic urbanization process fed by large-scale rural-to-urban migration (Lines 4–8). In all the countries— with the exception of Hungary—the urban population increased over the period by between 80% and 133% (line 9), or at an annual rate of between 3% and 6%.

In Hungary, while urbanization efforts (not the absolute level) are clearly behind those in the other socialist countries, the low figures may be partly a result of not reclassifying rural locations that became urban in character. That this is the case might be deduced from Konrad and

TABLE 16.3

POPULATION, URBANIZATION, AND MIGRATION IN FIVE EAST EUROPEAN COUNTRIES, 1950–1967[a]

			Hungary	Poland	Rumania	Bulgaria	Yugoslavia
A. Total population:							
(1)	1950	(in millions)	9.3	24.8	16.3	7.3	16.4
(2)	1967	(in millions)	10.2	31.9	19.3	8.3	19.8
(3)	(2)−(1) growth 1950–1967	(in millions)	0.9	7.1	3.0	1.0	3.4
B. Urban population:							
(4)	1950	(in millions)	3.3	8.9	3.8	2.1	2.9
(5)	(4) ÷ (1) 1950	(in percentages)	35	36	23	29	18
(6)	1967	(in millions)	4.5	16.0	7.5	4.0	6.8
(7)	(6) ÷ (2) 1967	(in percentages)	44	50	39	48	34
(8)	growth 1950–1967	(in millions)	1.2	7.0	3.8	1.9	3.9
(9)	(8) ÷ (4) Relative growth 1950–1967		0.38	0.79	1.00	0.90	1.33
(10)	Growth due to natural increase (in percentages)[b d]		24	40	25	23	—
(11)	Growth due to migration (in percentages)[c d]		64	36	29	61	—
C. Expected urban population:							
(12)	1950	(in millions)	4.5	11.9	7.0	3.1	6.7
(13)	(12) ÷ (1) 1950	(in percentages)	48	48	43	42	41
(14)	1967	(in millions)	6.3	19.5	11.6	5.0	11.5
(15)	(14) ÷ (2) 1967	(in percentages)	62	61	60	60	58
(16)	growth 1950–1967	(in millions)	1.9	7.6	4.6	1.9	4.8
(17)	(16) ÷ (12) Relative growth 1950–1967		0.41	0.64	0.66	0.64	0.72
D. Growth needed to close the gap:							
(18)	(14) − (4)	(in millions)	3.1	10.6	7.8	2.9	8.6
(19)	(18) ÷ (8) Relative growth 1950–1967		2.52	1.51	2.05	1.53	2.20

a Absolute figures are rounded off to 0.1 millions, which is the source of some discrepancies. Relative figures were calculated on the basis of more precise data.

b Natural increase of the urban population is a crude estimate. The calculation applies the rate of natural increase for the entire population to rate of increase for the urban population during the periods 1950–1960 and 1960–1967.

c Rough estimates based on Myers (see sources).

d The estimates do not include the natural increase among the migrants after they have moved to an urban location. Urbanization not accounted for by natural increase or migration is explained by the reclassification of rural into urban locations, either under an existing definition or as a result of a change in the definition of what constitutes an urban location. Here, however, the residuals include also errors in the estimates of natural increase and migration. The only available data on reclassification is for Rumania, where 1.6 million people were reclassified over the period (Myers, 1970, p. 102)—a figure that explains almost all of the residual—and for Poland, where an unspecified number of people in 103 workers' settlements were reclassified (Myers, 1970, p. 102). These workers' settlements must be very large in order to explain a residual of about 1.7 million people. The unexplained residuals for the other countries, Hungaria, and Bulgaria, are very small and can be explained by reclassification.

Sources:

Total population: See Urban population.

Urban population: See Sources for Appendix Table 1.

Expected urban population: Based on estimates of Eq. (1) as explained in the text. The basic data concerning natural increase and rural-to-urban migration are from Myers (1970, pp. 101–108, 125–136) and the sources cited by him in Footnote 38 on p. 106.

291

Szelenyi, who state that "Even in villages the heads of 64% of the households have their principal employment outside agriculture [Konrad and Szelenyi, 1974, p. 15]." The authors see this phenomenon as a consequence of the small effort directed toward the construction of urban areas.

In all the countries, the increase in the number of urban residents was at least equal to the overall increase in total population; urbanization absorbed the entire additions to the respective populations and more (compare lines 3 and 8), and the absolute number of rural residents declined. This phenomenon is especially impressive at early stages of urbanization, when most of the population, and thus its natural increase, are concentrated in rural areas and when the urbanization process is heavily dependent on rural-to-urban migration. Indeed, such migration represented two-thirds of the increase in urban population in Hungary and about 60% in Bulgaria (lines 11 and 8). In Rumania, where a large share of the incremental urbanization stems from reclassification of rural locations into urban ones, migration accounts for almost 30% of the total, but one-half of the nonreclassified, urbanization. The same is true with respect to Poland, where migration constitutes 35% of the total, but a much higher percentage of the nonreclassified, urbanization. Although part of the increased urbanization is due to reclassification—especially in Rumania and Poland[8]—and although reclassification itself is a costless act, it is important to emphasize that it reflects at least in part a de facto urbanization process (consisting of migration, investment in infrastructure, etc.) that has already taken place.

Let us now compare the socialist urbanization rates to what may be considered "normal" or "expected" rates based on observations of market economies. Lines (12) to (15) of Table 16.3 present estimates of normal levels of urbanization for the socialist countries, based on the equations of Table 16.1; on this basis we compute in line (16) the expected growth of their respective urban populations had they had initially normal urbanization levels and had they increased them at the same rate as the market economies in our sample having similar levels of GNP per capita. Corresponding expected relative rates of increase in *UR* are shown in line (17). Taking the absolute changes first, and comparing them with the actual changes that took place in the socialist countries, we see that for all these countries the estimates of increases in the urban population are higher than actually took place. The deficiencies range from insignificant ones of only 2% for Bulgaria and 8 to 9%

---

[8] See note (*d*) to Table 16.3.

for Poland to more significant ones of 20% to 25% for Yugoslavia and Romania and up to 50% for Hungary. Even the mere existence of such dynamic deficiencies indicates that, despite the forceful, much more than normally intensive industrialization drive of the socialist countries, the urbanization process did not proceed even at a normal rate, not to speak of narrowing or closing the initial gaps. Line (18) shows the absolute additions to the urban population that would have been required in order to close these gaps by 1967. Clearly, they are larger than the normal changes (line 16), and it could be claimed that these are the figures to which the actual figures of urbanization in the socialist countries (line 8) should be compared. As can be seen in line (19), the gap-closing figures involve urbanization rates that are larger by no less than 50%, and that in some cases reach levels of up to 150%, of what was actually achieved. Our conclusion, then, is that the socialist countries are indeed engaged in a policy of economizing on urbanization.

The same figures, together with others, may also inspire a second conclusion, that the economic implications of much higher rates of urbanization—as warranted by the normal trends—if they do not completely prohibit faster urbanization, at least pose serious difficulties for such a course. The source of these difficulties is, not surprisingly, the same factor that creates the need for intensive urbanization—the initial deficiencies in the level of urbanization itself.

The differences between the figures in line (18) and those in line (8), when looked at from the point of view of the economic and social costs involved, are impressive enough, as we have seen; but the actual costs of further urbanization are even higher than indicated by these figures. It seems reasonable to assume that the incremental costs per unit of urbanization increase with the amount of urbanization attempted at any given time, especially for intense urbanization efforts such as those undertaken in the socialist countries. An accelerated speed of urbanization involves first of all an increase in the proportion of rural-to-urban migration making up the incremental urban population, which means more dislocation, greater harm to the rural and agricultural sector, and higher costs in terms of human readjustment and economic retraining for the migrants. It also means having to move people who are relatively less prepared to move and relatively less fit for urban tasks and way of life. A faster urbanization process also means less efficient economic and social absorption, less thorough planning of the urban infrastructure and thus the less effective construction of new cities and unsatisfactory enlargement of old ones. In any case, higher speed means higher unit costs for the construction of the urban infrastructure.

Thus, if, historically, rural-to-urban migration contributed from one-third to two-thirds of the increase in the urban population in the socialist countries, a 1% further increase in the rate of urbanization, now totally consisting of migrants, would involve a 1.5% to 3% increase in the volume of such migration. At the rate of migration already achieved in the socialist countries, the increased relative contribution of migrants to urbanization would certainly be more costly per migrant in all the aspects mentioned above.

The capacity of the existing urban sector to absorb migrants is also a factor affecting marginal urbanization costs: The larger the initial urbanization base, the lower the incremental cost per unit. It may then be justifiable to examine the *relative* increase of the urban sector as compared to normal rates, in addition to the comparisons of absolute figures. Indeed such a comparison shows (compare lines 17 and 9) that, in relative terms, the urbanization effort of the socialist countries was—again with the exception of Hungary—larger than that experienced by the market economies: by only 6 points for Poland, but by about 30 points for Rumania and Bulgaria, and by some 60 points more than the normal (twice the normal level) in Yugoslavia. Obviously, the initial, abnormally low levels create this effect and for this reason relative growth cannot be a valid criterion for an overall comparison of various urbanization efforts. It is, however, a cost-augmenting factor, through its effect on absorptive capacity.

In addition to higher unit costs, an urbanization effort that aims at closing such large gaps over a short period of time would involve the allocation to urbanization—and away from more productive projects—of a very high proportion of total investment funds and a major share of the capacity of the construction industry. Such a shift may seem to be unreasonable for any economy; it is certainly inconceivable to the system directors of socialist countries, who are very sensitive to the distinction between "productive" and "nonproductive" investments.

We do not yet have the data for, and nor is there space here to go into, the precise calculations. Even rough ones, however, show what a closing of the urbanization gaps would mean for the investment and construction sectors.[9] During the period 1950–1967, all the East European countries devoted about 30% of their total investments in fixed capital to housing, communal services, trade, education, health, and so

[9] The basic data on the distribution of investments by branch and by type of asset are from the United Nations, *Yearbook of National Accounts Statistics* (various years), tables for individual countries.

on. (This figure does not include investment in transportation.) These investments made up between 50 and 60% of the entire investment in structures and buildings. True, part of the investments in housing and services—particularly with respect to schools, hospitals and the like— was directed to building up rural locations or to raising the level of urban services. Nevertheless, there are enough indications to show that the bulk of the "nonproductive" investments were connected directly with the construction of new urban facilities, either for migrants or for additional indigenous residents. To be on the safe side, let us assume that such investments made up only between one-half and two-thirds of the "nonproductive" investments. On this basis it can be estimated that doubling the rate of urban growth during the 1950–1967 period—roughly what is needed in order to close the urbanization gap (line 19 of Table 16.3)—would involve increasing the "nonproductive" share in total investments from the existing 30% to between 45 and 50% or more. The share of total construction would have to rise from between 50 and 60% up to between 70 and 100%.[10] The high proportions devoted to "non-productive" investments implied here are unacceptable and unattainable for the directors of a system that is, on the one hand, committed to high rates of industrial growth—involving large amounts of "productive" investment—and, on the other, very short of investment funds.

Two additional observations support this hypothesis about the difficulty of increasing the rate of urbanization beyond that actually achieved. First, in an earlier paper it was shown that even moderate plans for urban development and construction were very often not fulfilled, principally because scarce resources had to be reserved for the fulfillment of higher priority "productive" projects (Ofer, 1974b, pp. 61– 63). Urbanization projects were cut even though in many cases more people than planned for had to be brought into the cities to help fulfill urgent production plans. The unavoidable result was a two-directional squeeze on the level of urban services (housing, etc.) per urban resident. It follows that whatever potential there was to increase urbanization by reducing the standards of urban living had already been exhausted and could not have provided for additional urbanization.

Second, in most of the socialist countries, especially in Hungary, a mass movement of rural-to-urban commuters seemed to replace or

---

[10] That is, if total investment and total construction remained at their actual respective volumes. It is reasonable to assume that the share of investment in GNP was close to the attainable maximum. An increase in the urbanization effort, however, would involve an increase in the capacity of the construction industry.

substitute for unplanned, as well as planned and not fulfilled, urban development (Konrad and Szelenyi, 1974, especially pp. 16–18). Part of this development may have been intentional—an attempt to make up for scarce investment resources by using the "free" time of commuters and the already existing housing facilities in the countryside. Another part was, however, a manifestation of the difficulties faced in diverting enough resources to develop the urban infrastructure.

Much more work is still required in order to determine whether the policy of economizing on urbanization as followed in the socialist countries has justified itself from the economic and other points of view. What we have tried to show here is that while such a policy has many "socialist" elements and probably could have been followed given a variety of initial historical conditions, the initial deficiency of urban development in the countries of Eastern Europe at the time of the socialist takeover played an important role in the conception, development, and implementation of such a strategy. As shown elsewhere (Ofer, 1974b, pp. 47–49), very similar conditions prevailed in the Soviet Union prior to the period of the 5-year plans; there the strategy was developed some 20 years before Eastern Europe turned socialist.

APPENDIX TO CHAPTER 16

APPENDIX TABLE 1

BASIC DATA FOR TEXT REGRESSION: 23 NONSOCIALIST AND 8 SOCIALIST COUNTRIES, 1940–1967 (in percentages)

	1940								1950							
	UR	Labor shares			Product shares			GNP per capita (1964 U.S. $) Y	UR	Labor shares			Product shares			GNP per capita (1964 U.S. $) Y
		A	M	S	A	M	S			A	M	S	A	M	S	
United States	57	18.6	41.2	40.1	9	37	54	1,636	64	12.8	44.9	42.3	7	45	48	2,365
Sweden	44	29.2	43.0	27.8	—	—	—	—	48	20.5	49.1	30.2	12	52	36	1,415
Canada	54	29.6	37.8	32.7	13	46	41	1,040	63	19.6	44.2	36.1	13	51	36	1,575
New Zealand	45	28.5	26.6	35.9	—	—	—	—	56	21.6	43.6	34.7	24	40	36	1,430
Australia	67	—	—	—	—	—	—	—	75	16.6	47.8	35.6	29	39	32	1,395
Denmark	64	28.8	36.8	34.6	18	41	41	910	67	25.0	41.9	33.1	21	44	35	1,140
France	53	35.6	36.6	27.6	—	—	—	920	59	38.0	41.3	20.7	15	51	34	985
United Kingdom	79	6.0	54.4	40.6	—	—	—	830	79	5.1	57.1	37.8	6	58	36	1,090
West Germany	71	25.9	47.1	27.1	—	—	—	730	71	23.7	48.4	28.1	10	57	33	700
Norway	28	29.7	42.5	27.7	14	48	38	965	32	26.6	46.7	26.7	15	55	30	1,040
Belgium	61	17.0	54.5	28.4	—	—	—	735	63	12.5	57.4	30.1	8	49	43	980
Finland	23	61.9	23.9	14.2	35	36	29	630	32	46.6	33.6	19.8	26	47	27	800
Netherlands	52	20.8	48.5	30.6	11	47	42	615	55	20.7	42.4	36.9	14	49	37	805
Austria	46	39.0	37.3	23.7	—	—	—	550	49	32.2	47.5	20.2	18	55	27	490
Italy	45	48.7	32.4	18.9	27	37	36	340	46	42.2	36.1	21.7	23	43	34	445
Ireland	37	50.3	21.0	28.6	—	—	—	480	42	40.1	26.4	30.5	29	—	—	580
Argentina	60	—	—	—	24	31	45	520	65	26.7	36.5	36.8	14	14	42	622
Japan	38	50.6	23.9	25.1	20	45	35	251	38	48.7	26.3	25.0	21	39	40	250
Greece	32	—	—	—	38	25	37	—	37	51.3	25.8	22.7	31	29	40	269
Spain	—	53.8	28.4	17.8	—	—	—	190	37	49.6	29.5	20.9	22	13	35	240
Chile	52	35.7	30.2	34.1	18	31	51	—	60	31.2	35.1	33.7	14	32	54	346
Mexico	35	67.3	15.7	17.0	—	—	—	175	43	60.9	19.3	19.7	23	35	42	278
Portugal	31	52.6	24.1	23.2	—	—	—	180	31	51.6	25.0	23.4	33	41	26	194

Czechoslovakia	48	38.8	42.2	19.0	28.9	42.5	28.6	630	51	38.7	41.4	19.9	23.9	48.8	27.3	770
East Germany	67	20.2	54.8	24.9	—	—	—	710	69	21.4	54.5	24.1	11.3	51.9	36.8	549
Soviet Union	33	54.8	27.7	17.5	33.6	36.2	30.2	360	39	48.8	33.5	17.8	30.7	37.7	31.6	480
Hungary	36	50.3	26.6	23.2	37.3	30.0	32.7	485	35	49.0	29.2	21.8	29.7	41.0	29.3	450
Poland	29	66.6	18.0	15.5	36.6	26.3	37.1	320	36	54.7	31.3	14.0	36.9	32.2	30.9	450
Bulgaria	24	79.3	10.8	9.9	55.1	15.0	29.9	290	29	75.9	14.8	9.3	39.4	29.6	31.0	275
Rumania	24	76.2	13.2	10.6	—	—	—	320	23	74.9	16.1	9.0	31.3	29.9	38.8	305
Yugoslavia	15	78.5	13.5	8.0	—	—	—	250	19	70.6	21.3	8.1	27.6	37.2	35.2	270

General Note: In most cases the data refer to the date indicated at the head of the respective columns. In a number of cases, though, data for other years had to be used, usually not more than 2 years from the designated one; this occurs more often with data for 1940 (which in some cases refer to years as far back as 1936) and for 1967, where, in a significant number of cases, 1965 data were used. When possible, intrapolation of data was made to estimate data for the designated years.

Notes and sources: Nonsocialist (and non-East European) countries, 1950–1967:

Urbanization: Most of these data are from United Nations, *Demographic Yearbook 1970* (New York, 1971), Table 5. In a few cases data are from previous issues of ibid. and from the statistical yearbooks of individual countries. The data are according to the definition of urban population of the individual countries and thus technically nonconsistent.

Labor force: Mostly from two sources, International Labor Organization, *Yearbook of Labor Statistics* (Geneva, 1953, 1958, 1964, 1965, 1967, 1968); United Nations, *Demographic Yearbook 1964* and later years. A number of items for 1967 are from OECD, *Labor Force Statistics 1958–1969* (Paris, 1971). An attempt was made to use consistent data of "active employed population" but in some cases the data are of "total active population and in others they are of civilian labor data only.

Product shares: The industrial distribution by sector or origin is in most cases of GDP at current factor cost. In a few cases GNP or current market price is used. The source is, United Nations, *Yearbook of National Accounts Statistics* (New York, 1966, 1968, 1969).

Income per capita: Mostly GNP of factor cost per capita at 1964 U.S. dollars. Source: IBRD, *World Tables* (Washington, D.C., 1971), Table 4, Column 17.

Growth rates, 1950–1960, 1960–1967 were calculated on the basis of the above figures.

(Continued)

APPENDIX TABLE 1 (Continued)

| | | 1960 | | | | | | | | 1967 | | | | | | |
| | | Labor shares | | | Product shares | | | GNP per capita (1964 U.S. $) | | Labor shares | | | Product shares | | | GNP per capita (1964 U.S. $) |
	UR	A	M	S	A	M	S	Y	UR	A	M	S	A	M	S	Y
United States	70	6.8	42.2	51.1	4	45	51	2,720	73	5.3	41.2	53.2	3	43	54	3,410
Sweden	73	13.8	52.7	33.4	9	55	36	1,810	77	11.9	50.4	37.7	6	53	41	2,300
Canada	70	12.5	41.9	45.7	7	48	45	1,755	74	9.1	39.3	51.0	6	47	47	2,155
New Zealand	60	14.5	46.7	38.7	20	42	37	1,550	63	13.2	48.0	39.1	—	—	—	1,745
Australia	82	11.1	48.9	40.0	13	49	38	1,525	83	9.2	48.4	42.2	11	49	40	1,810
Denmark	67	17.8	44.4	37.7	14	49	37	1,415	46	17.9	45.6	36.6	10	50	40	1,800
France	63	20.0	43.6	36.4	10	53	39	1,375	70	16.4	45.1	38.5	7	52	41	1,855
United Kingdom	78	3.7	55.7	40.6	4	57	39	1,365	77	3.2	53.5	43.4	3	55	42	1,580
West Germany	75	11.8	54.4	33.8	5	59	36	1,340	75	10.0	53.5	36.3	5	57	38	1,705
Norway	32	19.6	48.5	31.8	11	56	33	1,290	41	17.5	45.6	36.6	8	56	36	1,735
Belgium	70	6.4	52.7	40.9	7	48	45	1,255	78	5.7	52.0	42.3	6	48	46	1,595
Finland	38	35.6	37.9	26.4	20	46	33	1,195	48	26.7	40.9	32.4	16	46	38	1,635
Netherlands	80	10.8	49.3	39.9	11	52	38	1,135	78	8.1	47.4	44.3	7	51	42	1,400
Austria	50	23.0	47.4	29.6	12	59	29	885	50	—	—	—	9	59	32	1,140
Italy	48	26.8	45.6	27.6	15	46	38	760	52	23.6	46.4	29.8	12	47	41	1,060
Ireland	46	36.1	29.8	34.1	25	30	45	685	49	31.0	33.8	35.1	20	—	—	870
Argentina	74	21.4	43.2	35.4	17	47	36	680	76	—	—	—	15	50	35	765
Japan	64	32.6	34.8	32.6	15	46	39	515	68	24.6	39.0	36.4	12	45	43	990
Greece	43	55.7	24.2	20.1	25	33	42	415	48	—	—	—	24	34	42	640
Spain	43	41.7	36.4	22.0	27	39	34	395	48	35.6	39.9	26.4	16	42	42	620
Chile	68	29.6	35.4	35.1	12	36	52	370	74	—	—	—	9	48	43	425
Mexico	51	54.6	22.3	23.2	19	38	43	350	60	—	—	—	16	40	44	450
Portugal	23	43.4	32.7	23.9	25	42	32	280	—	33.1	39.3	27.5	19	47	34	390

Czechoslovakia	57	25.9	51.7	22.5	15.7	62.1	22.2	1,120	61	19.9	53.3	26.8	12.4	65.5	22.1	1,350
East Germany	72	17.7	54.7	27.6	9.4	64.8	25.8	1,050	73	14.6	55.6	29.8	8.7	67.8	23.5	1,290
Soviet Union	48	38.8	39.8	21.5	22.6	54.8	22.6	770	55	30.5	43.1	26.4	21.1	58.5	20.4	1,000
Hungary	40	37.9	41.5	20.6	22.5	52.8	24.8	670	44	28.4	47.1	24.5	20.6	56.3	23.1	890
Poland	47	44.9	38.5	16.6	28.4	45.2	26.3	590	50	38.2	43.3	18.5	24.2	50.9	24.9	760
Bulgaria	38	56.9	29.5	13.6	28.1	46.7	25.2	480	48	39.5	42.3	18.5	15.6	62.4	22.0	720
Rumania	35	66.9	21.6	11.5	31.8	39.6	28.6	475	39	54.6	30.5	14.9	22.0	52.8	25.2	700
Yugoslavia	28	59.8	28.1	12.1	26.5	44.2	29.3	420	—	53.8	31.5	14.7	22.6	50.8	26.6	550

Nonsocialist (and non–East European) countries, 1940:

   Urbanization: Same sources as for 1950–1967.

   Labor force shares: International Labor Organization, *Yearbook of Labor Statistics 1948.*

   Product shares: United Nations, *Statistical Yearbook 1950, 1953.*

   Income per capita: Growth indexes for 1940 (or previous year) and a postwar year was mostly obtained from U.N., *Statistical Yearbook, 1950, 1953.* In a very few cases statistical annuals for individual countries were consulted.

Socialist East European countries: The following are the sources for all countries and dates, except for the cases specifically mentioned subsequently.

   Proportion of population in urban areas: United Nations, *Demographic Yearbook 1970* (New York, 1971), Table 5; Paul Myers, "Demographic Trends in Eastern Europe," in U.S. Congress, Joint Economic Committee, *Economic Development in Countries of Eastern Europe* (91st Cong., 2nd Sess., 1970), p. 102 (henceforth Myers, 1970). Also consulted were statistical annuals of Hungary, Poland, Rumania and the Soviet Union.

   Labor force shares: East European countries, 1950–1967: Andrew Elias, *Statistical Tables—Estimated Employment in Seven East European Countries, by Branch and Sector: Circa 1950 to 1970* (Foreign Demographic Analysis Division, U.S. Department of Commerce March, 1973).

(*Continued*)

Footnotes for Appendix Table 1 (*Continued*)

Prewar Period: Czechoslovakia (late 1930s): Intrapolated from the structures of 1930 and 1950. The 1930 data are from James N. Ypsilantis, *The Labor Force of Czechoslovakia* (U.S. Department of Commerce, Bureau of the Census. Foreign Manpower Research Office Series P-90, No. 13. Washington, D.C.: 1960), Table 4, p. 7. [Somewhat lower *A* share and higher *M* share would result if the calculation had been made on the basis of data by Andrew Elias, *Manpower Trends in Czechoslovakia: 1950 to 1990* (U.S. Department of Commerce, Bureau of the Census, Foreign Demographic Analysis Division Series P-90, No. 24. Washington, D.C.: 1972), Table 4, p. 19]. *East Germany* (1939): Wolfgang F. Stolper, *The Structure of the East German Economy* (Cambridge, Mass.: Harvard University Press, 1960), Table 12, p. 4. *Hungary* (1941): Samuel Baum, *The Labor Force of Hungary* (U.S. Department of Commerce, Bureau of the Census. Foreign Manpower Research Office P-90, No. 18. Washington, D.C.: 1962b), Table A-2, p. 30. *Poland* (1931): Zora Prochazka and Jerry W. Combs, Jr., *The Labor Force of Poland* (U.S. Department of Commerce, Bureau of the Census. Foreign Demographic Analysis Div. P-90, No. 20. Washington, D.C.: 1964), Table 6, p. 11. *Note:* No intrapolation for a later year was possible due to the marked structural changes in Poland during the war as a result of territorial changes. *Bulgaria* (1934): Zora Prochazka, *The Labor Force of Bulgaria* (U.S. Department of Commerce, Bureau of the Census. Foreign Manpower Research Office P-90, No. 16. Washington, D.C.: 1962), Table A-1, p. 32. *Rumania* (late 1930s): Intrapolated from the 1930 and 1951 structures. The 1930 structure is from Samuel Baum, *The Labor Force of Rumania* (U.S. Department of Commerce, Bureau of the Census. Foreign Manpower Research Office P-90, No. 16. Washington, D.C.: 1962a), Table 7, p. 10. *Yugoslavia* (late 1930s): Intrapolated from the 1930 and 1950 labor structures. The former is from: Andrew Elias, *The Labor Force of Yugoslavia* (U.S. Department of Commerce, Bureau of the Census. Foreign Demographic Analysis Division Series P-90, No. 22. Washington, D.C.: 1965), Table 7, p. 12. *The Soviet Union* (1940): *TsSU Narodnoe khoziaistvo SSSR*, 1967, p. 645; (1950–1967): U.N. Economic Commission for Europe, *Economic Survey of Europe 1969* (Geneva: 1972), Chapter 2, "Growth and Structural Change in Centrally Planned Economies," and Table 2.11, p. 18.

Product Shares: [GNP at factor costs in constant prices] *East European countries:* Most data are from Thad P. Alton, "Economic Structure and Growth in Eastern Europe," in U.S. Congress, Joint Economic Committee, *Economic Development in Countries of Eastern Europe* (91st Cong., 2nd Sess., 1970), Table 8, p. 54 (henceforth Alton, 1970). Prewar data for East Germany and Rumania were calculated on the basis of the industrial structure for 1955 in the above source, and indices of real growth of production of the various sectors prewar to 1955 as presented in Maurice Ernst, "Postwar Economic Growth in Eastern Europe—A Comparison with Western Europe," in U.S. Congress, Joint Economic Committee, *New Directions in the Soviet Union* (89th Cong., 2nd Sess., 1966) Tables 7, 8, 9, pp. 883–885 [henceforth Ernst, 1966.] *Soviet Union:* At 1955 factor costs, from Norman Kaplan: *The Record of Soviet Economic Growth 1928–1965* (Santa Monica: The RAND Corporation, 1969). The 1955 weights are from Table A-6.1, p. 123, Column 14, and the sectoral production indices (1955 = 100) are from Table 1, p. 5, Columns 2, 4, 5, 6.

GNP per capita: East European countries: For most countries and years based on growth rates as in Alton, 1970, Table 3, p. 47, and on GNP per capita levels for 1960 as derived from Gur Ofer, *Industrial Structure, Urbanization and Growth Strategy of Socialist Countries* (forthcoming), Appendix 1 [henceforth Ofer, forthcoming]. Prewar levels for East Germany and Rumania are estimated as above from GNP data in Ernst, 1966, Table 4, p. 880; and population data from Myers, 1970, Table 2, p. 73, and Table A-2, pp. 125–136. Prewar level for Yugoslavia is estimated roughly from the levels of Bulgaria and Rumania in a similar way as for 1960 (see Ofer, forthcoming). *The Soviet Union* (1960): See Ofer, forthcoming, Appendix 1; (other years): Based on Abram Bergson, *The Real National Income of Soviet Russia since 1928* (Cambridge, Mass.: Harvard University Press, 1961), p. 265, Table 55; and Stanley Cohn, "General Growth Performance of the Soviet Economy," in U.S. Congress, Joint Economic Committee, *Economic Performance and the Military Burden in the Soviet Union* (91st Cong.

Acknowledgments

Work on this paper was supported by the Russian Research Center at Harvard and by a grant from the Research and Development Authority, Hebrew University, Jerusalem. Part of the paper was read by Abram Bergson and Simon Kuznets. I am grateful for their comments.

References

Brown, A. Toward a theory of centrally planned foreign trade. In A. Brown and Egon Neuberger (Eds.), *International trade and central planning*. Berkeley and Los Angeles: University of California Press, 1968, pp. 57–93.

Brown, A., and P. Marer. Foreign trade in the East European reforms. In Morris Bornstein (Ed.), *Plan and market: Economic reform in Eastern Europe*. New Haven and London: Yale University Press, 1973, pp. 153–206.

Eckstein, A. *National income and capital formation in Hungary, 1900–1950*. Cambridge: Russian Research Center, Harvard University, 1956 (mimeograph).

Gerschenkron, A. Some aspects of industrialization in Bulgaria, 1878–1939. In A. Gerschenkron (Ed.), *Economic backwardness in historical perspective*. Cambridge, Mass.: Harvard University Press, 1962, pp. 198–234.

Hungary, Central Statistical Office. *Statistical pocketbook of Hungary, 1970*. Budapest, 1970.

Konrad, G., and I. Szelenzyi. Social conflicts of underurbanization. In A. A. Brown and E. Neuberger (Eds.), *Comparative urban economic and development models, issues, policies*. New York: Praeger, 1974.

Montias, M. J. *Economic development in Communist Rumania*. Cambridge, Mass.: MIT Press, 1967.

Moore, W. E. *Economic demography of Eastern and Southern Europe*. Geneva: League of Nations, 1945.

Myers, P. Demographic trends in Eastern Europe. In U.S. Congress, Joint Economic Committee, *Economic development in countries of Eastern Europe*. 91st Cong., 2nd Sess., 1970, pp. 68–148.

Ofer, G. Industrial structure, urbanization, and growth strategy of socialist countries. Research Report No. 53, Department of Economics, Hebrew University, Jerusalem, 1974. (a)

Ofer, G. Industrial structure, urbanization and socialist growth strategy: An historical analysis 1940–67. Research Report No. 54, Department of Economics, Hebrew University, Jerusalem, 1974. (b)

Rosenstein-Rodan, P. N. Problems of industrialization of Eastern and South-Eastern Europe. In A. N. Agrawala and S. P. Singh (Eds.), *The economics of underdevelopment*. Bombay: Oxford University Press, 1958, pp. 245–255.

United Nations. *Demographic Yearbook*. New York. (Various issues)

United Nations. *Yearbook of national accounts statistics*. New York. (Various volumes)

CHAPTER 17

Internal Migration and Economic Development under Socialism: The Case of Poland

Zbigniew M. Fallenbuchl

I. Migration at the Various Stages of Socialism

What pace and pattern of internal migration is to be expected under socialism? In order to answer this question even on a purely theoretical level, it is necessary to qualify it in several ways. Are we talking about a mature, well-established socialist system or one that is somewhere along the way to becoming established? Are we concerned with some ideal socialist system that has never existed in practice, a theoretical structure, or a real-life socialist system such as those that have been established, for example, in the Soviet Union and in the countries of Eastern Europe? Also of interest are the level of economic development that the particular socialist country has reached, the development and other policies that it has followed, and the strength of the demographic pressures—to mention only a few of the variables that need to be taken into consideration.

Theoretically, under socialism one can expect a lower propensity to migrate, other things being equal. To the extent that the system implies a greater degree of equality of incomes, the maintenance of full employment and extensive social services, a relatively equal distribution of social infrastructure and services throughout the country, and a

305

relatively uniform development of regions, there should be less incentive to move from one location to another.

This hypothesis must, however, be modified in the case of a country that is in the process of building a socialist system according to the Soviet model and, at the same time, attempting to accelerate its economic development in accordance with the Soviet-type policy of industrialization (see Fallenbuchl, 1974a). Such a country incorporates many features that differ from those to be expected under a mature socialist system. Material incentives are offered, and equality of incomes is regarded as less important than the fulfillment of the plan. Policies toward agriculture that are accepted as an integral part of the development strategy create a strong "push" effect for migration from rural areas. In all the socialist countries these policies have, at some early stage, included introducing the collectivization of agriculture and a relative neglect of that sector of the economy in order to increase investment in industry (see Fallenbuchl, 1967a). Even when a more balanced allocation of investment as between agriculture and other sectors was later introduced, agriculture remained a less important and a less prestigious sector, with incomes lagging behind those in other sectors of the economy, particularly heavy industry. Where decollectivization was allowed, as in Poland in 1956, various measures aiming at the introduction of the "socialist reconstruction of agriculture" and the threat of collectivization as a vaguely defined, long-term objective remained to affect adversely that sector, as did compulsory deliveries, which continued in Poland until 1972. At the same time, the emphasis on industrialization also prevented narrowing the gap between urban and rural infrastructures and remedying inequalities in the distribution of services. This strengthened the "pull" effect of the towns, which in any case is usually quite considerable at lower levels of development because of the status and the cultural and social amenities associated with urban life. With rural areas exerting a strong "push" effect and urban areas exerting a strong "pull" effect, one can expect a high rate of rural–urban migration (see Fallenbuchl, 1974b).

Other features of the Soviet-type of industrialization include a high priority on maximizing national gross material output, rather than on securing a more equal distribution of economic activity throughout the country; a stress on heavy industry, which tends to be concentrated in certain areas and induces, therefore, the growth of agglomerations; concentration of the limited funds allocated for the expansion of urban infrastructure, including housing, in a few larger cities, with the resulting neglect of small towns; attempts to increase self-sufficiency by exploiting domestic mineral resources, thus increasing manpower requirements in certain centers beyond the local supply. All these factors tend to increase the pace of internal migration, both interregional and intraregional (see Fallenbuchl, 1975).

At the same time, however, there are some obstacles to migration that tend to slow the pace. Administrative measures are used to limit movement into certain cities unless jobs in the priority sectors have been secured in advance. Housing and urban infrastructure in general have been neglected in order to expand so-called productive investment, and there is a shortage of amenities even in those cities that have enjoyed priority treatment. When more than one member of a family must work in order to secure a satisfactory standard of living, movement to another location involves finding jobs for all of them. Moreover, it is often necessary to have some established "connections" in order to obtain better—or even reasonably adequate—accommodation, food supplies, and other consumer goods. Newcomers are, therefore, at a disadvantage in comparison with those who have lived in a given locality for some time.

The interaction of conflicting forces, those that encourage and those that discourage migration, may induce migration substitution, in the form of rural-to-urban commuting—a phenomenon linked with the expansion of the dual-occupational (farmer–worker) group. Rural–urban migration will tend to be replaced in this situation by rural–rural migration: from villages in the remote parts of regions to those close to the industrial cities, in the same or in other regions, from which commuting is feasible.

At a higher level of development most of the forces connected with the industrialization drive tend to weaken. The process of growth tends to become more balanced, in both the sectoral and the regional sense, especially since the previously unbalanced pattern created some severe maladjustments. Further progress now may depend more on increases in labor productivity than on large increases in employment outside agriculture. At the same time, while the agricultural labor force will have considerably declined, the strength of the push and pull effects should also have declined. All these factors will tend to slow the pace of internal migration.

On the other hand, certain factors connected with gradual systemic changes and leading to some liberalization, and the achievement of a higher level of economic and social maturity, may act in the opposite direction. These factors include the relaxation of controls, the elimination of such obstacles as housing shortage, a greater awareness of opportunities existing elsewhere, and better education and improved skills—making workers less responsive to the family and other ties that tend to reduce their mobility. Migration substitution may now be replaced by an increase in outright rural–urban migration, and urban–urban migration will be stimulated.

As a result of the interaction of these forces, one can perhaps expect in a less-advanced socialist country to find a relatively high rate of internal migration in the early stages. It will then gradually decline and will reach a level below that experienced by nonsocialist countries, once the process of building socialism and industrialization is fairly well advanced. This trend will probably be accompanied by a change in the pattern of migration. In the early stages, rural–urban and rural–rural migration can be expected tó predominate. Over a longer period of time, the relative importance of these two types of migration should, however, decline and that of urban–urban and, eventually, of urban–rural migration can be expected to increase.

It may be useful to test this hypothesis and examine some empirical evidence in order to identify a "socialist pattern of internal migration." Poland provides a good case for study. It is a relatively large country, at a medium level of economic development among East European countries, and, with some minor modifications, it has followed basically the same policy as other socialist countries in that region (decollectivization in 1956 being the most important difference). Moreover, relatively good statistical data on migration are available; the subject has been studied by Polish scholars, and a considerable volume of literature exists.

II.   The Case of Poland: The Pattern and Pace of Migration, 1951–1973

In order to examine the pace and pattern of internal migration in Poland in a meaningful way, it is necessary to disregard those postwar movements of population that were connected with alteration of the national frontiers and with wartime dislocations. Some 2.7 million people moved to the western and northern territories and 1.2 million from rural areas to towns between 1945 and 1950 (see Dzienio, Opallo, and Welpa, 1973, p. 123), according to the official registration figures, which almost certainly were not all-embracing. By the end of that period the immediate effects of the war had ceased to affect migration. At the same time, postwar reconstruction had been completed and the transitionary stage in the process of building socialism had come to its end (see Fallenbuchl, 1967b).

Total migration seems to conform to a priori expectations (see Table 17.1). The largest number of people moved in the first half of the 1950s, which was the period of rapid industrialization, collectivization, and "sovietization" of the country. Total migration was only slightly less in

TABLE 17.1

INTERNAL MIGRATION IN POLAND, 1951–1973

Period	Total internal migration	Urban –urban	Rural –urban	Urban –rural	Rural–rural	Net migration into urban areas
A. *Number of migrants* (in thousands)						
1951–1955	6,904.5[a]	1,950.5	1,842.5[a]	1,250.0[a]	1,861.5	560.5[a]
1956–1960	6,717.7	1,558.1	1,610.4	1,190.7	2.358.5	419.7
1961–1965	5,030.7	1,128.7	1,303.8	800.9	1,797.3	502.9
1966–1970	4,324.3	947.0	1,265.4	567.7	1,544.2	697.7
1971–1973	2,609.4	590.8	835.3	331.1	852.2	504.2
B. *Annual number of migrants* (in thousands)						
1951–1955	1,380.9[a]	390.1	368.5[a]	250.0[a]	372.3	112.1
1956–1960	1,343.5	311.6	322.1	238.1	471.7	83.9
1961–1965	1,006.2	225.7	260.8	160.2	359.5	100.6
1966–1970	864.9	189.4	253.1	113.6	308.8	139.5
1971–1973	869.8	196.9	278.4	110.4	284.1	168.1
C. *Percentage share of various types of migration*						
1951–1955	100.0	28.2	26.7	18.1	27.0	8.6
1956–1960	100.0	23.2	24.0	17.7	35.1	6.2
1961–1965	100.0	22.4	25.9	15.9	35.7	10.0
1966–1970	100.0	21.9	29.3	13.1	35.7	16.1
1971–1973	100.0	22.6	32.0	12.7	32.7	19.3
D. *Average annual rate per 1000 of population*						
1952–1955	53.1	35.7	32.9	17.0	25.1	
1956–1960	46.7	23.5	24.3	15.3	30.4	
1961–1965	32.7	15.0	17.4	10.2	22.9	
1966–1970	26.8	11.6	15.4	7.2	19.5	
1971–1973	26.3	11.2	15.8	7.1	18.3	

[a] There are some conflicting statistics in different sources for this period.
Sources: *Ludność Polski w latach 1945–60* [Population of Poland in 1945–60] (Warsaw: G.U.S., 1966), pp. 112, 113, 115, 118; and *Rocznik demograficzny 1974* [Demographic Yearbook 1974] (Warsaw: G.U.S., 1974), pp. 258–259.

the second half of that decade (6.7 million as compared with 6.9 million); but it declined considerably during the first and, again, during the second half of the 1960s (5.0 million and 4.3 million, respectively). Average total internal migration per annum declined from one 5-year period to the next until the end of the 1960s. It slightly increased in the period 1971–1973. When measured per 1000 of population, the average annual rate of total internal migration declined steadily from one period to the next between 1952 and 1973 and the 1971–1973 rate was less than one-half of the 1952–1955 rate (26.3 and 53.1 per 1000, respectively).

Also as expected, during the period as a whole, rural–urban and rural–rural were the two predominant types of migration. Together they were responsible for about 60% of total internal migration. Rather surprisingly, however, rural–rural migration exceeded rural–urban migration (8.4 million and 6.9 million, respectively, out of the total of 25.6 million). In absolute figures, all four types of migration have been steadily declining since the beginning of the 1950s. The only exception is provided by a sharp increase in rural–rural migration between the first and second half of the first decade (from 1.9 million to 2.4 million).

When the relative importance of the four types of internal migration is compared during consecutive periods, the pattern does not conform to a priori expectations. The share of rural–urban migration declined between the first and second half of the 1950s (from 26.7% to 24.0% of total internal migration), when there was a slowdown in the process of industrialization and decollectivization. However, beginning in the next decade, its relative importance increased instead of declining; it was 25.9%, 29.3%, and 32.0% in the following periods. The share of rural–rural migration increased between the first and the second half of the 1950s (from 27.0% to 35.1%) and remained almost stable in the three subsequent periods (35.1% in both halves of the 1960s and 32.7% in 1971–1973).

On the other hand, the share of urban–urban migration, instead of increasing, experienced a series of declines from one 5-year period to the next until the end of the 1960s (from 28.2% in 1951–1955 to 23.2%, 22.4%, and 21.9% in the subsequent periods), and it was only at the beginning of the 1970s that it began to increase. In 1971–1973 it reached 22.6%—above the levels of the 1960s, but below those of the 1950s. The share of urban–rural migration, which can also be expected to increase eventually in an industrialized country when the movement to suburbia takes place, declined continuously from one period to the next, constituting: 18.1%, 17.7%, 15.9%, 13.1%, and 12.7% of total internal migration.

It is also interesting to compare the relative shares of the four types of migration in each period. In the first half of the 1950s, urban–urban migration was the largest (28.2%). It was followed by rural–rural (27.0%). Rural–urban, the type of migration one might expect to be the most important at that stage, was in third place (26.7%), with urban–rural, as expected, quite far behind (18.1%). In the second half of the 1950s, rural–rural migration became the largest (35.1%), with rural–urban far behind in second place (24.0%), followed by urban–urban (23.2%) and urban–rural (17.7%). This pattern was repeated in the three subsequent periods, although the gap between rural–rural and rural–urban migration steadily decreased and had almost closed by the early 1970s (32.7% and 32.0%, respectively).

From the point of view of urbanization and industrialization, it is net migration (rural–urban minus urban–rural) that is important. Its share in total internal migration was relatively small during the 1950s, and it declined from 8.6% in 1951–1955 to 6.2% in 1956–1960. It was not much larger in the first half of the 1960s (10.0%). It became, however, more important in total internal migration from the middle of that decade (16.1% in 1966–1970 and 19.3% in 1971–1973). The role of net migration has been increasing rather than decreasing over time. In all periods it was below rural–rural and urban–urban migration, although the gap declined in the second half of the 1960s and, particularly, at the beginning of the 1970s.

Net migration into urban areas was, however, far from negligible, even during the first decade. Although it represented less than one-fifth of the total increase in urban population during the first two 5-year periods, the net migration of people of working age represented 25.5% of urban population of that age in 1951–1955 and 27.5% in 1956–1960 (see Table 17.2). Even more important was the role of net migration of people of working age in comparison with average annual increases in employment outside agriculture and forestry. The ratio was 26.9% in 1951–1955 and 37.9% in 1956–1960. Nevertheless, all three ratios (net migration to increase in urban population, net migration of people of working age to increase in urban population of that age, and net migration of people of working age to increase in employment outside agriculture and forestry) show an increasing, rather than decreasing, trend.

To recapitulate, the pace of total internal migration in Poland declined, as expected on the basis of a priori considerations between the beginning of the 1950s and the end of the 1960s, but it increased in the early 1970s. Within this total, the share of rural–urban migration declined at first and then increased from one 5-year period to the next. The share of rural–rural migration increased at first, then remained approximately stable for 15 years, then began to decline at the beginning of the 1970s. In all periods it was larger than rural–urban migration. Urban–urban migration had the largest share during the first period, but it was smaller than both rural–rural and rural–urban migration in all subsequent periods. It declined steadily until the end of the 1960s and then began to increase. The share of urban–rural migration declined continuously, and in all periods it was considerably smaller than that of

TABLE 17.2

ANNUAL NET MIGRATION INTO URBAN AREAS AND ANNUAL INCREASES IN URBAN POPULATION AND IN EMPLOYMENT OUTSIDE AGRICULTURE[a]

Period	Average annual net migration into urban areas (in thousands)	Average annual increase in urban population (in thousands)	Net migration as a percentage of increase in urban population	Average annual net migration of people of working age (in thousands)[b]	Average annual increase in urban population of working age (in thousands)	Net migration of people of working age as a percentage of increase in urban population of working age (in thousands)	Average annual increase in employment outside agriculture and forestry (in thousands)	Net migration of people of working age as a percentage of increase in employment outside agriculture and forestry
1951–1955	112.1	564.8	19.8	77.1	302.8	25.5	286.6	26.9
1956–1960	83.9	466.8	18.0	56.6	208.0	27.2	150.2	37.9
1961–1965	100.6	256.0	39.3	65.2	157.2	41.5	228.2	28.6
1966–1970	139.5	281.4	49.6	92.2	224.8	41.0	282.8	32.6
1971–1973	168.1	353.3	47.6	113.3	365.7	30.9	377.3	30.0

[a] Calculated on the basis of data from Table 17.1.
[b] Assuming that the proportion of migrants of working age was, in each period, the same for net migration into urban areas and for in total internal migration.

Sources: *Rocznik demograficzny 1974* [Demographic Yearbook 1974] (Warsaw: G.U.S., 1974), pp. XX–XXIII, 16–19; *Mały Rocznik statystyczny 1974* [Concise Statistical Yearbook 1974] (Warsaw: G.U.S., 1974), p. 36; and *Rocznik statystyczny pracy 1945–1968* [Statistical Yearbook of Labor, 1945–1968] (Warsaw: G.U.S., 1970), p. 16.

the other three types of migration. Net migration to urban areas increased rather than decreased. It should be noted that the beginning of the 1970s witnessed a change in many of the trends, or, in some cases, acceleration of an existing trend.

By the 1970s there are, therefore, some clear differences between the anticipated and the actual pattern and pace of migration. In order to explain these differences it may be useful to examine the pace of urbanization and industrialization, the particular strategy of development that was followed and the administrative restrictions that were in operation. As there have been some variation in these variables over time, it is necessary to discuss these changes in chronological order.

III. The 1950–1955 Period

The fact that rural–urban migration was less important than urban–urban and rural–rural, and that net inflow into urban areas was only 8.6% of total internal migration during the rapid industrialization and collectivization drive in the first half of the 1950s, is quite unexpected. During that period urban population increased by 2.8 million and employment outside agriculture and forestry by 1.4 million (see Table 17.3).

TABLE 17.3

TOTAL URBAN POPULATION, URBAN POPULATION OF WORKING AGE AND
EMPLOYMENT OUTSIDE AGRICULTURE (IN THOUSANDS)

| Year | Total urban population (end of the year) | Urban population of working age[a] | | | Employment outside agriculture and forestry |
		Men 18–64	Women 18–59	Total	
1950	9,243	2,673	3,010	5,683	4,622
1955	12,067	3,427	3,770	7,197	6,055
1960	14,401	4,058	4,179	8,237	6,806
1965	15,681	4,463	4,560	9,023	7,947
1970	17,088	5,060	5,087	10,147	9,361
1973	18,148	5,635	5,609	11,244	10,493

[a] These figures were calculated by the author.

Sources: *Rocznik demograficzny 1974* [Demographic Yearbook 1974] (Warsaw: GUS., 1974), pp. 16–19; *Maly rocznik statystyczny 1974* [Concise Statistical Yearbook 1974] (Warsaw: GUS., 1974), p. 36; and *Rocznik statystyczny pracy 1945–1968* [Statistical Yearbook of Labor, 1945–1968] (Warsaw: GUS., 1970), p. 16.

An explanation may lie in the operation of three factors. There was, first of all, a marked increase in the participation in the working force ratio. Between 1950 and 1960 the ratio of urban population 18–59 years of age increased from 90.2% to 91.0% in the case of men and from 44.2% to 51.9% in the case of women (see Rajkiewicz and Zekonski, 1969, p. 165). As, during the same period, urban population of working age increased by almost 1.3 million, this was the major source of supply of labor for newly established industrial plants and for other nonagricultural activities. This would explain the very large urban–urban migration, which during the first half of the 1950s was the largest among the four types of internal migration. People moved from small towns, which, as a result of the social reforms and policies followed after 1945 had lost their role as a link between agriculture and the rest of the economy and found themselves in a state of chronic crisis (see Wysocki, 1974, p. 185; Nowakowski, 1967, p. 18; and Latuch, 1970), and the exodus from small towns was particularly strong during the period 1950–1955 (see Ginsbert, 1964, p. 7). There was also migration from those towns that offered fewer job opportunities to those that were developing more rapidly (see Jedruszczak, 1972, p. 224). As a result of these tendencies, during the 6-year plan period (1950–1955) the five largest cities alone absorbed 30.3% of the net migration into urban areas (see Dzienio, Opallo, and Welpa, 1973, p. 127). During the period of unbalanced growth and the emphasis on heavy industries—which were located in a relatively small number of urban centers, the participation ratio for the country as a whole could only increase significantly if accompanied by migration to these urban centers (see Jedruszczak, 1972, pp. 224–231).

The second factor was an increase in the nonagricultural employment, both in and outside urban areas, of workers who continued to reside in rural areas. As shown in Table 17.4, between 1950 and 1960, *rural* population with main sources of income outside agriculture increased by 1.5 million. This increase, which represented 29.6% of the total increase in population with main sources of income outside agriculture, should be compared with net migration into urban areas—which was 1.0 million during the decade. In other words, the number of people who depended on work outside agriculture but retained their residence in rural areas was 50% higher than the number of such people who left rural areas and moved to towns. As statistics are unavailable for the mid-decade year, it is impossible to know how much of this increase took place during the period 1951–1955. However, it must have been quite considerable.

This increase in the nonagricultural employment of people living in rural areas was probably associated, at least partly, with the very large rural–rural migration, which was the second largest type of migration in

TABLE 17.4

CHANGES IN POPULATION WITH MAIN SOURCE OF INCOME OUTSIDE
AGRICULTURE COMPARED WITH NET MIGRATION TO URBAN AREAS

| | Increase in population with main source of income outside agriculture | | | | | Net migration to urban areas |
| | In urban areas | | | In rural areas | | |
Period	Total (In thousands)	(In thousands)	(Percentage of total)	(In thousands)	(Percentage of total)	(in thousands)
1950–1960	5,109	3,598	70.4	1,511	29.6	1,012
1960–1970	4,785	2,780	58.1	2,005	41.9	1,201
1970–1973	1,467	1,100	75.0	367	25.0	504

Sources: *Rocznik demograficzny 1974* [Demographic Yearbook 1974] (Warsaw: GUS, 1974), p. 46; and *Rocznik statystyczny 1973* [Statistical Yearbook 1973] (Warsaw: GUS, 1973), p. 81.

the first half of the decade and by far the largest group in the second half (see Table 17.1). To a great extent this type of migration substituted for migration into urban areas.

Rural–rural migration has not been studied by Polish scholars as carefully as other types of migration. There are some grounds for believing that a large proportion of that migration is connected with marriage and other noneconomic motives (see Latuch, 1970, p. 125). However, the differences in the ratio of rural–rural to total migrants among various regions are of such magnitude that they cannot be explained in terms of regional differences in those factors. Regional statistics for 1950–1960 indicate that while in Poland as a whole rural–rural migration represented 31.1% of total migration, in *województwo* poznańskie, which surrounds Poznań City, the ratio was 45.0%, in *województwo* łódzkie, which surrounds Lódz City, it was 44.1%; and in *województwo* warszawskie, which surrounds Warsaw City, it was 40.8% (calculated on the basis of data in Latuch, 1970, pp. 205–206). In these regions there are large numbers of commuters, who live in the surrounding *województwo* but work in the city, which forms a separate administrative unit.

As a result of increased commuting, there was an increase in the dual-occupational group (workers–farmers). Between 1950 and 1960 this group increased from 4.5% to 5.8% of the total number of people active in the national economy and from 16.5% to 22.6% of the total number of individual farmers (see Table 17.5).

TABLE 17.5

DUAL-OCCUPATIONAL GROUP: THOSE EMPLOYED OUTSIDE AGRICULTURE WHO ALSO WORK ON THEIR FARMS

Year	Total number (in thousands)	According to size of farm				Percentage of total number of farms in each group			Percentage of total active in the national economy
		Up to 2 hectares		Above 2 hectares					
		Number (in thousands)	Percentage of total	Number (in thousands)	Percentage of total	Total	Up to 2 hectares	Above 2 hectares	
1950	525	413	79	112	21	16.5	50	5	4.5
1960	738	483	65	255	35	22.6	59	11	5.8
1970	1,398	724	52	674	48	41.1	64	30	6.7

Sources: K. Bajan, E. Gorzelak, F. Kolbusz, Y. Roszczypala, and B. Struzek, *Polityka rolna PRL* [Agricultural Policy of the People's Republic of Poland] (Warsaw: KiW, 1974), p. 174; and K. Dzienio, "Zasoby pracy w rolnictwie w latach 1950–1990" [Agricultural Manpower in the Years 1950–1990], *Gospodarka planowa*, No. 9 (1974), p. 573.

TABLE 17.6

URBAN POPULATION AND THE HOUSING SITUATION IN TOWNS

Year	Urban population (in millions)	Dwellings (in millions)	Dwellings per 1000 people	Persons per room
1946	7.5	2.0	260	1.67
1950	9.6	2.7	255	1.55
1960	14.2	3.6	257	1.53
1970	17.0	4.5	266	1.32
1973	18.1	5.1	278	1.22

Sources: A. Andrzejewski, "Ogólne kierunki rozwoju infrastruktury mieszkaniowej w Polsce w latach 1945–2000" [Main Tendencies in the Development of Housing Infrastructure in Poland in the years 1945–2000), in Polish Academy of Sciences, Committee for the Spatial Development of the Country, *Infrastruktura mieszkaniowa i jej zroznicowanie regionalne* [Housing Infrastructure and Its Regional Differences] (Warsaw, 1974), p. 18; *Maly rocznik statystyczny 1974* [Concise Statistical Yearbook 1974] (Warsaw: GUS, 1974), pp. 225–226.

The third factor that affected net migration into urban areas during the first half of the 1950s was the shortage of housing and the government policy that gave priority to other types of investment. As can be seen in Table 17.6 the number of urban dwellings per 1000 of population declined between 1946 and 1950. It increased slightly during the 1950s, remaining, however, below the 1946 level. The number of persons per room declined from 1.67 in 1946 to 1.55 in 1950 and remained almost

TABLE 17.7

DWELLINGS AND ROOMS COMPLETED IN TOWNS

Period	Dwellings completed		Rooms completed	
	Number (in thousands)	Rate per annum[a]	Number (in thousands)	Rate per annum[a]
1945–1950	260	43.3	615	102.5
1951–1955	219	43.8	619	123.8
1956–1960	370	74.0	1048	209.6
1961–1965	560	112.0	1626	325.2
1966–1970	717	143.4	2043	408.6
1971–1973	463	154.4	1534	511.3

[a] Author's calculations.

Sources: Instytut Gospodarki Mieszkaniowej [The Institute of Housing Economics] *Problemy mieszkalnictwa* [Housing Problems] (Warsaw: 1969), p. 21; *Maly rocznik statystyczny 1974* [Concise Statistical Yearbook, 1974] (Warsaw, GUS, 1974), pp. 226.

TABLE 17.8

INVESTMENT OUTLAYS IN THE NATIONAL ECONOMY (AT 1971 PRICES)

	1950–1955	1956–1960	1961–1965	1966–1970	1971–1973
A. *Investment (in billions of* zloty)					
Total investment	356.0	464.4	680.0	1002.0	922.5
"Productive" investment	255.2	310.9	485.8	751.5	716.8
"Unproductive" investment	100.8	153.5	194.2	250.6	205.7
Housing and "Communal					
Economy"	63.6	120.5	147.7	191.7	165.1
(Housing alone)	(49.0)	(101.2)	(122.4)	(155.6)	(127.0)
Industry	155.1	180.1	273.7	394.3	396.4
Agriculture	36.2	58.0	94.4	160.9	135.1
B. *Percentage of total investment*					
"Productive" investment	72	67	71	75	78
"Unproductive" investment	28	33	29	25	22
Housing and "Communal					
Economy"	18	26	22	19	18
(Housing alone)	(14)	(22)	(18)	(16)	(14)
Industry	44	39	40	39	43
Agriculture	10	12	14	16	15

Sources: *Mały rocznik statystyczny, 1974* [Concise Statistical Yearbook, 1974] (Warsaw, GUS, 1974), pp. 74.

constant throughout the decade (1.53 in 1960). During the period 1951–1955, only 219,000 new dwellings with 619,000 rooms were completed (see Table 17.7), while urban population of working age increased by 1.5 million, including 560,500 net migrants from rural areas. This situation reflected the priorities of the investment policy. Only 14% of total investment outlays were allocated to housing, and an additional 4% to the rest of the "communal economy" (public buildings, etc.) (see Table 17.8). As a result, towns were simply unable to absorb larger numbers of migrants from rural areas.

IV.   The 1956–1960 Period

In the years 1956–1960, following the "Polish October," there was a deceleration in the rate of industrialization as well as decollectivization and some liberalization of the system. Employment outside agriculture and forestry increased from 6,055,000 in 1955 to 6,806,000 in 1960.

Although we do not have data for the middle of the decade year, it can be assumed that the increase occurred mainly during the first half of the 1950s. Urban–urban migration declined more rapidly than rural–urban migration. Decollectivization did not increase urban–rural migration, which actually declined slightly. It was, however, at least partly responsible for a very big increase in rural–rural migration (from 1,862,000 in 1951–1955 to 2,359,000 in 1956–1960).

Average annual net migration into urban areas declined drastically (from 112,100 to 83,900). The ratio of net migration to average annual increase in urban population and the ratio of net migration of people of working age to average annual increase in urban population of that age both declined. However, because of the greatly slowed increase in employment outside agriculture and forestry, the ratio of net migration of people of working age to increase in employment outside agriculture and forestry increased and reached its highest level of the entire postwar period (see Table 17.2). This last development suggests that a number of workers who had remained in rural areas but worked in towns during 1951–1955 now moved to urban areas.

The shortage of housing and other items of urban infrastructure remained severe, but the situation improved somewhat. The number of completed dwellings rose to 370,000, as compared with 219,000 in the 1951–1955 previous period, and the number of rooms to 1,048,000, as compared with 619,000 (see Table 17.7).

On the other hand, a new restrictive factor appeared in the form of administrative limitations on movement into large cities and many other types of locality as from 1955 (see Ciechocinska, p. 7). Under the existing system, these limitations can be quite effective because (a) there is obligatory registration of every change of residence and housing administrators and janitors are responsible to make sure that all incoming tenants are registered; and (b) all accommodations, including those in private houses, privately owned apartment houses, and cooperative apartments are subject to allocation by the housing authorities on a prescribed basis, with additional space for special occupations. In order to be able to move to a city a person must obtain a job of sufficiently high priority and secure a support from his future employer (the state or local government or a firm or institution) for his application to the local authorities. As always happens under rigid controls, some "defensive mechanisms" have developed. However, the only effective weakness in the policy has been the preference of new enterprises to be located in large cities as well as the massive manpower demands of established firms and institutions.

V.   The Decade of the 1960s

From the beginning of the 1960s employment outside agriculture and forestry again increased rapidly—by 1,141,000 in 1960–1965 and by 1,414,000 in 1965–1970. However, rural–urban migration declined by 306,600 between 1956–1960 and 1961–1965, and by 38,400 between 1961–1965 and 1966–1970; and rural–rural migration declined by 561,200 and 253,100 although it still remained larger than rural–urban migration. Net migration into urban areas now became more important. It reached 10.0% of total migration in 1961–1965 and 16.1% in 1966–1970. The ratio of net migration to increase in urban population increased from 18.0% in 1956–1960 to 39.3% in 1961–1965 and to 49.6% in 1966–1970. The ratio of net migration of people of working age to increase in urban population of that age increased from 27.2% to 41.5% to 41.0%. On the other hand, the ratio of net migration of people of working age to increase in employment outside agriculture and forestry decreased f om 37.7% to 28.6% but then increased to 32.6% in 1966–1970 (see Table 17.2).

When the two decades are compared, it is interesting to note that although net migration increased from 1,012,000 in the 1950s to 1,201,-000 in the 1960s, the increase in rural population with main source of income outside agriculture was higher in the 1960s than in the preceding decade, and considerably above the net migration figure. For the 1950s rural population with main source of income outside agriculture increased by 1,511,000 which represented 29.6% of the increase in total population with main source of income outside agriculture. In the 1960s the increase was 2,005,000, or 41.9% of the total increase in employment outside agriculture.

The size of the dual-occupational group increased from 738,000 in 1960 to 1,398,000 in 1970, or from 5.8% to 6.7% of the total number of persons active in the national economy, and from 22.6% to 41.1% of all individual farmers. Moreover, while the dual-occupational group represented only 5% of farmers with farms above 2 hectares in 1950 and 11% in 1960, this proportion reached 30% in 1970 (see Table 17.5). The practice of workers combining employment outside agriculture with part-time farming on their own land appears to have spread rapidly and it ceased to be largely limited to farmers with very small holdings.

Commuting became a major problem. According to a study prepared by the Central Statistical Office, the number of commuters increased from 1,535,000 in 1964 to 1,722,000 in 1968. At the same time, there was a considerable increase in the distances and traveling time involved (see Dzienio, Opallo, and Welpa, 1973, p. 127). In the opinion of Polish economists, the productivity of the dual-occupational group is low while the social costs of commuting are very high (see Padowicz, 1973, pp. 337–338). The emergence of this group is regarded as a transitionary stage, and its members as potential migrants (see Padowicz, 1974, p. 814). On the other hand the policy of enlarging this group made it possible to keep housing investment down to a minimum. While in 1956–1960 investment on housing represented 22% of all national investment outlays, this share declined to 18% in 1961–1965 and to 16% in 1966–1970 (see Table 17.8). By 1970, the number of dwellings was only slightly higher than in 1946 and the number of persons per room had declined only from 1.67 to 1.32 (see Table 17.6).

Taking into consideration the combined impact of the housing shortage and the administrative restrictions that were in force from 1955 to 1970, it is indeed surprising that the average annual net migration into urban areas, which declined to 83,900 in 1956–1960, should have increased so substantially during the 1960s, reaching 100,600 in 1961–1965 and 139,500 in 1966–1970.

VI. The Early 1970s

It was noted in Section II that the early 1970s witnessed some important changes in respect of the pace and pattern of internal migration in Poland. Following the workers' riots of December 1970, Gierek's new development strategy, based on foreign borrowing and some relaxation of controls, resulted in the acceleration of economic growth (see Fallenbuchl, 1973). Between 1970 and 1973, employment outside agriculture and forestry increased by 1,132,000. Obligatory deliveries in agriculture were abolished in 1972, although many other controls remained in force in that sector. The policy of limiting migration was discontinued in 1970, although this change "is not tantamount to a full freedom of migration in Poland [Ciechocinska, forthcoming]."

There was an increase in average annual total internal migration (but not per 1000 of population, which slightly declined). Both urban –urban and rural–urban migration increased. Improvement in the conditions of agriculture and acceleration in the rate of growth of agricultural production did not, however, have any effect on urban–rural and rural–rural migration, which both continued to decline. Net migration into urban areas increased, and the ratio of net migration of people of working age to urban population of that age also increased; but the ratio of net migration to increase in total urban population and the ratio of net migration of people of working age to increase in employment outside agriculture and forestry declined (see Table 17.2).

The increase in rural population with sources of income outside agriculture declined as a percentage of the increase in that total group, from 41.9% during the 1960s to 25.0% in the early 1970s (see Table 17.4). However, the dual-occupational group continued to increase after 1970, both in absolute figures and as a proportion of the total number of people who live on individual farms.[1] There has also been a further increase in the numbers of workers commuting to towns from rural areas and from other urban areas.[2]

Changes in the pace and pattern of internal migration at the beginning of the 1970s are interesting as they throw some light on the relative importance of housing shortage and administrative restrictions as obstacles to migration. In the words of a Polish economist, ''At present, the chief obstacle to the internal migration of the population is the ever-persisting housing shortage, which is a consequence of the policy of industrialization of the country, giving an almost exclusive priority to the development of industry [Ciechocinska, forthcoming, p. 9].''

In this respect there has been no change. The share of investment allocated to housing declined to 14% of total investment outlays in 1971–1973, the same proportion as that allocated during the first industrialization drive of 1950–1955. Although the number of dwellings and rooms completed per year increased and there was again a slight improvement in the housing situation in urban areas at the beginning of the 1970s (see Tables 17.6 and 17.7), the 1973 statistics, both for dwellings per 1000 people and for number of persons per room, show very crowded conditions in towns. As a rough approximation we may, therefore, accept the acceleration in the pace of internal migration and changes in the pattern that occurred at the beginning of the 1970s as being related to the relaxation of administrative restrictions, rather than to the gradual amelioration of the urban housing shortage.

[1] Between 1970 and 1974 the total number of people who lived on individual farms declined from 13,658,000 to 13,351,000. During the same period, the number of people who lived on individual farms and earned their income from these farms as well as from other sources increased from 8,111,000 to 8,385,000, or from 59.3% to 62.8%, and the number of those who earned their income entirely from other sources increased from 427,000 to 448,000 or from 3.1% to 3.4%. Therefore, the number of people who earned their incomes mainly from individual farms declined from 5,120,000 to 4,518,000, or from 37.6% to 33.8% of the total population living on those farms (G.U.S., *Rocznik statystyczny 1975* [Statistical Yearbook 1975], Warsaw 1975, p. 278).

[2] In 1973 there were 2.9 million commuters in the country. Out of this total, 2.4 million commuted to towns either from rural areas (1.6 million) or from other urban areas (748,000). Commuters represented 27.4% of total employment. In 7 out of 22 administrative regions, the proportion exceeded 30%, the two highest being 47.8% in województwo Rzeszowskie and 41.4% in województwo Krakowskie (G.U.S., *Spis kadrowy 1973, część II* [Census of Manpower 1973, part II], Warsaw, 1975, pp. 16 and 33).

The increase in the average annual net migration into urban areas, together with a decline in rural–rural migration, indicate that some open migration replaced substitution in the form of rural–rural migration to places with better commuting facilities. On the other hand, the very substantial increase in the number of commuters suggests that this replacement was not sufficient to eliminate further growth of migration substitution.

It is expected that in the years 1970 to 1985, 1.5 million (and by 1990 more than 2 million) people will move from agriculture, with or without changing their residence in rural areas, with a further growth of the dual-occupational group (see Padowicz, 1975, p. 95). Discussing future trends, Polish economists refer to the danger of ''uncontrolled outflow,'' which could lead to a shortage and further demographic distortion (aging and feminization) of the agricultural labor force (see Dzienio, 1974, p. 579).

The acceleration in the annual rate of urban–urban migration, which increased for the first time since 1951–1955, suggests that this type of migration had been adversely affected by administrative restrictions. Probably it will accelerate further if the housing shortage is reduced.

To recapitulate, it seems that internal migration, and particularly rural–urban migration, would have been substantially greater in Poland in the absence of an urban housing shortage and administrative restrictions. The existence of these obstacles induced some substitution of rural–rural for rural–urban migration and migration substitution in the form of commuting from rural residence to urban employment. If rapid economic growth continues, the relaxation of administrative restrictions on population movement and gradual improvement in the urban housing situation should together induce a greater pace of internal migration in the future.

VII. Socialist and Nonsocialist Countries: Some Comparative Observations

It would be dangerous to generalize from the case of one country, and it would require further research to present a comparative study of all the socialist countries of Eastern Europe. However, a comparison of figures compiled by the Polish Central Statistical Office on total internal migration per 1000 inhabitants in some selected socialist and nonsocialist countries (see Table 17.9) makes the following observations possible:

1. In Czechoslovakia, the German Democratic Republic (GDR), and Hungary there is a downward trend in the rate of internal migration

TABLE 17.9

Total Internal Migration per 1000 of Population in Selected Countries

	Socialist countries						Nonsocialist countries								
Year	Poland	Czecho-slovakia	GDR	Hungary	Bulgaria	Rumania	Belgium	Denmark	Norway	Nether-lands	Spain	Finland	Italy	West Germany	USA
1950	50.3													62.3	
1951					18.5										
1952	53.1	48.9													
1953			49.7												
1954			41.7												
1955	52.8		43.0		18.0									65.6	
1956			42.3												
1957	46.7	32.7	40.2												
1958			38.8							43.9					
1959			36.9							43.1					
1960	42.3	29.4	36.1	33.9	22.4		60.1	96.0		44.1		49.6		60.9	64.5
1961	38.8	28.9	37.5	33.0	19.1		57.1	93.8		43.4		48.1		60.9	63.4
1962	34.1	28.2	31.8	33.5	17.8		56.9	92.2		42.9		47.5		59.7	61.4
1963	32.1	28.3	37.4	32.8	19.9		57.4	92.8		42.2	12.3	47.4		59.7	67.7
1964	29.9	28.8	31.0	31.4	19.5		56.3	96.2		43.8		47.9		62.0	66.0
1965	29.0	26.9	29.3	31.8	22.5		55.6	94.4		44.6		47.3		61.0	67.8
1966	26.5	27.3	21.7	31.1	20.4		54.6	91.7		46.3	8.6	45.9		61.9	65.9
1967	26.4	26.7	18.2	30.4	18.2		55.2	90.4	47.8	46.6	11.7	46.2	28.8	60.3	66.9
1968	26.7	25.0	16.7	28.3	17.6	14.6	54.9	89.8	49.1	48.6	11.2	43.7	29.2	60.1	70.1
1969	27.6	24.5	15.6	26.6		14.0	55.8	96.5	59.8	50.2	11.7	44.8	29.0	60.3	65.8
1970	27.1	28.2	15.9	26.3		14.5	52.7	85.7	49.0	49.5	11.3	58.1	29.1	60.4	66.9
1971	26.7	27.3	16.8	26.3	18.2	15.2		80.4					29.1	60.9	65.2
1972	27.1	24.7	15.4	24.5	17.6	16.4							28.4		
1973	25.0	25.6		23.9		18.0					6.0		30.3		

324

similar to that in Poland. It seems, on the basis of very incomplete figures, that in Bulgaria the pace of internal migration accelerated between the first half of the 1950s and the first half of the 1960s and subsequently declined. All that can be said about Rumania is that between 1968 and 1973 there seems to have been an increase in the pace of internal migration. The last two countries are the least developed of the East European socialist countries.

2. It seems that Poland had a somewhat higher rate of internal migration than either Czechoslovakia or the GDR during the 1950s (no data are available for that decade for Hungary). The rates of internal migration reached by Poland, Czechoslovakia, and Hungary at the beginning of the 1970s are quite comparable. In the GDR the rate of internal migration per 1000 of population was at first comparable to those in the above three countries, but then it declined much more rapidly.

3. At the beginning of the 1970s, the GDR, the most advanced country in Eastern Europe, and Bulgaria and Rumania, the two least advanced countries, had the lowest rates of migration. The pace of internal migration under socialism does not, therefore, depend mainly on the level of development.

4. The pace of internal migration under socialism does not seem to be affected by the size of the country.

5. During the 1960s and at the beginning of the present decade, the socialist countries of Eastern Europe had considerably lower rates of internal migration than most of the advanced nonsocialist countries, (Spain and Italy, the two least developed countries in the selected nonsocialist group, are an exception). On the other hand, the rates of internal migration achieved in Poland, Czechoslovakia, and the GDR in the 1950s are quite comparable to those achieved by the Netherlands, Finland, and Norway a decade later.

6. There does not seem to be a clear downward or upward trend in the rate of internal migration in the advanced nonsocialist countries during the period for which statistics are presented in Table 17.9.

Perhaps we may conclude, therefore, that socialist countries have lower rates of internal migration per 1000 of population than the advanced capitalist countries except during the early industrialization and collectivization drive, when the rates are more comparable with those of some advanced nonsocialist countries. Although the Polish case suggests that housing shortage and administrative restrictions have played an important role in reducing internal migration, it is impossible to say on the basis of the present study whether these two factors, linked with a particular strategy of development, are more important than some basic systemic differences as on explanation of the lower rates of internal migration in socialist countries than in advanced nonsocialist countries. However, this hypothesis can be advanced for further testing.

References

Ciechocińska, M. Internal Migration of Population in Poland. *Oeconomica Polona,* forthcoming.

Dzienio, K., M. Opallo, and B. Welpa. Procesy migracji ludności. Analiza i wnioski [Migration processes: An analysis and some conclusions). *Studia demograficzne* [Demographic Studies], No. 33, Warsaw: P.W.M., 1973. 123–134.

Dzienio, M. Zasoby pracy w roinictwie w latach 1950–1990 [Agricultural manpower in the years 1950–1990]. *Gospodarka planowa,* No. 9, 1974, 573–580.

Fallenbuchl, Z. M. Collectivization and economic development. *Canadian Journal of Economics and Political Science,* 1967, *33*(1), 1–15. (a)

Fallenbuchl, Z. M. Economic policy of the transitional period from capitalism to socialism. *Canadian Slavonic Papers,* 1967, *9*(2), 245–269. (b)

Fallenbuchl, Z. M. The strategy of development and Gierek's economic manoeuvre. In A. Bromke and J. E. Strong (Eds.), *Gierek's Poland.* New York: Praeger, 1973, pp. 52–70.

Fallenbuchl, Z. M. The Communist pattern of industrialization. *Soviet Studies,* 1974, *21*(4), 458–484. (a)

Fallenbuchl, Z. M. The impact of the development strategy on urbanization: Poland 1950–1970. In A. Brown, J. Licari, and E. Neuberger (Eds.), *Urban and social economics in market and planned economies.* New York: Praeger, 1974, pp. 287–318. (b)

Fallenbuchl, Z. M. The development of less developed regions in Poland, 1950–1970. In A. F. Burghardt (Ed.), *Development regions in the Soviet Union, Eastern Europe and Canada.* New York: Praeger, 1975, pp. 14–42.

Ginsbert, A. Ekonomiczne przeslanki rozwoju malych miast [The economic factors in the development of small towns]. *Biuletyn IGS,* No. 3–4, 1964.

Jedruszczak, H. *Zatrudnienie a przemiany spoleczne w Polsce w latach 1944–1960* [Employment and social changes in Poland in the years 1944–1960]. Wroclaw: Ossolineum, 1972.

Latuch, M. *Migracje wewnetrzne w Polsce na tle industrializacji (1950–1960),* [Internal migration in Poland against the background of industrialization: 1950–1960]. Warsaw: P.W.E., 1970.

Nowakowski, S. *Procesy urbanizacyjne w powojennej Polsce* [Urbanization processes in the postwar Poland]. Warsaw: P.W.N. 1967.

Padowicz, W. Perspektywiczna prognoza zmian w strukturze zatrudnienia [Perspective forecast of changes in the structure of employment]. *Gospodarka planowa,* No. 5, 1973, 331–338.

Padowicz, W. Kwalifikowana sila robocza w rolnictwie polskim: stan obecny i perspektywy [Qualified labor in Polish agriculture: At present and in the future]. *Gospodarka planowa,* No. 12, 1974, 810–817.

Padowicz, W. Wyksztalcenie kadr w rolnictwie w ujeciu prognostycznym [A forecast of labor education in agriculture]. *Gospodarka planowa,* No. 2, 1975, 94–102.

Rajkiewicz, A., and Z. Zekoński. Warunki zycia ludności [Living conditions of the population]. In K. Secomski (Ed.), *25 lat gospodarki Polski Ludowej* [Twenty-five years of the economy of people's Poland]. Warsaw: P.W.E., 1969.

Wysocki, Z. Uklad terytorialno-ekonomiczny malych miast w Polsce [The territorial and economic system of small towns in Poland]. In *Aktualne problemy demograficzne kraju* [Current demographic problems of the country). Warsaw: P.T.E. and G.U.S., 1974.

CHAPTER 18

Yugoslav Development
and Rural–Urban Migration:
The Evidence of the 1961 Census

Oli Hawrylyshyn

I. Introduction

The rapid economic growth of Yugoslavia after World War II has been regarded as one of a limited number of cases of successful development. In this process, the pattern of urbanization may have been rather unique. First, instead of growth of a single development node, as has often been the case in Latin America, Yugoslavia has experienced expansion of many intermediate centers. Second, stepwise migration from least urbanized to most urbanized areas has been considerably accelerated and perhaps even replaced by leapfrogging. Third, a very important phenomenon of daily commuting over long distances from rural to urban areas has developed in response to urban capital short-ages—perhaps even encouraged by social policies providing transportation for such a daily transfer of population as a substitute for urban capital stock expansion.

In this paper, I wish to elaborate on these three key aspects of the relation between economic growth and rural–urban flows within the framework of Ravenstein's well-known Laws of Migration. The remainder of this section presents an overview of the Yugoslav urban migration

329

process; Section II reviews briefly the Ravenstein laws and restates the main ones in an empirically testable form; Section III applies these hypotheses to the 1961 Census data for Yugoslav rural–urban flows; Section IV discusses the results in relation to the economic development process of Yugoslavia, while Section V summarizes the main conclusions.

Large migration into cities is common to most developing nations, as are the problems this movement occasions. In Latin American countries for example, this flow appears to have been funneled rather narrowly in waves or steps from smaller to larger urban areas and finally into one main city, resulting in an economic development illness that one economist has labeled "hypercephalism" (see Herrick, 1966). With the exception of Brazil and Colombia, the percentage of a country's 1960 population living in the capital (or largest) city, ranged from 10.4% to 40.7%. These high concentrations were to a large degree a result of migration flows, as evidenced by lower concentrations in 1950.[1] The magnitude of these flows is indicated by the example of Chile; of Santiago's population (in 1960, 25% of Chile's total) about 37% were nonnatives, that is, inmigrants (see Herrick, 1966, p. 46).

The situation in Yugoslavia provides a striking contrast. The extent of concentration is much smaller—in 1961 Belgrade had 4% of the country's total population, while the next largest city, Zagreb, had about 3%[2]—even though the relative magnitude of migration is much higher— the nonnative population of Belgrade and Zagreb being respectively 71% and 64% of the total. For the nine largest cities (100,000+) this figure is 64%, two-thirds of these nonnatives having migrated since 1946, as indicated in Table 18.1.

This suggests that Yugoslav rural–urban flow, though greater in magnitude relative to the urban population, has been somewhat more balanced in the sense of being directed toward several destinations, rather than a single large center. Ginić, writing on Serbian urbanization during the period 1953–1961 stated that "because of the ability to provide more easily housing and short travel distances for migrants, medium and small cities were able to attract more whole families, and therefore grew relatively more (see Ginić, 1966, p. 124). Fisher has shown that the gravitational orientation of economic activity and hence

[1] See Herrick (1966, Chapter 3) for a brief account of centralization in Latin America.

[2] The distribution of Yugoslav city sizes is intermediate between log-normal (the case for most developed nations) and primate (the case for most less-developed nations) (see Berry, 1961, p. 573). The rank size quotient for Yugoslavia is .94, which reflects a "balanced" distribution of city sizes.

TABLE 18.1

ORIGIN OF 1961 INMIGRANTS TO LARGE CITIES

	1961 population (in thousands)	Inmigrants as a percentage of 1961 population	Origin of inmigrants (in percentages)[a]		
			V	T	U
Belgrade	585	71	49	7	44
Ljubljana	134	58	52	17	31
Maribor	83	61	57	17	26
Novi Sad	103	68	56	6	38
Rijeka	101	65	44	17	39
Sarajevo	143	56	29	19	52
Skopje	166	60	53	7	40
Split	100	54	55	11	34
Zagreb	431	64	50	13	37
Total	1845	64	49	11	40

[a] V = village, T = mixed, U = urban.
Source: Computed from 1961 Census of Population of Yugoslavia, Book XII, *Characteristics of Migration* (Belgrade, 1966), Table 1.3, p. 19, and Table 2.1, p. 76.

population flows in Yugoslavia follows historical patterns—the existence of several very important "nodes" of development.[3] Thus, economic development and industrialization have *not* been largely confined to one or even two main cities; each republic has at least one industrialization node, and within each there has been a good deal of decentralization, at least in the case of Slovenia, Croatia, Serbia, and Bosnia (see Janev, 1968). In Serbia proper (excluding Vojvodina and Kosovo), there are at least three cities aside from Belgrade that can be considered as being of primary industrial significance (Kragujevac, Niš, and Smederevo) and at least four others of secondary importance (Pančevo, Leskovac, Šabac, and Loznica). As another manifestation of decentralized development, Yugoslav authors have pointed to the fact that the basic characteristic of migration has been the movement of the population into economic centers *from the surrounding regions* (see Gluščevič, 1968).

These facts do not, by themselves, tell the full story of rural–urban flows in Yugoslavia. They suggest, however, that the process was not a simple funneling of population in a wavelike or stepwise migration toward the main city. Hence, empirical analysis of flows cannot be

[3] See map in Fisher (1966, p. 52) indicating gravitational orientation of major Yugoslav cities.

based only on the evidence for the main city, as was justifiably done for Chile by Herrick (1966), but must rest on a framework that incorporates all population centers according to their degree of urbanization. Ravenstein's original Laws of Migration, respecified in a more rigorous analytical fashion, provide such a framework.

II.   Ravenstein's Laws of Migration—A Respecification

A. THE ORIGINAL STATEMENT

E. G. Ravenstein is justly credited with undertaking the first serious analysis of migration in his "The Laws of Migration" (see Ravenstein 1885, 1889). On the basis of 1881 British census data, he set forth a list of seven generalizations concerning the characteristics of migration, but he did not develop a "theory" of the causes of migration, other than two sentences, one in each of his two papers (see Ravenstein, 1885, p. 81; 1889, p. 286), suggesting a simple "economic gain" hypothesis.

The first two of these laws state:

1. The majority of migrants proceed only a short distance and there thus occurs a displacement of the population to the great centers of commerce and industry.

2. Migration is characterized by an absorption process whereby rapid-growth towns attract people from the surrounding area, the gaps left by these people then being filled by migrants from farther away.

The notions of displacement and of gaps filled in by other migrants have been more explicitly developed into a theory of "migration waves," being the underlying factor in the work of Arthur Redford on English migration in the period 1800–1850 (see Redford, 1964) and in the work of Herrick on recent Chilean migration (Herrick, 1966). In the latter, the author traces the movement from villages to towns to cities (each of these steps occurring over one generation, and "leapfrogging" from villages to cities being quite minimal), in order to test for the existence of what Redford called a "wave-like motion" (see Redford, 1964, p. 186). Herrick does in fact find such a pattern in Chilean migration, as discussed earlier.

B. AN EMPIRICAL FRAMEWORK FOR WAVE THEORY

As stated earlier, a cursory look at Yugoslav migration suggests important flows into many intermediate centers, hence a rigorous specification of the wave theory should first classify settlements by degree of urbanization. First, let me define: V = villages, T = towns, S = small cities, L = large cities; and VT = migration flow in a period from village to towns, VS = the flow from villages to small cities, and so on, whence a view of all migration is given by a square matrix of 16 elements (IJ) as follows:

DESTINATION (J)

		V	T	S	L
	V	VV	VT	VS	VL
ORIGIN (I)	T	TV	TT	TS	TL
	S	SV	ST	SS	SL
	L	LV	LT	LS	LL

Since the laws of Ravenstein are properly regarded as tendencies ("displacement" surely does not mean that the absolute number of empty spaces left in small cities by the flow SL are filled by the flow from towns TS), it is useful to transform the above into a matrix of percentages in each column—that is, a distribution of migrants into each destination type, by type of origin. Thus I define R, the "Ravenstein matrix" of 16 elements (ij):

DESTINATION (j)

	vv	vt	vs	vl
ORIGIN (i)	tu	tt	ts	tl
	sv	st	ss	sl
	lv	lt	ls	ll

where each element $ij = \dfrac{(IJ)}{\sum\limits_{I=V}^{L} IJ}$ (= migrants from I to J as a proportion of all inmigrants to J.)

: and $\sum\limits_{i=v}^{l} ij = 1.0$

1. The Strong Case of Wave Theory

A strong verification of the wave theory would be given by an ordering of column values that descended for origins further down the urbanization scale. That is, inmigration to settlements of a given urban type would be greatest from settlements of the next lower urban type, and lowest from the least urbanized types. For example, for large cities the percentage of inmigrants from small cities (sl) would be greater than the percentage from towns (tl), which in turn would exceed that from villages (vl). The lack of such an ordering need not necessarily disprove the wave theory, because the different population size of the origin groups surely has some effect on the numbers. The values can be normalized for this effect, and the normalized values can then be used to test a weak case of the wave theory, to which we will return later.

The above-stated hypothesis, testing the strong case of the wave theory, is summarized in two logical statements:

(a) $sl > tl > vl$
(b) $ts > vs$

What about the other off-diagonal elements? Ravenstein's fourth law states that for each main current of migration there is a countercurrent, which implies a reverse wave, hence a descending order of percentage values for origins further *up* the scale, for example, for villages, the percentage of inmigrants from towns should exceed that from small cities, which in turn exceeds that from large cities. Thus, to the above, we can add two statements:

(c) $tv > sv > lv$
(d) $st > lt$

No clear implications about the diagonal elements (vv, tt, ss, ll) can be drawn from the wave theory because flows among settlements of the same class do not contribute to the urbanization process and hence are not a test of a wave pattern in the process. These values are nevertheless useful, for they may suggest something about the *stage* of the urbanization process. At an early stage we might expect very low ll and very high vv values, and the reverse at a late stage of nearly "complete" urbanization. At an early stage, the first movement is from the many villages toward the few urban areas—a movement often limited to the few richer peasants working better lands. (For a discussion of this phenomenon in Yugoslavia, see Puljis, 1965.) Their places would then be filled with farmers from the poorer lands. In practice, this wave may take the form of movement into urban areas (and industrial occupations) from surrounding plains, followed by an even greater movement from the hills and mountains into the vacated plainlands.[4] In the later stages, most migration does not involve as much crossing of occupation lines but is rather a movement from one industrial job to a better one, hence a movement between two urban areas, hence a higher ll.

---

[4] This is discussed very often in the Yugoslav literature and was even more important in an earlier period when the geographer—anthropologist–ethnologist Jovan Cvijić wrote about the traditional currents of migration in the Yugoslav territory. See for example Lutovac (1968), and Sentic (1965).

2. The Weak Case of Wave Theory

If, in a given country, villages account for 60% of the population, towns for 20%, small cities for 15%, and large cities for 5%, it would seem unreasonable to expect the majority of inmigrants to large cities to have the most urbanized origins, particularly in a circumstance of rapid industrial growth demanding a large new labor force in the cities. A weaker wave effect might be more reasonable to postulate, with the share of migrants contributed by a given origin greater in proportion to its population base, the greater its degree of urbanization.

Formally, this can be done by transforming the R-matrix into a normalized matrix with elements defined by:

$$k_{ij} = \frac{ij}{\text{\% of total population in } I \text{ group}} \qquad (ij = \text{element of } R\text{-matrix}).$$

This normalized matrix can be used to test the weak case of the wave theory: for each destination type (J) the value of the normalized migration index k_{ij} varies inversely as the "urbanization distance" from that destination. That is, we would expect the same ordering of values along columns of N as the strong case implies for values of R. Note that if there were no systematic relation between the percentage distribution of inmigrants by origin and degree of urbanization of the origin, that is, if inmigrants were selected randomly from settlements of different types, then the normalized Ravenstein matrix would have all values equal to one.

Both the strong and the weak hypotheses may be summarized by the directional arrows in the matrix below indicating high to low cardinal ordering of element values. The letters in brackets refer to the logical statements of the hypothesis stated earlier.

These orderings in the R-matrix (share of migrants by origin for each destination) test the strong case of the wave theory, and those in the N-

matrix (R-matrix normalized by origin population base) test the weak case.

III. A Test of the Wave Theory in Yugoslavia

The 1961 Census of Yugoslavia provides the data necessary for a Ravenstein matrix (R), though not a 4×4 one as described, since the breakdown of inmigrants is given for three types of settlements: villages (V), mixed (T), and urban (U).[5] Data for a large-cities (those in Table 18.1) column are easily compiled from the census, and a column for small cities is then obtained by subtraction, since $VU = VS + VL$, etc. The separation of U into S and L cannot, however, be done on the basis of census information, hence we have a matrix of three rows and four columns. Table 18.2 shows the resulting computations, both in absolute terms and in percentages by type of origin. The figures are not, in fact, flows but 1961 stocks, which it is assumed (as must so often be done in migration analysis) are good proxies for the flows.

Perhaps the first point to note about the figures in Table 18.2 is the very high absolute value of migration VV; over 2.5 million of a 1961 village population of 11 million had moved from other villages. Of all the (known) migrants leaving villages, over half went to another village. Of the total migrant stock in 1961 (6.8 million = the sum of all elements in the matrix) over one-third is found to be in village-to-village movements.

Yugoslav research on migration has often stressed that "village–city migration became (after the war) the predominant characteristic of population movement [Sentić, 1965, p. 243]." It should be clear from Table 18.2 that, in absolute terms at least, the dominant stream of migration was not village–city $(VS + VL = 1.8$ million) but, rather, village–village.[6]

As indicated earlier, a high VV (and vv) suggests an early stage of urbanization, something clearly implied in the Yugoslav case. However, the expected concomitant low values for interurban migration are not found; rather, we find that urban–urban migration $(US + UL = 1.0$ million) is the third highest stream, and urban origins account for about

---

[5] The Yugoslav census classifies a settlement as village, mixed, or urban according to a scale combining size and percentage of nonagricultural population, so that large agricultural villages are not classified as cities and very small industrial towns are not classified as villages.

[6] This conclusion remains, even after one reduces VV by the organized colonization of Yugoslav peasants from the south into the Vojvodina lands left empty by the expulsion of the Volksdeutsch, a movement of about 250,000 people (see Stojković, 1961).

TABLE 18.2

RAVENSTEIN MIGRATION MATRIX, YUGOSLAVIA, 1961[a]

	Destination			
Origin	V	T	S	L
	(2591)	(584)	(1121)	(558)
V				
	88	68	57	49
	(94)	(81)	(175)	(122)
T				
	3	9	9	11
	(195)	(168)	(570)	(453)
U				
	7	20	29	39
Total[a]	(2939)	(859)	(1958)	(1186)

[a] Values in parentheses are absolute migration in thousands. Other values are percentage figures of R-matrix as described in test.

[b] Total for each column in fact includes a fourth row not shown: foreign and unknown origin; hence the precentage values add up to a little less than 100.

Source: V, T, U: Data from 1961 Census as summarized in D. Breznik, *Demografski i Ekonomski Aspekti Prostorne Pokretljivosti Stanovnistva* (Beograd: 1968), Chapter 10; S + L = U.

32% of inmigrants to small and large cities. Is this then a case of early urbanization or not? The answer is a qualified yes. By 1961 only 28% of the population lived in urban areas; but the process of urbanization in Yugoslavia has been a very rapid one, and by 1961 the economy had already begun to move into the stage of development in which interurban population flows became quite important. Urban–industrial opportunities for agricultural–rural populations were still expanding.

The figures of Table 18.2 contradict the hypotheses of the wave theory, perhaps because only three rows are available. It is possible to expand the matrix into four rows making an assumption that has a relatively neutral effect on the outcome of the test, namely that for any given destination, the relative percentage of inmigrants from the two types of urban areas (S, L) is proportional to the percentages of the total population in each of these two types: (= pop. S/pop. L). The ratio is about 2:1, and using this one obtains a hypothetical matrix as shown in Table 18.3.

In Table 18.3, the vertical arrows indicate the expected decreasing rank order of values in the matrix; for the less important cases of migration to less-urbanized from more-urbanized areas (columns V and T) the hypothesis is roughly supported. For migration to urban areas (S, L), the values generally contradict expectations, for the proportion of migrants from villages is higher than from more-urbanized areas (though note that, for large cities, the percentage from small cities is greater than from towns). These "unnormalized" values are consistent with the views of Section I on the multinode character of Yugoslav development.

This evidence suggests an important "population base effect," which can be incorporated using the methodology of Section II—the normalized matrix, which is given in Table 18.4. The arrows again indicate the expected direction of ordering of values—in this case for the weak statement. The evidence in the columns, though not overwhelmingly favorable to the wave theory, certainly does show the expected tendency of ordering, with the index values for village destinations decreasing down the columns and increasing for city destinations. Since only three values are available, there cannot be an a priori expectation for towns (T). The values in the table also point quite clearly to the dichotomous aspect of both a high rural–rural flow and a very high interurban flow—the implication being that Yugoslavia was experiencing the characteristics of an early and a later stage of urbanization at the same time. Since the k_{ij} value of Table 18.4 already incorporates the population base effect, one cannot apply the assumption used earlier to split row U of Table 18.2 into two parts; however, some independent

TABLE 18.3

MODIFIED RAVENSTEIN MIGRATION MATRIX,
YUGOSLAVIA, 1961

		Destination		
Origin	V	T	S	L
V	88	68	57	49
T	3	9	9	11
S	4.6	14	19.5	26
L	2.3	7	9.5	13

(a), (b), (c), (d) indicate arrows showing direction of ordering.

Source: V, T, as in Table 18.1; S, L, see text for explanation.

TABLE 18.4

NORMALIZED RAVENSTEIN MIGRATION MATRIX,
YUGOSLAVIA, 1961

Origin	Destination			
	V	T	S	L
V	1.24	0.96	0.80 (b)	0.69 (a)
T	0.33	1.0	1.0	1.12
U	0.35	1.0	1.45	2.0
		(c)	(d)	

Source: See text for explanation of k_{ij} values.

evidence does exist that implies something about the split of the element k_{ul} (2.0 in Table 18.4) into k_{sl} and k_{ll}.

The city of Belgrade data on official registration of inmigrants for the years 1964 to 1967, show that 13% to 14% of the inmigrants came from the provinces (*srez*) in which are included the cities comprising our L group.[7] Since this undoubtedly includes a good deal of rural–urban flow (especially in such cases as Novi Sad and Split, which have large, traditionally outmigratory hinterlands) it seems safe to say that the inmigrants from the L cities did not make up more than 10% of the total. Given the fact that Belgrade is the capital of Yugoslavia, we would expect this percentage to be higher than for other large cities. The percentage of the population in L was about 10% in 1961, thus the value for k_{ll} would be at the most about 1.0; since k_{ul} is a weighted average of k_{sl} and k_{ll}, with weights corresponding to the relative population, that is, about 2:1, this suggests a value $k_{sl} = 2.5$. On the basis of the latter, it would seem that the high interurban flow is not so much a movement among large cities as a movement from small to large and among small cities; this suggests that migration is not yet in the last stages of the urbanization process.

To summarize, it is clear that some amount of wavelike motion along the urbanization scale is occurring; however, it is not a predominant

[7] This is computed from unpublished data on the registration of newcomers to Belgrade which the author obtained from the city of Belgrade Office of Statistics in the fall of 1969, thanks to the kind efforts of Dr. Dusan Breznik, director of the Center for Demographic Studies in Belgrade.

pattern and shows up only in the weak test of the wave theory with the inmigrant share values normalized by population at origin. Further, a great deal of the village outflow went to large cities directly, leapfrogging the intermediate urban areas. Also, a tendency for large inflows into intermediate centers from both villages and other urban centers is evident in the figures of column S in Table 18.2. Finally, there is simultaneously a very high rural interchange of population, suggesting an early stage of urbanization, and a relatively high interchange of urban populations, suggesting a later stage. All of this points to an accelerated urbanization process in Yugoslavia, manifesting characteristics of both an early and a later stage of development.

IV. Migration and Labor Transfer in Development

Rural–urban migration is an important part of the development process because it is generally assumed to incorporate the transfer of labor from agricultural occupations to industrial-service ones. As industrial growth is generally located in cities, new labor demands not met by natural increase will have to be filled by geographical displacement from rural to urban areas. It is the purpose of this section to compare the magnitude of the occupational shift with the migration flows to see whether Yugoslav experience conforms to such a simplified view.

During the period 1953–1961, the agricultural labor force fell absolutely by about 600,000 and the nonagricultural labor force increased by almost 1 million, as seen in Table 18.5. The total population dependent

TABLE 18.5

LABOR FORCE DISTRIBUTION BY OCCUPATION, YUGOSLAVIA, 1953–1961

	1953		1961	
	In thousands	In percentages	In thousands	In percentages
Agriculture (including fishing and forestry)	5,361	68	4,731	57
Industry (including mining)	1,310	17	1,733	22
Services	1,177	15	1,676	22
Total	7,848	100	8,340	100

Source: *Yugoslavia, 1945–1964: A Statistical Survey* (Belgrade: Federal Statistical Bureau, 1965), pp. 52–53.

TABLE 18.6

POPULATION[a] DISTRIBUTION BY OCCUPATIONAL
DEPENDENCE, YUGOSLAVIA, 1953–1961
(IN MILLIONS)

	1953	1961	Change 1953–1961
Agriculture	10.3	9.3	−1.0
Nonagricultural	6.6	9.3	+2.7
Total	16.9	18.6	+1.7

[a] Workers plus dependents.
Source: As in Table 18.5.

on the two sectors changed by −1.0 million and +2.7 million, respectively (Table 18.6). How much of the shift to nonagricultural occupations was met by migration? This may be readily calculated.

The 1961 migrant stock data for all urban areas is available by period of settlement, hence migration for the period 1953–1961 from each type of area (V, T, U) into urban ones (U) may be calculated (call these VU, TU, UU). It is probably safe to assume that all of VU and TU involved shifting from agriculture to nonagriculture, any overestimate being compensation for the possibility that some of UU also involved such a shift. This sum yields a value of nearly 2 million ($VS + VL + TS + TL$ in Table 18.2), of which 1 million was in the period 1953–1961 (see Breznik, 1968, p. 84). Undoubtedly some of the movement into towns also involved an occupational shift, and I will assume that this is roughly given by VT. It was not possible to obtain the period breakdown for this, hence, I have assumed that the 1953–1961 flow in proportion to total 1961 stock was the same as for urban areas—50%—which gives a value of nearly 0.3 million. Thus, the upper estimate of rural–urban migrants shifting from agriculture to nonagriculture is 1.3 million, about 50% of the 2.7 million total occupational shift.

The remaining 1.4 million could not all have come from urban natural increase; given 1953 urban population, this would imply a growth rate of 2.5% per annum, compared to about 1.4% for all Yugoslavia. The actual urban rates were surely lower than this 1.4% (see Breznik, 1968 p. 2). The source of the shortfall is not difficult to find: It consists of people who shifted into nonagricultural occupations but continued to live in rural areas, commuting daily to urban industrial jobs. This group of *seljaciradnici*, or landed proletariat as I shall call them, has been the subject of a large literature in Serbo-Croatian (see Radovanović, 1968;

Bajić, 1966; and Fisher, 1966, pp. 73–74) which has explored both the causes and the effects of this phenomenon.

The number of landed proletariat is quite substantial; estimates for 1961 range from 800,000 to 1.3 million.[8] This phenomenon of "daily migration" (*dnevne migracije* as the Yugoslavs call it) has been analyzed as to causes and effects by many writers, with the main reasons usually given as: urban housing shortages, the possibility for large families on small plots to supplement their income by combining agricultural and industrial pursuits—with some members working the land, others commuting to factory work— and, finally, improved transportation (see Lutovac, 1968; and Vogelnik, 1966). But the large literature on the subject has failed to ask the important question, whether the not-so-obvious costs are worth the obvious benefits. What are these costs and benefits? It is rather clear that this situation reduces the influx of population into the cities and relieves the tremendous pressure on urban capital, particularly for housing construction. However, while less clear, it is undoubtedly a fact that there are considerable costs. Some of them are direct, such as the provision of commuter transportation (provided both by city governments and by individual enterprises); others are indirect, such as increased fatigue, wasted time (here the opportunity forgone is often part-time education), decreased participation in labor management, and so on.[9]

On this point, the socialist character of Yugoslavia becomes quite important, in that the ranks of the landed proletariat are surely swelled by the common socialist policy of underemphasizing the consumer sector, including housing construction. Though it may be that providing transportation as a substitute for urban housing for the incoming industrial work force proves beneficial to the process of development,[10] the question remains an open one.

Substantial literature exists on the problems arising from the large rural–urban migration: problems both at origin and at destination. The former is of the "How you gonna keep 'em in the *selo* (village) after they've seen the lights of Skadarlija" genre, and expresses a concern for

[8] The first figure is calculated from information on place of work and place of residence given in the *1961 Census of Yugoslavia,* Book VI, Table 1;8, p. 6; the second is found in Fisher (1966, p. 74).

[9] An excellent discussion of such costs, with some empirical information, is found in Krgović (1964).

[10] This may also be one of the facts behind the relative lack of the Latin American type of shantytown in most Yugoslav cities, although there does exist the practice of building "wild," that is on land outside the zoned areas encompassed by urban plans, as described in Antonijević (1962–1966), and Lutovac (1968).

TABLE 18.7

AVERAGE ANNUAL INMIGRATION
AS A PERCENTAGE OF THE TOTAL
POPULATION OF YUGOSLAVIA'S
LARGE CITIES, 1958–1961

Belgrade	2.9
Ljubljana	2.8
Maribor	2.5
Novi Sad	4.1
Rijeka	3.3
Sarajevo	3.1
Skopje	3.5
Split	3.5
Zagreb	2.9

Source: Inmigrants: 1958–1961 average; population in 1961 as given in Table 18.1.

the facts of rural depopulation and the discontinuity resulting from the outmigration of the potential young heirs to the family hectares.[11] The other problem, providing the social overhead capital for the expanding urban population is quite real, despite the safety valve of the landed proletariat. Table 18.7 shows that, for most large cities, the annual inflow between 1958 and 1961 made up about 3% to 4% of each city's population.

For the period 1964–1968 the figure for Belgrade (calculated from data described in Footnote 7) had risen to about 3.5%, and it probably would be safe to assume that a similar increase occurred in the 1960s for most of the other cities, particularly for the "boom towns" of Rijeka and Split (see Breznik, and Todorović, 1967).

In the capital city of Belgrade, this influx has been of the order of magnitude of about 30,000 annually, with outmigration of about 10,000 (see Footnote 7). With a natural rate of increase of about 1% per annum, this means that the increase in population each year is about 30,000, or 8000 families. Given that the number of new apartments constructed in a good year in the 1960s was 10,000, and that officially there were 50,000 Belgrade families waiting for them, it seems clear that the housing problem is going to be around for some time to come. The concern expressed by the authorites about the large inflow of people gave rise to

[11] The sociological, political, and demographic aspects of this "problem" are dealt with at length in Markovic (1966).

the rumor of instituting a "visa" requirement for inmigrants to Belgrade, a rumor that was only partially denied by Branko Pesic, mayor of Belgrade, in a newspaper interview in which he stated that Belgrade would remain an open city—for qualified workers.[12]

Clearly the problem of accommodating the entire new industrial labor force in urban areas continued to be an overwhelming one through the 1960s, suggesting that to encourage a "landed proletariat solution" would be a wise and appropriate policy in these circumstances of rapid economic growth.

V. Concluding Remarks

This paper has shown, first, that the pattern of rural–urban flows in Yugoslavia appears to take the form of a wave only in a weak sense, and far less than might be predicted by a strong interpretation of the Ravenstein theory. Instead, there is a good deal of leapfrogging from villages directly to cities, and some apparent acceleration of the entire process is indicated by the high interurban flow concomitant with a high intervillage flow and ongoing rural–urban flows. Second, the evidence on migration and other independent evidence on the intermediate size of cities suggests that industrialization is occurring with several growth poles, or nodes, and is not concentrated in the largest city. Third, industrialization is characterized by a phenomenon relatively unique to Yugoslavia and some other East European countries, such as Hungary and Poland, namely, a large amount of shifting out of agriculture by daily commuting to urban industries, instead of geographical relocation. This manifests an apparent policy of substituting commuter transportation for urban housing, in an attempt to alleviate the pressures on facilities caused by rapid growth.

References

Antonijević, D. Entnološka strukturriranost stihijnih naselja današnje imigracije Titovog Uzica. *Glasnik Etnografskog Instituta,* 1962–1966, *11–15,* 77–96.
Bajić, M. Dnevne migracije radne snage u Vojvodini. In: *Neke Karakteristike Geografskog Razvoja Vojvodine,* Sremski Karlovci: Zavod za Unapredenja Opsteg i Strucnog Obrazovanje, 1966, pp. 92–104.
Berry, B. L. City-size distributions and economic development. *Economic Development and Cultural Change,* 1961, 9(4), 573–588.

[12] *Politika,* December 6, 1969, p. 7; December 9, 1969, p. 8; and December 12, 1969, p. 11.

Breznik, D. *Demografski i Ekonomski Aspekti Prostorne Pokretljivosti Stanovnistva.* Belgrade, 1968.

Breznik, D., and G. Todorovic. Problemi Projekcija Stanovnistva Velikih Gradskih Podrucja. *Stanovnistno,* 1967, *2,* 95–102.

Fisher, J. C. *Yugoslavia: A multinational state.* San Francisco: Chandler, 1966.

Ginić, I. Demografski izvori i faktori urbanizacije u S.R. Srbiji. *Stanovništvo,* 1966, *4*(2), 116–126.

Gluščević, B. Regionalni problemi zaposlenosti i produktivnosti radne snage. *Ekonomska Misao, 1968, I,* 249–258.

Herrick, B. H. *Urban migration and economic development in Chile.* Cambridge: M.I.T. Press, 1966.

Janev, D. Mesto i uloga gradova u Srbiji u procesu migracije privrednih podrucja. *Ekonomska Misao,* 1968, *3,* 497–506.

Jugoslavija, Savezni Zavod za Statistiku. *Popis Stanovništva 1961,* Books VI, VIII, and XII. Belgrade, 1966–1969.

Jugoslavija, Savezni Zavod za Statistiku. *Jugoslavija, 1945–1964 Statistički Pregled,* Belgrade, 1967.

Krgović, T. Problemi Putujučih radnika. *Bilten Društva Socijalnih Radnika S. R. Srbije,* 1964, *9–10,* 10–19.

Lutovac, M. Migracioni procesi stanovništva Jugoslavije. *Cvijičev Zbornik Uspomen 100-god-njegovog rodenja,* 1968, 189–198.

Marković, P. *Uticaj migracija Poljoprivrednog stanovništva na Promene Agrarne Strukture.* Belgrade, 1966.

Puljiz, V. Mobilnost stanovništva u planinskim područjima. *Nase Teme,* 1965, *6,* 853–866.

Radovanović, M. O nekim pitanjima etnološkog proučavanja dnevnih migracija. *Cvijicev Zbornik,* 1968, pp. 207–215.

Ravenstein, E. G. The laws of migration. *Journal of the Royal Statistical Society,* 1885, *48*(2), 167–227.

Ravenstein, E. G. The laws of migration. *Journal of the Royal Statistical Society,* 1889, *52*(2), 241–301.

Redford, A. *Labor migration in England, 1800–1850* (2nd ed.). Manchester: The University Press, 1964.

Sentić, M. Znacaj Cvijičevog rada za savremena istraživanja Migracije. *Stanovnistvo,* 1965, *4,* 241–246.

Stojković, S. Naseljavanje Crnogroaca u A.P. Vojvodini. *Istorijski Zapisi,* 1961, *I,* 45–70.

Vogelnik, D. Makrodemografski aspekti formiranje urbanih regija u Jogoslaviji. *Stanovnistvo,* 1966, *4,* 261–281.

PART IV

Selected Case Studies

SECTION C

Special Constraints:
Causes and Consequences

The Demographic Effect of
Migration on an Urban Population:
Migration to and from West Berlin, 1952–1971

Frederick W. Hollmann

I. Introduction

In studies of the increasing percentage of the population living in cities, two major factors are cited as contributing to the growth of cities. The first (often erroneously considered the only factor) is the migration of people to the city from rural areas. The second is the changing pattern of natural increase in the city as compared to that in the rural sector. In the history of most developed countries, the typical pattern of rural–urban migration has consisted of the movement of the excess rural population, typically young adults, into the city, to compensate for the pressure of increased population on the system of inheritance. In the cities themselves, increased medical technology and the conquest of infectious diseases has caused a decline in the high urban mortality rate. Urban population has thus expanded both by the natural excess of births over deaths and through the inmigration of people from rural areas. Relatively low urban fertility is compensated for by the inmigration of a relatively youthful population with larger proportions in the childbearing ages. Correspondingly, the rural population, although it may continue to have a higher level of fertility, has its natural increase reduced by the outmigration of young adults.

The evolution of the population of West Berlin in the last 20 years can be seen as having some aspects in common with this general typology of urbanization and others that are very different. West Berlin, since World War II, has been the subject of considerable attention because of its special political status. From the end of the war until 1961, it was the main focus of a substantial migration from East Germany to West Germany. Since the cessation of legal migration from East Germany into West Berlin in 1961, it has ceased to serve this function at a demographically significant level but has become complete in its isolation from its natural surroundings. It thus plays a unique role in relation to its economic hinterland of West Germany. In regard to the general typology of urbanization, West Berlin has relied significantly on migration from the rest of Germany to sustain its rather unchanged population size. It has enjoyed the low level of mortality that characterizes modernized countries, but has had, in spite of this, a substantial excess of deaths over births. In addition, the city has had a unique age–sex selection of wartime mortality and timing of fertility changes, which has played a fundamental role in the city's postwar demographic history.

The most outstanding and best-known feature of this age–sex structure is the high percentage of elderly people of both sexes. As of December 31, 1970, 21.4% of the population was 65 years of age or older—15.8% of the male population and 25.8% of the female population. Also unique in West Berlin is the small percentage of the population, 15.2%, under 15 years of age—17.9% of males, and 13.2% of females. The sex ratio at this time was 77.5 men per 100 women, indicating a high preponderance of females.[1] This age–sex structure is even more striking when seen in juxtaposition to a predominantly masculine, youthful flow of migration to and from the city, at least in the last 20 years. The purpose of this paper is to analyze the pattern of this migration and how it has affected the size and age–sex structure of the population. From this analysis, two questions can be answered; first, the question of how a population can remain aged in the presence of youthful migration, and second, how the physical separation of a city from its hinterland affects the city's population through the migration pattern.

The migration to and from West Berlin in the last 20 years is viewed from several different angles. First, the trend in migration over 6-year periods is viewed from the standpoint of total in- and outmigrants, and the extent and manner in which East Germany (including East Berlin) and West Germany have been involved in this migration is analyzed.

---

[1] Berlin, Statistisches Landesamt, *Statistisches Jahrbuch Berlin, 1972.*

The migration trend is viewed both from the standpoint of overall magnitude and in terms of resultant net migration. In a situation such as this, where the volume of total migration is very large compared to net migration, interpretation of the difference between total and net migration is very significant to the analysis. Net migration, under normal circumstances, is a phenomenon that relates to the city itself and its attraction for outsiders, whereas total migration is largely a function of external circumstances. In West Berlin, the degree to which net migration is influenced by the amount of total migration is related to the effect of the city's isolation.

The second phase of the analysis concerns the demographic structure of the migrants at any given point in time during the period studied. The primary concern is the age–sex structure in the inmigrants, outmigrants, and net migrants. Of secondary concern is a comparison of the proportions married, by age and sex, among these classes of migrants since 1966 and among the population of West Berlin. The theoretical distinction between gross and net migration is also important for this phase of the analysis. For each of these first two phases of the analysis, comparisons are made with migration to and from the city of Hamburg, to pinpoint further those aspects that are unique to the Berlin situation.

In the third phase of the analysis, the cumulative effects of migration on the size and structure of West Berlin's population at different points in time are examined. This analysis, in contrast to the analysis of migration by period, must account not only for the age–sex structure of the population and of the net migrants, but also for the effects of aging on the population at the beginning of the period and on the net migrants during the period. Therefore, this portion of the analysis considers migration as it affects different birth cohorts over a 20-year period and addresses the question of how the population would have looked at a given time had there been no migration at all. In this way, the long-term effects of particular migration patterns can be studied.

II. The Trend in the Level of Migration

In evaluating particular periods of in- and outmigration, it is necessary to consider the changes in the political situation surrounding Berlin that have affected migration to and from the city. In particular, Berlin's involvement in the migration from East to West Germany in the 1950s, which so greatly affected migration into and out of West Berlin, was a function of the international political situation.

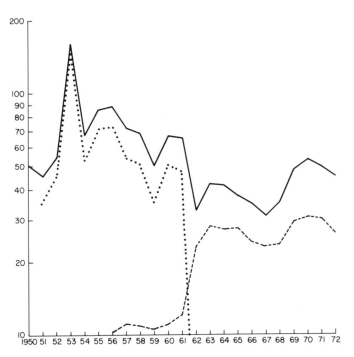

Figure 19.1. West Berlin: total inmigrants per 1000 population, 1950–1972. All inmigrants, ——; from German Democratic Republic (including East Berlin), ···; from German Federal Republic, – – –.

The pattern of inmigration rates into West Berlin shows considerable fluctuations over time.[2] It is evident from Figure 19.1 that total inmigration reached a very high level, 154.5 per 1000 population, in 1953, with secondary peaks in 1956 (88.4) and 1960 (66.9), dips in 1954 and 1959, and a serious drop in 1962. It can also be seen that a very substantial portion of the inmigration from 1951 to 1961 was from East Germany including East Berlin, which almost solely explains the time series variations during this period. The large peak in 1953 is primarily a result of the closing of the borders between East and West Germany, which increased the involvement of Berlin in the East–West migration. The decline in 1961 and the drop in 1962 are associated with the building of the Berlin Wall in August 1961, which thereafter prevented significant migration from East Germany and East Berlin.

[2] Berlin, Statistisches Landesamt, "Die Wanderungen in Berlin (West) 1950 bis 1955," *Berliner Statistik,* Sonderheft 55, and *Statistisches Jahrbuch Berlin,* 1953–1972.

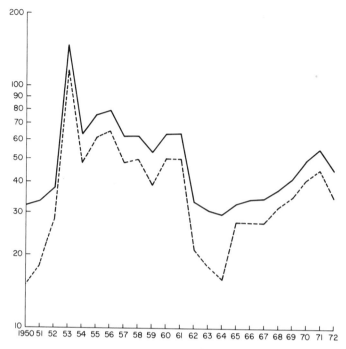

Figure 19.2 West Berlin: total outmigrants per 1000 population, 1950–1972. All outmigrants, ———; to Federal Republic, – – –.

Outmigration from West Berlin was an integral part of this movement; consequently, it follows very closely the overall trend of inmigration until 1961, with West Germany the major destination (Figure 19.2).[3] These facts indicate that the overwhelming majority of the migrants from East Germany did not remain in West Berlin but moved on to West Germany, in other words, the primary flow of migration was neither to nor from West Berlin, but through it. After 1962, in- and outmigration trends diverged, with outmigrants increasing nearly monotonically in contrast to a somewhat more fluctuating trend in inmigration.

These changing circumstances affecting migration in and out of West Berlin have also affected the sex balance of the migrants. From Table 19.1 it can be seen that every 6-year period has had more male than female migrants, and that the highest (most masculine) sex ratios were observed in the early 1960s, right after the building of the Berlin Wall.

[3] *Ibid.*

TABLE 19.1

WEST BERLIN: ANNUAL AVERAGE SEX
RATIOS OF MIGRANTS, MALES PER 100
FEMALES[a]

Years	In	Out
1950–1955	109.2	115.1
1956–1961	115.4	121.5
1962–1967	139.5	139.2
1968–1972	137.0	122.0

[a] From Statistiches Landesamt Berlin "Die
Wanderungen in Berlin (West) 1950 bis 1955,"
Berliner Statistik, Sonderheft 55; *Statistisches
Jahrbuch Berlin,* 1953–1972; as well as 1972
unpublished data of the SLB.

The extreme year was 1962, when the sex ratio reached a level of 159.8 males per 100 females. In addition, in the 1950s, the sex ratio was less masculine for inmigrants than for outmigrants, a trend that reversed itself in the late 1960s. Comparing the trend in sex ratios with the trend in the magnitude of in- and outmigration shows that the years of least mobility across the boundaries of West Berlin, the early 1960s, were the years with the most masculine sex ratios. This is best explained by the fact that males are generally more migratory than females, so that in periods less favorable to migration, the number of male migrants is less affected than the number of female migrants.

The trend in net migration, indicated by sex in Figure 19.3, presents a somewhat different picture than total migration, in that the positive relationship between the net migration trend and the total inmigration trend during the 1950s, although it exists, is considerably less clear than the relationship between inmigration and outmigration.[4] In this period, there was generally a slight excess of females in the net migration rates, suggesting that as far as the East–West movement is concerned, West Berlin acted as a kind of sorting mechanism. The East–West migration occurred in two stages, in which those who completed the second stage were more likely to be more mobile people, with a larger proportion of males. In other words, those who moved simply from East Germany to West Berlin could better represent the age–sex structure of the East German population. Those who continued to West Germany, having completed a greater move, tended to be composed of the more migratory

[4] *Ibid.*

males. Thus, although more males than females arrived in West Berlin, more males than females also left the city for the West; among those who remained females tended to predominate.

In contrast with the period before 1961, the period beginning in 1962 exhibited much greater fluctuation and also a greater predominance of males. As previously noted, the major source and destination of migration in this period was West Germany. Net migration occurred in waves, with large gains in 1963–1964 and again in 1969–1970, small losses due to outmigration during 1966–1968 and again in 1971, and a return to stability in 1972. This cyclical pattern, also noticeable in total inmigration, was much clearer for males than for females, leading to the hypothesis that each wave of migration resulted in increased competition in the labor force, which in turn weakened the pull of West Berlin for inmigrants. The sharpest change in the direction of male excess occurred in 1962, a result of the previously cited trend in total inmigration.

The unique aspects of the trend in migration levels for Berlin become clearer when compared to the corresponding trend for Hamburg.[5] The time series inmigration rates for Hamburg (Figure 19.4) show little fluctuation compared to the large fluctuations observed for Berlin, although the general magnitude of the rates and the direction of the year-to-year changes are similar. It can be noted, for example, that in the period 1953–1961, the rate of inmigration to Hamburg peaked in the

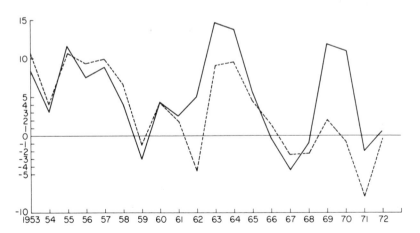

Figure 19.3 West Berlin: net migrants per 1000 population by sex, 1953–1972. Male, —
—; female, – – –.

[5] Hamburg, Statistisches Landesamt, *Statistisches Jahrbuch Hamburg*, 1952–1971 (see figures 4, 5, and 6 and all associated data).

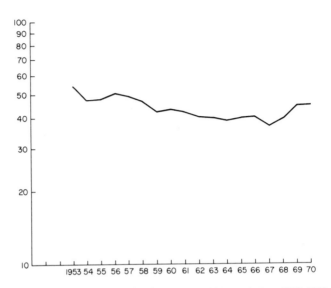

Figure 19.4   Hamburg: total inmigrants per 1000 population, 1953–1970.

same years that it did for West Berlin, although the peaks did not reach nearly as high a level. This demonstrates that Hamburg also received a significant number of people from East Germany, although they very likely arrived via West Berlin. In the more recent period, particularly in the late 1960s, similarity in the two trends is also evident, indicating that whatever economic factors were at work in causing migration from West Germany to West Berlin also affected migration to Hamburg. The migration rates out of Hamburg (Figure 19.5) also show similarity of trend with those of West Berlin the similarity is weaker than that shown by inmigration rates. The peak in 1953 and the dips in 1954 and 1959 are somewhat evident, although the fluctuations from year to year give way, for the most part, to a steadily increasing trend of departure from Hamburg until 1967.

   The net migration trend for Hamburg produced by this combination of in- and outmigration trends is one of steady decline from 1953 to 1967, followed by a rise, at least until 1970 (Figure 19.6). More significant in comparison to Berlin is the fact that net migration for Hamburg since 1956 has been consistently higher for males than females relative to the population of each sex, except for the most negative years, 1967 and 1968.

   The comparison of the Berlin migration trend with the Hamburg trend clarifies two aspects of Berlin's migration that are very likely related to

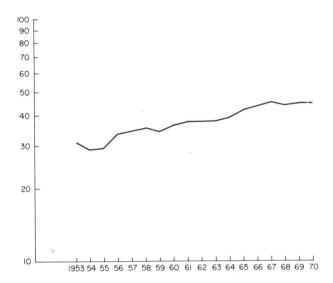

Figure 19.5   Hamburg: total outmigrants per 1000 population, 1953–1970.

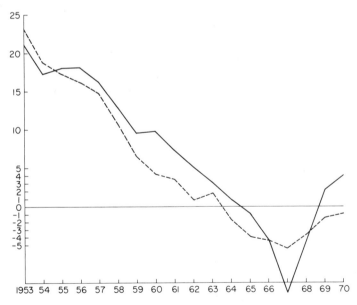

Figure 19.6   Hamburg; net migrants per 1000 population by sex, 1953–1970. Male, ———;
female, – – –.

the city's political status. The first of these is the relative steadiness of the trend over time observed for Hamburg. The explanation for this is obvious for the period before 1961; the role of West Berlin in the East–West migration caused the number of net migrants to be subject to political changes in which Hamburg was less directly involved. The fact that the trends in West Berlin continued to be somewhat irregular after 1961 indicates that, because of the city's political status, the decision to move there from West Germany was more strongly influenced by temporary economic circumstances, which changed from year to year.

The second aspect of the comparison worth noting is the fact that, in Hamburg, net migration in the late 1950s favored males more than females, in contrast to Berlin. This can best be explained by the fact that Berlin's migration in the 1950s involved families, hence a larger proportion of females. Since Berlin was the first stop in the move from East to West Germany it tended to catch the larger proportion of families. In Hamburg, on the other hand, migration was more voluntary and therefore tended to favor males. This constitutes a probable example of net migration being affected by external factors governing the mobility in and out of Berlin as a result of the city's separation from West Germany.

III. Age of Male and Female Migrants

Age of migrants is another factor that was strongly influenced by the changing circumstances of migration to and from Berlin. In order to analyze the variations in these trends, it is necessary to describe the age characteristics of the mobile population—typical of migratory populations in most Western societies. In this way, variations from the norm can be seen in their proper perspective. The general age category that consistently has the highest in- and outmigration rates in both Hamburg and West Berlin is that of young adults over 18 and under 25 years. Although rates in these ages are high for both sexes, males tend to predominate. The possible exception to this is the late teens, where females, under certain circumstances, are more mobile than males, probably because girls tend to complete their education at a younger age. The lowest rates of migration are observed for elderly people of both sexes; they generally make up a small proportion of total migrants, compared to their proportion of the German population. The relationship between the proportion of migrants in the young adult age groups and those of middle and preadult age, and how these relationships have changed over time, is the principal focus of this portion of the analysis.

TABLE 19.2

WEST BERLIN: AVERAGE PERCENTAGE OF MIGRANTS
AGED 18 TO 24[a]

Years	Males		Females	
	In	Out	In	Out
1950–1955	23.5	24.4	17.5	18.1
1956–1961	31.4	29.0	23.5	23.4
1962–1967	40.1	31.5	30.2	26.9
1968–1972	30.0	19.4	33.7	17.6

[a] From statistiches Landesamt Berlin, "Die Wanderungen in Berlin (West) 1950 bis 1955," *Berliner Statistik*, Sonderheft 55 and *Statistiches Jahrbuch Berlin, 1958–1972*, as well as 1972 unpublished data of the SLB.

The proportion of migrants aged 18 to 24, as shown in Table 19.2, has changed considerably over the period 1950–1972, but the magnitude of the change has varied both by sex and by direction of migration. For male inmigrants, the proportion in this age category increased steadily after 1958, with a jump after 1961. From 1962 on, there was a steady decline until 1967, by which time it was well below the 1960 level. For male outmigrants, the trend before 1961 was very similar, although the percentage in the category was generally lower. Unlike that for inmigrants, the percentage of outmigrants dropped somewhat in 1962, rose, and then declined again until 1969. For females, the trend was generally less clear. There was no dramatic change in 1962 for either in- or outmigrants, and the trend for the whole period was a rising one for inmigrants and a rising one for outmigrants until 1967, when a rather rapid decline occurred similar to that observed for males. The 6-year averages in Table 19.2 give a broad outline of these trends for the two sexes. The most significant observation about the periods before and after 1961 is that the difference between in- and outmigrants for this age category increased substantially after 1961. This further illustrates the fact that during the period before 1961, in- and outmigrants were fundamentally the same people, whereas after 1961, the social motivations for migration affected the inmigrants in this age group relatively more favorably than the outmigrants.

For people aged 25 to 39 (see Table 19.3), the pattern has differed in many respects from that for young adults. The average percentage of male inmigrants in this category for the period 1968–1972 was decidedly higher than in previous years. This, along with the reverse trend already

TABLE 19.3

WEST BERLIN: AVERAGE PERCENTAGE OF MIGRANTS
AGED 25 TO 39[a]

Years	Males		Females	
	In	Out	In	Out
1950–1955	21.6	22.4	25.0	26.3
1956–1961	23.4	25.2	22.0	24.8
1962–1967	34.1	40.2	24.6	29.9
1968–1972	43.5	45.4	28.7	30.1

[a] See Footnote a of Table 19.2.

observed in that period for the 18- to 24-year-olds, implies a general aging tendency in the late 1960s, that is, an increasingly large proportion of the young adult males migrating into Berlin were over 25 years of age. The same trend is observable for the male outmigrants, except that in this case, the change occurred in the early 1960s. For females, there has been very little in the way of a consistent trend, except that both in- and outmigrants showed a slight percentage increase after the building of the wall. Most important, outmigrants had a higher percentage in this category than inmigrants for both sexes, in clear contrast to the 18- to 24-year-olds, and the difference is, on the whole, somewhat greater after 1961. In the periods after 1961, the young adult inmigrants tended to be even younger than the corresponding young adult outmigrants.

The age groups that showed the clearest dichotomy in their contribution to total migration in the prewall and postwall periods were the categories aged 0 to 17 and, to a lesser extent, 40 to 64. For the former

TABLE 19.4

WEST BERLIN: AVERAGE PERCENTAGE OF MIGRANTS
AGED 0 TO 17[a]

Years	Males		Females	
	In	Out	In	Out
1950–1955	25.1	24.9	25.5	25.5
1956–1961	22.5	22.8	22.0	23.1
1962–1967	9.0	10.3	11.8	13.1
1968–1972	13.4	13.6	16.3	15.3

[a] See Footnote a of Table 19.2.

TABLE 19.5

WEST BERLIN: AVERAGE PERCENTAGE OF MIGRANTS
AGED 40 TO 64[a]

	Males		Females	
Years	In	Out	In	Out
1950–1955	26.9	26.0	27.2	26.3
1956–1961	19.7	20.3	26.1	23.9
1962–1967	11.8	14.0	19.1	20.5
1968–1972	10.1	15.2	13.9	23.9

[a] See Footnote a of Table 19.2.

category (Table 19.4), there is a marked rise in the 1968–1972 averages over those of 1962–1967 for both sexes and for both types of migrants, but this does not obscure the fact that the percentages were about twice as large during the years before 1961. The same is true to a lesser degree for those aged 40 to 64 (Table 19.5), although the direction of change in the late 1960s was a decline rather than an increase.

Although the percentages of migrants over 65 years of age are relatively small (Table 19.5A), and substantially smaller than the corresponding percentages for the population of West Berlin, it nevertheless is noteworthy that, until 1961, they made up a larger proportion of the inmigrants than of the outmigrants. This trend continued in the early 1960s; only in the late 1960s did it reverse itself, and then quite substantially. The latter change doubtless reflects the increasing proportion of elderly people in West Berlin during the late 1960s.

This age structure of total in- and outmigration produces an age

TABLE 19.5A

WEST BERLIN: AVERAGE PERCENTAGE OF MIGRANTS
AGED 65 AND OVER[a]

	Males		Females	
Years	In	Out	In	Out
1950–1955	2.9	2.3	4.8	3.8
1956–1961	3.0	2.7	6.4	4.8
1962–1967	5.0	4.0	14.3	9.6
1968–1972	3.0	6.4	7.4	13.1

[a] See footnote a of Table 19.2.

structure of net migration that is similar to total inmigration for some ages but quite different for others. Because net migration can be positive or negative, and those who constitute it cannot therefore be regarded as a population with an age structure, the following analysis cites age-specific rates as an index of measurement. The age groups having the most positive rates of net migration were again the 18- to 24-year-olds, in both the pre-1961 and the post-1961 periods. These rates are summarized in Table 19.6. It can be seen that there was a substantial jump in the rates for both sexes, particularly males, in the 1962–1967 period, which followed the increase in net migrants overall as well as the increasing concentration of migrants in these age groups. The further increase in net migration in these age groups after 1967, which was substantial for males and dramatic for females (having reached a high of 123.7 for the 18–19 age group in 1970) is in juxtaposition to a general reduction of net migration in these years, a result of the fact that the rates for all other age groups were either very small or negative.

In contrast to this, the 25- to 39-year-olds had the lowest or most negative net migration rates during the period studied. The highest rates for these age groups were observed in the 1950–1955 period (Table 19.7), followed by a substantial reduction during the late 1950s, until 1961. This was followed by a rise in net migration rates for these ages after the building of the wall which affected males only. The female rates of net migration were increasingly negative over the period, indicating that the women in these age groups continued to be very outmigratory. This is a further indication of the previously noted trend in gross migration, namely that although the young middle-aged women (aged 25 to 39) made up a substantial portion of the inmigrants, they were a more

TABLE 19.6

WEST BERLIN: AVERAGE NET MIGRATION RATES PER 1000 POPULATION FOR AGE GROUPS 18 TO 24 YEARS[x]

	Male		Female	
Years	18–19	20–24	18–19	20–24
1950–1955	24.3		23.7	
1956–1961	24.0	26.2	21.2	9.7
1962–1967	65.7	36.0	32.3	16.8
1968–1971	93.0	77.3	106.7	67.4

[a] See Footnote a of Table 19.2.

TABLE 19.7

WEST BERLIN: AVERAGE NET MIGRATION RATES PER 100 POPULATION
FOR BERLIN FOR AGE GROUPS FROM 25 TO 39 YEARS[a]

	Male			Female		
Years	25–29	30–34	35–39	25–29	30–34	35–39
1950–1955	14.4	11.1		12.9	10.8	
1956–1961	−.5	−4.5	−6.2	−1.7	−2.9	−.7
1962–1967	−1.7	2.0	.7	−5.0	−2.8	−2.2
1968–1971	3.8	6.1	8.8	−4.0	−6.8	−4.0

[a] See Footnote a of Table 19.2.

substantial portion of the outmigrants in the period after the Berlin Wall. This implies that when conditions were unfavorable to total volume of migration, the most substantial differentials in the net migration rates were among working-aged people. The contrast between the net migration of 18- to 24-year-olds and 25- to 39-year-olds, with women predominating, is also indicative of the fact that the conditions of life in West Berlin in the 1960s were unattractive to people of family-building age but very attractive to young working people.

With regard to the rest of the age pyramid, there was relatively little selection by age and sex. The net rates for people under 18 and over 39 tended to be small, and either positive or negative depending on the overall trend in the same year. This means that they were positive during the period before 1961 (with the exception of 1959, the only year in this period with overall negative net migration) and fluctuating after 1961. A notable exception to this trend was an increased negative net migration by older people in 1970 and 1971—which could indicate a new trend and might have long-term significance. (For a summary of the net migration rates by age and sex, see Appendix Table B, p. 378.)

The age structure of migration for Hamburg shows some differences from Berlin in terms of gross in- and outmigration which appear rather radical when translated into net migration. The most consistent difference relates to the migration of adults in the early middle years, 25 to 39, who have made up a consistently larger proportion of the migrants, both in and out, for Hamburg than for West Berlin. The 18- to 24-year-old migrants in and out of Hamburg have shown similar proportions, on the whole, to the migrants in and out of West Berlin, although somewhat higher for females before 1961, and somewhat higher for males after

TABLE 19.8

Average Net Migration Rates per 1000 Population Aged 18 to 39 Years
in Hamburg Adjusted to Level of Overall Net Migration Rate in
West Berlin

Years	Male				Female			
	18–19	20–24	25–29	30–39	18–19	20–24	25–29	30–39
1953–1955	34.3	40.5	18.2	7.8	45.5	32.3	13.4	7.5
1956–1961	36.4	39.6	19.9	3.2	34.7	23.2	6.7	1.4
1962–1967	26.1	21.8	11.4	4.3	27.1	12.0	−1.7	−1.3
1968–1970	32.3	42.8	20.8	8.3	40.6	26.2	1.4	−5.3

1961. What is more important, the sharp difference, favoring inmigrants, between proportions of in- and out-migrants in this age group which was observed in Berlin after 1961 did not occur in Hamburg, although there was some slight difference. Finally, there were relatively fewer females aged 40 to 64 in Hamburg for both types of migration.[6]

For Hamburg the net migration produced by this pattern shows less selection of the city by those aged 18 to 24 as compared with those aged 25 to 39. Table 19.8 is a summary of the age-specific rates of net migration for Hamburg adjusted arithmetically to produce the same overall rates of net migration observed in West Berlin, when applied to Hamburg's population age distribution. It can be seen that although the rates for 18- to 24-year-olds were higher in Hamburg than in Berlin before 1961, the situation was reversed in the early 1960s and this reversal became radical in the late 1960s. This is particularly exemplified by the rate of 40.6 per 1000 18- to 19-year-old women for Hamburg in the period 1968–1970, compared to a corresponding rate of 106.7 per 1000 in West Berlin in the period 1968–1971 (Table 19.6). The corresponding rates for males were 32.2 in Hamburg and 93.0 in West Berlin. A not quite so dramatic reverse comparison is evident for the 20- to 24-year-olds. It can also be seen, comparing Tables 19.7 and 19.8, that although the rates for Hamburg fell off substantially after age 25, they fell off less substantially than those for West Berlin. The age distribution of net migrants in the ages below 17 and above 40 were generally about the same for the two cities. This comparison of net migration by age indicates that the young migrants who remained in Berlin were excep-

[6] *Ibid.*

tionally concentrated in the ages under 25, at the expense of the prime family-building ages of 25 to 40.

IV. Marital Status of Migrants[7]

Marital status, along with age structure, is a measurable demographic characteristic which is relevant to the manner in which migration affects population characteristics. Insofar as marriage is associated with family ties, it inevitably affects the propensity to migrate. In a situation where the volume of youthful migration is fairly high, the marital status of the migrants can significantly affect the marital composition of the population. The following analysis demonstrates differences in the marital status of migrants by direction of migration and also by age, primarily for the most migratory ages. This is then translated into differential net migration by age, sex, and marital status (married versus never married, widowed, or divorced). Due to limitations of the data, this analysis is restricted to the years since 1966.

As might be expected, in the period 1966–1971, both inmigrants and outmigrants had less propensity to be currently married at the time of entering or leaving West Berlin than did West Berlin's population for almost all ages. The notable exception was the 15- to 19-year age group for both sexes (Table 19.9), where the reverse was clearly the case. Also of importance is the fact that there was relatively little difference between the in- and the outmigrants in terms of percentage married at each age. Clearly, more inmigrants than outmigrants of both sexes were married at the youngest ages, 15–19 years, although the proportions were small. It is apparent that this reflects the difference in the propensity to early marriage between Berlin and the areas supplying and accepting the migrants, which were on the whole less urbanized than Berlin. For females of all age groups above 20, a slightly higher percentage of outmigrants than inmigrants were married, indicating that marriage was more likely to provide a reason for leaving than for entering Berlin, although the differences were slight. The reverse was true for males in the groups 25 to 40 years old; above 40, slightly more outmigrants than inmigrants were married.

These small differentials in the marital status of in- and outmigrants produced a substantial difference in the rates of net migration for

---

[7] Computed from unpublished tables supplied by the Statistisches Landesamt Berlin giving migrants by age, sex, marital status, direction of migration, and place of origin or destination (West Germany as compared with the rest of the world) for the years 1966 to 1972.

TABLE 19.9

WEST BERLIN: AVERAGE PERCENTAGE OF INMIGRANTS, OUTMIGRANTS
AND POPULATION CURRENTLY MARRIED, BY AGE GROUP, 1966–1971

Age	Males			Females		
	In	Out	Pop.	In	Out	Pop.
15–19	1.1	.7	.2	13.8	11.6	5.7
20–24	11.0	11.4	18.4	28.8	31.0	44.9
25–29	36.1	34.8	53.6	52.7	54.4	70.9
30–34	57.8	55.7	74.5	65.9	66.9	78.7
35–39	68.5	67.9	82.1	70.1	70.5	73.9
40–44	72.4	74.4	85.5	68.5	70.5	73.9
45–49	72.8	77.2	86.8	63.6	65.8	67.1

married and single people (Table 19.10). For 15- to 19-year-old married
people, particularly males, there were very large migration rates and
moderate positive rates for unmarried people in that age group. This is
attributable to the very small population base of married people in this
age group, particularly males, and the demographic effect of this
differential is small. For the 20- to 24-year age group, there were
moderately large positive rates of migration for both sexes, but much
larger rates for the currently single than for the married. The age group
that, on the whole, showed the least gain from migration, the 25- to 39-
year-olds, showed substantially more loss due to migration among the
nonmarried than among the married. This relation held for both sexes,
although it was generally strongest for men 25 to 35 years old. Above

TABLE 19.10

WEST BERLIN: NET MIGRATION RATES PER 1000
POPULATION, BY MARITAL STATUS, 1966–1971

Age	Male		Female	
	Married	Single	Married	Single
15–19	388.9	39.6	132.8	38.4
20–24	35.1	54.7	29.1	62.7
25–29	1.7	−12.7	−6.7	−8.4
30–34	4.9	−6.1	−6.3	−7.2
35–39	5.9	5.9	−3.1	−3.6
40–44	−2.9	4.0	−7.9	−6.0
45–49	−6.3	.5	−10.3	−8.5

age 40, the tendency was again reversed. This indicates that, while West Berlin had little attraction for married people between 25 and 40 years of age, it had even less attraction for single people in those age groups. The best explanation for this phenomenon is that the young adult age groups, while the most migratory, also respond the most to the inertia created by marriage. In other words, where the net flow of migration is outward, married people have a greater propensity to remain than the unmarried, whereas where the net flow of migration is inward, the unmarried will predominate among those coming in.

V.   Cumulative Migration by Cohort[8]

The preceding analysis of migration by period leads to the important question of how migration has affected the age structure of the population as a whole over the last 20 years and to the third phase of the analysis, namely the cumulative effect of migration on birth cohorts. This approach aims at dividing the age structure of the population into two components—the first is derived from the January 1, 1952, population projected on the basis of vital rates, the second is the cumulative effect of migration. There are two principal differences in interpretation between this approach and the period approach. First, the cohort rates of increase show the effect of migration on different birth cohorts and therefore better represent the long-term effect of migration on the population, whereas the period rates show what age–sex groups are migratory at a given point in time and are therefore better suited to studying the effect of age on migration. Second, the cohort analysis is cumulative, in the sense that the base population is always projected from 1952, so that the migration being studied does not affect the denominator in calculating rates of increase; whereas, in the period analysis, the denominators of the rates are based on the actual population at a given point in time, which in turn is dependent on previous migration.

Given the available data, there are two methods of calculating age-specific cumulative migration. The first method involves projecting

[8] Raw data for the following analysis were obtained from unpublished tables for 1966–1972 (see footnote 7); migrants by age, sex, and direction of migration for 1955 to 1965, from *Statistisches Jahrbuch Berlin*, 1953–1972; and available life tables for 1949–1951, 1960–1962, and 1967–1969 (the latter for West Germany and West Berlin), obtained from Berlin, Statistisches Landesamt, "West-Berliner Sterbetafel, 1949/1951," *Berliner Statistik,* Sonderheft 40, *Berliner Statistik,* Heft 3, March 1965, and *Statistisches Jahrbuch für die Bundesrepublik Deutschland,* 1973, respectively.

cohorts by year (beginning January 1, 1952), using the observed age-specific fertility rates and estimated life table survivor ratios for each year, based on the available West Berlin life tables. Subtracting the projected cohort from the actual cohort yields the cumulative effect of migration on the cohort. The second method employs the number of registered migrants by cohort and computes the net migrants in the cohort, adjusting for mortality, using the same estimated life table survivor ratios. The second method has the advantage that it places less burden on the mortality assumption, since the number of migrants is smaller than the population in all cases. Thus, a given error in the survivor ratio will produce less error in the number of surviving migrants, which is important for the older cohorts where mortality rates are highest. The disadvantage of the second method compared to the first is that it is subject to accumulated error in the registration of migrants, which is of potential significance in the younger age groups where migration is heaviest. The first method is more realistic in this regard, since it takes into account the corrections in the actual population by age that resulted in the censuses of 1956, 1961, and 1970. The cumulative effects of migration are explored at four points in time at five-year intervals, December 31 of 1956, 1961, 1966, and 1971, and are based on the first method unless otherwise noted.

The cohort of 1947–1951, which achieved the ages of 20 to 24 years by the end of 1971, showed the sharpest rise of any of the 5-year cohorts analyzed. This rise, as can be seen from Table 19.11, occurred almost entirely in the late 1960s, reaching a cumulative level of nearly 46,000 surviving migrants on December 31, 1971, of whom 22,000 were male and 24,000 female. This indicates that although the migrants in these age groups were predominantly male when the analysis was by period, the net cumulative balance of the cohort was female. The chronological pattern of increase of the cohort due to migration shows a gain from

TABLE 19.11

WEST BERLIN: CUMULATIVE INCREASE DUE TO MIGRATION OF COHORTS BORN
1947–1951

Year	Age	Male		Female		Both	
		Absolute	%	Absolute	%	Absolute	%
1956	5–9	2892	5.8	2567	5.4	5458	5.6
1961	10–14	2854	5.7	2643	5.6	5497	5.6
1966	15–19	4992	10.1	4656	9.8	9648	9.9
1971	20–24	21,762	44.1	23,932	50.6	45,694	47.3

1952 to 1956 from 5% to 6% for both sexes, with similar gains from 1957 to 1961. As the cohort advanced into the late teens, from 1962 to 1966, there was a significant rise in the contribution of migration, 10.1% for males and 9.8% for females. Finally, between 1967 and 1971, when massive inmigration by the cohort occurred, the cumulative surviving net migrants increased by a factor of four for males and five for females, bringing the cumulative effect of the projected cohort to 44.1% for males and 50.6% for females.

Similar in its development but of a somewhat different magnitude was the cumulative increase for the cohort of 1942–1946 (Table 19.12). This cohort had reached approximately the same level in terms of percentage increase by the time it had reached the 15 to 19 age category in 1961 as had the 1947–1951 cohort 5 years later. As the cohort advanced into the 20- to 24-year age category, it increased substantially, although not as heavily percentagewise as the 1947–1951 cohort at the same age. Moreover, unlike the cohort of 1947–1951, females benefited much less from migration than males. It should be noted that the difference for males was due largely to the difference in the size of the cohorts at the base year, since the males in the older cohort enjoyed a somewhat greater increase in absolute numbers. For females, the number of surviving net migrants in the older cohort was less in terms of both absolute numbers and percentages. For the period 1967–1971, there was very little change of any kind due to migration, so the cumulative increase remained more or less constant. The differences between the 1947–1951 cohort and the 1942–1946 cohort are best explained by the fact that the latter, the older of the two cohorts, achieved the "boom ages" in the period 1962–1967, a time when the future of West Berlin was relatively uncertain, so that the less migratory females were less induced to stay in Berlin, a tendency noted in the period data. The

TABLE 19.12

WEST BERLIN: CUMULATIVE INCREASE DUE TO MIGRATION OF COHORTS BORN 1942–1946

		Male		Female		Both	
Year	Age	Absolute	%	Absolute	%	Absolute	%
1956	10–14	4527	7.3	3762	6.3	8289	6.8
1916	15–19	7302	11.9	6077	10.2	13,379	11.0
1966	20–24	22,617	37.0	13,801	23.2	36,418	30.2
1971	25–29	22,716	37.4	12,602	21.3	35,318	29.4

TABLE 19.13

WEST BERLIN: CUMULATIVE INCREASE DUE TO MIGRATION OF COHORTS BORN
1937–1941

Year	Age	Male		Female		Both	
		Absolute	%	Absolute	%	Absolute	%
1956	15–19	4425	5.6	7120	9.2	11,545	7.3
1961	20–24	16,079	20.3	13,432	17.4	29,511	18.9
1966	25–29	16,853	21.4	8602	11.2	25,455	16.4
1971	30–34	16,810	21.6	5494	7.2	22,304	14.4

younger cohort achieved these ages in the late 1960s, and the motivation
to remain in Berlin was apparently stronger for women in these years.

The oldest 5-year cohort to enjoy any substantial increase due to
youthful migration in this period was the cohort of 1937–1941, shown in
Table 19.13. This cohort achieved the ages 20 to 24 at the end of 1961,
so that its heaviest years of migration increase were the 5 previous
years, 1957 to 1961. The increase during these years was only 20.3% for
males and 17.4% for females, less than that for the younger cohorts
because the net migration in that period was substantially composed of
East German migrants, who were less concentrated in that age group. In
the years 1966 and 1971, there was a substantial decline in the cumulative increase of female migrants which was not observed for male
migrants—a result of the negative rates for females of these ages
observed in the period analysis. For the cohort of 1932–1936 (Table
19.14), the cumulative increase upon entering the 20- to 24-year age
group almost completely disappeared, with a total percentage increase in

TABLE 19.14

WEST BERLIN: CUMULATIVE INCREASE DUE TO MIGRATION OF COHORTS BORN
1932–1936

Year	Age	Male		Female		Both	
		Absolute	%	Absolute	%	Absolute	%
1956	20–24	1903	3.2	3727	6.1	5630	4.7
1961	25–29	4343	7.3	3688	6.1	8030	6.7
1966	30–34	5782	9.8	2958	4.9	8740	7.3
1971	35–39	8551	14.6	2632	4.4	11,184	9.5

1956 of only 4.7—3.2% for males and 6.1% for females. For this cohort, the increase did eventually occur for males, but not for females, reaching 14.6% for males by 1971, still a lot smaller than the cumulative increase for the younger cohorts.

The cohorts that showed the least gain (or most loss) due to migration during the period studied were those born after 1907 but before 1938. These cohorts formed the older section of the potential work force in 1971. By computing the survival of registered migrants (second method), there were in 1971 near zero or negative cumulative increases for all males aged 45 to 71 and all females aged 41 to 51, although the net decrease was small. These cohorts had, for the most part, gained small positive balances by 1956, but proceeded to lose them in the later years of the refugee period, until 1961. The oldest cohorts, born before 1900, showed, for both sexes, a cumulative gain due to migration, whereas the cohorts born between 1900 and 1906 showed a loss for males and a gain for females. These results are shown in Table 19.15, which gives a summary of the net cumulative gain for the cohorts that were 40 and over in 1971. These figures were inferred from population projections by cohort (first method) until the cohort reached age 50, and then by survival of registered migrants (second method) after age 50. It can be seen that the gains were universally more favorable for females than males after age 45, and that for females they tended to increase with age for ages over 45.

Also showing an increase due to migration, but for somewhat different reasons were the cohorts born since 1952. In evaluating these figures, it

TABLE 19.15

WEST BERLIN: CUMULATIVE INCREASE DUE TO MIGRATION BY DECEMBER 31, 1971, OF COHORTS BORN BEFORE 1932

Age	Birth Year	Male Absolute	%	Female Absolute	%	Both Absolute	%
40–44	1927–1931	2934	5.9	789	1.4	3723	3.6
45–49	1922–1926	−886	−2.2	−448	−.7	−1334	−1.3
50–54	1917–1921	−1260	−3.2	76	.1	−1184	−1.1
55–59	1912–1916	−295	−.6	2301	2.9	2005	1.6
60–64	1907–1911	111	.2	4018	3.9	4128	2.5
65–69	1902–1906	−1202	−2.0	4563	4.7	3361	2.1
70–74	1897–1901	108	.3	5319	6.7	5426	4.5
75–79	1892–1896	795	3.4	4648	7.6	5443	6.5
80+	before 1891	991	5.1	3943	7.5	4934	6.9

TABLE 19.16

WEST BERLIN: CUMULATIVE INCREASE DUE TO MIGRATION BY DECEMBER 31,
1971, OF COHORTS BORN 1952–1971

Age	Birth Year	Male		Female		Both	
		Absolute	%	Absolute	%	Absolute	%
0–4	1967–1971	6679	14.1	6237	13.7	12,916	13.9
5–9	1962–1966	4420	7.7	4088	7.4	8508	7.5
10–14	1957–1961	3769	8.2	3542	8.1	7311	8.1
15–19	1952–1956	5825	14.0	5660	14.5	11,485	14.2

should be noted that the cumulative effect is due not only to in- and outmigration of the cohorts themselves, but also to the effect of migration on the childbearing population. Table 19.16 shows the absolute and percentage increases due to migration by 1971 for the 5-year cohorts, born between 1952 and 1971. The increase is positive in all cases, and quite substantially so for the 1967–1971 cohort. This is due largely to the increase of young women, which caused a larger number of births than would otherwise have occurred, even in the presence of the same age-specific fertility. The only cohort that gained directly from migration was the cohort of 1952–1956, which was already into the late teens by 1971. All of the other cohorts in this group actually lost somewhat from migration in the long run because the net influx of children into West Berlin has been relatively so slight over the last 20 years.

Summarizing the cumulative effects of migration on the 1971 population of West Berlin by cohort, migration has primarily affected the cohorts of 1942–1951, which reached the ages of 20 to 29 in the year 1971. For males, the pattern has been manifested at a somewhat later age than for females, with substantial increases in the male cohort that was 30 to 34 years old in 1971. For the cohorts of 1902–1931, on the other hand, migration over the last 20 years has contributed virtually nothing. For the cohorts over 65 years of age, there has generally been an increase from migration, especially for females, although the increase has been somewhat less than that for the population as a whole. The figures for the total population showed an increase due to migration of 11.2% for males and 8.3% for females, with an absolute total of 181,000 surviving net migrants, male and female (see Appendix Table A).

VI. The Structure of the Population under the Assumption of No Migration[9]

A final aspect of the effect of migration on West Berlin's population is the size and age breakdown of the hypothetical population that would have existed if the population of January 1, 1952, had survived and reproduced as it actually did, but without any migration. This involves the assumption that age-specific fertility rates were the same as those which actually occurred, and that life table survivor ratios were the same as those which could be expected from available life tables throughout the period.

As of December 31, 1971, the estimated hypothetical population of West Berlin assuming no migration was somewhat smaller than the actual population and had a somewhat older age structure, as might be expected. Table 19.17 gives the actual and hypothetical populations by sex. The estimate of 91.3% for the hypothetical in proportion to the actual population means that 8.7% of the actual population was attributable to the effects of migration, either directly or through the effect of migration on natural increase. It can also be seen that, while both populations were predominantly feminine, the hypothetical population, compared to the actual, had a lower proportion of males. Stated in terms of sex ratios, the hypothetical population had 76.2 males per 100 females, whereas the actual population had 78.2 males per 100 females.

In terms of what might be expected with a youthful pattern of migration, the comparative findings regarding age structure are more surprising. As shown in Table 19.18, the hypothetical population was somewhat more aged than the actual population, but the difference was mostly contained within the working ages, rather than at the expense of the population over 65. Moreover, the difference was substantially greater for males than for females. The most significant difference was

TABLE 19.17

ACTUAL AND HYPOTHETICAL POPULATION OF WEST BERLIN, BY SEX

	Actual	Hypothetical	Difference	Hypothetical as % of Actual
Male	914,582	822,756	91,826	90.0
Female	1,169,330	1,079,935	89,395	92.4
Total	2,083,912	1,902,691	181,221	91.3

[9] See Footnote 8.

TABLE 19.18

AGE DISTRIBUTION OF THE ACTUAL AND HYPOTHETICAL POPULATION OF WEST
BERLIN, DECEMBER 31, 1971

Age	Male		Female		Both	
	Hypo.	Actual	Hypo.	Actual	Hypo.	Actual
0–14	18.4	18.2	13.4	13.5	15.5	15.6
15–39	35.1	39.8	26.1	28.4	30.0	33.4
40–64	29.0	26.3	33.8	31.8	31.8	29.4
65+	17.4	15.8	26.8	26.3	22.7	21.7
Total	100.0	100.0	100.0	100.0	100.0	100.0

for males 15 to 39 years of age who made up 39.8% of the actual
population and only 35.1% of the hypothetical population. This was
partly counterbalanced by a reverse relationship for the 40- to 64-year-
olds, who made up 26.3% of the actual population and 29.0% of the
hypothetical population. The rest of the difference was absorbed by the
over-65 group (15.8% versus 17.4%) indicating a slight amelioration
through migration of the aged character of the male population. For
females, the relationship was simpler. As a result of migration, there
was a somewhat higher proportion of 15- to 40-year-olds in the actual
population than there would otherwise have been (28.4% compared to
26.1% in the hypothetical population), and the exact opposite was true
for women 40 to 64 years old (making up 31.8% of the actual and 33.8%
of the hypothetical population). People over 65 and children under 15 in
each case comprised virtually the same proportions of the two populations, and this was so for females as well as males. Another measure of
the same effect is the dependency ratio, obtained by dividing the
population under 15 and over 65 by the population aged 15 to 64. This
was an estimated .620 of the population without migration (hypothetical)
and .594 of the population with migration (actual)—by no means a large
difference, given the time span involved. Thus, migration has done very
little to ameliorate the aged character of West Berlin's population,
although it has resulted in a more youthful work force.

VII.   Summary and Conclusions

The principal results of this study gravitate toward a number of basic
observations regarding migration to and from West Berlin. These

observations fall into two categories: those relating to the determinants of migration into West Berlin during the period studied, in terms of general magnitude as well as of age, sex, and marital status; and those relating to the accumulated effect of migration on the age–sex structure of the population.

The most prominent finding regarding the general determinants of migration relates to the effect of the location and political status of the city on the structure of migration. First, migration has most strongly favored young adult males and, to a lesser extent, young adult females in both the total and the net migration trends. Further, this concentration of migrants in the most mobile age groups was heightened by the effective curtailing of migration from the surrounding East German territory, which cast the political future of the city into some doubt. The impact of the Berlin Wall on migration occurred through the motivation to migrate. When a substantial portion of the migrants to and from Berlin came from East Germany, the less migratory age groups had a greater tendency to remain in Berlin, since it involved one less step in the movement from East to West. After 1961, the decision to go to Berlin, this time from West Germany, was much more voluntary, and a larger proportion of those who went there remained. This age concentration subsided somewhat in the late 1960's, but more so for males than for females.

A secondary result, rooted in the geographical isolation of the city, is the determination of which age groups tended to gain by migration at a given time and which did not. The preponderance of people in their early twenties among positive net migrants is not exceptional. However, there was an observed net outmigration tendency among people, especially females, in their late twenties and thirties, which suggests that the West Berlin situation is not appealing to these age groups. This can be explained by the theory that a city having geographical contact with the hinterland provides a better environment for raising families and becoming occupationally established, whereas the opportunities available in Berlin are better adapted to the more transient, younger people. The effect of the barrier to migration in keeping people in the city since 1966 was greater for married than for single people between age 25 and 35. Those who left in these ages tended to do so before marrying or remarrying.

A third fact which is of considerable relevance is the tendency until very recent years, of retirement-aged people to remain in West Berlin the increase in this age group from migration during the 1950s. Both of these phenomena can be explained by the geographical barrier: For the older migrants it was easier to remain in Berlin than to proceed from there to West Germany; for retirement aged residents, the separation of the city from West Germany created an added obstacle which diminished the motive to migrate.

With regard to the effect of migration on West Berlin's population, the most remarkable result is the failure of 20 years of youthful migration to reduce substantially the high proportion of old people in the city or to decrease the dependency ratio. This is partly due to the fact that those age cohorts that were over 65 in 1971 gained people from migration while the cohorts in the late working ages (40 to 59 for men, 30 to 54 for women) did not. The younger working ages gained very substantially, with more females than males among migrants in their early twenties. This, in turn, through childbearing, bolstered the childhood age groups somewhat. Thus, there has been a "juvenescence" of the working age groups without a substantial reduction of retirees.

This conclusion raises the question of whether the situation is likely to change in the future. The increasing outmigration of old people since 1967 suggests one possible change. Moreover, the cohorts that reached age 20 to 25 in the late 1960s—which gained so much from migration—will be growing older, and the younger cohorts should continue to swell, assuming no radical political or economic changes. Ultimately, the key factor will be the ability of West Berlin to hold on to those of its population in their late twenties and thirties. If these cohorts do not diminish too rapidly, the dependency burden will be relaxed, probably substantially.

The recent history of migration in West Berlin suggests some theorization about the geographical relationship of a city to its hinterland and the urbanization process in developed countries. First of all, the surroundings of a city normally provide a region into which the city can expand. This creates suburban areas of relatively low density within the city's influence which provide an outlet for the economically established people of childbearing age. This, in turn, acts as a hold on the portion of the population that has chosen to reside in the city as a means of becoming economically established. When this condition does not obtain, there develops a tendency for people to leave after they have passed the more transient ages, which offsets the gain to the work force by youthful migration. The integration of a city with its hinterland also provides a means by which retired people can move outside the city when they cease to be economically active, whereas if the city is physically separated from its hinterland, the geographical barrier tends to keep this naturally less-migratory age group in the city. On the basis of the data, West Berlin appears to have experienced both of these phenomena.

References

Berlin, Statistisches Landesamt, *Statistisches Jahrbuch Berlin,* Jahrgänge 1952–1972. Berlin: Kulturbuch Verlag.

Berlin, Statistisches Landesamt, Die Wanderungen in Berlin (West) 1950 bis 1955. *Berliner Statistik,* Sonderheft 55, November 1956.

Berlin, Statistisches Landesamt, Unpublished tables, giving migrants by age, year of birth, sex, and direction of migration with respect to West Berlin for each year, 1955 to 1965: as well as the same information but also for marital status and place of origin or destination (West Germany compared to the rest of the world) for the years 1966 to 1972.

Hamburg, Statistisches Landesamt. *Statistisches Jahrbuch Hamburg,* Jahrgänge 1952–1971.

APPENDIX

TABLE A

WEST BERLIN: CUMULATIVE INCREASE OF THE POPULATION DUE TO MIGRATION FROM JANUARY 1, 1952, UNTIL DECEMBER 31, 1971, BY 5-YEAR BIRTH COHORTS

Age	Birth Year	Male Absolute	Male $\%^a$	Female Absolute	Female $\%^a$	Both Absolute	Both $\%^a$
0–4	1967–1971	6679	14.1	6237	13.7	12916	13.9
5–9	1962–1966	4420	7.7	4088	7.4	8508	7.5
10–14	1957–1961	3769	8.2	3542	8.1	7311	8.1
15–19	1952–1956	5825	14.0	5660	14.5	11485	14.2
20–24	1947–1951	21762	44.1	23932	50.6	45964	47.3
25–29	1942–1946	22716	37.4	12602	21.3	35318	29.4
30–34	1937–1941	16810	21.6	5494	7.2	22304	14.4
35–39	1932–1936	8551	14.6	2632	4.4	11184	9.5
40–44	1927–1931	2934	5.9	789	1.4	3723	3.6
45–49	1922–1926	−886	−2.2	−448	−.7	−1334	−1.3
50–54	1917–1921	−1260	−3.2	76	.1	−1184	−1.1
55–59	1912–1916	−295	−.6	2301	2.9	2005	1.6
60–64	1907–1911	111	.2	4018	3.9	4128	2.5
65–69	1902–1906	−1202	−2.0	4563	4.7	3361	2.1
70–74	1897–1901	108	.3	5319	6.7	5426	4.5
75–79	1892–1896	795	3.4	4648	7.6	5443	6.5
80+	Before 1891	991	5.1	3943	7.5	4934	6.9
Total		91826	11.1	89395	8.2	181221	9.5

^{a} Percentages are based on hypothetical (projected, no migration) population. Cohorts projected for each year by method 1 until age 50, by method 2 after age 50 (see Section V).

TABLE B

WEST BERLIN: NET MIGRATION RATES PER 1000 POPULATION BY AGE AND SEX, 1950–1971[a]

Age	1950–1955		1956–1961		1962–1967		1967–1971	
	Male	Female	Male	Female	Male	Female	Male	Female
0–13	12.4	13.2	1.0	1.7	−.9	−.5	−1.0	−2.9
14–17	12.4	20.1	7.0	8.1	1.7	1.3	12.7	11.3
18–19	24.3	23.7	24.0	21.2	65.7	32.3	93.0	106.7
20–24	14.4	12.9	26.2	9.7	36.0	16.8	77.3	67.4
25–29			−.5	−1.7	−1.7	−5.0	3.8	−4.0
30–34	11.1	10.8	−4.5	−2.9	2.0	−2.8	6.1	−6.8
35–39			−6.2	−.7	.7	−2.2	8.8	−4.0
40–49	9.3	8.5	−2.0	5.2	−.9	1.8	−4.7	−11.7
50–64	9.1	6.5	2.1	6.1	−.8	1.6	−11.7	−13.2
65+	6.7	7.1	3.3	6.0	4.6	6.9	−11.8	−9.5
Total	11.4	10.5	3.9	5.0	5.6	2.9	4.9	−2.4

[a] From Statistisches LandesamtBerlin, "Die Wanderungen in Berlin (West) 1950 bis 1955," *Berliner Statistik*, Sonderheft 55, November, 1956. Rates for 1956 to 1971 computed from unpublished data of the Statistisches Landesamt on migrants by year of age and year of migration, as well as the population by age as given by the *Statistisches Jahrbuch Berlin*, 1957–1972.

CHAPTER 20

Ethnicity as a Barrier to Migration in Yugoslavia: The Evidence from Interregional Flows and Inmigration to Belgrade

Oli Hawrylyshyn

I. Introduction

Yugoslavia's mutlifaceted character is summed up in the description: one country with two alphabets, three religions, four languages, five nationalities, six republics, and seven surrounding nations.[1] Since World War II, Yugoslavia has changed from a largely agricultural economy to one with a substantial industrial sector, and in the process substantial internal migration has occurred. It is the purpose of this paper to determine whether the migration was simply a response to these economic developments or whether the flow was in any way affected by the multiethnic character of the nation.

The hypothesis that ethnic differences constitute a barrier to migration can be found stated explicitly in the literature; thus, Fisher (1966) states:

[1] Alphabets: Latin and Cyrillic; religions: Orthodox, Roman Catholic, Moslem; languages: Serbian, Croatian, Slovenian, Macedonian; nationalities: Serb, Croat, Slovene, Macedonian, Montenegrin; republics: Serbia, Croatia, Slovenia, Macedonia, Montenegro, Bosnia and Herzegovina; surrounding nations: Italy, Austria, Hungary, Rumania, Bulgaria, Greece, Albania. A few inaccuracies occur in such a simplification; for example, in the use of languages, Albanian and Hungarian are also important. A slightly different version is found in Fisher (1966, p. 8).

379

"Even though the North is economically more attractive than the South, ethnic, linguistic and other cultural differences restrict many southern workers from seeking jobs in the advanced North [p. 53]." Similarly, Breznik (1968) suggests that: "Because of [ethnic] differences migrations among regions of different language are of a lesser intensity [p. 18]."

In this chapter, I present two empirical tests of the "ethnic barrier" hypothesis, both of which give affirmative results. The first is undertaken in the framework of a regression model of interregional flows up to 1961 (Section III), and the second measures a Kuznets–Thomas-like "ethnic selectivity effect" for inmigration to Belgrade (Section IV). Section II first outlines the broad relationship between the migration flows and regional development patterns, to show that there was some reason for the suspicion of an ethnic influence evinced in the literature. In the conclusion (Section V), I return briefly to the migration-development link, to consider the implications for development of the ethnicity effect in migration.

II. Overview of Regional Development and Migration

In brief, the regional picture in Yugoslavia can be painted as follows: as one goes from northwest to southeast, one encounters less Latin, more Cyrillic; fewer Catholics, more Orthodox and some Muslim; less Western and more Eastern influences; and, finally, progressively less modernization and industry and greater poverty, as evidenced by the relative per capita income shown in Table 20.1.

The postwar growth of aggregate national income was generally high, but prior to 1962 the rates for the poor regions were in general lower or only slightly higher than the national average. Thus, although the evolution of the economy has not left the poorer center and south unaffected, the traditionally richer north and west have advanced equally rapidly, and their attraction to potential migrants was by no means diminished. One would therefore expect a migration pattern showing large flows (normalized for population) out of the poorest republics, into the richest—in effect a southeast to northwest flow.

The pattern to 1961 was not quite what economic developments might suggest. People were migrating out of the poorer republics of Bosnia and Montenegro, but net migration for the poorest, Macedonia, was almost zero. Nor were they going in the expected northwest direction—the richest republic, Slovenia, had no positive net migration; Croatia had a negative balance. Only Serbia, with an income below the Yugoslav average and a growth rate that was sometimes above and sometimes

TABLE 20.1

OVERVIEW OF MIGRATION AND REGIONAL DEVELOPMENT PATTERNS IN
YUGOSLAVIA: NET MIGRATION (IN THOUSANDS)

	Republic of 1961 residence					
	B–H	CR	MAC	MON	SL	SER
Republic of Origin						
Bosnia–Herzegovina	—	+89	0	−8	+5	+173
Croatia	−89	—	−3	−5	0	+143
Macedonia	0	+3	—	−3	+1	+5
Montenegro	+8	+5	+3	—	0	+58
Slovenia	−5	0	−1	0	—	+6
Serbia	−173	−143	−5	−58	−6	—
1961 net migration	−259	−46	−6	−74	0	+385
1961 net migration as % of 1961 population	−8.0	−1.1	−0.4	−15.7	—	5.0
Economic indicators						
GNP per capita 1967 (Yug = 100)	73	121	57	66	204	90
GNP Annual % Growth:						
1952–1957: (Yug = 10.4)	7.6	10.7	11.1	10.9	9.2	11.8
1962–1966 (Yug = 7.0)	7.4	6.8	5.2	8.2	8.6	6.5

Sources: Computed from data in "Internal Population Migrations in Yugoslavia,"
Yugoslav Survey, May 1968, pp. 1–10; and Jugoslavia, Savezni Zavod za Statistiku,
Jugoslavija Statisticki Pregled, (Beograd: 1965), p. 89.

below the national average, experienced a large positive net migration.
The north and west of the country appear to be overlooked by migrants,
despite high and rapid economic development.

The evidence of Table 20.1 at first sight seems to bear out the view
that "there is less interrepublic migration than might be considered
normal [Fisher, 1966, p. 53]," particularly as concerns the flow one
would expect into the rich north: Croatia and Slovenia. These two
republics appear to be set off from the rest by some kind of barrier, and
the attractiveness of the "ethnic barrier" hypothesis is clear, for this is
the old dividing line between East and West in Yugoslav history; it
separates religions, languages, cultures, and to some extent ethnic
groups. The Macedonians are a quite distinct group east of this line, and
their near-zero net migration in Table 20.1 is thus easily explained,
whereas the large net flow from Bosnia–Herzegovina to Croatia might
be largely a flow of Croats, who make up about one-fifth of the

population of Bosnia and Herzegovina.[2] As for the remaining migration from the less-developed regions, this is largely made up of Serbs and their very close ethnic brothers, the Montenegrins; it is precisely among the regions comprising this latter group that one finds very substantial transfers of population toward the richest of them, Serbia.[3]

However, the net figures may hide large gross flows responding to finer stimuli than are evidenced by the GNP data. Further, migration models[4] recognize the inadequacy of simple income comparisons; hence a convincing test of the hypothesis requires analysis of gross migration (place to place flows) in a more comprehensive causal framework. I turn now to the empirical tests.

III. A Regression Analysis of Interregional Migration

A. The Migration Model

The model used is of the "push–pull" variety[5] (although in fact only "pull" effects are explicitly included) stated in the form of a single equation explaining outmigration from a given region of origin (i) to all other regions (j) in the country, specifically:

$$OMR_{ij} = a + b \cdot D_{ij} + c \cdot UR_j + d \cdot YP_j + e \cdot LF_j + f \cdot EA_{ij} \qquad (1)$$

where OMR_{ij} is the outmigration from the given region to region $j(OM_{ij})$ divided by the 1961 population in region $j(P_j)$; D_{ij} is the distance from region i to region j; YP_j is the per capita national income of j in 1961; UR_j is the percent urban population in j, 1961; LF_j is the labor force participation rate in j, 1961; EA_{ij} is the percentage of j's population that is of the same ethnic group as the majority ethnic group in the region of origin, i (this is called the "ethnic affinity" variable); and a, b, c, d, e, and f are coefficient values.

For this analysis, the country is divided into 20 so-called demographic regions described in a Yugoslav study by the Institute of Social Studies

---

[2] Consider the following. Herzegovina (Region 18 in Figure 20.1) in the southwest of Yugoslavia has a majority of Croatians; of its outmigrants, 22% went to central and eastern Croatia. On the other hand, region 14, Northwest Bosnia, which bounds on Central Croatia, sent only 18% of its outmigrants to the same two regions. Northwest Bosnia's population is 60% Serb.

[3] In effect toward Central Serbia and Vojvodina, as other evidence clearly shows that the Kosovo is a net loser (see Hawrylyshyn, 1972, pp. 37 ff.).

[4] For a brief overview of economic theories of migration, see Hawrylyshyn (1972, Chapter 2).

[5] For a discussion of similar models of place-to-place flows, see Greenwood (1975) and Alonso (this volume Chapter 5).

in Belgrade (see Institut Društvenih Nauka, 1967). Place-to-place migration data for the 20 regions is found in Breznik (1968), while the independent variable data are derived from various documents as listed in the references. Twenty regressions were run, with nineteen observations in each.

Prior to discussing the results, a brief explanation of the variables in the model is in order.[6] The dependent variable to be explained is the *stock* of migrants in *j* from the region in question, rather than the ideally desirable flow. This is not unusual in migration studies; it is further clear in the Yugoslav case that the rate of migration has been accelerating in the postwar period (see Hawrylyshyn, forthcoming). Hence the 1961 stock is a very good proxy for flows in recently preceding periods.

Distance acts as a proxy for the transfer costs involved, which include more than simply transport; for example, the cost of keeping in touch with home is increased as the distance increases.

The urbanization variable reflects the attractiveness of a region in two respects: the greater opportunities for modern, industrial or service jobs in urban centers, and the attractiveness of urban centers for consumption opportunities: schools, health care, entertainment, and so on.

Per capita national income in 1961 is included to reflect the attraction of opportunities for higher earnings, and labor force participation rates are included to capture the "development of a labor market" effect,[7] or the job availability factor.

The ethnic affinity variable is much more complex than the others both in its theoretical role in the model and in the procedures for measurement, but what it may reveal is of much greater interest given my purpose—to test the hypothesis that ethnic differences constitute a barrier to migration. Let me therefore expand on the meaning of this measure.

One may consider the "ethnic barriers hypothesis" as consisting of three types of effect. First is what I shall call the *homoethnic climate* (or ethnic affinity) of the potential destination *j*; for the representative individual in *i*, what are the opportunities in *j* for living where the environment—schools, churches, community associations, radio and television, newspapers, official and professional contacts, personal friendships—is ethnically acceptable? Second, is the *heteroethnic climate* of *j* for the *i* individual: If *i*'s ethnic group is not the majority in *j*,

---

[6] A fuller discussion of the variables other than EA is found in Hawrylyshyn (forthcoming).

[7] See Renshaw (1970) for a discussion of the role of development of labor markets in explaining migration flows; also Greenwood (1975).

what particular group is? What indeed is the overall ethnic composition of j? Third is the *ethnic push* from within i upon the minority individuals in i, who may sense some degree of alienation.

The ethnic affinity measure used here (EA) is an attempt to quantify only the *homoethnic climate* type of effect, which may be thought of as a positive, or "pull," attribute in the migration decision. The other two bring into consideration possible repelling forces of an ethnic nature, analogous to "push" factors in migration analysis. I avoid these for two reasons. It is less clear how they influence the migration decision, and they are very difficult to quantify, requiring some sort of subjective perception and measurement of ethnic alienation—or "distance" as it has been labeled by sociologists. There has in fact been an attempt to measure "ethnic distance" among the groups in Yugoslavia,[8] but the results are not without controversy; it was thought best to limit the current analysis to the less questionable positive-attractiveness measure.

The homoethnic climate effect is akin to the "linkages" effects of Nelson (1959) whose "friends and relatives multiplier" explains that migration from i to j is greater the larger is the stock in j of former migrants from i because of (1) increased information flow, (2) easier adjustment, and (3) social attractiveness of a milieu where one is not a complete stranger but already has friends or relatives. One may think of an "ethnic affinity multiplier" acting in a way similar to (3): of all possible destinations for a potential migrant from i, the most attractive, ceteris paribus, is that in which the cultural, linguistic, religious, and habitudinal characteristics of the populace are most akin to his own.

To measure this, I begin by defining the ethnicity of each region (E_i) according to the ethnic group that is in the majority (see Figure 20.1). The great homogeneity of the regions makes this an acceptable procedure for all except three or four regions. In one case, Central Bosnia, there is a plurality of Muslims; three other areas in Bosnia have majorities of about 50% of a given group. But in 16 of the regions the majority comprises 60% or more.

Given the ethnicity of i, the ethnic affinity of another region, j, to potential migrants in i is defined as:

$$EA_{ij} = \text{percentage of population in } j \text{ that is}$$
$$\text{of the ethnicity of } i.$$

[8] See Pantić (1967). This study attempts to measure the "ethnic distance" among different groups in Yugoslavia through sample surveys posing such questions as: Would you consent to a person of X group (each ethnic group other than the interviewee's own) living in your republic, working with you, being your superior, being your friend, and—the acid test—marrying your daughter.

Figure 20.1   Ethnicity of demographic regions of Yugoslavia.

1. Šumadija (Serb, 93.2)
2. Old Serbia (Serb, 89.9)
3. Eastern Serbia (Serb, 98.0)
4. Southern Serbia (Serb, 89.8)
5. Kosmet (Šiptar, 67.1)
6. Eastern Vojvodina (Serb, 64.7)
7. Western Vojvodina (Serb, 49.6)
8. Eastern Croatia (Croat, 69.7)
9. Central Croatia (Croat, 86.0)
10. Northern Dalmatia (Croat, 75.3)

11. Southern Dalmatia (Croat, 83.8)
12. Western Slovenia (Slovene, 95.2)
13. Eastern Slovenia (Slovene, 96.2)
14. North-West Bosnia (Serb, 59.9)
15. North-East Bosnia (Serb, 50.8)
16. Central Bosnia (Moslem, 31.3)
17. Eastern Bosnia (Serb, 49.6)
18. Herzegovina (Croat, 50.9)
19. Macedonia (Macedonian, 70.9)
20. Montenegro (Montenegrin, 81.5)

Source: Breznik (1968), p. 127.

Thus, for example, Central Serbia is said to be of Serbian ethnicity; the ethnic affinity of Macedonia to Central Serbia is measured as the percentage of Serbs in the population of Macedonia.

As measured, the statistical evidence on the ethnic affinity effect will essentially be an answer to the following question a prospective migrant may ask himself: "All other things equal, is a place more attractive because it has relatively more people of my ethnic group?"

B.   RESULTS OF EMPIRICAL ANALYSIS

Table 20.2 presents the results of the regression analysis. The explanatory power of the variables is overall quite high as judged by the values of $\bar{R}^2$ and the F-test of the significance of the overall fit. High $\bar{R}^2$ does not of itself mean a good estimation, of course; thus it is gratifying to note that the fit of the individual variables is also quite good in the sense of being fairly consistent with respect to sign, value, and significance. Let me note very briefly the results for the "economic" variables before I discuss in detail the ethnic affinity evidence.

TABLE 20.2

OUTMIGRATION REGRESSION RESULTS, BY REGION (LOG-LINEAR FORM): COEFFICIENT AND $(t)^a$ VALUES FOR VARIABLES

Region	D	EA	UR	YP	LF	$\bar{R}^2$ (F)
1 Central Serbia	−0.96 (−5.10)	0.18 (2.27)	0.53 (2.25)	0.63 (2.57)	—	.8565 (20.9)
2 Old Serbia	−2.44 (−9.15)	0.08 (0.99)	0.58 (1.83)	0.70 (1.84)	—	.9082 (34.6)
3 Eastern Serbia	−1.65 (−6.78)	0.02 (0.16)	0.83 (2.69)	0.26 (0.86)	—	.8729 (31.9)
4 Southern Serbia	−2.40 (−8.51)	0.15 (1.67)	1.40 (3.84)	0.51 (1.18)	—	.9207 (40.6)
5 Kosmet	−1.84 (−6.02)	−0.03 (−0.32)	1.45 (3.39)	−0.35 (−0.74)	—	.8953 (29.9)
6 Eastern Vojvodina	−1.05 (−2.29)	0.27 (1.62)	0.53 (1.09)	0.67 (1.36)	—	.6894 (7.7)
7 Western Vojvodina	−1.16 (−2.89)	0.15 (1.10)	1.35 (3.43)	−0.05 (−0.13)	—	.7520 (10.6)
8 Eastern Croatia	−0.95 (−3.22)	0.33 (5.19)	1.03 (3.48)	0.05 (0.14)	1.65 (1.70)	.9140 (27.6)
9 Central Croatia	−0.85 (−1.69)	0.19 (1.94)	0.97 (1.69)	0.73 (1.11)	—	.7801 (12.4)
10 Northern Dalmatia	−0.49 (−0.66)	0.26 (2.04)	1.68 (2.23)	0.47 (0.49)	—	.7526 (10.6)
11 Southern Dalmatia	−0.03 (0.04)	0.47 (3.53)	0.92 (1.59)	0.40 (0.85)	—	.8092 (14.8)
12 Western Slovenia	−0.54 (−1.87)	0.34 (2.81)	0.21 (0.65)	0.82 (1.57)	—	.9282 (45.2)
13 Eastern Slovenia	−0.51 (−3.58)	0.48 (6.54)	0.32 (1.95)	0.77 (2.70)	—	.9868 (260.9)

14 North-West Bosnia	−1.56	0.50	1.00	0.93	−3.83	.7636
	(−3.12)	(3.08)	(1.69)	(1.07)	(−2.20)	(8.4)
15 North-East Bosnia	−2.27	0.22	0.46	0.83	−3.90	.8280
	(−4.85)	(1.23)	(0.86)	(1.04)	(−2.16)	(12.5)
16 Central Bosnia	−2.10	0.14	0.82	0.57	—	.9004
	(−7.43)	(2.25)	(2.76)	(2.11)		(31.7)
17 Eastern Bosnia	−1.93	0.40	0.35	1.23	−4.73	.7637
	(−3.22)	(1.95)	(0.44)	(1.42)	(−2.02)	(8.4)
18 Herzegovina	−1.66	0.24	1.38	−1.20	—	.5993
	(−2.04)	(1.43)	(1.79)	(−1.69)		(5.2)
19 Macedonia	−0.93	0.51	0.82	−0.35	1.61	.9568
	(−5.20)	(6.08)	(3.31)	(−1.30)	(3.31)	(57.5)
20 Montenegro	−1.21	0.41	0.41	0.45	−1.83	.8059
	(−3.06)	(3.14)	(1.23)	(1.08)	(−1.98)	(15.9)

[a] A t-statistic that is much lower than 2 indicates the coefficient estimate is not statistically significant. Precise statistical test values depend on the degree of significance one has in mind (1%, 5%).

The distance variable has a negative coefficient in all cases, as expected, and is highly significant, as shown by the high t-values, except for two cases—the very similar regions of the northern and southern Adriatic coast, which before 1961 had very poor transportation connections to the rest of Yugoslavia. Coefficients for the variable UR (percentage of urban population) are all of the expected positive sign, and a majority of them are significant. The insignificant cases (Bosnia, Montenegro) are regions in which much of the outmigration was not of the rural–urban type, but was rural–rural migration to better agricultural lands in the Pannonian Plain.

Income per capita has inconsistent sign and often insignificant coefficient values, but this may be due to the problem of collinearity between the two variables UR and YP ($r = .61$). Econometrics does not offer a "best practice" technique for dealing with multicollinearity except to suggest that two possible types of problems may occur. First, one variable may be a proxy for the other, and either fully captures the causal effect upon the dependent variable; in such a case it is probably best to leave in only one. A second case, however, is one in which the two variables each have a separate effect and are highly correlated through a different behavioral relationship. In this case, leaving both in precludes unbiased estimation of the coefficients but dropping one results in estimation bias for the whole equation through "omitted variable" effects.[9]

Migration theory suggests that both income and urbanization are important and distinct causal factors: greater income reflects greater economic benefits from migration; greater urbanization means greater opportunities for employment, job change, advancement, and education, and the consumption of material, cultural and other advantages. This argues for inclusion of both in the regressions.

Nevertheless, the problem of multicollinearity remains and biases all coefficient estimates, hence it is useful to probe the effects by attempting regressions with YP and UR left out in turn, both as a "test" of the theoretical justification given for including YP and UR, and as a sensitivity analysis of the effect on the EA coefficient of alternative specifications. To this end, Table 20.3 gives coefficients and t values for EA, YP, and UR only for each of the 20 regions. First, it is clear from a

---

[9] In such cases one may use a recently developed technique (Gramm–Schmidt Orthogonalization) which would first isolate the interrelationship between YP and UR, then use one of these plus the residual of the relationship in explaining OMR. This is described in A. Basilevsky, "A Multivariate Analysis of Consumer Demand in the United Kingdom, 1955–1968", Ph.D. Thesis, University of Southampton, 1973, p. 83. I am indebted to Gordon Fisher for pointing this out and for his advice on the multicollinearity problem.

comparison of Tables 20.2 and 20.3 that YP is an important variable—its coefficient and t-value are considerably greater when UR is left out, and in three of the four cases of negative sign in Table 20.2, exclusion of UR changes this to expected positive (and significant) values. That the effects of either variable are not fully captured by the other is suggested by the following: R^2 is higher with UR 15 times and with YP 5 times; the effect on EA of dropping one from Table 20.2 specification is not always the same—sometimes coefficient and t rise when YP is dropped, sometimes the opposite happens. In sum, there is no clear indication which of the two is "better," hence I conclude that the theory's suggestion of both being included is supported by this sensitivity analysis.

Finally, the impact on EA is clearly not great. In fifteen cases, the coefficient and t-statistic are little affected, while in three (1, 15, 16) they decrease perceptibly, and in two (5, 18) they improve perceptibly. The conclusion appears to be that whatever problems multicollinearity engenders, empirical support for the ethnic affinity hypothesis remains strong. Let me now return to analysis of Table 20.2.

The LF variable, rather than manifesting the expected effects of labor markets, coincidentally isolated the rural–rural migration flows. This is not the place to elaborate on this effect; suffice it to say that low participation coincided with high migration to fertile lands in regions with intermediate LF, and low migration to industrial areas with high LF.

The ethnic affinity variable shows consistently positive values and a high degree of significance for the coefficient in a majority of cases, suggesting that the ethnic affinity hypothesis should be accepted. For a given origin, the higher the percentage of the origin's ethnic group in a destination, the greater is the migration to that destination, ceteris paribus.

As indicated earlier, the variable does not test directly the ethnic push or heteroethnic climate elements of the "barrier hypothesis." However, the significance of EA does mean that migration may be somewhat less than it would be if people did not consider the strength of their group's ethnic milieu in their evaluation of the relative attractiveness of different regions. If this factor became irrelevant, then some of the people who had not migrated would find that the attractiveness of some regions would be greater than that of their own and would migrate. Also, there may have been migrants from i to j who in fact considered another region k to be slightly more attractive economically (perhaps only because of shorter distance to k) but j's ethnic affinity was enough to compensate. If ethnic factors were irrelevant, these people would have

TABLE 20.3

Alternative Specifications of Migration Equation[a]

Region	EA		YP		UR		R^2	
1	0.12	(1.32)	—		0.91	(4.16)	.788	(18.7)
	0.17	(1.93)	0.97	(4.47)	—		.805	(20.6)
2	0.06	(0.62)	—		0.99	(4.04)	.8859	(38.8)
	0.09	(1.02)	1.18	(4.05)	—		.8862	(38.9)
3	−0.01	(−0.1)	—		0.91	(3.83)	.8731	(34.3)
	0.003	(0.03)	0.84	(3.17)	—		.8499	(28.3)
4	0.13	(1.47)	—		1.71	(6.75)	.9128	(52.3)
	0.15	(1.20)	1.70	(4.17)	—		.8372	(25.7)
5	−0.03	(−0.3)	—		1.20	(4.56)	.8912	(40.9)
	0.18	(1.62)	0.90	(2.32)	—		.8095	(21.25)
6	.19	(1.18)	—		0.93	(2.38)	.6484	(9.22)
	.25	(1.50)	1.00	(2.56)	—		.6628	(9.82)
7	.15	(1.31)	—		1.32	(4.4)	.7517	(15.1)
	.15	(0.84)	0.82	(1.94)	—		.5932	(5.9)
8	.28	(4.86)	—		1.20	(5.12)	.8842	(38.2)
	.28	(3.98)	1.01	(3.51)	—		.8252	(23.60)
9	.16	(1.69)	—		1.46	(3.99)	.7607	(15.9)
	.24	(2.46)	1.60	(3.56)	—		.7349	(13.8)
10	.23	(2.08)	—		1.97	(4.58)	.7484	(14.9)
	.38	(2.87)	2.19	(3.45)	—		.6644	(9.9)
11	.48	(3.63)	—		1.21	(2.59)	.7995	(19.9)
	.57	(4.56)	0.85	(2.08)	—		.7747	(17.2)
12	.43	(3.87)	—		.57	(2.49)	.9156	(54.2)
	.34	(2.82)	1.07	(3.03)	—		.9260	(62.5)
13	.60	(9.0)	—		.59	(3.98)	.9799	(243.6)
	.47	(5.9)	1.12	(4.68)	—		.9832	(292.1)

14	.32	(2.52)			1.31	(3.17)	.6707 (10.2)
	.37	(2.18)	.97	(1.64)	—		.5341 (5.7)
15	0.02	(0.19)			.66	(1.6)	.758 (15.7)
	0.02	(0.12)	.24	(.49)	—		.7206 (12.9)
16	0.07	(1.22)			1.05	(3.4)	.8687 (33.1)
	0.11	(1.45)	.84	(2.80)	—		.8464 (27.5)
17	0.12	(0.77)			1.21	(2.15)	.6894 (11.1)
	0.15	(0.89)	.70	(1.26)	—		.6323 (8.6)
18	.16	(0.94)			.72	(1.02)	.5177 (5.37)
	.33	(1.98)	−.56	(0.85)	—		.5077 (5.2)
19	.58	(5.8)			.58	(2.85)	.9195 (57.1)
	.69	(7.5)	.48	(2.10)	—		.9040 (47.1)
20	.40	(2.5)			.54	(1.56)	.8006 (20.1)
	.51	(3.92)	.57	(1.53)	—		.7994 (19.9)

[a] t statistic in parentheses.

391

gone to k instead.[10] In these two senses, the significance of the ethnic affinity factor may be said to manifest the existence of some sort of "barrier" to interregional migration in Yugoslavia.

There is no reason to suppose that the ethnic affinity factor would be equally important for all ethnic groups or regions, nor even that it should *be* important for all groups. Hence it is instructive to look in more detail at the value and significance of the coefficient for the different regions.

First of all, it comes as no surprise that the coefficient for the Kosmet is not of the right sign and is quite insignificant. The 1961 population here was two-thirds Albanian (Šiptar)—the group undoubtedly furthest removed from all other nationalities in terms of language and culture.[11] Thus, it is also conceivable that they may be quite indifferent in choosing among regions in which other groups predominate and in which their numbers are extremely small, that is, the hetero-ethnic climate for Albanians is the same in all other regions. Much of this migration is of unskilled labor to large cities—particularly Belgrade—as suggested by the very high and significant value for the *UR* coefficient and the evidence of Table 20.3. For the large segment of the Kosmet population that is relatively unskilled, the great attractiveness of large cities is in the fact that the opportunities for peripheral, often temporary employment in labor-intensive jobs particularly in the tertiary sector (construction, snow removal, domestic odd jobs, marginal intracity haulage on bicycles or man-powered carts) are much greater than in less-urbanized areas.

The explanation for the unimportance of the *EA* variable in Western Vojvodina is of a somewhat similar nature: although 50% of the population is Serbian, there is a very large group of Hungarians in this area, comprising about one-third of the region's population. They too are ethnically quite far removed from the Slav groups in Yugoslavia, and though the region was classified in this study as being Serbian, it included a large group who may be relatively indifferent in their attitudes toward other ethnic groups[12] and perhaps also to the size of their own group outside this region, as their numbers elsewhere are very small.

Similarly, ethnic heterogeneity is probably the reason for insignificant *t*-values for the two Bosnian regions. Northeast Bosnia, which lies across the Sava River from the attractive fertile lands of Eastern Croatia

[10] One such possible real example is the case mentioned earlier of Serbs in Northwest Bosnia who migrated to Central Serbia instead of the equally attractive (economically) Central Croatia, perhaps because the former was considered more attractive once ethnic affinity was added to the decision function.

[11] A somewhat similar conclusion about the ethnic distance of Albanians is reached in the Pantić study of ethnic distance (Pantić, 1967).

[12] On the "distance" of Hungarians to others, see Pantić (1967).

(Slavonia) and Western Vojvodina (Srem and Bačka) has a population about one-half Serb and about one-fifth each of Croats and Muslims. Herzegovina, a barren land for the most part, is about one-half Croat and one-third Serb. Thus, even if the individual groups were taking into account the ethnic affinity factor in their decision to migrate, the lack of homogeneity is sufficiently great that the imperfect measure used here may not have been able to detect any ethnic effects. For all these hetreogeneous cases, the measure used here is too crude; a more sophisticated test should include similar ethnic affinity measures for the second- and perhaps even third-largest groups.

The very low value and insignificance of the *EA* coefficient in the case of Old Serbia and Eastern Serbia are not so easy to rationalize within the framework of the hypothesis. They are both extremely homogeneous, with the predominant Serbs accounting for 90% and 98% of the population, respectively. One might infer from this that in the case of regions that are predominantly Serbian the ethnic affinity variable does not play as great a role as hypothesized. In fact, there appears to be some relation between the size of the *EA* coefficient and the size of the ethnic groups within Yugoslavia.

The data in Table 20.4 are arranged in order of the average value for the *EA* coefficient of Table 20.2. The ordering by average is an excellent reflection of the values covered by the ranges, a slight disturbance of this relation being found only in the case of Bosnia. There appears to be a close clustering of the values when the regions are grouped into their respective republics, which suggests homogeneity in the effect among regions of the same ethnicity, and if one leaves out the values for Bosnia and the Kosmet for reasons mentioned earlier, the ordering of the

TABLE 20.4

VALUES OF *EA* COEFFICIENT BY REPUBLIC GROUPS

Republic	Regions	Range of values	Average
Kosmet	5	—	−0.03
Central Serbia	1, 2, 3, 4	0.02–0.18	0.11
Vojvodina	6, 7	0.15–0.27	0.21
Bosnia	14, 15, 16, 17, 18	0.22–0.50	0.30
Croatia	8, 9, 10, 11	0.19–0.47	0.31
Slovenia	12, 13	0.34–0.48	0.41
Montenegro	20	—	0.41
Macedonia	19	—	0.51

average coefficient values is closely correlated to the absolute size of the republics. As republics are proxies for ethnic groups, this suggests the following hypothesis: *the larger a group, the less it feels the need to consider ethnic factors as a separate element in the migration decision.*

IV. Ethnic Selectivity in Migration to Belgrade

Kuznets and Thomas (1957), in a study on migration and economic growth in the United States, hypothesized that migration preselects people by "sex, age, race, family status, education, health, and many other social and demographic characteristics [p. 3]." Thus, one usually finds that migrants are more educated, younger, more often male, and so on. The ethnic affinity hypothesis developed above suggests another preselection criterion: given the ethnic character of a destination, one might expect that relatively more migrants are of that ethnic group than would be a randomly selected group of migrants from each destination.

I test this proposition using the detailed migrant registry data for the city of Belgrade in the years 1964–1966.[13] The data provides information on gross inmigrants by destination, age, sex, marital status, education, occupation, and nationality, hence it is ideal for the application of a selectivity analysis. A selectivity ratio for each characteristic is defined as follows:

$$SR_{iA} = \frac{\% \text{ of migrants from } i \text{ having characteristic } A}{\% \text{ of population in } i \text{ having characteristic } A}$$

The ratio will be greater than 1 if having characteristic A increases the likelihood of migration, and less than 1 if it decreases it. A value of 1 will indicate that migration is unaffected by characteristic A.

Since Belgrade is a Serbian city, the ethnic affinity hypothesis can be tested by considering quite simply whether SR_i^{Serbian} is greater than 1.[14] Before I present and discuss these results, let me show briefly that Belgrade in other migration behavior respects shows the same selectivity effects as have usually been found.

Table 20.5 gives the values of SR for a number of characteristics. Clearly, the inmigrants into Belgrade in the mid-1960s exhibited the

---

[13] Obtained directly from the City of Belgrade Statistical Office by the author. The data were first analyzed in Paul Gosh, "Migration into Belgrade," Queen's University, Dept. of Economics, B.A. thesis, 1973, from which the values of the tables are derived.

[14] The reader will note the other two forms of the "barriers" hypothesis—ethnic push and an homoethnic climate—could also be tested using this data, for SR_i^A can be computed for each of A = Serb, Croat, Slovene, etc. For reasons mentioned in Section III, I have not done this here.

TABLE 20.5

CHARACTERISTIC SELECTIVITY RATES OF MIGRATION INTO
BELGRADE, 1964–1966[a]

A		SR^A	A		Sr^A
1.	Males	1.06	2.	Married	0.92
3.	Age:		3.	Education:	
	0–15	0.46		0–7 years	0.64
	16–20	2.94		8–11 years	6.34
	21–25	2.73		Polytechnic	14.65
	26–30	1.58		Vocational	0.29
	31–35	1.04		University	5.36
	36–45	0.94			
	46–60	0.34			

[a] SR given as average for all origins.
Source: Calculated from Belgrade Registry data obtained by the
author from City of Belgrade Statistical Office.

expected characteristics: they tended (though very slightly) to be male,
unmarried, in the age group 16–30, and to have more than eight years of
schooling. Again, no surprises occur; Yugoslav migrants are very
similar in their characteristics to those analyzed in numerous other
migration studies.

Let us turn to the test of the ethnic affinity hypothesis, the data for
which are given in Table 20.6. The implication is evident: Inmigrants to

TABLE 20.6

SERBIAN SELECTIVITY RATE FOR INMIGRANTS TO BELGRADE 1964–1966
BY REPUBLIC OF ORIGIN

Republic	SR of Serbs	Percentage of Serbs in origin population
Bosnia–Herzegovina	2.5	33.1
Montenegro	6.7	2.9
Croatia	4.7	15.0
Macedonia	8.9	3.1
Slovenia	63.3	0.8
Central Serbia	0.99	93.1
Vojvodina	1.2	65.3
Kosovo	2.4	23.5

Source: Belgrade data (unpublished): obtained by the author from City of
Belgrade Statistical Office. Percentage of Serbs Republic: from R. Petrović,
"The Numerical Strength and Territorial Distribution of the Nations and
Nationalities of Yugoslavia," *Yugoslav Survey,* February 1971, p. 3.

Belgrade tend to be Serbian in far greater proportion than is the origin population. The selectivity ratios themselves are far higher than for any of the demographic or economic characteristics noted, suggesting that the ethnic effect is perhaps stronger than any of these others.

This result was not changed by disaggregation from republic level to *srez* (province) level. Of 41 observations thus obtained, the *SR* for the characteristic "Serbian" was substantially greater than 1, except for Serbia iteslf, where it ranged from 0.94 to 1.03.

Furthermore, the results corroborate the suggestion made in Section III, that the ethnic effect is more important to smaller groups. There, it was the Serbs who, nationally, seemed least influenced, being the largest group. Here, it is Serbs only that are analyzed, and it is found that the lower the percentage of Serbs in a given region, the more are they represented in migration from that region; this is readily seen in Figure 20.2, which plots the values in Table 20.5.

One must stop short of saying that the lower the percentage of Serbs the higher the probability they will move, for this can only be verified by the data on all outmigrants from each region, whereas this data set looks only at those who came to Belgrade. Albeit unverified, the hint remains strong: the smaller a group's relative size, the more important the role played by ethnic factors.

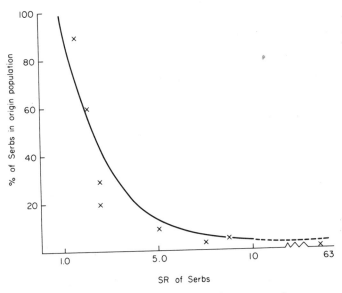

Figure 20.2 Relation of SR and Serb population in origin.

V. Conclusion and Implications

Empirical investigation of migration in Yugoslavia reveals the strong influence of an ethnic factor upon the migration decision. A strong positive attraction for a potential migrant is the existence in a destination of a large group of the same ethnicity as the migrant's. In Yugoslavia as a whole, it was found that this effect seemed most important for the smallest groups—Slovenes, Montenegrins, Macedonians—and least important for the largest group, the Serbs. But even for the Serbs, some evidence was found of putting more weight on ethnic considerations the smaller the relative size of their group in a region.

What does this imply for the economic problem of development? Inasmuch as migration is spurred by development and generally is found to follow it spatially, this factor in some degree modifies the pattern of migration flows that might be expected with development. This is of some importance only if social planning (new towns, schools, etc.) needs quite precise forecasts of such patterns, which seems not to be the case. On the other hand migration is also a cause of development, either as an enabling factor providing the needed labor force or because migrants tend to be more skilled and more dynamic and hence tend to stimulate growth, as suggested by the selectivity hypothesis of Kuznets and Thomas. Thus, if ethnic differences inhibit the flow of people among regions as dictated by economic pressures, the growth process itself may be impeded. In a static sense, such a "barrier" precludes an optimal factor allocation—the best Slovenian auto designer is not obtained by the new auto factory in Central Serbia, which has to make do with a less qualified one. Dynamic stimuli to growth may also be lessened because of such misallocation.

Though the evidence clearly suggests that migration patterns do not follow development in a conventional way, the feedback effect upon growth itself has not been measured—this would require a counterfactual exercise of some considerable ingenuity.[15] Certainly the rate of growth in Yugoslavia has been rapid despite this barrier. Were there perhaps enough capable and dynamic individuals within each group and region so that optimal factor allocation occurred within the confines of this barrier? Or might the growth rate have been higher in the absence of such barriers? Perhaps. But the forgone extra growth may have been the price individuals—and the collectivity—were willing to pay for the satisfaction of what is a noneconomic dimension of life.

[15] With little help from the literature, which, as Greenwood (1975) points out, has largely ignored the "migration causes development" side of the relation.

Finally, there is a possible link to development that may be of considerable future interest: Increasing economic development may break down many of the traditional ties, including the ethnic one, so that the importance given to ethnic affinity might decline with time and economic growth. This touches upon the subject matter of the contribution to this volume by Hammell (Chapter 21), who seems to find no evidence of a rapid breakdown in kinship relations, a view corroborated by the findings in Section IV above—that even in the mid-1960s ethnic considerations played a large role in the migration decision.

Let me conclude by suggesting that inasmuch as ethnic distinctions are made in countries other than Yugoslavia, it would be of some interest to investigate the existence of a similar influence there. Though some little work on this topic has been done in relation to blacks in the United States, and the French in Canada, this corner of the migration literature remains rather empty.

Acknowledgments

Sections II and III of this chapter are based on O. Hawrylyshyn (forthcoming). I wish to thank Egon Neuberger and Alan Brown for suggestions.

References

Breznik, D. *Demografski i Ekonomski Aspekti Prostorme Pokretljivosti Stanovništva.* Belgrade: SBPZ, 1968.

Breznik, D. Internal population migrations in Yugoslavia. *Yugoslav Survey,* May 1968, 1–10.

Fisher, J. C. *Yugoslavia: A multinational state.* San Francisco: Chandler, 1966.

Greenwood, M. J. Research on internal migration in the United States: A survey. *Journal of Economic Literature,* June 1975, pp. 397–433.

Hawrylyshyn, O. Patterns and determinants of internal migration in Yugoslavia. Unpublished Ph.D. dissertation, Massachusetts Institute of Technology, 1972.

Hawrylyshyn, O. Ethnic affinity and migration flows in Postwar Yugoslavia. *Economic Development and Cultural Change,* forthcoming.

Institut Društvenih Nauka. *Šema Stalnih Rejona za Demografska Istraživanja.* Belgrade, 1967.

Jugoslavija, Savezni Zavodza Statistiku. *Statistički Godišnjak Jugoslavije.* Several years to 1970.

Jugoslavija, Savezni Zavodza Statistiku. *Popis Stanovništva 1961,* Books VI, VIII, and XII, Belgrade, 1966–1969.

Jugoslavija, Savezni Zavodza Statisku. *Jugoslavija, 1945–1964, Statistički Pregled.* Belgrade, 1967.

Kuznets, S., and Thomas, D., (Eds.). *Population redistribution and economic growth*: *United States, 1870–1950* Vol. 1. Philadelphia: American Philosophical Society, 1957.

Nelson, P. Migration, real income, and information. *Journal of Regional Science,* Spring 1959, 43–74.

Pantić, D. *Etnička Distanca U SFRJ.* Belgrade: Institut Drustvenih Nauka, 1967.

Renshaw, V. The role of migration in labor market adjustment. Ph.D. dissertation, Massachusetts Institute of Technology, 1970.

Petrović, R. The numerical strength and territorial distribution of the nations and nationalities of Yugoslavia. *Yugoslav Survey,* February 1971, pp. 1–14.

CHAPTER 21

The Influence of Social and Geographical Mobility on the Stability of Kinship Systems: The Serbian Case

E. A. Hammel

A fundamental problem in our assessment of urbanization and industrialization is the effect that the underlying processes of economic and demographic change have on the conduct of social life in all realms, including those not strictly part of the productive process, and the effect that all such changes have on the ideology governing social relations in their extraeconomic aspects. That some changes indeed occur seems without question. Precisely what they are, their magnitudes, and the relationships between associated changes are matters far from clear. This paper will sketch some of these relationships for the limited case of urbanization centering on Belgrade in recent years.

A great deal of our expectation about the effects of urbanization and industrialization—indeed of any change—is negative. Much of social science is permeated by the idealization of Gemeinschaft and the stodgiest kind of functionalism. This Romanticist horse, although not quite dead, has been kicked with sufficient vigor and frequency so that I need not dwell on the false but common notion that urbanization, industrialization, and modernization inevitably mean decay of the social order and swift corruption of traditional ideology. Social order, the norms of agreement, and behavioral expectation can be extraordinarily robust to infrastructural change. This robustness and persistence may be particularly visible in the most intimate sectors of social life, namely those connected with the family and kinship.

An investigation of the relationship between economic and familial change in Serbia requires certain kinds of data and argumentation. First, it must be established that economic change occurred. Second, we must know or estimate the nature of familial life before the economic changes began. Third, we must measure the nature of familial life at some point after the economic changes have begun.

On the first of these points the picture is clear. In 1948, after the dislocations of occupation, war, and revolution, and after some rebuilding had already begun, 79% of the economically active population was still engaged in agriculture and fishing (see *Popis stanovništva 1948*, 1954, p. XXX). In 1953 that proportion had dropped to 75% and by 1961 to 64% (see *Popis stanovništva 1961*, 1970, p. XLIV). The decrease was accomplished largely by the migration of peasants to cities and towns, although of course a substantial proportion of industrial workers continued to live in their native villages and commute to work. In 1961 only 38% of the persons living in the county (*srez*) of Belgrade had been born in it. However, the remainder had come from not far away, an additional 29% originating elsewhere in inner Serbia (*uža Srbija*), another 8% from the Vojvodina, and 2% more from Kosovo and Metohija—so that 77% were from Belgrade and its Serbian hinterland (see *Popis stanovništva 1961*, 1967, p. 93). Ethnically, 87% were Serbs, some of them coming from outside Serbia, such as those from Bosnia or parts of Croatia (see *Popis stanovništva 1961*, 1967, p. 79). The picture of inmigration is even more sharply drawn if consideration is restricted to that portion of the population actively, rather than passively, involved, namely those over age 20. Only 27% of these residents of Belgrade county in 1961 were born in it (see *Popis stanovništva 1961*, 1967, p. 121). It is difficult to estimate the rate at which persons actually entered Belgrade, because of the effects of mortality and possible outmigration after initial inmigration. However, of the persons over age 20 living in Belgrade in 1961, about 73,000 had entered the county between 1958 and 1961, thus at a rate of about 18,000 per year (see *Popis stanovništva 1961*, 1967, p. 121).

Most of the people coming into Belgrade County, and thus into the city or immediate environs of Belgrade, came from villages, and their proportion has increased over time. Of the inmigrants to Belgrade County living in it in 1961 who had come before 1901, only 26% came from a village; many were from other cities or from provincial towns. Among those who arrived between 1920 and 1940, and who were still alive in 1961, the proportion originating in a village was 51%. With the exception of persons entering between 1941 and 1945, the proportion originating in a village continued to climb gradually, reaching 61% for those entering the county in 1961 (see *Popis stanovništva 1961,* 1967, p. 206). In short, the urban population is one that has been massively uprooted from the land, more than one-half of the population of the capital city and its environs having been born in a village.

The tempo of this migration has been sometimes rapid, sometimes slow, never regular and expectable. The occupational mobility of Belgrade workers and thus in large part their geographical mobility, given the rural origins of most of them, has been a response to the fluctuating cycle of economic development. In periods of economic stagnation and low investment, new workers were recruited into positions similar to or lower than those of their fathers. Thus, initial mobility was nil or even negative, only to be overcome by worklife mobility. In periods of economic growth, new workers were generally recruited into positions above those held by their fathers, so that initial mobility was usually positive. Table 21.1 shows some of the correlation coefficients between measures of initial mobility (the differentiation of fathers and sons) and of interfraternal differentiation on the one hand, and measures of economic growth on the other.

TABLE 21.1

CORRELATIONS BETWEEN ECONOMIC INDICATORS AND MEAN OCCUPATIONAL
AND MOBILITY INDICES FOR RESPONDENTS WITH DATE OF FIRST JOB IN A
GIVEN YEAR[a]

	Occupational index	Initial mobility	Total mobility	Interfraternal difference
National income	.25	.46	.38	.21
Fixed funds, true value	.22	.44	.35	.19
Growth of fixed funds according to new value	.27	.23	.41	.22
Growth of fixed funds, absolute increase	.22	.43	.41	.19

[a] Taken from Table 33 of E. A. Hammel, *The Pink Yo-Yo: Occupational Mobility in Belgrade, ca. 1915–1965,* Research Series No. 13, Institute of International Studies, University of California, Berkeley, 1969. The occupation index in this table is scaled in the reverse direction from that given in the source, so that the sign of the correlation coefficients is changed. Growth in the economic indicators leads to higher present jobs, higher initial and total mobility, and greater differentiation of job level between brothers. Initial mobility is the rank-order difference between a respondent's first job and his father's job at that point in time; total mobility is the rank-order difference between father's job at that time and respondent's current job.

Data on the second critical point of the argument, the base line of familial life, are less clear-cut because empirically oriented ethnography of the 1920s and 1930s paid rather little attention to details of family structure. A good deal of what we know concerns family ideology and expectation. The classic work of Bogišić at the end of the previous century provides information as good or better than that available from the first third of the twentieth century—but of course is too early in time (see Bogišić, 1874). Indeed, some of the most explicit data on household organization are from the Serbian census of 1863, but that is much too early to use in direct argument about the effects of economic change a half century or more later. Halpern's data on the village of Orašac in the 1950s are too late (see Halpern, 1967). My own data collected from Belgrade workers in 1965–1966 give some retrospective information on household composition in the mid-1940s, but that is also too late, coming after the dislocation of war and the beginning of intensive migration. We must therefore reconstruct the base line as best we can.

Although the fundament of traditional family life is held to be the *zadruga,* or communal joint family, censuses and tax lists show that Serbian households in the fourteenth, sixteenth, and nineteenth centuries were very frequently simple households of the structure familiar to Western European society—the nuclear family. In all the data examined thus far, the proportion of households that had a simple, nuclear structure (with no additional persons beyond the central married couple and their children or fragments of that structure, such as a widowed person and children) was always at least 40%. Table 21.2 displays data from several fourteenth-century tax rolls, a sixteenth-century Ottoman tax roll, and the Serbian census of 1863. Halpern has also shown that the proportion of households with nuclear family organization remained fairly stable until 1961, although joint family structure shifted toward lineally arranged combinations (fathers and married sons) at the expense of laterally arranged ones (coresident married brothers), as declining mortality increased the lifetime of familial elders (Halpern and Anderson, 1970).[1] The Belgrade workers interviewed in 1965–1966, who then averaged 35 in age, lived at age 15—and thus on the average in 1946—in households that were nuclear in arrangement in 70% of the cases. Of course, some of them were already living in the city, but this proportion is small, only about one-quarter of the total. In 1965–1966 these workers lived in households that showed nuclear arrangement in 75% of the cases (see Hammel and Yarbrough, 1973a, pp. 150–151).

---

[1] This analysis uses a different form of classification from that employed by the present author but there is nevertheless relative stability in the proportions as measured.

TABLE 21.2

CHARACTERISTICS OF SERBIAN HOUSEHOLDS

Census	Date	Number of households	Proportion of households of type [a]		
			Nuclear	Fraternal	Paternal
Sveti Stefan[b]	1313–1318	c. 500	.73	.22	.05
Dečani[c]	1330	c.2000	.41	.24	.35
Chilandar[d]	1315	127	.82	.09	.09
Beogradska Nahija[e]	1528	c.2000	.41	.27	.33
Orašac[f]	1863	129	.40	.20	.40

Source: Taken from Table 1 of E. A. Hammel, "Reflections on the Zadruga," *Ethnologia Slavica* (Bratislava) (in press).

[a] Nuclear households contain only one conjugal pair, with or without children, or a widowed person with or without children. Fraternal households contain at least one married or widowed person and at least one sibling of that person whether married or not, but no parents of such persons. Paternal households contain a conjugal pair or widow thereof and at least one other conjugal pair lineally related to it.

[b] See Lj. Kovačević, *Svetostefanska hrisovulja*, Spomenik IV (Srpska Kraljevska Akademija, Belgrade, 1890).

[c] See Miloš S. Milojević, *Dečanske hrisovulje*, Glasnik 12 (Section 2), Srpsko Učeno Društvo, Belgrade, 1880; also E. A. Hammel, "Some Mediaeval Evidence on the Serbian Zadruga," in *Communal Families in the Balkans*, R. F. Byrnes (ed.) (Notre Dame University Press, 1976).

[d] See Lj. Stojanović, *Stari srpski hrisovulji*, etc., Spomenik III (Srpska Kraljevska Akademija, Belgrade, 1890).

[e] See Hazim Šabanović, *Katastarski popisi Beograda i okoline* Belgrade, 1964; also E. A. Hammel, "The Zadruga as Process," in *Household and Family in Past Time*, P. Laslett (ed.) (Cambridge: The University Press, 1974).

[f] Joel Halpern and E. A. Hammel, "Serbian Society in Karadjordje's Serbia," paper presented at the conference *The First Serbian Revolution*, Stanford University, May 16–18, 1974.

Underneath these fragmentary figures and sketchy comparisons lie several conflicting trends. Family life changes in response to social and economic conditions but not in any simple unilinear fashion. Even in the medieval period there is evidence that ecological, economic, and political relationships, not to mention demographic ones, might have had strong effects on household composition and family life. The evidence from the Serbian census of 1863 demonstrates that land ownership was intimately linked to household size and composition, and suggests that migrational patterns might have affected families differently in different portions of their developmental cycle (see Halpern and Hammel, 1974). Ethnographic data also indicate that the advent of industry in the provinces encouraged the maintenance and even the development of extended and multiple households, providing a firm rural agricultural base from which some family members could venture forth to earn cash in industry without taking too many risks. Finally, it is expected that family size, and thus to a certain extent family complexity, would decrease in an urban locale simply because of the constraints of housing. What is surprising, then, is that household composition has changed so little in the period of acute industrialization and urbanization. Most of the changes from the traditional form (which itself displayed numerous examples of nuclear organization) seem to have occurred before the period of rapid economic change began.

Concerning the ideology of kinship and familial life, there is an abundance of opinion and loose characterization of prevailing attitudes but very little of a quantitative nature lending itself to precise comparison. Nevertheless, it is fair to say that traditional society in Serbia was characterized by intense interaction between kin, circumscribed local allegiance that was often coterminous with lineage membership, the supremacy of males in all public roles, and their primacy in statements about the importance of persons. The kinship system in all its aspects was extensive, fundamentally agnatic (male-focused), and often lineal. These aspects of the kinship system do not seem to have changed much from Bogišić's report at the end of the last century to the survey results obtained by Erlich in the 1930s on familial role relationships (see Erlich, 1966) and even to Halpern's observations in the 1950s, although some change was apparent at that point (see Halpern, 1967). Even in the data obtained in Belgrade in the mid-1960s and in an urban context with industrial workers, where one might have expected the greatest changes to have occurred, there is extraordinary persistence of the basic features of traditional kinship ideology. I will first address the matter of persistence of the kinship system and then turn to the hints of change.

Some evidence for persistence has already been suggested in discussion of household types. Of a sample of 326 male workers in 1965–1966, 72% had been born in a village and the majority had been in Belgrade less than 10 years, so that most of them were living in their natal villages in 1946. Their households in 1946 were nuclear in 70% of the cases, and their urban households in 1965–1966 were nuclear in 75% of the cases—a much smaller change than one might have expected.

One of the outstanding indicators of traditionality in Serbian culture is the expression of preference for male relatives, reflecting the historically important agnatic and male-centered quality of the kinship system. This preference exhibits itself in preference for relatives who *are* males and for relatives who are connected *through* males, and it is most strongly expressed by persons who are *themselves* male. For example, Table 21.3 displays data on expressed preferences for first cousins, matched

TABLE 21.3

PREFERENCE FOR UNCLE'S CHILD AND AUNT'S CHILD, BY SEX OF
RESPONDENT[a]

	Uncle's child	Aunt's child	Neither
Males			
N	217	84	38
Row percentage	64	25	11
Females			
N	33	21	1
Row percentage	60	38	2
Total			
N	250	105	39
Row percentage	63	27	10

[a] $X^2 = 7.52$, d.f. $= 2$, $p \langle .02$ (one-tailed)

on all characteristics except the sex of the connecting parent's sibling.
That is, respondents were asked to indicate whether they preferred the
uncle's or the aunt's child out of a pair consisting of a father's *brother's*
son and a father's *sister's* son, and out of a pair consisting of a mother's
brother's daughter and a mother's *sister's* daughter, and so on, keeping
the sex of the parent and of the cousin constant for each comparison and
restricting comparison to those informants who actually had the cousins
about whom to make the comparison. Table 21.3 also shows the
responses separately for male and for female informants. Out of a total
of 394 respondents, 250 preferred an uncle's child, 105 an aunt's child,
and 39 expressed no preference. Thus, 63% of all informants and 70% of
those expressing a preference chose an uncle's child. That bias is even
stronger for male respondents, for they expressed it in 64% of all cases
and in 72% of those showing a preference. Female respondents showed
this bias only in 60% of all cases and in 61% of those showing a clear
preference. The chi-square for this table is 7.52, significant at the 2%
level for the one-tailed test. (For a discussion of these data see Hammel,
1969.)

A weaker effect is seen in Table 21.4, where the preference for
children of consanguineal uncles and of consanguineal aunts is divided
according to whether these cousins are on the father's or the mother's
side of the family. The bias over the whole sample of 394 is again 63% of
all informants and 70% of those expressing a clear preference and
choosing an uncle's child. That choice was at the 67% level of all
respondents and 74% of those expressing a choice when the cousin was

on the father's side of the family but 60% and 66% when the cousin was
on the mother's side—a lower level of bias for cousins on the mother's
side. The chi-square value for this table is 2.62, not significant at the 5%
level.

Table 21.5 shows the distribution of preferences for male and for
female cousins where the cousin's parent was a consanguineal uncle or
consanguineal aunt. (The N for this table is lower because of the
impossibility of matching as many cousins in this particular set of paired
comparisons.) Sixty-four percent of all respondents and 69% of those
expressing a clear preference chose a male cousin, but this bias reached
70% of all respondents and 77% of those expressing a clear preference
when the cousin was the child of an uncle; it fell to 49% of all
respondents and 52% of those expressing a clear preference when the
cousin was the child of an aunt. The chi-square for this table is 22.69,
significant at the .001 level. These data support the contention that the
kinship system, as expressed in statements of preference, favors males
and persons related through males.

There is also some evidence in these same data suggesting that
respondents not only prefer males to females but that they remember
more males than females, and that this bias is stronger for male
respondents than for female ones. There are four different kinds of first
cousins: father's brother's child, father's sister's child, mother's
brother's child, and mother's sister's child. Each of these can be male or
female, and we would expect persons drawn at random to have on the
average as many male as female cousins in each of the categories.

TABLE 21.4

PREFERENCE FOR COUSINS BY SEX OF PARENT AND OF PARENT'S SIBLING[a]

	Parent's brother's child	Parent's sister's child	Neither
Father			
N	135	47	19
Row percentage	67	23	9
Mother			
N	115	58	20
Row percentage	60	30	10
Total			
N	250	105	39
Row percentage	63	27	10

[a] $X^2 = 2.62$, d.f. $= 2$, $p \rangle .05$ (one-tailed)

TABLE 21.5

PREFERENCE FOR COUSINS BY SEX OF COUSIN AND OF PARENT'S SIBLING[a]

	Male cousin	Female cousin	Neither
Uncle's child			
N	176	52	22
Row percentage	70	21	9
Aunt's child			
N	51	48	6
Row percentage	49	46	6
Total			
N	227	100	28
Row percentage	64	28	8

[a] $X^2 = 22.69$, d.f. $= 2, p \langle .001$ (one-tailed)

Among 375 male respondents, about 67% reported having at least one male cousin in each of the categories, while only 61% reported having at least one female cousin in each of the categories. Among 78 female respondents, the difference was smaller and the level of bias lower— 59% reporting at least one male in each of the categories and 55% reporting at least one female.

Further demonstration of this curious pattern of affect and remembering can be seen in the responses of several hundred respondents to questions concerning kinsmen who were, at several points in the respondents' lives, the most influential, or the most capable, or the most liked, or the least liked. If the responses are compared for minimal pairs of relatives differing only in their sex (that is, fathers versus mothers, brothers versus sisters, male cousins versus female cousins, etc.), male relatives are more numerous than female relatives on all criteria and for all pairs, with two exceptions. Mothers outranked fathers as the parent most loved when the respondent was age 15, and mothers outranked fathers as the more capable parent at the time of the survey (Hammel, 1969).[2] The male-centered bias of the kinship system is again evident.

My inference from these data is that the male-centered bias of the kinship system not only esists but that it *continues* to exist; that is, I assume that the traditional system was at least as biased in the directions shown as the modern system is. There is little information that can be

---

[2] That mothers were more loved than fathers when respondents were age 15 is not surprising, and that mothers were considered more capable than fathers when informants were adults may reflect only some disdain for fathers who were still peasants on the land or the fact that they had preceded their wives into senility.

adduced in direct support of this assumption, although Erlich's survey results from the 1930's and Bogišić's material on customary law, cited earlier, provide abundant indirect substantiation.

Another area of persistence is that of the strength and intensity of kinship relationships, regardless of their bias toward males. One way to explore this area is to examine the frequency of kinship contacts and, to avoid complications introduced by intersex differences, restrict the analysis to males. In the traditional kinship system, interaction and solidarity between fathers and sons and between brothers were frequent. They usually spent a portion of their adult married lives coresident in the same house, and after division of the family estate usually lived very near one another, in houses sharing a common yard or at least in the same ward of a village. They engaged in more cooperative labor activities than other neighbors, and, indeed, it is often difficult to say just when a family estate was truly divided in all aspects of social interaction. The sharing of rights to water mills, the continuance of certain ritual obligations, and political solidarity might persist for generations.

Patterns of personal visiting and postal contact were examined for 326 male workers resident in Belgrade. The analysis was restricted to contacts between them and their fathers and brothers who did not actually coreside with them in the same household. Of these 326 males, 38 appeared in the analysis only as sons, since they had no living brothers. Another 131 appeared only as brothers, since they had no living fathers. Another 157 appeared both as sons and as brothers. Thus, 195 of the respondents appeared as members of a father–son pair, and there are 195 patterns of father–son contact for analysis. Two hundred eighty-eight respondents appeared as members of a fraternal pair; however, some of them had more than one brother, and the number of fraternal pairs in which they were involved was 527. Because initial analysis showed the number of brothers a respondent had to be unrelated to the frequency of his contact with each of them, the unit of analysis was taken to be the fraternal pair, even if some respondents were members of more than one pair (see Hammel and Yarbrough, 1973a).

Table 21.6 summarizes information on the frequency of personal and written contact between kinsmen. Because geographical distance is so obviously a factor in such contacts, it gives data separately for respondents' kinsmen who lived in Belgrade, in a provincial town or another city, or in a village. Sons saw their fathers on the average about every 2 weeks and exchanged letters or packages about every 3 weeks; however, the median figures and the standard deviations show the distribu-

TABLE 21.6

FREQUENCY OF CONTACT FOR FATHER–SON AND FRATERNAL PAIRS

	Mean		SD		Median	
	Letters	Visits	Letters	Visits	Letters	Visits
Fathers						
In Belgrade	2.0	145.3	5.2	170.5	2	100
In city–town	17.1	4.3	22.1	4.5	9	2
In village	19.2	4.0	20.6	7.9	17	2
All	16.2	25.1	20.3	82.1	10	2
Brothers						
In Belgrade	1.2	158.8	4.20	195.0	0	62
In city–town	11.5	4.0	.216	8.5	9	2
In village	12.5	4.2	16.5	10.3	9	2
All	9.1	46.1	.316	122.6	6	3

Source: Taken from Table 1, E. A. Hammel and Charles Yarbrough, "Social Mobility and the Durability of Family Ties," *Journal of Anthropological Research*, 1973, *29*, 145–163.

tion to be markedly skewed. Respondents saw each brother almost weekly but exchanged letters or packages only about every 6 weeks; these distributions are also quite skewed. If the data are broken down by residence of the father or brother, it is seen that respondents have personal contact with their fathers practically every second or third day when the father is in Belgrade but with each brother a bit more often; the distribution for fraternal contacts is more sharply skewed. Respondents saw their fathers and brothers about every 3 months when these relatives lived outside Belgrade. The pattern of letter writing complements that of visiting. Written messages were rarely exchanged with relatives in Belgrade—perhaps once or twice a year. They reached an average level of one exchange every 3 weeks for fathers and sons, and one exchange every 4 weeks for brothers when these relatives lived outside Belgrade. From these data one could hardly conclude that the family and kinship system was being destroyed by urbanization. These are frequent contacts for any social system, and ethnographic evidence suggests that if the telephone network in Serbia were better developed they would be even more frequent: telephone contacts were not included in the investigation because telephones are so rare.

The strength of these contacts does not mean of course that they are impervious to change. Although we have no comparable historical data on kinship contacts, we can infer the direction and rate of change by

examining the variance in kinship contacts and its associated characteristics, using a multiple regression model. Distance is the primary source
of variation in contact frequency; the expense and inconvenience of
travel do more than any other factor to limit personal contact. If one
combines with distance whether a kinsman lives in or outside of
Belgrade (expressing thereby the relative ease of intracity travel in
addition to mere propinquity) and the length of time the respondent has
had in Belgrade to establish a firm base, these factors of material and
personal convenience account for 26% of the variance in written
contacts between fathers and sons, 37% of the variance in written
contacts between brothers, 30% of the variance in personal contacts
between fathers and sons, and 45% of the variance in personal contacts
between brothers. Other variables, such as those of age, marital status,
number of children, ethnicity, religious piety, occupational and educational level, and occupational and educational mobility have a lesser
effect. Taking all variables into consideration, including those of material and personal convenience, one can account for 42% of the variance
of father–son written contacts and of fraternal written contacts, 37% of
the variance in father–son visits, and 49% of that in fraternal visits.

The direction of these influences is very interesting. We would
expect, according to the usual assumptions about the effects of urbanization and industrialization, that mobility would dampen the frequency of
kinship contacts, as the highly mobile became gradually alienated from
the circle of kin and sought new contacts in a world of impersonal,
universalistic relations. The regression coefficients for personal contacts
onto occupational level are positive and onto written contacts negative;
highly placed respondents increase their personal contacts with kinsmen, trading off this increased activity against written contact. Conversely, lowly placed respondents rely more on written contacts. Educational level stimulates written contact as it increases, as does
educational mobility. Occupational mobility, for every level of occupational category, enhances personal contact, again with a tradeoff against
written contact. Generally speaking, highly mobile persons, successful
in their adaptation to urban life, visit their relatives more (and are visited
by them), but they write less, except for the general effect that increased
literacy has on written contact. Conversely, the unsuccessful urbanite
seems to diminish contact with kin, perhaps using written means as an
avoidance mechanism. These patterns of personal relationship would
appear to be no different than those occurring in more traditional times,
when successful rural migrants acted as magnets for following kin, while
the less successful disappeared from the kinship network.

Additional possibilities in inferring sources of change come from a more detailed analysis of the data on cousin preferences. Examining the genealogical structure of the first-cousin relationship, we see that it consists of four nodes, namely node 0 (the respondent), node 1 (the respondent's parent), node 2 (the respondent's parent's sibling) and node 3 (the respondent's parent's sibling's child, the cousin). Each of these nodes may be male or female. We may ask whether there is a tendency to report more cousin relationships according to the sex ratio at each of these nodes or across all of them, and what may account for the variance in such reporting. Further we may ask whether there is a tendency to prefer particular kinds of cousins, given that they are reported, and what may account for the variance in such preferences (see Hammel and Yarbrough, 1973b).

The expected proportion of nodes that are male, in remembering cousins, should conform to the sex ratio in the population for the appropriate age groups. For nodes 1, 2, and 3, these are .50, .50, and .47, and .49 across all nodes. Respondents do not deviate from the expected proportions significantly except at the third node and, partly in consequence of that bias, across all nodes. Both male and female respondents report cousins with a male proportion at the third node of .52, significantly different from the expected at the .0005 level. Male respondents have a male proportion across all nodes of .51, significantly different from the expected at the .005 level; female respondents do not differ significantly from the expected.

The expected preference for male or female cousins, for each of the four kinds of cousins, under the null hypothesis of no bias, should be zero—using a scoring system in which 1 is scored if a respondent prefers a male to a female cousin in a matched pair of cousins, −1 is scored if the respondent prefers the female of the pair, and 0 is scored if no preference is expressed. For each of the four types of first cousins, males show a bias favoring males, with mean bias scores ranging from .31 to .47 (thus favoring males, since they are positive scores); these differences are significant at the .0005 level. Female respondents show no significant departure from null expectation. Again, there is confirmation of the general bias and its greater strength for men.

There are some important sources of variance in these attitudes toward kinsmen, apart from the sex of the respondent. Educational mobility reduces bias. An ethnic background in a less traditional subset of society reduces bias, as does lack of religious piety. Coming from a small family reduces bias. Being unmarried or young (or both) reduces bias. Generally speaking, the effects of modernization reduce bias.

These effects are also markedly stronger for women than for men; that is, although women have less bias to begin with than men, they are even more susceptible to reduction of it under the influences of modernization. What emerges from this examination is the suggestion that subsets of a population traditionally excluded from networks of power and the distribution of important social privilege—in this instance women in an agnatic society—will adhere less closely to the ideological tenets supporting that system of power and distribution and will be more susceptible to the influences of change, however slight. This conclusion of course has implications for more than kinship ideology and urbanization, a fact not unnoticed by generations of political revolutionaries.

The picture that emerges is one of familial and kinship institutions that are extraordinarily robust in the face of massive social and cultural change, but in a flexible way. Kinship is still important in Serbian society; indeed it is fair to say that it is as important as it ever was, but its dimensions are beginning to change. There is more bilaterality in kinship relations now, and this tendency is more apparent in the highly mobile and urban. But there is no evidence that urbanization, migration, and economic growth have diminished the importance of kinship; on the contrary it is precisely those who have been successfully mobile who seem to have the highest frequency of kinship contacts.

In broader context, examining the now substantial body of evidence gathered by social anthropologists in areas as diverse as Europe, Latin America, Asia, and Africa, it becomes increasingly evident that the view of mobility and change as necessarily destructive forces is false. It is based in large part on the American experience, in which geographical mobility was enormous, spanning oceans or deserts or both in a historical period in which transportation was primitive. Most of the mobility we see in the modern world (and very likely most of that in history) has been more restricted in scope. Mobility is less a leap than an inching forward, keeping always some tie for a return to safe haven if the experiment should fail, testing one's way forward along links of social relationships. Kinship provides these links. When the network of kin is undifferentiated in social position, it provides little basis for mobility. As it begins to differentiate, so that some persons have moved forward while others have remained, its utility as a channel increases. When all members of a kin group have moved forward, the utility of the relationships will decline again. But of course stagnation at any level of mobility is a rarer state than change, and we should expect social relationships to be important in chaneling mobility. Friends may replace relatives, particularly when family size declines with changes in demographic rates, but in those countries in which mobility and population growth are vigorous, we should expect kinship to be a robust and active component of the social structure. These conclusions have important implications for social policy. Planners of change would do well to consider whether they want to strengthen or weaken ties of familial, tribal, and ethnic solidarity, and, given their policy decision, (with all its implications) they might then look to apparently minor factors—such as the price of bus and train tickets, the availability of vacation resorts for workers as an alternative to their home villages, and the difficulties of installing telephones and mailing letters. Social systems are often built of very small bricks.

Acknowledgments

The field research on which these analyses are based was conducted in Belgrade in 1965–1966 under the auspices of the Institut Društvenih Nauka, Belgrade and funded by the National Science Foundation (GS 689). Subsequent analysis was supported by NSF grants GS 2069 and 35766 and by supplemental grants from the Institute of International Studies, Berkeley. I am indebted to Charles Yarbrough for statistical advice throughout the entire span of the research, to Virginia Aldrich and Ruth Deuel for programming and computation, and to Djordje Šoć for help in coding.

References

Bogišić, V. *Zbornik sadašnjih pravnih običaja u južnih slavena.* Zagreb, 1874.

Erlich, V. S. *The family in transition: A study of 300 Yugoslav villages.* Princeton, N.J.: Princeton University Press, 1966.

Halpern, J. *A Serbian village* (rev. ed.). New York: Harper & Row, 1967.

Halpern, J., and D. Anderson. The Zadruga: A century of change. *Anthropologica,* 1970, n.s. *12,* 83–97.

Halpern, J., and E. A. Hammel. Serbian society in Karadjordje's Serbia. Paper presented at the conference, *The first Serbian revolution.* Stanford University, May 16–18, 1974.

Hammel, E. A., Structure and sentiment in Serbian cousinship. *American Anthropologist,* 1969, *71,* 285–293.

Hammel, E. A., and C. Yarbrough. Social mobility and the durability of family ties. *Journal of Anthropological Research,* 1973, *29,* 145–163.

Hammel, E. A., and C. Yarbrough. Preference and recall in Serbian cousinship. *Journal of Anthropological Research,* 1974, *30,* 95–115.

Popis stanovništva 1948, knjiga III, *Stanovništvo po zanimanju.* Belgrade, 1954.

Popis stanovništva 1961, knjiga VI, *Vitalna, etnička i migraciona obeležja stanovništva.* Belgrade, 1967.

Popis stanovništva 1961, knjiga II, *Ekonomska obeležja stanovništva.* Belgrade, 1970.

CHAPTER 22

Residence and Work Place in Dynamic Tension: A Study in the Dual Labor Market of a South African Plant

Arnt Spandau

I. Introduction

The legal and customary racial barriers affecting employment patterns prevent South African companies from optimizing labor input relationships. The result of these barriers is imperfections in the internal labor market that manifest themselves as follows:

1. The marginal rates of substitution of white for black workers do not equal the ratios of the wage rates of the two factors.[1]

2. Relative to their occupational abilities, whites are overrepresented in high-graded jobs, while blacks are overrepresented in low-graded jobs. During the growth of firms, there are certain intermediate occupations where the replacement of whites by blacks does actually take place. This process of replacement has certain elements of inertia. Abrupt and visible changes would be looked upon as being contrary to the "South African way of life." In the past, black occupational advance in South African manufacturing industries was cut off, by and

---

[1] The terms *white* and *black* indicate the polarization typical of a multiracial society. Persons of European descent are referred to as whites while members of the indigenous Bantu-speaking population are denoted as blacks.

large, at the level of operative machine minding. During recent years, blacks have also advanced into certain clerical, sales, supervisory, and control positions. With large employers of blacks, clerical personnel administration for nonwhites is nowadays largely done by blacks themselves.

3. In the intermediate occupations, whites tend to be paid wages in excess of, and blacks below, the value of their marginal labor product. Racial pay discrimination also percolates into the area of such fringe benefits as health protection and annual leave.

4. Legislation designed to control the mobility of black workers militates against the attainment of spatial equilibrium. To a certain degree this protects the urban resident from the competition of the migrant and results in tension between the two types of laborers.

It is the purpose of this paper to examine the factors that prevent the attainment of equilibrium in the labor market under conditions of South African racial discrimination. The data were collected during the months October and November 1972, when the writer spent some weeks on the premises of a bottling plant in the Transvaal.[2] In order to preserve the anonymity of those who freely supplied information—managers, workers, and informed outsiders—the plant in question will be called Company X.

The great variety of discriminatory practices makes the quantification and measurement of imperfections in the internal labor market a difficult undertaking. Genuine discriminatory practices can best be observed and measured where occupations held by whites and blacks actually overlap. Consequently, most of the evidence presented in this paper was collected on the shop floor where whites and blacks work side by side. In order to gain additional perspective, comparisons are also made between conditions prevailing in South Africa and conditions in overseas countries.

II. Competitive, External, and Internal Markets

Employment and wage rates are set on labor markets. Three separate labor markets are considered here—competitive, internal, and external. Under conditions of competitive markets, race is not a factor of wage or employment determination. A firm would achieve equilibrium in its hiring pattern if the ratios of the marginal productivities of all workers equaled their wage rates. Moreover, the differentials in the marginal

---

[2] The writer gratefully acknowledges the unfailing courtesy and cooperation of members of management and workers of the plant studied, without which this investigation would not have been possible.

productivities of various occupations would correspond to differentials in occupational skills, measured in terms of the costs necessary for their acquisition. If it is assumed that the costs of skill acquisition are borne by the worker, then the distribution of vocational skills among workers would be such that the discounted future income streams, net of the costs of education, are equal for all occupations, irrespective of the race of the worker.

While the competitive labor market is merely an ideal, both the internal and the external labor markets are observable, and the behavior of their parameters can be measured. Doeringer and Piore describe the internal market as "an administrative unit, such as a manufacturing plant, within which the pricing and allocation of labor is governed by a set of administrative rules and procedures [Doeringer and Piore, 1971, p. 5]." (For the term "internal labor market," see Dunlop, 1966.) They define an external labor market as one of "conventional economic theory, where pricing, allocating, and training decisions are controlled directly by economic variables [Doeringer and Piore, 1971, p. 2]." The internal and external labor markets are linked through ports of entry and exit (see Kerr, 1954). In many companies, administrative rules define entry and nonentry jobs, the latter being those which are filled only through internal promotion (see Ross, 1958).

III. Some Socioeconomic Data Concerning the Labor Force of Company X

Of the some 1400 workers in Company X, just under four-fifths are black. It is a direct outcome of South Africa's multiracial labor market that personnel problems experienced by Company X are different from those experienced by similar plants in other Western countries. Some major differences are:

1. Whereas in Europe the main labor supply problem is found on the level of the machine operator, in South Africa it is found in the supply of middle management personnel. Here is the boundary between (cheap) black and (expensive) white labor, and high rates of white absenteeism and labor turnover (particularly of shift workers) constitute a severe organizational problem.[3]

---

[3] During 1971, at Company X, labor turnover was 22% for (predominantly white) salaried staff, 74% for white weekly paid staff, and 56% for blacks, all of whom are weekly paid.

$$\text{labor turnover} = \frac{100 \text{ total separations per year}}{\text{average monthly labor force}}$$

2. The organized (white) trade union movement is weak. There is no militancy, and the relationship with management is good. In order to keep the union viable, Company X facilitates recruitment of members on its premises;

3. By contrast, race relations constitute a major problem. Conservative attitudes of whites toward blacks, poor leadership of first-line supervisory level, and poor communication between workers of different races (caused not only by racial discrimination but also by the language barrier)[4] are conditions likely to nourish potential labor conflict. Black trade unions are not officially recognized, but blacks may form a "works committee" to discuss labor grievances and conditions of work. Recent South African labor history has shown that works committees are a poor substitute for organized trade unionism.[5]

4. Whereas wages in racially homogeneous countries are relatively more uniform, the South African in-plant wage structure is widely differentiated, even for similar jobs. This makes the substitution of black for white labor an economic proposition.

5. The educational qualifications and skills of the labor force are low; in fact, more than one-half of Company X's black employees are classified as unskilled. Many of these persons are illiterate.

In contrast to whites, blacks are readily available at wage rates laid down by successive Industrial Council agreements. For Company X, there is, however, a strict legislative barrier against increasing the number of black workers, because the plant operates in an area covered by the Physical Planning and Utilization of Resources Act, 1967. In terms of Section 3(1) of this act, the firm requires the prior written approval of the Minister of Planning if it wishes to increase its Bantu labor force. This constraint has limited the growth of Company X during recent years.

There are two types of black laborers, those who are permanent local residents and those who are migrants. The migrant labor force—which predominantly is recruited in the Pietersburg area, where large unemployment prevails—is generally considered more reliable than local labor.[6] Of the total black labor force, about 40% are migrants. Because

---

[4] South Africa is a bilingual country with English and Afrikaans being the two official languages. Blacks speak their own languages, such as Xhosa and Zulu.

[5] A significant number of (illegal) work stoppages and strikes occurred at the beginning of 1973, particularly in Natal Province. Company X and its subsidiaries were not affected by this.

[6] In June 1972, the "avoidable" labor turnover (i.e., resignations, dismissals, and desertions) was 11.0% for local but only 3.9% for migrant labor.

of the high rate of migrancy, the ties to the work group are usually not close. But in South African manufacturing industries, lack of work commitment is penalized through strict administrative rules.[7] The punishment for lateness and absenteeism is usually severe. The penalty for insubordination is discharge, which, if inflicted upon a migrant worker, may cause him to lose his work permit. In general, the black work force is described as being docile and "easy to handle," mainly because of the fact that workable collective bargaining methods have never been allowed to develop.

Living conditions for urban blacks in South Africa are close to the Ricardian "physical subsistence level," with few "cultural" amenities. Most of the black workers employed by Company X reside in Tembisa, a rapidly growing township administered by the Germiston municipality. At the end of 1971, the population of Tembisa was about 100,000 persons, of whom some 30,000 were migrants—described by one observer as "temporary sojourners with no rights to remain or live with their families in town [Wilson, 1972, p. 195]." Migrants dwell either in three-bedroom houses each accommodating nine men or in huge hostels each housing some 4000 men. In these hostels, two to six men share a room. There are canteens that provide workers with breakfast and afterwork meals for a small charge (see Wilson, 1972, p. 45).

Due to the relatively abundant availability of employment opportunities on the highly industrialized East Rand (an industrial area of some 10,000 sq km), the average annual household income was R1130 in 1970, a figure that exceeded the secondary poverty datum line by approximately R375. Nevertheless, the expenditure pattern shows signs of poverty. A high proportion of income (about 37%) is spent on food, mainly on grain products, corn-meal, and white bread. There is no electricity in Tembisa. Battery-operated radios, recordplayers, and hand sewing machines are considered luxury items.[8]

Standards of education among the inhabitants of Tembisa are low.

[7] Piore reports for the United States that employers hiring ghetto workers may accommodate to their behavioral characteristics rather than attempt to change them. Unstable employment is reported to be tolerated, so is lateness, and, while the employer does not actually condone theft and the employee is fired if he is caught, the employer does expect a certain amount of theft and does not monitor it closely (see Piore, 1968b, pp. 5–10, 34). Similar observations would probably apply to the employment of domestic servants in South Africa. Yet in manufacturing, the writer has not observed similar lax employment patterns.

[8] 1 Rand = 1.40 U.S. dollars (December 1970). Average household income from Bureau of Market Research (1972). The secondary poverty datum line estimates the income needed by an individual household if it is to maintain a defined minimum level of health and decency (Potgieter, 1973).

The mean education of income earners is Standard 2.2; this corresponds to little more than 4 years of schooling (see Bureau of Market Research, 1972).

IV. Production Processes at the Plant of Company X

In the bottling hall, the writer, together with three staff members of the engineering department of Company X, studied work operations on one bottling and two canning lines. There was a great variety of different jobs requiring different skills, ranging from the simple mechanical handling of the product, on the one hand, to the monitoring of the running process, on the other. Blacks were employed both as production workers and as process operators. As production workers, they undertook repetitive and manual work where speed is of importance, such as in the handling of material. As process operators, they were responsible for the monitoring of such processes as washing, filling, and labeling. (For a competent discussion of bottling techniques, see Ruff and Becker, 1955.) The process operator is a controller, rather than a producer. With physical effort reduced to a minimum, operators are required to use their conceptual skills in a constant search for signs of departure from desired conditions—detectable through noise, odor, vibration, visible signs, or the kinesthetic senses. Occasionally, process operators also undertake certain manual functions, such as the filling of crowns into the hopper disc shaft or the removal of cullet. Often there are special and complicated procedures related to the starting up and closing down of a shift, and process operators have to be specifically trained in these.

During work, information about the state of the machinery should be passed on by the operators to the service technicians by word of mouth. A work-sampling study showed, however, that most communication that took place in the bottling hall was of an intraracial, rather than interracial, nature, and this was particularly damaging to the accomplishment of repair and maintenance jobs.[9] This is so because operators usually have intimate knowledge of the machinery and their failure to communicate with service technicians about the nature of machine faults is therefore likely to delay repairs particularly when inexperienced service technicians are put on the job.[10] It is a permanent dilemma in

[9] During several weeks of both day and night shifts, we recorded 20,175 work-sampling observations, covering black operators, white foremen, and the condition of machinery. The results are reported in Spandau (1973).

[10] Similar conditions have been reported for Nigeria before independence (see Kilby, 1969).

South African plants that the black machine operator is not trained and authorized to cooperate in the repair of machine breakdowns. The definitions of jobs laid down in Industrial Council agreements frequently curtail, rather than encourage, the use of latent skills. The following quotations may serve as examples:

> "artisan's labourer" means an employee who assists an artisan [service technician] . . . in all his duties . . . and may perform such duties delegated to him by the artisan . . . *provided that they do not involve the independent use of tools.*

> "bottling hall leading hand" means an employee who assists in the supervision of the bottling process . . . and *reports any difficulties to his superior.*

> "filler attendant" means an employee who operates a filler and . . . *stops the machine for any irregularities and reports them to his supervisor* [see Republic of South Africa, 1973—italics mine].

It is clear that such restrictive rules will supress the worker's initiative and consequently prevent him from acquiring the skills necessary for the adjustment and repair of machinery. On the personal level, the lack of communication between whites and blacks has produced a deep gulf between black operators and their white foremen. Most white foremen employed by Company X had paternalistic, domineering, and austere attitudes toward blacks. The relatively low pay and low status of their jobs (relative, that is, to other whites) and the knowledge that they are (technically) replaceable by blacks, attracts only a poor caliber of whites to the job of foremen.[11]

Inadequate black operator performance and poor interracial communication are among the reasons for low plant efficiency.[12] During the weeks of research, the average plant efficiency on the three lines we studied was 71%.[13] This standard of efficiency is well below what can be achieved with modern machinery and well-trained staff. In German bottling plants, average efficiency nowadays is between 90% and 95%.[14]

[11] Subsequent to the fieldwork of this study, the job of foreman was in fact Africanized.

[12] The principal reason for low plant efficiency stems, however, from the small size of the South African market, which made it rational for Company X to produce nine different brands of the product in no fewer than 46 different packs. On a single production line, we noted 16 changes in the size and shape of bottles. Moreover, 81 brand changes were recorded for the three lines observed.

[13] Average efficiency measures the quantity of beer that has been bottled or canned as a percentage of standard output.

[14] Schäuble (1971), Duchek (1971), and Berg (1972) report that efficiencies exceeding 90% are quite common, even for plants that bottle less than 60,000 bottles/hr. It is stressed, however, that these performances require highly trained staff.

One of the main arguments in the hypotheses of this paper relates to the acquisition of industrial skills. We shall now discuss the organization of skill acquisition at Company X.

V.   Skill Acquisition in the Bottling Hall of Company X

Skill acquisition in Company X takes the forms of formal in-plant training, informal on-the-job training, outside training, and learning by doing.

A.   FORMAL IN-PLANT TRAINING

Formal in-plant training is defined as the organized and planned arrangement to assist the trainee in the acquisition of industrial skills. At Company X the training department is responsible for a 2-day induction course, which is given to all black recruits, involving discussions, slide shows, and a factory tour. Technical training, however, is delegated to those departments that actually employ the recruits—because it is maintained that the supervisor of a department is the person most familiar with all technical operations—while the training department serves in an advisory capacity. It is the duty of the department's officers to devise training schemes, prepare and issue instruction manuals, and stimulate the discussion of and the demand for training. The training department, not being functionally responsible for the technical training process itself, becomes active therefore only at the request of line management. (This type of work division between the technical and the training departments is also common in the United States. See National Manpower Council, 1954). The training syllabus·worked out by the training department takes the form of training manuals. These manuals, which are prepared for specific jobs, originate in a three-stage process: (i) the training specialist studies the job and writes a task analysis incorporating photographs of task performance situations; (ii) overall performance objectives for the job are laid down; and (iii) the job is split into "trainable" sections in respect of which performance objectives are defined. In his training, the trainee is familiarized with the method of the experienced worker, whose speed becomes his target time (speed is of particular importance for manual and repetitive jobs). Separate parts of the job are then combined so as to form a complete work cycle. The objective is to train the worker to perform at the speed of an experienced operator. Lessons for specific jobs last 2 or 3 weeks and then end with a formal examination. Blacks who successfully pass the final examination are issued a certificate of competence. At Company X, all successful candidates are guaranteed the job for which they received specific training, and they are given the pay increase associated with the enhanced skill. There is therefore no training risk for trainees, nor is there excess training as far as the company is concerned.

B. INFORMAL ON-THE-JOB TRAINING

The second major means of skill acquisition is informal on-the-job training. This form of training is probably the most prevalent type in South African plants. (On-the-job training is also the prevalent means of imparting skills to blue-collar workers in many Western countries. See National Manpower Council, 1954, p. 208; U.S. Department of Labor, 1964; and Canada, Department of Labour, 1960.) Like (A), informal on-the-job training is usually highly specific and is directed toward immediate production needs. But, in contrast to (A), informal on-the-job training is not organized in any way whatsoever. The training meets spot needs and is applied when new processes are introduced or when a new worker joins a department. The instruction is incidental and frequently consists only of "Watch what I do" and "Now you try." As a rule, informal on-the-job training is not supplemented by class instruction or by lessons from vocational or technical schools. In a thoughtful discussion of the issue, Piore refers to the process as one of "osmosis," "exposure," and "hanging around" (Piore, 1968, p. 437). Learning through informal on-the-job training is a process similar to the passing on of social customs.

C. OUTSIDE TRAINING

Outside Training is obtained by workers who wish to acquire a driver's license. In November 1972, Company X had almost completed the Africanization of the heavy-duty driver's jobs. These men, who handle 18-ton trucks, acquire the necessary license at their own initiative, and they are not reimbursed the cost thereof (about R70 in 1972). Upon employment, drivers are given lessons in documentation, product knowledge, and organization of loading procedures. All in all, the trainees have to learn to distinguish among more than 20 different documents. As senior distribution drivers, they are also trained to handle cash.

D. LEARNING BY DOING

A skill is not innate, it is learned. The learning process may be initiated, either through a teacher–student relationship or through practice 'and experience on the part of the student. When practice and experience are the agents of the learning process, we speak of learning by doing. For this, time is the major explanatory variable. Learning by doing and informal on-the-job training are complementary. When the training process is informal, so that the worker acquires knowledge through trial and error or through occasional direction from his colleagues, the two methods of skill acquisition may become indistinguishable.

VI. The Hypotheses to be Tested

Most hypotheses are related to the issue of industrial training, the pattern of which is, in turn, closely influenced by the presence of a large migratory labor force. Let us look first at the latter phenomenon. (For the life history of a typical South African migrant, see Houghton, 1960.) Black migrants are not allowed to acquire permanent residence for themselves or their families in urban areas, and, in any case, their desire for permanent urban settlement is weakened through strong conservative links with their homelands and through the lack of town planning for blacks in urban areas. Although, of course, there is a wide range of attitudes, most migrants look upon their urban sojourns only as a means of earning the cash income needed to support their families. More often than not, the migrant's presence in town is interrupted at irregular intervals through obligations toward his extended kin (attendance at funerals, visits to the sick) and the need to plant his crop when the spring rains begin. For the employer, the instability of the migratory labor force produces many problems, one of which is that it inhibits the teaching of industrial skills. This becomes an ever more serious issue as the technical sophistication of industrial processes is enhanced. H. R. Burrows rightly observed that "the social disadvantages of sudden disruption have been avoided at the cost of delaying specialization. As a result, there is today no self-supporting peasant economy, nor permanent agricultural labour force, and no stable population [see *Native Laws Commission Report,* p. 23]."

Having noted that industrial training is offered preferably to local residents, rather than to migrants, what are the economic considerations that lie behind the firm's decision to offer training to workers? According to neoclassical theory, (i) each worker will be paid a wage equal to his marginal labor product, and (ii) the wage earned by a worker will be commensurate with what he could earn elsewhere. For various reasons the assumptions and conclusions of neoclassical theory are inapplicable under industrial conditions. A modern firm has to recruit, screen, and train new employees.[15] In other words, the firm incurs costs when attracting job candidates, when assessing their qualifications, and when enhancing their performance levels. These costs must be considered as fixed costs of employment, and in order to gain time for the recoupment of the outlay, the firm will have to devise policy measures likely to cut down on labor turnover. In the present context, fixed employment costs are the central focus and the curtailment of labor turnover is the derivative of it.

The formal implications of the issue under consideration have been examined by Oi (1962) and Becker (1964). Because of the presence of fixed employment costs, the neoclassical postulates regarding equality of wages and marginal labor product are inapplicable. Expenditures incurred on recruitment, screening, and training are nonwage adjustment costs that, over the period of time during which the appointee stays in the employment of the firm, must be recouped by paying the worker less than the value of his marginal labor product. This is so because, for the firm, fixed labor costs spent on a new appointee constitute an investment, the replacement costs of which must be incurred when the worker leaves the firm. The specific problem to be considered is that, in contrast to tangible assets, the worker does not become the property of the firm.

In order to lengthen the period of use to be had from invested money, the firm will work toward encouraging the permanency of employment of the appointee. The difficulty in which the firm finds itself is that it cannot pay the employee the full value of his marginal labor product if it wishes to recoup fixed employment costs. On the other hand, the employee himself, by virtue of fixed employment costs having been invested in him, often possesses bargaining strength (termed "rent") that enables him to ask for and actually obtain a wage even above his immediate marginal labor product—the value of the rent being equal to the value of fixed employment costs, discounted over the difference in time of the expected length of employment were the incumbent to be paid the rent and the length of employment were he not to be paid the rent. Assume, for instance, that if the worker does not receive the rent, he will resign after 2 years of service, whereas, if given the rent, he will stay for 14 years. In this case, the reinvestment of fixed employment costs is being delayed by 12 years if the rent is paid. In equilibrium, the discounted value of these fixed employment costs equals the discounted sum of rent payments.

---

[15] Even in a low-wage country like South Africa, areas of activity where fixed employment costs are negligible are fast disappearing.

For the reasons noted, the neoclassical principle of profit-maximization cannot be applied. According to Becker, provided that firms are compensated through the probability of receiving a marginal product that will exceed the wage rate in later periods, they will be prepared to pay workers more than their marginal labor product in early periods. Neoclassical theory does not, therefore, provide a theory of wages—at best it provides a theory of income (see Doeringer and Piore, 1971, p. 77).

On-the-job training enhances the skill of the worker and, with it, his expected marginal labor product. Whether on-the-job training will also raise the worker's bargaining power vis-à-vis management or whether the enhanced expected marginal labor product can be retained by the employer as a monopsonistic rent, depends on the degree of skill specificity. If the skills acquired by the worker are completely general,[16] they will raise the worker's marginal labor product in all firms employing workers in the kind of job for which he has been trained. Inasmuch as skill interchangeability makes the labor supply curve elastic, a rate for the job for a particular skill will emerge. In a competitive labor market it will then be impossible for the firm to recoup training costs. By contrast, if skill specificity exists,[17] training will not enhance the worker's marginal labor product in competing firms, and the firm will therefore be more likely to recoup training costs.

It is the function of the administrative rules of the internal labor market to shield firms from the competitive elements of external and competitive markets. More precisely, the internal market has to serve as a means of bringing about equality of the discounted values of expected cost and revenue streams over the expected lengths of employment of workers. The main force bringing about equilibrium on the external labor market, that is, labor turnover, has to be delayed. Failing this, no marketable skill investment in workers would ever be financed. It follows that the energy spent by the firm on establishing an internal labor market should be a function of the disadvantage associated with the resignation of particular groups of employees. When the recruitment,

---

[16] Only a few perfectly general skills can be conceived. Basic literacy and the ability to communicate constitute probably the most important general skills.

[17] On-the-job training is itself a condition for the mutation of plant equipment toward specificity. For U.S. plants, Doeringer and Piore (1971, p. 17) report that there is a tendency for line management to modify equipment, even if it is standardized, and thereby to improve overall plant efficiency. Normally no written records are made of these plant mutations; workers and company engineers tend to build up a certain "knowledge monopoly."

screening, and training of a particular type of worker is expensive, and when the skills involved are general, then a strong case will exist to individualize the position of that particular group of workers in the company. This could for instance be done by declaring the positions of high general skills, nonentry jobs. While this would protect job incumbents from external competition, it would also be of benefit to the company, inasmuch as the employee, if he resigned, would have to start in a lower-graded entry job of some competitive industry, rather than being able to move immediately into some sought after high-skill position. For the company, therefore, this strategy will lessen labor turnover, but it will only work if all (or most) labor-competitive firms instituted this system of declaring high-skill positions nonentry jobs.

VII. Evaluation of the Hypotheses

A sample from the company's black personnel files constitutes the empirical data. Of the total of 1070 black workers, a stratified sample size of $N = 291$ was made up as follows:

1. All machine minders of the bottling hall, both trained and untrained
2. All leading hands of the bottling hall
3. All forklift truck and heavy-duty drivers
4. Every third grade-1 worker, but all grade-1 and grade-2 workers who joined the company prior to 1963
5. Every second grade-5 worker
6. All grade-6 workers

The following data were collected: name of employee; code of initial job; code of present job; marital status; number of children; formal education; stamina; year of birth; year of employment with Company X; pay grade; type of training received; history of weekly pay since first employment with Company X; abode of worker.

Evaluation of the hypotheses required the quantitative measurement of factors influencing the pay structure. Multiple regression analysis was chosen to determine whether there are certain characteristics associated with pay and pay increases. Pay increase $(\dot{Y})$ is the compound annual growth rate of basic weekly pay between the year of employment of a worker and November 1972. Pay (Y) is the basic weekly pay in R, November 1972.

The model is specified as follows:

$$\dot{Y} = a_1 + b_{11}X_1 + b_{12}X_2 + b_{13}X_3 + b_{14}X_4$$
$$+ b_{15}X_5 + b_{16}X_6 + b_{17}X_7 + u_1 \quad \text{(1a)}$$
$$Y = a_2 + b_{21}X_1 + b_{22}X_2 + b_{23}X_3 + b_{24}X_4$$
$$+ b_{25}X_5 + b_{26}X_6 + b_{27}X_7 + u_2 \quad \text{(1b)}$$

X_1 = dummy variable for marital status (0 = married, 1 = single).

X_2 = stamina (ranging from 1 to 9. X_2 = 0 was used for seven newly appointed heavy motor vehicle drivers to whom the stamina test had not as yet been administered when the research was undertaken).

X_3 = standard of formal education:
  1 = Lower primary education (Subs A and B, Standards 1 and 2)
  2 = Higher primary education (Standards 3–6)
  3 = Junior secondary education (Forms I–III)
  4 = Senior secondary education (Forms IV and V)
  5 = Bachelors degree.

X_4 = age.

X_5 = length of employment with Company X, in years.

X_6 = training status (1 = informal on-the-job training, 2 = formal on-the-job training, 3 = outside training).

X_7 = Abode of worker (1 = local, 2 = distant, i.e., migrant worker)

The validity of calculated associations depends on whether or not multicollinearity is a serious problem. Two methods were employed to test for multicollinearity. First, a matrix of Pearson correlation coefficients was computed (Table 22.1).

Strong associations ($|r| > \frac{1}{2}$) prevail between age and length of employment (X_4/X_5), age and marital status (X_4/X_1), and length of employment

TABLE 22.1

MATRIX OF PEARSON CORRELATION COEFFICIENTS BETWEEN
INDEPENDENT VARIABLES ($N = 291$)

	X_1	X_2	X_3	X_4	X_5	X_6	X_7
X_1	1,00						
X_2	−0,01	1,00					
X_3	0,17	0,12	1,00				
X_4	−0,55	0,03	−0,38	1,00			
X_5	−0,35	0,12	−0,37	0,64	1,00		
X_6	−0,04	0,18	0,45	−0,07	−0,22	1,00	
X_7	0,25	−0,08	0,19	−0,44	−0,54	−0,10	1,00

and abode of worker (X_5/X_7). Significant correlations $(|r| \sim 0,45)$ are also found for the relation between training status and standard of formal education (X_6/X_3), and age and abode (X_7/X_4). For the rest, the correlation coefficients between independent variables are trivial.

The second method of testing for multicollinearity was that of successive veriable deletion. This test compares the full multiple regression equation which enters all independent variables in the equation with regression equations which omit one independent variable at a time from the number of variables being tested. To quote Melichar: "By observing the amount and direction of change in the coefficients obtained for a given factor as other factors are in turn added to or deleted from the regression equation, one can ascertain which intercorrelations masked the underlying relationship between the dependent variable and the factor being studied [Melichar, 1965, p. 382]."

Table 22.2 shows that training, formal education, stamina, and abode are the factors responsible for explaining the variation observed among different rates of income growth. By contrast, marital status, age, and length of employment turned out to be poor predictors. As successive variable deletions were made, there occurred some changes in parameter values but none of a size to cause concern.[18]

In order to determine the order of significance of independent variables, stepwise multiple regression was applied. This method provides the best possible prediction with the fewest number of independent variables. The first step is to choose the single variable which is the best predictor. Independent variables to be added to the regression equation in successive steps are those that give the best predictions in conjunction with the previous ones. At each step, only one new optimal variable is added, given the other variables already in the equation. According to this method, the statistical summary of the prediction of income growth $(\dot{Y})$ is:

$$\dot{Y} = -9,5685 + 7,1678X_6^{**} + 1,5954X_2^{**} + 4,3861X_7^{**}$$
$$\phantom{\dot{Y} = -9,5685 +} (1,4197) \quad\quad (0,3042) \quad\quad (2,0310)$$

$$+ 0,5342X_3^* - 0,5028X_1 - 0,0290X_5 \quad (2a)$$
$$(0,3288) \quad\quad (1,7457) \quad\quad (0,1620)$$

$R^2 = 0,2587$
F-ratio $= 16,5151$
*   significant at the 5% level
** significant at the 1% level

---

[18] The data were adjusted to the SPSS system: Nie, Bent, and Hull (1970). The writer is grateful to Mrs. C. Skjolde for the organization and coding of data for input into the SPSS system.

TABLE 22.2

TESTING FOR MULTICOLLINEARITY THROUGH SUCCESSIVE VARIABLE DELETION

Dependent variable	Intercept	b_{11}	b_{12}	b_{13}	b_{14}	b_{15}	b_{16}	b_{17}	F-ratio	R^2
$\dot{Y}$	-8,9539	-0,5695 (1,9395)	1,5946** (0,3049)	0,5283* (0,3378)	-0,0097 (0,1224)	-0,0228 (0,1802)	7,1802** (1,4308)	4,3713** (2,0431)	14,1072	0,2587
$\dot{Y}$	-12,0219	—	1,5918** (0,3043)	0,5292* (0,3372)	0,0058 (0,1102)	-0,0213 (0,1798)	7,2172** (1,4229)	4,3758** (2,0398)	16,4970	0,2585
$\dot{Y}$	-6,5240	-0,2577 (2,0265)	—	0,6792** (0,3518)	-0,0302 (0,1279)	0,1407 (0,1855)	8,3899** (1,4760)	4,5675** (2,1354)	10,8900	0,1870
$\dot{Y}$	-7,2625	-0,5953 (1,9444)	1,6353 (0,3046)	—	-0,0520 (0,1196)	-0,0397 (0,1803)	8,1038** (1,3066)	4,6319** (2,0415)	15,9692	0,2523
$\dot{Y}$	-9,5685	-0,5028 (1,7457)	1,5954** (0,3042)	0,5342** (0,3288)	—	-0,0290 (0,1620)	7,1678** (1,4197)	4,3861** (2,0310)	16,5151	0,2587
$\dot{Y}$	-9,0833	-0,5628 (1,9354)	1,5879** (0,2998)	0,5309* (0,3366)	-0,0164 (0,1101)	—	7,2311** (1,3706)	4,4787** (1,8545)	16,5129	0,2586
$\dot{Y}$	-4,0169	-1,4268 (2,0126)	1,8420** (0,3135)	1,2278** (0,3205)	0,0574 (0,1267)	-0,2773* (0,1801)	—	1,6323 (2,0510)	11,2989	0,1927
$\dot{Y}$	-0,0593	-0,6008 (1,9516)	1,6066 (0,3068)	0,5872 (0,3387)	-0,0337 (0,1226)	-0,1832 (0,1649)	6,3624 (1,3874)	—	15,5002	0,2467

* significant at the 5% level
** significant at the 1% level
$\dot{Y}$ compound rate of annual income growth
X_1 marital status
X_2 stamina
X_3 standard of formal education
X_4 age
X_5 length of employment
X_6 training status
X_7 abode

With an F-ratio of only 0.006, age is below the tolerance level and has therefore not been included as an independent variable.

Results pertaining to income in November 1972, expressed in terms of basic pay in R per week, are given by

$$Y = 6,9384 + 7,0756X_6^{**} - 2,5314X_7^{**} + 0,5587X_3^{**}$$
$$ (0,3607) \quad\quad (0,5171) \quad\quad (0,0855)$$

$$+ 0,1579X_5 + 0,0693X_4 - 0,0256X_2 \quad (2b)$$
$$(0,0456) \quad\quad (0,0279) \quad\quad (0,0771)$$

$R^2 = 0,7441$
F-ratio = 137,62

In equations (2a) and (2b), training status is the most important predictor of pay and pay growth (see parameters b_{16} and b_{26}). For the worker who successfully passes a formal on-the-job training course, the compound annual expected growth rate of income increases by 7.2%, compared with the worker who has received no formal training (equation 2a). (The parameter b_{16} should not be applied for the prediction of the income growth of heavy-duty drivers who received outside training. This is so because prior to 1972, this sought-after job was allocated through the internal labor market; it became an entry job only when, in 1972, the Africanization of this job neared completion.)

Training was also the most significant determinant of income in November 1972. Outside training raised the expected weekly pay by R7.08 over formal on-the-job training, which in turn yielded an identical expected premium over informal on-the-job training (equation 2b).

As with training, the standard of formal education is positively and significantly related to both income and income growth (parameters b_{13} and b_{23} refer). Advances in education from the lower primary to the higher primary standard, and from there to the junior secondary, senior secondary, and bachelors degree standards, are each associated with an annual expected increase in income growth of 0.5%. Looking at the effect of education on income from a static point of view (November 1972), the various steps of educational advance were valued at R0.56 per week.

While the influence of stamina on equations (2a) and (2b) is inconclusive, it emerges with clarity that age (X_4), length of employment (X_5), and marital status (X_1) are insignificant predictors of the income receipt structures.

It is of interest to note that the variable abode (X_7) is associated with a positive constant in equation (2a) but with a negative one in equation (2b). The explanation for this is that with the reduction of the black labor force which was gradually enforced during the years 1968 to 1972 under the Physical Planning and Utilization of Resources Act, the relative market power of local and migrant labor changed appreciably in favor of the former. Previously, the migrant worker had been the preferred employee because of his greater docility and because he could be "more easily handled." This argument became redundant, however, when, after the tightening of the labor market between 1968 and 1972, all efforts had to be directed toward keeping highly trained black staff. With the promulgations under the Physical Planning Act becoming progressively tighter, the risk of putting migrant workers into high-paid positions became too large; as a result, the migrants' position had considerably deteriorated by November 1972.

It also appears from the regression equations that for black employees, the income receipt and income growth structures are skill- rather than seniority-related.

Recall that the average standard of formal school education of the black work force is low. It is also known that Company X faces a situation of elastic *unskilled* black migrant labor supply at prevailing offer wages.[19] Moreover, the company cannot on the external labor market recruit workers with such specific skills, as those necessary to operate the filling, washing, or labeling machines (only heavy-duty truck drivers and, occasionally, forklift truck drivers, are hired on the external labor market). Because of the skill specificity of many jobs, therefore, training programs have to be undertaken on the internal labor market. But while we observed that formal in-plant training is generally outside the reach of criticism of the white lower line management or the white workers, cooperation is not forthcoming in respect of the informal on-the-job training needed after formal training has been finalized. For these reasons, the demand for and supply of skilled black workers must be considered as inelastic, at least in the short run. This leads to the following evaluation of the hypotheses:

1.In order to curtail labor turnover of black key operators, the company is prepared to pay trained operators a very significant relative wage premium, and this is found to be considerably cheaper than the opportunity cost of hiring and training whites for these positions. From the viewpoint of the worker, the disadvantage associated with a resignation is significant, as his skill-specific position would not constitute a means of entry into other companies.

---

[19] This statement is valid although the absolute maximum number of black employees is pegged in terms of the Physical Planning Act.

2. The correlation between training, education, and pay suggests that the company's relative wage structure is linked to marginal labor products, rather than to length of job tenure or seniority.

3. Within the pay structure of key operating jobs, there is no detectable differentiation according to whether skills are specific or general. The relative pay gradation of key jobs at Company X is done according to technical engineering evaluations, rather than according to the objective of minimizing labor turnover.

4. The congruence of the relative wage structure and the length of education and training suggests that the objective of allocative efficiency is observed. In racially homogeneous societies, there is usually a strong tendency to modify allocative optima so as to accommodate employee interest. Often this is done through restrictions imposed on entry into high-skill jobs or reliance on such criteria as seniority, length of service, and internal allocation of jobs (see Silznick and Vollmer, 1962). At Company X, black employee interests are accommodated only to a small extent. This is clearly shown in the regression equations, where neigher age nor length of service are significant predictors of the black income structure. The reason for this is that black workers are not effectively unionized and that the existing works committee does not have a notable impact on relative wage settings.

In order to quantify the hypothesis, 38 different jobs pertaining to the operations of the bottling hall were defined. Each of these jobs was given a job score based on object variety, motor variety, autonomy, required interaction, learning time, and responsibility. The job score measurement scale assigned task attribute scores of between 1 and 5 to each job.

With the cooperation of a large brewery and a technical university, both in West Germany, which provided information on skill classification and the hourly pay of different jobs, a comparison of the multiracial South African wage structure with its German counterpart became possible. Evaluation of the data showed that for the South African black who would advance from, say, a job score of 1.5 to a job score of 4.5, the predicted weekly wage would rise from R11.61 to R24.06, which is an increase of over 100%. This pay increase would allow the worker to advance from proletarian to middle-class status. In Germany, however, a similar skill advance would lead to a predicted wage increase of only about 15%, with relatively little bearing on the worker's standard of living.

5. Consider the parameter values b_{15} and b_{25} (length of employment with Company X, in years), and b_{16} and b_{26} (training status). The

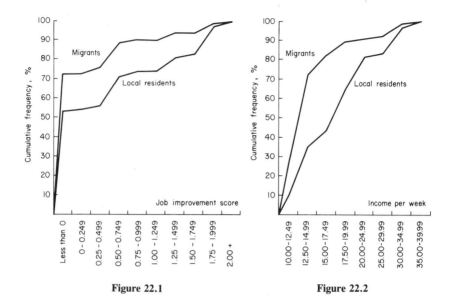

Figure 22.1   Figure 22.2

outcome of the regression model is that both formal on-the-job training and outside training yielded high rents for the workers who underwent vocational education. Moreover, informal on-the-job training and learning by doing (the length of which is given through the period of employment with Company X) have little predictive value for the structure of income and income growth. This underlines the thesis that white foremen and white rank-and-file hourly employees can do little to block formal training procedures for black employees, whereas they are able to withhold the assistance and encouragement needed to make informal on-the-job training and unorganized learning by doing a successful exercise.

Under South African conditions, the economic position of the untrained black worker is largely synonymous with that of the migrant. This is so because it does not pay the employer to invest in training unless he believes that the employee seeks permanent employment with him. Nor does the migrant see an inducement to excel because he knows that he is unlikely to be rewarded for it. The logic for these conclusions is substantiated by Figures 22.1 and 22.2, which give cumulative frequency curves for job improvement scores and weekly income, both for local residents and for migrants.

Figure 22.1 illustrates the magnitude of the migrant's retarded occupational advance. Of the sampled migrants, almost three-quarters have never experienced any occupational advance at all, while the same static employment position is observed for only one in every two of the local residents. On the upper end of the scale, we find that the job improvement score is in excess of one measurement unit for 26% of the local residents, but only for 10% of the migrants.

The migrant's retarded occupational advance is of course reflected in his low income. Thus in Figure 22.2 we find that the migrant is heavily represented in the low-income group of R12.50 to R14.99, whereas the income receipts of local residents are more regularly distributed between both low and high income ranges. At the upper end of the scale we find that approximately 20% of the local residents earn wages in excess of R20, while only 10% of the migrants achieve this income standard.

VIII. Conclusion

The one fact that emerges with clarity from the foregoing analysis is the lack of equilibrium in the South African labor market. Define a microeconomic equilibrium (or Pareto-optimum) as a situation where no person's welfare can be improved unless the welfare of some other person is diminished. Alternatively, if compensation payments are allowed, it is a situation where the "potential losers could not profitably bribe the potential gainers to oppose the change [see Little, 1963, pp. 98–105]." The compensation principle could profitably be applied to remove part of the imbalance of South Africa's labor market. This is so because there exists unused skill potential of black operators. If allowed vertical mobility, properly selected and trained blacks would aspire to more demanding positions. Blacks would then receive pay increases, and the productivity gain could be shared between the employers and the white employees.[20]

In spite of the all-around advantages of industrial training, the actual training achievement lagged behind what was considered optimal in the minds of the managers of Company X. Thus, it was one of the objectives of the personnel department of the company to give formal in-plant training to all black workers holding positions in grades 4, 5, and 6. Yet at the time when this study was carried out, only 28 of 319 workers employed in these grades had been trained. Although the monetary gains from black skill advancement and from Africanization are remarkeably high, there is a considerable underinvestment in formal in-plant training.

---

[20] Compensation payments to white employees were part of the 1973 wage agreement between the Chamber of Mines and the Mine Workers Union (Spandau, 1974).

Most South African blacks continue to live on bare subsistence wages. Their enforced abstention from consumption contributes to an immense waste of human potential. The tragedy is that South Africa possesses the physical wealth to produce a high income for all races. But the "schisms [of] a century-old ambivalence of ideas," as Professor S. Herbert Frankel has called it, is still with the country. It is the simultaneous fear of and dependence on the black man, the simultaneous desire for the "benefits . . . of drawing men together, [and] the fear that all will be lost if they are not kept apart (Frankel, 1960, p. 47]." South Africa continues to delay social decisions. Legislative and executive paternalism allocates the black man a permanent proletarian status, while economic forces have long since begun to work toward his social integration.

References

Becker, G. S. *Human capital: A theoretical and empirical analysis*. New York: Columbia University Press, 1964.

Berg, F. Wirkungsgrad und Ausnutzungsgrad von Flaschenkolonnen und ihre Auswirkung auf die Abfüllkosten. *Brauwelt, 1972, 112*(41A).

Bureau of Market Research, University of South Africa. Income and expenditure patterns of non-white urban households. *Tembisa Survey*. Report No. 27–13, 1972.

Canada, Department of Labour. Acquisition of skills. In *Research programme on the training of skilled manpower*. Report 4, Queen's Printer and Controller of Stationery, Ottawa, 1960.

Doeringer, P. B., and M. J. Piore. *Internal labor markets and manpower analysis*. Lexington, Mass.: Heath, 1971.

Duchek, P. Anlage bei der Lindener Gilde-Bräu, Hannover. *Brauwelt, 1971, 111*(65A).

Dunlop, J. T. Job vacancy measures and economic analysis. In *The measurement and interpretation of job vacancies: A conference report*. National Bureau of Economic Research, New York: Columbia University Press, 1966.

Frankel, S. H. The tyranny of economic paternalism in Africa: A study of frontier metality, 1860–1960. *Supplement to Optima*, Johannesburg, December 1960.

Houghton, D. H. Men of two worlds: Some aspects of migratory Labour in South Africa. *South African Journal of Economics, 1960, 28*, 177–190.

Kerr, C. The balkanization of labor markets. In E. W. Bakke et al., *Labor mobility and economic opportunity*. Cambridge, Mass.: MIT Press, 1954, pp. 92–110.

Kilby, P. *Industrialization in an open economy: Nigeria, 1945–66*. Cambridge: The University Press, 1969.

Little, F. M. D. *A critique of welfare economics* (2nd ed.). London: Oxford University Press, 1963.

Melichar, E. Least-squares analysis of economic surveys data. *Proceedings of the Annual Meeting of the American Statistical Association*, Business and Economic Statistics Section, 1965.

National Manpower Council. *A policy for skilled manpower*. New York: Columbia University Press, 1954.

Nie, N., D. H. Bent, and H. H. Hull, *Statistical package for the social sciences*. New York: McGraw-Hill, 1970.

Oi, W. Labor as a quasi-fixed factor. *Journal of Political Economy*, December 1962.

Piore, M. J. On-the-job training and adjustment to technological change. *Journal of Human Resources*, 1968, *3*(4), 435–449. (a)

Piore, M. J. Public and private responsibilities in on-the-job training of disadvantaged workers. Working Paper No. 23, Massachusetts Institute of Technology, 1968. (b)

Potgieter, F. J. The poverty datum line in the major urban centres in the Republic. Institute for Planning Research, University of Port Elizabeth, 1973.

Republic of South Africa. *Government gazette*, 1973, *101* (4093).

Ross, A. M. Do we have a new industrial feudalism? *American Economic Review*, 1958, *48*, 903–1920.

Ruff, D. G., and K. Becker. *Bottling and canning of beer*. Siebel Institute of Technology, Chicago, 1955.

Schäuble, R. Rationeller Flaschenkellerbetrieb. *Brauwelt*, 1971, *111* (65A).

Silznick, P., and H. Vollmer. The rule of law in industry: Seniority rights. *Industrial Relations*, 1962, *1*(3).

Spandau, A. The economics of Bantu operator training in a South African beer bottling hall. Johannesburg, 1973. (Mimeograph)

Spandau, A. Income policy and distributive justice. *Inaugural Address*, University of the Witwatersrand, Johannesburg, 1974.

Union of South Africa, Native Laws Commission, Report U. G. 28-1948, p. 23.

U.S. Department of Labor. Formal occupational training of adult workers. Manpower/Automation Research Monograph No. 2, December 1964.

Wilson, F. *Migrant labour. The South African Council of Churches, Johannesburg, 1972.*

PART V

Migration:
Disciplinary and Systemic
Comparisons

CHAPTER 23

Internal Migration:
A Comparative Disciplinary View

Joseph S. Berliner

Most people who write about migration are not interested in migration at all. They are interested in its consequences. Economists study migration because they are interested in income and employment, and migration of labor influences the spatial distribution of income and employment. Social psychologists study migration because they are interested in mental health, and migration appears to affect mental health. Anthropologists study migration because they are interested in culture, and migrants act as "culture brokers" in the process of culture diffusion. Sociologists study migration because they are interested in all aspects of social relations, and migration affects virtually all aspects— from stratification and mobility patterns to the stability of such basic social institutions as the family. I am not aware of research by political scientists on migration, but if it were done its aim would be to investigate such findings as that of the sociologist F. Musgrove—that migrants are overrepresented in the leadership of public organizations (see Musgrove, 1963, p. 12).

The only discipline in which migration is studied for the pure love of it is demography, the focus of which is the numbers of people of different kinds and their distribution in time and space. Since migration consists of a change in the spatial location of people, the subject is of primary interest. Somewhere between demography and the others lie the two disciplines for which space and time are the primary dimensions—

443

geography and history. Geographers are concerned with the principles that govern the spatial distribution of a wide range of things, from fauna and flora to factories and phonemes, and including people. Hence, like demographers, changes in the spatial location of people are of primary interest. Historians are concerned with the temporal sequence of events, and since people change their locations in time, along with their governments and their customs, migrations are a proper subject for historical study. To be scrupulously fair to the latter two disciplines, however, their interest is not confined to the explanation of events that occur in time or space, but extends to their consequences for the physical or social world as well.

In all the disciplines that deal with migration, the analysis of its causes is sharply distinguished from the analysis of its consequences. In the analysis of causes, it should occasion no surprise that the approaches of the several disciplines are very similar. Whatever the consequences one wishes eventually to investigate, one needs to know the answers to such questions as whether the phenomenon is of large or small scale and whether or not the rate has been changing, how many and what kinds of people tend to migrate and why, and what are the characteristics of the communities of origin and destination. One model, moreover, predominates in the effort to organize and explain the data—the "push–pull" model. It is a common-sense model that occurs naturally to intuitive and nonquantitative observers: "The centrifugal impulse doesn't have to be strong to take effect," writes the British autobiographer, Martin Green, "if the centripetal impulse is weak (see Musgrove, 1963, p. 8)." In the quantitative studies a number of variants have been developed: push models that attribute the forces to the negative characteristics of the communities of origin; pull models that identify the forces in the positive characteristics of the communities of destination; cost–benefit models that incorporate both pushes and pulls; and gravity models that postulate the forces to depend directly on the properties of both communities and inversely on the distance between them (see Alonso, this volume, Chapter 5; Bogue, this volume, Chapter 11; and Greenwood, 1975, p. 398). In seeking to discover who migrates, all investigate the same basic personal demographic characteristics of migrants: age, sex, race, and so forth. In asking why people migrate, all distinguish in some way "economic" from "noneconomic" reasons; the main finding seems to be that economic reasons—particularly employment opportunities at communities of destination—explain a large proportion but not all of the data (see Crowley, this volume, Chapter 15; Hall and Licari, this volume, Chapter 6, and Greenwood, 1975, pp. 410–412).

Within this broad picture of common features, there do occur some noteworthy differences among the disciplines in the analysis of causes. Most of them derive from the differences in the consequences of migration that the several disciplines conventionally focus on. Thus, in addition to the basic demographic variables that all investigate, social psychology is concerned with the various mental states of migrants relative to nonmigrants, economists pursue variables like occupation and income in rather great detail, anthropologists have a special interest in kinship structure and other cultural patterns of migrants and of their communities of origin and destination, and sociologists are concerned with social class background, social mobility of migrants' parents, and so forth. The common set of demographic characteristics also has a different significance in the models as they are employed in the various disciplines. Educational level serves, in economic models, as a basis for estimating the value of human capital, whereas in sociological investigations it serves as an indicator of social class and mobility.

When one turns from causes to consequences, the differences among the disciplines are clear and striking. Indeed, whatever the declared "scope and methods" of the disciplines as perceived by their practitioners, when one looks at the kinds of research actually done, it is the differences in the outcomes, or consequences, of social processes that distinguish the social disciplines from one another. A celebrated essay of Lord Robbins, for example, taught economists to think about their subject matter not as a subset of social activities dealing with the production and distribution of goods and services, but as the study of any social arrangements in which scarce resources are allocated among competing uses (see Robbins, 1952). In practical work like the study of migration, however, it is still the effect of migration on incomes, employment, and economic efficiency that is the basic subject of inquiry. For the social psychologist, if the subject of migration and its causes is interesting at all, it is because it has certain effects on mental health, attitudes, and other psychological states. Similarly for the anthropologist it is such consequences as the stability of the kinship structure that require investigation, and for sociologists it is social mobility and deviance. Thus if one examined a sample of scientific papers on migration and studied only their treatment of the causes, one might have difficulty detecting the disciplinary origin of each one. But if one studied the consequences with which they deal, their disciplinary origin would be unmistakably clear.

Since most of the social disciplines are interested in migration because of its consequences, one would expect that most of the research would be devoted to the analysis of those consequences. Yet it turns out that the opposite is true: research work has concentrated overwhelmingly on its causes.[1] The reason may be found, perhaps, in the great variety and complexity of the consequences. Techniques like regression are available, for example, to investigate a single outcome like the incomes of migrants. But to investigate several outcomes, general equilibrium techniques must be employed, like those developed by Hall and Licari in this volume. The state of the art and the data requirements are such that empirical investigations of that kind are not likely to be abundant. Moreover, migration rarely occurs in a pure form in nature but always in connection with other social processes, which complicates the analysis of its consequences. Until recently, for example, the predominant form of migration has been rural–urban (see Little and Leven, this volume, Chapter 13). The rural–urban migrant undergoes two social experiences simultaneously: he removes himself from one social system and enters another—this may be called the social effect; and he moves from a rural culture to an urban one—call this the cultural effect. Now, virtually all the studies that deal with the consequences of migration concentrate on the cultural effect. In fact the term "migration" is often treated as if it were synonymous with "urbanization," and studies of urbanization are often classified as studies of migration. This is particularly true of economists, as in Gur Ofer's intriguing analysis of the urbanization policies of socialist countries (this volume, Chapter 16). But it is also true of anthropological studies like that of E. A. Hammel, whose migrants moved from Serbian villages to urban Belgrade (this volume, Chapter 21). And in studies of the effect of migration on mental health, the problem is often the psychic consequences of moving from an ascriptive–particularistic rural society to an achievement–universalistic urban one. Thus most of the research on the consequences of migration tells us something about what happens to people and communities when they change from rural to urban. But it tells us very little about the effect of migration as a purely social experience.

Yet of all the consequences of migration, the social effect may be the most significant for human welfare. By the social effect, I mean the effect of a change in residence from one community to another, regardless of the specific characteristics of the migrants or of the communities. I shall develop the point first in broad intuitive terms, and then in terms of some fragments of social theory.

---

[1] Greenwood's survey emphasized the contributions of economists (Greenwood, 1975, p. 397), but the generalization may well apply to other disciplines, particularly in respect to quantitative studies.

The literature on migration abounds in mechanical metaphors—centrifugal and centripetal forces, and gravity and entropy models. Underlying these flights of fancy is a sense that the social world, like the physical, depends on certain constants, the stability of which makes that world orderly and predictable. The child discovers and internalizes the principle of inertia as he learns to walk, to throw a ball, and to place his shoes on the floor in the firm expectation that they will not float away. The eeriness of space travel as portrayed on TV reflects the disorientation in our perceptual world when the things we profoundly expect to stay in the same place fail to do so. The remarkable thing is that men can learn to live under these conditions. But it is a very different way of living.

The social world, like the physical, is characterized by something like the property of inertia, to which all our social interactions are attuned (see Lee, 1969, p. 291). When a person chooses an occupation, or a marriage partner, or a place of residence, he expects that choice to endure for some period of time. We have learned that it takes a force, of some magnitude we roughly understand, to induce a change. Suppose, then, that a cosmic change occurred in the size of the forces that have conventionally been required to change the location of people in space. A very small alteration in the balance of advantages of two jobs would induce a person to change from one to the other. If either of two marriage partners came upon another person with a slightly superior combination of characteristics than the present spouse, he or she would easily dissolve the old marriage and enter into a new one. On a particularly cold winter's day in northern Minnesota half the population may decide that they have had it and migrate to Florida. Like life in a space capsule, the population would be in constant physical and social motion. Possibly we could learn to adjust to these new properties of social existence. But it would be a very different kind of social life from that with which we have been familiar. It is impossible to predict what kind of new social arrangements might evolve under those conditions; we would have to rely on the imagination of the writer of social science fiction to describe it. Most people would expect it to be a rather awful society, though some exceedingly broadminded types may think it would be interesting.

The consequences of a high rate of migration, then, appear to have the potential for unhinging a society from its most fundamental constants. It is not too much to hope that the social sciences can provide some systematic understanding of the consequences of such massive phenomena and thus help to control our destiny. It is useful to distinguish those disciplines like economics and social psychology that deal with parts of the social process from those like sociology and anthropology that attempt to encompass a "holistic" view of society. The psychological literature concentrates not on social relationships directly but on the effect of social processes on individual psychological states. The research results appear to indicate that migrants contribute more than their share to mental illness—as measured, for example, by first admissions to mental institutions. There is also some evidence, however, that people with incipient or active mental disorders are overrepresented in the group that decides to migrate. It is not clear therefore whether an increase in mental illness can be counted among the consequences of migration as such. The present mood seems to be that while some part of the higher incidence of mental illness among migrants relative to nonmigrants must be attributed to selectivity at the point of origin, migration does contribute in some measure to mental illness. (see Malzberg and Lee, 1956, pp. 123–24). The absolute numbers are fairly small, however. The age-standardized rate of first admissions to New York State mental hospitals in 1939–1941 was 137 per 100,000 for native white males born in New York State, and 216 for native white males born in other states (see Malzberg and Lee, 1956, p. 84). The results suggest that the vast majority of migrants come through the experience with no significant negative effects, and many surely gain a great deal psychologically. For some persons migration may serve to remove them from social situations that entail large psychic strains, and it leaves them better off after the move. Migration thus serves as a safety valve, for the individual and perhaps for society as well. From the point of view of social policy, it suggests that facilities should be available for psychological assistance in communities experiencing immigration because immigrants are likely to require such services more than the nonmigrant population. But the psychological literature does not point to any major negative consequences of migration.

For practitioners of the dismal science, economists tend to be rather cheerful about migration. Migration was a vital facilitating factor in the large increase in per capita income and output of the last half century. Migrants enjoy higher incomes and a more satisfactory employment experience than those who remained in the community of origin, although by no means all of the increase can be attributed to the act of migration alone. The traditional view was that labor mobility contributes significantly to the efficiency of resource allocation. By migrating from regions of low marginal productivity and low wages to regions with higher marginal productivity and wages, mobile labor increases the total output of the society. Of two societies alike in all other respects, the one with the higher degree of mobility would enjoy the higher income. This traditional view of the consequence of mobility is now in dispute. If labor is regarded not as a homogeneous factor but as consisting of a variety of grades, and if it is the high-grade labor that emigrates, then productivity and wages in the community of origin will decline, rather than rise, following emigration. Migration in this latter case is no longer a Pareto-optimal redistribution, for some people are worse off as a result of the process.

It is perhaps because of the current uncertainty about the size and distribution of the economic consequences of migration that economists, who are not often shy about giving advice on public policy, are somewhat reticent in this case. But apart from that uncertainty, there is another reason why the normally powerful tools of economic analysis are somewhat fragile when applied to a social process like migration. The point is touched on in Ronald Crowley's allusion to the difficulty of establishing the nature of the social "wellbeing function"—or the social welfare function as it is often called (see Crowley, this volume, Chapter 15). The processes with which economists normally deal are such that it is often possible and reasonable to assert that those things which individuals regard as best for themselves are also best for the society. The burden of proving that in some cases this may not be so is implicitly held to rest with those who propose to interfere with individual choice. Hence if utility-maximizing individuals decide to migrate, that migration should be thought to increase the social welfare unless the contrary can be shown.

The literature on welfare economics, however, has now generated a long list of conditions that must be satisfied in a social system in order that individual choice can be shown to be consistent with the social welfare. Unhappily, a great many of them are violated in the case of decisions involving migration. Many of these conditions sail under the name of externalities, or conditions that create a divergence between private and social costs and benefits. The overriding form of externality in the case of migration may be shown by recourse to Abram Bergson's formulation of the nature of the Welfare Function (see Bergson, 1966, pp. 4–6). Economic Welfare is defined as a function of such variables as the amounts of each commodity consumed by each person, the quantities of each kind of labor employed in the production of each kind of good, and so forth. Social Welfare is also a function of these "economic" variables, but in addition it depends on certain "other" elements that affect the welfare of the society. An increase in Economic Welfare corresponds to an increase in Social Welfare only if it is not accompanied by a negatively-valued change in the "other" variables.

Now, the social processes with which economists normally deal involve "relatively small changes" in the economic variables, so that one may reasonably assume that the "other elements in welfare . . . will not be significantly affected." If many people change their fashion from worsted suits to double-knits, for example, that may be regarded as a relatively small change that is unlikely to affect the noneconomic elements of welfare. But if many people increase their incomes by changing the communities in which they live, it is not unreasonable to expect that there may be significant effects on the "other elements in welfare."

It is those other elements in welfare that Alfred Marshall had in mind when he proposed that economists restrict their investigations to the study of "mankind in the ordinary business of life (see Marshall, 1948, p. 1)." By ordinary business he intended the goods and services of normal commerce: shoes and coal and double-knit suits. But social activities that spill over significantly into religion or love or the stability of kinship and political systems are fragile materials for the tools of economic analysis. The profession learned later to think of its discipline as defined by its method rather than by its subject matter. Economics is the study of the allocation of scarce resources among competing ends, or even more generally, as the "logic of choice." In the latter formulation it would seem that in all social activity in which people make choices, or can be regarded as making choices, the methods of economic analysis should be able to shed some light on decisions made. Viewed in such broad terms, there is scarcely a department of social life in which choices are not made; we choose the church to which we belong and the faith to which we adhere, we choose to vote for one candidate rather than another, we choose to earn a living by being a dishwasher or a mugger, we choose our husbands and wives, our friends, and the community in which we decide to live.

It is always possible, of course, to regard the decision to migrate as a "choice" and thereby tailor it down to a dimension that makes it possible to wheel in the fine machinery of microeconomics. To the extent that it does indeed involve what we commonly think of as a choice, that method is productive of useful insights, and in the analysis of the causes of migration it has proven to be of significant explanatory power. Residuals that are left unexplained by the normal processes of reckoning of a utility maximizer have to be packaged under such rubrics as "psychic costs," for which magnitudes like distance or transportation costs then serve as proxies (see Greenwood, 1975, pp. 404–405). Here, incidentally, is the classic kind of analytic bind in which interdisciplinary research may be expected to make a contribution; social psychology does possess methods for measuring attitudes and anticipations, which might be turned to the development of more direct measures of psychic costs. In any case, the evidence is compelling that economic considerations like employment opportunities are dominant in the decision to migrate, and the tools that deal with the ordinary business of life have proven their power. The problem is not with the analysis of causes, however, but with consequences. All persons may well make choices on a personal calculus of utility, but the social consequences may be vastly different from what any of them intended. The least of the difficulty is the composition problem; that a decision which would maximize the utility of one person if he were the only one to make it would not maximize the utility of the group if all decided to make the same decision. That is a problem with which economists have learned to deal. The more general problem is that individual decisions made in the nonordinary business of life, even if based originally on economic motives, may have unintended consequences in such other parts of the society as the family or the political system, or in such social processes as socialization and class stratification,[2] and in such Durkheimian social facts as the crime rate, the rate of mental illness, or the rate of suicide.[3]

The power of the tools of economic analysis is due to the success with which the discipline has abstracted one subset of social relationships out of the total social matrix. The science of the economic subsystem is undoubtedly more highly developed than that of other subsystems like the family, the political institutions, or the arts. But the price economics has to pay for its success is a certain modesty in dealing with social processes the consequences of which transcend the limits of Bergsonian Economic Welfare. It is to the disciplines that seek a "holistic" view of society, like sociology and anthropology, that one must turn for an investigation of the broad consequences of migration.

Role theory provides a convenient language for examining the impact on a social system of a process like migration. Every society must provide for the carrying out of a set of basic functions like producing goods and services, socializing children, resolving disputes, and maintaining civil peace.[4] The functions are performed by persons holding various roles in social institutions. The society consists of persons, but

---

[2] Migration contributes to social mobility, but "internal migration in contemporary Britain is a process whereby the population is re-sorted into socially homogeneous groups; its results are socially divisive rather than cohesive (Musgrove, 1963, p. 105)." See also Little and Leven, this volume, Chapter 13.

[3] See Musgrove (1963, pp. 122–126 and Chapter 7—which reviews the literature on the social and psychological consequences of migration).

[4] These illustrations follow Talcott Parson's classification of the functional imperatives of a social system (see Parsons and Smelser, 1956, pp. 17–20).

the social *system* consists of the roles and the institutions. In a stable social system the persons who carry out the role functions may change, but the system does not. Now if there is a low rate of turnover in the personal incumbents of the roles, one can easily imagine that the system may not change; the king is dead but the new king reigns. But with a rising rate of turnover of the role incumbents, one can be less certain that the system itself will not change. That is why corporations do not permit all their executives to fly on the same aircraft. A neighborhood or a community can be expected to absorb a certain rate of turnover of its members without great change in the social system. But one can imagine a rate of turnover so rapid that the system will be unable to continue performing the social functions.

Even in the absence of migration the incumbents of social roles change over time. Over the time span of several generations, indeed, there is a total turnover of incumbencies. The original population of the society is totally replaced by a new one, but in a society exposed to few foreign contacts and little technological change the social system remains virtually the same. Even in the face of foreign influence and technological change, the fundamental social and cultural properties of the society, like kinship structure and language, persist with remarkable stability. How this occurs is, of course, one of the fundamental questions of anthropology and sociology.

The key processes are those of socialization and social control, by means of which new entrants into the society are taught to internalize cultural values and role expectations. Immigrants are thus formally similar to young children.[5] It does not follow, however, that a society whose techniques of socialization and social control are entirely successful with children will be equally successful with immigrants. One obvious reason is that immigrants have often already been socialized in a different culture. Less obvious, perhaps, is that the time-rate of admission of new children into the society is subject to biological and perhaps social limits, whereas there is no limit on the rate of immigration (or emigration) unless it is imposed externally. Among the general sources of instability in social systems are situations in which the frequency of a disturbance exceeds the speed of the system's response. There may well be a critical rate of migration below which the system can respond successfully to gains and losses in membership through migration, but beyond which the processes of socialization and social control cease to function adequately.

---

[5] The similarities between the psychodynamics of immigrants and young children are developed in Weinberg, (1961, pp. 222–223).

In functional theory, a social system whose capacity to perform the functional imperatives declines will in the limit "cease to exist as an independent or distinctive entity." [6] The expression has an apocalyptic ring, but the migration literature contains instances, the language of which is merely a sanitized version of the same concept. The "filtering" process analyzed by Little and Leven ends in neighborhood abandonment, (see Little and Leven, this volume, Chapter 13), and the Watts community in Los Angeles, according to recent reports, would not be inappropriately described as having ceased to exist as an independent entity. Normally, however, we expect social systems to adapt to external disturbances and to continue functioning, although in changed form. Migration indeed is one of the principal sources of social change. The task, then, is to anticipate and evaluate the kinds of social change likely to be induced by a rising rate of migration, rather than to expect societies to vanish.

There is not yet available a social input–output table for tracing through all the first- and higher-order consequences of disturbances to a social system (An essay toward this end may be found in Berliner, 1972). Most analysts are obliged to test general propositions about the whole by the study of individual sectors. E. A. Hammel, for example, holds the view that social systems are "extraordinarily robust to infrastructural change," and tests the proposition in his study of the stability of the Yugoslav kinship system under the impact of extensive migration (see Hammel, this volume, Chapter 21). Of the vast range of other social consequences that might be examined, I shall select one that is particularly interesting because it is derived from what I have called the pure social effect of migration; that is, the effect of an increasing frequency of change of the members of community, without respect to the specific cultural content or social organization. One of the fundamental elements in social cohesion is affect—the emotional attachment of people to their families, friends, and community. Affect is the principal source of the "psychic costs" that enter into economic models. One of the empirical laws of social behavior developed by George Homans, and later formalized into a model by Herbert Simon, is that affect is proportional to interaction (see Homans, 1957, Chapter 5). Social arrangements in which people are obliged to talk to one another frequently, hand things to one another, work together and see one another often, create an emotional relationship (positive or negative) between them. They think of each other more and relate to each other more closely. If the social arrangement is changed so that the frequency

---

[6] Johnson (1960, p. 52). The textbook follows the Parsonian theory of action.

of interaction is reduced, they are less aware of each other, care less, and think less often of one another. Hence the quality of social life and, therefore, the social nature of the members of the society, depends upon the frequency of interaction.

One of the consequences of migration is to reduce the rate of interaction among members of the family and of kin groups. The Yugoslav data show that family interaction varies inversely with distance, and migrants to distant places interact infrequently with members of their family.[7] In accordance with Homans' law, the degree of affect within families should be expected to decrease. What one makes of this depends on the role one sees for the family in the welfare of the society.

The family of orientation has traditionally been a major source of the social and emotional support of people. The weakening of the intensity of that relationship cuts people off from that source of emotional support, intimacy, and affect. It is possible, of course, that in a highly mobile society people develop new sources of such support in other primary groups like friends, clubs, and political organizations. One wonders, however, whether the nature or intensity of the affect relations is the same. As a corollary to Homans' law, it may be conjectured that affect is proportional to cumulative interaction—to the duration of an association—in addition to the frequency of interaction. That is, suppose two groups, the members of which interact with the same frequency per week; but in one group the members change every year while in the second group the members remain the same for long periods of time. One would guess that the affect would be of a much deeper quality in the second group. If that is so, then the substitution of new primary groups for family of orientation may nevertheless result in a different and lowered degree of affect. Suppose in one society the typical member has interacted in his lifetime with 10,000 persons, but with each for a period of one year. In the second the typical person has interacted with only 100 persons in his lifetime, but with each for 20 years. There must surely be a vast difference in the quality of the social life of a society in which one has many friends each for a year or two, and a society in

---

[7] In Hammel's data (this volume, Chapter 21), "When father and son were both in Belgrade, the annual mean frequency of personal contact was 145 . . . when the father was outside Belgrade, the mean personal contact frequency was 4." Hammel concludes from these data that "the evidence thus far adduced speaks strongly for stability." If Homans's law is valid, and if affect is a requirement for a stable kinship system, one comes to the opposite conclusion: The family of orientation is finished in Yugoslavia, though the family of procreation may be stable.

which one has a few friends of a lifetime's duration.[8] In this way, the changes in the rate of migration creep up on the society, changing the quality of people and their lives in ways that can hardly be perceived.

In all disciplines that deal with migration, there are bulls and bears. The bulls see migration as the conqueror of the "tyranny of space," as the champion of economic progress, as the corrector of imbalances, as the liberator of the individualist suffocating from the traditionalism of the village, as the vehicle of social mobility. The bears, as E. A. Hammel describes them, foresee "the decay of the social order and the swift corruption of traditional ideology (Hammel, this volume, Chapter 21)." This essay, it must be admitted, has been somewhat bearish on the subject and I should like to make partial amends by observing that there may be some optimal rate of migration. At very low rates of migration a society may well be exceedingly oppressive, and it would forgo the numerous advantages that come from moderate rates of migration. At rates of migration beyond the optimum the negative consequences that are the concern of the bears would take their toll. The notion of an optimum does appear in the urbanization literature, with respect to the size of a city, but I have not noted its use with reference to the rate of migration. With so many imponderables involved, no very precise statement ought to be expected about the size of the optimal rate of migration or about the conditions that must hold at the optimum. As Ronald Crowley writes with respect to the size of the city, however, the concept of optimality is of some use as a guide to the questions to be asked (see Crowley, this volume, Chapter 15).

The final question I should like to ask is whether the rate of migration tends to an optimal level. The answer cannot be gotten at directly, but it may be approached indirectly by examining the stability of social systems with respect to changes in the rate of migration. If they are stable, then an increase in migration would trigger off responses that would cause the rate to decline again or to level off. If they are unstable, however, then an increase in migration would set up responses that would cause it to increase even further. In a stable system there is no assurance that the rate at which migration stabilized after an initial rise

---

[8] The point was made in the sociological literature long ago by students of urbanization. Louis Wirth wrote in 1938 that urbanites know more people than the villager, but their knowledge is less intensive; they may restrict the depth and comprehensiveness of their contacts as a means of "immunizing themselves against the personal claims and expectations of others [quoted from Musgrove, 1963, p. 133]." To make the point is not necessarily to glamorize village life.

was the optimal rate. But there is some reassurance in the notion that it would eventually settle down. In an unstable system, however, since an increase in migration once begun tends to proceed indefinitely, one can be fairly sure that it will overshoot the optimum and there would be greater cause for concern.

It is not possible to offer a general answer to the question. But on a casual review of the literature it is difficult not to go bearish again. It is strikingly evident that analysts of migration, of all disciplinary persuasions, find themselves dealing explicitly or implicitly with elements of dynamic instability. I shall report a few such elements.

In the traditional economic theory labor is homogeneous and fully employed. The stimulus to migration is a disturbance that causes real-wage rates temporarily to diverge in two locations. The divergence in wage rates causes labor to flow from the low- to the high-wage location. The consequent changes in the marginal productivity of labor in the two locations diminishes the difference in wage rates and migration continues until the wage difference vanishes and migration then ceases. It is an ideal homeostatic process in which migration plays the role of equilibrator.

Possibly some small eddies of migration may be successfully modeled by the traditional theory, but many large streams clearly are not. Neither of the assumptions, of homogeneity and of full employment, can be held to apply, and the greater mischief may be with the latter. This follows from the evidence presented by D. J. Bogue and others that the major determinant of migration is the employment opportunities at location of destination (see Bogue, this volume, Chapter 11; and Greenwood, 1975, pp. 411, 419–20). For, in a world of full employment, employment opportunities would by definition be the same everywhere. Since it is primarily employment opportunities rather than wage differences that generate migration, the migrants consist, as Jerome Rothenberg points out, not of a random selection of homogeneous workers but of those members of a nonhomogeneous labor force best able to secure employment in the high-employment locations. These tend to be the more skilled, the younger, and the better educated. (see Rothenberg, this volume, Chapter 12). The effect of migration that conforms to this model is that the proportion of unemployed rises in the location of origin, with secondary effects that tend to reduce per capita incomes, thus accelerating both the rate of emigration and the rate of decline. The process is dynamically unstable and terminates in a "corner solution" in which the community has lost all its employables and ceases to be self-sustaining.

From a purely economic point of view such processes may be unobjectionable. Factors of production that have ceased to be valuable should eventually cease to produce, and it is dynamic processes like this that accomplish their euthanasia. If the productivity of a coal mine declines relative to that of newer sources of energy, it will continue to operate for a time, but it is eventually abandoned. The same may be said of communities. The only economic case that can be made for public policy to arrest the decline of depressed communities is based on the presence of externalities; for example, when a community that invests in the education of a young person fails to receive a return to that investment because he later migrates. But even if externalities of that kind were fully accounted for, a well-functioning economy maximizing its Bergsonian Economic Welfare must expect some communities to rise and others to decline and disappear; and the greater the rate of technological change the greater their number should be. If there is a basis for concern, it is to be found not in the economic effects but in the social effects.

Sociological and anthropological models are not as rigorously speci-fied as economic models, and their stability properties are not as sharply articulated. Most of them tend to be static, and the study of change takes the form of comparative statics. In Hammel's analysis, for example, the stability of kinship structure is studied by comparing various properties of families in which no one has migrated with those of families in which someone has migrated. Similarly, Homans's law tells us that if we disturb a social system by changing the frequency of interaction among its members, the volume of affect will diminish. Economists should find no objection to comparative statics as a form of analysis, for without it they would be largely out of business; at least out of what continues to be an important part of their business. But as Samuelson showed some time ago, unless the dynamic properties of a static model are specified, the analysis may not correctly describe the equilibrium to which the system will move following a disturbance. Moreover, if the disturbance is not merely a one-time shift in the value of some parameter but a continuing change—as migration is likely to be—one ought to be quite specific about the dynamic features of the model in order to trace through its consequences.

Perhaps because it deals with so fundamental a property of a social system as its inertia, migration seems to trigger off all manner of unstable dynamic processes. Consider a reasonably stable society with an unchanging technology. To isolate the social effect of migration from the cultural effect, suppose the society is neither rural nor urban—call it a rurban society. Migration in rurban society will conform to that pattern referred to by D. J. Bogue as "movement between similar environments" (see Bogue, this volume, Chapter 11). Persons who find their own communities oppressive for personal or social reasons will move to others. A community that has some distinctive feature, like a strong artistic tradition or a location on the seashore, will attract immigrants from other communities who place a particularly high value on those features. Prominent among the migrants will be people with mental disorders who change location out of fancied fears and hopes. Most people do not migrate, and the methods of social control are such that immigrants are easily reestablished in appropriate social roles.

Each community is characterized by what may be called a schedule of the propensity to migrate (see Spengler and Myers, this volume, Chapter 2). For each value of some parameter like transportation costs or employment opportunities elsewhere, a certain number of people will migrate per year; say 10 per 100 residents. Now suppose the system is disturbed by a one-time change in one of the parameters—perhaps a decline in transportation costs. In a static analysis, one would expect a rise in the rate of migration—to perhaps 15 per 100 residents per year. The community is operating at a point lower down on its schedule of the propensity to migrate. Each year 5 people who would not have moved with the original transportation cost now move with the lower cost.

A static analysis assumes, however, that the schedule of the propensity to migrate is unchanged by the increase in the rate of migration; the community moves to a new point on the same schedule and that is the end of it. But suppose the increase in migration leads to a change in the schedule itself. If the propensity to move depends on a person's ties to his community, then Homans's law leads to a dynamically unstable increase in migration. In the first stage, the effect of the decline in transportation costs is to increase the number of people who leave the community, from 10 to 15 per 100, and perhaps to replace them by inmigrants from other places.[9] The migrants were presumably those with the least intense ties to their communities of origin and were, therefore, on the margin of migrating initially. Since the nonmigrants interact with the inmigrants less than they did with their former neighbors who left, the quantity of affect in the community diminishes. The schedule of the propensity to migrate therefore shifts; for each level of transportation cost, more members of the community would now migrate than originally. In the second stage, some people who had not migrated initially

---

[9] "Where immigration is great, out-migration is also great. . . . Greenwood (1975, p. 413)."

now have less intense ties to the community and decide to migrate, and the migration rate rises from 15 to 20. The new outmigrants are again replaced by inmigrants from elsewhere, with a further decline in the quantity of interaction and affect, and a further shift in the schedule of the propensity to migrate. Each outmigrant leaves a hole in the network of social interaction. The more that leave, the weaker the hold of the debilitated community on those who remain, and therefore, a second wave of persons emigrate who might not have before the first did. In the absence of offsetting stabilizing elements, the society becomes one in which all social inertia has vanished, and with it the significant forms of social interaction. From week to week one's neighbors change. No one needs to tolerate an imposition upon him by another, or to work out accommodation with a testy neighbor. One simply splits and sets up a pad elsewhere. People flee that which makes them uncomfortable, and thereby flee that which makes them human.

I have discussed the dynamics of a rurban society in order to isolate the pure social effect of migration. If one added the specific cultural features that characterize actual migration patterns, the elements of instability are no less evident. In the suburban form of migration, Little and Leven consider a social arrangement in which households care about the identity of their neighbors. With no implausible assumptions, the dynamics lead eventually to the abandonment of entire neighborhoods (see Little and Leven, this volume, Chapter 13). The phenomenon of "hypermobility" reflects another destabilizing property. Migrating is like sinning; after you have done it once it is easier to do again. Hence, the finding that people who have moved once are more likely to move again than those who never tried it (see Lee, 1969, p. 291; and Morrison, this volume, Chapter 4). And also like sinning, it tends to be visited upon one's family and neighbors, in the form of the "siphon effect" and the "beaten path" (see Morrison, this volume, Chapter 4).

It is also visited upon the children, which introduces a longer timeframe into the process. In a British study, the highest average intelligence was found in schoolchildren from families who had moved most frequently (see Musgrove, 1963, pp. 130–131). The explanation is thought to be that mobile families exert a more demanding discipline on their children, which contributes to their higher intelligence. The consequence is that the children of migrants are more likely to be migrants because intelligence and education are related to mobility and because the inertia threshold is likely to be lower. The dynamic would then work like this: The children of migrants always migrate; but in each generation some people migrate whose parents did not migrate. In such a model, as long as there is some stimulus to migration other than the fact of having been socialized by migrant parents, the rate of migration will rise indefinitely. The time lag in this kind of process, however, is a generation, rather longer than the short-run analysis of the usual microeconomic kind. Time lags of that duration are not uncommon in the demographic literature; in Alonso's model, national income is lagged 20 years (see Alonso, this volume, Chapter 5). But when a generational time lag is involved, as it must be in processes involving socialization, empirical data are difficult to develop. In Hammel's Yugoslav data, for example, there is a sharp decline in the interaction rate between migrants to the city and their parents (see Hammel this volume, Chapter 21). These migrants, however, had been socialized in the village by nonmigrant parents. Their own children will have been socialized by mobile parents in an urban environment. One would, therefore, expect an even sharper drop in family interaction in the next generation. It follows that, since the rate of migration has accelerated sharply in the past generation, its full effect may not be known until another one or two generations have passed. Few of us are likely to be around long enough to collect the data, however. Such effects are difficult to study. Cigarette smoking became a widespread practice in the 1920s and 1930s, but it was not until the 1950s and 1960s that its relationship to cancer was established.

I have dwelt on the destabilizing elements in migration, but there are, of course, stabilizing elements as well. Migrants, for example, often form close relationships with other migrants, particularly from the same communities, and they build up their own subcultures and systems of social controls (see Philpott, 1970, p. 12). (Musgrove 1963, p. 14, reports, however, that the migratory elite are more isolated from each other.) Hence, the intensity of interaction in communities of destination may not diminish, although the patterns of interaction may change. There are also Malthusian-type stabilizers, like the decline in personal safety and other manifestations of social disorganization that reduce the pull of communities of destination and act to slow down the migration process. Furthermore, the exogenous factors that have contributed to rising migration in the past may diminish; energy costs may rise in the future and water supplies diminish, as Spengler and Myers point out (see Spengler and Myers, this volume, Chapter 2). It was not my purpose, however, to argue that social systems are in fact unstable in their responses to migration. It was rather to note that there are strong elements of instability associated with the migration process that should be a matter of some concern, and that the analysis of stability properties can benefit from the attention of all the disciplines that deal with migration.

References

Bergson, A. *Essays in normative economics.* Cambridge Mass.: Harvard University Press, 1966.

Berliner, J. S. *Economy, society and welfare: A study in social economics.* New York: Praeger, 1972.

Greenwood, M. J. Research on internal migration in the United States: A survey. *Journal of Economic Literature,* 1975, *13*(2).

Homans, G. C. *The human group.* New York: Harcourt Brace, 1950.

Johnson, H. M. *Sociology: A systematic introduction.* New York: Harcourt, Brace, 1960.

Lee, E. A theory of migration. In J. A. Jackson (Ed.), *Migration.* Cambridge: The University Press, 1969.

Malzberg, B., and E. S. Lee. *Migration and mental illness.* New York: Social Science Research Council, 1956.

Marshall, A. *Principles of economics* New York: Macmillan, 1948.

Musgrove, F. *The migratory elite* London: Heinemann, 1963.

Parsons, T., and N. J. Smelser. *Economy and society.* London: Routledge and Kegan Paul, 1956.

Philpott, S. B. The implications of migration for sending societies: Some theoretical considerations. In R. F. Spencer (Ed.), *Migration and anthropology.* Seattle: University of Washington Press, 1970.

Robbins, L. *An essay on the nature and significance of economic science.* London: Macmillan, 1952.

Simon, H. A. *Models of man.* New York: Wiley, 1957.

Weinberg, A. A. *Migration and belonging.* The Hague: Martinus Nÿhoff, 1961.

CHAPTER 24

Internal Migration:
A Comparative Systemic View

Egon Neuberger

I. Introduction

The English language literature on migration stresses the technological, resource, and social aspects of the problem of migration. It devotes much less attention to the role of the economic system in migration, and only a somewhat greater attention to government policies, as indicated in the recent review of this literature by Greenwood.[1]

In the literature on economic systems, considerable attention has been paid to the regional distribution of one key factor of production—capital. The problem of the regional allocation of investable resources in market and planned economies has not received as thorough a treatment as has the structural allocation among different sectors of the economy, but it certainly has not been neglected. On the other hand, there has been a relative neglect of the elements underlying the regional allocation of the other key factor of production—labor. One possible explanation for this difference is that the planned allocation of capital is ubiquitous in all planned economies and there exist various mechanisms for influencing it

---

[1] "What is perhaps most striking about the massive literature on the determinants of interregional migration is the lack of direct policy implications [Greenwood, 1975, p. 412]." The advantage of the simultaneous equations approach is that policy variables can be directly and explicitly introduced and thus the impact of policy decisions on migration can be clearly demonstrated.

463

even in most market economies. On the other hand, less stress has been placed on planning the regional allocation of labor, and labor—in market economies, and even in planned economies—has usually moved primarily on the basis of a push from the area of emigration or a pull from the area of immigration.

The fact that neither the migration nor the systems literature stresses the interrelationships between migration and economic systems has led us to try to take a step toward correcting this situation with the publication of this volume. Several chapters (including those by Berliner, Crowley, Fallenbuchl, Lucas, and Ofer) deal explicitly with the systemic variables, while others touch upon the policy options available to influence migration. In order to stress even more this heretofore relatively neglected aspect of migration, we are concluding the volume with this chapter exploring some of the interrelationships between migration and economic systems.

II. The Economic System and Migration

Following Neuberger and Duffy (1976), we define the economic system as consisting of the decision-making, information, and motivation structures, that is, the rules and institutions governing the allocation of decision-making power among the various agents, the information channels and languages needed to supply them with the data necessary to make their decisions, and the manner in which decision-making agents can get other agents to implement their decisions. Closely connected to the nature of a given economic system are the government policies conducted within the framework of that economic system.

What is the relationship between the economic system and migration? Migration involves the spatial redistribution of the population and thus of both the productive and the decision-making agents. The economic systems in the area of origin and area of destination are among the factors influencing directly or indirectly the strength of the pull or the push.[2] On the other hand, migration can in its turn affect the economic systems in the areas of origin and destination.

---

[2] Lucas (Chapter 3) discusses some of the contributions to the literature on economic development and migration that deal with systemic aspects, e.g., the effect of private versus communal property and of share-cropping arrangements on the benefits derived by a migrant. It is clear that such systemic variables have an impact on migration decisions. He also discusses the Harris–Todaro, Bhagwati–Srinivasan, and Stiglitz models for determining the optimal tax–subsidy policy mix for dealing with the interrelationship between rural–urban migration and urban unemployment.

The redistribution of population may be based on a national settlement policy, in which planners control the movement of population, or, as is more generally the case, on the voluntary action of individuals. In the former, relatively rare, instance, the economic system of the country plays a major role in the determination of migration movements. There must be sufficient centralization of decision making to enable the central planners to have control over settlement policies; they must have the necessary information to enable them to make rational decisions, and they must have access to appropriate motivation mechanisms to enable them to implement their plans. More on this later.

In the more usual case, where people move voluntarily in order to improve the economic, social, or other aspects of life, the economic system can enter into their decision framework either directly or indirectly. In some rare cases, the economic system itself can form one of the key arguments in the individual's utility function. For example, different individuals have different degrees of risk aversion; some prefer a free market system, in which anyone is permitted to become an enterpreneur, while others prefer a planned socialist system, in which they are guaranteed a job. The massive migration from East to West Germany before the erection of the Berlin Wall, discussed in Hollman's paper (Chapter 19), was clearly a response to differences in the economic and political systems themselves as well as in their respective levels of standard of living.

More usually, the economic system influences migration indirectly. It is the system's impact on wage rates, employment opportunities, supply of private and public goods, and general life style in two regions that makes the economic system one of the major determinants of migration. It is likely that this predominantly indirect effect of the system on migration explains, in good part, the relative neglect of the systemic variables in the migration literature. An econometric analysis of the causes of migration will in most cases yield a satisfactory explanatory power without the system itself being considered as one of the independent variables.

Similarly, in discussing the relationship between government policies and migration, it is necessary to distinguish between government policies that directly affect migratory flows and those that affect such flows only indirectly. Examples of the former are policies whereby the government raises or lowers the cost of transportation, subsidizes or taxes migrants, provides migrants with information on job opportunities and other key factors in other areas, or prohibits or licenses migratory moves. Indirect policies include all government policies with a regional bias, for example, investment allocation, allocation of R and D subsidies, welfare policies, policies dealing with structural unemployment, many types of fiscal policies, and even monetary policies that have an impact on particular areas, such as urban housing.

When we move from the causes of migration to the systemic consequences of migration upon the two areas, we again find that the indirect effects predominate. It would require an unusually massive rate of migration to bring about direct changes in some of the systemic variables. For example, if, due to a war or other catastrophe, the population of a given area were doubled or halved in a short period of time, this could cause a significant change in the economic system, such as the need to replace the market by a planned allocation of labor or of those commodities now in scarce supply. In addition, in such a case the set of decision makers might also change drastically and this could result in a change in the system to correspond to the objectives of the new decision agents. In the more usual cases of relatively slow emigration or immigration, neither the relative scarcities nor the set of key decision makers are likely to alter significantly, and therefore the migration would not directly cause changes in any of the systemic variables. Over time, however, even slow rates of migration could bring about systemic change, especially since migration tends to be highly selective, as pointed out by Spengler and Myers (Chapter 2), Greenwood (1975, pp. 406–408, 415), and others. One of Rothenberg's major contributions (Chapter 12) is his analysis of migrants as a self-selected, distinct subset of all decision agents. He discusses the various dimensions along which migrants differ from nonmigrants, such as differential "career trees," attitudes toward risk and differing life styles, prospective lifetime earnings (which vary with age), attitudes toward private versus public goods, ability to move (which depends on age, sex, familial connections, and available assets), attitudes toward the weakening of family and other social ties, and access to information.

The in- or outmigration of skilled, educated people of prime working age and with a relatively low degree of risk aversion can have an important impact on the set of decision makers, on the objectives that motivate them, on their ability to process information, and so on—each of which can bring about changes in some aspect of the economic system.[3]

An important concept in migration analysis is that of "distance." The points of origin and destination are separated by physical, economic,

---

[3] The impact of selective migration is felt not only by villages that lose their young men but also by mature central cities that lose their higher-income inhabitants and therefore suffer from fiscal decay, a point illustrated in the paper by Little and Leven (Chapter 13).

social, and other types of barriers. The greater this distance, the greater will be the economic, psychic, and other costs of migration.[4] Thus, one of the issues discussed below is the effect of various systemic variables on distance and, therefore, on the rate of migration.

III.   Interrelationships between Migration and the Three Systemic Structures

As indicated earlier, we define the economic system in terms of three component structures: the decision-making, motivation, and information structures.

A.   THE DECISION-MAKING STRUCTURE

The decision-making structure defines the allocation of decision-making power among various agents, including the extent of centralization or concentration of this power among a small subset of all agents, and the basis for that power (ownership, custom, coercion, information). For present purposes, the key question is the locus of the power to decide who has the right to move and under what conditions. If the decision-making structure is of a highly decentralized type, then each individual will have the power to decide whether he and his family will move to another area or not. Even if the decisions on certain issues, such as the rate of investment, its allocation among sectors and regions, the overall price level, and similar key magnitudes, are determined centrally, it is still possible for the migration decisions to be highly decentralized. On the other hand, if the decision-making structure is highly centralized and the center wishes to determine national settlement policies, then the migration decisions will have to be centrally controlled.

A very important aspect of the decision-making structure that will affect the distance between two regions is the division of a given geographic area into administrative units. This can have a strong influence on the effective distance between two points. For example, it is infinitely easier to migrate the 3000 miles from New York to San Francisco than the less than one-tenth of this distance from Leningrad to

---

[4] Rothenberg (Chapter 12) points out that geographical distance has at least four distinct, but probably mutually consistent, roles in influencing migration: A longer distance is positively related to moving costs, the utility significance of the "loss" of friends and relatives, and the net attractiveness of intervening destinations between the area of origin and the area of planned destination; but it is negatively related to the quality of information about the destination.

Helsinki. Even within the same country, a move within a given state or county or city is sometimes easier than a move to another administrative unit that is closer in physical terms. This would be the case where retirement, unemployment, and other welfare benefits as well as voting rights, and other rights or privileges were dependent on length of residence in the administrative unit. Thus, unless the whole country constitutes a single administrative unit or the migrant faces no obstacles and suffers no losses by moving from one unit to another, partitioning will result in adding "administrative" distance to the other aspects of distance. The effect of the administrative partitioning of cities or other geographic entities, with resultant differences in the supply of local public goods and in local taxes will itself cause migration as people's incomes or stages in the life cycle or both change.

One obvious aspect of the decision-making structure is whether or not a decision maker in the area of origin or in the area of destination has the power to increase or decrease the effective administrative distance. Must the would-be migrant obtain permission to move away from his region (as must the collective farmer in the Soviet Union) or to move into another area (as must anyone wanting to settle in a major city in the Soviet Union or some of the other socialist countries)? How does the system deal with the question of obtaining housing in the area to which the migrant moves? The rationing of scarce housing can prevent a would-be migrant from moving to a place as effectively as can an outright prohibition. Similarly, under what conditions can the migrant obtain a job?

B. The Motivation Structure

To examine the motivation structure, it is necessary to introduce two sets of concepts. First, all decision makers may be divided into two types: type A, those that directly choose among the acts into which any decision can be divided (e.g., to move from region i to region j or k), and type B, the agents that influence those who choose the acts. Second, this influence by type B decision makers may take the form of (1) limiting the set of feasible acts open to type A agents (e.g., you may move to region j but not to region k), (2) manipulating incentives in such a way as to make a move to j much more beneficial than a move to k (e.g., setting wages much higher or providing better housing in j than in k), (3) attempting to change the objective functions of type A agents so that they prefer moves to j to moves to k (e.g., if j is an underdeveloped frontier area, then planners can encourage people to move there by using propaganda that stresses nationalism and love of adventure), and

(4) controlling the flow of information (e.g., they can make the type A agent believe that their set of feasible acts is limited or that the incentives differ from those that actually pertain).

The first two types of influence are generally the most important, and they cover most of the motivations actually utilized. We may call the operation on the set of feasible acts administrative control and the operation on the incentives, which have the effect of altering the consequences of any given decision, manipulative control.

It should be noted that in a pure market system the invisible hand of the market will influence decision makers by manipulative control—by altering wage and price incentives—but never by administrative control. However, in many countries that may be considered market economies, some types of administrative controls are utilized, for example, zoning ordinances setting 2-acre minimum lot sizes effectively eliminate a move to these communities from the set of feasible acts of many potential migrants.

In centrally planned economies, the planners tend to use both manipulative and administrative controls, including actual prohibitions on migration, as discussed by Fallenbuchl (Chapter 17). However, even in planned economies, the major form of control over migration tends to be of the manipulative type, with differential wages and differential access to housing forming the two major incentives to influence people to move to areas that are considered to be lacking in labor.

C. The Information Structure

The third key structure—the information structure—enters into every facet of the migration problem. In a market system, would-be migrants require information on job opportunities, wages, and amenities in the regions to which they are considering a move, as well as on costs of moving, in order to calculate the costs and benefits of the move. The ability to obtain this information varies with the "distance" of the point of destination. While a potential migrant has considerable information about conditions in his present location, it is rather difficult and costly to obtain information about the place to which he is considering migrating.[5]

[5] Rothenberg (Chapter 12) provides a very useful discussion of the role of information in the potential migrant's decision-making process. He makes the important observation that more information about a region of destination does not necessarily increase the probability that this will be the region chosen. A risk-taking decision agent may actually choose to migrate to a region about which he has less information, on the optimistic assumption that it will provide better opportunities. On a more technical level, Rothenberg argues that the variance, as well as the mean value, of job and other opportunities enters into the decision process.

The least costly manner of obtaining such information is from friends and relatives who have already migrated to that place, and this is one of the factors that explain the "beaten path" syndrome, described by Morrison (Chapter 14). The other factor explaining this syndrome is the reduction in the cultural and social distance in such a case, as pointed out very clearly by Hawrylyshyn (Chapter 20) in analyzing the effect of the ethnic variable and Hammel (Chapter 21) in analyzing the kinship variables in Yugoslav migrations. If the individual does not have friends or relatives living in the area of potential destination, he will either have to travel there himself to investigate the place, which is rather costly if the physical and economic distance is great (with the latter depending on the costs of transport), or depend on official or other published information or on rumors. It is clear that a language difference between the areas of origin and destination will complicate greatly the task of obtaining the necessary information.

In planned economies, the information must be centralized so that the planners are in a position to reach rational decisions on settlement policies. In addition to the information needed to formulate the production and social plans that underlie plans for migration, planners also require some information regarding the preferences of would-be migrants in order to determine the best method of motivating them to move or, in the case of democratic planning, of maximizing individual utilities.

IV. Systemic Comparisons

A.   Optimum Migration: A Problem of Definition

Having discussed briefly the three structural components of economic systems and their relationship to migration, the next question is whether or not it is possible to make any a priori judgments as to the relative efficiency of different economic systems in achieving optimum migration flows. In order to answer this question, it is first necessary to define an optimum rate of migration.

As pointed out by Crowley (Chapter 15) and by Berliner (Chapter 23), the problem of defining an optimum rate of migration is a most difficult one. It is easier to determine the criteria for the allocation of goods or capital than for the allocation of labor: Goods and capital can be treated as inanimate objects with no utility functions of their own, and they can be transferred from region to region until some optimum allocation is reached. The same, of course, is not true of labor. Thus, in the case of migration, significant externalities, especially divergences between private and social benefits can easily arise, and the individual's welfare does not then correspond to the optimal settlement policy of the government. Even leaving aside this problem of private versus social welfare, no suitable solution has yet been formulated for developing national settlement policies and, therefore, for developing optimal migration policies. In this connection, it is important to stress that migration, like capital investment, is not a final good or process but, rather, an intermediate process aimed at achieving either individual utility maximization or a superior national distribution of population. It is the goods and services (including public amenities) that yield utilities for the individual, and migration is only one possible means to obtain more of the ones he wishes. Similarly, no national economic policy is interested in migration as such but, rather, in the population distribution among regions that is the end result of migration. On the other hand, as pointed out by Berliner, the rate of migration has significant social and psychic consequences, so that the process itself, regardless of the final consequences in terms of population distribution, has important policy implications.

Underlying much of the discussion up to this point has been the implicit dichotomy between efficiency and welfare (individual or social), two key goals for any economic system. Labor mobility, the alter ego of migration, has always been considered one of the major factors in achieving an efficient economy, and any economic system that placed barriers in the way of migration would be faulted on this score. Labor mobility is especially important in achieving long-run dynamic efficiency under conditions of technological change and major indivisibilities. Insufficient labor mobility requires excessive movement of capital or of goods and services or of both of these in order to compensate for this lack.

As indicated by Berliner, migration, even when improving the economy's efficiency, may not necessarily increase the community's total welfare, so that sole stress on productive efficiency may lead to faulty policy recommendations. After all, the decision to move any considerable distance is a much more serious decision than most other individual decisions. Probably the only individual economic decision with the same degree of potential impact is the choice of career. If the information made available to potential migrants is poor and the migratory move cannot be reversed without very high costs, a decision to migrate may even have long-run negative effects from the point of view of individual as well as of social utility.

B. INTERDEPENDENCIES, EXTERNALITIES, AND OPTIMA

Closely tied to the problem of the optimum are the problems of interdependencies and externalities. Migration has significant interdependencies of all types.[6] Outmigration will affect the labor productivity in the area of origin (generally raising it if labor was in excess there before, but frequently lowering it due to the selective nature of migration, since the predominant share of migrants usually consists of those in the prime working ages), and it will reduce the demand for all goods and services (unless the emigrants leave behind their families and send remittances to them), particularly the demand for housing and social overhead. The opposite effects will take place in the area of destination, and, if the area is a city, there will also result important external diseconomies in the form of congestion and environmental disruption. Under a completely free market system, these interdependencies will play a very important and completely uncontrolled role. The individual is the decision agent who initiates the migration decision and does it without interference from any other decision makers. He will generally take into account the direct effects of his migration, such as his probability of getting a job or a higher wage; he is likely to take account of the availability and cost of housing and amenities but not of the effect that he and other migrants, making their decisions independently, will have on the availability and cost of the infrastructural services nor of the congestion and pollution they will cause.[7] This is partly a function of the information that he is likely to seek and of the information he can reasonably expect to obtain. In a planned system, all of these interdependencies can theoretically be taken into account by the central

---

[6] One key reason, as pointed out by Berliner (Chapter 23), why economists are not able to provide policy guidance on migration is that migration movements tend to be accompanied by significant social and environmental externalities that are hard to measure, rather than by economic externalities more amenable to measurement. Many of the policies that economists analyze involve relatively small changes in economic variables and even smaller changes in noneconomic ones, so that it is possible to conduct the analysis in terms of maximization of the Bergsonian social welfare function by assuming that the noneconomic parameters of this function will not be significantly affected. This is much more difficult to justify in the case of migration.

[7] A good discussion of the problem of externalities in the growth of cities under free market conditions is found in the paper by Spengler and Myers (Chapter 2). They argue that the decision-making structure of a city is much less centralized than that of a firm or a plant which are subject to a single decision maker. Furthermore, the city in a free market economy is not able to control the movement of firms or individuals into or out of its territory and is unable to force them to pay the full cost of the external diseconomies they create for the city; the recent debacle in New York City is a vivid example of this problem.

planner and he can control migration movements in such a way as to balance the direct and indirect costs and benefits to society of any given level or composition of migration flow. In fact, this model of the omniscient, omnipotent, and all-wise planner does not really apply. Instead, there exist different bureaucratic organizations each controlling some part of the environment and the economic system and each trying to maximize its own utility function. Thus, the interdependencies are not fully taken into account and the externalities are often not internalized but continue to exist. What planners can do is to try to insulate certain factors and prevent the interdependencies from having full effect. For example, in a free market without any government interference, the migrant's demand for new housing would initially lead to a shift in investments—from industry to housing, trade, communal services, and so on. In a planned system, planners can prevent this from happening and can continue emphasizing industrial investment at the cost of these other sectors, even if they choose not to act by limiting migration as such. Furthermore, they can influence migration flows by providing information on the real nature of the interdependencies or by devising tax–subsidy schemes that individual migrants are forced to take into account in their migration decisions. In actuality, planners in existing planned economies have either interfered directly with the migration decisions or have cut the link between the migration flow and some of the other interdependencies, rather than merely affecting migration flows by the provision of information and/or internalization of the externalities by individual migrants.

In addition to the interdependencies problem, the attainment of an optimum is complicated by (1) the involvement of two different regions (the region of origin and the region of destination), which may be differentially affected by migration and (2) by the question whether social welfare should be maximized for a given region or for a given group of migrants (a point stressed by Morrison in Chapter 4). Assuming free migratory movement and fulfilled expectations about economic and noneconomic effects, it is clear that the migrants gain from a move. However, if the information provided to the migrants were incomplete or incorrect, or if conditions were to change rapidly, then expectations might not be fulfilled and migrants might not gain. In such a case, the proportion of the migrant's income used up in migration and potential reverse migration becomes a crucial variable.

As pointed out by Davis (Chapter 10), under certain circumstances both regions stand to gain—for example, where labor is overabundant in the region of origin and scarce in the region of destination. In such a case, where both regions gain and the individual migrants gain, we are clearly moving toward a Pareto optimal equilibrium. This would also result in a more efficient way of achieving factor price equalization than would the immobility of factors and trade in goods. Where migration is influenced primarily by job opportunities and wage differentials, this will also provide an automatic check on migration once it is no longer needed to equalize wages in the two regions.

Let us consider, however, the case where individuals are free to move but one region loses while the other gains. In this case, there is no longer a clear criterion for an optimum, unless we take the position that it is individuals and not regions that count. From the point of view of individual utility maximization, any migration that provided gains to the individual migrants would constitute a movement toward an optimum even if both regions were to lose thereby. For example, even if the "flight from the villages" were to ruin the economic and social base of part of the rural sector and create slums and other socioeconomic ills in the cities, as long as the individual migrants preferred to live in urban slums rather than in villages, we would have to consider the migration as a move toward an optimum.

In a planned system, the central planners would presumably guide migration by administrative or manipulative controls toward an optimum (in terms of their preference ordering) for the country as a whole. They would not be bound by the criterion of maximizing individual utilities or by the need to ensure that neither the region of origin nor the region destination suffered losses.

Thus, under both market and planned systems there exist potential mechanisms for achieving an optimal rate of migration. However, under either system there exist barriers to the attainment of such an optimum. In the market system, the primary obstacles are interdependencies and externalities and the problem of providing individuals with sufficiently accurate information at a cost they can afford. In a planned system, the obstacles consist of the inability of planners to formulate consistent goals, obtain and process information, and use effective motivating mechanisms to achieve the desired flow of migration.

C. The Problem of Norms

Closely tied to the problem of defining an optimum rate of migration is a question to which we have already alluded—What norms should be used in defining such an optimum? Should it be the norm (preference function) of a leader or group of leaders (the prevailing norm in the terminology of Koopmans and Montias (1971), the norm of the population (the unavailing norm in a dictatorship or the prevailing norm in a true democracy), or the norm of the person making a systemic comparison (the comparor's norm)? Although the choice of norm will obviously affect very strongly the selection of the optimum, there is no way of making such a choice without getting into normative analysis.

D. THE COMPARISON OF EXTREME PURE MODELS

Assuming that we have settled on some norm and have determined the optimum stocks and rates of flow of population, we could then compare the efficiency of various models of economic systems in achieving these optima. Given a norm of achieving a Pareto optimum, a perfectly functioning competitive market system with perfect information operating under the classical conditions (no nonconvexities, externalities, or indivisibilities) could achieve this optimum. Similarly, a model of a computopia, that is, a perfect system of central planning, with omniscient and omnipotent planners (i.e., a completely centralized decision-making structure and perfected information and motivation structures) could achieve an optimum based on the norm of planner utility maximization, including the maximization of the welfare of the population as one possible goal.

In terms of the efficiency of the information structure in providing the necessary information to guide migration within a country, it is clear that some central information agency, either a central planning board, or a private information-gathering agency, could gather and process the information on all possible areas of destination with less cost and greater efficiency than could any individual potential migrant. There exists a significant scale effect, and costs would be lower if the information were centrally gathered and processed. The choice between a central governmental information agency and a private organization selling this service would depend on the many well-known advantages and disadvantages of each type of agency, including the "free rider" problem for a private agency attempting to gather and sell the information.

E. A MIXED MODEL

In systemic analysis, a careful distinction must be made between the centralization of information and the centralization of decision making. Our analysis of the information structure has indicated that the centralization of information may be an efficient solution to the problem of providing information on all the potential places to which people may migrate. This does not necessarily lead to the conclusion that the movement of population should also be centrally controlled. If the costs of migrating are not very high, if migration is reversible, and if maximization of individual utilities is the norm by which we would judge migration policies, then the argument for a marriage between the equivalent of a purely competitive system, with its completely decentralized decision-making structure, and a centralized information system would seem quite strong. This mixed model would involve the gathering and processing by a central agency, governmental or private, of information on job opportunities, wages, housing, social amenities, and all other relevant variables for every location and the provision of this information to every potential migrant. The decision whether to migrate and where to migrate would be left to the individual, and the central government would not use either administrative or manipulative control to influence the migratory flows. It should be noted that if migration costs of all types (including the social and psychic ones) are very low, and migration therefore easily reversible, and if the information is very accurate and up to date, then this mixed model could also be used where the norm was productive efficiency for the country as a whole, rather than maximization of individual utilities. On the other hand, if the costs of migrating were high, and migratory movements therefore not easily reversible, or if it was not possible to have up-to-date information, then this mixed model would be less likely to yield optimal results as measured either by productive efficiency or by individual welfare. If the distance was great and the reversibility low, there might be insufficient labor mobility and the government might have to utilize incentives to persuade people to move. On the other hand, if the information supplied by the central information agency was out of date, then there might be either too much or too little migration. For example, information on excellent opportunities in a given area might take a long time to reach potential migrants, during which time no moves would take place. Then, once the information was available, migration might accelerate and bring about a change in the economic and social opportunities of the area, but without the information on these changes reaching other potential migrants; thus the region might continue to be flooded with migrants even after it was no longer short of labor.

V.   Migration and Government Policies

The nature of the economic system and the government's development and other policies have very important indirect effects on migration by affecting the variables entering into the migration decision. The two most important variables having a positive effect on migration rates are differential job opportunities and unequal wage rates. As Fallenbuchl (Chapter 17) points out, centrally planned socialist systems tend to reduce the effect of these two variables on migration since they maintain policies of full employment (even at the cost of inefficient use of labor) and relative equality of wages. He also points out, however, that during the early stages of the development process, planners in such systems use differential wages to get workers to move voluntarily to areas with labor shortages and set real incomes in industry higher than in agriculture, thereby encouraging interregional and rural–urban migration.

Working to reduce migration flows are the investment allocation policies in these systems. The emphasis on investment in industrial construction and equipment, and the corresponding deemphasis on investment in housing and communal services, decreases greatly the facilities available to house and care for potential migrants and thereby inhibits migration. This phenomenon, called "underurbanization" has been analyzed by Konrad and Szelenyi (1974), who have shown the social and economic consequences resulting from the more rapid development of urban industry than of urban infrastructure. One major result has been the emergence of a large class of peasant workers, who live in the villages, continue to participate in agricultural work during peak periods, and commute to the cities to work in industry (a phenomenon described by Hawrylyshyn in Yugoslavia and Fallenbuchl in Poland in Chapters 17 and 18). Although this commutation appears cheap in terms of investment (transportation costs less than new houses, schools, and utilities), it also has negative effects on labor productivity (Wiles, 1974).

We might note that the above factors do not result from the nature of the economic system per se. For example, there is nothing inherent in central planning that requires policies leading to underurbanization. A centralized planning system could emphasize current consumer welfare, including housing and urban infrastructure, at the expense of economic growth. It is just that most present-day centrally planned economies were introduced in relatively backward countries, where economic growth constituted a key factor in legitimizing the revolutionary regimes.

As the ample supplies of labor from previously unemployed urban workers, underemployed rural workers, and previously nonworking women gradually disappear, the emphasis necessarily shifts from extensive to intensive development. Thus, instead of attempting to achieve increases in industrial output through massive infusions of additional labor and capital, there has to take place a greater emphasis on increased productivity and technological change, or on "total factor productivity," in the jargon of aggregate production function analysis. Such a change in emphasis leads to a decrease in rural–urban migration and a possible increase in urban–urban migration. In order to make possible the necessary increase in labor mobility and to provide the necessary incentives for labor productivity, the policy of underurbanization must be abandoned in favor of a shift toward increased investment in housing and other urban services. Thus, it is important to differentiate between elements that are intrinsic to a given economic system and those that are a function of a given ideology or stage of economic development.

The danger of imputing the differences between existing centrally planned economies and market economies solely to systemic differences is illustrated in the paper by Ofer (Chapter 16). He shows that the low level of urbanization relative to level of industrialization in the East European countries can be explained by reference to their economic systems and development strategies, but that this leaves out one crucial explanatory variable—the historical legacies of these countries. Ofer shows that the conditions prevailing before the introduction of centrally planned systems, namely, the high concentration of population and labor in rural and agricultural sectors and the low level of development of urban infrastructure, were highly conducive to a policy of economizing on urbanization, a policy which is also a logical result of the Soviet-type of centralized planning and growth strategy.

Sometimes the policies pursued under different economic systems yield very similar results, even though the rationale behind these policies is quite different. An example of this is support for the construction of new housing at the expense of the repair and modernization of existing housing both in the United States and in USSR. As Little and Leven point out (Chapter 13), U.S. policy has been to require lower downpayments, longer repayment terms, and, frequently, lower interest rates for new housing than for the reconstruction of existing housing; trade union policies and local building codes have also favored new housing. In the USSR and other centrally planned economies, urban housing has been provided primarily by government agencies, so downpayments, repayment terms, and interest rates have played no role and neither have trade union policies. On the other hand, there exist strong bureaucratic preferences for new investment over reconstruction, in housing as well as in other areas, which yield the same results as do the completely different policies in the United States.

VI. Concluding Comments

This paper is in the spirit of the "new comparative economic systems," where the study of economic systems is tied to economic theory, and of the "new economic theory," where instead of taking the economic system as a constant the system itself becomes one of the variables, a trend highlighted in Leonid Hurwicz's Ely Lecture (1973). As indicated earlier, the application of these new approaches to the problem of migration is even less developed than its application to other aspects of economic and social life. We only hope that this book and this chapter have contributed in some small way to furthering this type of approach.

References

Greenwood, M. J. Research on internal migration in the United States: A survey. *Journal of Economic Literature*, 1975, 13(2).

Hurwicz, L. The design of mechanisms for resource allocation. *American Economic Review*, 1973, 63(2).

Konrad, G., and I. Szelenyi. Social conflicts of underurbanization. In A. A. Brown, J. A. Licari, and E. Neuberger (Eds.), *Urban and social economics in market and planned economies*. Vol. 1; *Policy, planning and development*. New York: Praeger Publishers and University of Windsor Press, 1974.

Koopmans, T. C., and J. M. Montias. On the description and comparison of economic systems. In A. Eckstein (Ed.) *Comparison of economic systems: Theoretical and methodological approaches*. Berkeley: University of California Press, 1971.

Neuberger, E., and W. J. Duffy. *Comparative economic systems: A decision-making approach*. Boston: Allyn and Bacon, 1976.

Wiles, P. J. D. Comments on Konrad and Szeleny. In A. A. Brown, J. A. Licari, and E. Neuberger, (Eds.), *Urban and social economics in market and planned economies*. Vol. I: *Policy, planning, and development*. New York: Praeger Publishers and University of Windsor Press, 1974.

Author Index

A

Abramovitz, M., 12, *30*
Adams, W., 11, 19, 24, *30*
Agrawala, A. N., *304*
Alonso, W., 25, 28, *30,* 63, *71,* 76, 86, *88,* 140, *143,* 219, 229, *233,* 237, *254*
Anderson, D., 404, *415*
Anderson, R. J., 29, *30*
Andrzejewski, A., 317
Annable, J. E., 92, *101*
Antonijević, D., 342, *344*
Apgar, W. C., 69, *71*
Arriaga, E. E., 106, *118,* 138, *143*
Arrow, K. J., 229, *234*
Ayensu, E. S., 25, *33*

B

Bachmura, F. T., 17, 24, *30*
Bajan, K., 316
Bajić, M., 342, *344*
Baranson, J., 20, *30*
Bardhan, P. K., 47, 48, 58, *59*
Barr, J. L., 27, *30*
Baumol, W. J., 26, *30*
Beale, C. L., 24, 26, *30,* 154, *166*
Beals, R. E., 131, *134*
Becker, G. S., 427, *438*
Becker, K., 422, *439*
Beckmann, M. J., 219, 226, *234*
Bellottis, O. C., 17, *33*
Bent, D. H., 431, *439*
Berg, F., 423, *438*
Bergson, A., 303, 449, *461*
Berliner, J. S., 453, *461*
Berry, B. L., 330, *344*
Berry, R. A., 16, *30,* 42, 43, *59*
Bhagwati, J. N., *11,* 12, *30,* 40, 42, 51, 55, *59, 60,* 205

Blanco, C., 23, *30,* 64, *71*
Blau, P. M., 66, *71*
Bogišić, V., 404, *415*
Bogue, D. J., *118,* 265, *273*
Böhning, W. R., I'9, *30*
Bornstein, M., *304*
Bourne, L. S., 24, *30,* 267, *273*
Bowles, G. K., 68, *71*
Bowles, S., 65, *71*
Bowman, M. J., 24, *30*
Bradford, D. F., 25, *30*
Brainerd, C. P., *134*
Brewis, T. N., 270, *273*
Breznik, D., 337, 341, 343, *345,* 380, 383, 385, *398*
Bromke, A., *326*
Brown, A., 279, *304, 326, 479*
Brown, L., 17, *30*
Buchanan, J. M., *31*
Burgess, E. W., 215, *234*
Burghardt, A. F., *326*

C

Cameron, G. C., 272, *274*
Cebula, R. J., 12, 22, *31,* 92, 94, *101*
Chakravarty, S., 40, *59*
Chen, C.-Y., 149, 150, *166*
Chenery, H. B., 25, *31*
Cheung, S. N. S., 47, 48, *60*
Chinitz, B., 11, *30, 33, 35*
Chisholm, M., 22, *31*
Chudacoff, H. P., 61, *71*
Ciechocińska, M., 319, 321, 322, *326*
Clapham, J. H., 15, *31*
Clark, C., 11, 15, 17, 18, 19, 21, 24, *31*
Clawson, M., 24, *31*
Cohn, S., 303
Collignon, F. C., 65, *71*
Courchene, T. N., 265, *273*

481

Crowley, R. W., 256, 267, *273*
Czamanski, S., 13, 23, 25, *31*

D

Dacy, M. E., 29, *35*
Dantzig, G. B., 24, *31*
Das Gupta, A., *118*
Da Vanzo, J., 68, *71*
David, P., 189, *205*
Davis, K., 147, 157, 158, *166*
Dean, W. H., 21, *31*
Deane, P., 13, 15, 21, *31*
de Jong, G. F., *31*
Demsetz, H., 42, *60*
Dewhurst, J. F., 17, *31*
Doeringer, P. B., 419, 428, *438*
Donnelly, W. L., *31*
Drake, R. L., 238, *254*
Duchek, P., 423, *438*
Duckworth, W. D., 25, *33*
Duffy, W. J., 464, *479*
Duncan, B., 65, *71*
Duncan, O. D., 25, *31*, 65, 66, *71, 273*
Dunlop, J. T., 419, *438*
Dzienio, K., 308, 314, 316, 320, 323, *326*
Dziewonski, K., 22, 29, *31*

E

Easterlin, R. A., *134*
Eckstein, A., 287, *304, 479*
Eldridge, H. T., *118,* 130, *134*
Elias, A., 302
Elizaga, J. C., *118*
Erlich, V. S., 406, *415*
Ernst, M., 303
Evans, A. W., 28, *31*

F

Fabricant, R. A., 12, *31,* 92, *101*
Fahte, V. L., 24, 29, *31*
Fallenbuchl, Z. M., 306, 307, 308, 321, *326*
Fals, R. L., 24, 25, *31*
Featherman, D. L., 65, *71*
Fei, J. C. H., 40, *60*
Fisher, J. C., 331, 342, *345*, 379, 381, *398*
Foley, D. L., 238, *254*
Forster, M. J., 17, *33*

Frankel, S. H., 438, *438*
Frey, W. H., 143, *144*
Friedlander, D., 19, *31*
Friedly, P. H., *274*
Fuchs, V., 22, 25, *32*

G

Galpin, C. J., 13, *34*
Gaude, J., 15, *31*
George, M. V., 149, *166*
Gerschenkron, A., 287, *304*
Ginić, I., 330, *345*
Ginsberg, R., 142, *143*
Ginsbert, A., 314, *326*
Gitelman, H. M., 61, *71*
Gluščević, B., 331, *345*
Goldstein, S., 143, *144*
Gomez-Pompa, A., 25, *32*
Goodrich, C., 17, *32*
Goodstein, M. E., 13, *32*
Gorzelak, E., 316
Gosh, P., 394
Greenwood, M. J., 22, 26, *32*, 69,71, 86, *88,* 92, 94, *101,* 140, 142, *143,* 183, *205,* 382, 383, 397, *398,* 444, 446, 450, 456, 458, 461, 463, 466, *479*
Guevara, S., 25, *32*
Gupta, M. L., 24, *32*

H

Hali, O. P., 94, *101*
Halpern, J., 404, 405, 406, *415*
Hamada, K., 55, *59*
Hamilton, C. H., *118*
Hammel, E. A., 403, 404, 405, 407, 409, 410, 411, 413, *415*
Hansen, N., *234,* 263, *273*
Harris, B., 28, *32*
Harris, C. D., 18, *32*
Harris, J. R., 49, 50, 51, *60,* 193, *205*
Harrison, D., 224, *234*
Haswell, M. R., 21, *31*
Hanfe, H., 16, *32*
Hauser, P. M., *273*
Hawrylshyn, O., 382, 383, *398*
Herrick, B. H., 49, 60, 330, 332, *345*

Hertzfeld, H. R., 24, 29, *31*
Higgs, R., 13, *32*
Hirsch, W., *89*
Ho, Ping-ti, 15, *32*
Hodge, G., 25, *32*
Holt, G. E., 213, *234*
Homans, G. C., 453, *461*
Hoover, E. M., 11, 24, 28, 29, *32*
Hoselitz, B., 23, *32*
Houghton, D. H., 426, *438*
Hoyt, H., 215, *234*
Huff, D., 80, *88*
Hull, H. H., 431, *439*
Hurd, L. E., 17, *33*
Hurwicz, L., 479, *479*

I

Ichimura, S., 12, *32*
Isard, W., 11, *32*

J

Jackson, J. A., *461*
Janev, D., 331, *345*
Janzen, D. H., 25, *32*
Jedruszczak, H., 314, *326*
Jensen, M. C., 230, *234*
Johnson, G., 41, *60*
Johnson, H. M., 453, *461*

K

Kain, J. F., 224, *234*
Kalbach, W., 262, 265, *273*
Kelejian, H. J., 25, *30*
Kennedy, R. E., 154, *166*
Kerr, C., 419, *438*
Kilby, P., 422, *438*
Klaussen, T. A., 22, *32*
Kolbusz, F., 316
Konrad, G., 284, 292, 296, *304,* 477, *479*
Koopmans, T. C., 226, *234,* 474, *479*
Koshel, P., 65, *71*
Kovačević, Lj., 405
Krgović, T., 342, *345*
Krugman, P., 55, *60, 205*
Kulski, J. E., 24, *32*
Kumar, J., 153, *166*
Kuznets, S., 12, 13, 15, 16, 17, 22, 23, *32,*
    134, 137, *143,* 394

L

Laber, G., 96, *101*
Lansing, J. B., 63, 64, 66, 67, 68, 70, *71, 72*
Lasuen, J., 25, *32*
Latuch, M., 314, 315, *326*
Lave, L. B., 24, 25, *33*
Lee, E. S., 62, *72,* 124, *134,* 141, *144,* 265,
    273, 447, 448, 459, *461*
Leven, C. L., 11, 27, *30, 33, 35*
Levy, M. B., 92, 94, *101, 134*
Lewis, W. A., 39, 40, *60*
Lianos, T. P., 96, *101*
Licari, J. A., 94, *101, 326, 479*
Lincoln, G. A., 24, *33*
Little, F. M. D., 437, *438*
Little, J. T., 217, 224, 228, *234*
Long, W. H., 11, *33*
Lot, F., 15, *33*
Lowry, I. S., 63, 64, *72,* 81, *88,* 215, *234*
Lucas, R. E. B., 56, *60,* 193, 204, *205*
Lutovac, M., 334, 342, *345*
Lyon, D. W., 238, *254*

M

Magoulas, G., *205*
Make, W. R., 25, *33*
Malzberg, B., 448, *461*
Mandelker, D. R., 233, *234*
Marer, P., 279, *304*
Marković, P., 343, *345*
Marsden, K., 20, *33*
Marshall, A., 11, *33,* 450, *461*
Marx, K., 13, *33*
Mathur, V. K., 13, *33*
Mazek, W. F., 64, *72*
McCloskey, D. N., 42, *60*
McKenzie, R. D., 215, *234*
McVey, W., 262, 265, *273*
Medrich, E., 237, *254*
Medvedkov, Y., 24, *33*
Meggers, B. J., 25, *33*
Melichar, E., 431, *438*
Mera, K., 25, 28, *33*
Miller, A. R., *134*
Miller, E., 64, *72*

Mills, E. S., 224, *234*
Milojević, M. S., 405
Montias, J. M., 287, *304*, 474, *479*
Moore, W. E., *143*, 287, *304*
Morgan, J. N., 68, *71*
Morrison, P. A., 26, *33*, 64, 65, 68, *72*, 137, 138, 139, *144*, 262, 268, *274*
Moses, L. N., 24, 25, *31*, *134*
Mueller, E., 63, 64, 66, 67, 70, *72*
Musgrove, F., 443, 444, 451, 455, 459, 460, *461*
Muth, R. F., 56, *60*, 69, *72*, 86, *89*, 141, *144*, 219, *234*
Myers, G. C., 19, *33*
Myers, P., 284, 285, 291, 302, 303, *304*
Myers, R. G., 24, *30*

N

Nagy, E. S., *119*
Nelson, M., 25, *33*
Nelson, P., 12, *33*, 384, *399*
Netzer, D., 219, *234*
Neuberger, E., *304*, *326*, 464, *479*
Neutze, G. M., 267, *274*
Newberry, D. M. G., 47, 48, *60*
Nie, N., 431, *439*
Nielsen, J., 20, *33*
Nowakowski, S., 314, *326*

O

Oates, W. E., 26, *30*
Odum, E. P., 25, *33*
Ofer, G., 278, 284, 288, 289, 295, 296, 303, *304*
Ohlin, B., 20, *33*
Oi, W., 427, *439*
Oka, I. N., 17, *33*
Olsson, G., 139, *144*
Olvey, L. D., 64, 69, 70, *72*
Opallo, M., 308, 314, 320, *326*
Owen, W., 24, *33*

P

Pack, J. R., 12, *33*, 92, *101*
Padowicz, W., 321, 323, *326*

Pantić, D., 384, 392, *399*
Park, R. E., 215, *234*
Parrish, W. L., 12, 16, *33*
Parsons, T., 451, *461*
Perloff, H., 29, *33*
Perlman, M., 11, *30*, *33*, 35
Peschel, K., *205*
Peterson, W., 137, *144*
Petrović, R., 395, *399*
Philpott, S. B., 460, *461*
Pierson, G. W., 61, *72*
Pimental, D., 17, 22, *33*
Piore, M. J., 419, 421, 425, 428, *438*, *439*
Plato, 15, *34*
Plummer, A., 11, *34*
Potgieter, F. J., 421, *439*
Power, E., 15, *31*
Pred, A. R., 24, *34*
Preston, L. E., 183, *205*
Price, D. O., 65, *72*
Puljiz, V., 334, *345*

R

Radovanović, M., 341, *345*
Rajkiewicz, A., 314, *327*
Ranis, G., 11, 24, *34*, 40, *60*
Rasmussen, T. E., 24, *34*
Ravenstein, E. G., 332, *345*
Ray, D. M., 271, *274*
Reder, M. W., 20, *34*
Redford, A., 332, *345*
Rees, P. H., 75, *89*
Reiner, T. A., 11, *32*
Relles, D., 137, 138, *144*
Renaud, M., *205*
Renshaw, V., 64, *72*, 189, *205*, 383, *399*
Richardson, H. W., 29, *34*, 272, *274*
Ridker, R. G., 25, *34*
Riew, J., 12, 22, *34*
Robbins, L., 445, *461*
Rodwin, L., 29, *34*, 272, *274*
Rogers, A., 75, *89*
Rosenstein-Rodan, P. N., 287, *304*
Ross, A. M., 419, *439*
Roszczypala, Y., 316
Rowland, D. T., 154, *166*
Rubin, E., 137, *143*
Ruff, D. G., 422, *439*

S

Savanović, H., 405
Sahota, G. S., 131, *134*
Samuelson, P. A., 38, *60*
Sauvy, A., 162, *166,* 256, *274*
Schäuble, R., 423, *439*
Schultz, T. P., 92, *101*
Schwartz, A., 56, *60*
Secomski, K., *327*
Sen, A. K., 42, 43, 44, *60*
Sentić, M., 334, 336, *345*
Shaw, R. P., 12, *34*
Shefer, D., 25, *34*
Sholes, O. D., 17, *33*
Siegel, J. S., *118*
Silznick, P., 435, *439*
Simon, H. A., 16, *34,* , *461*
Singh, S. P., *304*
Sjaastad, L. A., 12, 24, *34,* 56, *60,* 131, *134,*
   141, *144*
Smelser, N. J., 451, *461*
Smith, A., 13, 21, *34,* 39, 59, *60*
Smith, T. L., 19, *34*
Soligo, R., 16, *30,* 42, 43, *59*
Somermeyer, W. H., 13, *34*
Songre, A., 15, *34*
Sorokin, P. A., 13, *34*
Spandau, A., 422, 437, *439*
Speare, A., 143, *144*
Spencer, R. F., *461*
Spengler, J. J., 12, 20, *34,* 255, 262, *274*
Srinivasan, T. N., 47, 48, 51, *59,* 60
Sternberg, M. J., 20, *34*
Stigler, G., 27, *34*
Stiglitz, J. E., 41, 42, 44, 46, 48, 49, 51, 53,
   56, 57, *60*
Stojanović, Lj., 405
Stojković, S., 336, *345*
Stolnitz, G., 75, *89*
Stone, L. O., *119,* 265, *274*
Stone, R., 75, *89*
Streit, M. P., 25, *34*
Strong, J. E., *326*
Stouffer, S. A., 12, *34*
Struzek, B., 316
Sundquist, J. L., 267, 270, 271, 272, *274*
Suzuki, K., 22, 26, *34*
Svennilson, I., 17, 20, *34*
Szelenzyi, I., 284, 292, 296, *304,* 477, *479*

T

Taeuber, C. M., 213, *234*
Taeuber, I. B., 18, *35*
Tapinos, G., 19, *35*
Taylor, L., 25, *31*
Thernstrom, S., 61, *72*
Thomas, B., 12, 15, 19, 20, *34, 35*
Thomas, D. S., 13, 15, 20, 22, 23, *32, 35,*
   122, 130, *134,* 152, 394
Thompson, W. R., 25, 29, *35*
Thucydides, 15 *35*
Tisdell, C. A., 256, *274*
Todaro, M. P., 49, 50, 51, 55, *60,* 193, *205*
Todorovic, G., 343, *345*
Trott, C. E., 12, *35*

U

Ullman, E. L., 22, 27, 28, 29, *35*

V

Vázquez, C., 25, *32*
Vedder, R. K., 12, 22, *31,* 92, 94, *101*
Vogelnik, D., 342, *345*
Vollmer, H., 435, *439*
von Böventer, E., 25, *35*

W

Wadehn, M., *205*
Wadycki, W. J., 92, 94, *101*
Ward, B., 13, 20, *35*
Warner, S. B., 213, *234*
Warntz, W., 11, *35*
Warriner, D., 18, *35*
Weber, A. F., 16, *35*
Weinberg, A. A., 452, *461*
Weitzman, M. L., 42, *60*
Welpa, B., 308, 314, 320, *326*
Wertheimer, R. F., 68, *72*
Whitelaw, W. E., 41, *60*
Whitman, M. V. N., 28, *35*
Whitman, R. J., 17, *33*
Whitton, J. P., *274*

Wiles, P. J. D., 477, *479*
Williamson, J. G., 23, *35*
Wilson, A. G., 75, 82, *89*
Wilson, F., 421, *439*
Wingo, L., 29, *33*
Wolpert, J., 12, *35,* 143, *144,* 257, *274*
Wong, C. K., 25, *32*
Woods, P. D., *274*
Woytinsky, E. S., 15, 17, *35*
Woytinsky, W. S., 15, 17, *35*
Wrigley, E. A., 15, *35*
Wunsch, G., *119*
Wysocki, Z., 314, *327*

Y

Yamada, H., 22, *35*
Yap, L. Y. L., 183, *205*
Yarbrough, C., 404, 410, 411, 413, *415*
Yeates, M., 267, *274*
Ynzenga, B. A., 238, *254*

Z

Zachariah, K. C., 131, 133, *134,* 138, *144*
Zekoński, Z., 314, *327*
Zimmerman, C. C., 13, *34*
Zitter, M., *119*

Subject Index

A

Acephalous, 27
Administrative distance, 468
  unit, 467–468
Advanced countries, rural depopulation,
  153–156
Africa, 51, 160
  Central, 160
  North, 160
  South, 7, 417–439
Age, 140
  distribution, 239, 241, 242, 249–250
  structure, rural, 158, 159
  white, 248
Aged persons, 165
Agglomeration, 16, 23, 25, 306
Agrarian states, 148, 149, 150, 156
Agricultural
  economy, 379
  land, 262, 388
  produce, 286
  region, 147, 150, 158, 165
  sector, decline, 258
Agriculturalist output, 16, 17
Agriculture, 15, 19, 37, 39, 40, 41, 44, 46,
  48, 58, 151, 153, 158, 163, 311, 313,
  314, 321, 322, 402
  capital–labor ratio, 279
  collectivization, 157, 306, 308, 318, 325
  growth of, 16
  hand, 160
  marginal productivity, 51
  mechanization, 63
  policy, 306
  products, 16
  residual employment, 50
Air pollution, 92, 93, 94, 96, 97, 99
Air quality, 197
Alabama, 155
Albanian, 392
Alienation, 78

Alonso–Muth–Beckman model, 219, 460
Alonso, demographic model, 76–79
Altruism, 41
Amenities, 26–29
American city, density gradient, 223–224
American policy, 232, 233
American system, 211, 218
Analysis method, cohort, 130, 131
  econometric, 131
Apartheid, 7, see also South Africa
Arizona, 164
Arkansas, 148, 155
Asia, 160
Asset position, 200
Assimilation problems, 20
Australia, 154
  Victoria, 154
Automobile, 95, 232
  ownership, 213, 231
  technology, 223

B

Baltimore, 209, 236
Barrier, 184
Beaten path syndrome, 64–65, 470
Beckman model, 219–224
Belgrade, 330, 331, 339, 343, 344, 383, 392
  County, 402
  ethnic selectivity, 394–396
  migrant registry, 394, 395
  Serbs vs. non-Serbs, 395, 396
  urbanization, 401
  worker, 404
  occupational mobility, 403
Benefit, migrant view, 167–182
  private, 471
  social, 471, 473
Berlin Wall, 352, 353, 363, 376, 465
  prewall period, 360
  postwall period, 360, 363

Birth, 123, 153, 154, 159, 163
  control, 262
  migrant, 58
  place, migration estimates, 109–112, 113,
    115, 116, 117
  rate, 76, 78, 95, 98, 105, 106, 107, 161,
    163, 262
  rural, 58, 159
  United States, 77, 246, 250, 254
  West Berlin, 350
Blacks, 165
Bombay, 131, 132
Bosnia, Yugoslavia, 380, 381, 382, 384, 388,
  392, 393, 402
Boston, Massachusetts, 236
Brain drain, 12
Brazil, 131, 157, 287, 330
Britain, 272
Budget, local static, 218, 219
Buffalo, New York, 236
Building code, local, 232, 478
Bulgaria, 283, 287, 290–291, 292, 294, 324,
  325
  migration pace, 325

C

California, 26, 115, 116, 164, 238
  domestic migration, 240
  metropolitan structure, 253
  San Jose, 5, 64, 236, 237–243, 253
  SMSA, 239
Canada, 148, 258–265
  foreign investment policy, 271
  French population, 398
    growth rate, 258
    migration pattern, 263
    new community policy, 271
    regional development program, 270–271
  urban migration,
    parameters, 264
Capital, 20, 23, 38, 58, 59, 219
  allocation, 470
  formation, 18
  human, 11, 17, 19, 24
  immobility, 229
  investment, private, 270

  loss, 229, 230, 232
  market, 57, 212
  physical, 17, 19
  regional distribution, 463
  social overhead, 343
  urban, 329, 342
Career
  choice, 471
  profile, 187, 191, 192
  tree, 187, 188, 466
Census, 137, 138, 142, 170, 369, 404
  data, 121–134, 138
    age–sex, 121, 123, 124, 128, 129, 130,
      133
    birthplace, 125, 126, 1130, 131, 132,
      133
    residency duration, 125, 126, 127, 128,
      131, 133
    residency origin, 125, 126
    survival ratio, 124, 132, 133
  information, 105–109, 110, 111, 112, 113,
    114, 115, 116, 117, 336, 341
  Serbian 1863, 404, 405
Central business district (CBD), 219, 220,
  221, 222, 223
Chicago, Illinois, 236
  survey, 170–177
Children, 58, 108, 112, 113, 159
Chile, 157, 330, 332
  Santiago, 330
China, 14
Cincinnati, Ohio, 236
Citizen, disadvantaged, 250–251, 253
City, 26, 27, 28, 29, 332, 333, 334, 335, 336,
  337, 338, 339, 343, 344
  central, 209, 213, 222, 235, 253
    population decline, 236, 253
  correlates of size, 257, 266
  density, 213
  growth, 349
  input–output system, 256
  parasitic, 23
  size, 27, 28
    optimum, 255–258
  small, 78
  structure, 27
Cleveland, Ohio, 236
Cohort, birth, 368
  effect of migration, 368
  rates of increase, 368–374

Collectivization, Poland, 308, 313, 325
Colombia, 330
Commodity, 195, 198
  availability, 195, 196
  housing, 211
  private, 195, 197
  public, 195
Communal economy, 41, 43, 44, 46
  land, 46
  membership, 41, 43
  outmigrant, 41
Communication, 22, 23, 25, 26, 136
  interracial, 422, 423
  intraracial, 422, 423
Community, 23
  service, 173
Commuting, 315, 320–321, 322, 323, 329,
    342, 344, 402, 477
  cost, benefit, 342
  rural–urban, 307, 329, 341
Competition, 26
Competitor, monopolistic, 52, 53, 54
Computopia, 475
Congestion, 25
Consumer
  goods, 58, 59
  price, 194
Control, administrative, 469, 476
Correlates of size, city, 257, 266
Cost
  construction, 293
  coordination, 256
  direct, 68
  economic, 140, 467
  employment, 426–427
  goods and services, 212
  government, 28
  hiring, 51, 52
  information, 68, 475
  migrant view, 167–182
  migration, 56, 476
  modernization, 232
  movement, 139, 141
  moving, 469
  new construction, 232
  opportunity, 68, 168
  psychic, 68, 140, 450, 451, 453, 467, 476
  public service, 262
  relocation, 229
  repair, 232

  skill acquisition, 419
  social, 476
  technology, 236
  training, 428
  transfer, 383
  transition, 197
  transportation, 140, 212, 213, 219, 236,
    450, 458, 465, 477
  travel, 221, 412
  turnover, 52, 53
  urban access, 212
  urbanization, 279, 289, 293, 294
Cost–benefit
  analyses, 141
  matrix, 169, 170
  ratio, 27, 29
Cost of living adjustment, 196, 197
  indices, 194, 195, 197
Countries, high-fertility, 19
Countries, less developed, 193
Cousin, 408, 409, 413
Croatia, Yugoslavia, 380, 381, 392, 402
Cross-national comparability, 138
Cultural paroxysm, 78, 80
Culture, 381, 392
  Serbian, 406
Czechoslovakia, 283, 284, 285, 288, 289,
    323, 324
  labor force structure, 285
  migration rate, 325
  urbanization level, 285

D

Data
  census, 121–134, 138
  historical, 61, 62
Death rate, 76, 105, 106, 110, 123, 153, 163,
    286
  Canada, 262
  United States, 246, 250, 254
  West Berlin, 350
Decentralization, industrial, 236
Decision making, centralized, 465, 467, 475
  decentralized, 467
  structure, 464, 467–468, 476
Decollectivization, 310, 318, 319
Delaware, 164

Demographic accounting, 75–89
  Alonso model, 76–79
  characteristics, 121, 128, 133, 444, 445
    East European, 277, 278
    San Jose, Calif., 253
  distortion, 323
  factors, 91, 93, 94, 96, 101
  feature, 148
  model, 94
  multiplier, 76
  regions, 76, 77
  test, 138
  trends, 258–262
    fertility, 262–263
  variable, 77–79, 80, 81, 82, 85, 87, 92, 139
Density, 131
Department of Regional Economic Expansion (DREE), 270
Depopulation, 161
  rural, 343
    age structure, 158–159
  small communities, 24
  underdeveloped countries, 156–158
Depressions, 78
Destination
  pulling power, 80
  region of, 473
Detroit, Michigan, 236
Development
  decentralized, 331
  interactions, 2–3
  migration and labor transfer, 340–344
  strategy, 478
    Gierek's, 321
  socio-economic, 17
Differential, earning, 194–195
  job, 195
  opportunity, 195
  negative consequence, 197
Discrimination, 171
  pattern, information, 203–204
Dispersion, 22
Displacement, 22
  interstate, 22
Distance, 131, 140, 466–467
  economic, 140
  social, 140
  variable, 388
Distribution
  city, 23
  town, 23

Dual-occupational group (worker–farmer) 307, 315, 316, 320, 322, 323

E

Earning, 41, 44
  beginning, 194
  buying power, 194
  capacity, 132
  lifetime, 194, 466
    formulation, 191
  psychic, 57
East European countries, 157, 278–296, 305, 344
  socialist, 323, 325
  demographic characteristics, 277, 278
  interwar period, 287
  market economies compared, 280–289
  migration restriction, 268–269
East Germany, 283, 284, 285, 289
East north central states, 116, 117
East south central states, 116, 117
Economic
  activity, gravitational orientation, 330
  change, 402–404
  cycle, 12
    20 year cycle, 12
  development, 403
    effect of ethnic barrier, 397, 398
    effect of migration, 397
    mode, 329, 331, 338
  efficiency, 471
  equilibrium, city, 257
  factors, 91, 93, 94, 96, 97, 101
  gain hypothesis, 332
  growth, 321
    national, 69
  need, 62
  pull, 63
  stagnation, 86
  system, 463, 464–467
  variables, 80
Economies
  agglomeration, 256
  of decline
    growth, 143
    scale, 23, 25, 162, 279
  developed, 183, 184
  market, 277, 279, 280–289, 464, 478
    East European economies compared, 280–289

modern, 62
planned, 463, 464, 469, 470, 478
peasant, 39, 42
rural, 39
undeveloped, 183, 184
urban scale, 195
Economy
agricultural, 306, 379
closed, 59
communal, 41, 54
cost, 131
decline, 166
depressed, 63, 64
depression, 130, 131
expansion, 162
healthy, 63, 64
individualistic, 41, 44, 45, 46, 58
industrial, 137, 379
sector, 306
mixed, 41–42, 54
prosperity, 130, 131
returns, 131
shifts, 78
wage–labor, 48
welfare, 449, 451, 457
Education, 76, 80, 87, 128, 129, 131, 132,
140, 143, 197, 388, 421–422, 430,
431, 433, 434, 435, 436
benefit, 173
Egypt, 157
Electricity, 197
Emigration, 16, 19
rate, 153
Employee, black, 434
Employment, 19, 28, 50, 85, 86, 92, 94, 98,
99, 171, 172, 173, 175, 182, 187, 305
cost, 51, 52
distribution, 23
growth, 69, 98
layoff, 171
high-wage areas, 39
length of, 431, 433, 435
low-wage areas, 39
migrant, 12, 26
opportunity, 388, 456, 458, 465
pattern, South Africa, 417, 422, 423
Poland, 311, 312, 313
outside agriculture, 313, 314, 318, 319,
320, 321
outside forestry, 313, 314, 318, 319,
320, 321

rate, 49
scale, 209
time to find work, 178, 179, 181
urban, 16, 50, 51, 323
Energy, 24, 25
conservation, 24
cost, 24
England, 15
migration, 332
Entrepreneur, 21, 24, 69, 151, 465
Enumeration
birthplace, 109–112, 113, 115, 116, 117,
125, 126
census, 105–119
residency, 112–114, 116, 125, 126, 127,
128
Environment, 197, 256
air quality, 197
arable land, 24
biospheric, 23, 29
changes in, 12
climate, 24, 76, 77, 80, 182
condition of, 23, 26
congestion, 197
mineral, 24
natural, 262
objective characteristic, 168
social, 171, 172
socioeconomic, 11, 12
topography, 24
tropical areas, 25
water, 24, 197
Environmental factors, 91, 93, 94, 96, 98,
99, 101
Equilibration, type, 13
Estados, agrarian, 149, 150
Ethnic
affinity, 382, 383, 384, 385, 389–394, 392,
393, 394, 396, 397, 398
push, 384
group, 228
selectivity
Belgrade, 394–396
Kuznets-Thomas, 380, 394, 397
variable, 470
Ethnicity
migration barrier in Yugoslavia, 379–399
multifaceted character in Yugoslavia, 379
379
Ethnography, 404, 405
Euler's theorem, 42

Europe, 15, 16, 19, 20, 272, 286, 287
  medieval, 15
  population, 15, 16
  regional development program, 270, 271
European Common Market, 78
European Russia, 154
Exodus, 162, 165
  occupational, 151
  rural, 165
  rate, 157
  small town, 314
  U.S. central city, 257
  white, 235
Export, 16
Expressway, 224, 231
Externalities, 257–258, 266, 472, 473, 474

F

Factor price equalization, 38–39
Family, 213
  central city median income, 211
  communal joint, 404
  composition, 211, 213
  contact, 172, 173, 174, 179, 182
  estate, 410
  farm, 40
  high-income, 251
  interaction, 454
  low-income, 251, 262
  life, 402, 404, 406, 410, 415
    ideology, 406
  nuclear, 404
  relocation, 231
  resource, 179
Famine, 161, 162
Farm, 322
  family, 40
Farmer, 165, 320
Fertility, 19, 58, 62, 63, 76, 237, 250, 262
  decline, 19, 154, 155, 156, 157, 159
  rates, age-specific, 369, 374
    United States, 237
  ratio, 155
  rural, 153, 154, 155, 156, 157, 159, 160,
    349
  urban, 155, 156, 349
  West Berlin, 350
  white, 154, 155

Financial
  incentive, 271–272
  institution, 230
Finland
  migratory rate, 324, 325
  planning controls, 267
Fishing, 158, 163, 402
Florida, 115, 116, 164
Foreign investment policy, 268
  Canada, 271
Forestry, 158, 163
France, 15, 162, 272
  planning controls, 267
Freeway technology, 213
Function
  Benthamite welfare, 43
  household utility, 220, 221, 226
  housing production, 221
  migration, 55–56
  production, 47
  relational, 80, 84, 87
  Sen's production, 44, 45
  utility, 42, 43, 44, 220, 221, 226
  well-being, 256, 449

G

Geographic coordinates, 76
  subdivision, 131
Geopolitical factor, 286
German Democratic Republic (GDR), 323,
  324, 325
Germany, migration East–West, 465
Ghana, 131
GNP, 277, 278, 280, 292
  per capita, 280, 283, 284
  rates of growth, 278
  Yugoslavia, 382
Goods, allocation, 470
Government,
  agency dispersal, 270, 272
  central city, 211
  health standard, 94
    emission control standards, 96
  incentive, 476
  information agency, 475
  intervention, 87
  local, 211, 213
  policy, 464, 465
    regional, 465, 476–478

procurement preference, 272
  regulation, 165
Grant-in-aid programs, 211
Greece, 14
Gross national product, *see* GNP
Gross regional product, 92
Growth center,
  per capita, 15
  policies, 78
  strategy, 272

H

Hamburg, migration pattern, 351, 355, 356,
  357, 358
  age structure, 363–365
Harris and Todaro model, 49–51, 53, 193,
  194
Health care, 172, 197
Herzegovina, Yugoslavia, 381, 382, 393
Heteroethnic climate, 392
  effect, 383
Home, single-family, 235
Homeostatic mechanism, 257
Homoethnic climate effect, 383, 384
Household
  high-income, 219, 227
  income, 219, 222
  low-income, 219, 226, 227, 228, 229
  middle-income, 226, 227, 228
  nuclear structure, 404, 406
  organization, 404
  Serbian, 404, 405
    characteristics, 405
    composition, 405, 406
  urban, 406
  utility function, 220, 221, 226
Housing, 139, 196–197, 306, 473
  Act, 1949, 232
  asset value, 230
  choice, 212
  commodity, 211
  construction, 342
  cost, 472
  demand, 211, 212, 219, 221, 222, 224, 253
  finance, 232
  high access, 213
  investment, 294–295, 321, 478
  kind, 213

low density, 213
  market, 211, 227, 229, 251–252
  policy, 228, 232
  price, 219, 221, 222, 223, 225, 228, 232
  production function, 221
  public, 197, 224
  rationing, 468
  shortage, 317, 318, 319, 321, 322, 323,
    325, 342, 343
  single-family, 232
  space, 212
  spatial pattern, 211, 218, 220
  stock, 213, 215
  supply, 212, 220, 221
  urban, 197, 466, 478
  value, 215
    age effect, 215
    St. Louis, 215
Houston, Texas, 233
Human capital, 56–57, 190–191, 199, 445
Hungary, 157, 283, 287, 288, 290–291, 292,
  293, 294, 295, 323, 324
  ethnic distance, 392
  migration rate, 324, 325
  urbanization, 289
Hypermobility, 5, 459
  San Jose, 5

I

Idaho, 155
Illinois, 243
  Madison county, 243
  St. Clair county, 243
Immigrant, 20, 62, 127, 133
  employers of, 20
  foreign, 238, 263, 268
Immigration, 16, 137, 141, 263, 402
  Belgrade, 402
  Canadian, 263
Import, 16
Incentive, 48
  material, 306
  to quit, 53
  work-effort, 48
Income, 13, 15, 16, 43, 44, 45, 58, 64, 67,
  68, 76, 77, 78, 87, 94, 129, 131, 139,

151, 187, 189, 211, 212, 213, 215,
    218, 219, 231, 233, 235, 236, 388
aggregate, 219, 222, 380
city, 221, 223
SMSA, 222
benefit calculation, 191
communal, 41
differential, real, 194–195
distribution, 218, 219, 222
equality, 305, 306
family, 211, 231
flow, 187
growth, 16, 26, 141, 221
    rate, 222, 431, 433, 434, 435, 436
household, 219, 222, 421
individual, 42
interregional distribution, 79
levels, 141
lifetime, 187, 191
maximization, 41–42
median city family, 251
national, 460
neoclassical theory, 428
opportunity, 187, 188, 192
outside agriculture, 314, 315, 320, 322
per capita, 163, 380, 388, 448
    national, 382, 383
personal, 92, 98
propensity to move, 13
prospect, 188, 189, 190, 196
SMSA, 251
structure, black, 435, 436
transport cost dynamic, 219–225
India, 15, 122, 125, 127, 128, 132, 157, 287
Indicators, correlates of city size, 257, 266
Individualistic economy, 41, 44, 45, 46, 58
Industrial
    countries, 107
        rural depopulation, 153–156
    economy, 379
    growth, 335
    incentive program, 268, 270
    location policy, 268–269
    organization, 23, 25
    training, 424–426, 428, 430, 431, 433, 434,
        435, 436, 437
Industrialization, 6, 15, 16, 19, 258, 331,
    344, 401, 406, 412
    kinship, affect on, 412
    node, 331, 344

Poland, 307, 308, 310, 311, 325
    pace, 313, 318
    policy, 322
    socialist strategy, 277, 288, 293
        East European, 287
        Soviet-type policy, 306
Industry, 40, 128, 129, 209, 380
    Aerospace, 237
    Agriculture, 151, see also Agriculture
    capital–labor ratio, 279, 289
    decentralization, 236
    investment, 306
    marginal productivity, 51
    service, 237
    socialist construction, 294, 295
    transport-sensitive, 24
Information,
    agency, central, 476
    centralized, 470, 475
    media, 203
    discrimination pattern, 203–204
    structure, 464, 469–470
    system, centralized, 476
Infrastructure, 305, 402, 453
    housing, 307
    improvement, 268, 270, 271
    investment, 279, 292
    rural, 306
    services, 472
    urban, 306, 307, 319, 477, 478
Inmigrant, 330, 335, 336, 337, 340, 452, 458
    Belgrade, 394
    low income, 215
    registration, 339
    visa requirement, 344
    West Berlin, 352, 354
        marital status, 366, 367
Inmigration, 96, 98, 100, 104, 106, 107, 110,
    114, 115, 116, 117, 237, 238, 242,
    243, 333, 334, 466
    black, 252
    flow, 91
    foreign born, 116
    Hamburg, 355, 356
        age–sex structure, 358, 363, 365
    rate, 114
    West Berlin, 351, 352, 353, 355
        age–sex structure, 351, 358, 359, 360,
        361, 365
Input–output system, city, 256

Insurance, informal, 41
Interdependency, 472, 473–474
Interregional migration, regression analysis, 382–394
Intercensal period, 107, 110, 111, 116, 130, 133
Intercensus estimate, 209
Interest rate, mortgage, 230
Inter-republic migration, 381, 382
Internal migration, comparative analysis, 1–8
Interurban balance, 13
Interurban network, 23
Interwar period, East European, 287
Institutional benefit, 173, 181
Investment, 19
   allocation, 465, 477
   communal services, 477
   government policy, 317, 318
   housing, 321, 322, 473, 477
   industry, 306, 473
   productive, 307
   rate, 467
   skill, 428, 429
   socialist sector, 294, 295
      infrastructure, 279, 292
      nonproductive, 294, 295
      productive, 294, 295
   trade, 473
Iowa, 155
Ireland, 153, 154
   famine, 78

J

Japan, 18, 22, 121, 160, 161
Job Advancement, time profile, 192
Job
   choice, 187, 188
   market, 187, 200
   opportunity, 476
   prospect, 187–194, 200
      destination size, 190
      human capital, 190–191
      job sampling and variance, 189–190
      lifetime earnings, 191–192
      risk and active choice, 187–188
      search and experience, 188–189
      unemployment, 193–194
      wage rates versus earnings, 192–193
      training, 197

K

Kansas, 148, 155
Kansas City, 209
Kansas City SMSA, 243
Kinship system
   male-centered, 406, 407, 408, 409, 410
   migration effect, 401–415
   Serbian, 406, 407, 408, 409, 410, 411
      agnatic, 406, 407, 414
      cousin, 408, 409, 413
      traditional ideology, 406, 409, 410
Kinship variable, 470
Kinsmen,
   contact, 410, 411, 412, 413
   effect of industrialization, 412, 414
   effect of urbanization, 412, 414
   preference, 413
Kosmet, ethnic distance, 392, 393

L

Land
   reform, 287
   rented, 41, 42, 44, 47
   rural, 212
   sharecropped, 47
   use, 266
      control, 232–233, 267
Landed proletariat, 341, 342, 343, 344
Landlord, 46, 47, 48
Language, 379, 380, 381, 392
   new, 199
Latin America, 157, 329, 330
Laws of migration, Ravenstein, 6, 329, 330, 332–336
Legislation, minimum wage, 50
Leisure, 42, 44, 45, 46, 57, 58, 193, 219, 220
Less developed countries (LDC), 39, 49, 54, 193, 196–197, 233
Lewis' migration rule, 39, 46
Life cycle effect, 211, 218
Life style, urban characteristic, 195–196
Life table, 107, 124, 374
   survivor ratios, 374
   West Berlin, 369

Lifetime earning
  differential, 198
  formulation, 191
Loan payments, 41
Labor
  allocation, 466
  competition, 192, 193
  cost, 25
  demand, 63, 263
  force, 13, 68, 70, 95, 139, 148, 158, 162,
    165, 262
    age, 430, 431
    agricultural, 15, 16, 17, 18, 40, 45, 151,
      152, 153, 154, 156, 157, 158, 277,
      278, 280, 287, 307, 323, 340, 341, 426
    allocation, 37, 43, 54, 58
    American, 22
    black South African, 417–439
    blue collar, 222
    children, 58
    decline, 152, 153, 154, 157
    earnings, 66, 67, 68
    educated, 70
    elastically supplied, 42
    farm, 63, 151
    homogeneous man-hours, 43–44
    household service workers, 23
    industrial, 23, 40, 344, 402, 424–426
    interoccupational distribution, 21
    manufacturing, 277
    migrant, 420, 426, 427, 430, 431, 434,
      436, 437
    nonagricultural, 17, 18, 340, 341
    occupation distribution, Yugoslavia,
      340
    output, 26
    overaged, 70
    participation rate, 382, 383, 389
    productivity, 70
    ratio, 314
    reduction, 151
    resident, 420, 430, 431, 434, 436
    rural, 39, 41, 44, 45, 58, 63
    rural–urban, 38, 39
    seasonal, 44–46, 58
    size, 52
    skill acquisition, 424–426, 428, 430,
      431, 433, 434, 435, 436, 437
    skilled, 65, 70
    socioeconomic data, 419–422

  structure, Socialist countries, 282, 288,
    284, 285
  turnover, 427, 428, 429, 434, 435
  undereducated, 70
  underskilled, 70
  urban, 41, 44, 45, 49
  wage, 38, 39, 41, 42, 54, 55, 57
  white collar, 222
  young, 70
    low-cost, 163
  marginal productivity, 39, 42, 44, 45, 46,
    47, 48, 51
  market, 91, 92, 94, 96
    competitive, 418, 419, 428
    demand, 52, 53
    dual, 7
    external, 418, 419, 428, 429, 434
    internal, 417, 418, 419, 428, 433, 434
    San Jose, 243
    South Africa, 417–439
  maximization of output, 38, 40, 42, 44,
    45, 46, 47, 51, 53, 54
  mobility, 47, 182, 476, 478
  product, marginal, 426, 427, 428
  productivity, 44
  regional allocation, 463, 464
  surplus, 86, 160
  unskilled, 392
  turnover model, 51–54
Laissez-faire, 54
Land, 41, 42, 44, 47
  ownership, 405
Locational social capital, 199
Los Angeles, 238
  comparative forecast, 1971–1980, 98–100
  county, 218
  metropolitan area, 91, 94–100, 101
  model linkages, 94–96
  simulation result, 96–98
  Watts community, 453

M

Macedonia, Yugoslavia, 380, 381, 397
Macro aspects, 17–20
Manitoba, 149
Manpower, 19
  development-training program, 268
  diversified, 23

Manufacturing, 37, 44, 46, 49, 58, 277
wage, 49
Marital status, 128
Market basket
characteristic, 194
destination, 194
origin, 194
Market
economies, 280–289, 292
East European economies compared, 280–289
system, 469
free, 472
perfectly competitive, 475
value, decline, 229
Maryland, 164
Mental illness, 448
Methodology, 3
Metropolitan area, 63, 64, 94, 140, 151, 190, 209, 231, 235, 237
Canada, 263
Pittsburgh, 209
St. Louis, 212, 224
dispersal, 5
labor market, 63
outmigration, 63, 64
Mexico, 157
Michigan, 164
Micro aspects, 20–21
Microeconomic, 450
Middle Atlantic states, 116, 117
Migrant, 137, 184–185, 198
age–sex structure, 358–366
behavior, 137, 138, 139, 140, 141, 142, 168, 170, 182
black, 177, 179, 426
characteristic, 104, 127–129
age–sex distribution, 128, 129, 130
cross-tabulation, 128, 131, 133
children, 459
cross-classification, 121, 122, 128, 131, 133
decision, 142
demographic behavior, 153
demographic structure, age–sex, 351
enumeration, 108–117
employed, 26, 138
female, 171, 172, 176, 177
foreign, 137
help given, 174, 178, 180, 181

high-income, 141
individualistic, 49
internal, 103, 104
labor, 19
low-income, 141
male, 171, 172, 173, 174, 176, 177, 178–179
money resource, 173–174, 178, 179
motivations, 104
pool, 76, 81, 85, 85, 86, 87–88
professional, 140
remittances, 11
residency, 112, 115, 116, 117
registration, 319, 369, 372
rural, 21
rural–urban, 446
satisfaction, 179
South Africa, 426
survival ratio, 106–107, 114, 124
tax, 465
technical, 140
unemployment, 252
urban, 19, 49
Migration, 137
affect on birth cohort, 351
alternative choice, 204–205
analysis
cohort survival, 106, 107, 115, 116
of cause, 444, 445, 450, 451, 466
of consequence, 444, 445, 446, 447, 448, 451, 454
procedure, 114–117
analyst
anthropology, 443, 445, 452, 457
demography, 443
economist, 443, 445, 450, 457
geographer, 444
historian, 444
social psychology, 443, 445
sociology, 443, 445, 452, 457
barrier, ethnicity, 379–399
beaten path effect, 64–65, 470
Migration
benefit, 167, 168, 169, 170, 181, 182, 186, 187–198, 201, 204
housing quality, 186, 196–197
job prospects, 186, 187–194
life style, 186, 195–196
nonjob, 194–198
private commodities, 186, 195, 196

public commodities, 186, 195
real income differential, 194–195
utility significance, 195
Canadian case, 263–265
choice, information, 202–204
circulatory, 181
collective, 14
comparative
  disciplinary view, 443–461
  systemic view, 463–479
comparison, 7–8
constraint, 6–7, 185
control, 51, 53
cost, 14, 131, 167, 168, 169, 170, 173–174,
    175, 176, 179, 181, 182, 185, 186,
    194, 197, 204, 467
  life style change, 186, 198, 201
  lost friends, relatives, 186, 198, 200–
    201, 205
  moving, 186, 198–199, 205
  transition, 186, 198, 199–200
  uncertain prospect, 186, 198, 201–202
counterinfluence, 176–179
cultural effect, 446
cumulative, age-specific, 368–369
  by cohort, 368–374
cycle, 12
daily, 342, 344
data, 121, 122, 123, 136–138
  direct, 123, 124–127
  historical, 96, 101
  indirect, 123, 124
  subjective, 168, 182
decision, 92, 167, 168, 169, 170, 181, 182,
    184, 185, 187, 188, 190, 197, 202–
    203, 257, 262, 384, 393, 394, 449,
    450, 472, 473, 476
  cost–benefit approach, 167–170
  economic motive, 265–266
  labor market theory, 187
  push–pull approach, 167, 168, 169,
    177–178
  rule, 45, 56
destination, 80, 81, 190, 191, 198, 200
  city, 338
  urban, 197
  village, 338
destabilizing element, 460
determinant, 183, 196, 200, 376

developing countries, 37, 54
differential, 128, 129, 131
directional, 77
duality of growth and decline, 69–70
Eastern Europe, 6, 290–291
  rural-to-urban, 278, 279, 289–296
East to West Germany, 350, 351, 352,
    354, 358
econometric analysis of cause, 465
economic aspect, 212–219, 265–266
economic development, 37–60
effects, 78, 132
employment effect, 445
equation, 95, 390–391
evaluation, 57
evolutionary, 11
external, 20
factors, 130
  accumulation, 57–59
financial payoff, 175–176, 179
flow, 91–94, 100, 168, 236, 237, 330, 333,
    380, 473
  regional, 91–94
  San Francisco, 238
  San Jose, 242
  West Berlin, 353
  Yugoslavia, 336, 338
forecasting regional, 91–101
free, 45, 46, 51
freedom to locate, 21–23
function, 55–56
gross, 77
Hamburg, to and from, 351, 355, 356,
    357, 358
human capital, 66, 68
individual, 14
incentive, earning differential, 191, 194
income effect, 445
inducement, 185
information, 104–109, 465
  population census, 105–109, 110, 111,
    112, 113, 114, 115, 116, 117, 121–134
  population registers, 104
  spread, 11
  surveys, 104
interaction, 2–3
intercensal, 110, 111, 123, 126
internal, 37, 51, 122, 127, 199
  consequence, 130–132

determinant, 130–132
measurement, 135–144
microeconomic, 183–205
international, 19, 136, 149, 199, 237
intermetropolitan, 62, 63, 65
interneighborhood, 212, 230
interregional, 77, 91, 307, 477
regression analysis, 382–394
interrelationship between three systemic
structures, 467–470
inter-republic, 381–382
interurban, 12, 13, 336
intrametropolitan, 136
intraregional, 307
investment, 56–57
job prospects, 187–194
kinship effect, 445
land-settling, 14
leapfrogging, 329, 332, 340, 344
license, 465
lifetime, 109, 110
measurement, 123–127
direct, 108–118, 124–127
indirect, 105–107, 123–124
internal, 103–119, 121–134
mental health effect, 445
mixed, 14
model, 91, 139–143
aggregate, 185
aggregative econometric, 187
aggregative regression, 141, 142
Alonso, 76, 79, 140, 219
disaggregated, 185
equation, 141, 142
general equilibrium, 92, 93, 94
gravity, 77, 80, 81, 82, 86, 139
Harris–Todaro, 193, 194
interactive, 91, 93–94, 99, 101
macroanalytical, 139, 142, 143
microanalytical, 139, 143
multiplier, 143
neoclassical, 91
pull, 82, 85, 86
push, 80—81, 82, 85, 86
regional flow, 91–94
Wilson's entrophy, 82, 86
Wilson–Rees, 76
motivation, 228
movement type, 185

natural effect, 106
net, 77
nonseasonal, 46
objectives, 17–21
optimal rate barriers, 474
origin, 80, 81, 84
pace and pattern in Poland 1951–1973,
308–313, 321, 322
pattern, 224
leapfrog type, 224
peasant, 402
personal effect, 3–4, 62, 65, 66
personal satisfaction, 66, 67
population distribution, 22
prohibition, 465
pull factor, 167, 169, 170, 172–173, 177–
178, 179, 190, 306, 307, 382
push factor, 167, 169, 170, 171–172, 173,
177–178, 179, 306, 307
rate, 113, 114, 115, 218, 447, 452, 455,
458, 460, 466, 471
annual average, 111, 112, 113, 114,
115, 118
Belgrade, 402–403
Canadian, 263
low, 98
optimum, 455, 456, 470
Socialist, 307, 308, 319, 320, 321, 323,
324, 325
Yugoslav, 383
Ravenstein's Laws, 329, 330, 332–336
research, 80, 170, 446
reciprocal, 13
regional effect, 3–4
regional development, 380–382
restriction, 268–269, 319, 322–325
return, 133
reversibility, 55, 475, 476
staged, 199
streams, 262–264
rural, 16, 150
rural–rural, 307, 308, 310, 311, 313, 314,
315, 319, 320, 321, 322, 323, 338,
388, 389
rural–urban, 11, 12, 17, 19, 40, 44, 46, 47,
49, 51, 53, 58, 62, 63, 65, 67, 237,
306, 307, 308, 310, 311, 313, 319,
320, 321, 323, 329–344, 388, 446, 477
rurban, 458

seasonal, 44–46, 160
skill acquisition, 424–426, 428, 430, 431,
    433, 434, 435, 436, 437
social effect, 446, 459
social system effect, 451–454
Socialist pattern, 308
socioeconomic development, 11–35
stepwise, 329, 331
substitution, 308, 323
suburban, 459
systemic consequence, 466
time element, 55–59
total, 351, 354
    socialist and nonsocialist countries,
        324
transition period, 197
transoceanic, 17
trend, 12
    levels, West Berlin, 351–358, 365
unidirectional, 13
urban Canadian, 264
under Socialism, 305–327
United States, 235–254
urban–rural, 308, 310, 311, 319, 321
urban–urban, 308, 310, 311, 313, 314,
    319, 321, 323, 336, 338, 477
vectors, 13–14
war effect, 308
Wave theory, 332-336, 344
    Yugoslavia test, 336–340
West Berlin, 349–378
    age–sex structure, 351, 358, 362, 363,
        364
    cumulative surviving, 370
    effect of aging, 351
    marital status, 366–367
Migratory lag, 17
Milwaukee, 236
Mineral resource, domestic, 306
Miniaturization, 25
Mining, 163
Mississippi, 148, 155, 252
Missouri counties, 243
    Franklin, 243
    Jefferson, 243
    St. Charles, 243
    St. Louis, 243
Mobility, 21, 137, 138, 168, 170, 414–415
    geographic, 182
    interoccupational, 21

labor, 182
research, 170
threshold, 14
Model, Alonso–Muth–Beckmann, 219, 460
    Beckmann, 219-224
    comparison of pure, 475
    cost–benefit, 444
    entropy, 447
    gravity, 444, 447
    housing investment, 213
    push–pull, 382, 444
    Sjaastad's human capital, 56–57
    Stigilitz's labor-turnover, 51, 54, 56
Montana, 148
Montenegro, Yugoslavia, 380, 381, 382,
    388, 397
Mortality, 15, 106, 107, 114, 153, 154, 156,
    163, 404
    decline, 155
    rate, urban, 349
Mortgage finance, FHA-insured, 232
Mortgage insurance, 236
Motivation structure, 464, 468–469
Motive, 12
Mountain states, 116, 117
Moving behavior, decision, 61, 64, 65
    friend and relative influence on, 63, 64,
        65
    intent, 61
    labor demand, 63
    motive, 63
    "pull" vs. "push", 63–64, 65
    sequence, 61
Multicollinearity, 388, 389, 430, 431, 432
Muslim, 384, 393

N

National settlement policy, 471
Natural calamity, 165
Natural resources, 24, 25
Nazi Germany, 287
Nebraska, 148, 155
Neighborhood, 212, 213, 217, 218
    abandonment, 228, 229
    depopulation, 212
        downward filtering, 228, 229, 230
        income, 229
        low-risk, 230
    passive filtering, 228
    preference dynamic, 225–230

socioeconomic characteristic, 215, 218, 225
suburban, 229
Netherlands, 15, 121
    migration rate, 324, 325
    planning controls, 267
Net migration
    Hamburg, 356, 357, 363
        age–sex structure, 365
        sex ratio, 358
    West Berlin, 351, 354, 355, 363, 365
        age–sex structure, 351, 358, 362, 363, 364
        cumulative surviving, 370
        effect of aging, 351
        marital status, 366–367
Nevada, 164
New communities policy, Canada, 271
New England, 116, 117
New Mexico, 155
New World, 15
New Orleans, 236
New town development, 272
Nicaragua, 157
Nonmetropolitan residue, 77
Nonmigrant, 137, 184–185, 198
Nonmobility, 170
Norms, problem of, 474–475
North Carolina, 155
North Dakota, 148, 155
Norway, migration rate, 324, 325

O

Obsolescence, 29
Occupation, 128, 129
    agricultural, 340
    farmer, 307, 315
        dual (worker-farmer), 307, 315, 316, 320, 322, 323
    industrial, 334, 340
    urban, 151
Occupational composition, 139
Occupational mobility, 403, 412
Occupational shift, 341
Occupational structure, race, 417, 418
Oklahoma, 155
Opportunity, 184, 185, 187
    differential, 195
    employment, 193, 198
    inferior, 185

job, 198
    superior, 185
    urban-industrial, 337
Optimal migration policy, 471
Optimum city size, 255–258
    index of well-being, 256, 257, 258
    range of sizes, 256
Optimum population, 255–258
Oregon, 164
Organization for Economic Cooperation and Development (OECD), 259, 267, 269, 272
Outmigrant, 459
    West Berlin, 353, 354
        marital status, 366, 367
Outmigration, 16, 23, 63, 64, 96, 98, 104, 107, 110, 113, 115, 116, 117, 212, 219, 222, 223, 241, 242, 248, 251, 343, 382, 402, 472
    age structure, 158
    destination, 107
    economic consequence, 161–165
    economic stagnation, 69, 70
    effect on population growth, 153–158
    effect on region of origin, 147–166
    Hamburg, 356, 357
        age–sex structure, 358, 363, 365
    lifetime, 109
    local characteristics, 80–81
    rate, 64, 111, 114, 149, 150, 153
    rural, 16, 148–166
        cause, 150–153
        size, pattern, 148–150
    sex composition, 159–161
    social consequence, 161–165
    West Berlin, 351, 353, 355, 377, 378
        age–sex structure, 351, 358, 359, 360, 361, 362, 363, 365
Overpopulation, 19

P

Pacific states, 116, 117
Pareto optimal equilibrium, 474, 475
Pay structure, 433, 435
    determinant, 429, 430, 433
    South Africa, West Germany compared, 435

Peasant, 41
  economies, 39, 42
  farm, 44
  landless, 45
Per capita growth, 15
Permits
  residence, 87
  travel, 87
Personal information source, 203
Philadelphia, 236
Philippines, 157
Photochemical oxidant concentrations, 94
Photochemical smog, 94
Physical factor, city, 256
Physical Planning Act, South Africa, 420,
  434
Pittsburgh, 209, 236
Planning controls, physical, 267-268
Plantation, 44
Poland, 22, 152, 157, 283, 287, 290-291,
  292, 293, 294, 313-323, 344, 477
  dwellings and rooms in towns, 317, 318,
    319, 321, 322
  employment outside agriculture, 312
  housing situation, 317
  investment outlays in national economy,
    318
  migration and economic development un-
    der Socialism, 305-327
  urban area, 312
Policy
  national settlement, 465
  variables, 87
Political strength, 162
Political system, 465
Political units, rural, 148-150
Population, 24, 25, 94, 96, 99, 159, 162
  aged, 159, 160, 161, 165
  age structure, 106, 211, 358-366, 368
  agricultural, 20, 151, 153, 155, 156, 157,
    158, 159
  agricultural-rural, 337
  base effect, 338
  black, 171, 172, 246-247, 248, 250, 252,
    254
    replacement capacity, 249, 250
  census, 105-119, 121, 122, 127
  city, 157, 158, 349

classification,
  migrant, 125, 128, 129
  nonmigrant, 125, 127, 128, 129
concentration, metropolitan areas,
  OECD countries, 260-261
  rural, 278, 280, 287, 289
  through urbanization, 258-265, 289
contemporary, 136
cross-section, 184
decline, 12, 16, 21, 26, 69, 77, 78, 236,
  251-253
density, 96
displacement, 332, 333
distribution, 20, 21, 23, 218, 219, 231,
  250, 471
  occupational dependence, Yugoslavia,
    341
  perspective and policy, 255-274
East European, 290-291
East German, age-sex structure, 354
elderly, 248, 250, 251, 253, 350, 358
European, 16
farm, 148, 153
flow, 55, 137
  interurban, 337, 338, 339, 344
  model, 75-89
  Yugoslavia, 331
gaps, 332
growth, 12, 15, 18, 19, 21, 23, 27, 58, 69,
  97, 101, 106, 123, 124, 154, 155, 157,
  158, 161, 162, 163, 165, 209, 210,
  224, 236, 286, 343
  decline, 143, 154, 156, 157, 159, 161,
    162, 163, 166, 209, 224
  density, 163
  effect of outmigration, 153-158
  natural increase, 76, 77, 105, 106, 123,
    153, 154, 156, 158, 159, 162, 163,
    237, 238, 241, 246, 247, 253, 254,
    292, 340, 341, 343, 349
  percentage annual in selected coun-
    tries, 259
  rate, 148, 155, 161
  regional, 98, 101
  San Jose, 238, 242
  stability, 162, 262
hypermobile, 64, 141, 241, 253
internal shift, 211

metropolitan, 25, 210, 235, 236, 243
pressure, 15
registration, 104, 121, 122, 138
replacement capacity, 248–250, 253
rural, 16, 19, 23, 62, 148, 150, 151, 154, 156, 157, 158, 159, 160, 166, 284, 311, 322, 349
  rural to urban, 252
sex ratio, 413
size, 77, 80, 162
spatial distribution, 212
stability, prejudice against, 161–162
structure assuming no migration, 374–376
trend, urban formation, 252
  metropolitan dispersal, 252
urban, 18, 19, 20, 21, 25, 26, 61, 62, 149, 158, 160, 161, 258, 330, 337, 340, 343, 349, 382, 388
  Socialist countries, 277, 278, 292, 293, 294
urbanization, 289
West Berlin, 350, 351, 366
  age–sex structure, 351, 358–366, 375
  effect of aging, 351, 377
  effect of migration, 377
  hypothetical, 375–376
  marital status, 366, 367
  size, 350, 374
  white, 154, 172, 246, 247, 248, 250, 252, 254
  young, 159, 160, 349
Portugal, 157
Postmigration transition period, 194
Poverty, 161, 218, 251, 252, 380, 421
Present location, information, 202
  alternative location, 11, 203, 205
Presocialist, socialist periods compared, 280–289
  economies, 286–287
  labor gap, 284, 285, 286, 288
  urbanization gap, 284, 285, 286, 294, 295
Price differential, 218
Price equalization theorem, 38
Private goods, 465, 466
Private information agency, 475
Problem of norms, 474–475
Production, 94
  increase, 162

Productivity, factoral equipment, 13
Proebrazhensky dilemma, 58
Profit, 46, 47
Property rights, 42
Province, agrarian, 149, 150
Psychological variable, 181
Public goods, 465, 466
Public ownership of land, 266
Public sector, local, 219
Public service, 218
  benefit, 197
  improvement, 271
  local, 198, 200
Pull factor, 136, 138, 143, 306, 307, 382, 384, 464
Push factor, 129, 136, 138, 142, 143, 306, 307, 384, 464

Q

Quality-of-life
  indicators, 92–94
  ingredient, 198

R

Race
  composition, 217, 218, 228
    nonwhite, 218
  discrimination, South Africa, 418
  hostility, 171
  occupational structure, 417, 418
  pay discrimination, 418, 420
  restrictive work allocation, 422, 423
  wage, 417
Railroad, 213
Ravenstein's laws of migration, 6, 329, 330, 332–336
Ravenstein Migration Matrix, Yugoslavia, 336, 337, 338, 339
Real estate market, 227
Regional development, 306
  migration, 380–382
  patterns, Yugoslavia, 381
  policy, 268, 270–271
  population dispersal policy, 268–272
  Incentives Act, 270
Regional science, 11

Regulatory power, insufficient, 258, 266
Religion, 131, 228, 379, 380, 381
Religious paroxysm, 78
Rent, land, 41, 42, 44, 47
Residence, 112–114
  length, 468
  potential location, 189
  present location, 191
  region, 190, 191
Resident, newcomer, 188
  older, 188
Residential location model, Alonso–Muth–
    Beckmann, 212
Resource ratio, 165
Retirement, 468
Revenue, ecclesiastical, 22
  tax, 22
Revenue-sharing, federal, 211
Risk prospect, families, 187–188
Rome, 14
Rumania, 157, 283, 287, 290–291, 293, 294,
    324, 325
Rural area, 194, 195, 218, 262
  characteristic, 196
  impoverished, 252
  life style, 195
  land, 212
  resident, 292, 323
  outmigration cause, 150–153
  population, aging, 161
    sex distortion, 161
  pathologies, 39–48
Rural–urban balance, 13
Rurban society, 459
Russian Empire, 287

S

Saint Louis, 213, 214, 224, 236, 237, 241,
    242, 253, 254
  city decline, 243–252
  city population, 210
  county, 210, 218, 243, 247
  demographic change consequence, 248–
    251
  demographic trend, 243–248
  destination of migrant, 247
  disadvantaged citizen, 250–251
  neighborhood variable, 216–217

  population decline policy dilemma, 251–
    252
  replacement capacity, 249
  SMSA, 210
San Diego, 238
San Francisco, 236, 238
San Jose, California, 5, 236, 237–243, 252,
    253
  domestic migration stream, 241
  growth repercussion, 239–243
  migration flow affecting, 238–239
Saskatchewan, 149
School enrollment, 163
Search behavior, 188, 202
Seattle, 236
Security, loss, 201
Sen's production function, 44
Serbia, Yugoslavia, 380, 381, 382, 385, 393,
    397
  Case, 401–415
  kinship system, 406, 407, 408, 409, 410,
    411
    agnatic, 406, 407, 414
    cousin, 408, 409, 413
    traditional ideology, 406, 409, 410
Service
  investment, 294–295
  local government, 211
  public, 218
  urban, 295
Settlement policy, optimal, 471
Sewage, 197
Sex ratio, 159, 160
  hypothetical population, 375
  West Berlin, 350, 353, 354
Sharecropping, 39, 46–48
Shantytown, 197
Sjaastad's human capital model, 56–57
Skill, 12
  acquisition of, 12
Slovenia, Yugoslavia, 380, 381, 393, 397
Smith, Adam, 13, 21, 39
Smog, 94, 95, 96
Social behavior, Homans Law, 453, 454,
    457, 458
Social capital, 201
Socialist countries, 468
  economic system, 465, 477
  economizing on urbanization, 277–304

geopolitical factor, 286
growth strategy, 278, 283, 285, 286, 288
historical development, 286
Social disadvantage, 68, 71
farm, 184
Social relationship, 200
Socialism, 305–327
Social security data, 138
U.S., 138
Social services, 305
Social system, 451, 452, 453, 457
Social welfare, 46
function, 449
labor force structure, 282, 288
migrant group, 473
and nonsocialist countries, comparative
observations, 323–326
region, 473
Socialist system, 305, 306
Soviet model, 306
Society
agnatic, 406, 407, 414
agrarian, 287
low-income, 42
rurban, 458
traditional Serbian, 406, 409, 414
Western European, 404
Socioeconomic
characteristics, 121, 122, 128, 131, 133
factor, city, 256
structure, 12
Sociostructural changes, 12
South Africa
dual labor market, 417–439
Industrial Conciliation System, 420–424
Physical Planning Act, 420, 434
restrictive work allocation, 422–423
trade union, 420, 435
urban black living standard, 421
work committee, 420, 435
South Atlantic region, 116, 117
South Carolina, 155
South Dakota, 148, 155
Soviet Union, 16, 18, 278, 283, 285, 286,
296, 305, 468, 478
St. Charles County, 210, 211
Standard Metropolitan Statistical Area
(SMSA), 94, 209, 211, 215, 218, 219,
222, 223, 230, 231, 236, 238

California, 239
Kansas City, 243
Saint Louis, 243, 246, 247, 250
San Jose, 241, 242
United States, 244–245
Standard of living, 15
urban black South Africa, 421
States, development, 165
Static analysis, comparative, 38–55
Stigilitz's labor-turnover model, 51, 54, 56
Subsidy, 42, 50, 51, 53, 78, 272, 465
housing, 197
public, 231
Suburb, 210, 247, 248
low-density, 213
University City, St. Louis, 217
Suburbanization, 213
low-density, 262
Suicide, rate, 78
Surveys, 104, 138
Chicago, 170–177
community-based data, 170
Problems of Living in the Metropolis,
170–177
United Nations, 122
Survival probability, 124
Survivor ratios, life table, 369, 374
Sweden, 20, 121, 151, 152, 153, 154, 155,
156, 157, 159, 160, 267
Systemic comparison, 470–476
Syria, 287

T

Tax
base, 211
capacity, 211
collection, 211
concession, 272
excise, 46
inducement, 267
law, 236
property, 219, 233
rates, 87
roll, 404
subsidy, 473
Technological change, 258, 267
Technological progress, 15

Technology, 12, 256
  agrarian–handicraft, 147
  automobile, 223
  changes, 23
  communication, 136
  efficiency, 38
  engineering, 25
  expressway, 223
  freeway, 213
  transportation, 136, 233
  urban–industrial, 147
Telecommunications, 256
Tembisa, South Africa, 421
Tenant, 46, 47, 48
Thailand, 157
Todaro's urban wage formulation, 49
Topography, 24
Toronto, 267
Total migration, W. Berlin, 351, 354, 360
Town, 332, 333, 334, 335, 336, 338, 402
Trade, 38, 39, 42, 58, 59
  policy, autarkic, 288
  structure, East European countries, 287–288
  theory dictum, 42
  union policy, 478
    South Africa, 420, 435
Train, electric, 213
Transfer cost, 383
Transferral of development rights, (TDRs), 267
Transportation, 21, 22, 23, 24, 25, 26, 87, 94, 136, 256, 342, 388
  automobile, 94, 232
  commuter, 342, 344
  cost, 87, 140, 198, 219, 231, 450, 458, 465
  improvement, 87
  policy, 238
  system, 212, 213, 222
  technology, 233
  travel permits, 87
  urban, 232
Turkey, 287

U

Underdeveloped countries, delayed rural depopulation, 156–158
Underurbanization, 477, 478

Unemployment, 92, 138, 139, 141, 162, 193–194, 197, 199, 200, 468
  disguised, 39–46, 287
  rate, 52
  structural policy, 466
  urban, 49, 50, 51, 53
Union, 165
  policy, construction trade, 232
  South Africa, 420, 435
  trade, 478
Union of Soviet Socialist Republics (USSR), 478
United Kingdom, 153
  planning controls, 267
United Nations survey, 122, 125
Unites States, 18, 20, 26, 61, 76, 78, 80, 86, 115, 116, 117, 131, 137, 148, 149, 150–158, 163–165, 181, 183, 209, 478
  black population, 398
  geographical subdivision, 116, 117
  regional development program, 270, 271
  urban growth and decline, 235–254
University of Pennsylvania study, 130–131
Urban
  agglomeration, 266
  area, 193, 194, 195, 197, 209, 218, 262
    characteristics, 195–196
    population density, 213
    size, 222
  center, 13, 18, 26, 28, 49, 63, 64
  classification
    city, 332, 333, 334, 335, 336, 337, 338, 339, 343, 344
    town, 332, 333, 334, 335, 336, 338
    village, 332, 333, 334, 335, 336, 338, 340, 344
  decay, 211, 212
  definition, 284
  development policy, 232, 295, 296
  field, 263
  growth and decline, United States, 235–254
  infrastructure, 279, 280, 289, 293, 296
  land, price escalation, 262
    rent, 266
  pathologies, 49–54
  population
    demographic effect of migration, 349–378
    working age, 313, 314, 318

population growth, 258-269
  controls, 266-268
  and housing, 317
  problems, 262
  trends, 258-265
residence, 280, 283, 284, 292
  definition, 284, 285, 292
transport investment, 232
services, 279, 478
Urbanization, 5, 6, 12, 19, 22, 26, 28, 59, 65, 131, 148, 149, 156, 158, 236, 252, 388, 401, 412, 446, 478
  East European, 289-296
  economizing in Socialist Countries, 277-304
  level, Socialist and nonsocialist countries, 281
  literature, 455
  pattern, Yugoslavia, 329, 332, 333, 335, 336, 337, 338, 339
  rate, socialist, 292
  Serbian, 330
  typology, 349-350
  variable, 383

V

Venezuela, 149, 150, 157
Vermont, 164
Village, 332, 333, 334, 335, 336, 338, 340, 344, 402, 403, 410

W

Wage, 38, 39, 41, 42, 54, 55, 57, 131, 139, 162, 417
  costs, 52
  fixed, 48
  institutional urban, 49-51
  manufacturing, 49
  neoclassical theory, 427, 428
  rate, 192-193, 456, 476
  rural, 52, 53
  structure, South Africa, 420, 426, 427, 435, 438
  subsidy, 42, 50, 51, 53, 54, 55
  urban, 49, 50, 51, 52, 53
Washington, 164

Washington, D.C., 236
Water, 24, 25, 197
Wave theory, 332-336, 344
Welfare, 173
  function, 449
  human, 446
Welfare
  per capita, 28
  policy, 466
  private, 471
  service, 197
  social, 471
Well-being function, 256, 449
West Berlin, 350
  age-sex structure, 350
  hypothetical population, 374-376
  life table, 369
  migrants
    aged 0-17, 360-361, 363, 366
    aged 18-24, 359, 363
    aged 25-39, 359, 360, 363, 366, 368
    aged 40-64, 361, 363
    aged 65 and over, 361
    marital status, 366-368
  migration
    increase by cohort, 368-374
    pattern, 1952-1971, 349-378
    population structure assuming no migration, 374-376
  postwar demographic history, 350
West North Central region, 116, 117
West South Central region, 116, 117
West Virginia, 148, 155, 163
Western Countries, 267
  industrial nation, 161
  nation, 218, 231, 233
Western world, 159
World War I, 287
World War II, 236, 280, 287, 288, 329, 350, 379
  post period, 213
Worklife mobility, 403

Y

Yugoslavia, 6, 7, 157, 283, 287, 290-291, 293, 294, 329-344, 379-399, 477
  Belgrade, 330, 331, 339, 343, 344
  data, 454, 460

demographic region, 382–383, 385
development and rural–urban migration, 329–344
economic growth, 329
ethnicity as a barrier to migration, 379–399
kinship system, 453
outmigration regression results, 386–387
regional development patterns, 381

rural–urban flows, 1961 census data, 330, 336, 341
Zagreb, 330

Z

Zagreb, Yugoslavia, 330
Zero-migration property, 55
Zoning, 232–233, 267

A
B 7
C 8
D 9
E 0
F 1
G 2
H 3
I 4
J 5